BURT FRANKLIN: RESEARCH & SOURCE WORKS SERIES 806
American Classics in History and Social Science 204

A CONNECTED VIEW

OF

THE WHOLE INTERNAL NAVIGATION

OF

THE UNITED STATES

THE MAP

HAS BEEN ENGRAVED FOR THE PURPOSE, ACCORDING TO THE LATEST TOPOGRA-
PHICAL CORRECTIONS AND IMPROVEMENTS.—IT IS PROJECTED, ON A
REDUCED SCALE, FROM TANNER'S EXCELLENT FOUR SHEET
MAP OF THE UNITED STATES, RECENTLY PUBLISHED.

AND WITH

VARIOUS AUTHENTIC STATISTICAL DETAILS.

A CONNECTED VIEW

OF

THE WHOLE INTERNAL NAVIGATION

OF

THE UNITED STATES

NATURAL AND ARTIFICIAL, PRESENT AND PROSPECTIVE

CORRECTED AND IMPROVED FROM THE EDITION OF 1826, AND MUCH ENLARGED
FROM AUTHENTIC MATERIALS, DOWN TO THE PRESENT TIME

WITH

A SHEET MAP

GEORGE ARMROYD

BURT FRANKLIN
NEW YORK

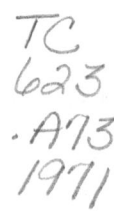

EASTERN DISTRICT OF PENNSYLVANIA, to wit:

(L. S.) BE IT REMEMBERED, That on the seventeenth day of April, in the fifty-fourth year of the Independence of the United States of America, A. D. 1830, GEORGE ARMROYD, of the said District, hath deposited in this office the Title of a Book, the right whereof he claims as author, in the words following, to wit:

"A Connected View of the Whole Internal Navigation of the United States; "Natural and Artificial, Present and Prospective : corrected and improved from "the Edition of 1826, and much enlarged, from authentic materials, down to the "present time. With a Sheet Map, and numerous engraved profiles, for the "illustration of the subject. The Map has been engraved for the purpose, ac- "cording to the latest topographical corrections and improvements.—It is pro- "jected, on a reduced scale, from Tanner's excellent four sheet map of the "United States, recently published. And with various authentic statistical de- "tails. By a Citizen of the United States."

In conformity to the Act of the Congress of the United States, intituled "An Act for the encouragement of learning, by securing the copies of maps, charts, and books, to the authors and proprietors of such copies, during the times therein mentioned." And also to the Act, entitled, "An Act supplementary to an Act, entitled, 'An Act for the encouragement of learning, by securing the copies of maps, charts, and books, to the authors and proprietors of such copies, during the times therein mentioned,' and extending the benefits thereof to the arts of designing, engraving, and etching, historical and other prints."

D. CALDWELL, *Clerk of the*
Eastern District of Pennsylvania.

Published by LENOX HILL Pub. & Dist. Co. (Burt Franklin)
235 East 44th St., New York, N.Y. 10017
Originally Published: 1830
Reprinted: 1971
Printed in the U.S.A.

S.B.N.: 8337-00642
Library of Congress Card Catalog No.: 77-146133
Burt Franklin: Research and Source Works Series 806
American Classics in History and Social Science 204

PREFACE.

"Shall I lead your astonishment to the verge of incredulity? I will: know, then, that one-tenth of the expense borne by Great Britain in the last campaign, would enable ships to sail from London, through Hudson's river, into Lake Erie. As yet, my friend, we only crawl along the outer shell of our country. The interior excels the part we inhabit, in soil, in climate, in every thing. The proudest empire in Europe is but a bauble, compared to what America *will* be, *must* be, in the course of two centuries, perhaps of one."—MORRIS, *Dec.* 1800.

THIS work was undertaken in the summer of 1825, and has since been added to, as new matter from time to time has occurred for insertion. The immediate object of it is, to present as clear and distinct a view as possible, of the past progress, and present state, of a particular class of improvements, whereof an enumeration at large, with detail of circumstances, is here attempted to be given; and, by inference, the present state and prospects of the country viewed in relation to that class of improvements, and their advancement towards a state of perfection in the internal intercourse of the whole nation.

The ultimate object of this undertaking, that of becoming, as it is hoped it may be, the occasion or instrument of a respectful suggestion, to whomsoever the talent and gratifying opportunity may be given, of a desideratum yet being to be satisfied, in regard to various topics of the highest import. *So*, not to this nation merely, but to the commonwealth of nations; namely:—

A literary performance, or series of performances, by an able pen, that can sink deep into the investigation of *causes*, and, with the fidelity and enticement of nature's way, can, at the same time, not the less entertain and engage attention, by a just and lively description of *matters;*—a pen that can reason as justly, as narrate pleasantly.

It (the desideratum) is a correct, and a minute, as well as comprehensive exposition of facts, so clear and convincing, and obviously authentic, as without comment or more explanation, to spread a knowledge of details as they really are, their true origin, and their proper bearings. Which knowledge, thus dispensed to the public and the world, necessarily in this, as in other cases, implies a dismissal of ignorance, and it becomes pleasant to anticipate it as superseding a certain alleged *existing* "*ob-*

scurity," that has hitherto been floating over and about this youthful creation.

Not only are we anxious that the present face, or physical superficies, of the country, should appear as fair to view as is consistent with truth, or, in other words, in the garb and colouring it has acquired, but moreover, that the hoped for new *light* should be made to penetrate and display the very energies,—the character of the operations, internal and external, of this rising and advancing republic, already become the aggregate of many independent states, and of still more extensive territories, incipients of additional states.

The effect *desired*, is that of opening to broad view the actual condition and character of this nation as a whole, her genuine history, which, though taken all together, is but brief in point of time, yet will be found to be impressively important, more and more so, as the few genuine particulars come to be more and more developed or explained;—the effect, in short, of displaying her acquisitions and attainments, physical, intellectual, and moral, compared with time and circumstance; her resources, as far as may be, commercial and political;—in so much, that, for the honour of the nation, and good of mankind in the cause of knowledge, combined, no portion of this sectional information may remain wanting, or in suspense, or the sum in toto be of rare occurrence among men of letters in the distant world; and especially, that, in the mind of no person claiming to be *well informed*, the name of the UNITED STATES may longer remain associated with an idea distorted, vague, or inadequate. It has been said abroad, and reiterated, that, in the document of true and genuine information regarding this section of the world, there is a hiatus or chasm that requires to be filled up, and requires the touch of a "gentleman" to do it—a gentleman too, who shall not belong to that class of philosophers who content themselves with the *surface of things*, but who shall be qualified to examine into and analyze the characters and constitutions of men and matters, and every way disposed, as well as qualified, to draw solid logical deductions, from accurate, well established premises, with an enlightened, unprejudiced mind;—a writer, in short, who shall not have viewed the institutions of the country as through an opera glass screwed to a wrong focus, but, if his survey be luminous and definite, then shall, besides, have his pen trimmed and dressed in such sort, as neither to expose the *gouty accoutrement of an invalid*, nor the light and unsubstantial apparel, or trim, of a mere tourist pen; on the contrary, be so cleanly shaved and polished at the sides, and nicely adjusted, as to transmit a clear, expanded, and intelligent view of the whole.*

---

* Captain Basil Hall's "Tour" through the United States and part of Canada, is not destitute of interest, nor without many judicious and instructive remarks,

In the interval, however, ere the social world can be thus ably and in extenso informed touching this great but youthful member of the commonwealth of civilized nations, and its component qualities and materials, the present inquiry and partial delineation will, it is hoped, present something of a satisfactory character. It will lay open to the intelligent reader at a distance, through a plain statement, a connected series of facts and circumstances appertaining to the one exclusive topic undertaken; and, being unmixed with other subjects, save here and there some incidental matters that have claimed to be noticed, may, perhaps, on that account, be the better suited for conveying a clear and impressive idea of what the particulars stated are intended to designate, namely—the precise point of advancement arrived at, and actual prospects of the country in this department of her career in prosperity.

But as the actual existence of the various works of improvement herein detailed, together with the mode and manner of their execution, necessarily implies, in the higher attributes of the nation, attainments, capabilities and views to correspond and harmonize, so there can be no doubt the enlightened reader and philanthropic economist and politician, will be enabled to elicit general conclusions nothing short of being satisfactory to his own mind, and some particular ones, and both perhaps not the less certain of an early verification for being on a scale of no inconsiderable dimensions. And in aid of his closer calculations as to particular points, it is hoped that a variety of authentic, statistical, and other information, and some remarks thereon, which will be found partly interspersed among the articles of this composition, and partly as an appendage, precedent to the General Rail Road article, the Canada article, and the Index, may be received with favour, and prove useful.

It will be perceived, that the succession of dates inserted at many of the enumerated articles of improvement, apply respectively to those articles, each one alone; by which method, an

such as might be expected from a sensible traveller; but much certainly might have been added by the gentleman; and more, perhaps, as profitably expunged from his notes.

The tour of a celebrated character through the United States, in 1824 and 1825, recently published in Paris, by A. Lavasseur, and now translated into English, has afforded an uncommon measure of gratification to readers in this part of the world.

"America, or a General Survey of the Political Situation of the several Powers of the Western Continent, with conjectures on their future prospects, by a Citizen of the United States," published in 1827, will be long consulted as a standard work on the subject treated.

The "Washington Papers" are soon to be spread before the public. They are in able hands for arrangement, and with or without commentary, will, no one doubts, afford, not only a rich repast for the political and domestic craving appetite, but instruction the most solid for the hour of reflection.

historical sketch, as well as description, is afforded to each article separately.

It will likewise be borne in mind, how short the period is which has sufficed for the achievement of what exists at the present day, in the various navigation improvements particularized. Not longer since than in the summer of 1817, it was, that the great Erie canal of New-York, for which, at the recommendation, and in a great measure through the influence of the late lamented Governor De Witt Clinton, the pecuniary resources of the state were pledged, had its commencement; and the success with which the prosecution of that work was attended, in realizing as it went on the objects of it, to a degree that outstripped every moderate expectation, and even surpassed the most sanguine anticipations of its supporters;—this it was which operated as a first effectual impulse, in bringing a deal of the country's capital suddenly forward, and the minds of men to bear intensely on the subject; it has served to bring into existence, of what now exists, all the rest nearly; that is to say, all nearly that now exists of great internal improvements, taken upon a broad national scale, in favour of universal intercourse. Without affirming that it created, we may safely say that it awakened, the general spirit of enterprise in this career of active industry, the true foundation of every other kind of prosperity; and the whole stock of the nation's now improved natural science, distributed as we find it among hundreds of favoured individuals, is in requisition and active service; and to thousands of the classes of labouring industry over the face of the country, substantial employment is actually afforded, in the prosecution of the many works of improvement, public and private, begun upon, and now more or less advanced; an activity this, that is in chief part, if not altogether, clearly to be traced to the impulse mentioned. Before that time, the Middlesex canal in Massachusetts, the Santee canal of South Carolina, and partial, but still very useful works at the rapids and falls of some rivers, particularly the Connecticut river and the Merrimack, adopted at an early epoch, were all the improvements which the navigation of the country had acquired; notwithstanding the circumstance often alluded to, which has become at the present day of striking notoriety, and has been termed an *inherent aptitude* in Americans generally for the works of mechanical and physical science, but, in truth, is nothing more nor less than the development of skill and progress therein, consequent on advances of population and freedom of institutions. It is, however, a skill not only in the various known applications of the science, but extended to the most important discoveries for facilitating the practical arts, incessantly calling upon and engaging the attention.

The states last mentioned, and other states of the Union, it must be allowed also, were not unendowed with acuteness of perception originally, in regard to their proper interests, nor unmindful of prosecuting their own particular objects ; but, as the expression implies, these objects were more sectional in their nature than general ; and the state of Pennsylvania, although especially conspicuous for her enlarged views, from the earliest periods, on the subject of trade and intercourse, and a persevering application of her valuable resources, manifested by a large amount of expenditure from year to year in the cause; yet, at the period of impulse above alluded to, Pennsylvania herself was, and had been for some time, "slumbering,"—slumbering under the slow operation of a *course of correctives*. In the years 1791, 1792, 1793, she had been bold and profuse ; but, after a while, and just in the midst of her overcalculated projects of achievement, was suddenly admonished that it was time for her to *draw in* and be prudent. She was, in fact, exhausting herself prematurely ; and though she possessed stamina within, and felt it, was not at that time strengthened and fortified with the proper aids and supports from without. The steps she had taken were loose, and miscalculated for stability. But she took the hint, and she adopted the wise plan of *sedatives* and *patience;* and under the operation of these it was that she slumbered herself into convalescence and vigour, as will be seen in the pages of this work.

This reserved preliminary page, the writer experiences no small gratification in occupying with a DEDICATION. He can obey no impulse more pleasing, than thus to inscribe his just acknowledgments to several most estimable and well-informed FRIENDS, for the generous interest they have taken in the hoped-for success of this his undertaking; and the many opportunities they have, to that end, improved, in both furnishing from their own stores, and causing him to be supplied from others, with much valuable materials suitable to his purpose. The which, he has freely made use of throughout the pages of the book ; and which he considers, wishing no concealment of the fact, to have mainly contributed to all that the public will be forward to recognise of *good* in the production. He is not fain to lay claim, avowedly or mentally, for his own particular share, to much, if to any merit, in the performance, beyond the motives which have actuated his assiduity, and not a little cheered him during the course of his labours from beginning to end ; the writer is but too well aware, notwithstanding the flattering nature of his aims, and although no pains nor any of his best faculties have been spared to acquire copious information, and to select from what he obtained, and render *all*, within admissible bounds, unexceptionably perfect, that yet there may still be found, both deficiency and error, in more than one instance of the subject matter, amongst the number of insertions, many of which having proceeded immediately, or exclusively, as it were—e ipse —from his own individual depôt, without receiving the benefit of new lights, to amend, qualify, or explain former information and impressions received into the *storehouse.*

Notwithstanding, however, the apprehensions here expressed, the reader is again respectfully assured, that exertions have not been omitted to prevent, as much as possible, deficiencies, and every kind of inaccuracy *throughout.* The main topic undertaken, and immediate incidental ones, are, so far as explorations extend, and data exist, susceptible of being treated with entire precision ; and the principal descriptions they embrace, at the several divisions of the work, are of a nature claiming of right to be *exact*, up to the technical meaning of the word, in order fully to accomplish the object in contemplation. This is truly what has been attempted ; and, if it so be, that the author has failed of succeeding, from within himself and his own proper resources, at some points, to the same extent and degree of precision his friends have succeeded for him ; and in virtue of their contributions, enabled him to be perfect at other points ; he is far from wishing that any of these his defects, laid open to public scrutiny, should not receive comment. He is, on the contrary, most heartily disposed to apply all "Reports" on the occasion, meant as salutary, in the way of so many *correctives.*

He invites, therefore, all *useful* information, from whatsoever quarter and in whatsoever shape ; acknowledging his special motive for this invitation to be, the hope of being enabled to *correct,* to *enlarge,* or to *modify,* and to present something, in a FUTURE EDITION, that shall be QUITE PERFECT.

INTERNAL NAVIGATION

OF

THE UNITED STATES.

NATURAL AND ARTIFICIAL, IN CONNEXION.

The connexion is designated in the map of the United States, by coloured lines, traced from point to point of one river to another, where such canals of connexion already exist, or are in contemplation; exhibiting, in consequence, (with the aid of some of the great river courses themselves,) one continuous, uninterrupted Inland Navigation, from sea to sea;—from the ports of outlet and inlet on the Atlantic, through the country, and by a variety of routes, to the ports of the Gulf of Mexico.

The *Red* coloured lines represent those canal works that are already finished, or well advanced; the *Yellow* lines, those that are either not yet commenced, or, if commenced, not as yet actively prosecuted. All which is attempted to be explained at the proper heads of the subject in this book.

The letters N, A, M, prefixed, one or other, at each of the articles, signify *Natural, Artificial,* or *Mixed,* in reference to the kind of navigation comprised in that article.

The articles of canal works are numbered consecutively throughout, beginning at New-England, and ending at Florida, from No. 1 to No. 159.

At the end of each division, into which the United States is here reduced, a summary is given of the Navigation, natural and artificial, comprised within the same; and at the end of the whole description, is given, a recapitulation, and grand summary, for the whole United States.

NEW-ENGLAND NAVIGATION.

M.—From the mouth of Merrimack river, below Newburyport, up the stream, by a ship passage, twenty miles, to Haverhill, Massachusetts, and thence, by a navigation rendered boatable, or to be so rendered, by canals and other improvements, at sundry rapids and falls, up to the mouth of Baker's river, near Plymouth, in Grafton county, New-Hampshire.

Distance, *Miles*, 130

No. 1.
MERRIMACK CANALS.

The particulars of these improvements are as follows:—
1. Bow canal, at Gardner's falls, 4 miles below Concord, New-Hampshire; 25 feet overcome by 4 locks and a dam; distance one-third of a mile. Expense, - - $19,000
2. Hooksett canal, at 7 miles below, 16 feet fall, overcome by three locks; distance two-thirds of a mile. Expense, - - - - - 13,000
3. Amoskeag canal, at 2 miles below, 45 feet fall, overcome by 9 locks and several dams; distance 1 mile. Expense, - - - - 60,000
4. The Union canal, immediately below, comprising 6 sets of falls, overcome by 7 locks; distance 9 miles. Expense, - - - - - 35,000
5. Cromwell's falls, 5 miles below, made passable by 1 lock. Expense, - - - - 9,000
6. Wiccasee falls, 15 miles below, made passable by 1 lock of 10 feet. Expense, - - - 12,000
7. Patucket canal, 4 miles below, 34 feet fall, overcome by 3 locks; distance 4 miles.

From Patucket falls to Haverhill, the descent is 45 feet; distance 36 miles.

Above the town of Concord, up to Plymouth, it is proposed that a new survey shall be made, with a view to a thorough improvement of the navigation between those points, whether to be effected for more or less of the distance upon the river stream, or by means of one continuous canal along the valley.

A.—From Baker's river last mentioned, near Plymouth, by canal, across the valley and the sources of Muscomy river, to a point on the Connecticut, at or near Hanover, or Lebanon, on the Muscomy; or otherwise, perhaps, up the valley of Baker's river, and down that of the Oliverian, which discharges into the Connecticut river, at Haverhill. Supposed amount of lockage, 500 feet. Distance, *Miles*, 35

No. 2:
BAKER'S RIVER AND OLIVERIAN CANAL.

This, together with some of the articles which follow, are projects now on foot for improving and extending the navigation of New-England, and especially in regard to the Connecticut valley, and the waters of the Connecticut river. A convention of the several states took place in January last, (1825) on the occasion, and committees were chosen, and commissioners have been appointed, to promote the objects, and superintend the works, for general utility. This article is to constitute, too, a small but important link of a general and most comprehensive chain.

1828. NOTE.

A survey of this canal route was gone into under an officer of the United States corps of engineers; according to which, the summit ridge was found situate at $11\frac{1}{2}$ miles from the Connecticut river; its height 683.45 feet above the same, and 549.45 feet above the Pemigewasset. Length of the whole canal, by the line surveyed, $39\frac{3}{4}$ miles. But it appears that some misunderstanding occurred during the operation, in consequence of which a re-survey is to take place, and then it is thought that not only some of the high ground gone over will be avoided, but the distance be somewhat shortened.

This prevents an exact plan of the canal from being laid down for the present. The resources for a supply of water to the summit, so far as yet ascertained, consist in the discharge from Baker's river, from the Tarlton or Eastman's two ponds, and the supply that may be derived from the latter as reservoirs.

This canal is planned to meet, at the point of intersecting the Pemigewasset, a line of canal passing from thence, through Squam lake and the Winnepiseogee lake, to tide water of the Piscataqua river, and connecting, consequently, by a direct line of navigation, the Connecticut river at Haverhill, with the seaport of Portsmouth, New-Hampshire, as described at article No. 4.

A route has been surveyed between the Connecticut river, at Sugar river, below Clairmont, and the Merrimack, near Concord, by way of Sugar river valley and the Sunapee lake; also by the valley of Blackwater river and the Conticook. The summit level here is the Sunapee lake, which is an immense body of water, insomuch that no doubt of an ample supply for a canal can exist. Distance of the lake from the Connecticut river, by the path of the survey, $25\frac{7}{8}$ miles, and from the Merrimack, $42\frac{5}{8}$;

together making, for length of canal, 68½ miles, besides 3¼ for crossing the lake. Total, 71¾ miles.

The lake is calculated to be not only the summit reservoir, but the summit pass also of the canal. Its level, 786.09 feet above the Connecticut river, and 859.04 above the Merrimack, making, for lockage, a total of 1645.13 feet.

M.—From the foot of Fifteen-mile falls, or head of M'Indoe's falls in Connecticut river, at Barnet in Vermont, by boat navigation, down to Hartford in Connecticut; rapids and falls in the way having been overcome, many years since, by improvements, to a certain degree. At present, additional improvements are on foot, to render the navigation more perfect.

Distance, *Miles*, 220

No. 3.
CONNECTICUT RIVER CANALS.

Improvements along the river, up to this point, or to a point above Newberry in Vermont, have heretofore been made; but not so as to obtain in low water season a good boatable navigation beyond the north line of Massachusetts, and the object now is to augment the facilities, and to render the whole of this distance passable for steam-boats of burthen, or steam-boats for towing loaded boats of burthen. Surveyors have been appointed, and the business is in progress. Moreover, the general government have undertaken to continue the examination of this river, upward from Barnet to its source in lake Connecticut, on the border of Maine and Lower Canada.

The descent of the river, from Barnet, to Hartford in Connecticut, is 420 feet. This, it is proposed to overcome by dams, and locks, and short canals, at the several places; extending together about twenty miles, and making, consequently, two hundred miles of slack water navigation. Estimate of cost for these improvements, including purchases of the existing locks and canals, 1,439,827 dollars.

In November 1825, the legislature of Vermont passed an act of incorporation in favour of a company, as "The Connecticut River Company," to embrace the object, and to take effect after being confirmed by the legislatures of New-Hampshire, Connecticut, and Massachusetts. Before which last, however, the matter is still pending; the two others have concurred.

The act goes to empower the company to receive a transfer of rights and privileges, from any and all prior associations incorporated for local improvements; and to raise by subscription a capital of 1,500,000 dollars, for the purpose of effecting the suggested improvements; which are as below stated, viz.

(Massachusetts has since concurred.)

1. At Enfield falls, 10 miles above Hartford, estimate of cost, $119,885
2. At South Hadley, various alterations, 194,027
3. At and near Hadley, 15,143
4. Below Montague falls, 13 miles, 36,005
5. At Montague falls, 89,000
6. At and near Miller's falls, 25,217
7. At Cooper's rocks, near the New-Hampshire line, 46,445
8. Opposite Brattleboro', a dam and canal, 57,420
9. At Clay's Island, 12 miles below Bellows falls, 27,504
10. At Bellows falls, 107,313
11. At the north of Charlestown, 46,610
12. At Dean's flat, 2 miles below Windsor bridge, 36,570
13. At Quechy falls, between Hartfield and Plainfield, 59,369
14. At White river falls, Lebanon, 85,709
15. Opposite Bradford, a dam and canal, 29,725
16. Near Newberry, 66,486
17. At Barnet, 19,286

Sundries additional, together with purchase of the old locks and canals, 378,113

Total amount up to Barnet, $1,439,827

The number of locks requisite will be 41. Dams 16. There will be 17 miles of the navigation through short canals, and 202 miles, or thereabouts, of river slack water navigation, the pools averaging 12 miles in length, more or less.

Above Barnet, the river obstructions are formidable. The descent from lake Connecticut is 1120 feet; thus,—

Level of the lake to Eames' dam at Stewardstown, Feet, 562
Thence to Sommers' dam at Dalton, the head of Fifteen-mile falls, 222
The Fifteen-mile falls, which includes 20 miles line of level, 336

Carried forward, 1,120

	Brought forward,	1,120
From foot of Fifteen-mile falls, to foot of M'Indoe's falls, between Barnet and Lyman,		50
Descent from the lake to this point, - -	Feet,	1,170

At Barnet, these improvements, contemplated by the Connecticut River Company, intersect the surveys now making by the general government, with a view of opening a communication between the waters of lake Ontario, and the Atlantic shore, through the Piscataqua and Kennebeck rivers, as noticed at Article 10.

But, besides the improvement of the Connecticut river navigation as here particularized, by locks and dams, up to Barnet, it is likewise under consideration to cause such additions to be made to the Farmington, and the Hampshire and Hampden canals, (hereinafter described,) as will go to form one continued line of canal up to the same point, a distance in all of 270 miles; that is to say, from New-Haven, through Connecticut and Massachusetts, to Barnet in Vermont.

NOTE.

As intimated above, a complete examination of the upper waters of the Connecticut, beginning at Barnet, the point where the New-England surveyors left off, and extending to lake Connecticut in the high lands bordering New-Hampshire, Maine, and Lower Canada, has been gone through with; as likewise an examination for an intended canal route between the Connecticut river and Lake Memphramagog.

These preliminary surveys are now reported to the war department of the United States, and as it thence appears that the project last mentioned is practicable, the article here following is in consequence inserted.

A.—From a point of the Connecticut river, at the mouth of the Nulhegan, or of the Pasumpsic, by canal, up the valley thereof, to a summit level at the Green Mountains, Vermont, and thence down to a point of Lake Memphramagog.   Distance, *Miles,* 50

No. 4.
CONNECTICUT AND MEMPHRAMAGOG CANAL.

The route from the lake to Connecticut river, by the Clyde

and the valley of the Nulhegan, presents, it is understood, less difficulty for the construction of a canal, than the route by the Pasumpsic valley. The principal feeder is Knowlton lake in the town of Random: summit level 495 feet above Lake Memphramagog, and 296 feet above the Connecticut at the mouth of Nulhegan river; together 791 feet, the lockage required.

The route to the Connecticut by the Barton and Pasumpsic river valleys, has Willoughby lake for feeder, in the town of Westmore. Summit, 523 feet above Lake Memphramagog, 755 above the Pasumpsic river mouth; together 1278 feet.

A route by Black river, and passing through Danville, was surveyed, but not found eligible; the summit elevated.

NOTE.

A survey of the Pasumpsic route has been made under an officer of the United States corps of engineers, from which it appears, that a summit has been established at a ground called Savannah pond, and this found to be 803 feet above the Connecticut level, also 572.69 feet above the Barton at the point where this river can be made use of, to Lake Memphramagog,—the adjacent country does not any where offer a convenient and sufficient supply of water for the proposed canal, except it be at Willoughby lake; and on determining the level of this lake, it was unfortunately found to be 58.88 below the Savannah pond summit; so that a canal is here impracticable, unless an extensive deepcutting at the summit be resorted to. Moreover, it has not yet been ascertained how the water can best be conducted from Willoughby lake to the summit; but if taken from the southern end, a tunnel of 1¼ mile may be necessary, besides a winding feeder of several miles in length. Further examinations are to be gone into. The distance from Savannah pond summit to the Connecticut river, by the line surveyed, 33¼ miles, and to the point of Barton river, 13¾ miles; together 47 miles.

Should the connexion of the Connecticut river and Lake Memphramagog be realized, as contemplated in the present article, it may possibly, in time, become an essential part of one direct line of navigable communication between Boston harbour and the River St. Lawrence; the line in question comprising improvements as here follows:—

1. The Middlesex canal in Massachusetts.
2. Canals around falls in Merrimack river.
3. The Merrimack and Connecticut canal, by the Baker and Oliverian river valleys.
4. A part of the Connecticut river improvements.
5. The Connecticut and Memphramagog canal, as here inserted.

6. Improvements of the St. Francis river of Lower Canada, between Lake Memphramagog and the St. Lawrence.

M.—From Lake Memphramagog, by the valleys of Black and La Moelle rivers, to the north of the latter on Lake Champlain, 8 miles north of Burlington. Distance by canal, or canal and river stream improved, *Miles*, 75

No. 5.

MEMPHRAMAGOG AND CHAMPLAIN CANAL.

A survey for this proposed connexion, as being the western division of a route from the Connecticut river to Lake Champlain, by way of Lake Memphramagog, has been effected, by a detachment from the United States corps of engineers, but the results have not as yet been reported upon in detail. It is however understood, that the construction of a canal along this route is shown to be not only practicable, but exempt from any unusual difficulty.

M.—From the tide water of the Piscataqua river, above the harbour of Portsmouth, New-Hampshire, or from the navigable water of the Cocheco, below Dover, by canal, up the valley, and across to Lake Winnepiseogee, through which, and across to Squam lake, and thence across to the Pemigewasset or Upper Merrimack river, at Holderness, below Plymouth Courthouse. Distance, by canal, 40, by lake navigation 20, together, *Miles*, 60

No. 6.

THE WINNEPISEOGEE CANAL.

The New-England committee on improvements have caused the principal section of this proposed work to be surveyed, for a commencement to be made in it; viz., from the Piscataqua, at tide water, to the mouth of Merrymeeting or Willey's river, south extremity of Lake Winnepiseogee; the distance, so far, on the route, being 28 miles ; the waters of the lake 501 feet above tide level, requiring lockage accordingly. It is proposed for this canal to be 30 feet wide, 4 feet deep, the locks 82 feet long, and of stone. The engineer's estimate of cost is 590,982 dollars; and, in addition, about 74,000 dollars for the continuation from Lake Winnepiseogee to Holderness, on the Upper Merrimack.

The lake will form a summit level, with an abundance of water to supply the canal on both sides.

A company, originally instituted in 1811, for this undertaking, have had their charter renewed. Capital stock, 600,000 dollars.

NOTE.

A resurvey of this canal route has been made, under an officer of the United States corps of engineers. It commences from a station on the Cocheco, at Dover, passing by the valley thereof, up to a summit table land between this and Willey's river, elevated 54 feet above the starting point at Dover ; and thence, after gaining a second summit, between Willey's river and Lake Winnepiseogee, it passes to Alten bay, which is found to be, by the line of route now surveyed, 29¾ miles distant from Dover ; and, according to the same, the highest land between Willey's river and Lake Winnepiseogee is at the 28th mile, say 564 feet above the said starting point, or 572.35 above low water mark, and this makes the level of Lake Winnepiseogee 517.21 feet above low tide water.

As stated above, it was intended to consider this great lake as the summit of the canal, from whence to draw the supply of water for the whole distance, after sufficiently deepening the level of the canal ; but this, it appears, would in fact be cutting through an extensive summit range of land, which, although clearly practicable, would prove costly in the extreme. And, it is in consequence recommended, with a view to obviate a part of the deep cutting in question, that a certain length of Willey's river, after being raised by means of a dam and lock, and furnished with a towing path, should be used as a canal. But it is also recommended so to alter the original plan, as to abandon the use of the Winnepiseogee water, and adopt the Merrymeeting pond, from whence the river Willey originates, as a source of supply for the canal navigation—a source which it is supposed cannot fail of being ample, the calculation being that the works can be so constructed as to ensure a supply at the rate of 260 cubic feet of water per second during the driest season.

No portion of the Cocheco stream, nor any of its tributaries, is contemplated as being applicable to the uses of this canal. All that valuable water-power is already taken up, and employed most usefully in supplying the flourishing cotton factories at Dover.

A.—From Portland harbour, at the mouth of Presumscut river in Casco bay, state of Maine, by canal, up the valley, to Sebago lake, and thence up to Bear pond in Waterford. Distance, *Miles*, 50

No. 7.
OXFORD AND CUMBERLAND CANAL.

For this proposed canal, or canals, the legislature of Maine passed an act of incorporation two years ago, but the work is not yet commenced; it is expected to be placed under contract in the approaching season, (1827.) The route was surveyed, and the expense of the work for the first 17 miles, viz. between Portland harbour and Sebago lake, estimated at 138,000 dollars.

Towards promoting the enterprise, some considerable privileges have been granted by the state in favour of the company. Bear pond is 143 feet above tide level.

A.—From Bear pond, the point last above mentioned, by canal, to a point of the Androscoggin river, at or near Bethel. Distance, *Miles*, 20

No. 8.
WATERFORD AND BETHEL CANAL.

This is projected as a continuation of the undertaking specified in the foregoing article; by which a communication between Portland harbour and the Androscoggin river is to be effected. No regular survey, however, for this extension, has as yet taken place.

A.—From the Kennebeck river at Gardner, by canal and by way of the Cobbassee Contee river, the Winthrop, the Wilson's, and great Androscoggin ponds, to a point of the Androscoggin river opposite the township of Leeds. Distance, *Miles*, 30

No. 9.
KENNEBECK AND ANDROSCOGGIN, OR THE COBBASSEE CONTEE CANAL.

The proposed connexion of the two rivers, has been the object of a company in Maine, long since organized for the purpose; but no advance in it hitherto is made, except the surveying of the ground. One survey was made many years ago, and another took place in the season last past, under an officer of the United States corps of engineers, reported upon to the war department.

Between the levels of the two rivers, the Kennebeck at Gardner or mouth of the Cobbassee Contee, and the Androscoggin river at Leeds, there is an ascent of 260 feet, one half of which occurs within the first 1½ mile; that is to say, between Gardner's wharf, Kennebeck river, and the Iron works pond dam, at 7200 feet above the Cobbassee Contee; and this, it has been suggested, might possibly be overcome by means of an inclined plane; in addition to which, it was thought, that by adopting a series of lock and dam constructions, and the clearing away of such obstacles in the Cobbassee Contee river and other natural channels along the route, as should prove susceptible of being cleared away, there might not be occasion for more than about 4 miles, or 4½ miles of excavation and regular canal works, to complete the entire navigable communication for freight boats; which expectation appears to be more than confirmed, by the recent survey alluded to above; except, however, that it is recommended by the United States engineers, the Cobbassee Contee *canal* should not extend eastward of the Iron works pond, but there terminate; and that from thence to Gardner, the improvements should consist in an excellent, well-constructed road, as a rail road.

In this proposed route of communication, the canal works are, viz.

1. Between the great Androscoggin and Wilson's ponds, distant near 2 miles, and much costly deep cutting requisite, averaging in ¾ of a mile not less than 60 feet.

2. To overcome a fall of 70 feet in 6200 feet distance, on Wilson's creek, between Wilson's and south Winthrop ponds.

3. At Cram's mills on the Cobbassee Contee river, 10 miles above the Iron works; a canal of 2000 feet, to overcome a fall in that distance of 13 feet.

The descent of 134 feet, existing between the Iron works pond and the Kennebeck river at Gardner, goes at present all to form water power, which, during the dry season of the year, and especially on the occurrence of any unusual drought, is needed in toto, by the numerous manufacturing establishments already to be seen in prosperous activity along the Cobbasse Contee stream.

The discharges of water from the several ponds, in August, were as follows:—

Great Androscoggin, - - 101 ⎫
Wilson's pond, - - - 27 ⎬ Cubic feet per second.
South Winthrop, - - - 49 ⎪
Cobbassee Contee, at Cram's mills, 93 ⎭

A change in the line of route, with a view of obviating some difficulty, has been recently suggested from a very intelligent quarter, and merits to be thoroughly examined into. It proposes entirely to avoid the Androscoggin pond, and to join the river above the township of Leeds.

But, besides thus connecting the Kennebeck and Androscoggin rivers, the company's object has been, and continues to be, to improve the navigation of the latter, above the point of connexion, and by canal to strike across to the Connecticut, as specified in the article which here next follows:—No. 10.

NOTE.

A project which has at times appeared, though of considerable importance, yet of doubtful execution, so as to embrace all the advantages desired from it, is that of uniting, by means of a short canal, the waters of Merrymeeting and Casco bays. It has been styled, the "Brunswick canal," and an accurate survey of the ground in reference to it is at present on foot.

There are two methods of effecting the union in question; namely, through a summit level, with the necessary locks, and a feeder canal taking its supply of water from the Androscoggin river, above Brunswick falls; and by a direct communication or thorough cut canal, by way of the "New meadows." But this latter route would not, as it appears, afford the essential requisites of a navigation intercourse between places situate on the waters of the two bays, free from sea exposure by the way. On the other plan, a route has been proposed, extending in distance from bay to bay $5\frac{1}{8}$ miles, the feeder canal from above Brunswick falls $2\frac{2}{8}$ miles in length, to intersect the same at a point $3\frac{5}{8}$ miles from Casco bay, and $1\frac{3}{8}$ miles from the Merrymeeting. Descent from summit level, to medium high tide of middle Casco bay, 38.61 feet, and from the same to low water mark on the Androscoggin 44.38 feet.

M.—From the point last above indicated, on the Androscoggin river at or near Leeds, up the course of the same, to the mouth of Dead river, above Shelburne, New-Hampshire, and thence, by canal, across, by the valleys of Dead river and upper Ammonosack, to the Connecticut river at Northumberland. Distance by canal, or by canal and stream improvements together, Miles, 130

No. 10.

ANDROSCOGGIN AND CONNECTICUT CANAL.

A survey upon this article at large, was expected to be gone into by the United States engineers, so as to form groundwork for an immediate decision, upon the great contemplated section of internal communication embraced by this and the preceding article: namely, from the Connecticut river at Northumberland, by the valley of the Ammonosack, to the Androscoggin, and down this latter to the point of junction with the Cobbassee Contee route, through which, to join the Kennebeck river at Gardner; but the two extremes only of this line, have as yet been surveyed; the long course of the Androscoggin itself, is yet untouched, except so far as a very cursory examination goes; from which, however, it would appear probable, that this river does not admit of being improved in its bed, by means of locks and dams, to obtain a good navigation; and consequently, the only plan remaining to be considered of for uniting the two extremes, is, that of an independent canal, lateral to the said river, and along its valley; with a view to which, a regular survey is recommended. It would be advisable also, to extend the survey of the Androscoggin valley down to Brunswick falls; as the result may have an influence on the projected canal route from thence to Casco bay, designated above.

The route of connexion surveyed between the Androscoggin river and the Connecticut at Northumberland, commences at the Dead river pond, which may be considered as a natural reservoir, and is nearly on the summit of the line. In a distance of 7160 feet, it is 141 feet above the Androscoggin level; but as this river rises precipitously, and at the head of a series of falls, and violent rapids, where the elevation is $41\frac{1}{2}$ feet above the Dead river pond level at low water, it is proposed a feeder shall receive water from the Androscoggin, to supply the canal summit. Length of this feeder 6100 feet.

The character of the country through which both feeder and main canal are to pass, is rugged in the extreme. Soil—clay, and granite rocks.

At $5\frac{1}{8}$ miles from the Androscoggin, by the route surveyed, the south end of the Ammonosack pond, the origin of the Ammonosack river, is struck, the north end whereof is nearly $24\frac{1}{2}$ miles from the Connecticut, making for the whole distance, as surveyed, $31\frac{1}{2}$ miles, length of the pond inclusive. The descent to the Connecticut level, taken at a low state of the water, is found to be 231.50 feet, and to the Androscoggin 154.32 feet, making a lockage up and down, of 385.82 feet, in case this pond, rather than the Dead river pond, be adopted for a summit level to the canal. The latter is 13.32 feet less elevated. It has been suggested to raise this by a dam at its outlet, to a level with the Ammonosack pond, and by a thorough cut to throw both into one, thus causing the whole extent of these ponds, and the thorough cut, to form a part of the canal, and be a summit reservoir.

The practicability of constructing this canal, and giving it a command of an abundant supply of water, is questionable, but if practicable, it is not a little desirable to have not only this and the Cobbassee Contee project both realized, but the two united by an intermediate navigable communication, by such means as shall be found to avail; if not by works of improvement in the bed of the river, according to the ideas that have been entertained on the subject; then, by an independent canal along the valley thereof. Besides the great importance of it to the immediate local trade, particularly in lumber, it will make an addition to the grand New-England chain spoken of, as may be seen on the map. The internal trader and navigator may then stretch from the Piscataqua in New-Hampshire, from Portland on Casco bay, and from Bath on Merrymeeting bay, state of Maine, direct to the St. Francis river, Lower Canada, equally as from Boston harbour already noticed, by way of the Connecticut river.

NOTE.

The improvements thus far designated; namely,—
> The navigation of the Merrimack, the Connecticut, and the Androscoggin rivers, or canals along their valleys.
>
> A connexion by canal, between the Upper Merrimack and the Connecticut rivers.
>
> Connexion by canal, between the Connecticut and Lake Champlain, via Lake Memphramagog.
>
> Connexion by canal, between the Merrimack and tide water of the Piscataqua.
>
> Connexion by canal, between the Androscoggin river and Portland harbour.
>
> Connexion by canal, between the Androscoggin and Kennebeck rivers.

These, together with,—
The canal connexion between Lake Champlain and the
River St. Lawrence, as designated at article No. 27,
being once accomplished, there will be laid open a number of
direct communications between the waters of Lake Ontario and
the Atlantic shores, across the states of Maine and New-Hampshire.

This is the object taken into view by the surveys made and
making by certain detachments from the corps of United States
engineers, of the Androscoggin, Kennebeck, and Upper Connecticut rivers, and the canal routes appertaining.

M.—From Augusta, on the Kennebeck river, up the
course of the stream, and, taking the western, otherwise named the Dead river branch, up to the Highlands between Maine and Lower Canada; there to
form a junction by canal with the waters of the Chaudiere river of Lower Canada, which discharges into
the St. Lawrence, above Quebec. Distance, by
stream improvements and canal navigation together,
Miles, 200

No. 11.
KENNEBECK RIVER CANALS.

Application was some time since made by the state of Maine
to the general government, for surveys to be made of the Kennebeck river: the which, as well as other surveys already noticed in the articles preceding, has in part been accomplished.
The dangerous pass of Lovejoy's narrows, in tide water, between the mouth of the river and the town of Gardner, has, in
the first place, had the engineer's attention. A plan of works
for removing the danger is reported, and an appropriation is, by
congress, made for its execution. Between Lovejoy's narrows
and the town of Gardner are situated two shoals, stretching
across, called the "Sands," over one of which there is not found
a depth of more than 6 to 7 feet of water in the channel at low
tide, which calls for improvement, if to be accomplished within
any reasonable bounds of expense. At Shepherd's landing, too,
Hallowell, the channel is narrow, and requires to be widened.
But between Hallowell and the bridge at Augusta, there is a
more urgent call for improvement, the river being at places so

shoal, as absolutely to restrict the present navigation to time of high water, or to a short space of time during each successive tide. Above the bridge at Augusta, where sloop navigation has terminated, and the tide ceases to act, up to Taconic bay, or the bridge at Waterville, is a distance of 18¾ miles of boatable navigation, but requiring to be facilitated by the removal of a number of existing obstacles along the channel. The Taconic fall and rapids immediately above, are not to be effectually overcome but by a continuous canal, extending from the vicinity above Kendall's mills to Taconic bay, below Waterville, a distance of 4½ miles, with a difference of 55 feet from surface to surface of the water for lockage in that distance. This important improvement once effected, and the river channel improved at several rapids, above Kendall's mills, as can readily be done by enlarging the gaps in the ledges of rocks, there will be laid open a fine continued boat navigation, from Taconic bay up to Scowhegan eddy, which is a fine deep basin of water, below the falls of that name, and 80 miles from the mouth of the river. The Falls of Scowhegan are very formidable; they have been surveyed, however, and at this point of the Kennebeck the surveys of the United States engineers have ceased for the present. It appears that the descent from still water above the rapids, to still water of the eddy below, is 26.05 feet, and would include, for a canal, an extensive deep-cutting. The river in this distance is confined to a narrow channel, its banks mural precipices, and current extremely rapid.

In Taconic bay the water level is 36 feet above high tide at Augusta bridge. Distance from Scowhegan falls up to Norridgewock 5 miles.

It is desirable that surveys on the upper parts of the Kennebeck should be made, to ascertain, with regard to the practicability and the expediency of such improvements thereon, by canal or other works, as may be likely to confer, amongst the advantages contemplated, the special one of leading to, and establishing, a connexion with the River St. Lawrence, by way of the Chaudiere, or Kettle river, as above suggested; that is to say, always with a proviso, that the Canadian government should see proper concurrently to promote the object. Its accomplishment would form a short and direct water communication between Quebec and the Atlantic, through the central parts of the state of Maine.

From Augusta, on the main Kennebeck, up to the confluence of the east and west branches, is about 100 miles; and thence, by the windings of the west branch, or Dead river, to the source thereof, at the summit, in common with the sources of the Chaudiere, the distance is about another 100 miles, or the same as by the east branch, through Moose Head lake.

It was by this route, then emphatically a wilderness, that the noted General Arnold, at the commencement of the revolution war, penetrated to Quebec. At that very period, too, there prevailed in *England* a strong opinion, that but for the death of General Montgomery, the great American enterprise would have been carried. For the solidity of which opinion, the writer (who was a witness) presumes not to vouch, but may say, in favour of *events as they are*, that in all probability it is a happiness to the world, and especially this western world, the bold attempt failed of being crowned with full success. No one will presume to affirm, what state of things, different from the present happy one, would have taken place, had the key of the St. Lawrence been lost to the British empire.

NOTE.

However the event may be, as to the internal communication by water with Lower Canada, as suggested in this article, there is little or no doubt at all as to the maintaining of a good road of communication between the settlements of the Kennebeck and the Chaudiere, being regarded as an object of interest on both sides. It will enlarge the scale of intercourse, to mutual benefit, and especially during the season of winter. The legislature of Maine have just voted a sum of 5000 dollars towards the object, and congress have now before them the measure of constructing a military road as far as the boundary line of the state.

A.—From the Penobscot river, at Bangor, at the mouth of the Kenduskeag, or near the same, by canal, up the valley, to Pushaw Great pond, or lake.

Distance, *Miles*, 6

No. 12.

THE PUSHAW CANAL.

This intended canal is somewhat detached in situation, from the general great continuous line of improvements herein undertaken to be described. It comes, however, into relation with the largest river of the state of Maine and its navigation, and is esteemed of much local importance. Its object is lumber; with which the country around the Pushaw lake is abundantly stocked.

The legislature of Massachusetts formerly passed an act of incorporation in favour of the project; but the work was delayed, and a new charter has now been granted by the legislature of Maine.

N.—From Hartford, on Connecticut river, down the stream, by a sloop and ship navigation, to the sea, at Saybrook, Long Island sound; whence, along the sound, and up to New-Haven, at the head of New-Haven bay. Distance, *Miles*, 85

A.—From the city and port of New-Haven, by canal, through the state of Connecticut, to the north line thereof, at Southwick, in Massachusetts; passing through the town of Farmington; and also from Farmington, up the Farmington river course, to the north line of the town of Colebrook, it being the state line; passing through the town of New-Hartford, Connecticut. Distance, from New-Haven to Southwick 50, from Farmington village to the Colebrook line 25 : together, *Miles*, 75

No. 13.

THE FARMINGTON CANAL.

For this canal, an act of incorporation was granted by the state of Connecticut, in 1822, authorizing subscriptions to a capital at the discretion of the company ; and it being understood that the state of Massachusetts would extend the line of the canal into that commonwealth, to a convenient point of the Connecticut river. The work will now go into execution with a prospect of being completed at an early period, being highly favourably reported upon as to facility of construction, and a plentiful supply of water, with a choice in the line of route : which, from Farmington to New-Haven, will probably be along the Southington and Cheshire valleys. In the distance from Southwick to New-Haven, about fifty miles, there will be required a ten foot lock for every three miles of canal, or nearly so.

NOTE.

These works are in progress. The excavation of the Farmington canal commenced in September 1825, and it is supposed the whole canal will be finished in 1827, or 1828. The engineer's estimate of cost, for the line between New-Haven and Southwick ponds, is 420,000 dollars; but the work is partly under contract, at twenty per cent. less than the estimate. Distance, according to survey, 58 miles; lockage, 218 feet. Over the Farmington river, there will be thrown an aqueduct of 280 feet, and in height 34 feet above the river surface. It is proposed, as to the branch canal up the Farmington, to carry it, for the present, only to New-Hartford, a distance of 15 miles; the estimate for which is 101,773 dollars. Width of canal to be 36 feet; depth of water, four feet; width at the bottom 20 feet: its commencement at New-Haven harbour, from a basin of 20 acres capacity. The construction of the dam across the Farmington river, at the head of the feeder, to be of stone laid in hydraulic mortar, and 11 feet high. The locks 80 feet long in the clear, and 12 feet wide: their construction, a wooden frame, planked water-tight, and supported by walls of dry masonry.

A.—From the ponds at Southwick above mentioned, by canal, northward, across the river Westfield, to a convenient point of junction with the Connecticut river, above Northampton.   Distance, *Miles*, 20

No. 14.
WESTFIELD AND NORTHAMPTON CANAL.

This, as above stated, is a proposed continuation, within the state of Massachusetts, of the Farmington canal.

NOTE.

The Westfield and Northampton, otherwise called the Hampshire and Hampden canal, is to be, as already stated, a prolongation, within the state of Massachusetts, of the Farmington canal. There has been a very recent survey; and the estimated expense of the work, from Southwick to its junction with the Connecticut river, at the Great Bend, about two miles above the village of Northampton, making large allowances, is 290,000 dollars; to which amount of stock, books for subscription are in consequence opened, at the different places most interested in the work. The width of the canal to be at bottom 20 feet, at the surface of the water 34 feet; the banks to be 6 feet high; locks, 12 feet in the clear, and 90 feet long. Distance measured at the survey, 29 miles; lockage, 298 feet.

The company associated for the work here specified, and the Farmington canal company, purpose applying to their respective legislatures, for an act of joint incorporation; so as to constitute the whole, in fact, but one canal. And it is to be noted, that the present view is, to extend this important canal upwards to the south line of Vermont state, near to Brattleborough, and thence into that state, along the banks of Connecticut river, as far as the mouth of Wells' river at least. The local facilities for this continuation are said to be not inferior to those afforded for what is already undertaken; and it is made clearly to appear, from facts known and stated, that to and from the port of New-Haven, along this canal, to whatever distance it may be carried, the trade will be very great and lucrative. The copious streams in the route, to be taken into service, will besides give opportunities of tapping this canal, along many miles of its length, almost at pleasure; so as to afford water power for machinery and manufacturing purposes, to an indefinite extent; perhaps, too, in a few instances, for irrigation.

A.—From a point on the Connecticut river, at or near Windsor, by canal, across the state of Vermont, and touching perhaps near the head waters of Otter river, or by Castleton and Fairhaven, and the Pulteney river, to Lake Champlain, at Whitehall; or otherwise, from a point of the Connecticut, at or near the mouth of White river, below Norwich, to a point of Lake Champlain, at or near Burlington.

Distance, *Miles*, 100

No. 15.

CONNECTICUT AND CHAMPLAIN CANAL. OR MONTPELIER CANAL.

At a meeting of delegates from the counties of Chittenden, Washington, Orange, and Caledonia, in Vermont, convened at Montpelier, in June last, (1825,) commissioners were appointed to ascertain as to the practicability of this connexion; and they have made a report, which states, as the result of their examinations—viz.

That the canal may commence at the shore of Lake Champlain, and pass up Onion river valley, through Williston and Richmond, to Bolton falls. Distance, 21 miles; rise, at the point of outset, in Burlington village, 220 feet.

From Bolton falls to Montpelier, is 16 miles; ascent, 174 feet.

From Montpelier, through Plainfield and Marshfield, to Onion pond, 21 miles; ascent, 877 feet.

From Onion pond to Connecticut river, at the mouth of Wells river. Distance, 19 miles; descent, 918 feet.

Or, from Montpelier, through Barre and Williamstown, to Cutter's pond summit; ascent, 363 feet. Thence to the Connecticut, at the mouth of White river; descent, 486 feet.

Or, from Montpelier, up the valley of Dog river, through Berlin and Northfield, to a summit in Roxbury: distance, 16 miles; ascent, 484 feet. Thence to the Connecticut, at the mouth of White river; descent, 590 feet.

In consequence of which reconnoissance and report, measures are taken, by the legislature, for an accurate and complete survey.

In regard to the southern route specified in the text above, there is proposed to be constructed along a portion thereof, a canal, as designated in the article which here follows:—No. 16.

NOTE.

A survey of this important communication has been made, under an officer of the United States corps of engineers, the route to have its termination on the Connecticut, at the mouth of White river.

The lowest place at which the highlands, between the Champlain and the Connecticut waters, in this direction, can be passed, is in that dividing ridge called the Hog's back, and through Cutter's pond; assuming which pond as a summit, the survey makes the distance thence, through Montpelier, the capital of Vermont, and through Onion river valley, to a debouche on the lake, in good water, near Burlington, $59\frac{7}{8}$ miles, 200 feet; the level of the lake 818.58 feet below Cutter's pond; and the distance to the Connecticut river $43\frac{3}{8}$ miles, 380 feet; difference of levels 579.34 feet. Total length of canal $103\frac{1}{4}$ miles, 580 feet. Total rise and fall 1397.92 feet.

But for the supply of this canal with water, it unfortunately happens that the examinations made, have ascertained the resources of the country as not being adequate. All that could be calculated on, even on the supposition of an expensive tunnel summit, made to accommodate the reception of a part of this supply, appears to be as follows:—

Discharge from Clarke and Cold ponds, 9.20 ⎫
               Pierce's pond, - - 1.55 ⎬ Cubic feet
               Second branch, - - 1.78 ⎱ per second.
               Stephen's branch, - 10.00 ⎭

Total supply for a tunnel summit of 4 miles, 22.53 cubic feet per second.

To secure, if possible, the execution of a work calculated to form so strong a feature in the general assemblage of improvements of the kind begun and contemplated, the engineer recommends that the summit of this route be passed by a rail road.

A.—From Rutland, on the Otter, by canal, westward, across the valley of Pulteney river, and through Castleton, or Pulteney, to Whitehall on Lake Champlain, head of the New-York canals. Distance, *Miles*, 25

No. 16.

RUTLAND AND WHITEHALL CANAL.

A charter has been granted by the legislature of Vermont, for the construction of this proposed canal, and concurred in by that of New-York. It being planned to form a junction with the New-York northern canal, the project lays claim to objects not a little interesting to both states.

As the stream of Otter river passes at some distance from the town of Rutland, it is proposed, in order to accommodate the trade of the place, to obtain a nearer position for the forming of a basin, and this, on the present occasion, presents itself in a natural enclosure, requiring but little to be done for an adjustment of it to the purpose; some embankment on one of its sides, by means of earth taken from the bottom, is the chief operation needed. It embraces an area of 10,000 square yards, and may conveniently be fed with water from East creek, within the distance of ½ a mile. From this proposed basin, to the east bank of Pulteney river, which forms the boundary between Vermont and New-York states, the distance by the line of route surveyed, is $18\frac{3}{8}$ miles; the difference of levels or descent, 184 feet; and from thence to the New-York and Champlain canal, in a distance of $7\frac{1}{8}$ miles, the descent is 220.98 feet; making together, for length of canal, 25½ miles, and for lockage thereof required 404.58 feet.

In regard to a supply of water, the streams along the route were gauged, and the following results obtained;—

East creek, - - 32.65 ⎫
Otter creek, near the
 crossing place, 264.00 ⎬ Cubic feet per second.
West creek, - 16.90 ⎪
Bombazine creek, 26.22 ⎭

M.—From the mouth of Otter river, at Ferrisburg, on Lake Champlain, up the stream, and (at points of improvement) by canal, to the head water of the Otter, in Bromley township. Distance through a mixed navigation, *Miles*, 100

No. 17.
OTTER RIVER CANALS.

For this projected work, an act of incorporation has been applied for to the Vermont legislature. The Otter river, or creek so called, furnishes, in general, excellent navigation between the falls, which are at Vergennes, Middlebury, Pittsford, and Rutland.

A.—From the head of Otter river in Bromley township, as inserted in the last article, by canal in continuation, to the upper water, and along the valley of the Battenkill to the New-York line, and thence to the Hudson river, or the Champlain canal, in Washington county, New-York, opposite Saratoga. Distance, 40 miles—deduct so much of it, lying within New-York state, as noticed at No. 34 of the New-York series, 20 miles, *Miles*, 20

No. 18.
THE OTTER AND BATTENKILL CANAL.

This is a continuation of the above line, and is referred to in the New-York series of canals.

A.—From Chelmsford, Massachusetts, on the river Merrimack, above Pawtucket falls, by canal, to Boston harbour. Distance, *Miles*, 29¾

No. 19.

THE MIDDLESEX CANAL.

A charter of incorporation for this undertaking was obtained from the Massachusetts legislature in 1789, but little was done in it by the company, till the year 1793 ; when Mr. Weston, an experienced engineer from England, was invited to run levels, and survey the ground. He did so; and confirmed, by his report, the favourable opinions already entertained. From that time, the work was carried on with an industry commensurate with its importance, through many striking difficulties attendant on its execution at the early period in question; and, in 1804, though not then fully complete, it was laid open for public use. Various additions were afterwards made, and there have necessarily been, from year to year, many repairs and renovations, besides a number of incidental constructions, as buildings, wharves, &c. to accommodate the trade; and purchases of some lands: the cost of all which, together, amounts to about 700,000 dollars. This canal is generally 30 feet wide at the water surface, and 20 feet at the bottom; depth of water 3 feet; height of the banks 4 feet. From the summit level at Concord river, there is a current down the canal of about a half mile per hour, in consequence of a descent or fall of 1 inch per mile. The boats of transportation, which carry 14 tons, are drawn by single horses, at the rate of 3 miles per hour; and the expense of transporting a ton, the whole length of the canal, is 3 dollars and 50 cents, whereof 1 dollar and 70 cents is toll, and 1 dollar and 80 cents freight. Packet boats pass the whole length downwards in 5 hours; upwards in 7 hours. The grant to the Middlesex Canal Company, is a perpetuity.

NOTE.

This canal falls short of the distance specified as above. The Concord, or Sudbury river, which affords a full supply of water in both directions, crosses the line of it at the summit level ; and from thence, by the most recent and accurate measurement, it is 22 miles to Charlestown, and 5 miles to the point of junction with the Merrimack river; together 27. From tide-water, at Charlestown, to the summit, the ascent is 104 feet, and thence to the Merrimack, the descent 32 feet; which is overcome by 20 locks of various lifts ; and these are 75 feet long in the clear, 10 feet wide at the bottom, and 11 feet at the top. The number of aqueducts, over rivers and streams, are 7 ; and there are 50 bridges across the canal, having stone abutments, 20 feet apart. As to aggregate cost, it stands at 528,000 dollars ; that is to say, this is the amount of assessments on the proprietors ; what has been, over and above, expended, was derived from income, appropriated at different times to the object.

During the last war, the timber used in repairing the Constitution frigate, and since then, the timber for building the Independence 74, (live oak excepted), was all brought down this canal to Boston ; and through the same channel, most of the masts, spars, &c. used there, in repairing and fitting out vessels of war, have been supplied. Without the Middlesex canal, this part of the country could not have furnished these articles for the occasion ; but now, there is no part of the United States, where the best white oak timber, for naval purposes, can be so easily, and so abundantly supplied, as from the central parts of New-Hampshire, through the Merrimack river and Middlesex canal. The resources of this quarter, in white oak timber, pine spars, and lumber of various kinds, are inexhaustible for ages to come, or will undoubtedly be rendered so, when the Winnepiseogee country, and the Connecticut river upper valley, come both to be united, by means of canals, with the Merrimack, as is soon to be the case.

Notwithstanding all this, however, and much more that might be said, touching the immense importance of the Middlesex canal, the time has not yet arrived, for the enterprising projectors and proprietors to receive any renumeration, in profit arising from the tolls thereof, or even to have the interest of their expenditure made thereby good to them. This is apparent, from the average annual income of the 3 years last past, not having amounted to quite 30,000 dollars. For 1825, it was only 27,930 dollars. Whereas the calculation is, that about 40,000 dollars income is requisite to yield a dividend of 6 per cent., after paying the expenses of management, and ordinary or average annual repairs. It is true, the corporation is possessed of mills erected at Charlestown, and others at Billerica, on Concord river, as also other real estate of value ; which may contribute to render the concern lucrative.

Moreover, the proprietors are the principal owners of the canals round the several falls of Merrimack river ; which at the present time is a far more productive property, in proportion to the capital invested, than the Middlesex ; the tolls from these canals yielding a large interest upon the cost of them.

Between Concord, New-Hampshire, and the entrance of the Middlesex canal at Chelmsford, the improvements in question, on the river Merrimack, long since effected, are as follows :

At Bow, 4 miles below Concord, a fall of 25 feet in $\frac{1}{2}$ of a mile; overcome by a durable canal with 4 locks, and a dam across the river, at the expense of 19,000 dollars.

Seven miles below this, are the Hooksett falls of 16 feet, running 50 rods; overcome by a canal with 3 locks. Expense 13,000 dollars.

Eight miles farther down, are the Amoskeag falls; overcome by a canal 1 mile in length, with 9 locks, and several extensive dams, at an expense of about 60,000 dollars.

Immediately below, commences the "Union Canal," extending 9 miles, and comprehending 6 sets of rapids or falls. These works have cost about 35,000 dollars; and for this distance of 9 miles, a toll is authorized at the rate of $7\frac{1}{2}$ cents per ton, per mile.

Finally, Wicassee falls, 4 miles above the entrance of the Middlesex canal. These have been locked, at an expense, including some incidentals, of about 12,000 dollars.

But, what is here perhaps most in point, is the very great accession of prosperity, which the Middlesex canal cannot fail to experience, when the great line of New-England connected navigation, at present under contemplation, as herein described, and every day advancing at different points, shall in a measure be realized.

A.—From Boston harbour, southward, across a part of Massachusetts, to communicate with Rhode Island, by way of Taunton river and the Narraganset. This is the route suggested for a canal in the well known report of Mr. Secretary Gallatin, in 1808; and is at the head of a then proposed series of Atlantic canals, adapted to the passage of sea coasting vessels, as at that time under consideration. Distance from Weymouth landing to Taunton, on Taunton river,

Miles, 26

No. 20.

BOSTON AND NARRAGANSET CANAL.

This desirable project was ascertained to be practicable, by an examination made previous to the report mentioned, by order of the Massachusetts legislature; and the ground was again viewed by commissioners of the state, conjointly with a board of United States engineers for internal improvement; which board reported favourably to the war department, under date 3d February

1825. Summit level at Howard's meadow, 133 feet above tide; which by digging 1 mile of distance, may be reduced to 123 feet. Lockage required, consequently, 246. Width of canal suggested, 60 feet; depth, 8 feet; supposed cost, 1,250,000 dollars.

NOTE.

The project of constructing a rail road between Boston and Providence Rhode Island, is at present on foot. As a preliminary on the part of Massachusetts, various courses of the route have been run by their engineer, and levels of the country taken: and plans and estimates are preparing for a proper selection to be made. Forasmuch as the jurisdiction of Rhode Island is concerned, the legislature of that state will, it is understood, pass a law, concurrently with Massachusetts, to promote the object; and if it be to be the undertaking of a corporation under charter, the company to have equal privileges in both states.

JULY, 1829.

The route proposed for this rail road, leaving Boston, passes through the towns of Roxbury, Dedham, Walpole, Foxboro', and across Sekonk plane and cove, to the India bridge, in Providence. Length, 43 miles; ascent, 381½ feet; descent, 378 feet. Difference of level, consequently, between Boston and Providence, 3½ feet. General course, S.S.W.

A.—From Barnstable bay, at the mouth of Scusset river, across the isthmus of Cape Cod, westward, by canal, to the mouth of Back river, on Buzzard's bay; or otherwise, from Barnstable harbour, across, southwardly, to Hyannis harbour. Distance, *Miles*, 7

No. 21.

CAPE COD CANAL.

A canal across this isthmus has long been a subject of speculation, and some years ago a company was organized for the object, in a canal that should be adapted to vessels drawing 10 feet of water; but hitherto obstacles of a formidable character have frustrated its execution. They consist materially in shoals, which obstruct a safe approach from sea, on one side or the other. In addition, the ground through which a canal would have to pass, is found to be porous and springy. Science and experience, it is possible, might overcome this latter obstacle, in case a good approachable harbour for vessels of the requisite draft of water could be found. The most advantageous passage for a canal, would be that between Barnstable and Buzzard's bays; and a survey was made in 1825, by engineers of the United States corps, from the mouth of Scusset to that of Back river; but it would appear, from the report, that a sufficient depth of water is not found over the bar, on either side, for coasting vessels.

An appropriation has been made by Congress, for the improvement of Hyannis harbour.

A.—From Boston harbour, by canal, across Massachusetts, to strike upon Connecticut river; suppose at or near Northampton or Springfield. Distance, *Miles*, 90

No. 22.

BOSTON AND CONNECTICUT, OR CHICKAPEE CANAL.

This is also a work proposed, and especially the object of a resolution of the Massachusetts legislature, at their last session, authorizing the appointment of commissioners, "to ascertain as to the practicability of making a canal from Boston harbour to Connecticut river, and to cause such surveys as they may deem necessary, to determine on the most convenient and advantageous route for the same."

An act of incorporation for a similar undertaking, was passed in the year 1792, in favour of the late general Henry Knox and associates; but, in those days, capital was wanting, and the period limited by the charter was suffered to expire, without the work having been commenced.

NOTE.

Since the above article was written, surveys of the ground have been made; and the engineer, appointed by the governor of Massachusetts to co-operate with the commissioners, having been engaged in this service during the summer and autumn, has just made an elaborate report, (9th Jan. 1826.)

By which it appears, that, as it is desired that this, and the canal in continuation, from Connecticut river to the Hudson, shall come into close connexion with the Erie and Champlain canals of New-York; and it having been ascertained, by reconnoissances, made by the Massachusetts commissioners, that the best route from the Connecticut to the Hudson, is up the valley of the Deerfield river, and down that of the Hoosack, it is in consequence requisite to take a more northerly course for this canal between Boston and the Connecticut, than the route by the Chickapee to Springfield. It may furthermore be requisite to take such northerly route, on account of certain water privileges already granted to the Blackstone canal company; as Worcester long pond, the Blackstone and all its tributary streams, which perhaps may be essential to the success of that undertaking. For these reasons, it has seemed expedient and proper to abandon the southern route; and a complete survey has been made of one, to terminate at the mouth of Miller's river on the Connecticut, and whereof Mud pond, in Ashburnham, forms the summit level, at 1066 feet above low water mark in Boston harbour, and 893 feet above the Connecticut, at the mouth of Miller's river.

From this summit, the route westward passes Pierce's millpond, Whitney's mill at the village in Winchendon, Hyde's bridge, Dennis' pond at New Boston village, in Winchendon, and thence, along by the course of Miller's river, to its mouth, below Durkee's mill-dam.

From the summit of Mud pond, eastward, the route is by the valley of the Brook stream to Gross's mill-dam, to Whitman and Farwell's mills, and along the left bank of the Nashua river to the road in Fitchburg; thence by the valley of Pearlhill brook and Wilder's ridge, and the ponds of Lunenburg, across to the Nashua again at Staple's mills; thence through Shirley, Groton, Littleton, Boxborough, and across Fort pond brook, to Elizabeth river at Sherman's mill-pond; thence to Concord river, above Lee's bridge, and over the high land which divides the waters of the Concord and the Charles, down to Waltham plain, at a point near the Schoolhouse: from thence to an eligible point of the harbour, hereafter to be selected. It is suggested, that the point of termination may be in a capacious basin, east of Washington street, where an easy communication can be had between sea vessels and canal boats, merely by forming an enclosure with lock-gates, for the admission of ships and other vessels to the surface of the water of the basin. The plan will probably be subservient also to the supplying the town of Boston with fresh water.

Distance, by the line of this survey.

Western section, from summit,	38
Eastern do. do.	62
Miles,	100

Fall, eastward and westward, 1959 feet.

The canal is to be 40 to 43 feet wide at the water surface, 28 feet at the bottom, 5 feet deep; and it is proposed that the locks shall correspond, in dimensions, to those of the Erie canal of New-York; say 90 feet long, by about 14 feet in width.

As to a supply of water, there is, considering the elevation of the summit, the means of an uncommon abundance at hand: independent of a number of great ponds, which may, any or all of them, be converted into reservoirs, and turned into the canal, as occasion is found to require, at very little expense, the sources of supply, found in the line of route, are not inconsiderable. The reservoir ponds alluded to, are in Ashburnham, Gardner, and Westminster, as follows:—

Upper Naukeag pond,	286 acres, 20 feet deep; giving,	249,163,200
Lower Naukeag pond,	208 acres, 10 feet deep,	90,604,800
East pond,	66 acres, 10 feet deep,	28,749,600
Wattatic pond,	27 acres, 10 feet deep,	11,761,200
Gardner pond,	139 acres, 20 feet deep,	121,196,800
Westminster pond,	152 acres, 20 feet deep,	132,422,400
	878 acres. Cubic feet,	633,898,000

So that there cannot be a doubt of an abundant supply of water forthcoming for the contemplated canal over the Mud pond level, answerable to the most extensive trade, at all seasons of the year, save the season of ice. Even the reservoirs alone, should it be necessary to resort to them, cannot but be sufficient, without using the natural streams passed on the line, in case such a thing is desirable.

The engineer's estimate of expense is, for the present, merely a rough one, because it is thought needful, at the next season, to re-examine parts of the route, in order to ascertain the means of avoiding certain difficult places, if possible, and how to overcome some other difficulties that are not to be avoided; also, it is proposed to make some lateral surveys, which time did not admit of at the past season; in consequence whereof, it may be presumed there may be deviations, more or less, from the general line marked out, that may affect materially the details of calculation. The estimate given in, applies to what is already known as feasible at least, and stands thus:—

For lands, water rights, &c.	$ 20,000
For lockage, 1959 feet, at $800 per foot,	1,567,200
Amount carried forward,	$1,587,200

Amount brought forward,	$1,587,200
For trunk of canal, including culverts, bridges, defence walls, &c., 100 miles, at $8000 per mile,	800,000
For aqueducts, deep cutting, &c.	300,000
For reservoirs,	20,000
For superintendence, and contingencies,	292,800
	$3,000,000

A.—From Northampton, or Springfield, on Connecticut river, by canal, continuing across Massachusetts to the New-York line, and thence into New-York state to the Hudson river, at or near the town of Hudson.

Distance, *Miles*, 60

No. 23.

CONNECTICUT AND HUDSON CANAL.

This may be regarded as a continuation of the project last above inserted; but its full execution is necessarily dependent on the concurrence of the state of New-York.

NOTE.

This, as already observed, is to be as a prolongation of the line, from the point where the canal of the preceding article terminates, on the Connecticut; so as to form one direct line from Boston harbour to the Hudson, and there to come into immediate connexion with the Erie canal of New-York.

Time did not allow of a minute survey of this canal route, or this section of the whole line being gone into by the engineer, during the past season; but the Massachusetts commissioners, in virtue of their preliminary examinations, have ascertained the fact of the practicability of constructing an eligible canal along the Deerfield and Hoosack river valleys.

The narrows and falls in the Connecticut, below Miller's river, it is proposed to pass by means of a dam, and a short canal along the left bank of the Connecticut, and across the bend, so as to debouche opposite to the mouth of the Deerfield. From that point, the route is up the Deerfield valley, to a summit-level, lying between the western branch thereof and the north branch of the Hoosack river, in Reedsborough; or, to a tunnel, as a summit-level, extending between the Deerfield great bend, and the Hoosack in Adams, through the base of Hoosack mountain; a length of 4 miles: which tunnel, if adopted, to be 20 feet wide, and $13\frac{1}{2}$ feet high.

After passing the Hoosack mountain, no formidable difficulty is discovered to exist, in the way to the Hudson. The route is down the valley of the Hoosack, as far as the falls in Pownal, and thence, either to continue down, on the right of the river, and strike for the Lake Champlain canal at Stillwater, 1 mile north of the mouth of Hoosack, and 16 miles distant from the Erie canal; or else, to take the left bank of the river Hoosack, from Pownal, to a point south of the Four Corners, and thence strike direct for the city of Troy, on the Hudson.

The following is given in by the engineer, as an "approximation" to an estimate of expense; to serve in some measure for a guide, until a full and minute survey of this canal route shall take place; which, it is understood, will be in the season that is coming.

Length of canal, 78 miles, at $10,000 per mile,	$780,000
Hoosack mountain tunnel, 4 miles in length, at $230,208 per mile,	920,832
Lockage east of Hoosack mountain, $611\frac{34}{100}$ feet, at $1,000 per foot,	611,340
Lockage west of Hoosack mountain, 711 feet, at $1000 per foot,	711,000
	$3,023,172

NOTE.

In the place of canals, it has lately been suggested, that a rail road should be constructed from Boston harbour to the Connecticut river, and thence, by continuation, to the Hudson; and plans for this project have been offered. It is thought at present, that along this line of the country, the rail road mode of improvement, besides being less costly than a canal one, may be productive of superior general advantages.

For a single track road, between Boston and the Connecticut, with sidelings at proper intervals, to allow teams to pass one another, and taking the distance at 100 miles, the estimate is as here follows:—

Purchase of land and of water rights,	$20,000
Levelling road, and fixing foundation stone, at $4000 per mile,	400,000
Amount carried forward,	$420,000

Amount brought forward,	$420,000
Cost of rolled iron bars, with expense of importation, exclusive of duty, at $2879 per mile,	287,900
Duty on rolled iron bars, in case it be not remitted,	141,000
Iron chains for securing bars,	73,900
Laying the rails,	34,000
Additional expense of the steep declivities, 9600 feet, at $6 per foot,	57,600
Wagons and carriages,	20,000
Superintendence and contingencies,	165,600
Total,	$1,200,000

Or, at the average rate of $12,000 per mile; which is thought to comprise large allowances in the principal items.

The routes suggested, are these; viz.

From Boston, by Waltham, Sudbury, Westboro', Worcester, Spencer, Brookfield, Palmer, Springfield, Westfield, to a point near the Hampshire and Hampden canal. Distance, — *Miles*,	108
Branching therefrom at Sudbury, and proceeding through Lancaster and Westminster to Miller's river at Winchendon; thence to the Connecticut above Miller's falls, and, by another branch, to Deerfield and Greenfield,	84
A branch from Palmer, proceeding through Granby and South Hadley, above the falls, to Northampton,	16
Whole distance of main road and branches, from Boston to the Connecticut river and vicinity, — *Miles*,	208

From either of which proposed points of termination, it may be eligible to extend the line into Berkshire county, and thence to the Hudson river; as, suppose from Westfield, through the valley of Westfield river to Stockbridge, and to Albany; or otherwise, from Northampton, through Goshen, Cummington, Windsor: or, through the Deerfield river valley to Hoosack mountain, and across to Williamstown, and to the Hudson.

For this continuation, the distance, in addition, may be,
Miles, 100

An appropriation for effecting surveys, has been passed by the Massachusetts legislature.

The construction of the Quincy rail road in Milton, has fully succeeded, and may be regarded as establishing principles in favour of other and more extensive works of the kind. It is at present in constant use, in conveying stone from the five granite quarries to the landing, at the mouth of Neponsit river, Boston harbour.

Not only has the action of the weather, during the past winter, had no injurious effect upon the work, but proved also not to occasion any impediment scarcely to the regular daily business going forward.

The length of road from the farthest quarry to tide water, is near 3 miles. It has a small, but not uniform descent; and it has for object, the transportation of large masses of granite; the cars for which, carry each about 4½ or 5 tons, either placed on a platform under the axle, or slung in chains.

Two of these cars make a load for a single horse, working through the day, and travelling at the rate of 3 miles per hour.

The sleepers are of granite, hewn from the same quarries; they are 7½ feet long, and laid 8 feet apart; the rails are of pine, 12 inches deep, with a covering of oak, and plates of iron over that.

The whole cost of the road is said to amount to $33,150, exclusive of $11,053, paid for the purchase of land, building of wharf, and some other accommodations.

NOTE.

The legislature of New-York, in virtue of the proceedings had in Massachusetts, have passed a law, providing for the appointment of commissioners, with concurrent power and directions, to explore routes, complete surveys, and locate a rail road, from the point of intersection with the line of the state, to its termination on the Hudson river; and have pledged the legislature, that if the state of Massachusetts shall, either directly or by incorporated individuals, construct a rail road from Boston to the eastern boundary of New-York, the state of New-York will then, either continue the construction to the Hudson, or grant corporate powers for its being so continued, on a footing of mutual and equal privilege as to all the objects of the road in both states.

The executive of Massachusetts, in addressing the legislature, observes;—

"Nothing short of a personal knowledge of the country, can furnish a proper and adequate estimate of its immense capacity for business and improvement. An interior trade, *ten fold its present amount*, might be had with the sea coast, but for the expense of transportation."

The address, along with a number of striking observations in point, further states:—

"It may safely be assumed, that, to many of the existing manufacturing establishments, the saving of expenses of transportation, by a rail road, would exceed the value of all the protection which the most liberal tariff of duties ever proposed could give."

NOTE.—1829.

A bill is reported to the Massachusetts legislature, authorizing the construction of a rail road, from Boston to the western line of the state, and the raising therefor a capital stock, to the amount of $3,300,000, whereof ⅓ part to be subscribed by the commonwealth.

The route adopted between Boston harbour and Albany, on the Hudson, is as follows; conformably to which an engraved profile of the road is given, along with the map illustrating this work.

Beginning at Boston, the route takes a western direction along the valley of Charles river, through Watertown, Newton, Needham, and Natick; and passes along the ravines of Concord river, by Sherburne, Holliston, Southboro' and Grafton, to the town of Worcester; thence through the town of Leinster, and over Grant's summit in Spencer, into the valley of Chickapee river, which it pursues to Ludlow factory, where the road crosses the Chickapee, and enters the town of Springfield. Continuing its western course along the banks of Westfield river, and passing through the towns of Westfield, Russel, Blandford, Chester, and Becket, it ascends Mount Washington, where the road attains its greatest altitude, 1480 feet; thence it descends into the valley of the Housatonic, through Dalton, to Pittsfield. Rising again in the town of Canaan, and crossing the dividing ridge between the waters of the Housatonic, and those of the Hudson, it descends the basin of the latter, through Chatham, Kinderhook, and Schoodic, and intersects the Hudson at Castleton landing; whence it pursues nearly a due north course along the left bank of the Hudson, to Greenbush, opposite Albany. Length of the road from Boston to the New-York state line, 160 miles; thence to Albany, 40. Total distance from Boston to Albany, 200 miles. Altitude at Grant's summit, 918 feet; Connecticut at Springfield, 38; and at Mount Washington, 1480 feet above the Atlantic ocean. General course, W.N.W.

N.—From Taunton, down Taunton river, to Mount Hope bay, down which, and up to Providence harbour, Rhode Island.   Distance. *Miles*, 50

A.—From Providence harbour, Rhode Island, by canal, along the Pawtucket, otherwise the Blackstone river valley, to Worcester in Massachusetts.

Distance, *Miles*, 45

No. 24.

BLACKSTONE CANAL.

Regular surveys for this work have been made, and preparations for its execution have commenced. The estimate amounts to 600,000 dollars, for which the stock of the company is about to receive an overflowing subscription.

In early times, the idea of opening a canal communication between Providence and the important town of Worcester, was formed, as of a thing that would very likely, in process of time, be done. It will now be realized, with an immense accumulation of collateral advantages.

Since the above was written, contracts have been made for excavating and embanking; and the work is now (1826). in active progress. It is expected the whole canal will be complete, and laid open for navigation, next year.

N.—From Providence harbour, down to Narraganset bay, and thence through Long Island sound to the harbour of New-York. Distance, *Miles*, 220

NOTE.—ON THE GREAT FISHERIES.

At Nantucket, from 1st January, to 31st December, 1828, there have arrived 20 ships from the Pacific, with 40,820 barrels spermaceti oil.

One do. from coast of Brazil, with 1100 barrels whale oil.

Whale ships from Nantucket, now at sea, viz.
Sailed in all 1828, 29
Sailed previously, 28
———57 ships.

At New-Bedford, from 1st January, to 31st December, 1828.

By 31 Ships, ⎫
    11 Brigs, ⎬ Importation from the Pacific, the banks of Brazil, and the Atlantic.
    3 Schooners, ⎭

Sperm oil, 25,923 barrels.
Whale oil, 28,502 do.
Whale bone, 262,310 pounds.

SUMMARY FOR NEW-ENGLAND.

ARTIFICIAL NAVIGATION.

Page.	No.		Miles.
10	1.	Merrimack river canals, and stream improvements,	110
11	2.	Baker's river and Oliverian canal,	39¾
12	3.	Connecticut river canals, and stream improvements,	220
14	4.	Connecticut and Memphramagog canal,	50
16	5.	Memphramagog and Champlain canal,	75
16	6.	The Winnepiseogee canal,	40
18	7.	Oxford and Cumberland canal,	50
18	8.	Waterford and Bethel canal,	20
19	9.	Kennebeck and Androscoggin, or Cobbassee Contee canal,	30
		Brunswick canal and feeder,	7⅜
21	10.	Androscoggin and Connecticut canal, and stream improvements,	130
23	11.	Kennebeck river canals, and stream improvements,	200
25	12.	The Pushaw canal,	6
26	13.	The Farmington canal,	73
27	14.	Hampshire and Hampden canal,	29
28	15.	Connecticut and Champlain canal, or Montpelier canal and rail road,	103¼
30	16.	Rutland and Whitehall canal,	25½
31	17.	Otter river canals, and stream improvements,	100
31	18.	Otter and Battenkill canal,	20
32	19.	The Middlesex canal,	27
34	20.	Boston and Narraganset canal,	26
35	21.	Cape Cod canal,	7
36	22.	Boston and Connecticut canal,	100
39	23.	Connecticut and Hudson canal,	78
44	24.	The Blackstone canal,	45

Total of artificial navigation, 1611⅞

NATURAL NAVIGATION.

10	Merrimack river, up to Haverhill,	20
16	Through Winnepiseogee lake,	20

Amount carried forward, 40

Page.		Miles.
	Amount brought forward,	40
26	From Hartford, on the Connecticut river, to New-Haven,	85
43	From Taunton, on Taunton river, to Providence, Rhode Island,	50
44	From Providence harbour, down to Narraganset bay, and thence to New-York harbour,	220

To which add :—

For all other streams and navigable waters; viz. Of the rivers, creeks, and bays within these six states, some of which are particularized below; there are about 500 capable of affording an average natural navigation of 10 miles each. This amounts to, 5000

Total of natural navigation, 5395
Total of artificial navigation, $1611\frac{7}{8}$

Total of both, Miles, $7006\frac{7}{8}$

Tributaries of the Connecticut river; viz.

In Massachusetts; the Deerfield, the Agawam, the Chickapee, the Millers.

In Connecticut; the Windsor, the Scantic.

In Vermont; the West, the Saxons, the Williams, the Black, the White, the Waterquechy, the Umpomponosack, the Waits, the Wells, the Pasumpsic, the Nulhegan.

In New-Hampshire; the Upper Ammonosack, the Lower Ammonosack, the Israels, the Johns, the Muscomy, the Sugar, the Cold, the Ashwelot.

Tributaries of the Merrimack river: viz.

In Massachusetts; the Concord, the Beaver, tne Shawsheen, the Spicket, the Powow.

In New-Hampshire; the Bakers, the Blackwater, the Contocook, the Souhegan, the Bowcook, the Cohas, the Suncook, the Piscataquog.

Charles river; rises in Middlesex county, Massachusetts, and falls into Boston harbour.

Mystic river; discharging on the north side of Boston harbour: it is connected with the Merrimack, by the Middlesex canal.

Ipswich river; rising in Middlesex county, and falling into the sea, below Ipswich.

Neponsit river; rising in Norfolk county, and falling into Massachusetts bay.

North river; from Plymouth county, falling into Massachusetts bay.

Taunton river; from several sources, falling into Mount Hope and Narraganset bays.

The Housatonick; rising in the valley of Berkshire, Massachusetts, and falling into Long Island sound, at Stratford, Connecticut.

IN THE STATE OF MAINE; VIZ.

Saco river, rises in the White mountains, New-Hampshire, enters the state of Maine at Fryeburgh, where it bends abruptly to the north, and then pursues a general south-east course, of more than 70 miles; receiving by the way, the Great and Little Ossapee from the west, and discharging into the sea, between the towns of Biddeford and Saco. Five or six miles from the mouth, are falls of 40 feet in height, precipitated over rocks, at Indian island : immediately below which, is a fine natural basin, open to ship navigation.

The Androscoggin river; has its source in the same ridge with the Connecticut, north of lake Umbagog, running south into the lake, and out thereof within the state of New-Hampshire, whence, at Shelburne, it re-enters Maine, and, after a winding course of near 200 miles, or a comparative course of 150, joins the Kennebeck at Merrymeeting bay, above the port of Bath. Navigation much obstructed by falls and rapids, but likely ere long to be improved.

The Kennebeck river, comprehends a western branch named Dead river; and an eastern branch, which is the main stream, rising in the same high lands between Maine and Lower Canada, opposite the sources of the Chaudiere, and flowing, (the main Kennebeck) by an intricate series of lakes and creeks, eastward into Moose Head lake; from whence, on the western side, it re-issues, and pursues a course south-westward to where the Dead river unites with it, at about 100 miles from the sources mentioned. After which, the Kennebeck pursues a general course, nearly south, of 150 miles, to the sea. It is navigable for ships of burthen to Bath, and for sloops 42 miles, up to Augusta, subject, however, to an impediment at low water. From Augusta, it is boatable 18 miles to Taconic falls, at Waterville, where the Sebasticook enters on the east, and constitutes much of the downward stream. At Norridgewock, 25 miles higher, the Sandy river enters from the west. The country along the upper part of the Kennebeck, as well as the river itself, calls for improvement.

The Penobscot river; is formed from two main branches, both passing through a number of lakes, the remote sources of the most western branch reaching to within 60 miles of the St. Lawrence, immediately below Quebec, and interlocking with sources of the Kennebeck, the St. John's, and the Chaudiere, in the high lands west and north-west of Moose Head lake. It flows by a general course of south-east, into the Chesuncook lake, a sheet of water 15 miles long by 5, and again issuing therefrom at the south-east angle, pursues the same direction to the influx of the Watawankeag river from the north-east, at 60 miles above Bangor. From the point of junction with the Watawankeag, the stream takes a general course westward of south to Penobscot bay. It receives, at 30 miles above Bangor, the waters of its great tributary from the west, the Piscataquis, which, in a general course of 50 miles, is composed of various branches, having their sources spread around the east and south of Moose Head lake, to the extent of 50 miles and upwards. The united stream meets the tide at Bangor, up to which point large sea vessels ascend, and at 30 miles below, it opens into Penobscot bay, between Castine and Belfast; which, at 30 miles still south, terminates in the ocean, between St. George's point and Fox island. Penobscot bay and river included, have a comparative course of 220 miles. The upper water of the river above Chesuncook lake, flows past and within 2 miles of the northern extremity of Moose Head lake. Here it is proposed to cut a canal, and thus form a union of the Penobscot and Kennebeck navigation from near the sources of these rivers.

To the great rivers specified, belong many tributaries, navigable for short distances, and communicating with lakes and ponds, which abound throughout this part of the country. And moreover, and besides what is here enumerated, the bay and harbour navigation along the sea border of the state, as well as the lower river navigation, is most extensive and commodious.

In the distance between the promontory of Portland, and the shore of New-Brunswick, at Passamaquoddy, the coast of Maine is indented by capacious bays, and these again are jagged into lesser ones, and strewed over with innumerable islands. Sheepscot river and bay discharge into the ocean east of the Kennebeck, the fine port of Wiscasset standing on the west of this river, which is navigable 20 miles, up to New-Castle.

Muscongus river, and St. George's river, each communicate with a number of small lakes, and enter the sea through the Bay of Muscongus, east of the Sheepscot; the Union river also, the Machias, and others, have all harbours at or near their mouths, and are for the most part navigable 10 to 20 miles upward.

The Schoodic, or St. Croix river; the boundary in part of the

United States and New-Brunswick, is formed of two branches, viz. the St. Croix proper, and the western branch, or Schoodic. The former, at latitude 45° 50', commencing in a congeries of lakes, and curving from south to east 40 miles, flows thence as a stream, southward, 25 miles, and receives the outlet of another series of lakes, composing the waters of the Schoodic branch; from whence the joint stream pursues a course southward and eastward into Passamaquoddy bay; the whole comparative course of the St. Croix being about 100 miles. It presents for the most part good navigation.

The St. John's river, and basin, are described as follows by Mr. Darby, in his "Geographical View."

"Sixty miles, a little north of east from the mouth of St. Croix, the great river St. John's enters the northern side of the Bay of Fundy. Geographically, the basin of St. John's extends from latitude north 45° 15' to 48°, and longitude from 6° 40' to 11° 40' east. Lying in a position from north-west to south-east, this basin is in form of a parallelogram, 240 miles long, and about 80 mean width, area 19,200 square miles. Independent of any artificial improvement, the St. John's is one of the most navigable of the Atlantic rivers, being much less impeded by rapids, shoals, or falls, than any other stream intervening between it and the Hudson. It is formed by two main branches; the St. John's has its extreme fountains in the north-west part of Maine, interlocking sources with those of the Penobscot and Chaudiere, at north latitude 46° 10', long. 6° 40' east. Flowing thence north-east, about 100 miles, nearly parallel to, and about 40 miles from, St. Lawrence river, it curves to the east, and receives from the south a large branch, the Alaguash. Assuming a course of north-east by east, in a distance of 6 miles below the Alaguash, the main stream is augmented by the St. François from the north, and at 40 miles, the termination of this course, by the still more considerable confluent, also from the north, the Matawaska.

"The St. François rises between Maine and Lower Canada, about 15 miles from the St. Lawrence, between Nare and Green islands, at north latitude 47° 45', and flowing thence about 40 miles, comparative course, falls into St. John's.

"The Matawaska is a stream deserving particular notice, as at and near its mouth extends, along St. John's, the settlement of the same name, now a subject of negotiation between the United States and Great Britain. See the map at that section of Maine.

"The Matawaska, the northern branch of St. John's, drains the extreme northern angle of Maine, and consequently, of the United States part of the Atlantic slope. The remote sources of this stream rise within 20 miles of the main volume of St. Lawrence, or about 30 due south from the mouth of Rimousky river, at north latitude 48°. Flowing south-east about 80 miles, the

Matawaska joins the St. John's. Below their junction, the united streams flow south-south-east 40 miles, and inflect to a little east of south at north latitude 47°, and pursue the latter course 80 miles. From some distance above the junction of St. John's and Matawaska, the main volume flows at a small distance from the eastern verge of its basin; the Restigouche, Nipisigic, and Miramichi, all rise near the St. John's, and flow north-easterly into the Gulf of St. Lawrence.

"The only confluent of St. John's below the Matawaska, which deserves particular notice, is the imperfectly known Aroostook. Interlocking sources with the Penobscot, the Aroostook follows the inflections of the St. John's, flows first 50 miles a little east of north, and thence about an equal distance north-east by east, and unites with its recipient at 46° 44' north.

"If a line be drawn along the earth's surface from the Saco river, where the stream traverses the White mountain chain, and extended thence north-east, it will pass over a series of bends in the Androscoggin, Kennebeck, Penobscot, and St. John's, which when viewed on a map, appear as if constructed from a given model, and afford conclusive evidence of a uniform structure in that section of the continent, and exhibit another instance, in the absence of mountain representation, of the defects of our maps.

"We have traced the St. John's to its great curve, where, in perfect accordance with the Saco, Androscoggin, Kennebeck, and Penobscot, it inflects to the north-east, which course it maintains 25 miles, and again turns to nearly east 50 miles. It is now a tide water river of great width and volume, and again bending, assumes nearly a southern course of 50 miles, and is lost in the Bay of Fundy, after an entire comparative course of 380 miles.

"As a navigable channel, the St. John's is much superior to any other stream of the United States north-east of the Hudson. The excessive high tides, and projecting rocks near its mouth, render it difficult of entrance except between the ebb and flow. The tides rise within its channel upwards of 80 miles. The mouth, between St. John's and Castleton, is narrow, and has only 17 feet water at low tides. Over this bar the incumbent mass of waters, above fifty feet, rush with prodigious velocity and eddying violence, particularly at the flow, when the ocean swell encounters the current of the river; but within, all is safety."

IN THE STATE OF NEW-HAMPSHIRE; VIZ.

Salmon-fall river, or Piscataqua; has many tributaries. From its source to its mouth, below Portsmouth, it is the boundary between New-Hampshire and Maine.

Besides the Piscataqua, the Connecticut, the Merrimack, the Saco, Androscoggin, and Upper and Lower Ammonosack, there are numerous streams contributing to water the state, in part navigable, and many lakes.

IN THE STATE OF VERMONT ; VIZ.

Lake Champlain; navigable in all its length, from Whitehall, its south extremity, to the Canada boundary, latitude 45°.

The Missisque, La Moelle, Otter, the Onion, and other streams, rise in the Green mountains, and fall into Lake Champlain; the Otter, at 20 miles south of Burlington, after a course northward of 90 miles: it has, between its falls, a bold navigation.

IN THE STATE OF CONNECTICUT; VIZ.

The Thames; formed of the Shetucket and Yantic rivers, uniting at Norwich; falls into Long Island sound at New-London. Vessels of burthen ascend to Norwich.

The Housatonick river; as well as the Connecticut, traverses the state from north to south, and branches into many short streams.

IN THE STATE OF RHODE ISLAND ; VIZ.

Providence river; formed of the Wanasquiatucket and Moshasuck streams, which unite above the town of Providence, 35 miles from the ocean.

Patuxet river; rises by two branches in the west of the state, and discharges into the Providence, 5 miles below the town.

Pawcatuck river; waters the south-west part of the state, and falls into Stonington harbour, Connecticut.

NEW-YORK NAVIGATION.

N.—From New-York harbour, by the Hudson river, which is navigable to Albany for steam and sail boats, and by some improvement, particularly at the Overslaugh near Albany, may be rendered so for larger vessels up to Albany. Distance, *Miles*, 145

A.—From Albany, by canal, (save in part where the Hudson stream is availed of, south of Fort Edward) to Lake Champlain, at Whitehall. Distance, from Waterford, or from the point of union with the Erie canal, south of the Mohawk river, *Miles*, 62

No. 25.

THE NEW-YORK CHAMPLAIN CANAL.

For this, and the grand Erie canal next below inserted, together with subsidiary works, the state of New-York has incurred a debt, amounting, down to the 31st December 1824, to 7,467,770 dollars : whereof the interest, by the terms of contract, partly at 6, and partly at 5 per cent., is 402,823 dollars per annum.

The revenue, from tolls, exclusive of other income, for the 12 months ending 31st December 1824, has exceeded 310,000 dollars, and it is expected, that in a year or two after all shall be finished and complete, the amount of tolls will be doubled, perhaps tripled.

N.—From Whitehall, through Lake Champlain, to the United States boundary line, north of the town of Champlain, lat. 45°. Whence, the River Sorel, or Richelieu, in Upper Canada, conducts to the St. Lawrence. Distance, *Miles*, 120

A.—From Albany, by canal, westward, passing Schenectady, Little Falls of Mohawk, Utica, Rome, Jordan, Montezuma, Lyons, Palmyra, Pittsfield, Rochester, Lockport, Blackrock, to Buffalo, on Lake Erie. Its junction with the Champlain canal, is formed south of the Mohawk river, the latter canal passing the town of Waterford on the north bank, and crossing the Mohawk. The distance, from Albany to Buffalo.

Miles, 363

No. 26.
THE ERIE AND HUDSON CANAL.

Of this, not much now remains to be done; a few miles only: and its full completion is expected with confidence, before the expiration of next year, 1826. The canal has a declivity of 4 feet between Buffalo and Rochester; and there will be, in the whole distance, 81 lift locks, embracing 688 feet of lockage, in 3 sections, thus:

West.	Buffalo to Montezuma,	158
Middle.	Montezuma to Utica,	96
East.	Utica to Albany,	109
	Miles,	363

West.	21 locks.	Descending		190
Middle.	7 do.	Ascending	62	
	2 do.	Descending	17	79
East.	51 do.	Descending		419
81 locks.			*Feet,*	688

Or, fall and rise, in the distance all together, 692 feet, and giving, consequently, 568 feet for the level of Lake Erie above the Hudson at Albany. From Syracuse to a little east of Utica, this canal has a summit water level of 67 miles; along which distance not a single lock therefore, nor any interruption. It is 40 feet wide at the surface, 28 feet at the bottom; depth of water 4 feet; and boats of 40 to 100 tons, laden with commodities, travel through its finished sections at the rate of 55 miles in 24 hours; boats with passengers at the rate of 100 miles in the same time. The locks are 90 feet long in the clear, and are of 15 feet width, a circumstance, which appears now to be regretted by some of our engineers, who think that had they been built of half that width or a little more, say 8 feet or 8½ feet, there would have been great advantage in it; but this is a controverted point.

A substantial and commodious harbour and basin have been constructing at Blackrock on the Niagara river, with a view to this canal having its termination there; that is to say, for it to enter that basin, and to receive its western supply of water therefrom; an additional canal from thence, passing on to Buffalo; but by an act of the legislature, 20th April 1825, it is now made the duty of the canal commissioners, to continue and complete the Erie canal, to Lake Erie at the mouth of Buffalo creek, *distinct from, and independent of the basin at Blackrock*, if in the opinion of the commissioners this plan will secure a more certain and permanent supply of water for the western part of the canal, or if, for any other reasons, they think it more for the public advantage, than the Blackrock plan.

By the same act of the legislature, the canal commissioners are authorized also, to cause such alteration and improvements in the "Champlain Canal," between Fort Edward on the Hudson and the dam at Saratoga falls, as they may deem necessary, to form a complete canal navigation from Fort Edward down to Fort Miller, 8 miles, and thence to Saratoga falls 2½ miles farther; along which intermediate space of 10½ miles, the channel of the river has hitherto been used: and for the expense of this alteration, the sum of 170,000 dollars is appropriated.

For the double purpose of insuring an abundant supply of water on the summit level of the Champlain canal, and of opening the navigation to a still higher point on the Hudson, the plan has been adopted of a navigable feeder, leading from the river at two miles above Glen's falls, through Glen's village and Sandyhill, seven miles, to the Champlain canal, entering it at two miles above the village of Fort Edward; and the work is commenced.

Total length of main canal, to its junction with the Erie canal, - - - - - - - - Miles, 63½
Glen's falls feeder, - - - - - - - 7

Together, Miles, 70½

NOTES.

A.

According to the eighth annual report of the commissioners, the New-York *canal fund*, on the 1st of January, 1825, consisted of the following items:—

The canals, estimated at cost, deducting the amount
of tolls received therefrom, - - $ 8,829,056
Lands given by the Holland Land Company, in the
county of Cattaraugus, 100,632 acres; valued at 35,221

Amount carried forward, $ 8,864,277

Amount brought forward, $8,864,277
Lands given by John Hornby, in Steuben county,
1,000 acres, valued at - - - - - 3,000
Lands given by G. Granger, in Steuben county,
1,000 acres, valued at - - - - - 5,000
Grand island, in Niagara river, 17,381 acres, - 48,423
Onondaga salt springs reservation, 540 shares, - 27,000
Bonds in hand for lands sold, of the canal fund, - 58,646

Amount of canal fund, - - - - $9,006,346

B.

The canal debt and revenue.

The receipts into the canal fund treasury, during the year 1824, were,

In revenue and loans, together, - - - $2,243,497
The disbursements in 1824, - - - - 1,984,140

Leaving, consequently, at the disposal of the commissioners, for the current year, a balance of - $259,357

The canal revenue for the current year, 1825, is estimated thus:—

Tolls, - - - - - - - - $400,000
Auction duty, - - - - - - - 186,500
Steam-boat tax, - - - - - - - 5,000
Salt duty, - - - - - - - - 120,000
Interest and principal on sales of land; in part, - 6,000

Amount, - - - - - - - - $717,500

The canal debt, as follows:—

$4,524,270 of stock, at 5 per cent. The interest whereon, - - - - - $226,213
2,943,500 of stock, at 6 per cent. The interest whereon, - - - - - 176,610

$7,467,770 $402,823

C.

Estimate to a full completion of them.

The Erie and Champlain canals, it is now pretty well ascertained, will be complete early in 1826. It was at one time expected they would be finished this year, 1825, except as to the alteration in the Champlain canal, between Fort Edward and Saratoga falls, which was lately authorized by law.

For a full completion of them, as also to satisfy all claims for damages, the commissioners estimate that there will be required the further sum of, - - - - - - $800,000

Add thereto,

The interest on the canal debt for this year, as is stated, B, - - - - - - - 402,823

Amount required for 1825, - - $1,202,823

The balance as stated B, at the disposal of the commissioners, is, - - $259,357

The canal income this year, is estimated, B, - - - - - - 717,500

These together make - - - - - - 976,857

So that the exigencies of the current year, which the legislature will provide for by a loan, amount to $225,966

The canal debt, to 1st of January, 1825, as stated, B, is, - - - $7,467,770
The sum required, as above, - - 225,966

These together, make the amount of debt to the 1st of January, 1826, when the canals will be nearly finished, - - - - - - $7,693,736

Deduct therefrom,

The donation lands, and Grand island, competent to reduce the debt, this sum, - - - - 91,644

Amount of debt to the 1st of January, 1826, to be extinguished by means of canal revenue, - $7,602,092

D.

Prospectus.

The commissioners observe, that when an uninterrupted water intercourse from the great lakes to the Atlantic ocean, by means of competent canals, such as it is hoped the Erie and Champlain and their accessories will prove to be; shall extend its influence into the almost boundless regions west and north, the effects produced, will be such as to make it not unreasonable to expect there will be, for some few years to come, an augmented proportion in the increase of toll amounts; great as that increase hitherto has actually been, since the works have been in progress. The auction and salt duties will be affected, too, by the event, in a like favourable manner. The commissioners think it quite a safe calculation, to compute, for the ten years next ensuing, after the manner which follows:—

The average amount of tolls for 10 years, commencing on 1st January, 1826: annually,	$700,000
The average amount of auction and salt duties, belonging to the canal fund: annually,	420,000
Making together; exclusive of steam-boat tax, and bonds in hand, and avails of unsold lands; an average annual income of	$1,120,000

From out of which, there will be required as follows:—

The average annual interest on the canal debt,	$410,000	
Expenses for repairs, and superintendence,	100,000	
		510,000

Leaving, consequently, an annual surplus revenue, to be applied to the payment of the canal debt of $7,602,092, this sum, — — — — — $610,000

Which, if the ground taken for accruing revenue, be assumed as solid premises, will, by being applied on the principle of a sinking fund, or in purchasing other stocks of the state, be adequate to an entire extinguishment of the said debt, on or before the 1st of January, 1836. And thereafter, if the same reasoning continue to hold good, and especially if it receive strength from the rapidity of the country's increase in population and general wealth, there will be a net amount of income of a million of dollars and more, and successive additions made to it; which may be turned into the treasury, and thereby may the government be enabled to remove from the people all burdensome taxation; to diffuse the blessings of education more and more abundantly; and accelerate by so much the increasing general prosperity of the state.

NOTE, ADDITIONAL, DECEMBER 31, 1825.

The work has thus early been accomplished. On the 26th of October, the Great Erie canal was in a navigable state; and vessels passed from that lake to the Atlantic ocean. In eight years and a little more, artificial communication of about 450 miles in length, have here been effected to the Hudson river; namely, from Lake Champlain, by the northern canal; thence to Lake Ontario, by the western canal and the River Oswego improved; and thence by continuation westward, to Lake Erie at Buffalo; opening, by the access they afford to other navigable waters in the west, the north, and south, an extent of inland navigation unparalleled in the world.

The expense of these works, in their actual state, including auxiliary and incidental matters, has been 9,267,234 dollars; which is exclusive of interest paid on loans: About 850,000 dollars of this sum is the cost of the Champlain canal.

The canal debt having been increased this year, 1825, by a loan of 270,000 dollars, at 6 per cent., stands thus:—

$4,524,270, at 5 per cent.
3,213,500, at 6 per cent.

$7,737,770

But, the said loan being to be reimbursed on the 1st of October next, 1826, the canal debt, from loans, will then return to its former point, viz. 7,467,770 dollars.

The amount of tolls received this year, 1825, it is now ascertained, exceeds half a million of dollars. It was estimated, in the foregoing statement, at 400,000 dollars. So that the real state of things at the present day, is much better than what was supposed in the calculation; and consequently anticipations being more than realized, we perceive, on taking our prospective view from hence, a still fairer and more encouraging aspect of the great concern, in its circumstances at large and results, than the anticipated prospectus, above laid down, was qualified to present. The ground is not shaken, for what is there predicted of it, from this time forward; but, on the contrary, strengthened and improved.

There are, however, as have been pointed out, many collateral, or additional improvements yet to be gone into, or to be completed; and of the work that is done, some of its parts are not without defects, which will require immediate remedy: but in the prosecution of these operations, which may possibly fill up a series of some years, there can be nothing to interrupt or retard the general prosperous tide of affairs; on the contrary, much to accelerate and advance it, by adding to existing facilities. The increase of transportation will, it is highly probable, "require a double set of locks, and perhaps a canal on the north side of the Mohawk, from Utica eastward." This, or railways, will very soon be required. At the present moment, a prospective view of the affairs of the Erie and Champlain concern, may be taken, as here follows :—

The canal debt, to the 1st of January, 1826, is
$7,737,770. After the 1st of October, it will
be, - - - - - - - $ 7,467,770
Which there is a competency to reduce, by donation
lands and bonds in possession, to amount, as particularized, of - - - - - - - 171,656

Making the amount of debt, to 1st of January, 1827,
to be extinguished, by means of canal revenue, $ 7,296,114

Revenue for the year 1826, *viz.*

Balance in hand on the 1st of January, as per statement of the commissioners, - - - - $ 226,672
Tolls. In 1824, the amount was $ 289,820 ; in 1825,
$ 511,280. This year, estimated at - - 750,000
Auction and salt duties, - - - - - 350,000
Reimbursement to be made to the commissioners, of
this sum advanced by them on account of the
Cayuga and Seneca, and Oswego canals, - - 58,727

Amount of revenue for the current year, - $1,385,399

Payments for the year 1826, *viz.*

Interest on the loan debt, $ 7,737,770, to the 1st of
October, and $ 7,467,770 from that date, - - $ 414,973
Estimated expense of repairing the canals, and collecting tolls, - - - - - - - 140,000
Improvements to be made on the Champlain canal, 100,000
Damages, estimated at - - - - - 50,000
Loan, reimbursable on the 1st of October, - - 270,000

Total expenditure, - - - - - - $ 974,973

So that, it appears the present year (1826) will have produced a surplus of 680,426 dollars, towards sinking or paying off the debt, besides 100,000 dollars appropriated to an alteration of the Champlain canal ; together, 780,426 dollars.

It is confidently expected, the surplus will, in subsequent years, amount to a million of dollars and more.

The following description of the two canal routes, has appeared in print.

The Erie canal commences at Buffalo, on Lake Erie, near the mouth of Buffalo creek, and proceeds for 10 miles along the shore of Lake Erie, and the bank of Niagara river, to Tonewanta creek, which it enters at its mouth. The channel of the Tonewanta is then made use of for 12 miles, after which the canal proceeds in a north-east direction, by a deep cut, $7\frac{1}{2}$ miles to Lockport, where it descends 60 feet by 5 locks, and proceeds in an easterly direction, on the south side of the Ridge road, and parallel to it, on a uniform level, for 63 miles, to Rochester, where it crosses the Genessee river by an aqueduct of 9 arches, each of 50 feet span, and immediately after receives a navigable feeder, or branch canal, 2 miles long, which connects it with the Genessee river above the Great falls. It then proceeds in an easterly direction, to Montezuma, $67\frac{1}{2}$ miles, in which distance it descends 126 feet, by locks at various places, and crosses Mud creek twice, by aqueducts, near the villages of Palmyra and Lyons. At Montezuma, the level of the canal begins to ascend, and between this place and the town of Salina, a distance of 27 miles, it rises 67 feet. In Salina, commences the 'Long Level,' which is preserved through the towns of Manlius, Sullivan, Lenox, Verona, Rome, Whitestown, Utica, and into Frankfort, in Herkimer county, a distance of more than 69 miles. From Frankfort, the canal descends, in the course of 12 miles, 49 feet, to the head of Little falls, where are 5 locks, each of 8 feet descent, and an aqueduct over the Mohawk, supported by 3 arches, connecting the Erie canal with the old canal at German flats. From the foot of Little falls, the canal continues its course for 70 miles, down the valley of the Mohawk, on the south side of the river, through Danube, Conajoharrie village, Charleston, Florida, Rotterdam, and the city of Schenectady, to Niskayuna, 4 miles below Schenectady, where it crosses the Mohawk, by an aqueduct 748 feet long, supported by 16 piers, 25 feet above the river surface. Descent from the foot of Little falls to Niskayuna, 86 feet. After crossing the Mohawk, the canal proceeds along the north bank thereof for 12 miles, and then re-crosses, by an aqueduct 1188 feet in length, and passes by the Cohoes falls, where, in the space of 2 miles, it descends 132 feet, by 16 locks. A little below the Cohoes falls, a feeder enters from the Mohawk, and connects the Erie with the Champlain canal, and the united work then proceeds to Albany, $8\frac{1}{2}$ miles, in which distance it descends 44 feet, and terminates in the tide waters of the Hudson.

Among the side cuts, or short branches of the Erie canal, are these: viz.—
1. One in Watervliet, opposite Troy, where a passage is opened into the Hudson, by 2 locks.
2. One proceeding from Syracuse, to the village of Salina, at the head of Onondaga lake, 1½ mile.
3. The one referred to, opposite Rochester, by which boats from the canal may ascend the Genessee river more than 70 miles.

The Champlain canal commences at the village of Whitehall, at the head of sloop navigation on Lake Champlain, and immediately rising, by 3 locks, 26 feet, proceeds on a level, 5½ miles up the valley of Wood creek, enters that stream, and follows its channel for 3 miles, to a lock of 4 feet lift, which extends the navigation up the creek 3½ miles farther, to Fort Anne village, where, after rising by 3 locks, 24 feet, it leaves the creek, and proceeds 12 miles on a summit level, through the towns of Fort Anne and Kingsbury, to Fort Edward. Here it receives the waters of the Hudson, above the great dam in that river, by a feeder of half a mile in length, and soon after descends 30 feet, by 3 locks, into the Hudson, below the dam. The great dam is 900 feet long, 27 feet high, and throws back an ample supply of water for the summit level. From Fort Edward, the navigation is continued for the present down the channel of the Hudson, 8 miles, to the head of Fort Miller falls, around which it is carried, by a canal taken out of the east bank of the river, half a mile long, and having 2 locks, of 18 feet descent. From Fort Miller, the river is made navigable for near 3 miles farther, by a dam at the head of Saratoga falls, just above which the canal is again taken out of the river, on the west side, and proceeds on a level for 17 miles, through Saratoga and Stillwater, Schuyler's flats, and over Fish creek by an aqueduct, to a point 2 miles below Stillwater village. From this point to Waterford, where the canal enters the Mohawk, a distance of 9 miles, it descends 86 feet, by 9 locks, 6 of which are in the town of Waterford. From Waterford, the Hudson is now made navigable for sloops to Troy, 3½ miles below, by a dam across the river at the latter place, 1100 feet in length, 9 feet high, and having a sloop lock at its eastern extremity, of 114 feet long, 30 feet wide, 9 feet lift. The cost of this lock and dam was 92,270 dollars. See the engraved profile of the Erie canal.

February, 1827.

The canal commissioners have rendered their report for the last year, ending on the 30th November, 1826. By which report it appears, that the tolls have exceeded the amount they were estimated at: they stand thus—

For the Erie canal,	$687,976
The Champlain canal,	74,191
The Cayuga and Seneca canal,	3,023
Tolls for 1826,	$765,190
Besides which, there has been received into the canal treasury, viz.—	
For auction and salt duties,	278,144
Sales of land, interest on bonds, and part of principal,	7,635
Balance of fund in hand at the beginning of the year,	226,672
Total received for 1826,	$1,277,641

Expenditure, as follows:—

Interest on the loan,—		
$2,943,500, at 6 per cent.	$176,610	
4,901,271, at 5 per cent.	245,063	
		$421,673
For various repairs, and new works of improvement on both the Erie canal and Champlain canal; as also payments on account of the Cayuga and Seneca canal, and the Oswego canal,		871,864
For the collecting of tolls and contingencies, not yet settled, but estimated at		30,000
Total expenditure for 1826,		$1,323,537

Which expenditure, consequently, has absorbed the whole of the year's income, and exceeds it by 45,896 dollars; this having been occasioned by some costly improvements which it was thought highly proper should take place, both on the Erie canal and the Champlain canal; together with sundry payments made by the commissioners in execution of the Oswego canal, and the Cayuga and Seneca canal. So that all these canals are now amalgamated, and brought under one head of account with the commissioners.

The construction between Fort Edward and Saratoga falls, to fill up the line of continuity of the Champlain canal, in lieu of that distance on the North river channel, is now nearly finished; and the Glen's falls feeder is under contract, to be completed this year, 1827.

The loan debt, it will be seen, in consequence of these heavy extra disbursements during the last year, has not been reduced, but amounts at present to 7,844,771 dollars. Whereof 2,943,500 dollars is at 6 per cent., and 4,901,271 dollars at 5 per cent.

It was thought of the highest importance to postpone for a season, the object of reduction, in favour of adding, by means of extra expenditure, to the security and stability of the works at large; thereby to enhance the prospects of the state in real solid permanent advantages, derivable from them. The immediate prospects of the state, founded upon what has here been stated, and which are not a little flattering, are according to what follows; viz.

Tolls expected for the present year, 1827,		$ 870,000
From other items of canal fund,		300,000
Total estimated income for 1827,		$1,170,000
Interest on loan debt, same as above,	$421,673	
For ordinary repairs,	100,000	
Disbursements required to complete the Oswego canal, and the Cayuga and Seneca canal,	330,000	
For new feeders, locks, bridges, and some other improvements yet to be added,	120,000	
For collectors and contingent expenses,	30,000	
For deficit of 1826,	45,896	
Total estimated expenditure,		1,047,569
Leaving for 1827, a surplus of		$ 122,431

By this time, should the expenditures on the Oswego, and the Cayuga and Seneca canals, all have been made to the full, these canals will have become productive of revenue: but, setting aside immediate expectations as to these last, an estimate for the year 1828, may fairly be stated, thus;—

Tolls for 1828,		$1,000,000
From other items of canal fund,		300,000
Total estimated income,		$1,300,000
Interest on loan debt, same as above,	$421,673	
For ordinary repairs,	100,000	
For walling, protecting of banks, renewal of bridges, and other improvements,	120,000	
Toll collectors and contingencies,	30,000	
Total of estimated expenditure,		671,673
Leaving a surplus of		628,327
Which, with the preceding,		122,431
Make together, the sum of		$ 750,758

Estimated, as applicable, at the expiration of the year 1828, to the reduction of the canal loan debt.

January, 1829.

By the annual report of the canal commissioners, now submitted to the assembly, it appears, that the aggregate result, as to finances, to the present period, has just about come up to expectations. In proof whereof, the loan debt is reduced to $7,780,156, and the commissioners have on hand in the canal treasury, and invested in other stocks, the sum of $625,982, to be applied to the object of reduction as early as possible. By contract with the lenders, no part of the above amount of debt is reimbursable before the year 1837.

As already noticed, the affairs of the Oswego canal, and of the Cayuga and Seneca canal, were, some time back, amalgated into one amount with those of the Erie and the Champlain canals. Of the joint canal fund, from all sources, including tolls, the revenue which has ensued, during the past year, 1828, amounts to $1,233,435.

And the whole of the expenditures, including interest on loan debt, and some payment in reduction of principal, together with temporary loans paid off; these have amounted to $1,002,287. The receipts of toll were $838,412, which does not quite come up to the mark expected; and this may be attributed to a deficiency in the last year's wheat crop. Wheat is the great staple of the western part of the state, and usually affords an amount of toll nearly equal to that of all other articles descending the Erie canal from thence.

Some additions and repairs of importance, and many substantial improvements, have been made to the works generally, at what may be considered as an extra expenditure. Nearly all the locks on the Erie canal have been furnished with additional culverts and gates; some locks have been rebuilt, as have many bridges, upon an improved plan; the locks at Glen's falls feeder of the Champlain canal, nearly finished; which feeder is to be navigable in the coming spring season. The Oswego canal, and Cayuga and Seneca canal, now prosecuted to the eve of a satisfactory completion, have each occasioned a larger amount of disbursements than was calculated on.

Prospects for 1829, *are stated as follows; viz.*

Taking the tolls at only the last year's amount, or thereabout, the other items of canal fund revenue added, will give, as the whole amount of receipts, $1,260,000

Amount carried forward, $1,260,000

Amount brought forward, $ 1,260,000
The expenditure, which, besides interest on loan debt, will probably not embrace any large sum beyond what may always be needed to defray current ordinary repairs, and a due superintendence of the works, it is thought quite sufficient to estimate at   757,443

Giving a surplus, in favour of the canal fund for the current year, 1829, of the sum of - - - $ 502,557

To complete the New-York communication between the Atlantic ocean and the great lakes; as also to spread the advantages of a canal navigation through the state conformably with the main design, it is strenuously recommended to the legislature, by the executive of this state, to take into consideration, and adopt measures for the early execution of the leading works essential to promote the objects contemplated. A series of undertakings are enumerated, as claiming, in this view, the attention of the New-York legislature; namely:—

A.—In the first place; a canal between the River St. Lawrence and Lake Champlain; at or near the boundary line of New-York with Canada. Distance, *Miles,* 75

No. 27.

ST. LAWRENCE AND CHAMPLAIN CANAL.

A survey of the route, applicable to this projected canal, has recently been made, and there is not found any formidable obstacle in the way, save that there is a ridge of 900 feet of elevation to pass; on account of which, as this mountain takes an abrupt descent within the domains of Great Britain, after passing the Canada line, it would be very convenient to run the canal through that territory, in case it were ascertained that the government of Great Britain were willing to agree upon conditions for such a measure. Distance, from the mouth of St. Regis river to the lake, near Champlain town, about 75 miles. It has been recommended, by a committee in congress, that measures be adopted on the part of the executive, (in establishing the northern boundary line of the United States,) to obtain from the government of Great Britain, a cession of a tract of land north of the 45° of latitude, 4 miles in width, and extending from Rouse's point on Lake Champlain, to St. Regis on the River St. Lawrence. The possession of this strip of land, it is affirmed, would enable the suggested canal to be constructed with facility, and at small expense.

Other routes have been proposed; particularly one from Plattsburg, Clinton county, running westward to a point of the St. Lawrence river at or near Ogdensburg.

The length of which last, according to a partial survey made thereof, would not be less than 130 miles, but where the summit could be supplied with water from the Lake Chateaugue.

A.—Secondly; a junction of the Great Erie Canal with Lake Ontario, through the River Onondaga, or Oswego.   Distance, suppose, *Miles*, 50

No. 28.
OSWEGO CANAL.

Some provision for this object, of distinguished importance in the list, was heretofore made by the legislature, but insufficient in amount. By an act passed 25th April, 1825, the commissioners of the canal fund are empowered, for the purpose of carrying on improvements along the river Oswego, and in order to connect, by a perfect navigation, the Erie canal with the waters of Lake Ontario—to raise forthwith, by means of loan, and to employ as the same shall be called for, to the extent of 227,000 dollars, this sum coming up to the engineer's estimates for the accomplishment of the works, taken in addition to what has been already expended. The distance, suppose from Rome, or more probably from Syracuse or near it, to the mouth of the Oswego, 40 or 50 miles, more or less.

The completion of this undertaking would seem to be an object of the highest importance, considered in the light of extending the benefits of the great Erie canal into the counties of Oswego, Jefferson, and St. Lawrence, and of giving a neighbourly access, by water, to Upper Canada, as the Champlain canal does, and will more and more, to Lower Canada.

A survey has been made of the route, commencing at Salina village, and passing through the valleys of Lake Onondaga, of Seneca river, and of Oswego river, to Lake Ontario. Fall 160 feet.

February, 1827.

The state commissioners have reported, on this canal, that the sum appropriated, of 227,000 dollars, has been expended, and that an additional sum of 210,000 dollars, by estimate, will be required in the course of the present year, to complete the work.

Pursuing a route on the northern shore of the lake, it will form a connexion with the Erie canal at Salina.

January, 1829.

At length this important work has reached within a mere trifle of being finished; and a good boat navigation obtained between the Erie canal and Lake Ontario, at Oswego harbour. The extent of it is 38 miles; one half this distance being canal, connected with Oswego river by locks and dams, the other half a slack water navigation on the river. Its structures consist of 22 bridges, 7 culverts, 1 aqueduct, 2 waste weirs, 8 dams across the river, 13 locks of stone, and 1 of stone and timber, overcoming 123 feet of descent. The sum of 505,115 dollars has now been expended on this construction, and about 20,000 dollars is still to be added; making the final cost, 525,115 dollars, or thereabout.

A.—From Great Sodus bay, Lake Ontario, by canal, through Wayne county, to strike the Erie canal, at a point where the latter may be entered by the Cayuga and Seneca canal, next below inserted.

Distance, *Miles*, 25

No. 29.

GREAT SODUS BAY CANAL.

The location of this proposed canal is dependent on a contingency, as above stated: it is probable, however, the point of intersection on the Erie canal, will be at Montezuma.

A.—Thirdly; it is recommended by the governor, to unite, in the most accommodating manner, the waters of the Lakes Seneca, Canandaigua, Cayuga, and others of the secondary class, with the Erie canal. Distance of one of the suggested communications, by the outlets of Seneca and Cayuga lakes, at which some works of improvement have heretofore been carried on, is, *Miles*, 21

No. 30.

CAYUGA AND SENECA CANAL.

An act has passed the legislature, 20th April, 1821, directing this work to be prosecuted. Besides the important navigation improvement implied, it has especially for its object, to drain and reclaim some extensive tracts of land, commonly known and designated as the "Cayuga Marshes." The engineer's report on the subject, proposes to locate the improvements in question, between Geneva, on Lake Seneca, and Montezuma, or near it, on the Erie canal, with some choice, open to contingencies, in the line of route to be adopted from Seneca falls to the Erie canal; and upon this point, it is made a duty of the commissioners, to cause such additional surveys and examinations to be made as are needful; and to have the works constructed on such levels, and on such a plan upon the whole, as to sink the waters of Lake Seneca and the River Seneca, so much below their natural levels, as to produce the effect of draining off the marshes at the head of that lake, and the various tracts of marsh and wet land at points lower down. What is proposed to be reclaimed, or partially improved in this way, is very considerable in the aggregate: the tracts are situate on both sides of the Erie canal, and mostly in the midst of a highly fertile district. An appropriation on this article is made, of the sum of 150,000 dollars. The distance, from Geneva, by the Seneca river, to Montezuma, is about 21 miles.

February, 1827.

The state commissioners have reported on this canal, that its execution has been unavoidably retarded, and that, in addition to the 150,000 dollars appropriated for it, the sum of 30,000 dollars, in the course of this year, will be requisite to its completion.

December, 1828.

On the 15th of last month, water was admitted into every part of this canal, from the foot of Seneca lake, to the Erie canal at Montezuma, and but little labour remains now to be bestowed on it, in the spring, to establish a thorough navigation. The works consist of 10 miles of independent canal, and 10 miles 24 chains of slack water navigation. There are 7 locks, embracing 73½ feet of lockage, 19 bridges, 5 safety gates, 5 dams, 6 culverts. And the total expense will be about 211,000 dollars.

NOTE.

On the subject of draining marshes, it may be noticed, that in France, an immense project is in actual contemplation, having for object, to redeem all the marsh land of that kingdom.

It is said to engage a number of great capitalists, and to have the patronage of government. Many a century may pass away from this time, before the ratio of population to territory, in these United States, will have been so raised, as to require and give encouragement to a similar *general* undertaking; yet, within this country, there are a few districts which may, before the lapse of many years, exercise profitably the mechanical genius of the inhabitants, in draining swamps and marshes, to an extent, perhaps, equal to all the waste land of that description in France, or more. The Mississippi delta, it is not improbable, will have very early attention paid to it.

A.—Fourthly; recommended by the governor, a connexion between the Delaware river and the Hudson.

Distance,	64
Continued to the Lackawaxen,	17
Miles,	81

No. 31.

THE DELAWARE AND HUDSON CANAL.

This work is likely to be forthwith executed. The company instituted for the purpose, have recently had new privileges attached to their charter by the state, and are now, moreover, privileged, by act of the state of Pennsylvania, to co-operate and be in union of interest with the "Lackawaxen Canal and Coal Company" of Pennsylvania.

A regular survey has been made of the whole line of the proposed improvements. It extends from tide water of the Waalkill or Rondout river, at Eddy's factory (near Kingston), through the Rondout and Neversink valleys, to the Delaware river, 17 miles below the mouth of the Lackawaxen river; up which, to the head waters thereof at Keen's mill-pond in Wayne county, Pennsylvania, 4 or 5 miles from the coal mines of Lackawannock. Distance in all, 117 miles, whereof 36 are in Pennsylvania state, viz:

From tide-water of the Rondout, to the summit level, at
the head of Sandberg creek, between the Hudson and

the Delaware, in Sullivan county, is 38 miles, and a rise of - - - - - - - - - feet 535
From summit level, down Neversink valley, to the Delaware river, at 4 miles above the mouth of Neversink, is 26 miles, and a descent of - - - - - 80
Up the Delaware river, to the mouth of the Lackawaxen, is 17 miles, and a rise of - - - - - - 148
Up the Lackawaxen, to head water at Keen's pond, is 36 miles, and a rise of - - - - - - - 668

So that, in these 117 miles, there will be 1431 feet of lockage, as requisite to overcome the rise and fall. The canal to be 32 feet wide at the water line; 4 feet deep.

The engineer's total estimate of expense, is 1,208,632 dollars.

Since the foregoing was written, this work has been carried on with great industry, and is much advanced. The greater part is under contract, and it is expected the whole canal, as far as the Delaware river, 64 miles, will be finished in the course of next year, 1826, in case the intervening winter should be mild, and favourable to the workmen.

January, 1827.

This canal was commenced in August 1825, and is reported on as being now finished, within a mere trifle, as far as the Delaware, 4 miles above the mouth of the Neversink. At the opening of the spring, it will no doubt be made ready for navigation. See Lackawaxen canal, article 59.

A.—From opposite the mouth of Lackawaxen river on the Delaware, by canal, up the Delaware valley, across part of Sullivan and Delaware counties, to the mouth of the Cookquago branch at the town of Deposite. Distance, *Miles*, 60

No. 32.

LACKAWAXEN AND COOKQUAGO CANAL.

Surveys are yet to be made in regard to this projected undertaking, as also the one in continuation of it, as next below specified. They are both recommended to the attention of the legislature, as a highly useful prolongation, in the state of New-York, of the Delaware and Hudson canal.

A.—From the point of the Cookquago branch, struck as above at Deposite town, by canal, westward, across to Bettsburg on the Susquehanna river, and thence, along the valleys of the Susquehanna and Tioga, and the Canisteo branch of the latter, to Hornellsville on the Canisteo.   Distance, *Miles*, 150

No. 33.

COOKQUAGO AND CANISTEO CANAL.

In regard to this article, like as the foregoing, regular examinations of the ground are yet to be made. If found of easy practicability, there is but little doubt of an early execution of the combined work : and one uninterrupted line of canal navigation may ere long be formed, extending from the Hudson to the mouth of Lackawaxen river on the Delaware, and thence up the Delaware valley to Deposite, and westward from thence across the southern counties of New-York, quite to Lake Erie at Portland harbour, and running for the most part nearly parallel with the Erie and Hudson canal, between Buffalo and Albany.

Thus these two great parallels of canal, having the Hudson on the east, Lake Erie on the west, and communicating with each other at various points on the way, will include within their influence the major part of the whole superficies of the state of New-York : and a prolongation of the line from Portland, through the Conewango and Alleghany valleys, will carry the intercommunication, by canal, as far as Pittsburg on the Ohio. The next inserted article, No. 34, is that of another contemplated communication between the Delaware and the Hudson. The great question in the present article is, as to the practicability of a communication, by canal, between the Delaware river at Deposite, and the Susquehanna at Bettsburg. The summit of the dividing land is found to be 497 feet above the Delaware, and 527 feet above the Susquehanna. If this apparent difficulty can be surmounted, it is understood for the rest, that nature has formed a valley, extending even from the foot of Otsego lake, to the western part of Steuben county ; through the whole of which, a distance of 220 miles, a canal might be constructed at a comparatively small expense.

NOTE.

In prolongation of the general canal system, it has moreover been suggested, as called for by the great interests of the country, that there should be a construction gone into, to encircle Lake Erie with a canal, from Buffalo quite to Detroit.

The table, below inserted, of the distance by stations, will present some idea of the magnitude of this suggestion, as also of the facilities to be found in the natural streams along the route, for a requisite supply of water; and Mr. Darby, in his Geographical View of the United States, has the following passage, in favour of the proposed undertaking :—

"Never did more circumstances combine, to excite to the performance of any undertaking, than to that of encircling Lake Erie with a canal, from Buffalo to Detroit. It would more than complete the chain already in-part executed in the Erie, and in progress in the Ohio canal, and the whole taken together, constitute one of the most useful and extensive lines of natural and artificial navigation, not only in existence, but which the earth admits to be put into existence.

"At the first view, it will no doubt to many persons appear extravagant, to propose bordering a navigable lake of above 300 miles in length, with a canal; but, if careful comparison is made between the safety and regularity of transportation by such a canal, and the very uncertain and tedious navigation of the lake, a decision would at once be made in favour of the former. The same canal boat which would be loaded in the Ohio or Hudson, could, without transshipment, be conveyed to the opposite extreme.

"The most remarkable circumstance, however, in such a canal, is, that it could be carried upwards of 300 miles on one level, if such a mode should be requisite; and, in any manner of construction, would demand less lockage, and be more secure of an uninterrupted supply of water, than any other canal line of equal length, which can be traced in the United States."

TABLE.

		Miles.
Buffalo harbour to Smoker's creek,		4
Cayuga creek,	9	13
Two Sisters' creek,	6	19
Cattaraugus creek,	9	28
Dunkirk harbour,	13	41
Fredonia creek,	1	42
Portland, mouth of Chatauque creek,	14	56
Northern angle of Pennsylvania,	10	66
Twenty mile creek,	1	67
Sixteen mile creek,	6	73
Twelve mile creek,	5	78
Erie town and harbour,	8	86

		Miles.	
Fair View, and mouth of Walnut creek,	5	91
Elk creek,	6	97
Crooked creek,	5	102
North-west angle of Pennsylvania,	4	106
Connaught village and river,	1	107
Ashtabula village and river,	14	121
New-market, and mouth of Grand river,	27	148
New-market creek,	9	157
Cuyahoga river and town of Cleaveland, where the Ohio canal debouches into Lake Erie,	18	175
Rocky river,	6	181
Black river,	18	199
Beaver river,	4	203
Vermillion river,	5	208
Old woman's creek,	10	218
Huron river,	3	221
Sandusky bay	10	231
Portage river,	20	251
Toussaint river,	8	259
Maumee river,	15	274
Raisin river,	9	283
Stoney creek,	5	288
Huron river,	10	298
Rouge river,	22	320
Detroit,	5	325

A.—From a point of the Hudson river, at or near Newburgh, by canal, along the Waalkill and Pauling's creek valleys, to the River Delaware, at the Water Gap.   Distance, *Miles*, 88

No. 34.

NEWBURGH AND WATER GAP CANAL.

By an act of the New-York legislature, 9th April, 1824, a company was instituted for this undertaking, and entiled the "Orange and Sussex canal company," and a concurrent act of incorporation was passed by the state of New-Jersey. The project has, however, been in some degree suspended; but at present examinations are on foot to ascertain with regard to its feasibility, and, in case of a favourable report, it is expected the company will receive aid from the state for a prosecution of the work.

A communication by canal, between the Hudson and the Delaware, at these points, is highly desirable ;—the route, between a continuation of the Catskill mountain on one side, and the Highlands on the other, passing through a valley of great fertility, and well replenished with minerals and lumber for transportation ; and, moreover, this route, striking the River Delaware at a point whence it is probable there will soon be a continuation of the route direct to the Susquehanna coal region. The ascent from the Hudson river to the proposed summit level, is stated at 430 feet; descent thence to the Delaware, 207 feet.

M.—Fifthly ; recommended by the governor, a connexion between the upper waters of the Alleghany, the Susquehanna, and the Genessee rivers.

Distance, *Miles,* 250

Nos. 35 and 36.

ROCHESTER AND OLEAN CANAL.

GENESSEE AND CHEMUNG CANAL.

By means of improvements at the natural obstructions, and of canals of communication from the Genessee to the other rivers specified, a line of navigation may be obtained, thus :—

Up the course of the Genessee, from Lake Ontario to Williamsburgh, and thence, on the one hand, up the valley into Cattaraugus county, to Olean, or Hamilton, and through Cattaraugus, to where the Alleghany river strikes on Pennsylvania ; on the other hand, from Williamsburgh, through Livingston and Steuben counties, down the Conhocton and Chemung valley, to the boundary line above Tioga point, or New-Athens. Regular examinations and estimates upon this article are directed by law, 20th April, 1825.

NOTE.

Examinations on this article are not yet gone through with ; but surveys have been partially made of several lines of route, for a canal between Rochester and Olean, or Hamilton, on the Alleghany. By the one proposed to pass through the valleys of the Genessee, Black creek, and Oil creek, the distance is 111 miles; lockage 1059 feet; estimate of cost, 875,588 dollars.

M.—Sixthly; recommended by the governor, a connexion between the Erie canal and the Susquehanna river, along the valley of the Chenango.

Distance, *Miles*, 150

No. 37.

THE CHENANGO CANAL.

The supposed route for this is from Utica, through Oneida, Madison, and Chenango counties, to Chenango point, in Broome, and thence down the east branch of the Susquehanna, to the Pennsylvania line, near Tioga point; and it comprehends a distance of 150 miles. Surveys and estimates directed by law, 20th April, 1825.

NOTE.

A survey has been had on this article, taking the route as commencing at Binghamton, below Chenango point, and proceeding up the Chenango valley, through Norwich, to the Erie canal at Whitesborough. Distance, by survey, from Binghamton to Whitesborough, 96 miles; lockage, 1032 feet; estimate of cost, 715,478 dollars.

A.—Seventhly; recommended by the governor, a connexion between Lake Seneca and the Susquehanna river, and Lake Cayuga and the Susquehanna.

Distance, together, *Miles*, 50

Nos. 38 and 39.

SENECA AND TIOGA CANAL.

CAYUGA AND OWEGO CANAL.

From the head of Lake Seneca, to Newtown, on the Chemung, or Tioga branch of Susquehanna, and from Ithaca, at the head of Lake Cayuga, to the East Branch of the Susquehanna, at or near the village of Owego :—these make together a distance of about 50 miles. Surveys and estimates directed by law, 20th April, 1825.

Another route of communication has been proposed, which appears to have great advantages to recommend it. It is from the head of Cayuga lake, direct across to the main Susquehanna, that is to say, commencing at the town of Ithaca, ascending the Cayuga inlet, and descending the valley of Shepard's creek, to Tioga point, or near the same. Distance 37 miles.

The canalling facilities are said to be good, and this line is a very direct one for transporting the New-York articles of plaster and salt into Pennsylvania. But, moreover than that, it approaches an extensive range of coal beds, situate on Towanda creek. This creek enters the Susquehanna in Bradford county, about 14 miles below Tioga point; and the coal is found in the Highlands, which terminate the forks thereof, at a short distance from the river, say 5 or 6 miles. It is of the bituminous kind, like the coal at the head waters of the Tioga river, and far more accessible for the consumption of New-York. As to abundance, those who have surveyed the ground, report that there is coal enough to supply all the state of New-York with fuel, and that they are of opinion, much the greater part of it will eventually be supplied from these beds.

Supposed lockage, between Seneca lake and the Chemung at Newtown, 504 feet. Estimate of cost, 239,118 dollars, including a navigable feeder from Painted Post to the summit level. Between Lake Cayuga and the village of Owego, lockage 760 feet; estimate, 320,000 dollars.

NOTE.

A company has been authorized by the legislature of New-York, to construct a rail road between Ithaca at the head of Lake Cayuga, and the Susquehanna river at Owego.

1829.

The legislature of New-York have authorized the construction of the Chemung canal ; that is, from the head of Seneca lake to the town of Elmira, or Newton, with a navigable feeder from the Chemung narrows, at the village of Painted Post, on the Chemung river, to the summit level : provided that the construction of both main canal and feeder can be accomplished at a sum not exceeding 300,000 dollars.

The proposed point of junction of the navigable feeder with the summit level, is at 13 miles distance from the head of Seneca lake; and the said feeder, commencing at Painted Post, will itself be 13 miles in length. From the Painted Post, it is proposed to carry a rail road up to the coal mines at the head waters of the Tioga, a distance of about 40 miles. Distance in all, 66 miles, to Seneca lake.

M.—Eighthly; recommended by the governor, a connexion between the Erie canal at Buffalo, and the Alleghany river at its confluence with the Conewango creek, and Lake Erie, at Portland.

Distance, *Miles*, 120

Nos. 40 and 41.

THE CONEWANGO CANAL.
PORTLAND AND MAYSVILLE CANAL.

This contemplated route of communication, through Erie county, and part of Cattaraugus and Chatauque counties, in a direction nearly south, to the Pennsylvania line, at the Conewango creek intersection; and thence to Maysville, at the head of Chatauque lake, and to Portland on Lake Erie, comprises a distance of about 120 miles. Surveys and estimates are directed by law, 20th April, 1825.

NOTE.

A survey has been had, with a view to the proposed works of this article: viz.

A canal from Portland, on Lake Erie, to the head of Chatauque lake. Distance, 10¼ miles; lockage, 724 feet; estimate of cost, 398,685 dollars.

A canal from Buffalo, through the valley of the Conewango, to the river Alleghany. Distance, 89 miles; lockage, 856 feet; estimate of cost to the Pennsylvania intersection, 503,312 dollars. This canal to communicate with Lake Chatauque, at Jamestown.

(There is now a handsome schooner sailing on Lake Chatauque; and a steam-boat is about being built, to be established thereon, and to ply between Jamestown and Maysville.)

Portland, on Lake Erie, is 60 miles from Buffalo: it has a pretty good harbour; and is becoming of importance as a landing place.

The engineer, who has recently surveyed the Conewango route, states that the proposed canal may be easily extended from the mouth of the Conewango, down the valley of Alleghany, to Pittsburg; and that the expense for the whole distance, of a canal by this route, from Buffalo to Pittsburg, would be less than 2,000,000 dollars. See the Pennsylvania article, No. 89.

M.—Ninthly; recommended by the governor, a connexion between Black river of Ontario, and the Erie canal, on one hand; the river St. Lawrence on the other.   Distance, *Miles*, 250

Nos. 42 and 43.
BLACK RIVER ONTARIO CANALS.
OGDENSBURG AND BOONSVILLE CANAL.

From Sackett's Harbour, Ontario, by the stream in part, and the valley of Black river, through Jefferson, Lewis, Oneida, and Herkimer counties, to the Erie canal, east of Utica; and from the waters of Black river, by a canal, to the St. Lawrence, at or near Ogdensburg: also from the Erie canal, west of the village of Rome, to intersect the aforesaid route. Surveys and estimates for all of which are directed by law, 20th April, 1825; and detailed reports are expected, that may enable the points of route to be decided upon.

The distance, by canal and river stream together, may be about 250 miles.

NOTE.

The New-York commissioners have effected in part the examinations here directed; and they report, as practicable, a route of communication between the Erie canal and River St. Lawrence, from Rome, through Boonsville, to Ogdensburg: distance, 114 miles; lockage, 1587 feet; estimate of cost, 931,014 dollars. Or through Camden to the same. Distance, 129 miles; lockage, 635 feet; estimate, 855,630 dollars.

A.—Tenthly; it is recommended by the governor to improve forthwith the upper parts of the Hudson river, so as to remove effectually the there existing embarrassments to its free navigation.

Distance, *Miles*, 10

No. 44.

THE OVERSLAUGH.

This is the impediment specially alluded to : it is situate a few miles below Albany ; that is to say, between Albany and New-Baltimore; and the removal of it is of so much greater importance, as it is now in a great measure ascertained to be profitable for canal boats to be attached to the canal exclusively, and transshipments of their lading consequently to be made, whenever they arrive at tide water, or other natural navigation.

It has been proposed to improve the bed of the Hudson at this place, partly by the use of machines, and partly by bringing together, or rather filling up spaces between a number of small islands, so as to confine the current if possible to one channel ; and thereby produce a greater velocity, and greater depth of water. By the which, or some other means, there can be very little doubt the object will ere long be attained ; not only will the sloop navigation be facilitated, but larger vessels find also a passage up to Albany, Troy, Waterford, and Lansingburg. Some transverse dams have indeed been constructed, and longitudinal ones will follow ; and, if such means as these alone have not the desired success, a deep lateral canal or two may possibly be next attempted : the distance is short.

NOTE.

The construction of a ship canal, from Albany to Coeymans, is suggested, and application about to be made for an act of incorporation. Capital, 1,000,000 dollars. The distance about 12 miles.

A.—Eleventhly ; recommended by the governor, several canals of connexion between the bays of Long Island. They are recommended as very desirable.

Distances, together, *Miles*, 50

No. 45.

LONG ISLAND CANALS.

The bays of this important island are directed by law, 20th April, 1825, to be surveyed, and their favourable points for a connexion to be defined; and the same to be reported upon, with estimates.

The bays in view are, particularly, Gravesend bay, Jamaica bay, Great South bay, and across the Canoe place, to Southold bay. The aggregate of canal works, perhaps, 50 miles.

An uninterrupted navigation along the south side of the island, and thence to the bays on the north, is an object of great moment.

NOTE.

The leading improvements suggested, are as follows:—
1. To join Southold bay with Southampton bay, at Canoe place. Estimate, - - - - - $30,913
2. Southampton bay, with Great South bay, - - 93,344
3. Shoals in Great South bay to be removed, - 20,000
4. From Hog island inlet to Jamaica bay, - - 63,837
5. Jamaica bay to Gravesend bay, - - - 54,124

This, comprising between Canoe place and Gravesend, a distance of about 11 miles of canal, and 75 miles of bay navigation; together, - - - - - - - Miles, 86

NOTE, (1829.)

An improvement at the dangerous pass of Hurlgate has long been desired. At present a project for effecting it is on foot, which derives encouragement from a survey that has been made of the ground. From this, it appears, that a ship canal, between Pot cove and Hallet cove, to avoid the present navigation difficulties, can be opened, and that the length thereof, so as to secure a depth of water in the coves sufficient for the largest vessels of war, will be 2439 running feet; whereof 470 feet will be excavation below high water; 1369 feet excavation of high upland, with indication of rock; and 600 feet of salt marsh. Two pair of gates at each extremity will be necessary. Dimensions of the canal, 137 feet in width from bank to bank, on the water surface, at high tide; 80 feet at the bottom, and 28½ deep. This will accommodate a line of battle ship; and for such a canal, including a drawbridge, the estimate of cost is $162,152. For a canal, 17½ feet deep at high water, 82 feet wide between the banks, and 40 feet at bottom, the estimate is $64,548.

And, moreover, by an act of the legislature, 20th April, 1825, surveys and estimates are directed to be made for the several canals designated, as next follows, viz.—

A.—From the Erie canal, at Syracuse, in Onondaga county, through Port Watson, to the projected Chenango canal. Distance, *Miles*, 65

No. 46.

PORT WATSON CANAL.

To be reported upon to the legislature, at their next session.

NOTE.

By a report made on this article, the projected route commences at Syracuse, near the village of Salina, and proceeds by the valley of Onondaga creek and Homer, to Port Watson; whence, by the Tioughnioga river, to Chenango point.

Length of canal, as far as Port Watson, 47 miles; lockage, 865 feet; estimate of cost, 432,000 dollars.

A.—From the Erie canal, at or east of Herkimer, by canal, to Lake Otsego, and down the Unadilla river valley, to the Susquehanna, east branch. Distance to Bainbridge, and thence down to the Pennsylvania line, *Miles*, 100

No. 47.

UNADILLA CANAL.

To be reported upon to the legislature, at their next session.

NOTE.

Application is making to the legislature to institute a company, for the effecting an improved slackwater navigation along the Susquehanna, from Cooperstown, on Lake Otsego, to the Pennsylvania line, near Harmony; with power to construct a rail road, from the head of Lake Otsego, to a point of the Erie canal, at or near Fort Plain.

A.—From the Alleghany river at Olean, by the Tonnewanta valley, and through the village of Batavia, to the Erie canal. Distance, *Miles*, 90

No. 48.

BATAVIA CANAL.

To be reported upon to the legislature, at their next session.

―――

A.—From Buffalo, on Lake Erie, by the valley of Buffalo creek and Ischua creek, to Olean point, on the Alleghany river. Distance, *Miles*, 75

No. 49.

BUFFALO AND OLEAN CANAL.

Examinations of a route for this projected communication, are to be made and reported upon.

―――

A.—From the Champlain canal, or the Hudson river, along the valley of the Battenkill, to the Vermont line. Distance, *Miles*, 20

No. 50.

BATTENKILL CANAL.

To be reported upon to the legislature, at their next session. A continuation of this canal, within the state of Vermont, to the head waters of the Battenkill, is proposed, as stated at No. 18 of the New-England series.

―――

A.—From Sharon, in Schoharie county, to the tide water of the Hudson, at or below the mouth of Croton river; or, from a point of the Erie canal, to the Hudson, at the mouth of Croton, passing through Sharon, in Schoharie county. Distance, *Miles*, 140

No. 51.
THE SHARON CANAL.

To be reported upon to the legislature, at their next session.

A.—From Catskill, on the Hudson river, along the valley of the Catskill and Schoharie creeks, to intersect the Erie canal, west of Schoharie creek.

Distance, *Miles*, 60

No. 52.
THE CATSKILL CANAL.

To be reported upon to the legislature, at their next session.

A.—From Lake Erie to Lake Ontario, by canal, along the Niagara river valley. Distance from Buffalo to Fort Niagara, 35 miles; or, from the mouth of Tonnewanta creek to Lewistown, *Miles*, 15

No. 53.
THE NIAGARA CANAL.

Application will be made to the legislature, at their next session, for an act of incorporation, to enable a company to make a canal round the falls of Niagara, in Niagara county, to terminate at Lewistown.

NOTE.

An act was passed, authorizing a boat canal and rail way, round the falls to Lewistown; but a bill, now before the New-York legislature, proposes to enlarge the object, by water, to a sloop lock navigation.

The company, by this, may hope to compete, in some measure, with their rival on the other side, the Welland canal company. Capital stock, 500,000 dollars.

SUMMARY FOR NEW-YORK STATE.

ARTIFICIAL NAVIGATION.

Page.	No.		Miles.
52	25.	The New-York Champlain canal, distance,	70½
53	26.	Erie and Hudson canal,	363
65	27.	St. Lawrence and Champlain canal,	130
66	28.	Oswego canal,	38
67	29.	Great Sodus canal,	25
68	30.	Cayuga and Seneca canal,	21
69	31.	Delaware and Hudson canal,	81
70	32.	Lackawaxen and Cookquago canal,	60
71	33.	Cookquago and Canisteo canal,	150
		Portland and Detroit canal,	269
73	34.	Newburgh and Water Gap canal,	88
74	35.	Rochester and Olean canal,	111
74	36.	Genessee and Chemung canal,	139
75	37.	Chenango canal,	96
75	38.	Seneca and Tioga canal,	
75	39.	Cayuga and Owego canal. Or Seneca and Tioga canal and rail road,	66
77	40.	Conewango canal,	89
77	41.	Portland and Maysville canal,	10¼
78	42.	Black river of Ontario canals and stream improvements,	136
78	43.	Ogdensburg and Lonsville canal,	114
79	44.	The Overslaugh canal,	12
80	45.	Long Island canals,	11
		The Hurl gate canal,	
81	46.	Port Watson canal,	47
81	47.	Unadilla canal; or Otsego canal and rail road,	100
82	48.	Batavia canal,	90
82	49.	Buffalo and Olean canal,	75
82	50.	Battenkill canal,	20
83	51.	Sharon canal,	140
83	52.	Catskill canal,	60
83	53.	Niagara canal,	15

Total of artificial navigation, 2626¾

NATURAL NAVIGATION.

Page		Miles.
52	The Hudson river, up to Albany,	145
52	Lake Champlain,	120
80	Bay navigation of Long Island,	75
81	Tioughnioga river, from Port Watson to Chenango point,	30

To which add:—

Lake George, situate south of Lake Champlain, and communicating therewith by a short outlet, at the old fort of Ticonderoga. It is 37 miles long; from 1 to 7 wide, - 37

Oneida lake, situate west of Rome, and discharging into the Ontario by the river Oswego. It is 25 miles long, by 5 in width, 25

The lakes, viz.—Otsego, the head of Susquehanna river, 9 miles long; Salina, or Onondaga, 7 miles; Owasco, 14 miles; Cayuga, 40 miles; Skeneateles, 15 miles; Seneca, 35 miles: Crooked, 20 miles; Canandaigua, 20 miles; Chatauque, 19 miles; together, - - - - - - - 179

The rivers; Oswegatchie, Grosse, Racquet, and St. Regis; which fall into the St. Lawrence.

The Big Chazy, Saranac, Sable, and other streams, tributary to Lake Champlain.

104 rivers in this state, 192 creeks and minor lakes, as enumerated below. Allowing to these an average natural navigation of 15 miles each; this makes - - - 4440

                Total of natural navigation, 5051
                Total of artificial navigation, 2626¾

                Total of both,   *Miles*, 7677¾

In the order of the counties of New-York, the rivers are as follow:—

IN SUFFOLK, L. I.

The rivers; Peconick, Connecticut, Patchogue, Nessaquague, Conetquot, Oriwanke; and Mattatuck creek.

The bays; Huntington, Gardener, Great Peconick, Great West, Great South, Shinnecaugh, Toad, Bullshead, Mecoa,

Quonic, Drownmeadow, Setauket, Stony Brook, Acaboutick, Three Mile; and ponds, Ronconcomb, Sagg.

IN QUEEN, L. I.

The bays; Rockaway, Parsonage, Merrick, Jerusalem, Cow, Jamaica, Oyster, Little Neck, Hampstead harbour, Oyster, Coldspring, Flushing; and creek, Newtown.

IN RICHMOND, L. I.

Freshkill, and other small creeks.

IN ROCKLAND.

The rivers; Hudson in part, Hackinsack, Passaick, Ramapough; and the Slate creek.

IN WEST CHESTER.

The rivers; Croton, Bronx, Mahanus, Mamaroneck, Hutchins, Sawmill, Hudson in part, Peekskill, Harlaem, Byram; and the ponds, Long, Byram, Rye.

IN PUTNAM.

The rivers; Hudson in part, Peekskill, Croton; and the ponds, Mahopack, Crumb.

IN ORANGE.

The rivers; Hudson in part, Waalkill, Neversink, Mongaup, Ramapaugh, Rutgers, Poplopenskill, Otter; the creeks, Shawangunk, Warwick, Chambers, Moordenars; the ponds, Thompson's, Wickham, Duxido, Cedar.

IN DUTCHESS.

The rivers; Hudson in part, Roeliff, Junsinskill; the creeks, Wappinger, Oblong, Wassnick, Sprout, Crumb, Elbow, Ten Mile; and the ponds, Saghkill, Londstmanskill, Slissing, Whaley's.

IN ULSTER.

The rivers; Hudson in part, Waalkill, Esopus, Big and Little Shandakin, Rondout, Saghkill, Plattekill, Goodherskill; and Shin's lake.

IN SCHENECTADY.

The river; Mohawk, in part; the creeks, Schoharie, Normanskill, Airplaatskill, each in part.

IN DELAWARE.

The rivers; Delaware, Susquehanna, Charlotte, each in part, the Cookquago, Popackton, Little Delaware; Oleont creek, and Beaver creek, in part.

IN SULLIVAN.

The rivers; Delaware, Neversink, each in part; the creeks, Beaver, Ten Mile, Kalkoon, and others.

IN ALBANY.

The rivers; Hudson, Mohawk, Catskill, each in part, Normanskill, Coeymanskill, Vlamanskill, Bozakill, Hacneraykill in part, Bethlehem and Black creeks, and Fox creek in part.

IN GREENE.

The rivers; Catskill, Kaatuskill, Schoharie, Hudson, each in part.

IN COLUMBIA.

The rivers; Hudson, Greene, each in part; the creeks, Kinderhook, Kleinskill, Abrams, Stone, Roeliff, Jansenskill, Dovekill, and Taghconic.

The lakes; Cookpake, Fish, Charlotte, and Whiting's.

IN SCHOHARIE.

The rivers; and creeks; Schoharie in part, Cobelskill, Fox, and head of Cookquago; Lake Utsayanthy.

IN RENSSELAER.

The rivers; Hudson, Hoosick, each in part, Poestenkill, Wynanskill; the creeks, Little Hook, Quackenkill, Tomhanick, Sunkomissick, Moordenaarskill, Tackewassickill, Tierkenkill; and Sand lake.

IN CLINTON.

The rivers; Big and Little Chazy, Little Sable, Saranac, Great Sable in part.

Lake Champlain in part, Chazyhead pond, Cumberland bay.

IN WASHINGTON.

The rivers; Hudson, Poultney, Powlet, Hoosick, each in part; the Battenkill, Wood creek, (North) Moses, East, White, Black creeks.

The lakes; George, Champlain, each in part; Big pond; South bay.

IN WARREN.

The rivers; Hudson, and North branch in part, Schroon, East Stony, and Halfway creeks in part.

The lakes; George, Schroon, each in part, Brandt lake, Friend's lake, Loon lake, French pond.

IN SARATOGA.

The rivers; Hudson, Mohawk, Sacondaga, each in part,

Snoekill, Anthonyskill, Dwarskill, Mournkill; the creeks; Kayadarassoras, Fish, Glowegee, and Chuckdenunda in part.

The lakes; Saratoga, Long, Round; and Oval pond.

IN FRANKLIN.

The rivers; Salmon, Little Salmon, St. Regis main and east branches, in part; head of Racquet, Trout, Chateaugay.

The lakes; Chateaugay, Saranac, Tupper's in part, and some ponds.

IN ESSEX.

The rivers; part of Great Sable and branches, Schroon river, part of Hudson north branch, Boquet river, Gilliland's creek; outlet of Lake George.

The lakes; Champlain, George, Schroon, each in part, Paradox lake; Augur, Rattlesnake, Worm ponds; the bays of Peru, and North-west.

IN BROOME.

The rivers; Delaware, Susquehanna, Chenango, Tioughnioga, each in part, part of Otselick, and of Owego creek, Nanticoke, Oghquago, and Cocoanut creeks.

IN MONTGOMERY.

The rivers; Mohawk, Sacondaga, Schoharie, each in part; part of East Canada creek; Garoga creek, Stoney, Otsquago, Chuckdenunda, West Stoney, Canajoharie, Nowndaga creeks.

The lakes, or ponds, at the heads of East Canada, and Garoga creeks, and others in the north-west part of the county.

IN HAMILTON.

The rivers; head waters of Racquet, of Moose, of Sacondaga, of Jessups, of some branches of the Hudson; Piseeka river, and many creeks.

The lakes, or ponds; Piseeka, Pleasant, Oxbow, and others.

IN OTSEGO.

The rivers; Susquehanna, Unadilla, Charlotte, each in part; the creeks, Butternut, Otsego, Shenevas, Cherry valley, Oaks, Fly, Wharton.

The lakes; Otsego, and Caneaderago, or Schuyler's lake.

IN COURTLANDT.

The rivers; Tioughnioga and its branches, Otselick in part. Skeneateles lake in part.

IN HERKIMER.

The rivers; Mohawk in part, West Canada creek and branches, East Canada in part; heads of Black, Independence, Beaver, Moose, Oswegatchie, Unadilla rivers.

IN TIOGA.

The rivers; Susquehanna, Tioga, each in part; the creeks, Cayuta, Butlers, Newtown, Cuttetant, and part of Owego, and others.

IN ONEIDA.

The rivers; Mohawk, Black, each in part; part of Oneida creek, and of Fish creek, and western branches, Oriskany creek, West Canada creek in part, Wood creek, Nine Mile, Cincinnati, Saghdequada creeks.

Oneida lake in part.

IN JEFFERSON.

The rivers; Black, Indian, Oswegatchie, each in part, Chaumont river; the creeks, Stoney, North and South, Big Sandy, and Perch.

Lake Ontario in part, and some small lakes; the bays, Hungry, Chaumont, Black river; Sackett's harbour, Henderson's harbour.

IN LEWIS.

The rivers; Black, Moose, Independence, Beaver, each in part, heads of Great Fish creek, and Indian river, of Great Salmon creek, and Mohawk river; of a branch of Oswegatchie; Deer creek, Otter Creek.

IN ST. LAWRENCE.

The rivers; St. Lawrence, Oswegatchie, Gross, Racquet, St. Regis, Indian, each in part.

The lakes; Black, Cranberry, and Tupper's in part, and small river head lakes.

IN OSWEGO.

The rivers; Oswego, and Salmon, Oneida in part; the creeks, Salmon, Grindstone, Catfish, Little Sandy, Scriba, and others, head of Fish creek.

The lakes; Ontario, Oneida, each in part, Fish lake; the bays; Sandy creek, Four Mile.

IN CHENANGO.

The rivers; Chenango, Susquehanna, Unadilla, Otselick, each in part.

IN STEUBEN.

The rivers; Tioga in part, Conhocton, Canisteo; the creeks, Mud, Canoe, Tuscarora, Conicodco, and others.

The lakes; Seneca, Crooked, each in part, Mud, Loon, and Little.

IN MADISON.

The rivers; head waters of Chenango, Unadilla, Otselick, each in part, Tioughnioga; the creeks, Comassaraga, Cowassabon, Chitteningo, and part of Oneida.

The lakes; Cazenovia, and part of Oneida.

IN TOMPKINS.

The lakes; Seneca, Cayuga, each in part.

The creeks; Fall, Six Mile, Cascadilla, and part of Salmon.

IN ONONDAGA.

The rivers; Seneca, Oswego, Onondaga, each in part; Salina and Skeneateles outlets; the creeks, Onondaga, Nine Mile, Butternut, Limestone; head of Tioughnioga, part of Chitteningo.

The lakes; Onondaga, Otisco, Skeneateles, Fish, part of Oneida, and the Green ponds.

IN CAYUGA.

The rivers; Seneca in part, Owasco outlet and inlet, part of Salmon creek, and others.

The lakes; Owasco, parts of Ontario, Cayuga, Skeneateles, Cross; Duck pond; Nine Mile bay.

IN ALLEGHANY.

The rivers; Genessee, and the heads of rivers and creeks which flow into the Susquehanna, into Lake Erie, into the Alleghany, into the Genessee.

IN SENECA.

The rivers; Seneca, Canandaigua, each in part, Seneca outlet, Tuckyhannock creek.

The lakes; Ontario, Cayuga, Seneca, each in part; the bays, Port East, Little Sodus, part of Great Sodus of Ontario.

IN LIVINGSTON.

The rivers; Genessee in part, Honeoye outlet in part; the creeks, Canaveraga, Casaqua, Canesus; the head of Conhocton.

The lakes; Canesus, and part of Hemlock.

IN ONTARIO.

The river; Canandaigua in part; the creeks, Red, Flint, Mud, and Salmon; the outlets of Hemlock, of Honeoye, of Crooked lake.

The lakes; Canandaigua, Scametica, Honeoye; parts of Seneca, of Crooked, of Ontario, and of Hemlock; and Great Sodus bay in part.

IN MONROE.

The rivers; Genessee in part; the creeks, Irondequot, Stone, parts of Black, of Allen's, of Salmon, of Sandy, and other creeks.

Lake Ontario in part; Irondequot and Braddock's bays.

IN NIAGARA.

The rivers; Niagara, Tonnewanta, each in part; the creeks, Wilkins, Howell's, Tuscarora, Cayuga, and others; and part of Lake Ontario.

IN GENESSEE.

The river Tonnewanta, and all its head waters; parts of Allen, of Black, of Cattaraugus creeks; the creeks, Anyocheeca, Oakorchard, Johnson, Sandy, and three branches of Buffalo; the heads of Ellicott's, and of Sulphur spring.

Lake Ontario in part; the Silver, the Jefferson, and some smaller lakes.

IN CATTARAUGUS.

The rivers; Olean, and parts of Alleghany, and Connemaugh; the creeks, Oswaya, Tusquiatossee, Tuniauguant, Oil, Ischua, Great and Little Valley, and part of Cattaraugus.

IN ERIE.

The rivers; Niagara, Tonnewanta, Cattaraugus, each in part; the creeks, Seneca, Cayuga, Cazenovia, (forming Buffalo,) Ellicott's, Cauquaga, Two Sisters, Sulphur spring, Ransom's, Smoke's, Conjockeda, and others.

IN CHATAUQUE.

The river Conewango; the creeks, Cosdauga, Walnut, Chatauque, Canadaway, French; and parts of Cattaraugus, of South Branch, and Chatauque outlet.

The lakes; Chatauque, Cosdauga, Bear, and part of Erie.

NOTE.

In the several shipyards of the port of New-York, there are now building, as follows:—

        2 Line of Battle ships.
        2 Frigates.
        2 Sloops of War.

And repairing:—
        1 Line of Battle ship.

The above are for foreign account. There are, besides, on the stocks:—

        12 Merchantmen.
        8 Steam Vessels.

And on the stocks of the United States Navy Yard:—
        2 Frigates.
        2 Sloops of War.

NOTE ADDITIONAL, 1828.

1. Since the year 1826, no state tax has existed in New-York, of any description. The expenses of government are charged upon a fund denominated the "General Fund," the capital whereof is 1,670,740 dollars, and the revenue derived from it, though at this moment not quite equal to the charge in question, is likely to be rendered equal.

2. There exists in New-York a "Literature Fund," of 331,609 dollars, the management whereof, and distribution of revenue, are intrusted to the regents of the university.

3. A "Common School Fund," amount 1,700,000 dollars, in productive capital; whereof the income is about equal to an annual appropriation of 100,000 dollars.

4. A "Canal Fund," the income whereof for the 12 months last past, has amounted to 1,233,435 dollars.

Thus the public funds of the state of New-York, are composed of,

>A General Fund.
>A Literature Fund.
>A Common School Fund.
>A Canal Fund.

NEW-JERSEY, DELAWARE, MARYLAND, PENNSYLVANIA, AND OHIO NAVIGATION.

N.—From New-York harbour, through Rariton bay, and up the river, to Brunswick, in New-Jersey.

Distance, *Miles*, 35

A.—From Brunswick, on the Rariton river, by canal, to the Delaware, below Trenton falls. This line is the one marked out for a water communication, in Mr. Gallatin's Report of 1808, alluded to. The location of the canal now to take place, will probably not differ widely from the plan at that time.

Distance, *Miles*, 28

No. 54.
DELAWARE AND RARITON CANAL.

A charter for the execution of this projected work, was granted, by an act of the New-Jersey legislature, on the 30th December, 1824, conditionally, that the concurrence of Pennsylvania should be given touching one of its provisions; which has in consequence been given, but under certain limits and stipulations, by an act of the legislature, passed on the 6th April, 1825.

Upon a joint examination, made by commissioners of New-Jersey state, and a board of engineers of the United States appointed to that object, it was decided as most eligible, if not indispensable, that a feeding canal should be constructed, drawing from the Delaware itself a supply of water for the summit level of the main canal; that appearing to them the only certain source for obtaining an abundance, proper to facilitate a passage, such as the intercourse is likely to require, and adapted to such vessels as navigate the great rivers and bays of the sea-coast. This therefore has been adopted into the plan: the feeder to enter the River Delaware, at or near Bull's island falls, 23 to 26 miles above tide, at Lamberton, and to terminate, and enter the main canal, within a mile or two of the latter's debouche at Lamberton.

The capital stock of the company, which is 800,000 dollars, with privilege to augment to a milliom if requisite, and an option on the part of the state, of being one-fourth proprietor, if its legislature so determine, has been subscribed with eagerness, and preparations for the work are gone into.

The engineers' estimates are,

For the main canal, taking the length thereof at 30 miles, and making, it is said, large allowances,	$475,000
For the feeder, taking it at 25 miles, and large allowances, - - - - - - -	375,000
Together,	$850,000

The location of this canal will, it appears, differ somewhat from the above specification. It is in agitation to run the line from the Rariton, at some miles below Brunswick, or between Brunswick and Washington, and to make it strike across, not to Lamberton, but to Bordentown, at the mouth of Crosswick's creek; to which point, in such case, the feeding canal will necessarily be extended downward; that is to say, extended to Long Bridge Farm, 5½ miles distant from Trenton. But it is besides in agitation, to lengthen this feeder upwards; that is to say, for it to commence, and take its supply of water out of the Delaware, at within a short distance of Easton, in place of taking it out at Bull's island falls. In consequence of which alteration, if it take place, there will be an enlargement of the company's capital stock, to quadrate with the increase of expense.

A still further consideration òf the subject, seems to have brought back the original intention of terminating this canal at Lamberton, after a course by Millstone valley, somewhat circuitous in comparison of the other. The New-Jersey commissioners report the following line of route as agreed upon.

The main trunk. Along the Rariton valley, and the Millstone river valley, to near its junction with Stony brook; passing south of Princeton, and through the Lawrence meadows, to the city of Trenton, and thence to Lamberton, and its point of connexion with the channel of the Delaware. The feeder to commence opposite to Durham, or the confluence of the Delaware and Musconetcong; passing along the margin of the Delaware, through Trenton, to its termination in the main canal, within a mile of Lamberton, direct across, and by the canal itself, 2¼ miles from the Delaware, below Lamberton. Width of the feeder 40 feet; depth of water 5 feet. It has a descent of 117 feet; the head of Durham falls being 130 feet above tide level, and the Rariton river, a little below Brunswick, 13 feet above tide. The summit level 48 feet. Width of the main trunk to be 60 feet, and depth of water 8, to correspond with the Chesapeake and Delaware canal. Whole length of the canal and feeder, 84 miles. Length of the locks on the main canal, 100 feet, measured between the hollow quoins. Width at bottom, and between the hollow quoins, 22 feet.

To avoid the shoals of the Delaware below Lamberton, it is proposed to extend the main canal into Pennsylvania, by a construction from Biles creek, opposite Lamberton, across the alluvial soil of Bucks county, to Tullytown wharf, distance 5¾ miles; a cut that will moreover be advantageous, in reducing the distance between Lamberton and Philadelphia to 28 miles only, in place of 40.

A new estimate is given as follows:—

Main canal, to 59th section, near the mouth of Millstone river,	$313,897
Lockage, and work connected with the locks,	187,600
Continuation of main canal, from 59th section to New-Brunswick,	164,000
Aqueducts and culverts,	72,300
Grubbing and making roads,	12,856
Fencing 60 miles of canal and feeder,	38,400
Road and farm bridges,	66,000
Protecting banks of main canal with stone,	20,680
Feeder to Eagle island, 5 feet deep, 40 feet wide; 20 miles,	212,592
	1,088,325
Contingencies, five per cent,	54,416
	$1,142,741
Continuation of feeder from Eagle island to Durham, $256,875	
Extension of main canal in Pennsylvania, or Pennsbury manor canal, 87,384	
	344,259
Total,	$1,487,000

Notwithstanding which, however, a law has finally passed the Pennsylvania legislature, to this effect;—that the company be obliged to make their canal below those points, in both rivers, where there is not at all times 8 feet of water, and below all shoals, sand bars, &c., allowing them, however, the right to remove those obstructions in the channels of the rivers, if they prefer that to carrying the canal below them; and allowing them also to make the canal across Pennsbury manor. Pennsylvania stipulates also some other conditions.

The expense of constructing the canal, under the conditions of this law of Pennsylvania, will, it is supposed, amount to little short of 2,000,000 dollars.

January, 1827.

In consequence of the occurrence last above stated, the undertaking altogether is suspended for the present; the canal company not deeming it advisable to prosecute the work, subject to the conditions of the Pennsylvania law here mentioned.

This suspension is much to be regretted; possibly, however, it may have the effect of accelerating another enterprise; which, if not of quite equal importance with the canal as projected, will in many respects be an excellent substitute; namely; a rail road across New-Jersey state, between the Rariton and Delaware rivers; which there is great likelihood will be undertaken, if not forthwith, as soon as the art of constructing rail ways shall be somewhat better understood with us, in its several details, than can be said as yet to be the case.

A short lapse of time, with the public attention turned, as it now is, to the subject, and in particular to the actual results in the instances of two or three of the rail way constructions in England, will be sufficient, with what information is already possessed, to make up the requisite stock of science on the subject, to proceed with upon safe ground. And now assuming for a fact, that a substantial work of the kind, with double tracks, can be constructed, of permanent materials, at an expense not exceeding the estimate for a canal such as has been projected, over about the same length of ground, there is scarcely a doubt, even in case the New-Jersey legislature should determine to leave the thing entirely to individual enterprise, but the subscription for it will eagerly be filled up, as soon as it shall be proposed on the solid footing alluded to.

No district of country can be found, offering a line of road of a like moderate length, better, if so well, adapted to the purposes of a general transportation; nor much better calculated for the effecting a rail way construction along its distance; and consequently, there is offered the fairest prospect of success; a success which perhaps will not be greatly interrupted even by the concurrent operations, at a future day, of the projected "Delaware and Rariton canal" itself.

A plan for a rail road between Camden and Amboy bay, is submitted to the New-Jersey legislature.

A plan for one from Patterson, on the Passaic, eastward, to the

Hudson, is likewise submitted, and an act of incorporation applied for.

JANUARY, 1829.

As time advances, and improvements of the country at large are every day receiving accessions, in degree more or less accelerated, the anticipated views still taken of the accomplishment of this canal, lose nothing of their former vividness. The several great branches of the country's inland navigation, as now established, and every day growing in importance and value, constitute a dependence, that leaves no doubt upon the mind, of a very ample income being in store, to remunerate for the execution of the project, viewed even in the mere light of a separate individual or corporation enterprise.

On the north-eastern side of the Rariton—we have

1. *The East river navigation to Providence, Rhode Island.* Into which flows: 1. The Eastern coasting trade. 2. The trade of the Middlesex canal, extending from Boston to Concord in the centre of New-Hampshire. 3. That of the Blackstone canal from Providence to Worcester in Massachusetts, 45 miles. 4. The Farmington canal, leading through a rich agricultural country to New-Haven—together with the trade of the navigable rivers of New-England, which empty into the East river, or sound—and

2. *The New-York Canals:* Connecting Lake Erie and Lake Champlain with the Hudson, embracing a trade, the tolls from which have amounted during the past year to 838,412 dollars—a trade constantly increasing with the progressive improvement of the country, and which will speedily be swelled to an immense amount by the completion of the numerous additional canals contemplated by the legislature of that great and enterprising state.

By these mediums, the immense trade of a population of several millions of our most enterprising citizens, scattered over a large agricultural and manufacturing country, embracing seven states, have access to the Rariton. But its progress is bounded by the southern shores of that river—thus far it can go and no further. It is still 28 miles from the Delaware.

Passing over this narrow strip of land, to the shores of the Delaware—we have

1. *The Lehigh Canal,* opening an outlet from the inexhaustible fields of coal at Mauch Chunk into this river, with the certain prospect of a continuation of this navigation to the Susquehanna, and Lake Erie, in reversion.

2. *The Central Pennsylvania Canals,* uniting the Delaware and Susquehanna with the Alleghany and Lake Erie, connecting

the various navigable streams of Pennsylvania, and opening an avenue by which her immense agricultural and mineral trade will flow into the Delaware.

3. *The Chesapeake and Delaware Canal*, connecting the Delaware with, 1. The Chesapeake bay and its tributary rivers and populous cities—The Susquehanna, Patuxet, Rappahannoc, Potomac and James—Baltimore, Annapolis, Norfolk, Petersburgh, Fredericksburgh, Richmond, Alexandria, Washington, &c. 2. The Dismal Swamp Canal, soon to become navigable to Newbern in North Carolina. And 3. The splendid canal and rail road projects, uniting the Ohio river with the Chesapeake.

Such is a brief view of the two great sections of country and their internal navigations, which the Delaware and Rariton canal is to unite. It is to form a junction between the East river navigation and its canals and the New-York canals *on one side;* and the Lehigh, central Pennsylvania, and Chesapeake navigations and canals *on the other.* A view before which, in the opinion of the committee, the mere fact that this proposed canal will open a navigation between Philadelphia and New-York, sinks almost into insignificance.

But, the inquiry with us, now particularly in hand, is as touching a minor interest, compared with the great national concernment alluded to: it is, *as to the probable revenue of the proposed Delaware and Rariton canal.* On the 15th of this month, was made a very able and circumstantial report, to the New-Jersey legislature, by a committee appointed to review the whole ground. They strenuously recommend the execution of the work, by the state, as a public concern, and set forth with great clearness, in a series of details, the many advantages, both public and private, that may in all reason be expected, and which, indeed, for the most part, must infallibly flow out of it. The committee recommend it, not only on the broad principle above stated, but as a measure calculated well to reward the state, in her yearly finances, if she assume the proprietorship of the enterprise. The revenue of the canal, to arise from tolls on merchandise, and personal passage along the same, is predicated on a comprehensive review taken by the committee, and stated to the legislature, of the branches of this country's trade and intercourse, embraced in the inquiry.

An estimate of revenue is likewise reported, through the governor of New-Jersey, in compliance with a resolution of the legislature, authorizing and requiring the governor to obtain an accurate estimate of the quantity of merchandise, and productions of all sorts, constituting the coast and inland trade, between the cities of New-York and Philadelphia, and the ports and places on the waters of the Chesapeake; as follows:—

Supposing the canal and feeder are to be 60 miles in length, and that 100,000 tons of coal from the Lehigh, to pay only a cent a ton per mile, shall yearly pass through it, will give - - - - - - $60,000

From the great facility of communication which this and the Chesapeake and Delaware canal (now nearly finished) will afford, between New-York, Philadelphia, Baltimore, and other ports on the Chesapeake bay, the intercourse will be immensely increased; for a very small variation in the price of any article, in any of these markets, would cause shipments through these canals, where insurance would be unnecessary, and certainty of time could be calculated on, so that the estimated amount of the coasting trade between New-York, the Delaware river and bay, and the Chesapeake bay, as now furnished by the corporation of that city, namely, 212,000 tons, may safely be assumed as the minimum on which toll would be collected; to which must be added, what now passes inland, say 10,000 tons more, making an aggregate of 222,000 tons, to pass through the canal, and pay a cent and a half a ton per mile, or sixty cents per ton through, will give 133,200

The toll on the transit of passengers, from the very cheap, easy, and comfortable manner they may, through the canal, be conveyed from city to city, will in a little time be a considerable source of income. Upwards of 80,000 passengers in the steamboats and stages have passed between New-York and Philadelphia during the past year, and will probably be nearly, if not quite doubled, when this cheap and very convenient mode of conveyance shall be afforded, and it is believed may safely be set down at 20,000

The lumber, grain, flour, with various other articles of agricultural produce, and manufactures, which will pass through both feeder and canal, from each side of the Delaware above; from the transit of merchandise carried back; and from the lime, marl, and other manures; with the wood, timber, stone, brick, and other articles, to be shipped on the line of the canal, which would presently be set in motion, may, it is presumed, be estimated at a like sum of 20,000

Making a sum total of annual toll of $233,200
To which add:—
For the East river, &c. trade with Philadelphia, 38,562
For the East river, &c. trade with the south, &c. 33,333
Total estimate of revenue from tolls, $305,095

In the present view of things, the dimensions of the canal have been assumed, at 60 feet by 8, the feeder 40 feet by 5; and the estimate already exhibited, with reference to the Millstone route, taken as a basis; but the same not intended to preclude or discourage any re-examination or reconsideration, either as to route or dimensions, that may be deemed advisable, before the one or the other shall be absolutely decided on and fixed. Taking the estimate as it stands, and the feeder not supposed to extend higher up the Delaware than Eagle island, we have an amount of 1,142,741 dollars, for canal and feeder together; length of the two 60 miles, or about 19,000 dollars average rate per mile. But this estimate was made two years ago, and since that time, materials being considerably reduced in price, and contracts for canal labour having been made at one half the former rate of this most expensive item in the work, to wit, 6¼ cents per cubic yard of excavation, it is thought, in consequence of this, that 13,000 dollars per mile, or the sum of 780,000 dollars, may be considered an ample estimate of cost, for the whole 60 miles of canal and feeder; it being admitted, that along the line of route traced, there exist not *any unfavourable circumstances for construction.*

Commissioners are forthwith to be appointed, by the states of New-Jersey and Pennsylvania, respectively, with a view to their coming to an amicable arrangement, for the reciprocal use of the waters of the Delaware, in relation to this canal, and the Pennsylvania state canal; and also for milling and manufacturing purposes, to the mutual benefit of the states.

N.—From Rariton bay, at Perth Amboy, up the Arthur Kull, and Newark bay, and Passaick river, to the entrance of the Morris canal, as next below specified, at Acquacknack. Distance, *Miles,* 30

A.—From Acquacknack, on the Passaick river, by canal, across the state of New-Jersey, to the Delaware river, opposite Easton. Distance, *Miles,* 76

No. 55.
THE MORRIS CANAL.

For this canal, across the state of New-Jersey, north of the one last specified, a charter was also obtained; and the stock of the company has been filled, with a great excess of subscriptions. The work is to commence forthwith. The route surveyed is through Warren, Morris, and Essex counties, making a general course of east and west nearly. It commences at Philipsburg on Delaware, or opposite the mouth of Lehigh river; taking along the north side of the Pohatcung river; after crossing which, it proceeds along the north of Musconetcong valley, to Stanhope, and thence, on the south, to Brookland. Here is the crown, or summit level, deriving water from the lake, or great pond Hopatcung, in the vicinity: from whence the route is down the valley of Rockaway river to its mouth; thence to Little falls of the Passaick, to Patterson, and to Acquacknack.

The details of the route, however, are not yet quite fixed; nor can they be, some of them, but as the work advances. The crown, as above, will give the bottom of the canal an elevation of 888 feet above tide at the Passaick, and 739 feet above the Delaware level at Easton; of the which rise and fall, it is proposed that 1400 feet shall be overcome by the use of inclined planes in place of lockage. The canal to be 30 to 32 feet wide at the water surface, 16 to 18 feet at the bottom, and 4 feet deep, calculated for boats of 3 feet draft. The engineers' estimate is 809,813 dollars; or, on the supposition of locks being used in the construction throughout, then the estimate amounts to 1,148,103 dollars. At present, the sentiment is in favour of the experiment of inclined planes.

May, 1827.

This canal was commenced in July 1825, and, by an official report of the president of the company, just now given in, there appears to be such satisfactory progress made, that the whole, from the Delaware opposite Easton, to the Passaick, extended to Powles Hook, or Jersey city opposite New-York, may be complete and in operation, in the course of next year, 1828, or the year following.

An important change has been made in the route, by extending it from the Passaick to the Hudson; it was laid out first to Acquacknack, and secondly, to Newark, still on the Passaick, in the belief that the high rocks of Bergen ridge could not be passed. There has, however, since then, been discovered a falling off of the ridge, precisely at a spot where a ravine exists and passes quite across the ridge. Through this the canal will be carried, with considerable facility, and so as to be on a level with tide water all the way from Newark to Jersey city, which, as the canal is to go, is between 11 and 12 miles. Locks of masonry, and an extensive dam, together with a collection of machinery, have been completed at the Hopatcung lake, and the result goes to indicate that there is a supply of water 5 times greater than will be necessary for the locks along the whole line of canal. Nevertheless, it has been thought expedient to adhere to the plan of "inclined planes," on a part of the route, for the sake both of economy in the construction, and of superior expedition in the conveyance to be afforded. And from an experiment made recently at Rockaway, where the difference of level amounts to 52 feet perpendicular, there is reason to believe the plan will succeed to perfect satisfaction, although the experiment itself was not quite as conclusive as could have been wished, owing to certain deficiencies in some of the preparatory steps taken for the occasion.

Research is at present making, after the most efficient machinery that can be adopted into these works, according to the latest improvements in mechanics, and the needful preparations of the ground are making, for the application of the same at the several places where inclined planes are to come into use. The highest lift to be encountered is 90 feet; it is at Boontown falls.

The western division of this canal, from the summit level, embraces 75 sections of half a mile each; and the eastern division, as far as the Passaick, 90 half mile sections; which, consequently, with the 12 miles additional to the Hudson, makes the whole canal distance 94½ miles, or thereabout, besides a navigable feeder at the summit, of ¾ of a mile, which opens a navigation of 9 miles upon Lake Hopatcung.

The cost of all the work done, down to the 1st of this month, amounts to 417,917 dollars, and this is considered as having been by far the most difficult portion of the whole; so that it is confidently expected the entire canal, including its extension from the Passaick to the Hudson, will not exceed the cost of 1,250,000 dollars, but rather fall within this sum.

The company's canal stock, agreeably to charter, and subscribed for, was to the amount of 1,000,000 dollars; but circumstances of defalcation amongst subscribers, caused the company afterwards to resume more than half the number of shares, and of these, the company are at the present day still holders of a portion to be disposed of, say 3204 shares, which, if the company can immediately dispose of at par, would enable them to finish the Morris canal as far as Newark, by the month of July or August 1828.

The directors are sanguine as to a highly beneficial revenue from this canal, when once it shall come into full operation, and apparently are so with reason, considering the various productive sources from agriculture, from manufactures, and from the mines, which its location will command, for a great transportation; and more especially, after a water communication with the

Susquehanna river shall be laid open through the Lehigh, a project that is now on foot. In the mean time, the proprietors of the Lehigh coal mines, it is stated, have offered to come under contract, to deliver annually, for a number of years, 50,000 tons of coal, at the entrance of the Morris canal, at the price of 3 dollars per ton ; which would include considerable profit to the Lehigh company, besides paying them the charge of transportation.

October, 1829.

These works have continued to be steadily prosecuted, and as it would seem, with great judgment, and not a little skilful contrivance on the part of the engineers employed ; though not with that rapidity, altogether, which was at one time intended, owing in part to some disturbance the company experienced in financial operations, a natural consequence of their resumption of a large portion of their capital stock, as has here been stated; and in part also, owing to a willingness to gain adequate and confirmed experimental knowledge in regard to the inclined plane system, which the company contemplated from the beginning to adopt into their plan, as already stated. Accordingly, there is now the best ground for believing, that the system will, in this undertaking, prove completely successful ; and if so, the time is not far off, when a new era may commence, as for the intercourse improvement principle acquiring accelerated force; and the late Fulton's known saying on that head come to be greeted as a true prediction, applicable to the country at large. It is computed that the difference in cost of inclined planes, compared with locks, is as 8 to 1 ; and, as to time in the act of passing, as 16 to 1 in favour of planes.

There remains not now, on both divisions of the route, more to be done, than can with facility be accomplished in the ensuing working season, if nothing new occur to prevent. In the course of operations thus far, some slight alterations have been made as to sites and distances: the whole route, as it now exists, runs as follows :—

Western division, from the feeder at summit level, near Lake Hopatcung, to the Delaware opposite Easton, comprising 74 sections, of 42 chains each, - - - say 74 sections.
Eastern division, from feeder at summit, as far as
Newark on the Passaick river, comprising, 97 do.
From Newark, to Jersey city on the Hudson, 21 do.

Together equal to 100 miles 64 chains; to which, adding the navigable feeder from the lake, 60 chains, this makes in all a navigable distance of 101 miles 44 chains. And this includes the sections passing through the town of Newark, to the west bank of the Passaick, not included in former estimates.

There will be on the western division, 7 locks, overcoming a difference in level of 67 feet, and 11 inclined planes, overcoming 691 feet. On the eastern division, between summit level and the Passaick, there will be 17 locks, overcoming a difference of 156 feet, and 12 inclined planes, overcoming 743 feet.

Total ascent and descent, 1657 feet.

There will be within these limits, 4 guard locks, 5 dams, 30 culverts, 12 aqueducts, 200 bridges and upwards.

The aqueducts are all complete; that across the Passaick river at Little falls, is especially worthy of notice, as superior to any work of the kind in America. It is a beautiful structure, all of cut stone, finished with architectural skill and taste; the duct resting on a single arch of 80 feet, with 50 feet radius, and measuring 52 feet perpendicular above the water level, that is, up to the coping of the side walls, above which, will be the balustrade. Extent, from wing wall to wing wall, over 200 feet; say 215.

The inclined planes are situated thus; viz.

On the western division:—

	Feet.	Inclination.		Feet.
1 At Great meadow, elevation	58	$\frac{1}{10}$	making	580
1 At Stanhope,	70	$\frac{1}{11}$	"	770
1 Near Sager's,	55	$\frac{1}{12}$	"	660
1 At Old Andover,	80	$\frac{1}{8}$	"	640
1 Near Anderson,	64	$\frac{1}{12}$	"	768
1 At Montrose,	50	$\frac{1}{10}$	"	500
1 At Pohatcong,	73	$\frac{1}{10}$	"	730
1 At Hulziser's,	62	$\frac{1}{11}$	"	682
1 Near Bridleman's creek,	100	$\frac{1}{10}$	"	1000
1 Near Green's mills,	44	$\frac{1}{12}$	"	528
1 At Delaware river,	35	$\frac{1}{12}$	"	420

On the eastern division; viz.

	Feet.	Inclination.		Feet.
1 At Summit level,	50	$\frac{1}{12}$	"	600
1 At Drakesville,	80	$\frac{1}{10}$	"	800
1 Near do.	38	$\frac{1}{12}$	"	456
1 At Baker's mills,	52	$\frac{1}{8}$	"	416
1 At Dover,	63	$\frac{1}{9}$	"	567
1 At Rockaway,	52	$\frac{1}{12}$	"	624
1 At Boontown falls,	80	$\frac{1}{10}$	"	800
1 At Montville,	76	$\frac{1}{11}$	"	836
1 At do.	74	$\frac{1}{11}$	"	814
1 Near Pompton,	56	$\frac{1}{12}$	"	672
1 At Bloomfield,	52	$\frac{1}{12}$	"	624
1 At Newark,	70	$\frac{1}{12}$	"	840

23 Planes, together surmounting 1434 feet.

Were it not that two or three of the eastern planes, and as many locks, remain to be finished; and that, on one or two other of the planes, some experimental improvements are yet going forward, the whole 50 miles of this eastern division, from the summit down to Newark, would at the present time be navigable and in use; preparations are making to lay open, and give activity to all the unobstructed parts thereof, in a few days from this.

The present estimated cost, for the whole of the works, from the Delaware at Easton, to the Hudson at Jersey city, including consequently the Bergen division, when completed, is 1,242,275 dollars. There has been expended by the company, down to the 29th of last month, the sum of 912,393 dollars, which includes payments for lands purchased, water privileges, &c.

The company's affairs appear to be in a prosperous condition, a consequence of great prudence in the management, at a critical period of time, and since; and the prospects, touching their not hitherto productive enterprise, to be now very bright.

The present suspension of the Delaware and Rariton project, though regretted as to itself, will, however, confer considerable advantages on the Morris, at its outset, not only as the latter will have, for some time at least, the unrivalled transportation across the state of New-Jersey, to the city of New-York, of the Lehigh coal, but as forming a connexion with the great natural and artificial water communications of the states of New-York and Pennsylvania in general. The Lehigh canal terminates on the west bank of the Delaware, at a point directly opposite to where the Morris begins; the two canals may in fact be considered as one, and a word may here be said of the economy observed, or to be observed, in the Lehigh coal transportation; this substance being taken up at the mine, or rather coal quarry, above Mauch Chunk, without being handled by man, from the time it enters the coal wagon there, until its delivery in New-York. It is put by the miner into a wagon, at the mine, and is drawn 800 yards by animal power, to the apex of the self acting plane; thence the wagon descends 9 miles to the schute on the Lehigh river, and there discharges itself into a boat, in which the coal is brought to the wharves of New-York; and were it not for a certain indirection which the Morris route takes, for the sake of passing near the important manufacturing town of Patterson, the distance by the canal, and that by the ordinary road, between New-York and Easton, would be nearly the same. The state of New-York is now engaged in effecting a canal communication between the great Erie canal and the River Susquehanna, as specified at Article 38; and the project of opening a canal by the Nescopec valley, between the Susquehanna and the Lehigh, as specified at Articles 62 and 63, and the general Pennsylvania state article, it is probable will also succeed. Now it may be seen, that when these designs are accomplished, New-York city will have the following route, both to the coal districts and the great lakes, at command; namely:—

Through the Morris canal, to Philipsburg opposite Easton.
Through the Lehigh canal, up to Wright's creek.
Through the Nescopec canal, to Berwick.
By the Pennsylvania canal, up to the New-York line.
By the Chemung canal, and the Seneca canal, to the Erie canal at Montezuma.

Which will be nearly as direct a route, to that point on the Erie canal itself, and so far towards the great lakes, as the route at present pursued, up the Hudson and the Eastern part of the Erie canal; and be a far more direct route to the extensive coal districts of the line; besides affording another advantage, which in years of severe weather accruing, may be great, viz. that this will be a navigation opening earlier in the spring, and continuing open later in the fall, than the navigation near Albany.

M.—From the junction of the Rariton canal with the River Delaware, up the stream of the Delaware, to the mouths of the Lehigh and Lackawaxen rivers, and thence up to the New-York boundary line, north of Wayne county, near the forks of the Popachton and Cookquago. Distance, *Miles*, 220

No. 56.

UPPER DELAWARE CANALS.

In the Delaware river, there are no precipitous falls. It well accommodates a downward navigation, and this distance of its upper water can, sometimes, in the season of flood, be also ascended by boats. To render it passable at all times, it is proposed to clear out and deepen the natural channel; to cut down the heads of the falls and pitches; so as to make the descent more gradual and uniform: then, to dam up all, or many of the lakes and ponds about the tributary streams, so as to save water, to be let out only when wanted in the dry season; and lastly, in case of necessity, to construct lateral canals at particular passes. The execution of which, it is expected, will so far improve the navigation of the Upper Delaware, as to enable craft of some burthen, and possibly steam-boats, to navigate nearly all the summer through, quite up to the forks.

NOTE.

The particulars of existing falls, and rapids, and shallows, between tide water and Easton, are described from actual surveys, as follows; and, in so far as they obstruct the river's navigation, there is reason to believe effectual improvements will forthwith be made. The states of both New-Jersey and Pennsylvania are highly interested in the measure.

	Distance below the mouth of the Lehigh in miles.	Length of each in feet.	Fall of each. Ft. In.	Head of each above tide. Ft. In.
Trenton falls,	49	3500	9 8	9 8
Gould's falls,	46½	3000	4 5	16 8
Scudder's rift,	44	2500	4 2	24 8
Knowles' Point rift,	39¾	500	3 1	33 6
Bucktail rift,	36½	500	1 5	36 5
Wells's falls,	35½	4780	12 1	49 9
Greenbank rift,	32	500	1 9	58 9
Galloper's and Howel's rift,	31	1500	7 6	68 3
Bull's falls,	27½	800	4 5	72 2
Cutson's rift,	25½	1000	3 10	85 4
Tumbledown falls,	24 to 25	5000	11 1	89 1
Marshall's island rapids,	21 to 23¾	1000	11 5	100 7
Man of war rift,	20	500	1 5	102 3
Stuhl's falls,	18	350	1 8	107 2
Freeman's falls,	17	700	3 7	110 11
Noxmixon falls,	14	1700	4 11	117 6
Linn's falls,	12	2300	7 4	127
Durham falls,	9½	350	2 9	130
Gravelly falls,	8	1500	1 3	133
Rocky falls,	7	2000	2 9	136
Ground Hog rift,	6	1700	1 11	138 1
Old Sow rift,	5	750	2 4	145 5
Clifford's rift,	3½	2000	5 1	150 10
Bixler's rift,	½	2000	7 5	160 5

In addition to which, are the following shallows, where the water, without sensible fall, has but little depth: viz.

Limestone shallows; these occur at a short distance above New-Hope, and 32⅓ miles below the mouth of the Lehigh. They have 15 inches at low water.

Lowrey town shallows; at 16¾ miles below the Lehigh; these are formed by a sand bar in the pool, through which a channel is cut near the Pennsylvania shore.

Whippoorwill shallows; at 2½ miles below the Lehigh; this is a small gravel bar, at the head of an island of same name near the Jersey side.

And moreover, many shallow spots in the different pools, formed by sand bars, or by rocks lying near the surface.

March, 1827.

A bill is now before the Pennsylvania legislature, which goes to empower the canal commissioners to commence the construction of a navigable communication, by canal or canals, between Philadelphia and Easton, on the River Delaware, and by continuation, between Easton and Carpenter's point; provided such canal or canals can be constructed in the Delaware valley, and fed by streams within the state; and provided it shall appear, by proper estimates, that the cost of constructing an uninterrupted navigable communication between the said points, shall not exceed the average rate of 12,000 dollars per mile.

NOTE.

This line of canal will be embraced in the grand Pennsylvania state canal, as forming a section thereof. See Article 84.

N.—From Trenton rapids, down the river stream and bay, to the Capes of the Delaware.
Distance, *Miles*, 155

A.—From the mouth of the Schuylkill river, below Philadelphia, by a series of lock and dam improvements, up the river, to Mount Carbon, in Schuylkill county, about 50 miles above Reading.
Distance, *Miles*, 117

No. 57.

SCHUYLKILL CANAL WORKS.

On the 8th March, 1815, the legislature, by act of incorporation, instituted a new company, to take up, or resume the works on this river; and out of the procedure, a series of constructions have arisen, and are become united in their present elegant and *useful* forms; and the whole undertaking is now nearly complete. It has been prosecuted to the eve of a conclusion, with much taste, by the "Schuylkill Navigation Company." It comprises 31 dams, commencing at Fair Mount water works, near

Philadelphia, by which is produced a slack water navigation of 45 miles; also 23 canals, of 32 to 40 feet width at the water surface, 3 to 4 feet deep, and extending together 64 miles: 588 feet is the fall, overcome by 125 locks; which are 17 feet wide, by 80 feet in length, and of which number 28 are guard locks: there are 17 arched aqueducts; a tunnel of 450 feet, cut through and under solid rock; 65 toll and gate houses. Taking the works as commencing at the Lancaster Schuylkill bridge, Philadelphia, and ending at Mount Carbon, the whole extent is about 108 miles, whereof 63 or 64 consists of canals, 45 of pools in the river: along which pools, channels and towing paths are at present made and making. The dams, 31 in number, vary from 3 to 27 feet in height; the towing paths are 6 to 10 feet wide at top, covered with gravel, about 4 feet above common water: he sides of which are built at an angle of 33°, and are faced with stone. In some places, extensive canals are made, inland, from one dam to another; in others, the dams connect, next to the land, by one or more locks, 17 feet wide by 80 long. The channels are intended to be kept at about 4 feet in depth, and have been cleared out accordingly, next the towing paths, to 35 or 40 feet wide at the bottom. See engraved profile of these works.

Single horse boats, it is calculated, will pass the whole distance, from the coal mines to the city, in 4 days, with convenience, and return in the same time; packet boats, with passengers, in half the time. Toll from Mount Carbon to Philadelphia, 6 cents per bushel of coal. The cost of these works will amount to 1,800,000 dollars, and upwards.

The whole is now nearly brought to a conclusion. There are as yet a few desirable improvements going forward, and some points are yet to be strengthened and finished off; but, the whole extent has been laid open for use, and already there is an active navigation carried on, promising what it is to become by and by, from the accessions it will receive. From the 16th of March to the 19th of December, 1825, the descending trade has amounted to - - - - - - - Tons, 15,573
The ascending trade to - - - - - 2,636

Total, - - - - - - - Tons, 18,209

Which, it is probable, will appear but small, a few years hence, when it comes to be compared with the tonnage that will then pass through the Schuylkill locks, within a similar period. And if the proportion here shown, of about 1 to 6, should be maintained, as there is room now to suppose will be the case, the ascending trade, by this route, in comparison with the descending, will much exceed what has been calculated on. It is thought probable, that a deal of merchandise will ascend the

Schuylkill from Philadelphia, and be transported from the head of the present navigation, with an advantage, in time and expense, over other routes, to several points calling for it.

The annual report, for 1825, has been made; and the following statement exhibits the company's financial situation:—

Statement of the receipts and expenditures of the Schuylkill Navigation Company, from the commencement, to the first day of January, 1826.

Amount received from subscribers,		$1,037,796 26
Do.	for tolls,	23,099 81
Do.	rents,	10,994 69
Do.	interest,	3,837 09
Do.	real estate,	893 04
Do.	on loan,	843,273 60
Do.	for premiums on loans,	5,589 40
Do.	from the city corporation, for removing the restriction on the surplus water at Fair Mount,	26,000 00
		$1,951,483 89

Amount paid for improvements,		$1,704,948 80	
Do.	land,	63,405 64	
Do.	damages,	39,701 73	
Do.	interest on loans,	80,911 41	
Balance on hand, in securities,		$60,848 89	
In cash,		1,667 42	
			62,516 31
			$1,951,483 89

Received,

In 1818, tolls.	$233,	ho. and gr. rents,	$15		
1819, do.	1,202	do.	60		
1820, do.	803	do.	25,	water rents,	$300
1821, do.	1,792	do.	130	do.	296
1822, do.	1,055	do.	243	do.	684
1823, do.	1,964	do.	274	do.	1,164
1824, do.	635	do.	645	do.	2,482
1825, do.	15,415	do.	435	do.	4,275
	$23,099		$1,827		$9,201

By which it appears, that the cost of these works, exclusive of interest on loans, may finally be taken at about 1,850,000 dollars. Of course, to bring in, at the rate of 5 or 6 per cent. on this disbursement, there will be required a net revenue of from 95,000, to 110,000 dollars; which it is hoped will, within a few years, be much more than realized.

It was not until the latter part of September, that a thorough navigation, between Mount Carbon and Philadelphia, became established; yet, the tolls down to the end of the season, (about the 19th of December,) have amounted to 15,415 dollars, and it is conjectured, that in all the present year, 1826, the amount of toll will not fall short of 70,000 dollars, besides the income from ground and water rents, which now is about 5,000 dollars. The coal trade is increasing with great rapidity; the demand for coal being, just now, much beyond the means of transporting it from the mines; and the income from general transportation, that is, from other articles than coal, seems likely far to exceed what was anticipated by calculators: the produce of the Susquehanna, it is remarked, is "seeking a conveyance to market, through the Schuylkill." The Union canal, when finished, will be the means of bringing in no small addition to the Schuylkill company's revenue; and it seems, moreover, at this moment, to be a favourite project, to construct a *rail way*, between the head of the Schuylkill works, and some point of the Susquehanna river, not far from Sunbury.

The annual expenses, for superintendence, after the present year, it is supposed may amount to 13,000 dollars. Of the average annual expenses for keeping the works in repair, there is not, as yet, sufficient experience to speak with any precision; but the sum of these two items, deducted from the amount of tolls and rents, will give, of course, the company's net annual income.

JANUARY, 1827.

Another yearly report has been made to the stockholders; and the present situation of the company's affairs, is shown by the "general statement;" thus:—

Amount received from subscribers, 20,970 shares, at 50 dollars,	$1,048,500	
Outstanding, deduct,	727	
		$1,047,773
Amount received for tolls,		66,208
Amount received for rents,		17,366
Amount received for interest,		4,442
Amount received for sales of real estate,		2,177
Amount received on loan,		945,074
Amount carried forward,		$2,083,040

Amount brought forward,	$2,083,040
Amount for premium on the loan,	8,732
Amount for stock forfeited,	3,649
Amount from the city corporation, for a removal of restrictions on the surplus water at Fair Mount,	26,000
	$2,121,421

Amount paid for improvements, including all contingent expenses,	$1,858,985	
Amount paid for real estate,	65,650	
Amount paid for damages,	58,063	
Amount of interest on loan,	133,704	
		$2,116,402
Balance in hand,		5,019
		$2,121,421

Tolls received for 1826; viz.

Descending,	$32,969	
Ascending,	10,140	
		$43,109
Water and other rents,		6,372
		$49,481

From which it appears, that the tolls for the year expired, have not amounted to the sum it was thought they would amount to: yet their actual amount nearly triples that of 1825, although there happened, in the height of the season, an interruption of business, occasioned by the unfinished state of the works at a few points; and these are yet to be made perfect against the opening of business in the spring ensuing.

As to *proportion*, in ascending, compared with the descending tolls, it has risen from as 1 to 6, (its ratio in 1825,) to as 1 to 3¼, its ratio shown as above; which is a favourable circumstance of no small account.

It appears that the whole cost of these works, including real estate and contingencies, down to the present time, amounts to 1,987,828 dollars; that is to say, 1,992,847 dollars, is the aggregate amount of capital and loan debt invested, with a balance of 5,019 dollars cash, in hand, towards the payments of next year.

In how short a period from this time, the accruing revenue will have come up to the work of enabling the managers, with propriety, besides discharging the annual interest on the amount of loan, to declare dividends in favour of the stockholders, remains yet to be ascertained. It possibly may be thought most advisable to postpone this measure yet for a season, for the sake of some further improvements to the works, calculated to render them more lastingly beneficial than otherwise they might be. The gross amount of tolls and rents, 49,481 dollars, for the past year, makes about 2½ per cent. on 1,987,828 dollars, the whole sum disbursed. Strong hopes are entertained that the stock will become a profitable one to the company. Recent occurrences have satisfactorily confirmed every favourable idea indulged in, as to the great public utility of these works; and the greatest activity now prevails, in extending local conveniences, such as warehouses and other buildings, and various establishments to accommodate the trade that offers;—a trade, in fact, waiting to be accommodated. The rate at which the coal trade has increased with us, and the likelihood of its going on more and more to increase, indicate, that before many years pass away, a second line of transportation may very possibly be needed, between the Schuylkill collieries and the wharves of Philadelphia.

It is in contemplation to extend the navigation from Mount Carbon to the mouth of Mill creek, and likewise in the direction of West branch, Schuylkill: which will give 3 leading avenues to the collieries; viz.—

Eastward, by Mill creek,
Westward, by West branch,
By the centre, or turnpike.

Which last, may be improved into a rail road.

January, 1828.

The report on the Schuylkill navigation company's affairs, for the year now expired, shows that the tolls of 1827 have amounted, as follows:—

Descending, $42,865 00
Ascending, $15,284 00

Together, $58,149 00

And that the tonnage passed through the locks, has
been, descending and ascending together, tons, -   65,501
In 1826, the whole tonnage was - - - -   32,404

So that the year's trade has actually more than doubled the preceding one. It does not give double the amount of tolls, by reason, chiefly, that the managers, for the sake of future as well as present encouragement, have thought it advisable to make a con-

siderable reduction on the material article of coal. At this reduced rate of toll, the sum received on coal has been, $31,360
On all other articles, descending, - - $11,505
Ascending, - - 15,284
26,789

Total, as above, $58,149

In 1825, the amount of ascending tolls, compared with the descending, was as 1 to 6. In 1826, the proportion rose to as 1 to $3\frac{1}{4}$. For the last year, it appears to be as 1 to $2\frac{4}{7}$ths.

The whole cost of the company's works, including real estate and contingencies, down to the present time, is 2,067,016 dollars.

The extension up to Mill creek is now under contract, to be executed forthwith. It is $2\frac{1}{2}$ miles above Mount Carbon, and is a prolific coal quarter.

The aspect of this concern is not a little promising: the stockholders are looking forward to be well remunerated for their patient advance of capital.

January, 1829.

The annual report of the president and managers of the Schuylkill navigation company, notices, that, in the past year, many substantial improvements and repairs have been added to the works. The extension of the navigation to Mill creek, is finished in a manner quite satisfactory; the works generally have been improved in solidity; and the year's operations are gone through with, free from accidents to impede their steady progress.

The quantity of coal brought to market this season,
has been, - - - - - - - 47,284
In 1827, the quantity was - - - - - 31,360

Increase, more than 50 per cent., Tons, 15,924

Tonnage passed through the locks in 1828,—
Descending, 84,134
Ascending, 21,329
105,463
In 1827, it was - - - - - - - 65,501

Increase, 61 per cent., Tons, 39,962

The tolls of 1828 have amounted, viz:—
Descending, whereof 46,202 dollars is derived from
coal, - - - - - - $64,001
Ascending, - - - - - 23,170
                                            ———————
                                            $87,171
The tolls of 1827 amounted to   -   -   -   -   58,149
                                            ———————
                        Increase, 50 per cent., $29,022

Of the tolls of 1828, as above, the sum of 12,214 dollars was received from boats navigating the Union canal.

The income of the company from real estate, ground rents, and water rents, continues advancing; and, it may here be observed, that the new town of Pottsville, at the head of the works, is rapidly growing up to a place of consequence.

NOTE.

The following statement serves to show, that an enormous expenditure has in reality been incurred on the Schuylkill improvements generally; but, granting the position, it may as truly be said, that the advantages purchased are, in point of value, incalculable. In that point of view, the community has got a great bargain, and got it consequently cheap enough; but the fact is, in another point of view, that 15 years ago this country was young, if not in the *theoretical*, at least in the *practical*, of such like works; and were the whole ground to be, *de novo*, gone over at the present day, there is not a doubt but that a conspicuous economy of cash might take place, for the acquisition of equal benefits; and not only so, but a plan differing rather widely, as to details, from the present existing one, would perhaps now be adopted. However, the statement appertaining to the present state of things, stands thus:—

Sums expended by the present company,   - $2,190,176
Expended by the city corporation on the dam and
  canal at Fair Mount, exclusive of the water works, 300,000
Expended by the old Delaware and Schuylkill canal
  company, on the abandoned route, about   -   -   210,000
Legislative appropriations, and private expenditures
  on the river, prior to 1815, supposed   -   -   20,000
Sum to be expended by the company to complete the
  works,   -   -   -   -   -   -   -   -   50,000
                                            ———————
                        Total amount, $2,770,176

The Fair Mount dam is 1478 feet long.

One of the objects to be effected by the old Delaware and

Schuylkill canal company, was to supply the city of Philadelphia with water. Which privilege, on the dissolution of that company, devolved on the Union canal company ; and finally, by agreement, the city corporation undertook, and they have well executed, the noble enterprise. Of this, a detailed analysis is here given, viz.—

FAIR MOUNT WATER WORKS.

Cost of ground at Fair Mount, including the vacation of streets, and sundry restrictions,	$116,834 00
For the water power purchased of White and Gillingham,	150,000 00
For the dam, canal, buildings, and machinery,	300,000 00
For the payment of damages for lands overflowed by the dam,	40,000 00
For a new pump and iron water wheel, &c.,	12,000 00
For the erection of reservoir No. 3,	25,000 00
For the 20 inch iron main, now in use, and for the necessary branches and feeders required to supply the city and districts with water,	120,000 00
For reservoirs No. 1 and 2, formerly used for the steam engine works,	50,000 00
For an extra 20 inch iron main, to be laid in 1829,	65,000 00
For erecting reservoir No. 4, now in hand,	60,000 00
For 172,792 feet of iron pipes, laid through the city,	337,920 00
For 52,800 feet of wooden pipes, and hydrant pumps,	52,800 00
Together amounting to,	$1,329,554 00

Statement of iron pipes laid in the city and districts:—

In the city,	172,792	feet.
In Spring Garden,	15,298	
In Northern Liberties,	38,323	
In Southwark,	26,233	
Making,	252,646	feet.

Or upwards of 48 miles.

Number of dwellings, manufactories, &c. supplied with water:—

In the city,	6775
In Spring Garden,	357
In Northern Liberties,	1066
In Southwark,	572
Together,	8770

The above dwellings, factories, &c. consume daily, an average quantity of water, equal to 160 gallons each, after making due allowance for the additional quantity of water used from the public hydrant pumps, which exceed 300 in number.

Amount of water rents assessed in the city and districts.—

In the city,	- -	$35,791 50
In Spring Garden,	-	2,508 75
In Northern Liberties,	-	8,426 50
In Southwark,	- -	4,293 25
	Together,	$51,020 00

Being on the average less than 6 dollars for each family or manufactory.

Independent of the advantages of the Schuylkill water for private comfort, the difference of losses by fire between New-York and Philadelphia may be attributed to it, as by a late publication it appears, that the amount of losses sustained by fire in Philadelphia during the last year, was less than 100,000 dollars, when in New-York it was upwards of 600,000 dollars.

NOTE.

From the head of the Schuylkill navigation company's works, a rail road is proposed to be constructed along the Norwegian and Mill creek valley, over a tract of about 10 miles, and through a rich body of coal land. Books for subscriptions to the undertaking, to be opened on the 9th February, 1829, at Pottsville, and at Philadelphia. *See article* 67.

Moreover, a company is organized, as the "Mine hill and Schuylkill haven rail road company," for the object of constructing rail roads between those points, and along the valley of the Schuylkill west west branch, to the coal mines in that direction. The route from Schuylkill haven, passes up the valley of west branch to the confluence of that and the west west branch, and thence divides, taking the direction of each of these streams to the foot of Broad mountain, a distance in all of 17 miles.

This coal district, taken at large, has a length from east to west of 70 miles, with an average width, between Sharp mountain and Broad mountain, of 3 miles, consequently covering a surface of about 210 square miles. It comprises the Schuylkill mines in the middle, the Swatara and Susquehanna mines on the west, and the Lehigh mines on the east. The veins of coal average about 10 feet in thickness: their depth, on the inclined plane, stretching beyond any experiments hitherto made.

SUMMARY.

The Schuylkill navigation company's works; consisting of canal and slackwater navigation, between Philadelphia and the mouth of Mill creek,   Miles, 110½

To which may be added, viz:—

Rail road, as above, commencing at Pottsville, and passing, by the Norwegian and Mill creek valley, to a rich body of coal lands, - - - - - - -   10

The proposed rail road to be carried by the "Schuylkill valley company," from the head of navigation, as above, to Reber's mill, or Port Carbon. See article 67. -   10

Rail roads along the valley of west branch, and west west branch, from Schuylkill haven; each to the foot of Broad mountain. Together, - - - -   17

A rail road between the navigation, as above, and the Pennsylvania north branch canal, at the town of Catawissa, passing round the heads of Great and Little Mahanoy creeks. See Pennsylvania state canal and rail road article, - - - - - - - -   58

A branch rail road, from the summit of the last specified, to communicate with Little Schuylkill river. See the same, - - - - - - - -

Another branch rail road, from said summit, to communicate with the Lehigh navigation, by way of Quacake valley. See the same, - - - - - -

An improved slackwater navigation of the Little Schuylkill river; or else, a continuation of rail road, down to its junction with Big Schuylkill. See article 66, -   22

     Aggregate connexion when complete, Miles, ...

January, 1830.

By a fresh annual report, now made to the stockholders, the public are confirmed in the fact of the business of this company, for the year last past, having been quite equal to what was anticipated of it; and in the expectation, that great prosperity is from the present moment to be looked forward to, as for these noble works terminating in making liberal returns to the worthy projectors and proprietors of them, for all the skill and perseverance exerted from the beginning to this epoch; and, what is more, as terminating in advantages to the community at large, such as are not, in point of extent or amplitude, susceptible of being by any means calculated with precision beforehand. The company's charter being soon to expire, they have obtained from the state legislature, a renewal, or supplement, whereby all needful powers are continued to them, for the term of fifteen years, from the eighth day of March next; and security in consequence given, for undertaking, without reserve, all such enlargements, extensions, and improvements of the works, as are or may be in contemplation, and the good of the community now or hereafter may require. The official report of the president and managers contains these words; viz:—

"The importance of this improvement to the city and state, can scarcely be now appreciated; but there is every reason to believe, that the utmost extension which can be given to the exercise of the privileges and powers of the company, will not go beyond the demands of trade."

The quantity of coal brought to market in the season just closed, has been,	79,973
In 1828, it was	47,284
Increase, near 70 per cent., Tons,	32,689

Tonnage passed through the locks in 1829.—

Descending, Tons,	112,704	
Ascending,	21,820	
		134,524
In 1828, it was		105,463
Increase, 27½ per cent., Tons,		29,061

The tolls of 1829 have amounted, viz:—

On descending, whereof 77,032 dollars is derived from coal,	$92,186	
Ascending trade,	27,853	
		$120,039
The tolls of 1828 amounted to		87,171
Increase, 37½ per cent.,		$32,868

Total cost of the improvements, 1st of January, 1830, - - - - - $2,236,937

A.—From Reading, on the Schuylkill river, by canal, called "the Union Canal," westward, to Middletown, or confluence of the Swatara and Susquehanna rivers.   Distance, *Miles*, 71

A.—From Middletown, as above, by canal, to the mouth of Paxton creek, and taking along the rear of Harrisburg, thence up to the mouth of Juniata river, or thereabout. This is a contingent supplementary work, to be decided upon by the result of inquiries and examinations now on foot; but, in the mean time, " the Harrisburg canal company" have obtained a charter, to improve a part of the distance; namely, from Paxton creek, to a point of the Susquehanna river above Hunter's falls. The latter is for the purpose, in particular, of supplying the town of Harrisburg with water. Distance, *Miles*, 30

No. 58.

THE UNION CANAL.

This great work, denominated "the Union," from two former companies, chartered in the years 1791 and 1792, to open a canal between the waters of the Susquehanna river and the Schuylkill, and another between the Schuylkill and the Delaware, having united, and being now the company prosecuting this work, is, according to a report made by the managers, expected to be finished, so as completely to join the Susquehanna and Schuylkill rivers, early in the year 1827. One-half of it in distance, and about two-thirds as regards difficulties, labour, and expense, may be considered as done : this consists of a summit level, at Lebanon, length 2¾ miles, (which the engineers have a project of extending,) and nearly all the eastern section, or the descent from Lebanon, to the mouth of the Tulpehocken, at Reading, 34 miles. The canal is 24 feet wide at the bottom, and gives, at 4 feet depth of water, 36 feet surface : the locks are 8½ feet, differing in that respect from the New-York canal locks, and those of the Schuylkill, which are wide. The canal has a towing path of 10 feet on the south margin, and the number of locks in this descent is 52, overcoming a fall of 300 feet. Along the western section, to the mouth of the Swatara, the fall to be overcome is 210 feet. The whole canal distance, will be best adapted to boats of 20 to 25 tons burden, which, with one horse, a man, and a boy, to each, will transport their lading at the rate of 2½ to 3 miles per hour.

Further, it is in contemplation, as already stated, to extend the line of this communication from the Swatara to Paxton creek, and thence upward to a point of the Susquehanna river, opposite the mouth of Juniata, or thereabout; which, however, is a contingency resting on the adoption of the Susquehanna and Juniata rivers, as one of the great thorough water communications from east to west. The Union canal, not including this adjunct, was estimated at 1,000,000 dollars cost.

Since the above was written, the annual report of the president and managers has been laid before the stockholders, 15th November, 1825, which exhibits a fair prospect of this canal being finished, and in use, early in the year 1827, if not by the end of 1826. Nothing material of the eastern section now remains to be done, except in front of Reading, and that will be completed next spring. It is proposed to erect a dam across the Schuylkill river, at the mouth of the Tulpehocken, and extend the canal about 2 miles downward from Reading, thereby rendering more perfect and commodious, a union with the Schuylkill navigation works, and giving to the borough of Reading a fine harbour, that will be of vast consequence to her.

On the western section, the valley of the Quittapahilla, at first intended for the route, has been abandoned, and a more advantageous one taken up; which passes from the west of the old summit, first to Snavely's farm; thence, by a tunnel of 286 yards, to the valley of Clarke's creek, and to the Swatara; over which, passing by an aqueduct, it continues on along the western side thereof, to the Susquehanna. From the western extremity of the old summit, to within a mile of the Swatara mouth, at Middletown, there are 74 half-mile lengths, all under contract, and the contractors are obligated to complete these portions by the 1st October, 1826. The mile still in reserve, (which is to crown the whole,) will be disposed of, so as to meet the other work. Making allowances, therefore, the entire of the Union canal will probably be finished, and in use, by the spring or summer of 1827. In consequence of the alterations mentioned, the distance, altogether, will be increased to about 77 or 78 miles.

On the eastern section, including the summit level, the expense incurred amounts to 524,979 dollars: and for the western section, it is estimated now at 550,000 dollars.

The plan of this canal, as now fixed, is thought to possess great advantages; insomuch, that at a future day, when the trade of the country shall require it, a double set of locks may be constructed; with the practicability of raising, by mechanical power, at a moderate expense, the whole contents of the Swatara river into the summit level, if it shall be needful; and by this operation, together with, in case it be found needful, an extended feeder, taken from a point as near the river head as the coal region at the Blue ridge, have at command an abundance of water, to answer occasions, when things shall have advanced to the state anticipated.

A bill, to authorize the Union Company to extend the present navigable feeder of the canal, from near Weidman's forge, up towards the head of the Swatara, or the coal beds at the Blue ridge, is before the state legislature. (It has passed.)

November, 1826.

Another annual report to the stockholders has just been made. It is in the highest degree favourable; going to confirm previous expectation in the completion of the work by the time specified, or thereabout, in a manner, as the report expresses it, to give entire satisfaction. This is grounded on the masterly workmanship, and, to all appearances, by a careful inspection, on the solid and durable structure of the several parts that are now finished.

The report goes farther: it gives strong hopes of advantages accruing to the company, superior to what was of late calculated on, or than could in fact, until now, be anticipated as so immediately to follow the completion of the work; for present expectations are founded, in a degree, on a new combination of circumstances;—in the first place, by virtue of agreement with the "Schuylkill Navigation Company," boats of the Union will pass the Schuylkill locks down to Philadelphia, and in consequence, there has been effected, or soon will be, a prolongation of the canal, to about 4 miles below Reading, so as to form a convenient junction at the head of what is called the "Girard section." In the second place, a similar advantage, and greater in degree, is to be derived from a connexion with the Pennsylvania state canal, now constructing from the termination at Middletown of the Union, and to be continued to Pittsburg. In the third place, an economical and never failing measure has been adopted, for gaining an additional and prompt supply of water at the summit level, whenever occasion shall so require, by means of the use of steam; and an engine of 100 horse power, with pumps of 20 inches diameter, is bespoke: which, whenever wanted, will throw up from the river Swatara, (94 feet,) at the rate of 670,000 cubic feet, making the aggregate supply of water to the summit, from the various sources specified, equal to 307 locks full per day; and this of course may still be augmented by the erection of another water wheel, as originally intended; or the application of a second steam-engine, as most probably may take place. In the fourth and last place, the plan adopted by the engineers, in the construction of this canal throughout, is such, that at a future day, as soon as the trade of the country shall require it, it will be competent to the company to enlarge the capacity thereof for transportation, by merely raising, as can very conveniently be done, the banks and locks, and applying such further steam or mechanical force as is above suggested, or circumstances may call for, to raise the summit supply to any required extent.

The whole length of the main canal, from the Schuylkill works, near the head of the Girard canal, to the great basin of the Pennsylvania state canal on the Susquehanna, is reported at 82 miles 6 chains, and the navigable feeder on the Swatara, as at present, up to near Weidman's forge, in the direction of the coal mines, 7 miles 40 chains: the locks are of cut stone ; in number 93, with 2 guard locks of wood ; and are so constructed as for the average time required to pass the boats through, not to exceed 5 or 6 minutes for each ; so that a passage between the Susquehanna and Reading for loaded boats, is expected to be compassed within 40 hours. The reservoirs on the summit level, now complete, are 2, containing 12 millions cubic feet of water.

What chiefly remains to be finished, is the tunnel, and the section of canal which is to connect it with the great basin of the state canal, near the junction of the Swatara river with the Susquehanna ; and the managers feel confident of having the entire line open to the public, for the transportation of property, in the ensuing season. The tunnel alluded to, will be an excavation through solid rock ; the dimensions of it $17\frac{1}{2}$ feet wide, 12 to 14 feet high, 850 in length.

In regard to an extension of the Swatara feeder as far as the coal region, for which, authority of the legislature is obtained, the measure is before the stockholders for their determination : the act authorizes the carrying this feeder up the Swatara, as far as the south-eastern foot of Broad mountain, in Schuylkill county, if requisite.

The following is a summary description:—

Beginning at its eastern end in the Schuylkill works, about 4 miles below Reading, it ascends along the western bank of the Schuylkill, to the valley of the Tulpehocken ; and passes up that valley to the east end of the summit level, within 5 miles of Lebanon, rising 311 feet, by 54 locks of various lifts, 8 to 4 feet. The summit extends 6 miles 78 chains, part whereof is a tunnel of 850 feet, opening into Clark's creek valley, along which the canal descends to the Swatara ; and continuing along this river valley, terminates in Middletown on the Susquehanna, where it joins the east end of the Pennsylvania canal. Descent from summit $208\frac{1}{2}$ feet, overcome by 39 locks ; whole length of the canal 82 miles, exclusive of the navigable feeder of $7\frac{1}{2}$ miles, leading to the Swatara coal beds. It has 43 waste weirs, 49 culverts, 135 road and farm bridges; 12 aqueducts, 1 of which is 276 feet in length; 2 guard locks of wood, 93 lift locks of cut stone, cemented principally with the water lime of Pennsylvania. There are, besides, solid protecting walls to the extent of 14 miles, constructed against the pressure of contiguous streams. (See engraved profile of this canal.) At the water works, one of the wheels for raising the water of the Swatara to the summit, is 36 feet in diameter, working 2 pumps; and there are to be 2 steam-engines, viz., one that is now erected of 100 horse power, and a second one, similar, or of 120 horse power. By which arrangement, it is understood, most ample provision will be made, in the way of guarding against any stoppage or interruption of the current trade, from the contingency of any portion of the water works happening at any time to give way, or requiring to be repaired. The engine now erected is to work at 60 pound pressure to the square inch, but is affirmed to be of sufficient strength to sustain a pressure of 200. The cylinder is 23 inches diameter; length of stroke 6 feet; number of strokes per minute 20. The boiler 32 inches in diameter, and adapted to anthracite coal for fuel. Cost of this engine, complete, Pittsburg manufacture, 5000 dollars.

A lock of 2½ feet lift, connects the basin of the Union with the basin of the Pennsylvania canal, and between the latter and the Swatara river is a lock of 9 feet, which is connected with the outlet of the Union canal into the Swatara.

November, 1827.

Tne Union canal, it appears from official report, is now complete in all its parts, save only the planking on the summit, which is to be finished within a few days. So that this canal will be in readiness for service throughout, at the opening of next spring.

The summit excepted, the whole canal, including its navigable feeder, is at present filled with water, and used for conveying articles from place to place.

The boats of the Union canal are necessarily *narrow*, to suit the locks; those already in use are of 25 tons burthen, and found to be easily drawn, each by a single horse, and to pass through one of the locks in 5 to 6 minutes.

Upon a supposition, therefore, of the locks meeting employment equal to the passing 8 of these boats through per hour, this makes, for the day of 24 hours, 4800 tons; and if the year be taken at 250 effective days, we find, from these data, that the capacity of the Union canal will be equal to 1,200,000 tons of goods passing through the locks annually, part eastward, part westward.

But it will, at any time hereafter, be competent to the company, should the trade of the country require it, to augment the capacity of this canal, by raising the banks and locks 1 foot; so that boats of 40 tons may then navigate it, and then it will have the competency of passing 1,920,000 tons annually. A double set of locks may also be resorted to, to accommodate the trade and prevent detention.

A second steam-engine, of 100 or 120 horse power, and another great water wheel, are constructing, and are forthwith to be erected.

November, 1828.

Another annual report, by the president of the company, is now made. On the 20th of December, last year, the planking of the summit of the canal, in the extent of 6 miles, was finished; and the weather of the season continuing mild, there passed, on the 25th of that month, a boat and cargo of Susquehanna coal, through the entire canal, to its port opposite Reading. With the opening of spring it was in readiness for use, and has been, and is at the present time, in successful operation; that is to say, free from accidents or interruptions not incidental to new canals generally, during the first season of trial. Not more or greater leaks than are usual to new works have declared themselves; and these, on drawing off the water, when the current season for navigation shall have closed, may then be effectually stopped: 18000 tons of goods have already passed through the locks since spring, notwithstanding every impediment likely to be encountered in a first season; of which, the want of boats in this instance proved a material one. An abundance of them, it is not doubtful, will be, by private enterprise, prepared for the trade, against the ensuing spring.

Great additional improvements, as formerly suggested, have latterly been decided on by the company, to widen the scope of accommodation for a vast expected course of business through this canal, and to guard especially against any casual interruption of it, by the occurrence of any unusually dry season reducing the volume of water in the Swatara river below the standard calculated on. In consequence, there will be formed, and the work is now under contract, a new reservoir, of prodigious capacity, in the mountainous country, and in the very bed of the river. It will be compassed by means of a dam of 40 feet high, at the gap of the Blue mountain, where the ravine through which the Swatara passes, has been found to be 430 feet wide, with rocky banks. Up to this point, the present feeder from Weidman's forge is to be extended, and the construction of this dam will have the effect of setting the water back above the mouth of Fishing creek, and making a pool of 6 miles in length, thereby, in addition to the main object of forming a great reservoir for the summit, perfecting so much of the Swatara navigation towards the coal mines of that quarter, and approaching them to within the distance of 4 miles. This part of the navigation, it is ascertained, can be so arranged, as to admit of the water being drawn down as much as 10 feet, for the uses of the summit, if ever occasion should so require, without interrupting the passage of boats.

In the second place, it is determined, not only to sheathe the sides of the summit, but to raise them so as to attain a perpendicular depth of 5 feet.4 inches of water, producing an extra quantity equal to 700 locks full; a provision, consequently, in readiness to be used in times of drought, as a reduction of the 5 feet 4 inches of water down to 3 feet 4 inches, may at any time be made, without interrupting the navigation.

These great matters accomplished, and a few slight improvements, perceived to be called for on the two sections, east and west, being also once made, it is confidently hoped the Union canal may be regarded as a fixed and solid establishment, being at the same time the direct occasion of a large accession of prosperity to a district of country secondary to none in importance, and a direct channel, through which the trade is *uninterruptedly* to circulate, between the Susquehanna river, on one hand, and the Delaware, with its port of Philadelphia, on the other.

The erection, however, of dams, at various points of the Susquehanna, now going forward, some of them quite across the stream, and the rest more or less obstructive to navigation, whilst building, together with the yet unfinished state of other portions of the "Pennsylvania" canal works, it is true, may operate so as to interrupt business, and delay any great activity of the Union, as a thoroughfare of the trade to the Delaware, for a season or so.

It is the purpose of the company, sanctioned by an act of the legislature, amending the clauses of the charter, to extend the feeding canal, as above stated, from the present head, at Weidman's forge, up to the proposed basin, or Swatara gap, at the foot of the Blue mountain, and further, to extend a navigable canal, from the northern extremity, or head of said basin, up to a point at or near the village of Pine grove; connecting the whole by means of locks, and making the distance of feeder, and prolongation, in all, about, - - - - *Miles,* 23
To which, adding length of main canal, - - - 82

This makes a total of, *Miles,* 105

From different points of the Great basin, and Branch canal,

thus described, there will hereafter be carried short rail roads along the valleys of the Swatara river, and its several branches, up to situations in this "coal region," found to be most favourable for coal excavation; but whether these contemplated rail roads are to be undertaken by the Union company, or by other individuals, is at present uncertain. In either case, as it is believed, the Swatara coal will enter upon a competition in the market with the coal of other districts, on about equal terms; so this goes materially to strengthen the hope entertained, that the Union canal will enjoy the constant transportation of this important mineral to a large amount. It is affirmed, that the mines of the Swatara, or depôts of coal there, soon to become mines, can be wrought as easily and economically as those of Mount Carbon.

A.—From the mouth of Lackawaxen river, on the Delaware, by canal and slack-water improvements, up the course of the former to its head waters, situate 4 or 5 miles from the coal mines of Lackawannock.

Distance, *Miles*, 36

No. 59.

LACKAWAXEN CANAL.

By an act of the state of Pennsylvania, passed on the 1st of April, 1825, the "Lackawaxen canal and coal company," instituted to improve the navigation of the River Lackawaxen, are authorized also to act in union of interests with the "Delaware and Hudson canal company" of New-York. By which union, the projected works of improvement in both states make one whole, extending from the sources of the Lackawaxen to the Hudson river, at or near Kingston, as is particularized in the "Delaware and Hudson" article, already inserted, and whereof 64 miles lie in New-York state, 36 miles in Pennsylvania, besides 17 miles common to both, in case the stream be used. Rail way along the route, is, equally with canal, authorized by the charter.

The Lackawannock coal mines, (to be termed, with a tract of land annexed, "Carbondale,") are 32 miles distant from Wilkesbarre, or 22 from Pittston, and 16 miles from the Dyberry fork of the Lackawaxen; to which last, a rail road from the mines is in agitation; and this canal, up the Lackawaxen valley, to stop, by consequence, at the Dyberry point.

NOTE.

The company have had it latterly in contemplation, to construct a rail road, to hold the place altogether of this projected canal; i. e. a road to run between the termination of the Delaware and Hudson canal, at 4 miles above the mouth of Neversink, on the Delaware, and the Lackawannock coal mines above designated. Distance 58 miles.

Nevertheless, (December, 1828,) this important canal has been prosecuted, and the work is now finished; that is to say, from the mouth of the Rondout river, on the Hudson, to Port Jervis, near to Carpenter's point on the Delaware, and thence along the eastern bank of the Delaware, to a point opposite the mouth of Lackawaxen river : distance 81 miles, as described at article No. 31, and as being so far the "Delaware and Hudson canal;" from which point, to the western bank of the Delaware river, a dam having been erected across, the Lackawaxen canal commences thence, and is continued up the Lackawaxen river valley to the Dyberry forks, at the village of Honesdale : distance 25 miles.

Between Carbondale and this point, the distance whereof, as already stated, is 16 miles, the construction of a rail road, for conveying coal from the mines so far for embarkation, is actually in considerable forwardness, and promises to be in use by the end of next summer ; in the mean time, transportation between Carbondale and Honesdale, by the common road, has commenced, and the New-York market will thence be supplied with coal in large quantities.

The structure of the rail road is to be of timber, with iron plates screwed to the timber rails. Both stationary and locomotive steam-engines are to be used.

Summary, between the Hudson, near Kingston, and the Carbondale coal mines on the Lackawannock river, viz :—

Canal, by the valleys of the Rondout river, the Neversink, and the Delaware, to a point opposite the mouth of Lackawaxen, and thence, by dam, across, - - - - - - - - Miles,	81
Canal, by continuation, up the Lackawaxen valley, to the Dyberry forks, or village of Honesdale, -	25
Rail road, thence to Carbondale, - - - -	16
Total, Miles,	122

Total estimate of cost, 1,916,704 dollars.

A.—It has been proposed to extend the canal last above specified, to the Susquehanna river; that is, from the head water of the Lackawaxen, at Keen's pond, down the Lackawannock valley, to Pittston; 33 miles.

But the mountain to be passed in this route, is 250 feet above the level of Keen's pond, which is 1431 feet above tide; and Pittston is 496 feet above tide; so that there would be an abrupt lockage of 1435 feet; likely to set aside the attempt at present, even supposing there is no want of water for a summit level, without a long tunnel; which does not appear to have been regularly ascertained as yet.

Distance, *Miles*, 33

No. 60.

LACKAWAXEN AND PITTSTON CANAL.

A proposed communication between the Lehigh and the Susquehanna, at Wilkesbarre, by way of Solomon's creek, is said to present more facility of execution: the route is the one in the following article.

NOTE.

It is proposed to erect a rail road from the Dyberry forks of the Lackawaxen, to a point of the Lackawannock coal district, to be termed "Carbondale;" distance 16 miles. Distance from Carbondale to Pittston, 22 miles.

A.—From Lausanne, on the Lehigh, to Green Mount run, otherwise called Sandy Island run. Ascent 495 feet. Distance, 21 miles.

Green Mount run to summit level, in which the use of inclined planes is suggested. Ascent, 361 feet. Distance, 6¼ miles.

Summit level, through a tunnel, to Solomon's creek. Distance, 8½ miles.

Solomon's creek to Wilkesbarre, in which also the use of inclined planes is suggested. Descent, 894 feet. Distance, 4¼ miles.

Rise and fall, 1750 feet. Distance, *Miles*, 40

No. 61.

THE LAUSANNE AND WILKESBARRE CANAL.

As above particularized and noticed in the article preceding; but this projected communication is not promising.

A.—From Stoddartsville, on the River Lehigh, another coal region of Pennsylvania, by a series of slack-water improvements, accomplished and to be accomplished, to the mouth of that river, at Easton, on the Delaware. Distance, *Miles*, 84

No. 62.

THE LEHIGH NAVIGATION.

An act of the state, dated 20th March, 1818, authorized navigation improvements along this mountain stream, the fall of which, in the course of 100 miles, is not less than 1650, or 1700 feet: from Stoddartsville to Easton, 1184 feet; and to overcome this last, is within the undertaking of the "Lehigh coal and navigation company." They are obligated to render this distance navigable; and Messrs. White and Hazard, the superintending engineers, have already succeeded in the work, so far as to carry improvements up to Laurel run, which is 17 miles above Mauch Chunk, or within about 20 miles of Stoddartsville. They have, by means of dams and falling locks, rendered the stream navigable for their coal vehicles, called arks, from Mauch Chunk, the seat of the coal beds, downward to Easton, which is 46 miles, and has a fall of 364 feet; and this degree of their success, has opened an active and increasing transportation of anthracite coal, to a market for its consumption, particularly to Philadelphia.

Still, however, the actual navigation is no more than a downward one on the Lehigh. Thoughts are entertained of effecting an upward navigation, and the able engineers of the company do actually promise that they will effect it, from Easton as high as Mauch Chunk, so soon as the River Delaware itself shall be improved, by canal or otherwise, for its ascending navigation to reach up to Easton.

Any ascending navigation of the Lehigh, much higher than the coal beds, although not impracticable, would be difficult and expensive. But, it seems probable, that there will be accomplished, ere long, some kind of connexion between the waters of the Lehigh and the Susquehanna, in favour at least of a descending transportation of bulky commodities; in particular, of coal.

From a very recent, but not altogether conclusive, examination of the ground, it is conjectured that a cut, of but a few miles in length, is practicable, as in the article next following; the summit commanding, it is thought, a sufficient supply of water.

NOTE.

From the mouth of Mauch Chunk creek, a road of 9 miles conducts to the coal mines; which are situate at the summit of the mountain, about 1000 feet above the level of the Lehigh, at the mouth of Mauch Chunk creek.

The mountain from which this creek derives its name, is a spur of the Blue ridge, and divides the waters falling into the Schuylkill and Lehigh rivers.

The entrance to the mine, or, perhaps, more properly to speak, *quarry*, presents to the eye a stupendous and a beautiful spectacle. "One entire mountain of coal, black and glossy as jet," from beginning to end of the excavation; not separated by intervening strata of other matter, but one continuous mass of the same material for fuel; all finely polished, and in places scintillating with the colours of the rainbow, according as the light admitted from the entrance happens to fall upon its various surfaces, raised upon the blackest ground. This is the kind of coal denominated *anthracite*, and, perhaps, only to be found in the state of Pennsylvania. Of it there are several varieties. It gives out, as is now well known from daily experience, a most powerful heat, when once thoroughly ignited; nevertheless, it remains as yet undiscovered how to use this coal to advantage in the furnace, a desideratum the more eagerly sought after, as in the very vicinity of the anthracite coal, are situated inexhaustible beds of the finest iron ore.

The legislature of Pennsylvania, it may be hoped, will pass a law, to entitle whosoever may be the successful discoverer of a mode of using anthracite coal advantageously in a blast or air furnace, for reducing ore into metal, on a large scale, to a generous premium.

January, 1827.

The engineers and managers of the "Lehigh coal and navigation company," have just made an elaborate and an interesting report on the present situation of the company's works and property; and as to prospects which they appear to possess, of extraordinary advantages and profit to the company, being the immediate consequences of certain new improvements pointed out, in case these shall be pursued to a completion, according to a plan adopted latterly, and already carried partially into effect.

It is stated, that the Lehigh coal and navigation company are proprietors of nearly all the eastern end of the southern coalfield, embracing its whole width of 7650 feet, for about 10 miles in length, commencing at the Lehigh; its depth unascertained, but at the least 60 feet.

A rail way, which has been commenced, is to convey the coal from the mine down to the Mauch Chunk landing; and this to be done free of any propelling power, other than its own gravity, except for the first half mile, which distance is an acclivity to the summit level; from whence the descent of the rail road, $8\frac{1}{2}$ or $8\frac{3}{4}$ miles, to terminate at the commencement of a *chute*, or inclined plane, and this latter to terminate in a depôt for coal, sufficiently elevated above the edge of the water for the coal to be expeditiously shot into the arks and boats, as they arrive to receive it. The whole elevation of the summit above the Lehigh, is 982 feet; height of the upper part of the chute, about 200 feet; the sleepers of the road to be, in this instance, of timber, laid 4 feet apart; the rails likewise of timber, covered with plates of iron.

The lands of the company have a front on the Lehigh of 3 miles, 1 mile of which can be converted into coal landings. The Beaver meadows coal range, which lies parallel to the company's, is at least 30 feet thick, and 5 miles wide: of this also, the produce may chiefly descend, on rail ways, by the power of gravity, to the Lehigh landings. And the Northern, or Wilkesbarre and Lackawannock coal range, lying in veins 6 to 18 feet in thickness, can also, or a good portion thereof, reach the Lehigh, by rail ways of 6 to 18 miles long.

The stores of coal, therefore, at this place, in readiness for transportation by water, will doubtless at all times be very great. It is probable, as the report intimates, that one half of all the anthracite coal excavated from the mines of that description, hitherto discovered in Pennsylvania, will find its way to market, most economically, through the waters of the River Lehigh, considering particularly that the business so carried on is not likely to be affected in its limitation, by any deficiency of water in this river, at the driest season of the year. It has been ascertained, say the engineers, that at 17 miles above Mauch Chunk, there is at command a quantity sufficient to fill one of the largest locks of the Lehigh every 7 minutes; and from Mauch Chunk downward, the locks can be filled and passed, either way, in 5 minutes each; but allowing for a boat of 150 tons, 10 minutes to pass a lock each way, equal to 3 boats or 450 tons per hour, it gives 10,800 tons per day, or for the year of 250 days, 2,700,000 tons descending, and the same quantity ascending. This is the computed capacity of the River Lehigh.

To connect the Lehigh and Susquehanna, it is suggested, in the engineers' report, as expedient to throw a dam across at 1½ mile above Bear creek, or 6 miles below Stoddartsville, by which the Lehigh river water will be made to flow into a feeder canal, to the summit between Wright's creek and the Nescopec: and a main canal to be constructed in conformity to these premises. This is proposed as one of the eligible means of rendering the Lehigh a great thoroughfare from and to the northern parts of Pennsylvania and the state of New-York; and regular examinations of the ground, are in a train of being made and reported upon, as stated in the article which next follows, No. 63.

The calculation, in reference to the Lehigh itself, is, that when the additional improvements which are begun shall be finished, the company will have it in their power to place their coal to any extent that may be required, upon the wharf at Philadelphia, at the cost of 145 cents per ton, exclusive of tolls.

Now, as to tolls, answering to the repairs of works and maintenance of a canal navigation, they will, generally speaking, be in proportion to distance and lockage: taking which for a criterion, the Lehigh establishment possesses, from situation, an obvious advantage over some other establishments, in the conveyance of their coal respectively to market. This is made apparent to the eye, by a scheme, or diagram, of the sundry routes, drafted by the engineer of the Lehigh company, thus:—

DRAFTS

Of the comparative Heights and Distances of the principal Districts of Anthracite Coal, in Pennsylvania, to Market.

To Philadelphia Market; viz.

	Feet.
Lackawaxen—317 miles; from the coal landing at Keen's pond, - - - - Lockage,	1583
Wilkesbarre—275 miles; via Chesapeake and Delaware canal, - - - - -	550
Wilkesbarre, via Lehigh—170 miles; from sum-	

		Feet.
mit level of the proposed Susquehanna and Lehigh canal,	*Lockage,*	1325
Lehigh—132 miles; from Mauch Chunk coal landing,		524
Schuylkill—108 miles; from Mount Carbon coal landing to Philadelphia, west side,		588

To New-York Market; viz.

	Feet.
Lackawaxen—217 miles; from the coal landing near Keen's pond,	1431
Wilkesbarre—375 miles; via River Susquehanna, the Chesapeake and Delaware canal, and Delaware and Rariton canal,	650
Wilkesbarre, via Lehigh—192 miles; from summit level of the proposed Susquehanna and Lehigh canal,	1325
Lehigh—162 miles; from Mauch Chunk coal landing,	524
Schuylkill—208 miles; from Mount Carbon coal landing,	738

New-York, for the present, relies principally for a supply of coal to her great emporium, on the mines of the Hudson; on those of the country situate near the margin of her canals; and on the Lackawaxen or Lackawannock mines in Pennsylvania; to which last, the Delaware and Hudson canal, and the works along the Lackawaxen valley, conduct: and for the present, the wants of Philadelphia are supplied from Mount Carbon and Mauch Chunk together, through the Schuylkill and Delaware rivers and canals; the two latter sources being both looked to for a large supply, passing into and along the contemplated New-Jersey canals, so soon as they shall be in existence, and prepared to receive it. Moreover, in regard to this mineral, it is believed, that for reasons stated at Article 93, the period is not very distant, when the produce of the Potomac banks may be brought to a tolerably successful competition, at most of our coal markets, not excepting occasionally those north of the Chesapeake, with the other supplies eventually to be found at them for sale.

The navigation improvements spoken of as yet to be perfected, embrace 52 large locks on the Lehigh, of 100 to 130 feet in length, and perhaps 27 dams, and a certain length of canal; 6 of these locks, with the necessary proportion of dam and canal, for ascending navigation, being already finished; and when all this shall be done, there will be a complete ascending as well as descending navigation upon the Lehigh river, to and from Mauch Chunk, for steam-boats as burthensome as 150 tons, or other vessels up to 200 tons each. And the scheme of improvements further embraces a series of lock and other constructions along the bank of the Delaware river, from the mouth of the Lehigh at Easton, down to tide water, so as to overcome the rapids in this distance, or 160 feet of descent. Added to which, a commodious rail road, as above described, for conveying the coal, very economically, from the mine to the water side.

When all shall be thus complete, a steam-boat, as above, will make the trip, from Mauch Chunk to Philadelphia and back, in 7 days, allowing 1 day for loading and unloading by the power of the engine.

Five of the locks already finished, are 130 feet long; 30 feet wide; and by some peculiarity in their construction, may, notwithstanding these large dimensions, be passed through, either up or down, in less time, it is said, than the common locks can.

The company's valuation of their present stock, and the improvements as projected, all together, is as here follows; that is to say, when all shall be thus complete, it is estimated the whole amount of cost will have been 2,000,000 dollars; viz.

For improving the Lehigh river, from Mauch Chunk to the Delaware; and the Delaware navigation from Easton to tide water,	$1,200,000
For a rail road from the coal mine, down to the Lehigh river landing, and all other expenditures,	800,000
Total amount; which includes the company's whole property,	$2,000,000

The quantity of coal dispatched from Mauch Chunk, in the course of last year, was 31,280 tons: and preparations are now making for the dispatch of 40,000 tons between the opening of spring and December next.

In the year 1830, if against that time the navigation works, in the manner described, shall all be finished, as it is expected they may be, the company purpose bringing to market 100,000 tons of Lehigh coal; and will be able to increase the quantity at the rate of 100,000 tons annually, for a number of years thenceforward, if the demand for it shall call for such increase.

The mines of the Lehigh and of the Susquehanna together, may be regarded as inexhaustible; at least, are more than adequate to any supply that can be needed for centuries to come, great and increasing as may, and to a certainty will be, the demand for coal. The capacity of the Lehigh waters for transporting the article from the mines, has been shown to be equal to 2,700,000 tons per annum.

NOTE.

In regard to improving the navigation of the river Delaware, from tide water up to Easton, although the supposed expense thereof, as proposed by the Lehigh company engineers, is included in their statement, as above, yet, being a concern of the state of Pennsylvania at large, the legislature are petitioned on the subject, and prayed to cause the needful improvements to be effected. Or, it is not improbable, that a branch section, or new division, of the Pennsylvania state canal, may be made to take this course, and supersede other projects. (This is now fully realized, and the Delaware valley adopted into the *one* great state enterprise.)

JANUARY, 1829.

By a report of the board of managers, now made to the stockholders, it appears, that, notwithstanding some accidental occurrences, tending to retard the execution of the proposed additions and improvements to the works, so as not to come up, in point of rapidity, with first expectations, yet, on the whole, the progress of operations is found to be very satisfactory; and withal, notwithstanding all embarrassments of the work going forward, and hindrances of the weather, the company succeeded in sending down to market, during the past season, upwards of 30,000 tons of coal.

The rail road at the mine, it is stated, continues an effective auxiliary to the business of the company; and, it is hoped, that the whole of the works now in progress on the Lehigh, will be thoroughly complete before the expiration of the coming season.

Then, there will be finished, a navigation from Mauch Chunk to Easton, made up of 37 miles of canal, and about 10 miles of slackwater pools, having 5 feet depth of water, and a well-constructed towing path along the whole distance, faced with a permanent slope-wall, from the top of the bank to the under water line; being a facing of 16 to 18 feet; the ponds connecting the several lengths of canal all cleared out in the channel, to the width of 50 feet; the canals, at their surface, all 60 feet wide at least; the first mile of distance, commencing at Mauch Chunk, and long since complete, has a bottom width of 60 feet; this large area having been planned for a capacious basin or boat harbour; it is formed by a dam and guard lock, and comprises 4 lift locks, of 130 feet length in the chamber, by 30 feet wide: after which, the several distances of canal, down to Easton, will all be 45 feet wide at bottom, and the bank walls mostly sloped 1½ foot base, to 1 foot rise, so as to give, for 5 feet depth, a water surface of 60 feet wide; where sandy soils occur, the bank slope to be 2 base to 1 rise, and the water surface consequently 65 feet in width at such places. These canals are, or will be, furnished with 43 locks, from 6 feet lift to 9, whereof 2 are at the same time guard locks, besides other 5 guard locks at the pools respectively; dimensions 22 feet wide, and 100 feet long between the gates.

Eight dams, substantially built across the river at as many points, and varying in height from 6 to 16 feet, will supply the canals with water; and the whole line of navigation, both canal and pool, is intended to retain a depth of 5 feet, so as to accommodate boats of the burthen of 134 to 150 tons, or pairs of boats of 67 tons each. Whole difference of level to be overcome by lockage, as the same is now measured, 360.87 feet. The lock walls are constructed, and constructing, of rough stone, laid in hydraulic cement, and planked stoutly on the inside; the stone for which cement, was luckily discovered in the vicinity of the river, and has proved to be of excellent quality.

The plan embraces also four aqueducts; one built over the Monococy at Bethlehem, having 3 stone arches of 18 feet span each; one over the Aquanshicola creek at Lehigh gap; one over the Hackendoque; one over Burtsh creek.

Twenty-two culverts; 4 of which double, and all laid in hydraulic cement; 22 waste weirs of wood, from 50 to 100 feet in length. About 23 bridges; 7 whereof for public roads, 21 feet wide, and 50 feet span generally, erected on stone abutments of dry walls. (See the engraved profile of the Lehigh work.)

It is observed, on the supply of water, that, over and above all that can be required for the purposes of navigation, it will afford very important power for machinery, in advantageous situations, especially the one at Easton.

About one-eighth part of the whole work remains to be finished; and a recent estimate, delivered in by the company's acting engineer, runs thus; viz:—

Contracts, completed and accepted, amount to,	$152,038 47
Monthly estimates on unfinished work, do.,	425,487 75
Lumber, cement, and iron work furnished by the company,	174,194 56
Work remaining to be done, materials to be furnished, and amount due on contracts,	178,775 38
Add for contingencies,	30,000 00
	$960,496 16

The board of managers conclude their address to the stockholders, in the following terms:—

When these magnificent improvements are completed, nothing

will remain but the finishing the Delaware division of the Pennsylvania canal, to enable this company to come into the market with an ample supply of coal, of the first quality, and at the most reduced price. And when it is recollected how much of the Delaware canal is already excavated and under contract, no reasonable doubt can exist that the whole might be completed in the course of the present year; and if the legislature should hesitate about making the necessary appropriation, their fears might be dispelled by a knowledge of the fact, that tonnage is already waiting, sufficient, at a moderate rate of toll, to produce a handsome income to the state. And surely improvements of a similar character elsewhere, could not be more effectually promoted, than by speedily finishing a division of canal, that would at once demonstrate the wisdom and profit of such investments.

Your managers might here expatiate upon the prospects of advantage to arise from the completion of the Morris canal, and from several other important works, intended to connect with the improvements on the Lehigh, which, beside increasing the profits of the company, would greatly swell the revenue of the state upon the Delaware division of their canal; among these may be mentioned the proposed connexion of the Susquehanna with the Lehigh, through the valley of the Nescopec; and the Delaware and Rariton canal. The former has been recently surveyed by a skilful engineer, appointed, under the authority of the state, to explore the district of country lying north of the Blue mountain, and between the Susquehanna and Delaware; and we have had the satisfaction to learn, that his opinion is decidedly in favour of this route, as the only practicable line, in this region, where sufficient water can be brought to the summit to supply a canal of any importance; and that here an abundance can be obtained; and no serious difficulty presents to making the improvement. Believing, as we do, that this channel would furnish the best outlet for the trade of the North branch of the Susquehanna, and equally convenient with any other now made, or which can hereafter be made, for the trade of the West branch, we are fully persuaded that the strongest inducements exist for its construction; whether this should be done by private companies, or by the state, is perhaps an important question. If the state should desire to make it, no difficulty ought to be presented by the company, respecting their right to improve that part of the upper grand section of the Lehigh, not necessary to perfect their arrangements in the neighbourhood of Mauch Chunk. But whether this connexion be made or not, we presume that sufficient evidence exists to justify the stockholders in the settled conviction, that nothing but steady perseverance and energy are required, to crown their own enterprise with complete success.

The rail road, from the principal mine to Mauch Chunk landing, which has been completed since May, 1827, is found to be an effective adjunct to the other of the company's works, and even materially essential to the great success that attends their operations. This, then, being in proof with regard to a rail road operated upon in part by horse power, it has suggested an improvement, and given occasion for measures to be taken in the vicinity, and a situation to be selected, whereon to erect a steam-engine, for the purpose of drawing up the wagons loaded with coal, from the mouth of the mine to the rail way summit, whence they will continue to descend by their own gravity to Mauch Chunk. The selection of site is such, that from the engine station, a convenient connexion can be made with a point to which the wagons will run by gravity, with their lading of coal, not only out of the great mine already opened, but also out of such as may hereafter be opened, within a range of 2 miles; and horse power will thenceforward only be needed to drag the empty wagons, after discharging their coal, up the inclined plane.

The rate at which the horses and mules now travel with the empty wagons up the inclined plane, is 5 to 7 miles per hour, which experience has taught to be more favourable to the health of the animals than a greater speed; and, so strong is their attachment to *riding down*, that, in one instance of their being sent up with the coal wagons, without the mule carriages, the hands were not able to drive them down, but were actually obliged to drag up their carriages for the animals to ride in!

The rail road now possessed, and in use, by the company, stands thus:—

Length, from Mauch Chunk to the west end of the coal mine, 9 miles, or feet,	47,520
Lateral, or branch roads to the mine,	8,069
Roads, and branches of the same, in the mine,	11,437
Total length of single tracks, $12 \frac{7}{10}$ miles, or feet,	67,026

The cost whereof,	$38,726
Cost of reservoir, brake, chute, and fixtures,	9,500
Total cost,	$48,226

On the important question of *economy*, in rail roads and canals compared, the acting manager's report contains the following passage:—

Perhaps some remarks on our experience with our rail road, on which has been transported upwards of 60,000 tons, may settle the question, with some of our stockholders, who have doubted the policy of canalling the valley of the Lehigh, in place of making a rail road. I therefore now give the cost of transportation on our rail road, and also on the Erie canal; data for the latter I obtained from the superintendent of the east division of the Erie canal, and also from a gentleman, largely engaged for three years, in the making of hydraulic lime, or cement, and transporting it on 152 miles of this canal : both are given, without tolls or repairs of road or canal.

Cost of transportation on our rail road, for the year 1828.

Mules and horses, cost	$1\frac{1}{3}$ cent per ton a mile.
Hands,	$1\frac{1}{3}$ do.	do.
Repairing wagons,	$\frac{2}{3}$ do.	do.
Oil for do.	$\frac{1}{5}$ do.	do.

Total, $3\frac{53}{100}$ cents per ton a mile, full load one way, and the whole cost divided into the distance one way only.

Cost of transportation by the Erie canal.

For boats of 40 tons burthen, 1 cent per ton a mile: full loads one way, and returning empty. Calculated as per the rail road.

Calculating on same data as above, on a boat of 67 tons, such as will be adapted to the Delaware canal, will cost seven-tenths of a cent per ton a mile : and for a boat of 134 tons burthen, adapted to the Lehigh canal, one-half cent per ton a mile ; the latter being less than one-sixth the cost per mile, as per our rail road, notwithstanding the favourable circumstances attending that rail road.

A rail road, well made, is attended with little expense for repairs and decay at first; but all its essential parts begin, though slightly, to decay at its existence, and its decay gradually increases to its final annihilation.

A canal is attended with expensive breaches, &c., in the first instance, but every repair makes the work better, and most of its constituent parts are as durable as time.

January, 1830.

The official report now issued, commences in these words, namely :—

"It is with great pleasure that the managers congratulate the stockholders on the entire completion of the Lehigh canal, from Mauch Chunk to the harbour of Easton, on the Delaware. The high and permanent character of the works, as given by the commissioners who were appointed by the governor of the state, under the provision of the act of assembly, to inspect the improvements made by the company, preparatory to granting them the right to assess toll, has since been fully sustained and confirmed by the minute inspection of the line, in one instance, by the whole board of managers, and by frequent visits of committees of the board, and of their officers.

"The managers wish not improperly to vaunt the merits of the work thus spoken of, but they believe they may, with perfect truth, state, that there is no work of the kind in our country, of equal length, that can compare with it in point of magnitude, permanency, and efficiency. In the words of the acting manager, 'there has been no money expended for ornament, though no money has been spared to render the work sound and permanent.'

"As before stated, the length of our line of improvement is 46¾ miles, and has cost, including the whole of the river improvement, from its commencement as a descending navigation, to its final completion, as above, including also the amount paid to White and Hazard for their property, rights, and privileges, and the extinguishment of Hauto's claims, about 1,558,000 dollars. The managers have spoken of their work as finished; this was strictly the case until the middle of the last year, when it was deemed expedient, by the canal commissioners, to direct an additional dam to be thrown across the Lehigh at its mouth, below the company's present outlet lock, consequently making a new outlet lock necessary. This was done with a view to procure a feeder for the Delaware arm of the Pennsylvania canal, from our jurisdiction on the Lehigh, in place of procuring it, as previously intended, from the waters of the Delaware, by damming that river below Easton. The work pertaining to the plan of which we have spoken, is rapidly completing, and it is believed that no injury to the interests of the company, or detention on that account to the navigation of the Lehigh, will take place.

"As relates to the full success of our past labours, in yielding to the stockholders their fair expectation of profit on their investment, of which the managers are exceedingly sanguine, they proceed to remark, that the speedy prospect of an ample outlet to the trade of the Lehigh, is now brightening in their view. As soon as the company shall have a free navigation for keel-boats, which they can return to Mauch Chunk by the Pennsylvania and New-Jersey canals, and reach the tide waters of the Delaware, New-Jersey, and New-York, an immense business will be thrown open to our company, possessing as we do an ability to supply coal, bounded only by the demand."

On account of the works still in hand, during the forepart of the past season of business, the company's shipments of coal from Mauch Chunk did not commence before the latter end of June, and from that time to the closing of the season, the quantity loaded at their premises, and sent down, by the company themselves and others, has amounted to 27,150 tons.

The report of the company's acting manager, contains the following very interesting passages:—

"In addition to the extensive examinations which took place previous to my last report, explorations have been made, which prove we can uncover and quarry our coal in a continuous opening, about 2 miles in extent, *east* and *west*, having our present quarries about in the centre. We have uncovered coal at the summit of the mountain, 320 feet *north* and *south*, across the strata of coal, which is of a quality similar to that in the great quarry; so that we have, beyond all doubt, enough coal that can be *quarried*, without *mining*, to last more than one generation, even supposing our shipments exceeded 1,000,000 of tons a year, and *that*, without extending our quarries more than 1 mile from the summit. And when our successors have done quarrying, they may follow the veins *under ground* eastward to the river about 7 miles more, and 5 miles in a western direction.

"On the supposition that we should have to raise some of our coal up to a summit from 40 to 160 feet, I have been induced, by way of experiment, to put up a set of propellers to uncover the coal, which answers my most sanguine expectations. The result of 1 day's work with the propellers is as follows; viz.

"In $10\frac{3}{4}$ hours, 3 horses drove the machinery and raised 204 wagons loaded with $1\frac{1}{2}$ tons each, or including the weight of the wagons, 2 tons each, up a plane of 35 feet rise and 210 feet in length. As the propellers require no more attention, in passing a wagon, than a piece of common rail road, and there being no gudgeons or machinery to grease except the driving part, the expense of going up hills is reduced to a mere trifle, being confined pretty much to that of the driving power. In a country like ours, where coal can be had for 50 cents a ton, the expense of a steam-engine, with the necessary attendance, would not exceed one twentieth the cost of horse labour. The peculiar situation of the company's coal lands, makes this an exceedingly valuable discovery, as the mountain extends from the river on the side of all our lands, so that by the aid of the propellers, and 2 or 3 engines, a coal business to the extent of 500,000 tons can be effected *by gravity* to and from the coal mines to Mauch Chunk, and thus avoid all animal power.

"We have made some very satisfactory alterations in the rail way, for the purpose of preventing the early decay of the timber and the jolting of the wagons. We now run the wagons at the average rate of about 6 miles an hour, and find this motion produces much less wear both of the wagons and road than a greater velocity. I have demonstrated, to my satisfaction, that the wear and tear of the road and wagons is in proportion to the motion, and that in the end, a motion exceeding 20 miles an hour (which we tried in the first months of our business) will make the transportation on rail roads more expensive than that on our graded turnpike, on which the rails were laid.

"It is expected the Delaware division of the Pennsylvania canal, and the Morris canal, will both be ready for use by midsummer of the present year. Should this expectation be realized, so far as to give full confidence that they can be used without interruption in the succeeding year, we can readily make such arrangements as to give each of those canals 100,000 tons of freight for the year 1831."

Some time ago, specimens of the Lehigh anthracite, and mineral powder, were sent over to a scientific gentleman at Manchester, England, for the purpose of undergoing analysis there, and practical or familiar experiments, with a view to elicitation of discovery; for the hope is always entertained with us, that a discovery will sooner or later be made, by which one at least of these very cheap and abundant substances, and both, perhaps, may be brought to use, for the furnace, upon the most extensive scale, profitably, consequently, to multitudes concerned in the *desideratum*.

The shipment from hence spoken of above, produced the information and inquiries contained in the extract here inserted.

"The black matter sent by Captain Dixey, appears, from my experiments upon it, to be almost wholly vegetable charcoal, in the state it reached me (rather damp),—by exposing 600 grains for a few hours, to a temperature of 200 to 212, Fahrenheit, it lost in weight 120 grains, or 20 per cent., leaving 480 grains. 80 grains, or one sixth, thus dried, then infused for some hours in distilled water, frequently agitated, then separated by filter, and dried, weighed as at first, 80 grains,—so that no part was dissolved, nor was the water at all altered in its specific gravity. The same weight (80 grains), infused in dilute sulphuric acid, then washed and dried, lost no weight, nor was the acid coloured or altered in specific gravity;—treated the same way with dilute nitric acid, and with dilute muriatic acid, the result was the same. When deflagrated with nitrate of potash, the nitrate is decomposed, and there remains sub-carbonate of potash, resulting from the decomposition of the nitrate; and a small quantity of earthy matter, resulting from the charcoal and its impurities. Such being the result of these experiments, it appeared to me not worth further pursuit, as it is evidently nothing but vegetable carbon, or charcoal, with a small portion of earthy admixture. Its value of course is small—not enough to pay freight to this country; I wish, for your sake, that gold had been a component part; but alas! neither dollars nor cents present themselves to my chemical view.

"The sample of Lehigh coal, is the most beautiful and pure anthracite I ever saw, but it would not suit my or Englishmen's taste for parlour fuel; we like a blazing fire. Is it used in your smelting furnaces? I think it would do well for that purpose, and for malting; or for any purposes where a strong fire without smoke is necessary. It requires a pretty strong draft to burn it to full effect. Does it occur near Philadelphia? Is it in a mountain, or under low ground? Do they mine it by perpendicular or horizontal shafts? The difference of cost in cash and labour of the two ways, is immense."

Alluding again to the coal dust, the writer proceeds:—

"It is a very curious geological discovery. You say any quantity may be had. I should like to know how it lies; whether horizontal—to what extent—what it lies upon, and what stratum or strata cover it, and what depth under the surface of the earth, and what is the thickness of its stratum. By its being in the form of powder, I think it cannot have been formed where it now lies, but that it is there an alluvial deposite, brought from some higher country, perhaps, at a very remote period, by rain, or the overflowing of rivers and lakes on a higher level; it may originate from the spontaneous burning of some large forest, or a great surface of grass, reeds, &c. Does it contain no large pieces of charcoal, or *any other* organic remains, as bones, shells, &c.? I think a paper well drawn up, descriptive of its localities, and every visible circumstance attending it, would be an acceptable contribution to the transactions of the London Geological Society."

Upon the appearance of which, the editor of this book made application to the gentlemen at the head of the "Lehigh coal and navigation" establishment, for a statement of *further facts;* and he has, very obligingly, been furnished with a letter on the subject, in the following terms;—

"I received thy favour of the 7th instant, with the inclosed queries.

"Query 1. Have experiments been made, giving a probability that anthracite coal may be used for smelting iron ore?

"Answer. We pulverized anthracite coal, and mixed it with iron ore, and put the mixture in a close crucible, which we put in a furnace, and kept it there under a cherry red heat; say we had 4 close crucibles, thus filled, and kept in the fire for 24, 12, 6, and 2 hours each. Part of the contents of those subjected to 24 and 12 hours heat, were put in other crucibles and melted down by a smith's fire in 15 minutes, and produced good grey iron, soft enough to be cut with a penknife. That subjected to 6 hours heat, melted down also, into white cast iron. That subjected to 2 hours carbonating, was also melted, but the iron *did not separate from the other matter*.

"Hence we infer, there is no chemical difficulty in the way of its general application for smelting iron ore, and in the most perfect manner.

"Our mining of anthracite coal, is carried on in the same way as Cooley quarried his stone at Fair Mount, when he built the Fair Mount dam. The coal is loaded in the mine into the wagons, which bring it to Mauch Chunk; the wagons, thus loaded, pass out of the mine by gravity, and so does the water drain out.

"2. What is the condition of the fine black matter, and how is it found?

"Answer. It usually forms the upper covering of the coal, say 3 to 6 feet in thickness; it appears to be decomposed coal. Whenever the coal crops out to-day, the *finest* black matter is on the top, and it gets coarser as we descend; same as in a common stone quarry, when good plough land is on the top, and as they dig down, it gets coarser to the rotten rock, and next comes soft rock, that can be barely handled, and then comes the hard rock; just so with our coal. Our fine black matter contains small pieces of pure hard anthracite coal, but no organic remains. We have some veins that fracture like wood, but it is more *troublesome* in a fire than slate itself. We have appearances of "fern," &c. in our small veins, but never or very rarely in our great mine."

A.—From Berwick, on the Susquehanna, through the Nescopec valley, to Lowrytown, on the Lehigh, 16 miles above Mauch Chunk; or to Lausanne. Summit, 948 feet.   Distance, *Miles*, 35

No. 63.
THE BERWICK AND LEHIGH, OR NESCOPEC CANAL.

An act of incorporation, 25th March, 1826, has passed the legislature of Pennsylvania, for this undertaking; by which the company are empowered to enter on the Nescopec creek, at or near the falls thereof, and to construct a canal, or a slackwater navigation, or both, from thence to a convenient point of the Lehigh. Capital stock 600,000 dollars, with power in the company to augment, should the cost of the works require it. The company, on being organized, to receive their charter of incorporation from the governor, as the "Susquehanna and Lehigh canal company."

This, together with some of the preceding projects of communication, here inserted, whether the same be executed throughout in the form of navigable passes, or, as it appears at present probable, by means, in part, of *rail roads*, will evidently be much stimulated by the progress and completion of the Rariton canal; if the latter, as it is hoped, shall speedily be set on foot; in consequence of a close connexion of interests. There will be established a transportation direct across to New-York, not only of the Lehigh coal itself, but also of that produced from the ranges of coal beds, situate on the Susquehanna and neighbouring waters; as thus:—

From Wilkesbarre, by canal or rail road, to Lausanne, on the Lehigh,	*Miles*, 40
Lausanne, to the mouth of the Lehigh, at Easton,	49
Easton, passing down the Delaware, and through the feeding canal, and the main canal, to Rariton river,	80
Thence to New-York,	35
Distance,	*Miles*, 204

A canal has also been proposed, from the mouth of the Lackawannock, at Pittston, on the Susquehanna, through Northampton, to the Delaware, at the Water Gap, 24 miles above Easton, as is inserted in the article which here follows. This route, continued on to New-York, would be still more direct, viz.

From Pittston to Water Gap,	*Miles*, 60
Water Gap to Easton,	24
Easton to New-York,	115
	Miles, 199

NOTE.

By an act of the legislature, passed on the 3d April, 1827, the board of commissioners for internal improvement, are required to make examinations, to ascertain as to the practicability and cost of constructing a canal, or a rail road, between the North branch of the Susquehanna and the River Delaware, by the head waters of the Lehigh, and by Broadhead's creek valley; and to report thereupon.

NOTE.

Accidents have occasioned a postponement of these examinations, by the Pennsylvania commissioners, to the season of 1828.

December, 1828.

It appears, by report of the commissioners, that the construction of a canal along the Nescopec valley, is not at all impracticable, but would be attended with an inconvenient amount of lockage. A rail road is recommended. The opinion, however, of the Lehigh Company's engineers, is still in favour of a canal between Berwick and the Lehigh upper waters. They think it probable, that transportation from Berwick, as far as Mauch Chunk, may, by means of a canal, be afforded at one third of the price a rail road would require to be paid per ton. They represent, moreover, that it is the only line for a water communication, north of the Blue mountains, that can connect the Susquehanna river with the Delaware and Philadelphia; furnishing the best outlet to the important trade of both the North branch and West branch of the Susquehanna. Water, the engineers state, is in abundance, and, by resorting to a tunnel of only 175 poles long, and a dam of 10 to 13 feet high, across the Lehigh, at the mouth of Bear creek, the River Lehigh will flow into the summit.

It is proposed that the Nescopec canal be adapted to boats of 67 tons, to correspond with the Delaware division of the Pennsylvania canal.

A.—From the mouth of the Lackawannock, at Pittston, on the Susquehanna, by canal, across the head waters of the Lehigh river, through Stoddartsville, and through Northampton county, down the Pocano, or Broadhead's creek valley, to the Delaware river, at the Water Gap.   Distance, *Miles*, 60

No. 64.

PITTSTON AND WATER GAP CANAL.

This proposed canal route, like one or two others, to connect the waters of the Susquehanna and the Delaware, has not yet been satisfactorily surveyed; but the importance of the project will not fail to bring it forward. It will open a very direct communication between Philadelphia and all the Wyoming district of country, abounding in coal of the anthracite kind. The intended improvements in the bed of the Delaware, on its upper waters, will take place, to meet the occasion. This route is shown too, in the preceding article, to be more direct than by the Lehigh route, across to the city of New-York. It will, moreover, become a leading route to and from the counties in New-York state, south of the secondary lakes.

In the latter point of view, indeed, an easy and commodious communication, between Pittston and the Delaware river, appears to be an object extremely desirable; more so, perhaps, than on every other account; and might fully warrant the construction, not only of a canal, but of a rail road also, upon the very best plan, to accommodate the probable transportation trade. This route will, there can be no doubt, become a most active thoroughfare for much of the produce of a very rich wheat country, and the return trade; and Pittston and Wilkesbarre will rise in importance, as places of depôt on an extended scale.

Since the above was written, application has been made to the legislature of Pennsylvania, for an act of incorporation, as "The Delaware and Susquehanna canal and rail road company;" capital stock, 1,500,000 dollars. The works to commence at Lackawannock, and proceed to the Delaware Water Gap, and to Easton. Application also, for another act of incorporation, constituting "The Wilkesbarre and Delaware central rail way company;" capital, 1,000,000 dollars, to make the connexion in a line from Wilkesbarre to the Delaware Water Gap. Likewise, another act of incorporation for "The Lackawannock and Susquehanna rail road company;" capital, 150,000 dollars. The line of connexion, from the Susquehanna to the Belmont coal beds.

NOTE.

By an act of the legislature, 3d April, 1826, the governor is authorized to institute a company, as the "Delaware and Susquehanna canal and rail road company," empowering the same to make a complete canal navigation, or a rail road, from a point of the River Susquehanna, at or near the mouth of the Lackawannock, to a point of the River Delaware, at or near the Water Gap, and thence to another point of the River Delaware, opposite the mouth of the proposed Delaware and Rariton feeder canal, suppose near to Durham creek, Bucks county; or, perhaps, to Easton merely. Empowering the company also to construct a branch canal, or rail road, from the main canal or rail road aforesaid, to the borough of Wilkesbarre, if they, the company, shall decide so to do.

Capital stock, 1,500,000 dollars, with power in the company to augment if requisite.

The company at liberty to construct, at their option, either canal or rail way, along any part of the route.

December, 1828.

By surveys made in the past season, with a view to connecting the Lackawannock river with the Delaware, at the Water Gap, through Broadhead's creek valley, either by means of canal or rail road, it does not appear that the routes surveyed and reported upon by the state engineers, furnish needful facilities for either the one or the other construction. *See summary on the Pennsylvania canal and rail road.*

A.—From the Lehigh river, near Allentown, by canal, along the Jordan and Perkiomen valley, to the river Schuylkill. Distance, *Miles*, 40

No. 65.

THE PERKIOMEN CANAL.

As to this formerly projected undertaking, surveys have been suspended.

M.—From the River Schuylkill, at a point above Kittatinny mountain, and below Orwigsburg, by the East branch, or Little Schuylkill valley, and that of the Catawissa creek, through Schuylkill and Columbia counties, to the Susquehanna river, near Danville. Distance, by canal, or the stream improved,
Miles, 50

No. 66.

THE CATAWISSA CANAL.

An act has passed the Pennsylvania legislature, empowering the governor to grant a charter for a portion of this projected work; that is to say, for effecting a lock navigation along the East or Little Schuylkill river, to the coal mines: subscription books to be opened on the 11th June, 1826, by commissioners appointed for the purpose.

NOTE.

The said act passed on the 20th February, 1826, by which the company are styled the "Schuylkill East branch navigation company," and are empowered to make a complete navigable canal, or a slackwater navigation, as they may deem most eligible, between the point of junction of said East branch, or Little Schuylkill river, with the Big Schuylkill, up to the point where the Wilkesbarre state road crosses the river; or, to the foot of Broad mountain, if found expedient by the company, with privilege and right to connect this improvement at the junction of the two branches, with the improvement already formed, or forming, by the "Schuylkill navigation company." Capital stock, 250,000 dollars, with power in the company to enlarge it in case of need. Distance for a rail road, along Little Schuylkill valley, 22 miles.

It is further made the duty of this company, to cause a survey to be made of the ground, and of the waters from the head of said navigation, by the Catawissa valley, to the Susquehanna river; with a view of completing the connexion of the waters of the Susquehanna and the Little Schuylkill. And, in case of not succeeding in a practicable route for canal communication, then to cause a survey and estimate of cost to be made for a rail road of communication.

The company are authorized to purchase and hold coal lands, to the extent of 5000 acres.

NOTE 2.

An act of incorporation has passed, in favour of the "Pottsville and Danville rail way company," for the object of constructing a rail road, from the head of the Schuylkill navigation, at or near Pottsville, to the most eligible point of the Susquehanna river. Also, by an act of the legislature, March, 1828, the board of canal commissioners are required to effect surveys from points of the Schuylkill river canal, to a point or points on the Susquehanna river, between Catawissa and Sunbury, with a view to the construction of a rail road of connexion, and to report to the legislature, with estimates, and all particulars.

December, 1828.

It appears, by report of the commissioners, that, from Catawissa, a rail road, suited to locomotive steam engines, except at the summit, where stationary power is needed, may be carried either through Quacake valley to the Lehigh river; or carried to the Schuylkill at Pottsville; or, by the head of Little or East Schuylkill, to the point of junction with Big Schuylkill. And that a rail road, adjusted for the use of horse power, may be constructed between Pottsville and either Danville or Sunbury.

Sunbury being situated on the verge of the pool, in which the trade of the North and that of the West branch Pennsylvania canals meet, ought, it would seem, on this account, to be preferred.

A.—From the mouth of Mill creek, on the Upper Schuylkill, by canal, or other navigation improvements, up to the mill of George Reber. Distance, *Miles*, ...

No. 67.

SCHUYLKILL VALLEY CANAL.

By an act of the legislature, 20th March, 1827, the governor of Pennsylvania is authorized to institute a company, as the "Schuylkill valley navigation company," for the purpose of effecting this work of improvement; not to interfere, however, with the rights and privileges heretofore granted in favour of the Schuylkill navigation company. Capital stock, 150,000 dollars.

NOTE.

A rail road is proposed to be constructed over this tract of 10 miles, more or less, for the transportation of coal; as also another rail road, of about the same distance, commencing from the Schuylkill navigation company's works, at Pottsville, and passing by the Norwegian and Mill creek valley, to a rich body of coal lands: and books for subscription to this undertaking are to be laid open at Pottsville, and at Philadelphia, on the 9th February, 1829.

A.—From the mouth of Mahanoy creek, on the Susquehanna river, Northumberland county, by canal, or slackwater, or other improved navigation, up the course of said creek, and up that also of the Little

Mahanoy, and of Serby's brook, to the coal mines, on and near the latter.   Distance, *Miles*, ...

No. 68.

MAHANOY CREEK CANAL.

By an act of assembly, 22d March, 1827, the governor of Pennsylvania is authorized to institute a company, as the "Mahanoy creek navigation company," for the purpose of effecting this work of improvement; and the company to have power to construct a rail road, from the coal mines along the route, or any part thereof. Capital stock, 60,000 dollars.

A.—From the mouth of Shamokin creek, on the Susquehanna river, Northumberland county, by canal, or other improved navigation, up the course of said creek, to the coal mines, situate on or near the same.
Distance, *Miles*, ...

No. 69.

SHAMOKIN CREEK CANAL.

By an act of assembly, 14th April, 1827, the governor of Pennsylvania is authorized to institute a company, as the "Shamokin creek canal company," for the purpose of effecting this work of improvement; with power in the company to construct a rail road from the mines, along the route, or any part thereof, at their option. Capital stock, 60,000 dollars.

A.—From Newbold's landing, soon to become "Delaware City," on the River Delaware, nearly opposite to Fort Delaware, Pea Patch island, 45 miles below Philadelphia, westward, across the peninsula, to Back creek, Maryland, on the Chesapeake, 4 or 5 miles south of Frenchtown, and near the mouth of Long creek.   Distance, *Miles*, 14

No. 70.
THE CHESAPEAKE AND DELAWARE CANAL.

This work commenced on the 5th of April, 1824, and is in such vigorous prosecution, that, barring casualties, it will be complete for navigation before the year 1828. It is to be 60 feet wide at the water surface, 36 feet at the bottom, 8 feet depth of water, and at every half-mile, to have recesses for the passing of vessels, where the width will be increased to 110 feet. There will be no more than 2 lift locks, one tide lock at the Delaware, and another at the Back creek termination. Dimensions of the locks, 100 feet long, by 22 wide in the chamber.

The line of canal is divided into 7 sections; Nos. 1, 2, 3, to St. George's town, distance 4½ miles, to be made on the thorough cut plan, the bottom 10 feet below the level of common high tide on the Delaware; Nos. 4, 5, 6, as far as Broad creek, 7¾ miles, to have, for the present, the bottom on a level with common high tide; No. 7, which is through Broad creek to Back creek, 1¾ miles, to have the bottom 6 feet below the common high tide level of the Chesapeake.

The section No. 5, comprises a deep cut of 3¾ miles, and of 76 feet in depth at its highest part; and this summit, which is 8 feet above common high tide, is plentifully supplied with water from the drainage of the adjacent country, or the creeks on either hand, which empty into the Chesapeake and the Delaware respectively. An extensive reservoir, measuring at least 100 acres area, by an average depth of 10 feet, will therefore here be formed; or, if needful for the occasions of the canal, more than one reservoir.

The peculiar and very interesting feature of the arrangement, is, that it may be regarded as provisional; for it contemplates an enlargement, at a future day, whenever it shall be decided to make this canal into a passage for ships: a project which can readily be executed, on the thorough cut plan, by deepening the sections Nos. 4, 5, 6, 10 feet, and the western section, No. 7, 2 feet; and then there will be a canal throughout, with a command of the Atlantic ocean for its reservoir, to give constant passage to large vessels, as well as to small.

Furthermore, details have been submitted for the improvement of this canal, at some future day, to such a scale as for it to be adapted to the passage of ships of war, drawing 20 feet of water, and so far to correspond with the great Caledonian canal. In which ultimate improved state, the engineers' estimate of cost for it, has been given in at 2,000,000 of dollars; not, however, to say, but that a larger expense might be needed for such a work.

On the plan of its immediate execution, it will be sufficient for a passage to our coasting vessels, or boats of equal draft, and will, at the least, in this respect, equal in accommodation the Dismal Swamp canal, between Virginia and North Carolina, as also the Delaware and Rariton canal, as at present projected.

In regard to cost, on this provisional scale, the estimate is 1,250,000 dollars. Towards which, the general government is, by virtue of an act of congress, a subscriber to the joint stock of the company, for - - - - $300,000
The state of Pennsylvania, a subscriber for - - 100,000
The state of Maryland, for - - - - 50,000
The state of Delaware, for - - - - 25,000

Connected with the work, there is constructing, at the eastern debouche of the canal, on the Delaware river, a capacious harbour for shipping. Form of the harbour, semicircular; with an opening of 150 feet, at that part of the arch where the main current of the river forms a tangent to it, and where vessels will be received and delivered in 20 feet of water, near upon the edge of the river channel. The whole, for solid security, no less, but rather much more, than for beauty even, to be finished with facings of stone, from the top of the embankments to the bed of the river.

The Delaware tide lock of the canal, which is 100 feet in length between the gates, and 22 feet wide in the chamber, and containing 40,000 feet of solid masonry, is finished. It opens into a capacious basin. The Back creek lock will correspond in dimensions.

The summit level, above noticed, makes, in consequence of the deep cutting there, an elegant site for a bridge, that will be thrown across, with a span of 200 to 250 feet, and the under side of the arch 90 feet above the bottom of the canal.

December, 1826.

Great and unlooked for difficulties have been encountered at section 3 of this undertaking, a distance of about 3½ miles, extending to the lock at St. George's town, through Cranberry and St. George's marshes.

On arriving at, and attempting to carry the works over this ground, marsh land though it was known to be, yet, at this late period only, it was, and never before, that the worst of its circumstances, in relation to canal purposes, came to be discovered. It was found to be infinitely less suited for canal construction, than had been supposed; in so far, as where stiff clay had been thought to prevail, at a certain depth of the earth, and to offer consequently at that depth the resource of a compact foundation, upon digging into those very places, no clay was found : and, in this dilemma, no alternative presented, but the one of *making* a foundation of 3½ miles long, from materials at a distance ; which was wisely resorted to, and the work proceeded ; and it is now well advanced through this formidable pass.

This, however, the managers have necessarily not been able to effectuate, short of a great increase of expense; and therefore, as this occurrence was not foreseen, the ultimate cost of the Chesapeake and Delaware canal, it is understood, will exceed the early estimate of it, by a considerable amount.

At other points, the work has been advancing satisfactorily, as appears by an official report ; and it does not appear that the completion of the work, in toto, will, from what has occurred, be much, if at all delayed beyond the appointed period ; viz. 1828.

NOTE.

It is not unworthy of being remarked, that the Delaware and Chesapeake communication, *has been* considered as the parent of all canal projects in this country ; having, from certain causes, attracted the attention of the commercial and enterprising community of Philadelphia, at a period very soon after the time when canals commenced in England. We find, that as early at least as the year 1767 or 1768, the matter was seriously taken up, and prosecuted by Mr. Thomas Gilpin and other gentlemen; who were at great pains in accomplishing a number of surveys, and giving estimates to the public, for a canal from Duck creek to the head of Chester. In 1769, a condensed view of all that had been done, was presented by Mr. Gilpin to a committee of merchants, formed in Philadelphia, for the purpose of improving the trade of the province; as also to the American Philosophical Society : and this was soon followed by a survey, and remarks upon another route ; viz. from Bohemia river to Appoquinimink; which, by the by, might perhaps have been a preferable route for a canal to the present one. After which, the Elk route was also examined. These and many other particulars of what was done, previous to the revolution, to promote the object in question, and again subsequent to that event, when the time had come round for the subject to be taken up anew, have been given to the world, by a descendant of the gentleman above named, in an historical work, not long since published. And it is curious to observe from it, how intimately the idea of this very improvement could identify itself, at that early day, with the country's best interests and future prosperity, in the minds of many patriotic individuals. They were, however, not a little enlightened, as it would seem; nor a little zealous in the cause ; and not a little, perhaps, of the present day's success, in the accomplishment of their wishes, is to be attributed to their own diligent efforts, followed up and persevered in to the end, by some of their descendants, successively, through every change of circumstance.

We have said above, that the Chesapeake and Delaware communication *has been* regarded as the first canal project in this country; so saying, however, without any intention to disregard the most accurate chronology in such an important point of history, or any wish to be instrumental in dealing "first honours" otherwise than in strict conformity to the true order of those long past events; and if it be not within our power, at the present day, to determine the point in question, with all the precision it merits, it is no less an act of justice here to state, that what is now termed the "Union canal," starts up in importance for the honour of a precedence. It has been affirmed, that as early as 1762, David Rittenhouse, the celebrated astronomer, and at or about the same time, Dr. William Smith, provost of the University of Pennsylvania, effected a survey, or surveys, and levelled a route for a canal, to connect the waters of the Susquehanna and Schuylkill rivers, by the Swatara and Tulpehocken; and, what would not be credible, did it not seem to be well authenticated, is, that these conspicuous characters, together with some others, their contemporaries, and particularly residents of Philadelphia, actually viewed this project, great as it was in itself, still as nothing more than a part of something greater; a preliminary step to something farther. These gentlemen had at that day in their "mind's eye," a thorough commercial communication between the east and the west, and the waters of Lake Erie reciprocally, in a line of route 582 miles long; which they actually traced for it, between the Delaware river, and the Ohio at Fort Pitt, and the lake at Presque isle. This, not by means of one continuous navigation, it is true, but by the projection of judicious improvements, the times considered, along the great water courses, such as locks, and dams, and walls, with here and there a short canal, and a good turnpike road across the Alleghany mountain.

All this, it is to be remarked, was in agitation here in the minds of several eminent men, at a time even when the Duke of Bridgewater's canal, in England, was hardly finished, and turnpikes but just got into vogue; and the "Union canal," now so called, identifying itself with what was then to be the first effective part of the whole gigantic project, may, perhaps, without the smallest intentional injustice, file a claim for seniority over every other canal project of the country, whether acted on by works, or not; a seniority over even the Chesapeake and Delaware communication; which, however, is a point not here undertaken to be absolutely decided on.

William Penn, in one of his papers, of the year 1690, says something of the *feasibility of a passage, by water, between the Susquehanna river and a branch of the Schuylkill;* but the brevity of the passage renders it unintelligible, as canals were not then practically known in England.

June, 1827.

The president and directors of the Chesapeake and Delaware canal, have just made a new general report; which, taken all together, is highly gratifying. It is so, in the view that it gives of the actual situation of the works; and likewise in the probable inferences to be drawn as to the quantum of their approaching efficiency. Nothing of the kind can, according to the tenor of the report, be more promising. The most sanguine expectations are at present entertained, as to those great public benefits, which necessarily must follow a successful opening of this canal navigation; and of individual enterprise, in the case, being besides, remunerated to a liberal extent.

This is the present encouraging aspect of things, notwithstanding that the managers have had, for some months last past, a series of difficulties to surmount; such, in fact, as have called for the exercise of all their zeal and industry on the occasion, as well as an extra application of science.

Unfaithfulness and failure on the part of some of the contractors, along with the occurrence already noticed, have conjointly been the cause; but no greater detriment has ensued, than some delay, and a considerable augmentation of expense; both which, it was desirable to have avoided; but, on the other hand, it is not improbable that the entire work will have derived advantages, in point both of stability as a structure, and usefulness in its general objects, from the very circumstance of the deliberation observed in finishing and testing some of the parts where accidents have occurred; and, at some other points, the incidental changes made, in regard to plan, from the one originally laid down. The slipping and sinking of banks over marsh and quicksand ground, claimed repeatedly extra attention towards the obtaining of a solid foundation; and there has been taken, on each of these occasions of repairing, or of reconstruction, the most deliberate measures for the purpose of not leaving in any doubt the security and permanency of the work. The same caution having been adopted likewise in regard to other important parts of this great undertaking, it has occasioned altogether an immense quantity of stone work, additional to that originally contemplated in the plan. In the construction of the Delaware harbour, solid wharf-work has been adopted in lieu of earthen banks: 220 feet of wharf on the north side, and the same on the south, with 500 feet on the river bank, connecting the two sides, are finished as to timber work, and nearly filled up with stones and clay.

The scale of the canal itself, is so materially changed, that instead of 8 feet depth of water, as at first intended, it is now constructed for a retention of 10 feet throughout; and the Chesapeake and Delaware canal is a canal of 10 feet navigable depth in ordinary tides: in spring tides, occasionally the depth will be increased to 12 feet.

Section 3, which has proved so difficult and expensive in its execution, can now be said to have yielded to labour and perseverance. The water of the Delaware has, by way of experiment, been passed into it. The banks, however, of this section, are yet to be wrought upon.

Section 1 is finished.

Section 2, likewise so, excepting some small matters of facile accomplishment.

Sections 6 and 7, both finished.

Sections 4 and 5, including the deep cut, and summit level, comprise therefore what chiefly remains to be finished, and it is all in a satisfactory train: 1900 and odd workmen and labourers are at this moment industriously employed on it; and, before the close of the present season, should no sinister accident happen, great progress will have been made towards a completion of the whole canal. The span of the bridge across the deep cut, is 235 feet. (See an engraved profile view of this canal.)

PROSPECTS OF INCOME, VIZ:—

Capacity of the Chesapeake and Delaware canal.

This canal will be competent to the passage of boats of more than 100 tons burthen.

Now, allowing 3 boats, of 100 tons each, to pass the locks from east to west, and the same number the other way, every 10 minutes each, it gives 600 tons within the hour, or 14,400 tons per day: or, for the year, taken at 300 days, 4,320,000 tons. This is the computed capacity of the Chesapeake and Delaware canal.

But, supposing a tonnage equal to 5 boats only, averaging 75 tons each, should pass the locks per hour; and supposing the canal to be employed at this rate during 15 hours of the 24, this gives 5625 tons per diem, or 1,687,500 tons for the year of 300 days.

GENERAL ESTIMATE OF INCOME,

On a supposition of employment equal to the above computed trade, of 1,687,500 tons passing through the canal locks in the course of a year; viz:—

The present rate of carriage for a barrel of flour from Elkton to Newcastle, varies, according to circumstances, from 25 to 37½ cents; this latter being in general the packet price; which, at 10 barrels to the ton, makes the rate of carriage $2 50 to $3 75 cents.

Now, looking to this rate of transportation, it has been supposed, that the toll for passing the Chesapeake and Delaware canal might, in reason and moderation, be fixed at 80 cents per ton as a maximum, and 40 cents as a minimum, according to bulk and kind of the merchandise. If, then, constant employment should take place; or rather, if only such a run of employment should take place, as will, in the course of the year, amount to the tonnage here supposed, of 1,687,500 tons; and, if we suppose one-half of this as appertaining to the maximum description of goods, and the other half to the minimum description, we shall, upon these suppositions, obtain for the Chesapeake and Delaware canal, an annual income as here follows:—

  843,750 tons, at 80 cents, $ 675,000
  843,750 tons, at 40 cents, 337,500

Amount of tolls for a year of 300 days, $ 1,012,500

An amount, this, which may be startling at first sight, but which it does not at present appear impossible should be realized, provided the rates of toll here supposed were absolutely established. There is a large margin, therefore, for allowances, as to the quantity of trade that may be forthcoming, and great prospects will still remain.

In the following statement of "calculations," the scale is not otherwise contracted, than by a supposition of the canal having, not a full and constant, but a partial, employment.

CALCULATIONS,

To show the probable income of the Chesapeake and Delaware canal, by particulars likely to pass through the locks at the early stages of its operation; viz:—

The produce of the Susquehanna, in grain, flour, iron, whiskey, &c., 60,000 tons, at 80 cents per ton, $ 48,000

      Amount carried forward, $ 48,000

Amount brought forward,	$48,000
Lumber of the Susquehanna, 3,000,000 cubic feet, at 75 cents per 1000,	2,250
Coal of the Susquehanna, 20,000 tons, at 40 cents per ton,	8,000
Tonnage, between ports of the Delaware and the Chesapeake, 64,000 tons, at 80 cents,	51,200
Probable tonnage to and from eastern ports, passing the canal, to avoid the longer navigation by sea, 15,000 tons, at 80 cents,	12,000
Annual income, according to these premises,	$121,450

Which, provided the present state of our internal commerce prove not to be overrated in these calculations, will, in the course of a few years, it is not unreasonable to conclude, double itself, and triple itself, and go on to do more. The capacity of the canal is shown above to be equal to that, and much more, without any probable inconvenient pressure of business upon it. In the end, lateral locks may have to be constructed to accommodate the trade.

In corroboration of the present estimate, it may be remarked,

1. That the downward commerce of the Susquehanna river for the year 1826, conveyed in rafts, keel boats, and arks, has been computed at 5,000,000 dollars in value, and the tonnage or bulk thereof equal to   tons. A great proportion of which, and nearly all perhaps that portion of the trade composed of the bulkiest commodities, such as coal, lumber, &c., it is probable will continue still to find its way, by the river channel, to tide water, notwithstanding those canals which will present themselves on the passage down; so that of this trade, a good deal may be expected to enter the capacious locks of the Chesapeake and Delaware canal, leading to the Delaware river. It appears, from registers taken, that between the 3d day of March, and the 3d of July, 1826, there passed the town of Columbia, bound to tide water,

>   1037 Arks,
>   164 Keel boats,
>   1090 Rafts.

2. As to the item of trade, or the tonnage between the ports of the Delaware and the Chesapeake:—In the first place, there are now 3 lines of packets, exclusive of steam-boats, employed between Philadelphia and Baltimore alone:—one by way of Wilmington, one by Newcastle, and one by Appoquinimink; which 3 lines, comprise 8 vessels, of 40 to 45 tons each, dispatched each way every week, and their freights deposited, or delivered over, respectively, to an intermediate over-land conveyance. Now,

if we suppose the double freight of each trip to amount to 50 tons, and that the year averages 40 weeks merely of navigable weather, we shall have 400 tons, as the weekly tonnage of merchandise, by these over-land packets, or 16,000 tons per annum, between Philadelphia and Baltimore alone. These packets transport principally the lighter and more valuable articles of commerce; besides them, there is, in the second place, a regular line by sea, sailing weekly between Philadelphia and Baltimore; and, in the year 1826, the clearances at the Philadelphia customhouse, for the several ports of the Chesapeake, Baltimore included, appear to have amounted to 10,280 tons. How much the tonnage the other way amounted to, does not appear; but the sum of these quantities taken together, it is not improbable will be found to bear no more than a limited proportion to the tonnage of the trade from port to port, which hereafter is to be carried on, through so convenient, safe, expeditious, and, consequently, economical a channel, taken in every sense, as the Chesapeake and Delaware canal.

The able report of the managers has, for a concluding paragraph, the words as here follows:—

"When we take into view the immense trade of the Susquehanna, and its tributary streams; the vast amount of produce which must arrive from the *west*, by the Pennsylvania state canal, so happily commenced; and the increased intercourse which will be opened with the eastern shores of Maryland and Virginia, and the various other thriving and extensive districts connected with the Bay of Chesapeake, we may be induced to doubt, not indeed whether *one* canal will lack employment, but whether it will be possible for it alone to accommodate all the trade which will present itself at the gates," (for a passage through.)

JUNE, 1828.

The ninth annual report of the president and directors is now issued. The tenor of it goes to confirm previous expectations; and, it is expressly stated, that a doubt does not exist, of the entire canal being complete and navigable in the ensuing autumn. For some weeks past, the water has been let into sections No. 1, 2, 3, 4, and a lively scene of business already prevails all along the eastern division, from the River Delaware to the company's wharf, near the summit bridge; and it is found that the depth and the expanse of water are such, as to enable vessels to proceed along this splendid canal, at the rate of 6 or 7 miles an hour.

The work upon the deep cut of the summit, is advancing rapidly to a close; the stoning extends along the whole 3½ miles.

by a wall somewhat more than 11 feet perpendicular, 16 feet on the slope, on each side, and descends 1 foot below the bottom of the canal. It is from 18 inches to 5 feet in thickness at the base, according to the nature of the soil over which it passes; at the top, from 1 to 3 feet thick; and under the summit bridge, this wall is carried up, on both sides of the canal, until it is met by the abutments, which of course it will serve to protect. Of 44,000 perches of masonry which this wall will contain, 18,000 only now remain to be built.

The present water-arrangements on the summit, are these:—

500 acres overflowed, which it is computed will yield, - - - - - - cubic feet,	43,560,000
Lum's mill pond, 100 acres, average depth 6 feet,	26,136,000
Jones's mill pond, 25 acres, average depth 5 feet, and may be increased, - - - - -	5,445,000
Additional 3 feet, which Lum's pond can be raised,	21,780,000
Cubic feet,	96,921,000

This, it is to be observed, is independent of the supplies to be derived from the inexhaustible reservoirs formed of the Delaware river and Chesapeake bay, whenever the demands of the canal shall render it needful to resort thereto.

An act of Congress has passed, authorizing the secretary of the treasury to subscribe in behalf of the United States, for 750 shares additional, or 150,000 dollars, to the stock of this company.

The whole expenditure on this canal, is now upwards of 2,000,000 dollars.

July 4th, 1829.

This day, a thorough navigation of the canal, from the Chesapeake waters to the Delaware, has taken place, and the event of a passage through is celebrating.

The canal will shortly be laid open for general navigation.

October 18th, 1829.

Yesterday, by appointment, the ceremonies appropriate to the great event, were observed; and the chairman of the committee, on the occasion, announced, to a numerous assembly of visitants, passing through the canal from state to state, in ceremonious style, that "the work is finished;" all is now complete, and a thorough navigation laid open to the public.

NOTE.

The legislature of Delaware state are applied to for an act of incorporation, for the construction, by a company, of a rail road, between Newcastle, on the River Delaware, and Frenchtown, on Elk river, Maryland.

N.—From Frenchtown, (Maryland,) down the River Elk, to Chesapeake bay, and up the Patapsco river, to Baltimore. Distance, *Miles*, 60

A.—From Baltimore, or tide water of the Patapsco, by canal, northward, to the Susquehanna river, above Conewago falls. Distance, according to a survey made of the ground, *Miles*, 92¾

Whereof 36. 75. Across the valley, to near Havre de Grace.
        14. 12. Thence, along the margin of the Susquehanna, to the Pennsylvania line.
        41. 51. Thence, to the head of Conewago falls; this section being wholly within the state of Pennsylvania; and, therefore, requiring its concurrence in the construction; for which, application will be made to the legislature.

Total lockage, 335 feet.

No. 71.

THE BALTIMORE AND SUSQUEHANNA CANAL, OR YORK-HAVEN CANAL.

This proposed canal, surveyed by commissioners of the state of Maryland, and reported upon to the legislature as practicable, although for nearly 56 miles it must run along the margin of the river, and be of expensive construction, has for object, to augment the trading intercourse between Baltimore and the various and distant tracts of country watered by the Susquehanna and its branches; and may be considered, in relation to the city of Baltimore, as an object of interest, to about the same degree, for the upward as well as downward trade of the river, as the contemplated Pennsylvania canal, below inserted, through the counties of Chester and Lancaster, on the east side of the Susquehanna, in relation to the city of Philadelphia. The engineer's estimate of expense, for the 92¾ miles, is 2,600,000 dollars.

A vote has passed the Maryland house of Delegates, appropriating 500,000 dollars towards the execution of this work.

January, 1827.

At a meeting of the citizens of Baltimore, a new plan for a company, and the execution of a canal, has just been adopted. The company to be styled "the Pennsylvania and Maryland canal company," and the proposed canal to be divided into 2 sections, north and south: the north section to begin at the mouth of Swatara river, the termination of an eastern section of the Pennsylvania state canal, and to terminate at tide water on the Susquehanna; the south section to begin from the point last mentioned, and to terminate at the city of Baltimore. Capital stock, 2,500,000 dollars.

The states of Maryland and Pennsylvania invited to patronize and subscribe.

March, 1827.

An act of incorporation, in conformity to the above, has just passed the Maryland legislature, in such sort, that not Yorkhaven, but the mouth of Swatara river, is to be the commencing, or northern point of this canal; always, however, provided, that a concurrent act be passed by Pennsylvania. Liberty is left for either side of the Susquehanna to be availed of in the construction, according to whichever shall be found to be most eligible. Distance to Baltimore, about 100 miles.

This act also confirms the grant of 500,000 dollars made at the last session; providing that this sum shall be at the disposal of the present company, so soon as 800 shares of the stock shall have been, *bona fide*, subscribed for.

The act confirms, moreover, the grant of 500,000 dollars in the way of subscription, in favour of the Chesapeake and Ohio canal, so soon as the congress of the United States shall have subscribed for 10,000 shares in this canal stock, and guarantied to the state of Maryland, the privilege of intersecting the said canal through the district of Columbia.

NOTE.

An act of incorporation has also passed the Maryland legislature, for a rail road, to be constructed from Baltimore to the Ohio river; and the state of Virginia has passed a law, confirming this charter, with a proviso, that the said canal shall not strike on the Ohio at any point lower than the Little Kanhaway river. The company is styled, "The Baltimore and Ohio rail road company." Capital 5,000,000 dollars.

The estimated distance of this proposed road from Baltimore to Wheeling, or to some other suitable point on the Ohio, is 250 miles; along which, the tolls for conveyance of goods, it is assumed, may be fixed at the rate of $2\frac{1}{2}$ dollars per ton, or 1 cent per mile, per ton, from west to east, and 3 cents per mile from east to west. At which presumed rates, the company anticipate a revenue of 750,000 dollars, to be derived from 150,000 tons descending, 50,000 tons ascending, per annum.

In regard to cost, the highest estimate, in the rough, for a road of double tracks, is 20,000 dollars per mile; giving, for 250 miles, 5,000,000 dollars, the amount of the company's capital stock.

Regular surveys are to be immediately gone into. Locomotive engines are to be applied.

It is supposed that the 250 miles upward, may be travelled at the average rate of 4 miles per hour; making $62\frac{1}{2}$ hours.

NOTE.

A rail road is suggested, between the city of Baltimore and York-haven on the Susquehanna; as thus:—

From Baltimore to Western run,	*Miles*, 15
Western run to Gunpowder creek,	10
Gunpowder, to summit at Strasburg, and thence to Codorus valley,	18
Codorus to Yorktown,	14
Yorktown to York-haven,	12

Length, *Miles*, 69

The act of Maryland, incorporating the "Baltimore and Susquehanna rail road company" for this object, is, however, not concurred in by Pennsylvania, as regards the portion of said road proposed to be located within the state of Pennsylvania; and the consequence, it is supposed, will be the construction of a rail road, by the company, from Baltimore, to terminate at the Maryland and Pennsylvania line.

The 4th of July, 1828, the 52d "American anniversary," is appointed the day for a splendid ceremonial, to attend an actual commencement in the construction of the Baltimore and Ohio rail road, whereof the first corner stone is then to be laid, with masonic observances, and sanguine are the expectations formed as to the success of this great enterprise!

DECEMBER, 1828.

An examination of the ground for this undertaking, between Baltimore and the Ohio river, by a party of the United States corps of engineers, detailed for the purpose, has been gone through with, and reported upon favourably; and surveys are on foot for the location of the entire eastern division of the road, extending from Baltimore to Cumberland, whereof about 25 miles, beginning from the Baltimore corner stone, are under contract, and already well advanced in the preparatory work to the laying of the rails. Subscriptions to the capital stock of the company, have been made to the amount of 4,000,000 of dollars; there remaining, as yet, 1,000,000 to be filled up; which it is expected will, in whole or in part, be done by the general government. A collision in regard to pre-emptive rights, on certain portions of the ground bordering the Potomac, has occurred, between the company and the "Chesapeake and Ohio canal company," but this matter is in a train for judicial arrangement, and it is supposed will be adjusted without any material delay having been occasioned to the operations of either party, in the location of their works.

The road, commencing from the "corner stone" at the southwest angle of the city, and crossing Gwyn's falls, strikes into the valley of the Patapsco, by a deep cut through the dividing ridge, and proceeds up the said valley; whence, in the direction of Bennet's bush, or Linganore creek, it passes to "Point of Rocks," where the Potomac breaks through the Catoctin mountain; from which point, the projected route, as far as Cumberland, lies generally along or near to the margin of this river. From Cumberland, the passage of the Alleghany ridge, and thence the whole western division of the road, down to the River Ohio, are as yet confined to preliminary examinations, on the part of the company's engineers. The examinations go no farther, as yet, than to ascertain the practicability of the undertaking; and a choice in the direction is still open. It is suggested, however, that facilities of location are to be obtained, by entering the territory of Pennsylvania, and, after passing the Laurel hill by the valley of the Youghiogany, proceeding with the route, in the direction of sundry tributaries of the Monongahela and Ohio rivers, as far south as the Pennsylvania line on the Ohio, or even to the mouth of the Little Kanhaway in Virginia; or the line of route may be carried down the Youghiogany and Monongahela valleys, to Pittsburg.

The actual location of the road, approaches at present to Parr spring ridge, or high land between the waters of the Patapsco and the Monococy, 40 miles distant from Baltimore; and this ridge, in pursuance of the plan of operations adopted, is assigned as the first occurring point on the road, for the construction of an inclined plane, and stationary power to be applied. The governing principle, at the very outset, which was thought to be indispensable; namely, that of *"accommodation to the city of*

Baltimore, as now improved," has led to the maintenance of a level of 66 feet above mean tide, for the distance of about 6½ miles; because, with this elevation of the great avenue or main rail road, brought within the limits of the city, the line may be so continued, as that, diverging branches, or single track roads, may from thence strike off, in any requisite number, through any or all of the principal streets of Baltimore, and be made to proceed to any point or points of navigable water, at pleasure, from Harris creek to Carroll's point inclusive; but this capital object will not have been accomplished without a very extraordinary expense being incurred, owing to natural circumstances of the road at its commencement. Upon the natural conclusion, that the immediate great flow of trade must be *eastward*, it became evident, upon true engineering principles, that all ascents in that direction were to be avoided, in order to economize the motive power intended to be applied; and this, therefore, it was, that determined the adoption of a *level*, to extend from the city boundary to the valley of the Patapsco, and up the said valley to some point, whence, by an equable ascent within the limit prescribed, of 30 feet rise to the mile, the route might be conducted across the Frederick road, at Ellicott's mills, at such an elevation, as to admit a passage for that road under the rail road. Ellicott's mills are by this way 11¾ miles from Baltimore. At contract prices, it appears that the cost of bridging and grading this section, in readiness for the reception of rails, will amount to 17,000 dollars per mile, or a total of 200,000 dollars; whereof 157,000 dollars will be absorbed in the first half of this distance.

Strenuous efforts may be expected, on the part of the company's engineers, to accomplish, in all the season of 1829, the entire bridging and grading of about half the distance from Baltimore to the Parr spring ridge, and a final location of the residue of that distance, if not as far quite as the Potomac valley, a distance of 66 miles; and to procure and lay the rails, with all their adjustments, along some part of the distance graded. See engraved profile of the work, as far as Williamsport, on the Potomac.

December, 1829.

The location of the route has now taken place, as far as Lower Point of Rocks, 69 miles from Baltimore, along which distance, the works are in as promising a train, and forward a state, as could, with a due regard to their proper execution, be desired.

Starting at Pratt street, at 66 feet above mid-tide, they maintain, agreeably to the plan laid down, a dead level to Dorsey's run, from whence the road has a gradual ascent of about 13 feet per mile, until it reaches the top of Parr spring ridge; a gradual descent runs on the western side of this ridge to Williamsport, on the Potomac, as may be seen on the profile; and proves, according to the survey now made, to be of the same favourable character as far as Cumberland, or the vicinity of the great coal districts. It is therefore ascertained, that in all the distance of 180 miles, there is but the single point of Parr spring ridge, requiring to be supplied with stationary power; and consequently, that it will afford remarkable facility for the transportation of coal, and other commodities, to market at Baltimore, at all seasons of the year.

The section of road between Baltimore and Ellicott's mills, or division No. 1., which, together with the city division, embraces 13 miles and upwards, is now completed, and the width graduated to 26 feet, with the exception of an unimportant point or two; that is to say, all is ready so far, for the work of laying the rails, which is to commence forthwith, and be prosecuted through the winter, except as to some places, where the road is entirely of earth, or the embankments too fresh. The aggregate of excavation and embankment, on these 13 miles, amounts to 1,274,403 cubic yards.

The Carrollton viaduct over Gwyn's falls, is a work very much admired for solidity, beauty, and grandeur. The whole exterior of which, is composed of dressed blocks of granite; and very many blocks of the same material, of prodigious size, have their place in the interior. The length of this structure is 312 feet; height, from foundation to top of parapet, 63 feet 9 inches; from the surface of the water to top of parapet, 51 feet 9 inches. Width of the rail way travelling path, 26 feet 6 inches. Eastern abutment 19 feet thick. Western abutment 20. Chord of the arch, springing from the abutments, 80 feet 3 inches; height, from the chord line to top of key stone, 33 feet. From the water to top of key stone, 47 feet 3 inches. To relieve this arch from pressure, parallel spandrel walls are built on each side, and connected with transverse brick walls, having cells or openings 2 feet wide, by 5 feet 3 inches long, and a coping of 6 inch stone flags, immediately below the bed of the road. Wing walls 15 feet thick at their base each, with as deep a foundation as the abutments, on the eastern side for 30 feet distance, on the western side for 100 feet.

There are, along with the essential parts of this viaduct, or bridge, and the many contrivances for its greater security, a great variety of architectural embellishments interspersed, and the whole is thought to be finished with extraordinary taste.

It was commenced, no longer since than about the middle of May last, and on the 7th of November, within the lapse of 6 months, was passed over.

A.—From Baltimore, or tide water of the Patapsco, by canal, through the district of Columbia, to the Potomac river, at the Little or the Great falls.

Distance, about *Miles*, 55

No. 72.

THE BALTIMORE AND POTOMAC CANAL.

This is contemplated as a continuation, across to the port of Baltimore, of the proposed grand opening, by water, to be effected between Washington city and Pittsburg, by way of the Potomac valley, as described in the article below inserted.

Surveys, as to this supplementary work, from Little falls, Potomac, through Columbia district to Baltimore, have not been as yet completely made; they were gone into, and calculations made, incidentally to examinations that were then on foot, for a canal, to enter the Potomac at a different point. The examinations will be completed, in connexion with those for the primary work, now going forward.

Taking the distance at about 40 miles, and the lockage between Little falls and tide water of the Patapsco, at 323 feet, the engineers' estimate was 719,213 dollars; but, allowing the distance and the lockage to be in reality both greater, according as one only, or as two summit levels may be found to be requisite, the expense of construction will, of course, be greater; but it is said can hardly, from what is positively known, come up to 1,000,000 of dollars.

The Little falls, Potomac, is 37 feet above tide; consequently, presents a saving of 74 feet in lockage, for a canal to Baltimore, taken from thence, compared with one, if the work were commenced at the tide water below; for it is ascertained that at this level of 37 feet above tide, a canal can pass through the city of Washington, north of the capitol, with facility.

A route different from this has been proposed, for a canal communication with the Potomac; namely, from Baltimore to the mouth of the Monococy river, about 50 miles above Georgetown; and as yet it is not certain, which of the two may, in preference, be adopted.

NOTE.

The Maryland house of delegates have passed a vote, appropriating 500,000 dollars, as a subscription of the state, towards effecting "a canal communication between Baltimore and the Potomac river."

January, 1828.

A survey has been made of the route, by a party of the United States engineers. It contemplates a junction with the Chesapeake and Erie canal at Georgetown; and is on the plan of a single summit level; which, if adopted, will involve an enormous expense, as it appears, for deep cutting, through Waterloo, Middle, and Snowden's ridges, a distance, the 3 together, of 6 miles. The report states; viz.

	Distance.		Feet.
Georgetown to Bladensburg	$9\frac{3}{8}$	descending	18
Thence to Summit Level,	$9\frac{1}{4}$	ascending	130
Summit Level,	$12\frac{7}{8}$		
Thence to Elk ridge landing,	$5\frac{3}{8}$	descending	122
Thence to Baltimore,	$7\frac{7}{8}$	descending	24

Total distance, therefore, $44\frac{3}{4}$ miles. Lockage, 294

The canal calculated to be 48 feet wide at the water surface, 33 feet at the bottom, and 5 feet deep: the locks 104 feet long from heel-post to heel-post, 14 feet wide in the clear, and to be constructed of faced stone.

Estimated cost 2,980,815 dollars.

May, 1828.

A charter has been granted by the Maryland legislature, for the construction of a rail road between the cities of Baltimore and Washington; and the same is now confirmed by Congress, for as much as respects its passing into the district of Columbia.

The charge to be made by the company, on all goods by this road, for the whole distance, not to exceed 1 cent per ton per mile, toll, and 3 cents for transportation; and the charge for passengers not to exceed 3 cents per mile.

M.—From the mouth of the Susquehanna, below Havre de Grace, up the river stream, in its contemplated improved state, and by lateral canals at particular rapids, through the Pennsylvania counties of Dauphin, Northumberland, Columbia, Luzerne, Bradford, to Tioga point, otherwise called New-Athens; and thence to the New-York line, either by way of the Tioga branch, towards the head of Seneca lake, or by the Owego branch, towards the head of Cayuga lake; a junction being proposed with one or other of these lakes, or perhaps with both, as is already inserted at the New-York article.

Distance, to the New-York line, *Miles*, 275

No. 73.

THE SUSQUEHANNA RIVER, MAIN AND NORTH ROUTE.

By an act of the legislature of Pennsylvania, 25th March, 1825, the governor of the state was empowered and required to make additional appointments of commissioners, for the purpose of ascertaining with precision, the navigable capabilities of the River Susquehanna throughout, and of carrying into effect such measures as may realize the local facilities discoverable, for opening communications, through the Susquehanna, with the west and the north.

Towards improving the navigation of these sections of the river, an appropriation was, at the same time, made by the legislature; and this work, which has reference to the bed of the river, between the towns of Columbia and Northumberland, or the mouth of West Branch, is now in active prosecution: contracts have been made with individuals, and much is expected to be done before the present season closes, of what is contracted for; and preparations made for increased operations upon it during the next season.

The lower points of the river, that is to say, from Columbia down to tide water, are also attended to by the commissioners, under an act of 1823, conjointly with a board of commissioners of the state of Maryland. In their report, made last December, 1824, details are given, as to several obstacles to the descending navigation having been, during the past season, removed. The report contains, likewise, an opinion, that an *ascending* navigation, from tide water to Columbia, may be effected, if the expense of it, consequent on the difficulties of the ground, does not prevent.

But there are, likewise, taking place, from day to day, improvements in the construction of steam-boats, which possibly may result in vastly curtailing the labour, requisite otherwise to be bestowed upon the other class of river improvements; that is to say, what is at this moment a particular object of research is, to reduce, by mechanical means, the boat's draft of water, and to communicate, at the same time, to paddles, or other essential part of the boat's movement, an increase of power, whereby some rapids may be stemmed, which hitherto have been quite impassable. A steam-boat, named the Susquehanna, launched not long since, on experiment, was brought to navigate, upon an even keel, at a draft of 18 inches fore and aft; but this, in the present state of things, will not clear the shallow rapids; and another boat is building at present, in Baltimore, on a plan to draw less water than the "Susquehanna."

Moreover than this, there is a sheet iron vessel building at York, of the dimensions of 60 feet keel, 9 feet beam, 3 feet depth; the weight of iron employed to be 3400 pounds, and the weight of wood work, for cabin, deck, &c., to be 2600 pounds. Weight together, 6000 pounds, or suppose 3 tons; the steam-engine, boiler included, to weigh 2 tons; making, for the whole weight, 5 tons; which is to have no more than 5 inches draft of water, and for every ton of lading, or weight of any kind, taken on board, the boat's draft to be 1 inch additional. The engine is upon the high pressure principle, calculated to bear 600 pounds to an inch; but is to be worked with not more than 100 pounds to the inch. The power of the engine to be that of 10 horses, and the space for it to occupy in the boat, 10 feet, by 3 feet 4 inches; anthracite coal to be used exclusively, for the production of steam.

All these circumstances taken together, warrant a conclusion, that the course of the main Susquehanna, and north-eastern branch, will become completely and conveniently navigable, for all the purposes of descending navigation and transport; and possibly for the ascending also, without an interruption. Little or nothing is now wanting for the object, as far downward as the Conewago falls, even from the head of Otsego lake, in the heart of New-York state, except occasionally, at certain points, deeper water; the upper parts of the river, in many places, spreading out into shallows; but for which the remedy, in general, will not be very difficult; the channel can be contracted, and thereby deepened: it can be cleared, at particular places, of a few obstructing rocks.

From Otsego to the Conewago falls, the distance is 400 miles; and from the head of Conewago falls to tide level, at Port Deposite, distance 60 miles, the descent is 272 feet.

During the revolution war, the whole distance, between the head of Otsego lake and Tioga point, was navigated by a brigade of the army, with all their artillery, their horses, and munitions of war, free from any loss or accident, though this was in the latter part of summer. It was done by means of an artificial freshet or flood, produced from a head, which the men had succeeded in raising, by the labour of about 6 weeks, in damming up and watching. A project that was conceived, and brought to bear, by the enterprising spirit of a soldier of distinction, (the late general James Clinton, on being ordered to join general Sullivan at Tioga point,) although not one man of the brigade, such was the wild state of the country down to that period, had ever before so much as seen that branch of the Susquehanna river.

Great attention has been paid, this last year or two, in Europe, and particularly in Scotland, with the most promising beneficial effects, to the *saving water system;* it is not merely by a damming up, temporarily, of the outlets of remote head collections, and streams of water, to be let out occasionally, as required, but likewise by embanking valleys for the preservation of rain water, and forming artificial reservoirs thereof in the immediate vicinity, and even within the actual boundaries of cities and seaport towns; the same creating water power, which so far displaces, to much advantage, the steam-engine power that was previously made use of for the same objects, but used in certain cases at greater expense, or to a more limited extent, as is very aptly exemplified, by comparison, in the circumstance of our Fair Mount water works, which have so happily replaced the former steam power, in supplying the city of Philadelphia with water from the Schuylkill.

The aqueduct for carrying Shaws Burn water to Whin hill, immediately south of Greenock, is, including flexures, about 7 miles long. A great reservoir is constructed, by means of an embankment across the valley, and the ground submerged has an area of 315 acres; the highest water of which is 56 feet, and the quantity contained, 250,000,000 of cubic feet; which, together with the contents of some smaller dams, amounts to 300,000,000 of cubic feet. An ample store this, derivable from the floods of the Burn, to supply the Greenock works, during 4 months of the year; that is to say, by detention of water in the reservoirs in wet weather, and its discharge in dry weather, to the full extent of turning the mills, or to the extent of any deficit in the supply from other quarters. This will be regulated by *weather sluices;* and *wasting sluices*, placed along the aqueduct, at intervals, will secure against overflowing or rupture.

The discharge of water from the reservoir, being estimated at 300,000,000 cubic feet of water, in 4 months, or 105 days; and the fall from the aqueduct on the Whin hill, to high water mark on the Clyde, being $512\frac{1}{2}$ feet, it follows, that, deducting $12\frac{1}{2}$ as declivity between the contiguous mill seats, there will still be an aggregate of 500 feet, as an effective head of water; and this affords a power, according to professor Leslie's formula, equal to that of 8,234 horses, working at the rate of 8 hours per day.

This great amount of mechanical power, obtained, as it would seem, at something less than the expense of 20,000 pounds sterling, the estimated cost of the whole work!

It has been stated, as remarkable, that Scotland, producing but few of the staple articles for exportation, and presenting obstacles not a little formidable to the construction of canals; moreover, deeply indented, as is the whole western coast, from Solway Frith to the Orkneys, with arms of the Atlantic sea, and on the north-east and the east, having the spacious estuaries of the Dornach, Cromarty, Murray, Spey, Don, Dee, South Esk, Tay, and Forth rivers, all affording more or less navigable facilities; and besides, having no part of the country, perhaps, at a greater distance from tide water than 45 miles;—all these circumstances considered, it has been stated as remarkable, that Scotland should possess any canals at all; yet, in point of fact, she is both splendidly and usefully supplied with canal works; as shown by the following specifications:—

The Forth and Clyde Canal.

Beginning at tide-water at Grangemouth, on the Forth, and terminating at Bowling bay, on tide-water, below Glasgow; length 35 miles, height of summit level 156 feet; having 20 locks on the east side of the summit level, and 19 on the west side, (the same state of tide being 9 feet higher in the Clyde than in the Forth); width 30 feet in the bottom, and 50 at the water line; locks 74 feet long, and 20 feet wide; depth of water on the sills, 8 feet; [have understood that the depth has been increased to 10 feet,] has 18 draw-bridges, and 15 large aqueducts; has 1 artificial reservoir of 50 acres, and 24 feet deep, and another of 70 acres and 22 feet deep, for supplying the summit level; cost, 200,000 pounds sterling. The revenue raised in 1823, 50,000 pounds sterling, or about 25 per cent. on the original expense. The principal articles of thoroughfare, are grain, timber, West India produce, and passage-boats. Engineer, the celebrated John Smeaton.

The Monkland Canal.

This canal connects the Forth and Clyde canal with the city of Glasgow; length 12 miles, width 24 feet at bottom, and 34 at the water line; depth 4½ feet; raises 119 feet from the point where it strikes the Forth and Clyde canal, and terminates in a basin in the suburbs of Glasgow. Revenue, 12,000 pounds sterling per annum. Articles of transportation, coal, iron, and manure. Engineer, the celebrated steam-engineer, James Watt.

The Glasgow and Androssen Canal.

Beginning at Glasgow, and runs on the same level to Pauley and Johnston, then ascends 64 feet, and, on that level, passes the villages of Loughwinnoch, Beith, Dalzey, and Kilwinning, to near Saltcoats, where it descends 100 feet to tide-water at Androssen. Length 30 miles; size of boats 70 feet long and 7 feet beam.

Canal connecting Glasgow with Edinburg.

Beginning at the lock No. 16, on the east side of the summit of the Forth and Clyde canal, and raising 110 feet by 11 locks, and, proceeding on that level, terminates in a basin in the suburbs of Edinburg.

This canal is proposed to be connected with the summit level of the Forth and Clyde canal, by an ascent of 6 locks, which will connect the cities of Edinburg and Glasgow, by 2 levels, 1 of 26 and another of 28 miles, separated by 6 locks near Falkirk. Has 1 small tunnel and 3 large aqueduct bridges. Engineers, Messrs. Hugh Baird and Thomas Telford.

Crian Canal.

This canal is 9 miles long, summit 62 feet above tide water, and is passed by 15 locks, each 96 feet long and 24 feet wide, and connects that arm of the Atlantic called Kilbramin Sound, and Loch Fine, which separates the long peninsula of Kintyre from the main land, with Jura Sound, near the north-east end of that island.

From an inspection of the map, it is evident, that, by this canal, and the Caledonian canal, without being exposed to the billows of the Atlantic, a vessel may sail from the mouth of the Clyde to the German ocean, at the Murray Frith, completely land locked. Engineer, Mr. Telford.

Caledonian Canal.

This work is, perhaps, not surpassed by any thing of the kind in the world, and connects the Northern ocean, at the mouth of the Murray Frith, with the Atlantic, at Fort William; beginning at the Murray Frith, where there is a sea-lock of 170 feet long, 40 feet wide, and has a lift of 8 feet. Opposite the town of Inverness, there are 4 locks of 8 feet lift, which raises it to the level of Lough Ness; then, by a canal $6\frac{1}{2}$ miles long, to Lake Darfour, which is $1\frac{1}{3}$ mile long, and has from 5 to 9 fathoms of water. The entrance to this lake is secured by a regulating lock; thence, by Lough Ness, 22 miles, with a depth of water varying from 5 to 129 fathoms, and without a rock or shoal. At the south end of the lake, the canal crosses part of the Glacis of Fort Augustus, and ascends 40 feet, by 5 locks, to the level of Lough Oich, which is about 5 miles in length, and ¼ of a mile in width. This lake is the summit level of the canal, and is 94 feet above the level of the sea. From Lough Oich to Lough Lochey, a distance of 2¾ miles, the digging is 40 feet deep; near the end of this deep cut, there is a descent to Lough Lochey of 9½ feet, by 2 locks, 1 of which is a lift of 7 feet, and a regulating lock having a lift of 2½ feet. The surface of this lake is raised 12 feet above its original level, to avoid excavating rock. From Lough Lochey, to Lough Eil, is a descent of 64 feet, by 9 locks, 1 of which is a guard or regulating lock; thence to the Atlantic by 3 locks, which descend 22 feet 9 inches. The locks are 170 and 180 feet long, 40 feet wide, and have 20 feet water on the sills: the width of the canal is 50 feet at bottom, and 100 feet at the water line, and 20 feet deep. The lock gates are plates of cast iron, 4 inches thick, and form segments of a circle, and each pair of gates weighs about 200 tons; they work on wrought iron rollers, and are opened and shut by machinery. The whole length of the canal is about 69½ miles, 30 of which is excavated, and 39½ through deep lakes. Cost, 1,000,000 of pounds sterling. Engineer, Mr. Telford.

To return to the Susquehanna;—since the above was written, the sheet iron boat, Codorus, was launched at York; and after passing the locks at Conewago, was directed up the Susquehanna river. She passed the rapids on her way successfully, and is now at anchor opposite Harrisburg. She stemmed, with great ease, the ripples opposite M'Claysburg, and passed through Miller's ripples, to Cockstown. Her draft of water, with all her machinery on board, is 6½ inches; and for every subsequent ton of lading, or of passengers, 1 inch more. She can accommodate about 70 passengers.

The channel of the Susquehanna is under contract for improvement, at the several rapids upwards from Conewago, undertaken so as that there may be afforded at least 12 inches of water in depth, by 50 feet in width: and as soon as this shall be effected, a boat, on the plan of the Codorus, may then pass up, with 70 or 80, or more passengers on board, or other equivalent weight.

The Codorus experiment has determined with precision, the depth and width of channel requisite to accommodate vessels of this construction. It has determined that rapids, provided they have 12 inches of water, and a straight channel of 50 feet, can be passed up by such vessels, with at least 5 tons of lading.

Still subsequently to the above: there is now issued a report of the commissioners of Pennsylvania, acting under the two laws for improving the River Susquehanna; viz. one taking it from Columbia upwards, to Northumberland town; the other, from Columbia downward, to tide water. The report is dated 17th November, 1825, and states,

That, from Columbia upwards, the commissioners have this year (1825) carried their examinations as far as Liverpool, and issued contracts for works upon the bed of the river, at the principal rapids, and most difficult places in the way; leaving, however, many others to be attended to hereafter; some of which contracts are already fulfilled, the rest in progress; and so far, improvement is accomplished. A new appropriation, required of the legislature, will enable the commissioners to extend their operations from Liverpool upward, as contemplated, and also to take in, and place under contract, those situations, which, for this season, they were obliged to pass over. It appears, that in addition to clearing and sinking the river bed, a certain number of wing dams must necessarily be constructed, in order to secure a navigable channel, at every point, throughout the dry season of the year.

From Columbia downward, contracts *in toto* have been issued, and the most of them have been fulfilled; which has already improved this passage, rendering places, before dangerous to navigate downward, now easy.

In the next season, (1826) wing dams are to be constructed at a number of places between Columbia and the head of the Maryland canal; and the remaining contracts on the river bed will, no doubt, be complied with. All which being accomplished, it is asserted, there will not then be any further improvement practicable upon the natural stream, from Columbia down to tide water.

March, 1827.

There is now before the legislature, the report made to the governor of Pennsylvania, by the engineer appointed to explore and survey the River Susquehanna in its main and north channel, more particularly than heretofore; that is to say, through all the distance lying between the Maryland and the New-York boundary lines, with a view to such improvements, if found practicable and expedient, as will give effect to a thorough and constant navigation, both ascending and descending, by the river stream, without the aid, if possible, of lateral canals; and upon such a scale as to give passage to steam-boats, arks, and large river craft, for an unlimited transportation of the trade up and down.

The examination commenced at Harmony, in Susquehanna county, where, at the distance of 15 miles 47 perches along the Great bend, the river returns into New-York state ; so that the examination again commenced, at the point of the line where it re-enters Pennsylvania, which is 4 miles above Tioga point.

The examination proceeds by sections, as below stated ; and the engineer reports, that the improvements along the river stream, to the desired extent, can be effected; and the engineer's plan is as follows :—

To excavate a channel, and form a towing-path along the margin of the river, the width of the channel to be, in the main river, 60 feet, in the branch, 50 feet, and throughout 3½ feet deep. In addition to this,—

To erect a sufficient number of dams, of 3½ feet in height each, with an equal number of sunken locks, of 6 to 8 feet lift.

By which mode, a continuous channel, of 6½ feet in depth, will be obtained at the lowest stage of the water, sufficient to afford a safe and spacious navigation at all times of the year, when not obstructed by ice; nor will it, in the times of freshets, interfere with the present mode of descending the river. The work of erecting dams, it is remarked, will be greatly assisted by numerous islands, strewed over the river in every direction. At the Nescopec falls, at the town of Berwick, it may be best, it is remarked, to give place to a side lock, of about 1000 perches in length ; and, at Conewago, where the fall is 19½ feet in ¾ of a mile, it may be found expedient to have recourse to Hopkins's old canal,—to excavate this 3 feet deeper, and then, by 3 locks, sink into the pond at the lower end of the falls.

Estimate of expense, according to the annexed expose.

Section, from the state line north of Tioga point, to Northumberland, - - - - - - $573,227
Section, from Northumberland down to the Maryland line, - - - - - - - 750,351

Total, $1,323,578

Which, however, is exclusive of the dams, locks, guard walls, breakwaters, &c., to be estimated hereafter.

EXPOSÉ OF IMPROVEMENTS,

On North-east branch, in part, and the North branch of Susquehanna river, to Northumberland.

Section.	Distance in Miles and Perches.	Fall in feet and parts.	Average fall per mile.	Ripples in each section — The number	Ripples — Average depth ft. in.	Ripples — Length in Perches.	Composition.	Irregular natural channel excavation, requiring pilots for steam-boat and craft navigation, adapted to 2 feet low water. Cubic yds.	Price 18 cts.	Total cost.	Regular margin excavation, with towing paths, requiring no pilot for craft and steam-boat navigation, calculated for 3¼ feet in lowest water seasons. Cubic yds.	Price 15 cts.	Total cost.	The part of North-east branch. It includes Comstock's rapids.
1	15.47	59.089	3.900	30	0.7	1528	Gravel.	39.200		$7,056	284.352	15	$32,652	
2	20.26	63.859	3.179	29	1.1	1295	Gravel.	79.139	18	14,242	392.700	15	$58,905	
3	37.31	86.840	2.340	27	2.0	1350	do.	82.500	18	14,850	715.444	15	108,816	This includes Wyalusing falls.
4	34.69	74.797	2.187	25	1.0	1220	do.	74.555	18	13,420	688.661	15	103,299	
5	26.218	41.024	1.542	19	1.0	1485	do. & shistus.	36.483	37½	10,648	521.766	20	104,353	{ This includes Nanticoke falls, and the longest ripples.
6	25.90	40.648	1.616	11	1.0	1556	Gravel.	95.088	37½	35,658	491.944	20	98,388	This includes Nescopec falls.
7	22.280	30.142	1.316	18	1.0	560	do.	34.222	37½	12,833	457.333	20	99,466	
	166.74	337.310	2.030		1.17	7466		401.987		$101,651	3267.848		$573,227	Total for North branch, or New-York line to Northumberland.

On the main river, from Northumberland, to the Maryland line.

8	20.40	35.947	1.788	20	1.0	680	Gravel & shistus.	49.866	50	$24,933	472.260	25	$118,066	This includes M'Kee's half falls.
9	21.80	60.751	2.855	19	1.0	1230	do.	90.200	50	45,100	498.666	25	124,666	This includes Berry's falls, and Forster's falls.
10	19.160	43.127	2.211	17	1.9	680	do.	4,933	50	4,933	453.896	25	113,474	This includes Hunter's falls.
11	18.195	49.351	2.686	13	0.9	420	do.	30.800	50	15,400	460.179	25	120,911	This includes Conewago falls.
12	28.40	157.900	5.615		1.0		soft rock.	-	-	-	546.469	50	273,234	This includes Strickers, Turkey hill, Wissingers, Eshelman's point fall, Indian step, Cully's falls.
	107.195	347.076											$750,351	Total.

Making together, Distance, - - - 273 miles, 269 perches.
Fall, - - - - 685 feet.
Estimated expense, $1,323,578.

} Exclusive of the detached Harmony section, and not including dams, locks, guard walls, break waters, &c. to be estimated hereafter.

Extract from official report of 1828.

It would be difficult to form any thing like an estimate of the quantity and value of the produce which will descend the valley of the Susquehanna in a few years, but a clear view of the kinds of these commodities is shown, and thence, perhaps, some conjecture may be formed as to the future magnitude of them, by a reference to the account stated of the arks, rafts, and boats, which descended the river last spring, under all the inconvenience, and at all the hazards attending this perilous navigation in the bed of the river.

From an account kept at Harrisburg, it appears, that, between the 28th of February and the 23d of June, 1827, there passed that place, 1631 rafts, and 1370 arks.

The rafts supposed to contain, on an average, each,

25,000 feet of lumber, - - Amount, feet, 40,775,000
Two hundred of the arks, laden with coal, each 55
   tons, - - - - - Amount, tons, 11,000
Remainder of the arks, laden principally with flour
   and whiskey for the Baltimore market, average,
   400 barrels, - - - Amount, barrels, 468,000
About 300 keel boats descended during the same period, with wheat, average, about 900 bushels, - - - - Amount, bushels, 270,000

The latter enumerated articles, after finding their way over the difficult and dangerous navigation from York-haven to tide, at Port Deposite, were then transshipped into bay-craft for Baltimore.

Under an act of the legislature, 11th April, 1825, the canal commissioners were moreover required to effect a survey along the valley of the Susquehanna river, North branch, with a view to the construction of a canal, from Northumberland up to the New-York line. Which survey was, in the past season, gone through with; and the engineers' and commissioners' report is this; viz:—

That the board have found the ground generally favourable for the construction of a canal, which may be effected at a less expense than 8000 dollars per mile, average rate; making, consequently, for the whole distance of 161 miles, about 1,288,000 dollars. This is the outside estimate. Lockage, 337 feet. The article here follows.

A.—From Northumberland, on the Susquehanna river, by canal, up the valley thereof, to the same point as in the article preceding; that is to say, to the New-York boundary line, between Lake Seneca and Tioga point. Distance, *Miles*, 161

No. 74.

NORTHUMBERLAND AND TIOGA CANAL.

It is much to be desired, that this work were speedily gone into. The New-York state project of a canal, from the head of Seneca lake to Newtown, is in a fair way of being executed; so that, when both shall have been accomplished, and the eastern division of the Pennsylvania state canal continued from the mouth of Swatara river as far as Northumberland, there will then need only to be added, one short cut of about 16 miles, in New-York state, to fill up the line of canal navigation from the mouth of Swatara river to Seneca lake, a distance of 254 miles; and Seneca lake will communicate, by canal, with the great Erie canal at Montezuma.

The ascending lockage required from Seneca lake to Seneca summit, is 443 feet; and from that point to the mouth of Swatara river, the descent is 552; together 995 feet of lockage, whereof 477 feet lies within the state of Pennsylvania. It is a line of canal communication, through which the states of New-York and Pennsylvania will have active intercourse.

NOTE.

By an act of the Pennsylvania legislature, 3d April, 1827, the board of commissioners are required to make further examinations, surveys, and levels, for the most favourable location of this projected canal, and to report the result, with estimates.

A.—From Tioga point of the Susquehanna, by canal and slackwater navigation on Tioga river, to the coal mines, at Peter's camp. Distance, *Miles*. . . .

No. 75.

PETER'S CAMP CANAL.

By an act of the Pennsylvania legislature, 20th February, 1826, the governor is authorized to institute a company for this proposed work, and to be styled the "Tioga canal and navigation company."

Power in the company to make a complete navigable canal, or a slackwater navigation, up and down the River Tioga, between the New-York line, at or near Lawrenceville, and the coal beds, at or near Peter's camp; also, by Crooked creek, to Pine creek, if the company deem this latter to be eligible.

Capital stock, 125,000 dollars, with power in the company to augment, should the cost of the works require it.

A.—From Port Deposite, on the east bank of the Susquehanna, along a line of rapids, north, to the boundary line of Maryland and Pennsylvania.

Distance, by canal, *Miles*, 10

No. 76.

PORT DEPOSITE CANAL, MARYLAND.

This was constructed several years ago, by the state of Maryland. Canal works on the west side of the river, as high at least as Columbia, will, according to report made, be carried up ere long; being now ascertained to be practicable at no very uncommon expense.

A.—From Safe harbour, Susquehanna river, at the mouth of Conestoga creek, by canal and slackwater passage, up the course of the creek, to Lancaster city.

Distance, *Miles*, 18

No. 77.

THE CONESTOGA CANAL.

By an act of the state, bearing date 28th March, 1820, Mr. James Hopkins was empowered to improve this navigation. The citizens of Lancaster have the thing now in progress. The works will comprise a canal and 8 dams, with their locks, overcoming 70 feet of fall. An act of incorporation passed the legislature for it, on the 3d March, 1825.

It appears, that a contract has been entered into with the company, for a steam-boat navigation, to be effected from the city of Lancaster to the Susquehanna river, by the 4th day of July, 1827. Consideration, 53,240 dollars.

Were a canal accomplished upon a large scale, along the valley of the Conestoga, down to the Susquehanna river, there would then only remain to be constructed the extreme eastern section, through Chester and Lancaster counties, of the Pennsylvania state canal, (hereinafter described,) in order to unite, through Lancaster city, the waters of the Schuylkill and Susquehanna rivers; and lay open, consequently, an enlarged, and, in some respects, new scene of business through that city, of the highest importance.

But, the Chesapeake and Delaware canal, as well as the present course of improvement on the Conestoga navigation, once finished, and provided success attends the operations now going forward to improve the channel of the Susquehanna, there will already be laid open a great increase of navigable communication along the line, between Philadelphia and Lancaster, and the western counties.

Another class, too, of advantages, will naturally attend the improvements suggested, and partly on foot, along this line, to no small amount; namely, the creation of water power, and establishment successively of numerous manufactories.

December, 1828.

The work of improvement along the Conestoga, has been successfully completed, and a good navigation is now open for arks and boats, from Safe harbour up to the city of Lancaster. It is effected by a series of locks and dams; the pools affording never less than 4 feet depth of water; the locks 100 feet long, by 22 in the chamber. Towing path on the south side of the river. The pools present beautiful sheets of water, of a width generally from 250 to 350 feet.

A.—From foot to head of Conewago falls, west side of Susquehanna river, York county, Pennsylvania; and the same, east side, Dauphin county; by canals.

Distance, together, *Miles*, 2¼

No. 78.
CONEWAGO CANALS.

Both these, under the authority of legislative acts, were long since constructed. Two dams, one of 800 feet, the other of 500 feet, are connected with the works The fall surmounted is 21 feet, by 1 guard and 3 lift locks, each 110 feet long, by 18 wide.

NOTE.

An act has passed the Pennsylvania legislature, authorizing the governor to grant a charter of incorporation to a company, as the "Codorus navigation company," for the object of improving the navigation of this stream, from its mouth on the Susquehanna, up to a point above the borough of York.

A.—From a point on the River Schuylkill, at or near Valley Forge, by canal, through the Pennsylvania counties of Chester and Lancaster; or, perhaps, through Delaware, Chester, and Lancaster, to the Susquehanna river. Distance, viz.

From Philadelphia, up the River Schuylkill, to Valley Forge, - - - - - - ...
Thence, along the valley, north side, to the Gap, 16 miles east of Lancaster city, - - - 38
From the Gap, passing by Lancaster, and up the course of the Susquehanna, across the Chickesalungo creeks, and the Coney, and the Conewago, to the Swatara river, at Middletown, - - - - - - - 45
From Middletown upwards, to the mouth of Paxton, or Hunter's falls, or other higher point of the Susquehanna, convenient for crossing it by an aqueduct, as is already inserted at the Union canal article, - - ...

Miles, 83

No. 79.

THE DELAWARE AND SUSQUEHANNA CANAL.

This is to be viewed as one section of an entire Pennsylvania line of canal, from Philadelphia to Pittsburg; the practicability of which first section, and in part as to the others, has been ascertained, as appears on the face of a report, made by the state commissioners, dated 2d February, 1825.

In consequence whereof, and to obtain further and more specific information, the legislature resolved to proceed in the research by an increased board of canal commissioners, and passed a law, under which the governor has made appointments accordingly; five characters were by him selected for the duty; and more comprehensive examinations are in consequence now on foot, to be reported upon, when accomplished. In the mean time, the line of communication, as it has been contemplated, may be stated to run thus:—

Section 1. From Philadelphia, to the River Susquehanna at or near Harrisburg, to be determined by the best plan for taking the water out of that river, and crossing it by an aqueduct.

Section 2. From the east bank of the Susquehanna, across to the west, and up the course of the Juniata river to the upper fork of the Frankstown branch, below Holydaysburg, in Huntingdon county.

Section 3. From the Juniata forks, over the Alleghany mountain, to the forks of the Little Conemaugh river, in Cambria county.

Section 4. From thence, down to Pittsburg.

But, in consequence of the expected, and apparently very successful completion of the Union canal, being now near at hand, it is to be observed, that the execution of the extreme eastern section of the "Pennsylvania canal," here under consideration, will not form the first in order as to time, but the second great artificial channel of communication across between the Susquehanna and the Delaware. It is, however, well understood at the present day, that the accomplishment of the one, need be no bar nor hindrance to, but rather, on the contrary, will aid in giving scope for furthering the execution of the other. For many years to come, this trade of mutual and reciprocal internal interests will grow, as opportunities are afforded for its expansion, in the way of cheap and easy modes of transportation, for the commodities of the country to a market; and, where possible, to a choice of markets. This is now well understood. In what is here incidentally observed, there is meant no attempt at promulgating novelty. The riches of the country, yet in a latent state, are known to abound; and there is nothing required but a certain growth of the country's intelligent population, and, concurrently, the facilities of internal commercial intercourse to be advanced, for those riches to be developed, and brought, step by step, into a state of cheering activity.

So, the projected portion of the Pennsylvania state canal, lying between the cities of Philadelphia and Lancaster, will, it is likely, be forthwith executed; and from the latter city, probably, be so carried forward, as to strike the Susquehanna river at Columbia. Or, should it so happen, after further examinations, which are now to be made, that along the whole of this route, canal construction be fully ascertained to be too difficult and expensive, then, probably, a rail road, for the distance between Philadelphia and Columbia, through Lancaster, will at once be resorted to.

NOTE.

By an act of the legislature, 3d April, 1827, the board of Pennsylvania commissioners are required to make examinations, surveys, and levels, along the whole route from Philadelphia to Middletown; with a view to the construction of a canal, to meet, and unite with, the "eastern section" of the Pennsylvania canal, now in progress. They are likewise required to make examinations for a rail way, with locomotive steam-engine, &c., along this route, and to report upon both modes of improvement, with estimates. A rail road between Philadelphia and Columbia, will, in all probability, take place.

A.—From a point of the intended canal last above specified, by canal, down the Brandywine valley, to a point north of the Delaware state line, and thence, across the ridge to Chester creek valley, and down the latter to the River Delaware.

Distance, *Miles*, 25

No. 80.

CHESTER CREEK CANAL.

By the act last above mentioned, the Pennsylvania commissioners are also required to make examinations for this proposed branch canal, out of the foregoing main section. Or, in case the waters of the Brandywine cannot be diverted from their natural channel, then, examinations to be made, for a rail road across the dividing ridge; and to report all particulars.

NOTE.

It being now ascertained, that a canal between the Susquehanna and Delaware rivers, through Chester and Delaware counties, is not practicable, therefore this proposed branch canal does not take place. But, a rail road probably will.

A.—From the mouth of Paxton creek, or such other point of the Susquehanna river, as may be struck by the canal last above specified; across by an aqueduct, and from thence up the Juniata valley to a situation on the upper waters thereof, whence a navigable communication can be formed with the waters of the Kiskimenetas, and so by the course of that river, and the Alleghany, downward, reach the Ohio, at Pittsburg. Distance, by canal altogether, or perhaps, in part, by river stream, as follows: viz.

From the mouth of Paxton creek, below Harrisburg, to the Juniata, and thence, through Perry, Mifflin, and Huntingdon counties, to the Frankstown fork, taking the courses of the river, is	142
From the Juniata forks, across the ridge, to the forks of the Little Conemaugh river,	27

Thence, by the courses of the rivers, to Pittsburg;—

Little Conemaugh,	10	
Big Conemaugh,	48	
Kiskimenetas,	25	
Alleghany,	30	
		113
	Miles,	282

No. 81.

JUNIATA CANAL.

This, which comprises sections 2, 3, 4, of the great Pennsylvania contemplated undertaking, whereof section 1 is specified above, will, if the line of route here designated be retained and adopted, make the canal pass across the Alleghany ridge, by the aid of a tunnel of 4 miles, at 754 feet below the crown, the elevation of which is 2585 feet above tide water; and this being assumed as a summit level, makes about 1075 feet of fall, to be overcome by lockage between the mountain and Pittsburg, taking the Ohio there at 756 feet above tide. For such a canal, the estimate given in is as follows:—

East section, No. 2,	$ 961,548
Mountain section, No. 3,	1,086,735
West section, No. 4,	749,344
	$ 2,797,627

Or, in round numbers, 3,000,000 of dollars, for a canal, taking it to commence at the mouth of the Swatara, and to terminate at Pittsburg.

NOTE.

According to recent intelligence from the Pennsylvania commissioners, it is stated, that the western section of this work, fixed upon to be recommended to the legislature, is as follows: and that drafts and estimates will be prepared accordingly, viz.

From the highest point of navigation on the Juniata, across to the highest point of navigation on the Conemaugh river; this to be, not canal, but a *road*, which can be constructed at a cheap rate, and so laid as not to exceed an angle of one degree with the horizon. Distance,	19¾
From the point last mentioned, that is, from Ben's creek harbour, on the Conemaugh, *a canal*, down to Pittsburg. Distance,	120
To which add, for the eastern section, from Harrisburg,	130
Total distance, for canal and road together, from Harrisburg to Pittsburg, *Miles,*	269¾

JANUARY 20, 1826.

A bill has been introduced into the Pennsylvania legislature, and will no doubt pass, for the commencement of the "Pennsylvania canal" without further delay; that is to say, for the construction of two sections, very important of themselves, even as independent canals, and essential as parts of the whole line in contemplation: namely, an *eastern section*, from the present extremity of the Union canal at the mouth of the Swatara, to a point of the Susquehanna river, opposite the mouth of Juniata; the distance perhaps 25 miles, and the lockage about 28 feet. A *western section*, extending from Pittsburg to the Kiskimenetas river, length about 30 miles, and lockage 44 feet.

300,000 dollars is the estimate for constructing these sections, and is proposed, by the bill, to be appropriated by the legislature.

The whole great work, including these sections, it is proposed shall be a *State Canal*, to be kept in the hands of the public.

February 3, 1826.

The Pennsylvania commissioners, under an act passed 11th April, 1825, have now reported in full to the governor of the state, with plans and estimates. They report two routes as practicable, between the Susquehanna and Alleghany rivers; viz. the Juniata route, and a northern route; but with regard to the first of these, it does not appear that a supply of water can be relied on for the pass across the dividing mountain, so as to admit of a constant navigable communication; and, in consequence of this, it is suggested to pass the mountain by a *rail road*. The particulars, including estimates, are as follow:—

The Juniata Route:—267 *Miles* 173 *Perches from the Mouth of Juniata.*

From the Susquehanna river to the Frankstown branch of Juniata. Rise 582 feet; locks 73; culverts 36; aqueducts 6.

Basin, capable of containing 100 boats, at the junction of the Frankstown and Beaver dam branch,	$15,000
Store houses, cranes, &c.	12,000
28 miles of rail road, with sidelings and brakes, on the east and west sides of the mountain, communicating with the south fork of Conemaugh,	330,000
Basin at junction of the south fork,	15,000
Store houses, cranes, &c.,	12,000

From the south fork of Conemaugh, to the mouth of Kiskimenetas; fall 653 feet; locks 81; culverts 32; aqueducts 2.

From the Kiskimenetas to Pittsburg; fall 46 feet; locks 6; culverts 10; aqueducts 2.

1281 feet, rise and fall.

160 locks,	800,000
78 culverts,	117,000
10 aqueducts,	40,000

Amount carried forward, $1,341,000

	Amount brought forward,	$1,341,000
238 miles of canal: width at the top and water line 40 feet; at bottom 28 feet; depth of water 4 feet; towing path 6 feet above the bottom; at 6,000 dollars per mile, grubbing included,		1,428,000
		2,769,000
Contingencies, 10 per cent.,		276,900
		$3,045,900

January, 1827.

The commissioners of the state of Pennsylvania, under act 11th April, 1825, had still, at the opening of last season, to perfect the several surveys as here follows:—

1. A survey of the "Northern route," by the Susquehanna West branch, the Sinnemahoning, the Clarion, and the Alleghany rivers, from the mouth of Juniata to the mouth of Kiskimenetas.

2. A survey of the Alleghany river valley, from the mouth of Kiskimenetas to that of French creek, with a view to a connexion with Lake Erie.

3. A survey of the "Juniata route," from the mouth of Juniata river, to that of the Kiskimenetas.

4. A survey of the Susquehanna river North branch, from Northumberland up to the New-York state line.

5. A survey of routes, through Cumberland and Franklin counties, for a junction-canal between the Susquehanna river and the Potomac, by the Conecocheague valley, or by the Monococy and the Conewago.

Which surveys have chiefly been accomplished, but the engineers' and commissioners' reports on them are not yet prepared.

The commissioners, under the same act, were invested also with these duties; namely,

1. To perfect the survey of a route, between Philadelphia and the Susquehanna, through Chester and Lancaster counties.

2. To survey a route, to connect the "Juniata route" with the proposed Chesapeake and Ohio canal, hereinafter described.

But upon these two objects, and especially the latter, any proceedings of the Pennsylvania board of commissioners are now postponed for a while, until the works, of which they are appendages, shall have been caused in some degree to advance.

Under the act, 25th February, 1826, the commissioners received this object in charge; viz.

The location and construction of two canals, to form an eastern and a western section, and become parts of one grand Pennsylvania canal, after intermediate spaces shall have been filled up. That is to say:—

1. A canal from the mouth of the Swatara river, to a point of the Susquehanna opposite the mouth of Juniata, at Clark's ferry.
2. A canal from Pittsburg, to the mouth of Kiskimenetas, on the Alleghany river.

Which two canals are at present in active progress of execution. The specification here follows.

A.—From the mouth of the Swatara river, as above stated, to a point of the Susquehanna opposite the mouth of the Juniata, at Clark's ferry.

Distance, *Miles*, 23½

A.—From Pittsburg, by canal, up the Alleghany valley, to the mouth of Kiskimenetas, on the River Alleghany. Distance, including navigable feeder, *Miles*, 39

No. 82.
MIDDLETOWN AND JUNIATA CANAL.

No. 83.
OHIO AND KISKIMENETAS CANAL.

The first of these was located, and given out to contractors, in June and July last, by sections of a half mile each, 47 in number. Length, consequently, together, 23½ miles. Some of the sections are now nearly finished. The cost of as much of the work as was done to the 2d December, appears to amount to 56,517 dollars, and there will be requisite, according to a report presented by the engineer, the additional sum of 296,400 dollars, to complete the whole; which is expected to be accomplished in the course of this year, 1827.

The general dimensions of the canal are,

40 feet, width of water line.
28 feet, width at bottom.
4 feet, depth of water.

But, to afford some local accommodation, and a certain quantity of surplus water for machinery, 3 feet in addition have been given to the width, and 6 inches to the depth, from Harrisburg up to the mouth of the Juniata. The locks, 17 feet wide, 90 feet long, within the chamber. At Harrisburg, the basin, which is now nearly finished, has an area of 3½ acres. The level of this canal is carried to the upper reef of Foster's falls, near Clark's ferry.

The other canal was, after some time employed in examining both sides of the Alleghany river, located on the west side, from the mouth of Kiskimenetas down to the mouth of Pine creek, 5 miles above Pittsburg: from whence it is proposed, either to continue the same down, so as for it to enter the Alleghany immediately opposite the city; or else, to cross this river at the mouth of Pine creek, by an aqueduct, and so proceed down the eastern side to Pittsburg, and there enter the Alleghany; or, pass through the city, and enter the Monongahela; or, enter both these rivers, according as the state legislature shall decide upon the point. The question involves a considerable difference of expense.

A navigable feeder from the Kiskimenetas, at about 9 miles above the mouth of this river, is to pass down the north bank thereof, and cross the Alleghany by an aqueduct at the main canal.

The main canal, from the mouth of Kiskimenetas as far as Pine creek, was placed, by the commissioners, under contract, in August last; and since the beginning of September, the work has been carried forward with spirit: it is all to be completed by the month of December next, and the aqueduct in May, 1828. What is actually finished of the work, the engineers' report sets down at 40,000 dollars cost; and for what is to be done, the estimate is as here follows:—

For excavation and embankment,	$96,972
Locks, culverts, and the small aqueducts,	50,044
Large feeder aqueduct over the Alleghany river,	70,000
Bridges,	5,045
Under contract,	$222,061
To which, on a supposition that the Alleghany be crossed by the main canal at Pine creek, there is to be added, For the aqueduct,	85,000
For the 5 miles distance between the aqueduct and the termination of the canal, in Pittsburg,	46,946
Total estimate, exclusive of damages to property along the line,	$394,007

Total of lockage, from the head of the aqueduct on Kiskimenetas river, down to Pittsburg, 81 feet.

No. 81. JUNIATA CANAL. (CONTINUED.)

February, 1827.

The report now made, exhibits the Juniata route as more favourable than any other one yet explored, for a canal from east to west. Still, however, the localities do not admit of the mountain being passed by water. A rail road, or a turnpike, must necessarily be resorted to over that portion of the route. The following summary of the survey, comprises the few particulars, essential, at present, to be known of it; viz.

1. From the mouth of the Juniata to Frankstown, distance 132 miles; lockage 594 feet; estimate, $1,262,000
2. Thence to Johnstown on the Conemaugh river, by a rail road, or a turnpike, distance 41 miles.
3. Thence to the head of the Kiskimenetas feeder canal, according to the present location thereof; distance 64 miles; lockage 368 feet; estimate, 836,138

Total estimate of cost, exclusive of the road, $2,098,138

Total distance 237 miles. Lockage 962 feet.

It is proposed that a location of the road shall take place as early as possible; and then an estimate of the cost of construction may be formed. The line already run, should no alteration be made, has determined the length of road to be as above, and that it will have an ascent of 1591 feet, and a descent of 1348 feet; for which a uniform inclination is proposed to be given, of 1° with the horizon, or nearly so.

The board of commissioners, in their report, strenuously recommend to the state, the construction, without delay, of the works as here follows:—

1. A canal from the mouth of Juniata river, or a point opposite thereto, up the Susquehanna valley to Northumberland, and thence up the valley of West branch, as far as the mouth of Bald Eagle, Lycoming county. Distance stated in survey 107 miles. Estimate of cost, - - - - $1,294,000
2. A canal from Northumberland, as already particularized, up the North branch valley, to the New-York state line. Distance 161 miles; estimate, 1,288,000
3. The Juniata canal, and land portage, as above specified, to join the present location of the "western section" canal, at the head of the Kiskimenetas feeder. Distance of canal, 196 miles; estimate, 2,098,138

The aggregate estimate, for these 464 miles of canal, being, - - - - - - - $4,680,138

NOTE.

A bill has passed the legislature of the state, 3d April, 1827, by which the board of canal commissioners are authorized to carry into execution the Juniata line of canal; also to enter upon examinations, and take the necessary steps for various other proposed works. They are required; viz.

1. To locate and contract for the works, beginning at the "eastern section," now in progress, and passing up the valley of the Juniata, to a point at or near Lewistown, in Mifflin county, Pennsylvania.

2. To locate and contract for canal works, beginning from the "western section," now in progress, and passing up the Kiskimenetas and Conemaugh valleys, to a point at or near Blairsville, in Indiana county.

3. To make examinations and surveys, from Frankstown, on the Juniata river, to Johnstown, on the Conemaugh: to determine in respect to the best mode of passing the Alleghany mountain; whether by rail road, or other kind of road, and all attendant circumstances, including the consideration as to using the power of steam-engines, locomotive and stationary, in case a rail way be adopted to complete the communication across.

4. To locate and contract for a canal, beginning at the said "eastern section," and passing up the Susquehanna valley, as far as the town of Northumberland; having, in this location, due regard to the accommodation of the trade flowing from both branches of the Susquehanna river.

5. To make further examinations, surveys, and levels, with a view of ascertaining precisely as to the practicability and cost of a thorough navigable communication between the West branch of Susquehanna, and the Alleghany river.

6. Further examinations, surveys, and levels, for the location of a canal, from Northumberland, up the Susquehanna North branch valley, to the New-York state line; and estimate.

7. Examinations, surveys, and levels, for the location of a canal, from the said "western section," at or near the mouth of Kiskimenetas, by the Alleghany river and French creek valleys, to a point on Lake Erie, at or near the town and harbour of Erie.

8. Examinations, surveys, and levels, for the location of a canal, from the city of Pittsburg, by the valleys of Beaver and Shenango, to the same point of Lake Erie.

9. Examinations, surveys, and levels, for a canal, from Philadelphia, through Chester and Lancaster counties, to Middletown, at the mouth of Swatara river; there to meet and unite with the section of canal now in progress; also to make examinations for a rail road, with locomotive steam-engine power, or without, along this route; and to report upon both modes, with estimates.

10. Examinations, surveys, and estimates, for a canal, to strike from the foregoing canal, down the Brandywine valley, to a point north of the Delaware state line, and thence across the ridge, to the valley of Chester creek, down which to the River Delaware : or, if the waters of the Brandywine cannot be led from their natural channel, then to make examinations for a rail road across the ridge; all which to be reported upon.

11. Examinations, &c., to ascertain as to the practicability and cost of forming a connexion between the North branch of Susquehanna river and the Delaware, by the head waters of the Lehigh, and down Broadhead's creek valley, by means of a canal, or of a rail road; and to report.

12. Examinations, &c., to ascertain as to the practicability, and the expense, of extending the "Pennsylvania canal," from the mouth of Swatara river, down the line of the Susquehanna, east side; as also on the west side, as far as the Maryland boundary line; and to report thereupon.

Towards the fulfilment of all which requirements, and the accomplishment of their several objects, appropriations are made to the extent of 1,200,000 dollars; that is to say, this sum has been voted by the legislature, to answer engagements for the present year's occasions in the furtherance thereof.

A.—From a point of the River Delaware, at Philadelphia, by canal, up the Delaware valley, to Easton, at the mouth of the Lehigh, and thence in continuation, up to Carpenter's point, at the north-east line of the state.

Distance, *Miles*, 150

No. 84.

THE PENNSYLVANIA CANAL;—DELAWARE LATERAL SECTION.

A regular survey of the whole of this route is in forwardness, to be reported upon to the legislature. In the mean time, the commissioners, acting under the authority already stated, have this day, 27th October, 1827, broken ground and commenced the work, at the town of Bristol; and contracts are entered into for several of the lower sub-sections from Bristol upward.

For the distance between Bristol and Easton, 60 miles of canal, with a depth of 5 feet water, the engineers' estimate of cost is 686,596 dollars, including a dam across the River Lehigh; lockage 170 feet. Canal 40 feet wide at the water surface, and of proportionate width at bottom, with 5 feet depth of water. The locks to be 100 feet long in the clear, by 14 wide. For the distance between Bristol and Philadelphia, 17½ miles of canal, 200,799 dollars, including aqueducts over the Neshamony, Poquiston, Pennypack, and Tocony creeks, and a capacious basin at Kensington. Termination of the canal at Kensington, near Dyott's glass factory.

Were it requisite for the locks in all the distance between Easton and Bristol, to be supplied, in toto, with water from the Lehigh, this stream is considered as being quite sufficient.

NOTE.

The survey between Easton and Carpenter's point has been finished; and the engineers' estimate for a canal along this distance, 70 miles, amounts to 1,430,699 dollars.

An act has passed the Pennsylvania legislature, March, 1828, authorizing and requiring the board of canal commissioners, to locate the distance of canal between Taylor's ferry and Easton, and to place immediately, or in the course of this year, from 15 to 45 miles of the same, under contract for execution.

The board of commissioners are, by this act, moreover required to make further examinations between Easton and Carpenter's point, with a view to the construction of a canal along this distance, of smaller dimensions than the general scale, and with locks of 9 feet width; and to report a location of the same, with estimates of cost, and all particulars, to the legislature, at their ensuing session.

M.—From Sunbury, 35 miles above the mouth of Juniata, up the Susquehanna, West branch, to a point on its upper waters, whence a navigable communication may be formed with the Alleghany river, and thence down to the Ohio at Pittsburg. Distance, by canal, or by a mixed navigation of canal and river stream, viz.

By the courses of the West branch, through Northumberland, Lycoming, Centre, and Clearfield counties, to its extreme source in Indiana, at the dividing ridge,	170
Acrosss to the Alleghany river, at or near Kittaning, below the mouth of Mahoning creek,	35
Thence, downward to Pittsburg,	50
Miles,	255

But, according to a report of the Pennsylvania commissioners, this West branch route, taking it to commence from the mouth of Juniata, is by actual measurement 365 miles in length, including 14 miles of rail road, which, should ever this route be adopted, it is recommended to substitute at the pass across the dividing mountain, owing to an apparent scantiness of water for lockage.

The report is dated February 3d, 1826, and the survey is stated as follows:—

From the mouth of the Juniata, to West branch, and up the same to the mouth of Clearfield creek; rise 732 feet.

Thence, up to the Cherry Tree, below the mouth of Cushing creek; rise 283 feet.

14 miles of rail road, from the Cherry Tree to the forks of Two Lick creek.

Down Two Lick to Black Lick, and thence to Newport; fall 261 feet.

Newport to mouth of Kiskimenetas; fall 275 feet.

Thence down to Pittsburg; fall 46 feet.

Rise and fall 1597 feet.   Distance, *Miles*, 365

No. 85.

SUSQUEHANNA WEST BRANCH CANAL.

The commissioners of the state of Pennsylvania, are specially required to review this line of route, and cause surveys on it, to ascertain whether it may not have a preference over the Juniata route to the Ohio, last above specified; or whether both may not hereafter be executed with advantage, and be connected one with the other.

From near Blair's Gap, at the Alleghany mountain, where the head waters of the Juniata and the Conemaugh rivers approach, there strikes out a ridge to the heads of the Sinnemahoning branch of the Susquehanna, which may be considered in its extent as the dividing summit between the eastern and western streams. It will be ascertained by the commissioners, through accurate surveys and levels, and measurement of streams, whether any, or what point or points of this ridge, can be advantageously passed, for the purposes of navigation; and they will compare the circumstances of such passage, or passages, with those of the Juniata summit.

FEBRUARY 3, 1826.

A "northern route," has been reported on by the commissioners, which differs in circumstance from the one by the Juniata summit, in passing the mountain by a continuous navigation, and not by rail road; that is to say, with the aid of a tunnel 482 perches in length, at 140 feet below the ridge; but the distance of this route exceeds the Juniata route by 85 miles. The particulars, including estimate, are as follow:—

Northern Route:—

Distance from mouth of Juniata to Pittsburg, 353 miles 11 perches; viz.

From the mouth of Juniata to Northumberland, rise 86 feet; locks 11; culverts 20; aqueducts 5.

Up West branch to the Sinnemahoning, rise 277 feet; locks 34; culverts 44; aqueducts 8.

Up which, to the tunnel, at the head of West creek, rise 896 feet; locks 112; culverts 16; aqueducts 5.

Tunnel 482 perches in length, and 140 feet below the surface,	$180,000
5 dams and feeder, at the head waters of Toby and of Elk creek,	32,000

From tunnel, to the mouth of Clarion river, fall 708 feet; locks 89; culverts 14; aqueducts 5.

Thence, down the Alleghany to Pittsburg, fall 116 feet; locks 14; culverts 36; aqueducts 8.

Rise and fall, 2083 feet.

260 locks, at $5000,	1,300,000
130 culverts, at $1500,	195,000
31 aqueducts, at $4000,	124,000
350 miles of canal, at 6000 dollars per mile, grubbing included,	2,100,000
	3,931,000
Contingencies, 10 per cent.,	393,100
Amount of estimate,	$4,324,100

This route deviates from that by the main sources of West branch, in its taking a more northerly course from the mouth of Sinnemahoning creek to the Alleghany river. It is also shorter by 12 miles.

February, 1827.

The "northern route" is now further reported upon, after a more ample examination; from which it appears, that a thorough canal along this line of route, is not practicable, on account of a deficiency of water at West creek summit.

If this route were adopted, a road of about 25 miles from the mouth of West creek to a point of Clarion river, would have to be substituted for canal. This route is, besides, long and difficult, and the work would be costly.

Here follows a comparison of particulars, as they present themselves on this route and on the Juniata route.

Whole distance to the mouth of the	North.	Juniata.
Kiskimenetas,	337 miles	249 miles.
Length of canal,	310 do.	208 do.
Portage,	27 do.	41 do.
Rise and fall of portage,	1130 feet	2939 feet.
Lockage,	1080 do.	962 do.
Cost estimated exclusive of the portage,	$4,592,000	$2,098,138

A canal, however, embracing a portion of the route, is recommended as eligible, and, in connexion with other proposed works, deserving of the immediate attention of the state. It is as here follows:—

A.—From the mouth of the Juniata river, or point opposite thereto, by canal, up the Susquehanna valley, to Northumberland, and thence up the West Branch valley, as far as the mouth of Bald Eagle creek, Lycoming county. Distance, *Miles*, 107

No. 85. BALD EAGLE CANAL;—SUSQUEHANNA WEST BRANCH.

It is expected that the board of commissioners will be directed by the legislature, to make an actual location of this canal, and to commence the work. The engineers' estimate for it is 1,294,000 dollars. But, by adopting a slackwater navigation at two or three places, where the river passes through narrows, a saving of 263,000 dollars may be made, reducing the estimated cost to 1,031,000 dollars, or, about 9650 dollars per mile. Lockage 255 feet.

APRIL, 1827.

By an act of the legislature passed on the 3d of this month, the board of canal commissioners are authorized and required to locate immediately, and contract for the construction of a canal, along so much of this route as lies between the mouth of Juniata river, and Northumberland, on the Susquehanna; and an appropriation is made for the purpose.

Moreover, they are authorized and required to cause such further examinations, surveys, and levels, as may be sufficient to determine with precision, in regard to an entire navigable communication between the West branch Susquehanna river and the Alleghany, being, or not being practicable, and if practicable, the cost thereof.

NOTE.

The commissioners report, that these further examinations have been prosecuted unsuccessfully, the engineers not having discovered a summit commanding a competent supply of water, or, at least, a supply that could permanently be depended on ; so that the former opinion is confirmed, that a thorough navigable communication between the eastern and western waters of Pennsylvania, adapted to the useful purposes contemplated, is not, at any justifiable expense, practicable.

An act has passed the Pennsylvania legislature, March, 1828, authorizing and requiring the board of canal commissioners to locate the section of canal between Northumberland and the mouth of Bald Eagle river, and to place immediately, or in the course of this year, from 20 to 25 miles of the same under contract for execution.

NOTE.

A company has been chartered by the legislature, as the "Lycoming navigation, rail road, and coal company," capital 250,000 dollars. They are empowered to hold coal lands as a body corporate, and to improve their premises as expressed in the charter.

The company's tract of coal lands consists of 3000 acres, situate on the head waters of Lycoming creek. A commencement has been made in mining, and some of the coal sent to market, which is of the bituminous kind. It is stated that the veins lie horizontally, and are easily wrought upon. It is proposed by the company, in furtherance of the objects of their charter, to construct a rail road from the landing place up the creek valley to the mines, a distance of 20 miles; by the aid of which improvement, and as soon as the Pennsylvania canal shall have reached the mouth of Lycoming creek, they purpose entering largely into the transportation of coal.

The company look forward to their means of supplying the article on very advantageous terms ; and state the following as the easy routes along which it will have conveyance to the several markets for it. The miles, however, as extended, vary somewhat from the exact distances these routes will present when perfected.

1. Lycoming rail road, - - - - - Miles 20
   Pennsylvania canal, Union, and Schuylkill, to
      Philadelphia, - - - - - - - 240
                                                    ———
                                                    Miles 260

2. Lycoming rail road, - - - - - Miles 20
    Pennsylvania canal to Columbia, and thence, by rail
        road, to Philadelphia, - - - - - 197
                                                    ─────
                                                    Miles 217

3. Lycoming rail road, - - - - - Miles 20
    Pennsylvania canal to Berwick, - - - - 73
    Nescopec and Lehigh canals to Easton, - - - 80
    Morris canal to New-York, - - - - - 90
                                                    ─────
                                                    Miles 263

4. Projected rail road, from the Lycoming coal mines, to
    the head of Seneca lake, in New-York, Miles 58

M.—From Pittsburg, by the course of the Alleghany river, through the counties of Alleghany and Armstrong, to French creek, at Franklin, in Venango, and up French creek to the mouth of the outlet of Conneaught lake, ten miles below Meadville: from which point, two routes for canals offer, to lake Erie, of about 48 miles each, to the town of Erie; either of them requiring much lockage, but the supply of water to be had from French creek, it is said, may be ample for a summit level.

Distance from Pittsburg to the French creek
    ford, - - - - 165
        Thence to Erie town, - - 48
                                        ─────
                                        Miles, 213

No. 86.

LAKE ERIE AND OHIO CANAL.

The Pennsylvania Route.

A detachment from the United States corps of engineers have been, and still are engaged in preliminary examinations along this route; and the commissioners appointed by the state, will carry their inquiries and surveys to the needful extent upon this article, so as to frame a circumstantial report to the legislature; which, however, it appears, cannot be accomplished before the season of 1826, owing to other objects, as enumerated; on which last, the engineers' and commissioners' attentions are employed.

But, the Alleghany river, in all the distance from Pittsburg to the New-York line, about 240 miles, it is understood, is susceptible of having its bed so thoroughly cleared, and its natural channel so well improved, and in consequence supplied with water, as that a regular uninterrupted navigation, for steam-boats of burthen, or boats of burthen towed by steamers, may be there established, for both the descending and the ascending trade; and that this can be effected at a moderate expense; for, the works proper to accomplish it, are of easy execution.

Should the improvement of the Alleghany channel be thus realized, in its course from the New-York line to Pittsburg, through the counties of Warren, Venango, Armstrong, and part of Alleghany; and through the towns of Warren, Franklin, Lawrenceburg, and Kittaning, in length 240 miles; it will include 140 miles, the distance between Pittsburg and French creek fork at Franklin, out of the 213 miles specified in this article as the projected canal route. Should it, however, be preferred to have a continuous line of canal independent of the river channel, the improvement of the latter must, notwithstanding, prove to be of very high importance; and it is estimated, that the moderate sum of 400,000 dollars would be sufficient to accomplish a complete navigation for steam-boats, on the Alleghany river, between Pittsburg and Warren. Distance 220 miles.

The only source to be relied on, for a competent and permanent supply of water to a *Pennsylvania* canal, between the Ohio river and lake Erie, is French creek, whether it be that the route commence by the Alleghany valley, or by the valley of the Big Beaver.

The works of improvement now carrying on at Erie harbour, it is expected, will render it the best harbour on the south shore of the lake, for easy access, as well as security within. A cut through the bar at the entrance of it, is requisite.

January, 1827.

By the act of the legislature, 11th April, 1825, the Pennsylvania commissioners were required to effect a survey of the Alleghany river valley, from the mouth of Kiskimenetas to the mouth of French creek at Franklin, with a view to the connecting of Pittsburg with lake Erie, by a continuation of the line of "Pennsylvania canal." Which survey has been completed in the past season; and the engineers' and commissioners' report is as follows:—

That the ground presents great difficulties to the construction of a canal along this valley, but that it is practicable. Distance between the two points mentioned, 88 miles; Lockage, 235 feet; and the cost estimated at 1,754,000 dollars, or about 20,000 dollars per mile.

A survey and location, made at the same time, for a navigable feeder canal, from French creek to the intended summit level at Conneaught lake, is also reported upon; and this report is to perfect satisfaction. There appears not to be any formidable impediment in the way of this object, and not only will the supply of water from this feeder be most ample for any future communication between the Alleghany river and lake Erie, but it is computed, that even in the driest season, after every allowance made for the wants of the summit, there will remain a considerable surplusage, to be applied to purposes at pleasure.

It is proposed to construct this feeder on the same dimensions as the main canal itself, in the two sections already commenced. Length, from a point of French creek to the foot of Conneaught lake, 21½ miles. Estimate, including a large aqueduct over French creek, and several extra conveniences at the two extremities, 231,820 dollars, namely;

Works at Bemis's mill on French creek,	$ 13,690
Construction of feeder down the French creek valley, eastern route; aqueduct included,	117,047
Construction of feeder from French creek to Conneaught lake, and works at the latter,	77,803
Fencing, at 240 dollars per mile,	5,280
Engineering and superintendence,	18,000
Total estimate,	$231,820

SPECIFICATION;—

A.—From a point of French creek, by canal, down the valley thereof, and thence to Conneaught lake. Distance as above. *Miles*, 21½

No. 87.

CONNEAUGHT SUMMIT;—FEEDER CANAL.

Under the Pennsylvania act, 25th February, 1826, the board of canal commissioners are empowered to construct this feeder canal, as soon as they shall find it advisable to do so.

NOTE.

By an act passed 3d April, 1827, the commissioners are required to cause further examinations, surveys, and levels, for the best location of a canal, from a point of the Kiskimenetas river as above, by the Alleghany and the French creek valleys, to a point of lake Erie, at or near the borough of Erie; and required to report upon the same, with estimates.

—•))»⊙⊙⊙⊙«((•—

A.—From the city of Pittsburg, by canal, passing up the Beaver and Shenango river valleys, through Alleghany, Beaver, Mercer, Crawford, and Erie counties, to a point of lake Erie, at or near the borough of Erie.   Distance, *Miles*, 175

No. 88.

THE SHENANGO VALLEY CANAL.

By the act 3d April, 1827, referred to in the foregoing article, the Pennsylvania commissioners are further required to make examinations, surveys, and levels, to determine as to the expediency of a canal along the route here specified, and to report upon the same, with estimates.

NOTE.

It is now ascertained, that this canal route, passing through the Shenango valley, will be adopted as the *Ohio and Lake Erie section* of the Pennsylvania state canal. *See article* 86.

—•))»⊙⊙⊙⊙«((•—

A.—From a point of the Pennsylvania state canal, Kiskimenetas section, by canal, to the New-York state line, at the intersection of Conewango creek.

Distance, *Miles*, 150

No. 89.

KISKIMENETAS AND CONEWANGO CANAL.

Application is made to the Pennsylvania legislature, for an act of incorporation, authorizing the construction of a canal, to commence from a point of the state canal, and to proceed northward, and strike the Conewango creek at the New-York line. This route, from the said point of commencement, at or near the mouth of Kiskimenetas, passing through the counties of Armstrong, Venango, and Warren; at which extremity it will meet the proposed New-York Conewango canal, and communicate with both Lake Erie, and the Erie canal of New-York.

NOTE.

By an act of the legislature, 16th April, 1827, the governor of Pennsylvania is authorized to institute a company as the "Alleghany and Conewango canal company," for the purpose of constructing this canal. The point of commencement, however, to be, not at the Kiskimenetas, but at the mouth of French creek, or near thereto; and thus, the route to pass by the Alleghany and Conewango valleys, to the New-York line.

Capital stock, 250,000 dollars, with power in the company to increase it to the amount the work may require. Distance, 70 miles.

By a supplementary act of the legislature, 8th April, 1829, the company *are empowered* to use their discretion in the mode of this improvement, and to substitute for canal, if they think proper, a slackwater navigation, from the mouth of Conewango creek up to the New-York line.

A.—From the west bank of the Susquehanna river, opposite Harrisburg, or from such point, as where the proposed aqueduct, towards the Juniata, shall strike the west side of the Susquehanna; by canal, diverging to the Potomac river; suppose through the Cumberland and Conococheague valleys; to the mouth of Conococheague river, at Williamsport, 94 miles above tide water of the Potomac. Distance, *Miles*, 90

No. 90.

THE CONOCOCHEAGUE CANAL.

This proposed Susquehanna and Potomac connexion, is another object, pointed out to the attention of the Pennsylvania commissioners of survey, and may probably receive it in the season of 1826.

JANUARY, 1827.

By an act of the legislature of Pennsylvania, the 11th April, 1825, the canal commissioners of the state are required to effect a survey of routes through Cumberland and Franklin counties, for the object of a connecting canal between the Susquehanna and Potomac rivers, by the Conococheague valley, or by the Monococy and the Conewago. Which survey was, in the past season, effected; and

The report of the Engineers and Commissioners is as follows;

That the most favourable summit between the Conococheague and the Conodogwinnet, is at Green village, Franklin county, where a supply of water, equal to 43 cubic feet per second, may be had through short convenient feeders. The measured line, between the mouth of Conodogwinnet and Green village, is 75 miles; ascent 365 feet.

The South mountain, which is found to be 823 feet in height above the mouth of the Conodogwinnet, intervening between the waters of the Conewago and the Conococheague, no canal communication between the two latter appears to be practicable: and, in regard to the Conewago and Monococy project, the summit level, which is at Gettysburg, is found not to command a sufficient supply of water.

So that, the Conodogwinnet and Conococheague route, as above stated, is, it would appear, the only one to be adopted for a canal between the Susquehanna and Potomac rivers. Distance, from the mouth of the Conodogwinnet, by way of Green village summit, to the mouth of the Conococheague, at Williamsport,

Miles, 120

NOTE.

By an act of the legislature, 3d April, 1827, the board of commissioners are required to make further examinations, with a view to the construction of this proposed canal.

Also to make examinations of the ground from Harrisburg bridge, west end, to the borough of Chambersburg, Franklin county, and from the west end of Columbia bridge, through York and Gettysburg, to Chambersburg; with a view to the construction of a rail road; and to report upon the same, with estimates.

NOTE.

Accidents have occasioned a postponement of these further examinations, to the season of 1828.

M.—From Washington city, up the River Potomac, to the head of tide water, and thence still up the river stream, by a navigation rendered boatable by a series of canal and other improvements, to Cumberland, in Alleghany county, Maryland. Distance, by a mixed navigation, *Miles*, 182

No. 91.
POTOMAC RIVER CANALS.

The Potomac company, in pursuance of the powers vested in them by charter, have executed the following works.

1. Large canals, taken out of the river, and conveyed through locks, round the principal falls.

At Little or Lower falls, about 3 miles above Washington; a canal of 2½ miles long. Difference of level 37 feet 1 inch, surmounted by a series of 4 sets of locks, of solid masonry, 80 feet in length, and 12 in width.

At Great falls, 9 miles above; a canal of 1200 yards long, lined with walls of stone. Difference of level 76 feet 9 inches, surmounted by a series of 5 sets of locks, of solid masonry, each 100 feet long, and varying in width from 10 to 14 feet; of lift from 10 to 18 feet, and of the cubical contents of 18000 to 25000 feet: a set of guard locks, and an extensive basin. Of the lockseats, the 2 lower pair have been excavated entirely out of the solid rock, and exhibit a lasting and handsome specimen of skill and perseverance. Both here and at Little falls, the canal dimensions are, 25 feet wide at surface, 20 feet at bottom, 4 feet deep.

At Seneca falls; at Shenandoah falls; at House's falls; canal works on a lesser scale.

2. Erections of walls, and excavations in the body of the river, in order to confine the passages of water within canals of widths varying from 16 to 25 feet.

Dams of stone run across the river, leaving openings or sluices of similar width, to raise the water in the river above them.

Removals of large stones, and masses of rock; which obstructed the passing of boats along many parts of the river channel. Similar to these, works have been executed on the Monococy, the Autictam, and the Conococheague rivers; and very extensive operations upon the Shenandoah.

Notwithstanding, however, the extent, and in general the skill manifested in the erection of these works of the secondary class, on the Potomac, at an enormous expense, it is apprehended that very little additional facility, has ever, in consequence, been, or is yet, afforded to the navigation up and down the stream; and although the Potomac company are required, by their charter, to give a low water navigation of at least a foot deep throughout the year, yet it is chiefly to floods and freshets that the navigation at present used is indebted, and of course is of limited duration, not exceeding, perhaps, for the two seasons, from 35 to 50 days during the year.

Under these circumstances, therefore, and in order to combine the present, as also any future stream improvements it may be thought advisable to construct, with the more improved mode of navigation; namely, by independent or continuous canals, and to place the whole under one general administration, it has been resolved, at a meeting of the stockholders of the Potomac company, 16th May, 1825, to make a surrender in favour of the lately instituted "Chesapeake and Ohio canal company," of the charter of the Potomac company, and to convey (for considerations acknowledged) all the property, rights, and privileges of the latter, to the said Chesapeake and Ohio canal company, specified in the article next below inserted.

This surrender and conveyance, to take place immediately upon the due organization of the Chesapeake and Ohio canal company, agreeably to the terms and requirements of their charter.

The river's descent, in the distance of 182 miles from Cumberland, is 578 feet; and, taken from the mouth of Savage river, it is 890 feet to tide-level.

According to an official report, rendered in the year 1808, the sums expended for improving the Potomac navigation, and that of the Shenandoah together, down to that period, amounted to 444,652 dollars.

The sums expended by the "Potomac company," down to the
31st July last, 1827, and actually paid, amount to $739,205
And there was due by the company, for work done, 201,398

Together, $940,603

Amount of tolls and rent, for the year ending at the
same date, 31st July, 1827, - - - - $10,947

NOTE.

This company received a charter in the year 1784, by concurrent acts of the Maryland and Virginia legislatures; a measure in no small degree promoted by the influence and active exertions of General Washington.

But, as early as February 1773, a project of improving the navigation both of the Potomac and of James river, from tide water upward, by John Ballendine, of Fairfax county, Virginia, was published in the city of London, in reference to a proposal then under consideration by the British government, to establish a "new colony on the Ohio, in North America."

It was proposed by Mr. Ballendine, to effect these works of improvement on each river, by means of locks and otherwise, and to carry them up to the highest points practicable, so as to communicate, by a short and easy wagon road, each, the Potomac with the Monongahela, and James river with the great Kanhaway. The locks and canals along each line, always to have at least 4 feet water, and the barges to be used in the trade, it was proposed should be, at first, of 60 feet keel, 15 feet width, and 3 feet depth, so as to draw 2 feet of water, but might, in process of time, be replaced by barges of 150 or 200 tons, differently constructed.

The commerce of the Atlantic ports, with the then contemplated *new colony on the Ohio river*, through these two avenues, it was believed, would soon grow into great importance; and calculations were stated, whereby large profits were assigned to the boats and barges to be employed in the transportation.

Of the success that would have attended, however, a prosecution of Mr. Ballendine's bold and spirited projects at that epoch, there exists not, perhaps, any difference in opinion now, considering all that has since taken place, in the way of improvement along both of the Atlantic rivers in question, and how the case stands at the present moment with these interesting matters.

COPY OF ORIGINAL DOCUMENTS, VIZ.—

"*Proposals for opening the navigation of the River Potomac —printed in London, in* 1773, *by John Ballendine.*

"Whereas the removing the obstructions in the rivers James and Potomac, in the colony of Virginia, in North America, and thereby making a more easy and *cheap* communication, than there is at present between the several seaport towns on these rivers, and the numerous and populous settlements upon the upper parts thereof; and also between the said seaport towns, and the rivers Monongahela and Great Kanhaway, *in the proposed new colony, upon the back of Virginia and Maryland,* will greatly increase the yearly demand for, and consumption of, British manufactures, and promote the culture and importation of hemp, tobacco, flax, &c., into this kingdom: And whereas John Ballendine, of the county of Fairfax, in the said colony of Virginia, gentleman, being well acquainted with the said rivers, and having skill and judgment in water works, and having already made several useful improvements on and in the said River Potomac, did, in the beginning of the year 1772, represent to the respective governors and councils, and general assemblies of the colonies of Virginia and Maryland, and to the other principal inhabitants thereof, that if they, by their several donations and otherwise, would countenance and encourage his undertaking, he would engage to remove the obstructions in, and render more navigable by locks, &c., than are at present [for *large* boats and barges] the said rivers James and Potomac, from the tide waters of the same to the heads thereof. And to the end that he, the said Ballendine, might receive every necessary information for the perfect completion of the business aforesaid, he did undertake to embark for the kingdom of Great Britain, and examine the canal in Scotland, from Carron to Clyde, and the canals, locks, &c., of the Duke of Bridgewater, &c. And whereas his Excellency the Earl of Dunmore, Governor of the colony of Virginia, his Excellency Robert Eden, Esq. Governor of Maryland, the Right Honourable Lord Fairfax, and most of the principal gentlemen of the said provinces, were so fully convinced of the knowledge and integrity of the said Ballendine, and of the facility and great utility of rendering the said rivers Potomac and James more extensively navigable than they are at present, *did*, therefore, on the 9th day of May, 1772, promise and oblige themselves, and their heirs, &c., by a certain instrument of writing, bearing date the same day, to pay to the said Ballendine, and his assigns, the respective sums of money therein written, opposite to their several names, as upon reference being had to a copy of the said instrument (authenticated under the seal of the county of Prince William, in the said colony of Virginia) will more fully and at large appear. And whereas the said Ballendine, in conformity to his engagement as aforesaid, did embark for this kingdom, and has, since his arrival therein, examined the great canal in Scotland, and several others in England, and has obtained plans and models of many necessary machines and works, and has engaged several ingenious mechanics to go with him to North America, for the purpose of opening and rendering more easily and extensively navigable, the said rivers James and Potomac. And whereas we, the subscribers, being willing and desirous to co-operate with our fellow-subjects in Virginia and Maryland in so beneficial and public-spirited an undertaking, do promise and oblige ourselves, and our executors, and administrators, (each for himself, and not one for another,) to pay to the said John Ballendine, his heirs and assigns, the following respective sums, written opposite to each of our names, and at the times, and under the conditions and limitations hereafter mentioned; that is to say :—

"First, That the sums of money hereunto subscribed, and all such farther and other sums as have been or shall be subscribed, either in North America or elsewhere, shall be faithfully and solely applied to, and disposed of, for removing the obstructions in, and rendering more open and extensively navigable, than are at present (as aforesaid) the said rivers Potomac and James, from the tide waters of the same, (or as far as sea vessels do *now* sail *up* these rivers) to such parts of the *heads* of the said rivers; as from *thence*, the shortest and most convenient wagon roads can be made, to the rivers Great Kanhaway and Monongahela, in the intended new colony aforesaid.

"Secondly, That the said rivers, from the tide waters thereof to such parts of the *heads* of the same, as aforesaid, shall be *so* opened, and rendered more easily and extensively navigable, as that the intended locks and canals shall *always* have 4 feet water in them [that being the general depth of the said rivers James and Potomac]—and barges, of at least 50 tons burthen, may also, when laden, be employed on the said rivers, from the tide waters thereof, to the heads of the same, as aforesaid.

"Thirdly, That inasmuch as it is intended that the said rivers shall be *so* rendered more open and extensively navigable, by the voluntary subscriptions of gentlemen both in North America and in Great Britain, it is, therefore, expressly covenanted and conditioned by the subscribers, to and with the said John Ballendine, that no other tax, duty, or impost, shall, at any time hereafter, be laid or levied upon any articles or commodities going up, or being sent down, the said rivers Potomac and James as aforesaid, except such only as the respective legislatures of the colony of Virginia, and province of Maryland, shall, by concurrent acts of Assembly, charge the said commodities with, for the sole purpose of paying the expenses attendant on the said locks and works, and keeping the said rivers, and the channels thereof, *free* from logs or other obstructions, which may occasionally be brought down the same, in the time of freshets.

"Fourthly, That the said John Ballendine shall keep a fair and just account of all the particular costs and expenses, which shall arise and be incurred in the removing of the obstructions, erecting locks, &c. in the rivers Potomac and James, (as aforesaid) until the same is finished.

"Fifthly, That all the said accounts of the costs, expenditures, and charges, as aforesaid, with their several and respective vouchers, shall be submitted to the examination and final adjustment of six gentlemen, to be nominated and appointed as follows:—Two thereof to be nominated and appointed by and under the hand and seal of the governor of the colony of Virginia for the time being; two to be nominated and appointed by and under the hand and seal of the governor of the province of Maryland for the time being; and the remaining two to be nominated and appointed under the hand and seal of the honourable Thomas Walpole, of the county of Middlesex, in the kingdom of Great Britain; any four of which said commissioners, from time to time, meeting, adjusting and settling the said accounts, and delivering a copy thereof, when so settled, signed by each and every of them, to the governors, severally, of the provinces aforesaid, to be lodged and deposited by them, in the respective Rolls Office, or Office of Registry in the said colonies, shall be deemed final and conclusive; and in and by such accounts, and no other, the said Ballendine shall be credited for the costs, expenditures, and charges, as aforesaid, (and also for his expenses to and from this kingdom, and a compensation for his services, &c. as mentioned under the sixth head,) and therein likewise shall the said Ballendine be debited for such sum or sums of money, as he shall have received or may receive, in and by virtue of subscription made, or to be made, in Great Britain, or North America, for the purposes aforesaid.

"Sixthly, That the said John Ballendine shall be paid out of and from the money so subscribed as aforesaid, such reimbursement for his expenses to and from this kingdom; and also such compensation and reward for his skill, judgment, and industry, in directing, managing, and completing the business of rendering the said rivers James and Potomac more easily and extensively navigable, as aforesaid, as they, the said commissioners, or any four of them, shall certify under their hands, to the respective governors of Virginia and Maryland, for the time being, that the services of the said John Ballendine do merit and are entitled to.

"Seventhly, That so soon as it shall appear, by a certificate signed and sealed by the governors of the colonies of Virginia and Maryland, respectively, and by two of the council of each of the said colonies, that the said John Ballendine has rendered complete and sufficient, by locks and otherwise, as aforesaid, one half of the whole intended navigation of the said rivers James and Potomac, and that barges, of at least fifty tons burden, can pass loaded up and down the said rivers, from the tide waters thereof, to the end of the said finished and completed navigation; that then, we, the subscribers, do oblige ourselves, severally, and not jointly, and our several executors and administrators, to pay to the said John Ballendine, his executors, administrators, and assigns, the one moiety or half part of the several following sums of money, written by us opposite to each of our names; and, so soon as the whole of the said intended navigation, on the said rivers James and Potomac, shall be fully made and completed, by locks and otherwise, as that barges of at least fifty tons burden shall, when loaded as aforesaid, pass up and down the said rivers, from the tide waters thereof, to the heads thereof, as is specified and particularly mentioned under the first head; and so soon, likewise, as the same shall be certified to us under the hands and seals of the governors of the colonies of Virginia and Maryland, respectively, and of two of the council of each of the said colonies; that then, we, the subscribers, do, as aforesaid, oblige ourselves, and each and every of our executors and administrators, (severally, and not jointly,) to pay to the said John Ballendine, his executors, administrators, and assigns, so much, and *no more*, of the remaining moiety of our following respective subscriptions, as shall, (together with the money that may be collected in North America, for the purpose aforesaid,) be sufficient to pay the amount of the liquidated and settled accounts of the said Ballendine, as mentioned and described under the fifth head.

"In testimony whereof, we have hereunto set our hands and seals, in Great Britain, this ——— day of ———, one thousand seven hundred and seventy-three."

"*Transcript from an original contract between Thomas Walpole, W. Pownall, B. Franklin, and Samuel Wharton, relative to the colony here alluded to.*

'We the committee of the purchasers of a tract of country for a new province, on the Ohio, in America, do hereby admit the Ohio company as a co-purchaser with us, for two shares of the said purchase, in consideration of their agent, Col. ****** to withdraw the application of the said company, for a separate grant within the limits of the said purchase.

'Witness our hands, this 7th day of May, 1770.

'THOMAS WALPOLE,
'W. POWNALL,
'B. FRANKLIN,
'SAMUEL WHARTON.

'The whole being divided into seventy-two equal shares; by the words 'two shares' above, is understood, two seventy-second parts of the tract, so as above purchased.

'THOMAS WALPOLE,
'W. POWNALL,
'B. FRANKLIN,
'SAML. WHARTON.'"

"*In a printed advertisement, dated* 'London, February 25, 1773,' *of the* '*cost of carriage from the seaports of Georgetown, in Maryland, and Richmond and Alexandria in Virginia, to the proposed new colony on the Ohio, in North America, by John Ballendine, of Virginia,*' *the following particulars are narrated:*—

"It is proposed by Mr. Ballendine that the locks intended to be erected in the rivers James and Potomac, shall *always* have four feet water in them, as that is the general depth of these rivers, except in the spring and autumn, (which are the great periods of exportation and importation from and into Maryland and Virginia,) when these rivers usually have from 6 to 8 feet water in them.

"Mr. Ballendine is thoroughly convinced, from an experience of fifteen years, in transporting merchandise up and down the River Potomac, that all kinds of British goods can be carried from Georgetown (which is a seaport on that river, at least twelve miles above Alexandria, where General Braddock landed his troops,) to the head of the north branch of the navigable waters of Potomac, at 6*d*. sterling per hundred weight; and at the same price, also, goods can be carried from Richmond, (a seaport town,) on James river, to the head of that river. He proposes, at first, to employ barges of only 60 feet keel, 15 feet wide, and 3 feet in depth, which will not draw more than 2 feet water. But when the country on the Ohio is thickly settled, barges of 150 and 200 tons can (as is now done on the Thames) be properly made use of on the rivers James and Potomac.

"It requires but 3 days for the barges to go down the stream, from the head of the north branch of the navigable waters of Potomac, to the seaports of Georgetown and Alexandria; and only the same space of time, from the head of James river, down stream, to the seaport of Richmond, in Virginia; and from thence back again, up stream, to the head of James river, only 8 days; and the same time from Georgetown, or Alexandria, up stream, to the head of the navigable waters of the north branch of Potomac."

A.—From tide water of the Potomac river, above Georgetown, by canal, along the meandering course of the river, up to Wills' creek at Cumberland, and still upward as far as the mouth of Savage river; whence, by the course of this and Crabtree creek, to the dividing ridge; across which, and taking the valley of Deep creek to the falls, pass, by the ravine of the Youghioghany river, through Smithfield, and Connelsville, to the Monongahela river, at 15 miles above Pittsburg.   Distance as follows;—   *Miles*, 360

Eastern Section.

From head of tide water to Great falls,	9
Great falls to Harper's ferry,	96
Harper's ferry to Conococheague,	39
Thence, to Cumberland,	38
Thence, to mouth of Savage river,	33
Savage river, to summit level,	13
	Miles, 228

Western Section.

From the dividing ridge, to the Narrows,	6	
Thence, to falls of Deep creek,	9	
Thence, to Smithfield,	24	
Smithfield to Connelsville,	38	
Thence, to Monongahela river,	40	
Down to Pittsburg,	15	132
		Miles 360

No. 92.

CHESAPEAKE AND OHIO CANAL.

Final surveys of the ground, for this proposed communication with the west, in a line passing through the seat of the general government, are now making by the United States engineers, and commissioners of the states of Virginia and Maryland, appointed thereto; and a report upon all matters in relation to the subject, it is hoped may be made at the next session of congress.

Congress, on the 30th April, 1824, made an appropriation for the object; and directed that a detachment from the United States corps of engineers should examine and survey between the tide water of the Potomac and the head of steam-boat navigation on the Ohio river; and between the Ohio river and Lake Erie; for the purpose of determining as to the practicability of a communication, by canal, between those points; of designating the most suitable route; and of forming plans and estimates for its execution.

To carry which act of congress, in reference to the present

and other suggested objects, into the more complete effect, a board of internal improvement was instituted by the executive; and three brigades of the United States engineers have been, since then, and still are, engaged on this ground. They are expected to report after the close of the present season, 1825.

The partial examinations and inquiries, hitherto made, give expectation that this grand and highly interesting project can be carried through; and possibly, in this case, it may be done, with no very great variation from the line of route here designated, although the ridge to be passed across, or through, which is called the Little Backbone, or Little Savage mountain, is 2486 feet above tide water, and 1730 feet above the level of the Ohio river at Pittsburg.

The crown of the ridge has 116 feet of elevation from the bed of Deep creek, at the Narrows; from whence it has been proposed to commence the cutting. Now, this cutting is, in five and a half, or six miles, to reach the east side of the mountain; and having received the water of Deep creek, will convey it to the eastern descent, conducting to the Potomac waters.

A summit level, therefore, is here proposed, of five and a half or six miles long, at a depth of 116 feet, where it subtends the highest part of the ridge; and it may be formed, either by an open cut through the whole, or else by an open cut in part, and a tunnel of about a mile and a half, immediately under the crown, which last will probably have the preference.

It is supposed that a good summit level can be obtained at this place, to be amply supplied with water from Deep creek; which is fed chiefly from glades, or mountain meadows of great extent; and these, it is said, send forth water throughout the year.

Estimates of expense, predicated on what is here laid down, have been formed, and submitted, as follow:—

The eastern section, 228 miles, comprising 2400 feet of lockage,	$3,342,250
Summit level, for tunnel and excavation,	343,750
The western section, 132 miles, comprising 1600 feet of lockage,	1,880,560
Total,	$5,566,560

The preparatory examinations are stated thus;—

From tide water in the Potomac, to Cumberland—Moore and Briggs' survey,	Miles 182
From Cumberland to mouth of Savage river—Abert's survey,	27½
Amount carried forward,	209½

                    Amount brought forward,   209½
From mouth of Savage river to mouth of Bear creek, by
 the Deep creek route—surveys of M'Neill and Shriver,   41
From mouth of Bear creek, to Pittsburg—Schriver's
 computation, - - - - - - -   100
                                          —————
                              Distance, Miles 350½

Rise to Cumberland, - - - - Feet 537
  to Savage river, - - - - -   327½
  to base mark on Deep creek, - - - 1432
                              Ascent, ———2296½
Fall to mouth of Bear creek, - - -   956
  to the Ohio at Pittsburg, - - -   584½
                              Descent, ———1540½

                              Lockage, feet, 3837

But, with regard to this calculation, as the more elaborate surveys of the ground, which are now on foot, may bring new facts and circumstances to light, so there may be occasion to make many alterations in the details of construction, if not in the general plan, or line of route; and to modify accordingly the estimate.

For the execution of the work, a charter, dated 27th January, 1824, was granted by the state of Virginia, to the "Chesapeake and Ohio canal company," upon conditions of confirmation on the parts of Maryland and Pennsylvania, and of congress in behalf of Columbia district, as also of the concurrence of the old "Potomac company," in the provisions of the act of incorporation.

In conformity to which, the legislature of Maryland passed an act in January, and congress one in February, 1825; also, the old Potomac company, by a resolution of the stockholders, have, for as much as they are concerned, given in their concurrence. At a general meeting, 16th May, 1825, it was resolved to surrender up the charter, and make a conveyance to the Chesapeake and Ohio canal company; which is accordingly to be done. The Pennsylvania legislature have a bill of assent before them, and it most likely will pass.

The capital stock proposed, and authorized by the charter to be subscribed, is 6,000,000 dollars, with power to augment, should the work eventually be found by the company to require it.

A convention of delegates from the states of Virginia, Maryland, Ohio, Pennsylvania, and district of Columbia, have empowered a committee to open books and receive subscriptions.

The corporate powers are perpetual; and the canal, and all its appurtenances, are, for ever, exempted from taxation.

It is also, and every part thereof, to be for ever esteemed and taken as a public navigable highway, free for general transportation, on payment of such tolls only, as are stipulated by the act; nor is any additional toll or tax, for the use of the canal or works belonging, ever to be imposed, without the consent of the states through which the canal passes, and of congress of the United States.

The act provides, that the right to the waters of the river Potomac, for the purpose of any lateral canal or canals, which the state of Virginia, or of Maryland, may authorize to be made in connexion with this canal, is reserved to the said states respectively, and a similar right reserved to the state of Pennsylvania in relation to the rivers and streams within the territory of that state, the waters of which may be used in supplying the western section of this canal: also provides, that the government of the United States shall retain the power to extend this canal, in and through the district of Columbia, on either side, or both sides, of the River Potomac.

The house of delegates of the state of Maryland, have passed a vote, appropriating 500,000 dollars, as the state's subscription to the stock, if the work goes into effect.

NOTE.

On the present article, a remark occurs, that is not without interest in canal history. At the tumultuous, and, for this country, (then colonial,) critical period of 1769, the celebrated Richard Henry Lee, brought a bill into the Virginia house of burgesses, for the purpose of *opening and improving the navigation of the river Potomac, from tide water up to Fort Cumberland.* The details of which bill have been considered as no less remarkable for a display of statistical knowledge, and economical views in regard to the country, at that early day, than for exemplifying the indefatigable industry, and versatility of a mind, known to be incessantly intent upon furthering the political objects of his country, at the momentous epoch in question. It is, besides, a striking instance, in addition to one already noticed, of the rapidity with which comprehensive ideas, touching a new class of important improvements, adopted in the mother country, could travel across the Atlantic, to be received and adopted here. Ballendine's project followed on the heels of this legislative proceeding.

JANUARY, 1827.

The board of United States engineers for internal improvement, have reported upon this article.

Truly, they have taken a magnificent view of their subject, and treated it on a scale accordingly. Their report, dated 23d October, 1826, is now before congress. It states, that the objects of the survey, now gone through with, were;—

"To determine the route to be recommended ; and, to obtain the data necessary to frame a general plan of the work, and a preparatory estimate of the expense."

And the result is, that the route selected, as having appeared to be the most eligible one, and the estimates of cost, for a canal of the character described, are given in as here follows;—

Eastern Section.

From Cumberland to Georgetown, along the valley of the Potomac, on the Maryland side; the minima resources of water on this line, being from, viz.

The south branch;—

Great Cucapon,
The Shenandoah,
Evitt's creek, Licking creek,
Great Conococheague,
The Antietam, Monococy, Seneca,

} together, affording at the rate of 457 cubic feet per second.

Distance, $185\frac{5}{8}$ miles. Descent, 578 feet, by 74 locks. Estimate 8,177,081 dollars.

Middle Section, 70 miles 1010 yards.

From Cumberland, or west end of the eastern section, to the mouth of Casselman's river, on the Youghioghany, keeping on the right side of the valley, which gives to the canal a southern exposure.

This section includes the summit level, where a tunnel of 4 miles 80 yards long, passing under a ridge of the Alleghany of 856 feet elevation, is needful, with a deep cut of 1060 yards long at the western end, and another deep cut of 140 yards at the eastern end, each of these cuts opening into a basin of 880 yards in length, 64 in width.

The tunnel, deep cuts, and 2 basins, form together the summit level, the length of which, therefore, is 5 miles 1280 yards. At the termination of each basin is a lock.

The stream of the Casselman is chiefly relied on, to supply the summit and the portions of canal contiguous; and, by computation, deduced from a series of observations, it appears, the minimum supply, during the expected 8 months of navigation, will be at the rate of

2,750,000 cubic yards from reservoirs,
1,728,000   do.   from the river stream,

4,478,000 cubic yards per month,

Which is supposed to be more than sufficient, grounded upon calculations detailed in the report.

Estimate for the Summit Level.

Tunnel shafts,	$233,033
Heading,	383,535
Side heading,	7,704
Tunnel,	2,495,243
Draining,	159,469

For the tunnel, 4 miles 80 yards in length,	$3,278,984
The eastern basin,	26,741
The eastern deep cut,	18,733
The western do.	141,841
The western basin,	5,668

Total for summit level, $3,471,967

On this same section, the canal proceeds from the summit;—

1. Eastward to the mouth of Little Wills' creek, and thence to where the eastern section terminates, a little below Cumberland. Distance, 29 miles 240 yards. Descent, 1325 feet, by 166 locks. Estimate for this portion, including a feeder from the Potomac, and aqueduct and guard lock thereto, also a capacious basin and levees around, - - - $3,856,624

2. Westward, from summit at a basin in Flagherty's creek valley, the termination of a feeder from the reservoir in the Casselman's valley; to the mouth of Middle Fork creek, and thence to that of the Casselman on the Youghioghany river. Distance, 35 miles 1250 yards. Descent, 636 feet, by 80 locks. Estimate, - - - - - - - $2,699,532

Middle section, total Distance, 70 miles 1010 yards. Lockage, 1961 feet. Estimate, $10,028,123

Western Section.

From the Youghioghany river, at 440 yards below the mouth of the Casselman, along the right of the valley, to the Monongahela river, and thence, by the right bank of this stream, down to Pittsburg; the resources of water on this section, being,

From the Casselman river, } giving, at their minima, at the
Laurel Hill run, } rate of 70 cubic feet per second.
Youghioghany river,

To which running water, is to be added the water of the reservoirs; viz.

	Cubic yards.
From Indian creek,	210,370
Mountz creek,	323,889
Jacob's creek,	356,357
Big Sewickly creek,	1,750,580
Dunbar,	214,464
Reservoirs, cubic yards,	2,855,660

The means exist also of forming other reservoirs, should occasion require an addition of them to these. Distance, on this section, 85 miles 348 yards. Descent, 619 feet, by 48 locks.
Estimate, - - - - - $4,170,223

For the whole canal, therefore, as follows;—
Distance, 341 miles 676 yards.
Lockage, 3158 feet, by 398 locks.
Estimate of cost, $22,375,427

(See engraved profile.)

The dimensions adopted in this statement, are these;—
Width at bottom, 33 feet.
Width at water surface, 48 feet.
Depth of water, 5 feet.
Towing path, 9 feet wide.
Guard locks, 5 feet at the top.
Surf beams, kept on a level with the water, 5 feet wide, each.
Towing path and top of the guard bank, 2 feet above the canal surface.

These dimensions, however, to be modified, in carrying on the construction, where local circumstances so require; but the depth of 5 feet water to be preserved throughout. The locks to be 102 feet between the hollow quoins, and 14 feet wide in the clear, adapted to boats of 60 tons.

Taking various data, more or less plausible, as a ground, the board of engineers compute that the annual revenue of the canal, when its trade, by virtue of the increase of population and the action of the canal combined, shall have reached their maximum, will amount to the enormous sum of 5,570,791 dollars, or about one fourth of the aggregate construction at the estimates here specified.

This, truly, is a flattering perspective of things; but, when the happy period of a maximum trade shall have arrived, it may well be expected, that the opportunities for the conveyance of commodities to and fro, will have multiplied, and the vastly augmented amount of receipts for transit through every considerable district or section of the country, will not then remain to one establishment alone, but have to be distributed amongst a plurality, whether of the canal or the rail road description.

The appearance of so large a sum in the engineers' report, as the estimated cost of this great canal, has caused surprise; and not a little regret has been expressed, that so able scientific a report should not have been framed upon better local information, in regard to the *prices* of *labour* and *materials* along the tract of country surveyed, than those gentlemen appear to have obtained. A thorough acquaintance with these particulars, it has been shown, would have afforded a basis for the otherwise valuable calculations of the report, so different from the one assumed, that it would have resulted in an estimate of total cost, not approaching within several millions the sum above transcribed from the report.

Difference in the statement of prices considered, and all things else the same, it has been affirmed, that this canal, between Georgetown and Pittsburg, can be constructed for less than one half, perhaps for *one third* of the above sum of 22,375,427 dollars.

An adjourned meeting of the convention of delegates on this projected work, took place at Washington on the 6th of December. Delegates from the states of Virginia, Maryland, Pennsylvania, Ohio, and the district of Columbia, all present; at which a committee was appointed to prepare, and the committee appointed did prepare, an estimate of cost, founded upon data in their possession, deemed good, although hastily collected together; and which estimate of the committee was to the effect above signified. Whereupon the convention passed resolutions as here follows:—

Resolved, That an extension of the Chesapeake and Ohio canal to lake Erie, at such points and by such route, either in Pennsylvania or Ohio state, as shall be considered most advantageous to the company, or to intersect the Ohio state canal, if deemed more expedient;—is within the view and contemplation of the friends of internal improvement, and therefore entitled to the favourable consideration of this convention.

Resolved, That the president of the United States be, and he is hereby requested to cause, under the act of congress, 30th of April, 1824, surveys and estimates to be made on the several routes embraced within the foregoing resolve.

Resolved, That the president of the United States be requested to cause a survey to be made from the mouth of Kiskimenetas river to the harbour of Presqu' Isle, on Lake Erie, by way of the Alleghany river and French creek, with a view to ascertain as to the practicability of a canal between those points; and also of a route from the Ohio, at the mouth of Beaver river, by the way of Little Beaver, to intersect the Ohio state canal near the mouth of Sandy creek.

Resolved, That it will be expedient to obtain such amendment of the charter of the Chesapeake and Ohio canal company, as shall authorize the company to terminate, if they deem proper, the eastern section of the said canal, at or near the town of Cumberland ; and to extend, by any route therefrom, the western section, across the Alleghany mountain to Pittsburg ; or to substitute therefor a rail way, or a turnpike road, along that portion of the route, or any part thereof, designated in the report of the board of internal improvement, dated 23d of October, 1826, as the "Middle Section;" or on that part of the route by Savage river, which corresponds therewith ; and in the event that such a change shall be deemed expedient in the route now prescribed by the charter, to defer the extension of a canal along the Potomac, from Cumberland to the mouth of Savage river; or to reduce the dimensions thereof, and give it a breadth less than that now prescribed.

Resolved, That a committee be appointed to memorialize the congress of the United States for a subscription to the stock of the said canal, and to present like memorials to the legislatures of Virginia, Maryland, and Pennsylvania, and that application be made to the cities of Washington, Georgetown, Alexandria, and Baltimore, to aid by their subscriptions the stock of the company.

Which resolutions being passed, and an acting committee appointed, the convention adjourned, on the 9th of December, *sine die.*

It remains, therefore, yet to be ascertained, whether it be most advisable to adopt the route last surveyed, for as much of it as lies between Cumberland and the Youghioghany river, at the mouth of the Casselman, or to adhere to the original plan of continuing along the margin of the Potomac, as far as the mouth of the Savage, at the base of the Alleghany mountain, and thence by way of Deep creek to the Youghioghany. This latter, passing through an extensive body of coal land, has, in consequence, much importance attached to it.

But a survey has been additionally made by the United States engineers, along the Potomac valley, between Cumberland and the mouth of Savage river, with a view to this being constructed as a branch canal to the main one. Estimate for this adjunct, $1,794,903.

SPECIFICATION:—

A.—From Cumberland, or west end of the eastern section of the article as above, by canal, up the Potomac valley, to the mouth of Savage river, at the base of the Alleghany mountain.

Distance, *Miles*, 30

No. 93.
SAVAGE RIVER BRANCH CANAL.

Should the Casselman summit be adopted into the route of the Chesapeake and Ohio canal, as above inserted, then it is probable, for reasons stated, that this branch will be added. Lockage 312 feet, by 39 locks. Estimate of cost, by the United States board of engineers, as above.

The coal trade is relied on as a source of income to the company in no inconsiderable proportion. An expectation grounded on the well known excellent quality of the Potomac coal; on the extraordinary facility there will be of reaching the *elevated* banks which supply it, by the proposed canal boats; (for it will be found along those very banks, in parallel strata, with but a small horizontal dip;) on the moderate charge, consequently, of toll and freight, at which it will thence be quarried, taken on board, and conveyed to market; and, finally, on the various multiplied uses to which this kind of coal is applicable. When the boats of this proposed canal shall arrive at these coal-beds, it is believed the article will be delivered on board at something less than the rate of one cent per bushel.

From the enlarged dimensions of the Chesapeake and Ohio canal, designed, as has been seen in a former note, to give to the boats the advantage of floating on an indefinite expanse of water, the freight cannot be computed at more than four, or, at most, five cents the bushel. The tolls charged on this commodity, in the early operations of the canal, will be required to be large, in order to yield a sufficient income upon the stock of the canal: they will, of course, be reduced, when the resources of the country through which the canal passes, and the territories which it is designed to unite, shall be fully developed. If the toll for the first years be computed at $6\frac{1}{4}$ cents the bushel, then the price of the commodity in the district of Columbia will be $12\frac{1}{2}$ cents, exclusive of the mercantile profit of the dealer, which may make it fourteen cents.

On various parts of the line of the canal, it will be much lower. At Pittsburg, coal is delivered into the cellars of the houses of the inhabitants, after transportation from the neighbouring mines, distant from one to five miles, at three cents the bushel.

If the district of Columbia, the states of Maryland and Virginia, the river Potomac, or the shores of the Chesapeake, shall, hereafter, rear a city of but secondary rank, or all their cities together shall be equivalent to but one such emporium of arts and commerce; if this emporium shall not surpass the single city of Glasgow, in Scotland; the future profit accruing to the Chesapeake and Ohio company from coal alone, will reach the *maximum* income limited by its charter, as the following extract from a work of unquestioned authority will clearly demonstrate:

"In the suburbs of Glasgow, there are *eighteen collieries*, containing 58 engines, amounting in all to 1,411 horse power.

"Taking the average of three years, ending the 31st of December, 1824, *exclusive of what came from the suburbs*, 1,690,653 tons of coal were brought, annually, to Glasgow, by the Monkland canal." The tonnage of this canal, at three cents toll a bushel for its coal, would amount to $1,420,148 43, or near a million and a half of dollars.

On the 11th of April, 1825, there were in Glasgow 176 engines used in manufactures, amounting, in whole, to 2,970 horse power, average of engines $16\frac{275}{1000}$ horse power.

"The first boat propelled by steam, in Europe, was made in Glasgow. It began to ply on the Clyde, in January, 1812. On the 11th of April, 1825, there were 53 steam-boats plying on the Clyde, containing 68 engines, amounting to 1,936 horse power. Total steam power, viz. engines in Glasgow and on the river Clyde, 244, equivalent to the power of 4,906 horses.

"The population of Glasgow, in 1801, was 83,769; in 1821, 147,043. The population of the suburb parishes of Barony and Gorbals, are included in these estimates. The Royalty alone contained, in the last year, 72,765 souls."*

Throughout Great Britain coal is found, not on the sides of mountains, as along the Potomac, but beneath, and sometimes very far below the general surface of the country, as on James river in Virginia. It is, consequently, brought to the surface there, by the application of great power, and at heavy cost. Almost as much labour is exerted in pumping water from the mine, and in raising the rock and earth loosened in excavation, as in elevating the coal to the surface of the earth; and the health of the labourers, immured in sulphurous and damp pits, while getting it, is exposed to a danger, which will not be encountered on the banks of the Potomac. Some estimate of this advantage of the Potomac coal mines, over coal pits, so circumstanced, may be formed, from the fact, that the bushel of coal now costs at the summit of the shafts sunk near the James river, considerably more than the computed expense of raising and transporting it to the markets of the Potomac, exclusive of toll. Every branch of American manufacture is destined, hereafter, to expe-

---

* Sinclair's Analysis of the Statistical Account of Scotland.

rience this advantage, in a competition with Great Britain, for the supply, not only of American consumption, but of that of all other nations. Great Britain owes her superiority, in manufactures, eminently, to her abundant mines of this valuable mineral, and that nation which shall hereafter obtain it, on the cheapest terms, all other circumstances being alike, must surpass her in the mechanic arts, as she has hitherto done the rest of the world.

When the forests of a country have been thinned or exhausted by the various uses to which wood is applicable, the cost of the manufacture of both lime and iron depends on the price of other fuel or mineral coal, if to be had at all.

Russia has been sometimes induced to prohibit or suspend the exportation of timber, for the sake of her iron manufacture, to the serious injury, and indeed almost total ruin, of a part of her subjects. Ireland, which early manufactured iron, at one time ceased to do so, because its forests would no longer supply necessary fuel. The quantity of iron annually supplied by the English mines, was, after the middle of the last century, reduced, from the same cause, to but 28,000 tons, when Dudley discovered that it could be smelted by the substitution of coked coal for common charcoal. In consequence of this discovery, the annual production of iron in Great Britain had risen, in 1803, to 300,000 tons. Such will be the result in America, of pushing internal navigation from the Atlantic to the bases of those mountains that supply, in the same neighbourhood, iron ore and mineral coal. The foreign importation of this necessary commodity will then cease, and an immense stock arise for exportation, on terms cheaper than any other country now known can supply it to the world.

Pit coal, freed, by coking, from its bitumen, and made to resemble, as nearly as possible, the charcoal of wood, is consequently diminished in gravity. Coke is, therefore, transported in great quantity on the British canals, and is applied to various uses as well as to the smelting of iron ore, for which it is so extensively employed, that it may be said to be the basis of the British iron works. The bitumen, which is separated in a fluid form in this process of coking, defrays its cost, and is applicable to many of the uses of vegetable tar. England, however, continues to import into New-Castle and Hull large quantities of Swedish iron for the manufacture of steel, and especially of that species which, being anciently used to make sheep shears, is called shear-steel, in her manufactures.

Iron has not been found in any considerable quantity on the Erie canal of New-York. It is manufactured in the Highlands on the Hudson, and procured from Lake Champlain, of excellent quality, by the Northern canal. It abounds, in every quality, on the Potomac, in the vicinity of the Coal Banks, and on the navigable streams of Virginia, which empty their waters into that river. The flux, essential to the manufacture of the crude ore, is abundantly supplied by lime stone and other minerals in the vicinity of the ore banks.

The mountains which seem to impede the progress of the Chesapeake and Ohio canal, will, therefore, become the fruitful source of its income; which must surpass that of any canal which yields neither coal nor iron.—*Report to Congress.*

No. 92. CHESAPEAKE AND OHIO CANAL. (CONTINUED.)

What with the mass of valuable information upon this great undertaking which the managers are now furnished with, and the measures taken for obtaining a confirmation in regard to various details in many parts of the construction as contemplated, from practical experience had in neighbouring quarters, the managers appear to be in a train for arriving forthwith at that point of confidence which may ensure subscriptions, and be followed up by a judicious location of the work.

Such a report of the subject, probably, will be made to congress, as may induce a subscription, on the part of the United States, to the extent of one million.

NOTE.

A re-survey of the whole Chesapeake and Ohio route is immediately to take place by civil engineers, under appointment of the United States war department, or as much of the route as may be found necessary, for the purpose of reconciling disparities in the estimates made as above, and of arriving at the real or most probable truth as to what will be the cost of this canal. It will be grounded upon actual comparison by the engineers, of what has been done and is doing, both in New-York state and the state of Pennsylvania; and a circumstantial report on the subject will be expected, for the information of congress. In the mean time, books will be opened, by the committee authorized, in Washington and other places, for subscriptions to the capital stock of $6,000,000.

MAY, 1828.

On the 10th of March last, the civil engineers' report was made to the war department, and by the latter submitted to congress, of a re-examination of this canal route, as far as near Cumberland, and of a revision of the estimates; by which it is confirmed that this "eastern section" can be constructed at an expense of less than one half the sum contemplated in the report of 23d October, 1826; viz.

Estimated cost of a canal, to be made along the valley of the Potomac, on the Maryland side, from 1 mile below Cumberland, to tide water at Georgetown, 186 miles 1353 yards.

For a canal of 40 feet water surface wide, and 4 feet
depth; the locks 90 feet in the chamber, by 15
feet wide, - - - - - - $3,643,641
If 10 per cent contingencies be added, 364,364

It makes, $4,008,005

For a canal of 48 feet water surface, 33 feet at bottom, and 5 feet depth; the locks 102 feet in the
chamber, by 14 feet wide, - - - $3,937,265
Contingencies 10 per cent, 393,726

Makes, $4,330,991

For a canal of 60 feet water surface, 45 feet at bottom, and 5 feet depth; the locks 102 feet in the
chamber, by 14 feet wide, - - - $4,072,133
Contingencies 10 per cent, 407,213

Makes, $4,479,346

The latter enlarged dimensions to extend 126 miles out of the 186. Along the other 60 miles, which includes all the deep and river embankments, and steep hill side cutting, the estimates still keeping a canal of 40 feet water line width in view.

In these estimates, 7 great feeders are embraced, all, except one from the Great Conococheague, drawn from the Potomac itself: from which, as great a quantity of water can be drawn as can conveniently move in the canal, without obstructing the ascending river navigation.

The distance to be supplied by each of these feeders is as follows; beginning at sub-division No. 1, which is to be supplied by a feeder from the Potomac and Mills creek on the middle section, to

	Miles.	Feet.		Feet.
Feeder The south branch of the Potomac,	16	5076	descent	104
No. 1. From Potomac below South branch,	31		do.	96
2. From Potomac to Williamsport,	39	2271	do.	80
3. From Great Conococheague to Harper's ferry,	38	4068	do.	112
Amount carried forward,	126	855	do.	392

Feeder.		Miles.	Feet.		Feet
	Amount brought forward,	126	855	descent	392
No. 4.	From Potomac below Shenandoah, to head of Seneca falls,	39	1551	do.	64
5.	From Potomac to head of Great falls,	7	3300	do.	32
6.	From Potomac to head of Little falls,	9	2799	do.	110
7.	From head of Little falls, through the existing canal, to Georgetown,	4	834	do.	37
	Total distance,	186	4059	do.	635

In consequence of which official information, and especially, in consequence of congress having just passed an act authorizing a subscription, on the part of the United States, of 1,000,000 dollars to the company's stock, the work is immediately to be gone into.

Other subscriptions; viz. by the state of Maryland, by the three corporations of Columbia, and by a number of individuals, which had taken place conditionally, already amounted to 2,600,000 dollars. So that, here is nearly, if not a full and entire, provision now made for a thorough accomplishment of the section of canal from Georgetown up to Cumberland. During the prosecution of which, deliberate measures will be taken for what regards the proposed continuation of the work, in carrying it across the mountain, and entering on the "western section." This will be done, with immense advantages in possession, derived from practical experience.

To the engineers' new estimate for the eastern section, may be added the following, in regard to the middle and western sections, as forming together, for the present, a brief summary for the entire canal.

The cost of summit level, including a tunnel of 4 miles, is estimated upon given data, at - - - - - $1,539,000

Lockage of the whole middle section between Cumberland and the mouth of Casselman river, embracing 1961 feet of ascent and descent, at 1000 dollars per foot lift, - - - - - 1,961,000

Lockage of western section, between the mouth of Casselman river and Pittsburg, 85 miles, embracing a descent of 619 feet, at 600 dollars per foot of lift, - - - - - - - 371,400

Amount carried forward, $3,871,400

Amount brought forward, $ 3,871,400

The construction in other respects than lockage, of about 150 miles of canal, between the summit level and Pittsburg, at 13,500 dollars per mile, which is considered a fair, if not a large average estimate. For 100 miles of the work next above Pittsburg, an offer has been made to construct at the rate of 10,000 dollars per mile,   -   -   - 2,025,000

Total estimate for middle and western sections, $ 5,896,400

It being to be observed, that if the middle, or mountain section lockage shall derive its stone from the adjacent excavation, as may be expected, then it will be found that the cost thereof, is overrated above, near 1,000,000 of dollars.

It is observed by the committee in congress, that, if the elements of a just calculation be derived from the numerous tables of ascertained facts produced; and a fair comparison be instituted, between the simple deductions inferable from them, and the scientific conclusions of the United States engineers, the result of that comparison must be, that those learned officers have overrated the cost of the Chesapeake and Ohio canal, in the aggregate, much more than 100 per cent; and that this work can be accomplished, on a more enlarged scale than their own, at less than 10,000,000 dollars.

On the 20th of next month, June, a meeting of the stockholders takes place at Washington; in order to a choice of directors being made, for a term not exceeding 3 years.

It is provided by act of congress, that, for the supply of water to any other canal, which the state of Maryland, or state of Virginia, or congress, may authorize to be constructed in connexion with the Chesapeake and Ohio canal, the section leading from the head of Little falls of Potomac, to the proposed basin next above Georgetown, shall preserve the same tide elevation throughout, and have a width at the water surface of not less than 60 feet; a depth of water not less than 5.

July, 1828.

The 4th day of the present month, on which fell the 52d anniversary of *America*, was the day appointed for an actual commencement in the work of this great undertaking; and the operation of breaking ground, with the first stroke of the spade, was assigned, by the president and managers of the canal company, to the president of the United States.

Accordingly this task has been ceremoniously performed, and

a beginning of the excavation made, at the spot marked out by the engineer in chief for it to begin; namely, at the head of Little falls, Potomac, a short distance east of the existing canal there. It was hailed, as being thought to be, in its several attendant circumstances, auspicious of a final and glorious fulfilment of the celebrated Bishop Berkeley's prophecy, of the last century,

"Time's noblest empire, is the last,"

in allusion to the gigantic empires of conquest, by man over man, which have successively subsisted and vanished, in the ancient world; and to the transplantation of *learning and the arts* to this hemisphere, as destined to become, in time, a "nobler" and more lasting empire than the others;—the dominion of learning and the arts, over the natural imperfections of man's condition.

The first great and essential step, observes the president, towards the accomplishment of the bishop's prediction, was, the acquisition of the *right of self-government* by the people of the British North American colonies, achieved by the Declaration of Independence, and the acknowledgment thereof by the British nation.

The second step; more arduous than the first; that of *forming a union* of all the separated colonies, under one general government, effected by the adoption of the actual Constitution of the United States.

And the third step; more arduous and difficult still than either of the other two, or both; is now most happily gained, as exemplified in the ceremonies of the day, not alone at the particular spot here designated, but besides, within the precincts of a neighbouring city, on the occasion of a commencement in the execution of another vast enterprise, different in mode and form, but similar in its objects. This third step is the all-important one gained, of an adaptation of the powers, physical, intellectual, and moral, of this *whole union* to the successive improvement of its own condition politically, physically, and morally, both as a whole, and as regards the many distinctive parts of which the whole is composed.

Such works as these, will not, it is to be hoped, or rather, it may be affirmed of them, cannot, through any vicissitude short of a convulsion in Nature, present to distant future generations of men, a mere detached solitary spectacle or two of astonishment and wonder, like the pyramids of Egypt, or some fragments of aqueducts; memorials of power and grandeur passed away! But that, being the victory of human genius, over the tyranny of ignorance, now, apparently for the first time, so directed as to subserve the good of *all* classes of the community, whether proximate as to place, or remote; in short, the good of man at large,—the principle will necessarily grow into a "noble," and glorious "empire," still in remote future ages retaining inherent energies, to swell the tide of human knowledge, and still enlarge the sphere of human happiness.

The subjoined highly wrought passage from a recent European publication, may perhaps be allowed a place, and read without reluctance, as a quotation illustrative of certain facts not inapposite to the present point of the subject.

"The world has not witnessed an emigration like that taking place to America, so extensive in its range, so immeasurable in its consequences, since the dispersion of mankind; or perhaps since the barbarians broke into the empire, when the hunter or pastoral warrior exchanged the lake of the eagles, or the dark mountains, for the vineyards and olive yards of the Romans. As attraction in the material world is ever withdrawing the particles of matter from what is old and effete, and combining them into newer and more beautiful forms; so a moral influence is withdrawing their subjects from the old and worn-out governments of Europe, and hurrying them across the Atlantic, to participate in the renovated youth of the new republics of the west; an influence which, like that of nature, is universal, and without pause or relaxation; and hordes of emigrants are continually swarming off, as ceaseless in their passage, and crowded, and unreturning, as the travellers to eternity. Even those who are forced to remain behind, feel a melancholy restlessness, like a bird whose wing is crippled at the season of migration, and look forward to America as to the land of the departed, where every one has some near relative or dear friend gone before him. A voice like that heard before the final ruin of Jerusalem, seems to whisper to those who have ears to hear—'Let us depart hence.'"

RECAPITULATION.

The president and directors have fixed the width of the canal, at the water surface, at 60 feet, except for a few portions of no great extent altogether, but where the expense would be excessive; at these places the surface width to be reduced to 50 feet, but no where on the whole line to be less than 50. Width at the bottom, generally 45 feet, but to depend, in a degree, upon the quality of the earth through which the canal passes, and the facilities that may be afforded for the inner pavement of its slopes as it advances along. Depth of water, for the present, not less than 5 feet throughout, and having in view a depth ultimately of 6 feet. The inner lining of the banks to be of stone; at least so far as this material for it can be furnished from the excavations. The locks, of stone throughout, with chambers 100 feet by 15 in the clear; and it is under consideration to establish a double set of these, along the first 60 miles of canal, that is, up to the mouth of the Shenandoah river.

Hopes are entertained, from the known disposition of *contractors*, and other circumstances, that these 60 miles, or at least as far as the Catoctin mountain, which is 50 miles, may be completed by the spring of 1830. With a proviso, however, that a collision of interests, or an apparent collision of interests, which has intruded itself between this company and the Baltimore and Ohio rail road company, on the point of a priority of right to use the Maryland bank of the Potomac, shall be speedily removed, by a legal decision.

The lowest feeder on the line, will be taken from the river immediately above Little falls, and this feeder it is intended shall be 80 feet in width, and 6 feet deep, with a view of a plentiful supply of water being had from it, not only for the several sub-canals which are in contemplation, as extensions from the main; as one to the navy yard, one to Annapolis, one to Alexandria, one to Baltimore; but besides, a large volume of surplus water to be used hereafter for manufacturing purposes within the district of Columbia, in case it shall be found expedient so to use it. With regard to the eastern termination of the main canal, it has been proposed, after entering the basin above Georgetown, to carry on the works into the city of Washington, first to the mouth of Rock creek, and then to the mouth of the Tiber, there entering a basin to be constructed at an elevation of 3 feet above common high tide of the Potomac. This to be the point of termination; and sub-canals to be extended to the navy yard, to Alexandria, to Annapolis, and to Baltimore.

The Alexandria connexion to be by means of an aqueduct across the Potomac river.

A.—From Pittsburg, by canal, ascending by the course of the Big Beaver river, to a summit level, near Warren, in Ohio state; and from thence, descending through the valley of Grand river, to Newmarket or Fairport, on Lake Erie; or, otherwise, descending through the Cuyahoga valley, to Cleaveland. Distance, from Pittsburg to Cleaveland, *Miles,* 154

No. 94.

OHIO AND ERIE CANAL;—BY BIG BEAVER.

This is to be considered as a continuation of the Chesapeake and Ohio canal line, last above inserted; the two canals constituting, together, one grand national project; and they will be decided upon in conformity to such connected reports as shall be made by the United States engineers, now engaged in the examinations.

The summit level here pointed out, which is a small swamp, situate north of Warren, at about 60 miles from Lake Erie, between the sources of the Big Beaver, the Cuyahoga, and Grand rivers, and which offers, within a small compass, much variety of route, is 342 feet above the level of the lake, and 218 feet above the level of the Ohio river at the mouth of the Big Beaver, or thereabout.

NOTE.

It is probable, however, that a route different from this, will be reported on by the United States engineers, so as to strike Lake Erie shore more to the east, either in Ohio state, or in Pennsylvania. Four brigades of topographical engineers, and one brigade of civil engineers, have been engaged upon the Chesapeake and Ohio canal and this canal together, and they have completed their labours of surveying. Minute accounts of the whole, with estimates appertaining, are in course of preparation, to be reported to the war department, in the summer of this year, 1826, but not before the rising of congress. The estimates for the whole great project, it is understood, will vastly exceed what has heretofore been supposed.

JANUARY, 1827.

The completion of surveying referred to above, it now appears, regarded only the Chesapeake and Ohio canal, reported upon 23d October, 1826, as in the foregoing article. The surveys on the line from Pittsburg to Lake Erie, were delayed; and no report on the subject, except merely the preparatory examinations in 1824, as to the practicability of such a canal, has yet been made, by the United States board of engineers.

They pointed out a variety of routes, to be considered of, and out of which regular surveys are yet to decide which is to be the chosen one; as

1. From Pittsburg, to follow the right bank of the Ohio river, to the mouth of Big Beaver; whence, up the valleys of Big Beaver, Shenango, and Pymatuning; and to descend to Lake Erie, at the mouth of the Ashtabula river. Summit level to run to the east of Pymatuning swamp, and be supplied by a feeder from French creek, through Conneaught lake.

2. From Pittsburg, as above, to the forks of the Shenango and Mahoning, whence up the Mahoning valley to a summit level at Champion swamp, and thence down to Lake Erie, either following the valley of Grand river, or turning to the mouth of

the Ashtabula, through the townships of Bloomfield and Austenburg. Summit to be fed from Cuyahoga river and Silver creek.

3. From Pittsburg, up to the same forks, whence up the Shenango valley to Greenville, and the Shenango creek valley, or else, Crooked creek valley, to Conneaught lake summit level; from whence, to descend to Lake Erie at the mouth of Elk creek; summit to be fed from French creek and the reservoir of Conneaught lake.

4. From Pittsburg, to ascend the valley of the Alleghany to Franklin, and of French creek and Conneaught creek, to the summit level of Conneaught lake, and thence down to Lake Erie, as in the route last suggested.

Such are stated as being four routes which may connect the Ohio river at Pittsburg with Lake Erie, by the shortest distance and least elevation of summit level. Exact surveys, however, can alone give true distances and true heights.

Other terminations for the canal, at Lake Erie, are likewise suggested, and are yet to be considered of; as,

The Cleaveland termination, from a summit at the rapids of the Cuyahoga; or otherwise, by uniting with the northern section of the Ohio state canal, descend from the Ohio portage summit, to Cleaveland: and the eastward suggested termination of Presque Isle or Port Erie, from a summit level at Beaver dam swamp, where rises Lebœuf creek of the Alleghany, and Walnut creek of Lake Erie.

At a meeting of the canal convention of delegates at Washington, on the 9th December, a resolution on this subject, along with others, was passed, and a committee was appointed, to address the president of United States thereupon, as is stated in the article above inserted.

May, 1828.

Definitive examinations and surveys, in regard to a location of route, for a continuation of the Chesapeake and Ohio line of canal from Pittsburg to Lake Erie, are still postponed, and now not intended to take place until after the eastern section of the said Chesapeake and Ohio line shall be well advanced, and some progress made in the middle and western sections towards their execution.

A recent discovery, of the highest importance in regard to these canals in particular, and of proportionately favourable bearing on the construction of canal works generally, consists in the existence of inexhaustible quantities of hydraulic lime-stone on the Potomac river; this now well ascertained fact, taken in connexion with its being also discovered in corresponding situations along James river and along the Susquehanna, seeming not to leave a doubt of this precious material being eventually found to exist in abundance, on every long line of canal, leading from the seaboard towards the mountains, through the lime-stone region of the middle states of the Union.

An improvement, of the mechanical kind, has likewise just been made, likely to cast a most favourable influence over the success of all future canals. It is the happy invention of artists lately employed on some of the New-York canal locks; and consists in increasing the number of paddle-gates, and so placing them as to fill and empty a lock in one half the time hitherto required. The expense of this improvement will be small; the advantage, equal almost to doubling the number of locks!

A.—From Lake Erie, by canal, to the Ohio river, through the state of Ohio; several routes for which seem naturally pointed out; as the following:—

> By the sources of the Cuyahoga river, and the Tuscarawas branch of the Muskingum.
>
> By the sources of Black river, and the Killbuck branch of the Muskingum.
>
> By the sources of the Sandusky and the Scioto rivers.
>
> By the sources of the Maumee and the Great Miami rivers.

All which having been examined, and the circumstances separately and connectedly considered, a compound canal, upon a broad scale; or, rather, a plurality of canals and feeders, has been adopted; so as to comprehend a great proportion of all the navigable distance specified above. Distance, according to surveyors' report, exclusive of feeding canals,

Miles, 572

Nos. 95 and 96.

OHIO STATE CANALS:—THE MUSKINGUM AND SCIOTO DIVISION; THE MIAMI VALLEY DIVISION.

This is an enterprise of the state, entered upon by the government, after due consideration, and a course of surveys made of the ground, by their commissioners and engineers.

The plan is comprehensive, and nothing now is wanting, save a series of circumstances to favour the execution of it, in the same spirit as that in which it is gone into: if which should take place, we may behold, not the prospect merely, but the actual and sudden creation of a very great increase of prosperity to this section of the country.

To meet the expense, in the mean time, it is proposed to have recourse to the loan system; and a fund of 400,000 dollars, raised against an issue of state stock, bearing an interest of 5 per cent. per annum, answers to the present year's occasions, 1825.

Other loans will take place, from year to year, to defray the expense, as the work proceeds: and to pay the annual interest of the sums so borrowed, as well as to secure the redemption of the debt, a state land tax is to be assessed, until such time as the improvements, having become productive, shall supersede its continuance.

On the part of the general government, there stands assigned 100,000 acres of the public land, in aid of the object.

Portions of both the Muskingum and the Scioto river valleys are to be included in one great canal, as now it is decided on, and the work begun: another great canal, which is also commenced, takes within it the Miami river, and a portion of the Maumee, terminating below the rapids thereof, near Lake Erie; so that the improvements from a point as near to the eastern extremity of the state, on the Erie shore, as has been thought advisable, with reference to securing a good harbour at the lake, and a summit with plenty of water; that is to say, at Cleaveland, or mouth of the Cuyahoga river; and the line, in its progress, strikes diagonally; and again, beginning at the south-west angle of the state, and taking a direction northward, from the Ohio river at Cincinnati, the improvements will here embrace the whole of the western border.

The plan and estimates of the engineers are given in as follows:—

Route by the Tuscarawas and the Cuyahoga.

No. 1. From the mouth of Scioto river to Cochocton,	*Miles*, 176	23
No. 2. From Cochocton to Old Portage bridge,	92	2
No. 3. From Old Portage bridge to Lake Erie level, at Cuyahoga,	38	23
Length of the main line,	*Miles*, 306	48
Length of Columbus and Raccoon fork feeders,	15	45
Canal and feeders,	*Miles*, 322	13

No. 1. Expense of construction,	-	-	$1,675,240
No. 2. Do. do.	-	-	610,563
No. 3. Do. do.	-	-	446,033
Additional, at the feeders and harbour,		-	69,873
Total expense of canal and feeders,	-	-	$2,801,709

Amount of lockage, 1185 feet.

Route by the Great Miami and the Maumee.

From the Ohio river, at Cincinnati, to the Loramies summit, - - - - - - *Miles*,	145	66
From the summit to the foot of Lower rapids of Maumee, - - - - - -	119	56
Length of main line, - - - - *Miles*,	265	42
Length of feeders, from the Miami and Mad rivers,	25	20
Canal and feeders, - - - - - *Miles*,	290	62

Amount of lockage.

South of summit,	*Feet*, 511
North of do.	378
	Feet, 889

Expense of construction.

From the Ohio to the crossing of Mad river, near to Dayton,	$566,837
From the crossing of Mad river, to the south end of the Loramies summit,	846,973
From the south end of summit, to the crossing of the Maumee, below Fort Defiance,	682,309
From the crossing of Maumee to the foot of Lower rapids,	406,375
Main line,	$2,502,494
Feeders,	427,463
Canal and feeders,	$2,929,957

Total expense, for the whole on both routes, 5,731,666 dollars; and if 10 per cent. for contingencies be added, it makes the sum of $6,304,832.

It is calculated, that the line first above specified, together with so much of the other line as reaches from Cincinnati to

Dayton, 67 miles, will all be finished by the year 1831. On the 4th day of July, 1825, the commencement was made.

The said first mentioned line of route may run thus, viz.

From Portsmouth, on the Ohio, at the mouth of the Scioto river, which is 474 feet above tide level, and 94 below Lake Erie, up the valley of this river, east side, to the vicinity of Pikestown; there crossing the river on its surface, and proceeding northerly, to near Chilicothe, where it again crosses the river, and continues along the eastern bank to the Big Belly creek, near the dividing line of Pikeaway and Franklin counties, where it receives a feeder of 10 miles in length, from the Scioto at Columbus. After this, leaving the Scioto valley, it passes, eastward, up the valley of Walnut creek, to the Licking and Walnut creek summit, between the head waters of those streams.

To supply which summit with water, feeders are to be cut to the north, to the south, and the Raccoon forks of the Licking, besides a large reservoir to be established near the canal.

From the summit, the line proceeds down the valley of Licking creek to Rocky fork, and thence across the valley to the Tomaka, and down the course thereof to near its junction with the Muskingum river. From this point the ascent commences; and the line passes up the Muskingum valley to White Woman's creek, near the junction thereof with the Tuscarawas at Cochocton. Crossing the creek at its surface, it proceeds up the valley of the Tuscarawas fork, first on the western, then on the eastern side of the river, to a point where its two head waters unite, near the south-west angle of Portage county. This is the centre of the Portage summit, extending 10 miles, viz. 5 miles on the bank of the Tuscarawas, and 5 miles across to the Cuyahoga river. It receives an abundance of water from the Tuscarawas, at this point, where it crosses the stream.

From the north of the Portage or Akron summit, which is 499 feet above the Ohio river, at Portsmouth, 973 feet above the Atlantic level, and 405 feet above Lake Erie, the line passes down the Cuyahoga valley, first on the west, after on the east side of the river, to within 6 miles of the mouth thereof, at Cleaveland; for which 6 miles, the river channel is to be used, with a towing path annexed.

Such is the plan formed; but in the prosecution of this extensive work, many local deviations from these particulars, it is not impossible, may be made, for the better completion of it, under all occurring circumstances. See the engraved profile of this canal.

That portion of the Miami line of canal of immediate execution, begins from a large basin at Cincinnati, on the Ohio, and passes northward, up the valley of Mill creek, and across to that of the Miami, at Hamilton; whence up to Middletown, where a short cut is to enter the Miami river, and receive its water. From Middletown the line proceeds 23 miles, up the eastern bank, to Mad river, at one mile from its confluence with the Miami at Dayton. In this distance of 67 miles, the ascent from the Ohio, at low water, is 108 feet, to be overcome by lockage. For a supply of water, the Mad river is abundantly equal thereto, for the whole distance.

From Dayton, the line will hereafter extend through the valleys of the Miami, Loramies creek, the Anglaise, and the Maumee, to Lake Erie. The summit level, which commences about 18 miles north of Dayton, extends 60 miles within a single lock; and this level, together with 75 miles of the line north of it, must receive all its water from feeders from the Mad and the Miami rivers.

Width of canal, at the water surface, 40 feet; depth 4 feet.

NOTE.

At Cleaveland, on account of an obstruction at the mouth of the harbour, occasioned by sand thrown up by the waves, a remedy is proposed, by erecting a pier, to extend 1056 feet in length, from the shore into the lake.

The commissioners have been authorized by the Ohio legislature, to make surveys for the purpose of ascertaining as to the practicability of a canal from the mouth of Little Beaver on the Ohio river, to a point of the main canal at Tuscarawas, at or near the mouth of Sandy creek, and near the line which divides Stark and Tuscarawas counties. This would at once connect Pittsburg and Lake Erie.

Besides which, there is to be a convention of delegates from the counties of Portage and Trumbull, in Ohio state, and of Beaver, Butler, Mercer, and Alleghany, in Pennsylvania, to be held soon; in order to adopt measures for ascertaining as to the practicability of carrying a canal direct from Pittsburg to the said Ohio canal, at the Portage summit, the centre of which summit is at the south-west angle of Portage county; and it extends five miles along the banks of the Tuscarawas, and five miles across the portage, to Cuyahoga river.

In regard to the Miami valley canal, it will be so abundantly supplied with water from its two sources; the Mad river above Dayton, and the Miami river at Middletown; that the commissioners anticipate very extensive establishments of hydraulic works, through them, at Cincinnati. They calculate on water sufficient for 60 pairs, at least, of four and a half feet mill-stones, to be kept in constant operation, without at all injuring the banks of the canal, or impairing the mill privileges on the Miami river.

A.—From the Ohio river at the mouth of the Little Beaver, by canal, westward, through Columbia county, Ohio, to a point of the Ohio state canal, at or near the junction of Sandy creek with the Tuscarawas river.   Distance, *Miles* 60

No. 97.

SANDY CREEK CANAL.

The canal commissioners of the state of Ohio, have been authorized, by a resolve of the legislature, to effect preliminary surveys for this projected communication. It is connected in some measure with the project specified in the next inserted article.

A.—From the river Ohio, at Pittsburg; or, from the mouth of Big Beaver, by canal, north westwardly, to strike the Portage summit of the Ohio state canal.
                               Distance, *Miles*, 75

No. 98.

PORTAGE SUMMIT CANAL.

In addition to the proposed route of communication, as specified in the article last above inserted, a convention of delegates from the counties of Trumbull and Portage, in Ohio state, and of Beaver, Butler, Mercer, and Alleghany, in Pennsylvania, have before them the object of ascertaining in regard to the practicability and expediency of a canal communication, direct, between Pittsburg and the Portage summit, as expressed in this article.

NOTE.

A company has been instituted by the state of Ohio, as the "Pennsylvania and Ohio canal company," for the execution of this proposed work; and a concurrent act has been passed by the legislature of Pennsylvania. The point, however, of this canal's eastern termination, to be fixed by a board of Pennsylvania commissioners, and the waters of French creek not to be made use of to supply this canal.

No. 95, No. 96.—OHIO STATE CANALS. (CONTINUED.)

January 1827.

By a report of progress during the past year, rendered by the canal commissioners to the legislature, it appears, that, from the Portage summit to the basin near Cleaveland, a distance of 37 miles of canal will be navigable in June next; also from the said summit southward, as far as Goshen, in Tuscarawas county, a distance of 61 miles, is under contract, to be finished in July, 1828. Or, together, about 100 miles; which, it appears, will be accomplished at a cost considerably within the general estimate. Also, that about 35 miles of the middle division of this canal, is under contract, to be completed in the summer of 1828. This comprises the Licking summit level, the deep cut, the great reservoir, and feeder.

Of the Miami line of canal, the distance of 43 miles from the Ohio river below Cincinnati, up to Middletown, is in such forwardness, as to leave no doubt of being complete for navigation in the course of the ensuing summer. And all the remaining sections of both lines, are to be prosecuted in that order which will best ensure their being laid open to use, and to consequent income from tolls, in degree as they shall successively be finished.

On this plan, it is expected by the commissioners, that there will be open a connected line of canal navigation, between Lake Erie, and the deep cut on Licking summit, distance 183 miles, as early as the month of July, 1828.

Of this same line, and the Miami line together, upwards of 100 miles, probably, will already be navigable in the summer of this year, 1827.

Experience, thus far, both as to the several portions of the work actually finished, and those now under contract, warrants a belief that these canals will be accomplished at an expense considerably within the aggregate estimate.

Surveys in regard to the Sandy creek and Portage summit canal routes are still pending.

May, 1828.

To give aid to the state of Ohio, in these her great undertakings, and accelerate their completion, an act has just been passed by congress, authorizing grants of public lands; as follows;—

To aid the state, in extending the Miami valley canal, from Dayton to Lake Erie, there is assigned, of the public lands which the same shall pass through, a quantity equal to one half of 5 sections in width on each side of the canal, between Dayton and the Maumee river at the mouth of the Anglaise; the United States reserving to herself each alternate section of the said land, from one end to the other; provided this extension be commenced within 5 years from the approval of this act, and finished within 20 years; and the canal to be for ever a public highway for the United States, free from toll.

Further, there is assigned of public lands within the state, to be selected by the governor thereof, the quantity of 500,000 acres, for the purpose of aiding the said state of Ohio in the construction and completion of canals generally, as well those already in progress, as others, if any, in extension of the same, yet to be commenced: provided, however, that the same be completed within 7 years from the approval of this act by the legislature of Ohio; and the said canals, all and every of them, to be public highways, for the use of the government of the United States, free from toll, for ever.

January, 1829.

Owing to various accidental and natural causes, the works of this article, taken at large, have not advanced altogether with that rapidity which was for some time expected; but on the other hand it is shown, by the annual report of the commissioners just made, that what has been accomplished proves to be of the most solid character, and that every hope subsists of the most sanguine anticipations in regard to the whole being ultimately realized, and every object of the great state undertaking attained.

The aqueduct over the Tuscarawas river, near the south line of Starke county, has been finished, and is considered a fine piece of architecture; all the foundations of aqueducts, culverts, and other structures, between the Licking summit and Massillon, have been placed and secured, and the masonry resting upon these is in a good and forward state; as it appears that most of the other heavy jobs of contractors on the unfinished line north of the Licking summit, likewise are. The works at the mouth of the Cuyahoga, designed to secure a commodious channel from Lake Erie into the river, leading to the canal, have been prosecuted in a satisfactory manner by means of an appropriation from congress. The supply of water on the Portage summit, is found so far to be more than ample, and no doubt is harboured but that it will prove, in future, equal to the demands of the most active commerce.

Much the greater part of tolls collected during the past season, has accrued upon the 38 miles of canal between Akron and Cleaveland. Under authority of the legislature, act of 11th February last, a side cut, to connect the canal with the Muskingum river, near the town of Dresden, has been traced, and is now under contract, to be finished by next September. It is 2½ miles in length, to cross the Tomaka creek on an aqueduct, and descend to the River Muskingum by 3 locks, with 28.79 feet of lockage. Estimate of cost, 35,400 dollars.

South of the Licking summit, an aqueduct for crossing the Scioto river near Circleville, and lines of canal extending to and across Deer creek, are now placed under contract, the whole to be finished by the 1st of June, 1830. They embrace, in a distance of 55¾ miles, 240.75 feet of lockage, divided into 34 locks. On the whole canal, the total length of line finished at present, or under contract, stands thus;—

From Cleaveland to Massillon,	*Lockage*,	67 *Miles.*	
Massillon to Caldersburgh,		68 do.	39 ch.
Caldersburgh to Deer creek,		114 do.	69 ch.
		250	28

and between Cleaveland and the Massillon lock, a distance of 67 miles, the navigation has been laid open. This section has cost the sum of 737,521 dollars, including sundry important improvements, grafted upon the original plan; it comprises 49 locks, all of stone, overcoming an ascent and descent of 436 feet.

Moreover, the board of commissioners have decided, for reasons stated, on continuing the location from Deer creek downward, along the west side of Scioto river; in consequence whereof, the canal to terminate at a point immediately opposite the narrow isthmus formed by the Scioto and Ohio rivers, at the lower end of the town of Portsmouth; and the said isthmus to be cut through; in this way forming a capacious harbour on the Scioto, for the meeting there of canal boats and steam-boats in any number.

In relation to the Miami canal, the entire line from Cincinnati to Dayton is complete, with the exception of a dam on Mad river, and a small side cut at Hamilton, and the whole is now filled with water; this division, which embraces 22 locks, overcoming a descent of   feet, stands thus, as to extent and cost; viz:

Length of canal according to survey made since its completion,			-	-	-	65	20	34
Hamilton side cut,	-	-	-	53	62			
Miami feeder,	-	-	-	42	00			
Mad river feeder,	-	-	- 1	40	00			
						2	55	62
		Total length, Miles,				67	75	96

Cost, including side cut and feeders, and repairs of all damages, 746,852 dollars.

The Still Water and Killbuck creeks are in a course of regular examination, with a view to the improvement of their navigation.

December, 1829.

It is officially reported, that the residue of the entire line of eastern canal is now under contract, to be completed in the year 1831. The navigation has actually advanced as far as near Newark, on the Scioto, 180 miles from Lake Erie. It is expected to reach Chilicothe, or thereabout, some time next year; and, in 1831, its termination at the Ohio river.

No. 83. (CONTINUED.)
THE PENNSYLVANIA CANAL; OHIO AND KISKIMENETAS SECTION.

The final location of the Ohio residue of this section, took place in May 1827, and on the 21st June it was, by the commissioners, placed under contract. The section, in consequence, continues from Pine creek down the western bank of the river Alleghany, to a point opposite Washington street; thence, by an aqueduct across, and, by a tunnel through Grant's hill, to the Monongahela river at the mouth of Suke's run; but, on the western side, it is to be connected also with the Alleghany by means of locks, and therefore it will have a double outlet and inlet. The estimate of cost is, viz.—

For the canal from Pine creek to its junction with the Alleghany river,	$129,604
For the aqueduct across to Pittsburg; contracted for,	100,000
For the works thence to the Monongahela river, including a tunnel of 800 feet through Grant's hill, and locks,	61,000
Total,	$290,604

The feeder aqueduct, across the Alleghany, at the mouth of Kiskimenetas, and the canal thence down to Pine creek, are now well advanced to a completion: and the cost of these portions of the work, it now appears, will be 396,223 dollars, making, with the sum above, the amount of 686,827 dollars.

This section, therefore, of the Pennsylvania canal, is rendered more costly, by something considerable, than was presumed by former estimates. Alterations made in the line of route, and additions to what was at first proposed, have materially contributed to cause the difference; and some accidental hill-slips upon the Alleghany river, in consequence of severe weather, have been a further cause.

No. 85. (CONTINUED.)
JUNIATA AND NORTHUMBERLAND CANAL.

By an act of the legislature, 3d April, 1827, the Pennsylvania commissioners were authorized to locate, and contract for, so much of a projected canal, as lies between the mouth of Juniata river and the town of Northumberland on the Susquehanna. Pursuant to which, after a due examination of both sides of this river, for a selection of the best, the canal route was, by the commissioners, laid out on the west side, beginning at Duncan's island, and passing up the river valley to a point opposite Northumberland. The work was placed under contract, and immediately commenced, and the whole distance, which is 37½ miles, between the two points mentioned, is to be completed by the 1st December, 1828. At contract prices, the cost of these 37½ miles of canal, including 60,000 dollars for the erection of a dam at Shamokin ripples, will be 441,350 dollars.

No. 81. (CONTINUED.)
THE PENNSYLVANIA CANAL;—DUNCAN'S ISLAND AND LEWISTOWN SECTION.

By act of the legislature, 3d April, 1827, the Pennsylvania commissioners were authorized to proceed to the location and construction of this portion of the Juniata section of canal; first, however, causing strict examinations to be made on both sides of the river, in order to fix on the most favourable location.

In virtue whereof, and measures being taken accordingly, the line of route was, by the commissioners, determined, so that, between Lewistown and North's island it should be on the north bank of the Juniata; crossing which by a dam, it should thence proceed along the south bank, down to the head of Duncan's island, at the mouth of Juniata.

The work was placed under contract; and the commissioners expect this distance of canal, which is 44½ miles, to be laid open for navigation in the spring of 1829, and at the cost of 597,775 dollars. This is the estimate.

At Duncan's island, the Susquehanna will be crossed by a dam, and the communication of this section of canal, and of the Northumberland section, with that of the eastern division opposite the mouth of Juniata, will be made through the pool of the dam, and by means of a towing path and a turnpike bridge.

NOTE.

The location of the road across the Alleghany mountain, has

necessarily been postponed to the spring or summer of 1828. A hope is entertained of some change being effected in the plan, by which the distance of road may be shortened to about 30 miles.

An act has passed the Pennsylvania legislature, authorizing and requiring the board of canal commissioners to locate the section of canal from Lewistown to the highest point expedient and practicable for a canal on the Juniata; and to place immediately, or in the course of this year, 1828, from 15 to 45 miles thereof under contract for execution.

Moreover, the board of commissioners are by this act required to locate and contract for the construction of a rail road across the Alleghany mountain, by the shortest or most eligible route, to connect the Juniata and Conemaugh sections of canal.

No. 81. (CONTINUED.)
THE PENNSYLVANIA CANAL;—KISKIMENETAS AND BLAIRSVILLE SECTION.

Pursuant to act of the legislature, 3d April, 1827, the commissioners caused this portion of the Pennsylvania canal line to be marked out; and on the 20th October, 1827, it was all placed under contract, a distance of 51 miles, between the mouth of Kiskimenetas river and Blairsville, in Indiana county: the cost whereof, at the contract rates, will be 552,789 dollars.

Some of the work is done; and it is expected the whole distance of canal between Blairsville and Pittsburg, will be navigable by the month of November, 1828.

An act has passed the Pennsylvania legislature, anthorizing and requiring the board of canal commissioners to locate the section of canal from Blairsville up to the highest point expedient and practicable for a canal on the Conemaugh river; and to place immediately, or in the course of this year, 1828, from 15 to 45 miles of the same under contract for execution. Moreover, the board of commissioners are to locate, and contract for, a rail road across the mountain, as stated in the article last above inserted.

No. 82. (CONTINUED.)
THE PENNSYLVANIA CANAL;—MIDDLETOWN AND JUNIATA SECTION.

This portion of the great canal is far advanced, and would ere now have been quite complete, but for a delay at the upper extremity, in order to ascertain the precise point for crossing the Susquehanna river. And it being now decided that the Juniata section, likewise the Northumberland section, are both to communicate with this section, through the pool of a dam to be erected across at Duncan's island, there is consequently required an extension of this section from Forster's falls up to the said point; which is in progress. It is expected, that in all the distance from Fishing creek down to the mouth of the Swatara, water will be admitted, and a junction formed with the Union canal, in the coming spring. The entire cost of this section is now estimated at 478,738 dollars.

No. 74. (CONTINUED.)
NORTHUMBERLAND AND TIOGA CANAL.

As directed by act of the legislature, 3d April, 1827, the board of Pennsylvania commissioners have caused a re-survey of the route for this proposed canal, along the north branch of the Susquehanna, between Northumberland and the New-York line; and, by the engineers' report thereof, now given in, it appears, that, for the whole distance, which is 161 miles, the estimate of cost amounts to 1,820,587 dollars.

This supposes a location of the canal, partly on one side of the river, and partly on the other, crossing and re-crossing at several points, so as to take advantage of the most favourable ground for economy in the execution. Nevertheless, this estimate is considerably higher than the former one. For 56 miles of the distance, that is, from Northumberland to the Wyoming valley, keeping on the west side of the river, the expense will not exceed 8,500 dollars per mile.

NOTE.

An act has passed the Pennsylvania legislature, March, 1828, authorizing and requiring the board of canal commissioners to locate this section of canal, between Northumberland and the New-York state line; and to place immediately, or in the course of this year, from 15 to 45 miles of the same, under contract for execution.

No. 79. (CONTINUED.)
THE PENNSYLVANIA CANAL;—DELAWARE AND SUSQUEHANNA SECTION.

Pursuant to act of the legislature, 3d April, 1827, the Pennsylvania commissioners proceeded to cause surveys to be made towards conclusive information and decision upon this proposed section ; and the result is, that, having established a summit level at the gap of Mine ridge, which divides the waters proposed to be connected, the engineer found the means of an adequate supply of water for the summit to be decidedly wanting, and therefore, that a navigable connexion is impracticable.

Which being ascertained, the engineer, in conformity to instructions contained in the said act, next proceeded to survey the ground for a canal, from the mouth of Swatara river as far as Columbia on the Susquehanna, and for a rail road along the remainder of the distance to Philadelphia. The line of road accordingly projected, reaches the north of Lancaster city, very direct, and thence, crossing the Conestoga, the Pequea, and some other streams, arrives at the Gap; whence it descends into Chester valley on the north side, and, crossing the Brandywine branches, reaches the valley summit, and passes to the south side, at the White Horse. It thence crosses the country to a point of the Lancaster road about one mile from Philadelphia. At this point, it is left, for the present moment, for consideration, as to whether or not it shall pass the Schuylkill river; and then, the location to be completed.

For the proposed canal from the mouth of Swatara to Columbia, the engineers' estimate amounts to 192,000 dollars. And a rough estimate for the rail road as above, from Columbia to Philadelphia, makes it probable that 1,000,000 dollars will cover the expense, or thereabout.

From the bank of the Susquehanna, where a stationary engine will be requisite to surmount the declivity, it is stated, that the graduation adapted to locomotive steam-engines, may be preserved along the whole distance to the city of Philadelphia.

NOTE.

A survey of the ground has been made, in reference to a continuation of canal down to the Maryland line, the construction of which, it appears, would be attended with formidable difficulties, if at all practicable; particularly so, on the west side of the Susquehanna. On the east side, for a canal along the 61 miles distance between the mouth of Swatara and the Maryland line, the cost is estimated at 1,245,408 dollars. Of which sum, the distance below Columbia would require 1,053,408 dollars.

An act has passed the Pennsylvania legislature, March, 1828, by which the board of canal commissioners are authorized and required to locate the section of canal between the mouth of the river Swatara and Columbia, and to place forthwith, or in the course of this year, 10 miles of the same under contract for execution. Moreover, the board of commissioners are by this act required to locate, by the most eligible route, a rail road from Philadelphia, through the city of Lancaster, to Columbia on the Susquehanna, and thence to the west end of the borough of York, in York county ; and to place that portion of the road east of the Susquehanna immediately under contract, with a view to its being completed within two years, or as early thereafter as practicable. Distance of rail road, 84 miles.

And further, the commissioners are by this act required to effect surveys between the borough of Columbia and the mouth of Conestoga river on the Susquehanna, with a view to an improved navigable communication from one to the other, whether by canal or by other means; and to report upon the same, with estimates, and all particulars.

No. 87. (CONTINUED.)

CONNEAUGHT SUMMIT AND FRENCH CREEK FEEDER CANAL.

The Pennsylvania commissioners, under act of the legislature 25th February, 1826, caused a commencement on this feeder; that is to say, upon a selected portion, 9 miles in length, which is common to all the suggested canal routes between the Ohio river and Lake Erie ; and therefore will be applicable, and come into service, which one soever of the routes may be adopted.

The work was placed under contract on the 15th August, 1827. It begins at Bemis's mill on French creek, and passes down, 9 miles, to the Conneaught outlet. Some of the work is done, and according to contract prices, the cost of this portion of feeder will be 80,768 dollars.

No. 86. (CONTINUED.)

THE PENNSYLVANIA CANAL;—OHIO AND LAKE ERIE SECTION.

The commissioners, as directed by act of the legislature, 3d April, 1827, caused a course of surveys, applicable to this section of canal, to be made, in order to determine as to the line of route, to be preferred, under all circumstances, for accomplishing the proposed connexion. From the results of several surveys and correspondent estimates, combined with what was already ascertained and reported on last year, it appears, that—

1. Commencing at the mouth of Kiskimenetas, and passing by the Alleghany valley and French creek, through Waterford, to Erie harbour, there would be 162 miles of canal; 1103 feet of lockage. The estimated cost, $2,339,427.
2. Commencing at the same point, and passing by the Alleghany valley and French creek, and Conneaught summit, and thence by Elk creek to Erie harbour. Distance 166 miles; lockage 837 feet. The estimated cost, $2,667,373.
3. Commencing at Pittsburg, and passing by the Beaver and Shenango valleys, and the Conneaught summit, and thence by Elk creek to Erie harbour. Distance 167½ miles; lockage 852½ feet. The estimated cost, $1,730,015.
4. Commencing at the same, and passing by the Beaver and Shenango valleys, and by the Conneaught lake, French creek, and Waterford, to Erie harbour. Distance 186 miles; lockage 1118 feet. The estimated cost, $1,576,131.

And considering all which, the board of commissioners are, for various reasons, decided in recommending that the No. 3 line of route be adopted. This canal, therefore, to commence from the Ohio at Pittsburg, and, striking from the Shenango valley upon a point near to Conneaught lake, cross the Conneaught summit, and thence proceed to strike across the valleys of Elk and Walnut creeks, for the harbour of Erie, or Presque Isle.

NOTE.

An act has passed the Pennsylvania legislature, March, 1828, requiring the board of canal commissioners to effect a survey of the valley, as also of the stream of the Monongahela river, between Pittsburg and the Virginia state line; with a view to a navigable communication, either by canal or a slackwater navigation; and to report on the same, with estimates, and all particulars.

This improvement will meet the Virginia navigation improvements on the upper waters of the Monongahela.

Moreover, the board of commissioners are, by this act, authorized and required to effect additional surveys and examinations, along the valley of the Alleghany river, from the mouth of Kiskimenetas to that of French creek, to ascertain as to the practicability and probable cost of, viz.

1. Constructing a canal between those points.
2. Improving the navigation of the river, by dams and locks, for steam-boats, between those points.
3. Improving the same, for common boats, between those points.
4. Effecting an improved navigable communication, partly by canal, and partly by dams and locks, between the said two points.

And also are required to effect further examinations, from Pittsburg to the mouth of Beaver river on the Ohio, to ascertain whether, or not, the navigation of the Ohio river can be adequately improved, at a less expense than the expense of a canal, between the points last above referred to; and to report to the legislature, upon all these matters, with estimates in detail.

The engineers' estimates for the whole of the "Pennsylvania canal and rail road," amount to something above 8,000,000 of dollars. With contingencies, it is thought probable the whole cost will not fall short of 10,000,000; and may be considerably more, much of the route proving very difficult; but, however costly it may be, there exists, at the present day, a high degree of public confidence; and experience goes to prove, on the most mature principles of analogy, that a thorough accomplishment must have the effect, not confined to a scanty or even a liberal remuneration, but that of enriching the commonwealth, successively, in a ratio not to be reduced to calculation or estimate beforehand.

At the spirited rate at which the works are now advancing, it is supposed the whole may be complete in 4 or 5 years. The appropriation for the service of the present year, is 2,000,000 of dollars.

This most comprehensive project in the catalogue of improvements, to become, by and by, a magnificent, if not wonderful, continuous structure, comprising, as it were, a chain and platform of moving industry, over a line and area of unprecedented dimensions, may be said to have originated in a certain bill brought into the Pennsylvania legislature, by Mr. William Lehman, the Philadelphia member, in the session of 1817, being the very year in which the New-York Erie canal was commenced,—a bill *for a board of commissioners to be appointed to take preliminary steps for making canals and rail roads.* To the persevering and intelligent industry of this gentleman, from that time forward, through a laborious collection and arrangement of facts, out of doors, and incidental statements, at each succeeding session, it is no more than strictly just to say, is mainly owing that the measure of *state improvement* was at length carried, and acts have passed accordingly, as already noticed, in succession, and that the project has been improved and perfected, into the connected and comprehensive system, which the foregoing specifications claim to exhibit;—a matter, truly, for no feeble, or lukewarm public gratulation!

December, 1828.

From the respective engineers' reports, made to the governor, and by him communicated to the Pennsylvania legislature, it

OF THE UNITED STATES. 253

appears, that, in addition to the several sections of canal; namely,

From Pittsburg, up the Alleghany, Kiskimenetas, and Conemaugh valleys, to Blairsville,	80
Part of French creek feeder, from Bemis's mill to Conneaught outlet,	9
From the mouth of Swatara to that of Juniata,	24
From the mouth of Juniata river, up the valley thereof, to Lewistown,	44½
From the mouth of Juniata, up the Susquehanna valley, to Northumberland,	37
From Bristol, up the Delaware valley, to Taylor's ferry,	18
Together, Miles,	212½

which, prior to the present year, authorized by acts of the legislature, of 1826, and 1827, were already under contract, and in progress of execution; the following have, in the course of the past season, been placed under contract also, and the work of each is, more or less, advanced;—

Along the Delaware division, from Taylor's ferry up to New-Hope,	7
Along the same, from New-Hope up to station south of Easton,	28½
Adjunct to the Juniata and Susquehanna divisions, in order to unite these at an eligible point on Duncan's island,	4½
Along the Susquehanna division, part of 54 miles, between Northumberland and Nanticoke falls,	45
Along the West branch division, from Northumberland up to Muncy hills,	23
Along the Juniata division, from Lewistown up to Smith's mills above Huntingdon,	45
Engineers' estimate for this section, 890,229 dollars.	
French creek feeder; extension thereof, terminating at Muddy run, two miles short of Conneaught lake,	10½
Along the Conemaugh section, from Blairsville up to near Johnstown,	27
Along the Susquehanna division, part of the distance between Middletown and Columbia,	10
Together, Miles,	200½

Making, in all, 413 miles of canal, whereof one half the distance, or thereabout, is nearly finished; and, should the means continue to be provided on a liberal scale, and the same spirit be exerted during the ensuing year, the residue will by that time be respectably, and, it is hoped, (in regard to tolls) profitably advanced, together with such further sections of the great work as may, wholly or in part, have been placed likewise under contract.

Minute examinations were made, preparatory to a rail road location between Columbia and Philadelphia, whereby it was satisfactorily ascertained, that such a construction, graduated within the limit of locomotive machinery, from the bank of Susquehanna river, to the bank of Schuylkill, will not be difficult to effect; each end of this road, however, being to terminate at an inclined plane, supplied with stationary steam power, by which to reach the water level. It is proposed, according to the view at present taken, to cross the Schuylkill river by a bridge near the seat of the late Judge Peters, and carry on the rail road thence, to and along the line of the old Union canal, to the intersection of Broad and Vine streets, in Philadelphia; leaving it to be decided, by circumstances, hereafter, as to the construction of short branch roads, leading to and through the city and adjoining districts, to the Delaware river. A location has been made, according to the following designation, accompanied by a series of observations, which still keeps the question open, for inquiry and decision, as to any means there may be of adopting partial improvements into the plan.

1. From the Mine ridge gap summit fixed on, at Henderson's, down through the north-east corner of Lancaster, to the Big and Little Conestoga, passing north of Mount Pleasant village, to the head of the inclined plane near Columbia bridge; or otherwise, a position at the southern extremity of the town. Height of plane 90 feet; length thereof 660 yards. The engineers' estimate, for levelling and other works on the road, preparatory to laying the rail way, amounts to 131,285 dollars. Distance, 29 miles.

2. From the summit as above, eastward, crossing the west and east branches of Octoraro creek, and winding on, through Chester and Delaware counties, to a point north of the seat of the late Judge Peters; whence, by an inclined plane of 180 feet to the Schuylkill river; crossing which, and following the bed of the old Union Canal, the line, arrived east of Bush Hill establishment, curves southwardly and enters Broad street, proceeding to the intersection of that and Vine street in Philadelphia. A company is proposed as the "Northern Liberties and Penn township rail road company," with the object of constructing a branch which shall pass on to Front street, Philadelphia, by the way of Willow street, Northern Liberties; and another branch, if the company think proper, to pass westward, and strike on the Schuylkill river, at a point north of Vine street. The graduation of the whole road, from level distances to a maximum ascent and

descent of 30 feet in one mile. Engineers' estimate, for road forming from Columbia to Vine street, Philadelphia, 495,557 dollars. Distance, from the head of inclined plane at Columbia, to the Schuylkill river, 79½ miles; distance to Vine street, 82$\frac{8}{10}$ miles.

Estimate for rail way.

Supposing the use of iron and stone only.

Malleable rail; for double tracks; weight per yard 28 lbs.; is 88 tons per mile; delivered at 65 dollars,	$5720 00
For sidelings,	143 00
Chairs of cast iron, 18.267 tons at 45 50	831 14
Iron pins for fixing chairs, &c.	36 00
	$6730 14
United States import duty, 25 per cent.,	1682 53
Broken stone for paving and embedding,	970 00
Blocks of stone for fixing rails, &c.	1835 00
Contingencies,	280 11
	$11,497 78

Making, for 79.42 miles,	$913,143	
Amount for bridges, using wooden rails plated with iron,	10,066	
For 2 steam engines,	14,000	
Total cost of rail way from Columbia to the river Schuylkill,		$937,209

This, consequently, being in addition to the grading and bridging the road, above estimated; which preparatory work, may, however, be reduced $\frac{1}{12}$th in expense; in case the use of iron and stone be exclusively adopted in the rail way, according to the supposition in this estimate.

Very extensive surveys have also been made, during the past season, at the Alleghany mountain, in reference to the portage between the Juniata and Conemaugh levels; but the subject is not yet quite matured for a decision as to the precise line of route to be adopted. Besides a rail road, and in combination with it, the project of carrying across, an easy, graduated, M'Adamized turnpike, between the eastern and western heads of the canal, is at present in contemplation, and strongly recommended by the engineer; not, however, with any view of its entering into competition with the rail way conveyance in the transportation of country productions and of merchandise, but to subserve the convenience of travellers, whose numbers, passing and repassing, will necessarily be multiplied by the scenes of business created along the canals and rail roads, and at the places they connect. The routes surveyed, and submitted for a selection, embrace 2 summits, as follows;—

1. From Bob's creek summit, eastward, by way of Newry, to the canal basin near Frankstown; descent 1591.30 feet, - - - - - 21 Miles. 79 Chains.
Westward, to basin as proposed, on the Conemaugh, at the north branch junction; descent 935 feet, - - - - - - - 10 20

Total ascent and descent 2526.30,   distance, 32 19

Estimate for formation of road, 333,895 dollars, or 10,543 dollars per mile.

2. From same summit, eastward, by way of Newry, to basin, near Poplar run, 1552 feet, - 18 Miles. 16 Chains.
Westward, to the Conemaugh basin, as above, 935 feet, - - - - - - - 10 20

Total ascent and descent, 2487 feet,   distance 28 36

Estimate for formation of road, 302,655 dollars, or 10,652 dollars per mile.

3. From same summit, eastward, by the south side of Blue Knob, to Cove basin; descent, 1515.17 feet, - - - - - - - 16 Miles. 46 Chains.
Westward, to the Conemaugh basin, as above; descent, 935 feet, - - - - - 10 20

Total ascent and descent, 2450.17 feet,   distance, 26 66

Estimate for formation of road, 283,584 dollars, or 10,571 dollars per mile.

1. From Sugar run gap summit, eastward, to the canal basin near Frankstown; descent, 1381.655 feet, - - - - - - - 15 Miles. 00 Chains.
Westward, to the proposed Conemaugh basin; descent, 758.175 feet, - - - - 14 48½

Total ascent and descent, 2139.83;   distance, 29 48½

Estimate for formation of road, 248,341 dollars, or 8,341 dollars per mile.

OF THE UNITED STATES. 257

2. From the same summit, eastward, by the north side of the turnpike, to the Frankstown basin; descent, 1419.281 feet, - - - - 18 Miles. 54 Chains.
Westward, to the Conemaugh basin, as above; descent, 788.175 feet, - - - - 14 48½

Total ascent and descent, 2177 feet; distance, 33 22½

Estimate for formation of road, 318,155 dollars, or 9,559 dollars per mile.

3. From the same summit, eastward, by the south side of the turnpike, to the Frankstown basin; decent, 1417½ feet, - - - - 18 Miles. 66 Chains.
Westward, to the Conemaugh basin, as above; descent, 758 feet, - - - - 14 48½

Total ascent and descent, 2175½ feet; distance, 33 34½

Estimate for formation of road, 345,185 dollars, or 10,325 dollars per mile.

To which one soever of these routes that may be selected, they all terminating at the North branch junction, is to be added, viz.—

From the said point of junction, down the Conemaugh valley, to Johnstown; descent, 380 feet. Distance, 17 miles 40 chains.

Estimate for formation of road along this adjunct, 166,250 dollars, or 9,500 dollars per mile. Also, the amount of *rail way* is to be added; the average cost whereof, per mile, is estimated, according to the following proposed plan, at $7,820 30.

Plan.

Stone supports, or sleepers, 20 inches square, by 30 inches long, properly cut and drilled to receive a wooden plug; these placed in 4 parallel lines, 5 feet apart, and on them to be placed side rails of locust timber, 6 inches by 10, secured to the stone supports. Upon the inner edges of these side rails, plates of rolled iron, 2 inches by half an inch, to be secured.

Estimate.

4224 stone supports, cut, drilled, and set, at 70 cents, $2956 80
1418 pieces of locust timber, prepared and delivered, at 75 cents, - - - - - - - 1063 50
30 tons iron plates, drilled and delivered, at $100, 3000 00
4 tons iron bolts, delivered, at $150, - - 600 00
1 ton spikes, - - - - - - - 200 00

Cost per mile, workmanship included, $7820 30

K k

As directed by law, a further examination of the Delaware line of canal, from Easton up to Carpenter's point, has been made; and estimates have been formed on two several scales; namely— allowing to this distance of canal, the same capacity as to the section below Easton, the engineers' estimate of cost, in that case, appears to amount to 13,309 dollars average rate per mile; but for a canal of smaller dimensions, if such should be determined on, it is calculated that the average of 11,678 dollars per mile, may suffice for its construction. The point is undecided for the present, and no part of the section yet under contract.

The new survey was prosecuted, as here follows;—

From a dam at Peters' rift, three quarters of a mile above Carpenter's point, down the Delaware valley, to Easton; crossing in its course the Bushkill, and Broadhead's creek, the Sawkill, Ranny's kill, Dingman's creek, Cherry creek, Cobuskill, the Lower Bushkill, and other streams, also passing the Walpuck bend, the Water gap, and the Wygaat ranges of mountains; this last not far from Easton. Descent, from station at the dam, 259 feet, by 28 locks. Distance, $66\frac{4}{10}$ miles. The engineers' estimate, for a canal 40 feet wide at the water surface, 25 at the bottom, 5 feet deep, with locks of 11 feet wide, and calculated for boats of 40 tons, is 885,502 dollars. Estimate for one of 32 feet wide at surface, 20 feet at bottom, and 4 feet deep, 776,798 dollars.

For the sections between Philadelphia and the station $6\frac{1}{2}$ miles below Easton, the engineers' estimate, at contract prices, amounts to 626,571 dollars. For the section thence up to Easton, 137,028 dollars.

On the Susquehanna north branch division, the section of 27 miles, from Nanticoke falls downward, is estimated, at contract prices, at 283,097 dollars; and the 27 miles in continuation, down to Northumberland, estimated at 129,250 dollars.

According to survey effected on the "West branch," along the eastern side thereof, from Northumberland up to a proposed dam on Bald Eagle creek, 2 miles above the mouth thereof, the distance of this canal route is found to be 68 miles 85 perches; and the engineers' estimate of cost for the canal, amounts to 723,311 dollars.

A survey of the Ligonier section, between Blairsville and Johnstown on the Conemaugh, makes the distance thereof 28 miles 52 chains; and the cost is estimated at 500,413 dollars, including a basin and harbour.

The surveys authorized by law, to determine as to a rail road location, from some point of the Schuylkill canal, to Sunbury, Danville, and Catawissa; also for canals, and rail roads, between the Lehigh river, and North branch Susquehanna, by the Nescopec valley; and for a connexion by canal or rail road, from the

Lackawannock to the Delaware, by Broadhead's creek, and other projected routes;—have all been executed; and the result is;—

1. That it appears probable, a canal by way of the Nescopec valley, between the Lehigh river at the mouth of Wright's creek, and the North branch canal at Berwick, is not impracticable, but the execution attended with difficulties very expensive to be overcome, particularly in point of lockage: the survey traces the routes, from a summit between the respective waters, down the valley of Wright's creek, to the Lehigh, distance 2.23 miles, in a descent of 209.217 feet; and from the same point, down the Nescopec valley, to a point of junction with the North branch canal, at 96 feet below the bridge at Berwick, distance 35.05 miles, in a descent of 829.284 feet; and it proposes that the summit should be reduced 70 feet, by means of a tunnel 175 poles long, with some deep cutting: which, however, will still leave a rise and fall of 898.501 feet to be overcome by lockage, and for an extension of the canal from the mouth of Wright's creek, down to Mauch Chunk, 597 feet in addition; together, 1495½ feet. The other difficulties consist, in much rock excavation, in long stretches of embankment and slope wall, and in forming a connexion with the North branch canal, by an aqueduct of 1230 feet long, elevated 20 feet above the water of the river. Yet, as the supply of water for the summit level, to be had from Wright's creek, from Pine run, and especially from Bear creek, is ascertained to be abundant; so the canal, though of difficult construction, is considered to be practicable. Whole distance, according to survey, 37.28 miles.

A careful examination of the whole dividing country, between the North branch of Susquehanna, and the tributaries of the Delaware river, proves, that, excepting by the valley of the Nescopec, no route is presented for a canal, with facilities of construction deserving of consideration. *(See article 63.)*

2. That, in regard to a rail road between a point or points of the Susquehanna from Sunbury to Catawissa, and a point of the Schuylkill canal, there are difficulties in the way, arising from the depth and the direction of the Mahanoy and Little Mahanoy valleys; the junction of the two Mahanoy streams presents a gulf 700 feet lower than the most depressed part of the Broad mountain, requiring to be passed; which, and the subsequent difficulties, found on the line from the said fork, by the Shamokin valley, to Danville, and to Sunbury, made it nearly conclusive for an abandonment of it; and other experimental lines were resorted to. In consequence whereof, a route has been traced as follows;—

From the Schuylkill navigation, near Pottsville, or from Potts's furnace, passing up the valleys of Norwegian creek, east branch, and Mill creek, to the most depressed point of Broad mountain, at an elevation of 900 feet, and thence along the northern slope thereof, rising from 10 to 20 feet per mile, to a summit at the head of the Mahanoy creek, and the dividing ground between that stream and Little Schuylkill; from which point, a level is established to the most depressed point of the dividing ground between Little Schuylkill and the south branch of Catawissa. Here is a descent of 600 feet, in less than 4 miles, to be overcome by inclined planes; after which, a graduated descent of $27\frac{1}{2}$ to 13 feet per mile, reaches the North branch Susquehanna canal, at the town of Catawissa. This route, in length 58 miles 13 chains, according to the survey, is calculated for locomotive steam-engines, except at the Broad mountain and Catawissa summits, where stationary power is needful. And it is proposed that branches be extended both to Little Schuylkill, as presenting the most direct feasible line of route from North branch Susquehanna to Philadelphia, and to the Lehigh river, by the way of Quacake valley. Of both which branches, the examinations made have determined the practicability, but surveys for their precise location remain yet to be made.

From the Schuylkill navigation, near Pottsville, to the Broad mountain summit as above, and thence to the forks of the Mahanoy, and to the Susquehanna river at Sunbury, the distance is 49 miles 70 chains; but, although shorter, as already intimated, is much less favourable to graduation than the Catawissa route. In case, however, horse power, in place of locomotive engines, be adopted, it is understood that a rail road may be adjusted to it. *(See article* 66.)

3. That, in regard to other routes for rail way communication, and particularly, one proposed by way of Black creek and Little Schuylkill, and another between the Susquehanna, at Wilkesbarre, and the Lehigh navigation, it appears to be ascertained, by a line of levels run, and critical examination made, from the Catawissa and little Schuylkill summit, along the whole of the dividing ground between the North branch Susquehanna and the Lehigh river, as far north as the Wilkesbarre and Easton turnpike,— that such routes are to be considered as impracticable, by reason of the great elevation of their summits, and other obstacles. *(See article* 61.)

4. That, in regard to a connexion between the Lackawannock and Broadhead's creek, either by canal or rail road, for which two routes had been suggested; viz. One passing up the valley of Roaring brook, crossing the Lehigh and Tobyhanna rivers near their source, and descending from that table land, to the valley of Broadhead's creek;—the second route, leaving the valley of Roaring brook at a point where it approaches the West branch of Waalenpaupack, and then retaining a level, after cross-

ing the dividing ridge, for a descent into Broadhead's creek valley; the examination of the first route proved unfavourable, on account of its elevation of 1900 feet above tide level, and great difficulties in crossing the Lehigh and Tobyhanna rivers. The second line of route could not be examined with instruments, on account of a fall of snow intervening, but so far as a partial reconnoissance could go to decide the question, proved not as favourable as had been expected. *(See article 64.)*

On the result of a fresh survey along the Alleghany river, as directed by law, from the mouth of Kiskimenetas to the mouth of French creek, embracing different modes of improvement, it appears, that,

1. For an entire canal between those points, traced along the east side of the river, 28 feet wide at the bottom, the towing path 12 feet wide at the top, the river banks to be supported by a wall of stone, aqueducts with stone abutments and wooden superstructures; distance 93¾ miles; descent on the river 223 feet, (differing from former surveys); the first supply of water taken from French creek, the rest, by 3 feeders, from the Alleghany; from the 81st mile, the canal to be continued on a level, down to its intersection with the Kiskimenetas canal; lockage 205 feet. For this, the estimate amounts to 2,100,559 dollars.

2. For an improved stream navigation, by locks and dams, combined with a length of canal, and adapted to the use of steamboats; thus;—from French creek down to Fort Run ripple, 3 miles below Kittaning, it is proposed to construct 18 dams and 28 locks, with ponds between, wherever two locks are required by the height of any dam; at this point the slackwater improvement to terminate, and a connexion to be formed with the Kiskimenetas line, by a canal. Locks to be 120 feet, by 20 in the chamber, and built of stone; these dimensions assumed as being adapted to the size of the low water steam-boats in use on the Ohio. These boats introduced, it is calculated, will carry each 60 tons of freight, with 3 feet draft of water, and will travel, each one with 2 canal boats in tow, of 40 tons freight each, at the rate of 5 miles per hour, or average, including lockage, of 4 miles per hour.

For the improvement after this plan, the estimate of cost is as follows:—

Cost of the dams,	$346,035
Ponds and short canals,	25,623
Removing of rocks and gravel bars, below the locks,	5,275
Amount carried forward,	$376,933

Amount brought forward,	$376,933
Cost of 12¼ miles of canal, from Fort Run to Kiskimenetas,	219,697
Guard lock at head of canal,	2,050
Lockage, 185 feet, at 1,300 dollars per foot lift,	240,500
	839,180
Contingencies, 10 per cent,	83,918
	$923,098

This, from its saving in some measure the construction of dams, and the advantages offered for its connexion with the Kiskimenetas canal, seems, at present, best adapted to the river.

3. For an improvement, adapted to steam-boat navigation, by means of locks and dams, without the aid of canals. Estimate, 873,343 dollars.

4. For an improvement, by locks and dams, adapted to the use of common boats; the formation of towing path, on this plan, very expensive, arising from circumstances of the river. Estimate 1,708,275 dollars.

A thorough examination was made along the valley and the stream of the Monongahela river, from Pittsburg up to the Virginia state line, with a view to the effecting an improved navigation, by means of a canal or otherwise. By the report upon which, it appears, that a canal construction is not practicable, on one side or the other, within the limits of any reasonable expense; but, that a slackwater navigation on this river, may be advantageously carried into effect. The distance between the Virginia line and Pittsburg, is 89 miles, along which the river falls 75 feet; it is proposed, by erecting 8 dams, with 10 appropriate locks, at proper intervals, as designated in the report, to create, along the said distance, a complete steam-boat navigation, with 4 feet depth of water.

The dams here proposed, are those known by the name of crib and frame dams; the bottom to be built in the form of crib work, the top of frame work, and the whole to be filled in with loose stones.

Estimate of cost, as follows;—

For the 8 dams, including wing walls, excavation, &c.,	$156,916
Ponds,	5,553
Lockage, 75 feet, at 1,300 dollars,	97,500
Amount carried forward,	$259,969

Amount brought forward,	$259,969
Grubbing and clearing along the banks,	6,350
Removing some wing dams,	1,676
Damages of mills,	8,500
Walling below locks,	2,400
	$278,895
Contingencies, 10 per cent.,	27,889
Total cost,	$306,784
Or, in case crib locks be used, the cost,	$265,534

An examination of some distance on the Ohio river, was moreover made, with a view to improving the navigation thereof; namely, from Pittsburg down to Stone's island, immediately below the mouth of Beaver; distance 25¾ miles; and the object, it appears, may be accomplished by the erection of 4 dams, with their locks, as below specified. By which, a continued steamboat navigation, to the extent of 4 feet depth of water, at the lowest stages of the stream during the dry season, will be obtained. Plan of the dams, the same as that proposed for the Monongahela river; the locks to be built of stone, and to be 140 feet, by 40 in the chamber, as calculated for the largest boats that come up to Pittsburg. Descent to be overcome, 34 feet; with a foot proposed for the dam to raise at Pittsburg; this makes 35 feet.

Dam at Neville's island, two parts,	$37,685
Dam at Wolrey's Trap ripple,	31,210
Dam at Dead Man's ripple,	34,505
Dam at foot of Stone's island,	39,650
Lockage 35 feet, at 1,600 dollars,	56,000
Excavation below locks Nos. 3 and 4,	2,130
	$201,180
Contingencies, 10 per cent.,	20,118
Total estimate of cost,	$221,298

Upon the surveys directed in reference to proposed rail roads, from the west end of Harrisburg bridge, to Chambersburg, Gettysburg, and York, no report is yet made.

In consequence of the contracts now entered into, and the works respectively more or less advanced, estimates of expense, claiming mostly to be provided for in the ensuing year, (1829) are given; together with some observations by the board of commissioners, as here follows:—

Delaware,	$520,000
North branch,	330,000
West branch,	151,000
Juniata, (Lower line,)	315,000
Do. (Upper line,)	890,000
Susquehanna division, including dam and bridge over the river,	284,000
French creek feeder,	76,000
From Middletown to Columbia,	245,000
Conemaugh, from Blairsville to Johnstown,	500,000
Part of Pennsylvania rail road,	200,000
	$3,511,000

It is estimated, from the experience of former seasons, that supposing the utmost activity to be used upon all the lines within the approaching year, at least 700,000 dollars of the aggregate, exhibited by this statement, will remain to be expended in the year 1830, so that the amount required for the operations of next year, making full allowance for the sums yet to be paid on the eastern and western divisions, cannot materially exceed 3,000,000 dollars, and may probably fall short of that sum. In as much, however, as the faith of the commonwealth is already pledged for the contracts made, it will probably be desirable, that a precise limit should not be fixed, and that full scope should be given for the execution of such contracts as early as possible.

That this statement presents a scene of operations of great extent, is readily admitted;—but it is equally certain, that a vigorous effort for another year, will so reduce its magnitude, as to place the success of the whole system of internal improvement beyond a reasonable doubt. By the month of August next, 47 miles on the Juniata, 41 miles more on the Susquehanna, and 28 miles on the Delaware, will certainly be completed, reducing the whole distance to 184 miles. By the month of December next, the North and West branch divisions may be ready for navigation, the Delaware line to Easton will be nearly completed, and the obligations of the commonwealth, for lines now under contract, will have been reduced to a sum considerably short of 1,000,000 of dollars.

Upon the view thus presented, the board would propose a system of proceeding, recommended at once by its extreme simplicity, its tendency to sustain the confidence of the public, and the certainty it affords, that the whole scheme of internal improvement adopted by the state, embracing a complete communication, from Philadelphia to Pittsburg and Lake Erie, and the projected lines along the Susquehanna, its branches, and the Delaware, may be triumphantly executed within a reasonable period.

It is based upon the supposition, that the whole expenditure of the coming year will be 3,000,000 of dollars, which, added to 3,300,000 dollars already borrowed, makes 6,300,000 dollars; and also that the income from the eastern and western divisions, next year, will equal the interest of the excess of the canal debt above 6,000,000 of dollars, at the end of that year. Upon these suppositions, it is proposed:—

1. That the revenue at present applicable to the interest of canal loans, be so increased by legislative provisions, as to produce, annually, the interest of 6,000,000 of dollars, independently of all receipts from the canals.

2. That all further extensions of the lines of improvement beyond the cost of 6,000,000 of dollars, shall be made by loan, upon the credit of receipts, from the finished canal, and shall be limited by the sufficiency of those receipts to discharge the interest of such further loans.

3. That as the finished portions of the canal increase in revenue, so as to exceed the interest of the loans to which they are pledged, the excess shall be applied as a sinking fund, or as a fund for the making of other valuable improvements, not included in the present system.

The board, in offering these suggestions, desire it to be understood, that they mean not to diminish the extent of the system, as already adopted, but, on the contrary, that they calculate upon its early and effectual completion. They entertain no doubt, that the receipts from canal tolls, within the year 1830, will justify the expenditure of $3,000,000 that year, if such a sum be required; and will increase from that time, in a ratio fully equal to the further wants of the commonwealth, in executing its system. In proof of this, they remark, that during the whole of next season, 103 miles of valuable canal will be in full operation; that at the commencement of the year 1830, the extent navigable will be 290 miles; and that within the last mentioned year it will be extended to 350 miles, embracing sections equalled by none other in promise and importance.

1829.

SUMMARY OF PARTICULARS ON THE "PENNSYLVANIA CANAL AND RAIL ROAD,"

Embracing the divisions and subdivisions as below stated; which are in part finished, in part under contract for execution, and the rest in a course of preparation or preliminary arrangement.

No. 84.

DELAWARE DIVISION;

Connecting the Delaware navigation at Philadelphia, with the same at Carpenter's point, at the north-east boundary of the state, by canal, along the valley of the river; viz.—

		Miles.
Philadelphia and Bristol section; distance according to survey,		17½
Bristol and Easton section; viz.—Bristol to Taylor's ferry, Miles, 18		
Taylor's ferry to New-Hope; ascent by locks, feet,	7	
New-Hope to station south of Easton; ascent by locks, feet,	28½	
Latter station to Easton; ascent by locks, feet,	6½	
		60
Easton and Carpenter's point section; ascent to dam at Peters's rift, ¾ of a mile above the point, by 28 locks, 259 feet. Distance, by the survey,		66½
	Miles,	144

Nos. 86, 88.

OHIO AND LAKE ERIE DIVISION;

Connecting the Ohio navigation at Pittsburg, with that of Lake Erie at Presque Isle harbour, by way of the Beaver and Shenango valleys, and across the valley of Elk creek; being one of the routes surveyed between the said points; viz.—

From Pittsburg, by the Beaver and Shenango valleys, to Conneaught summit. Lockage, 345 feet, - - - - - Miles, 120½
From said summit to Erie harbour. Lockage, 507½ feet. - - - - Distance, 47
Miles, ——— 167½

No. 87.

FRENCH CREEK AND CONNEAUGHT SUMMIT FEEDER;

From Bemis's mill on French creek, along the eastern side thereof, 9 miles, down to a point opposite the Conneaught outlet; and thence passing across by an aqueduct, westward 12½ miles, to the said lake; so much of this route as extends to Muddy run, within two miles of Conneaught lake, having been laid off and placed under contract. Descent,   feet. Distance, Miles, 21½

Nos. 73, 74, & 82.

SUSQUEHANNA OR MIDDLE DIVISION;

Connecting the Susquehanna navigation at Columbia, Lancaster county, with the same, at the New-York state line, 4 miles above Tioga point, by canal, along the river valley, comprising the several sections as here follows ;—

Columbia and Middletown section; ascent, by 8 locks, 70 feet, - - - - - Miles,	18
Middletown and Duncan's island section; ascent, by locks, feet, - - - -	24
Duncan's island and Northumberland section; ascent, by 9 locks, 62 feet, - - -	37½
Additional, in order to unite this division and the Juniata division, at an eligible point of Duncan's island, - - - - -	4½
Northumberland and Nanticoke section; ascent, by 9 locks, 77½ feet, - - - -	54
Nanticoke and Tioga section; ascent, by locks, feet, - - - - - -	107
	——
	245

No. 81.

JUNIATA, OR EASTERN PART OF TRANSVERSE DIVISION;

Connecting the Susquehanna navigation at Duncan's island, with a rail road communication across the Alleghany mountain, and through this latter, with the Alleghany or western division, by canal, along the valley of the Juniata river, up to Frankstown; this division comprises the sections as follows;—

Duncan's island and Lewistown section; ascent, by 11 locks, 95.3 feet, - - - Miles,	44½
Lewistown and Huntingdon section; ascent, up to Smith's mills, by locks, feet, -	45
Huntingdon and Frankstown section; from Smith's mills, upward; ascent, by locks, feet, - - - - - -	42½
	——
	132

(See engraved profile.)

Nos. 81 & 83.

ALLEGHANY, OR WESTERN PART OF TRANSVERSE DIVISION;

Connecting the Ohio navigation at Pittsburg, with a rail road communication across the Alleghany mountain, and, through this latter, with the Juniata, or eastern division, by canal, along the Alleghany, Kiskimenetas, and Conemaugh river valleys, up to Johnstown; this division comprising the sections as here follows;—

Grant's Hill tunnel section,—
 From the Monongahela river at Suke's run, through said tunnel, to the Alleghany aqueduct, at Washington street, Pittsburg. Ascent and descent, by 4 locks, 39 feet, *Miles*, 7/8
The Alleghany section,—
 From Pittsburg, across by the aqueduct, and up the Alleghany river valley, to the mouth of Kiskimenetas river.
   Ascent, by   locks,   feet,   30
 (This section includes a connexion with the Alleghany river, west side, opposite Pittsburg, by a line of communication 60 chains in length. Lockage 45 feet).
Kiskimenetas section,—
 From the Alleghany line, along the valley of the Kiskimenetas, up to the head of the Salt works. Ascent, by locks, feet,   24
Conemaugh lower section,—
 From the terminating point last mentioned, up the Conemaugh valley, to Blairsville.
   Ascent, by   locks,   feet,   27
Conemaugh upper section,—
 From Blairsville, as above, up the said valley, to Johnstown.
   Ascent, by 30 locks, 234 feet,   28½
   ——— 110⅜

(See engraved profile.)

No. 81.

MOUNTAIN RAIL ROAD, OR MIDDLE PART OF TRANSVERSE DIVISION;

Connecting the east and the west head navigation; namely;—
According to one of the several routes surveyed;
From the Juniata level at Frankstown, by the north side of the turnpike, to a summit at the Sugar run gap. Ascent, 1419 feet; distance,   *Miles*, 18¾
From said summit, down to a basin at the North branch Conemaugh junction.
   Descent, 758 feet,   distance,   14½
From the said point of junction, down the valley, to Johnstown.
   Descent, 380 feet,   distance,   17½
   ——— 50¾

(See engraved profile.)

No. 85.
WEST BRANCH OF SUSQUEHANNA DIVISION;

Connecting the navigation at Northumberland, with the navigation of the Bald Eagle river, which discharges into West branch, in Lycoming county; viz.

From Northumberland, by canal, up the West branch valley, east side of that river, to a dam above the mouth of the Bald Eagle, and thence, across the small peninsula there formed, to a dam on the Bald Eagle, erected to a level the same as the other dam. Ascent, by 14 locks, 101 feet.

Distance, according to survey, *Miles*, 68¼

No. 79.
PHILADELPHIA AND COLUMBIA RAIL ROAD DIVISION;

Connecting the Delaware navigation at Philadelphia, with that of the Susquehanna at Columbia, by a rail road passing through the counties of Delaware, Chester, and Lancaster; viz.

From the Mine ridge gap summit, at Henderson, westward, to the head of inclined plane, at Columbia.

Ascent and descent, 848½ feet, *Miles*, 29

From the said summit, eastward, to the head of inclined plane, at the Schuylkill river.

Ascent and descent, 940 feet, 50

From head of inclined plane, across the Schuylkill, to the intersection of Broad and Vine streets, in Philadelphia, - - - - 3¾

———— 82¾

(See the engraved profile.)

Length of "Pennsylvania canal and rail road," *Miles*, 1022⅛
Whereof 888⅝ miles composed of canal,
133½ miles composed of rail road,
Subject to any alterations that may take place, on and along the sections not yet definitively located, particularly the Delaware division, relative to which, commissioners on the part of Pennsylvania and New-Jersey jointly, are to examine, and report.

Sub-Recapitulation.

Delaware division, - - - - *Miles*, 144
Ohio and Lake Erie division, - - - 167½
French creek and Conneaught summit feeder, 21½
Susquehanna division, - - - - 245

Amount carried forward, ———— 578

Amount brought forward, *Miles*, 578
Juniata, or east part of transverse division, 132
Alleghany, or west part of transverse division, 110¾
Mountain part of transverse division, 50¾
West branch division, to Bald Eagle, 68¼
Philadelphia and Columbia rail road, 82¾
───── 1,022⅛

To which may be added; viz.

The several particularized works in contemplation, which are to be regarded, either as integral parts, or as coming, when finished, into immediate connexion;—they are, as designated herewith, No. 1 to 9, about 450

Together, *Miles*, 1,472⅛

It is not, of course, to be expected, that of this gigantic undertaking, every section throughout will be immediately begun upon; prudence, and the true interests of the public, rather require that the means of the state, in this matter, should be concentrated and applied with full energy, to complete, in the first instance, those parts already commenced, and render them profitable, ere any heavy disbursements be gone into upon the remote sections. A somewhat gradual extension of the works, will best ensure the successful and even speediest accomplishment of the whole grand enterprise, according to its original design.

Proposed works in connexion with the Pennsylvania canal and rail road, referred to above;—

1. A canal between the Lehigh navigation at Wright's creek, and the North branch canal, at Berwick, by the Nescopec valley, as already stated. Lockage, 898½ feet. Tunnel, 175 poles. Distance, according to survey, Miles, 37¼

2. A rail road, between the Schuylkill navigation at Pottsville, and the North branch canal at the town of Catawissa, passing round the heads of Great and Little Mahanoy, as already described. Adapted to locomotive steam power. Distance, according to survey, 58

3. A branch rail road, from the summit of the latter, to communicate with Little Schuylkill river; the practicability of which is ascertained, but the route not yet regularly traced, ..

4. A branch rail road from said summit, to communicate with the Lehigh navigation, by way of Quacake valley, also

ascertained to be practicable, but the precise route remaining to be traced, - - - - . .

5. An improved navigation of the Alleghany stream, between the mouth of French creek and the mouth of Kiskimenetas, by means of locks and dams, combined with 12¼ miles of canal, as already described. Adapted to steam-boat trade. Decent, 223 feet. Distance, according to survey, 93¼

6. An improved navigation of the Monongahela river stream, from Pittsburg, up to the Virginia state line, by means of dams and locks, as already described. Adapted to steam-boats. Ascent, 75 feet, to be overcome by lockage. The distance, according to survey, - - 89

7. An improved navigation of the Ohio river stream, from Pittsburg, down to Stone's island, below the mouth of Beaver, by means of dams and locks, as already described; to admit the steam-boat trade at the lowest stages of the water during the dry season. Descent, 34 feet. Distance, according to survey, - - - - - 25¼

8. Extension of rail road from Columbia to the mouth of Conestoga river, on the Susquehanna, and from the same to the west end of the borough of York, in York county. Locations for these, not yet accomplished, - - . .

9. A rail road from the Susquehanna navigation opposite Harrisburg, through Cumberland and Franklin counties, to the borough of Chambersburg. This has just been reported upon. The country between Carlisle and Chambersburg admits of two distinct lines of location, according to the route surveyed and detailed in the report, and taking it to commence, not at Harrisburg bridge, but at the river bank, 1 mile 14 chains below, and to terminate in Chambersburg, near the market-house, is 54½ miles; and supposing the road plan as suggested to be followed, which is this;—

After levelling and grading, locust sleepers 3 by 6 inches, to be laid 8 feet apart, and embedded on broken stone. Locust blocks to be pinned on these, their upper surfaces level with the horse path. Upon these, oak scantling to be secured, and the iron rails spiked to the timber. Iron, 2 inches by $\frac{3}{8}$ of an inch;—then, the engineers' estimate of the total cost of a road on this plan, with double tracks, and including turn outs, amounts to 418,964 dollars, or the average rate of 7673 dollars per mile, - - - - 54½

NOTE.

A rail road from Chambersburg, through Gettysburg, to the borough of York, is reported on as not practicable, within any admissible expense.

1829.

Efforts are at present directed, and are to be additionally enforced, to accomplish navigation upon parts of the "Pennsylvania canal," in the following order; namely,

Middletown and Duncan's island section,—
   Navigation throughout to be laid open on the
   1st September, - - - - - - *Miles*, 24

Grant's hill tunnel section, - - - *Miles*, $\frac{7}{8}$
The Alleghany section, - - - - - 30
Kiskimenetas section, - - - - - 24
Conemaugh lower section, - - - - 27
   These 4 sections, from Pittsburg to Blairsville, inclusive. Navigation throughout to
   be laid open on the 1st September, - —— $81\frac{7}{8}$

Duncan's island and Northumberland section, and
   connexion, at the island, with the Juniata
   section,—
   Navigation throughout to be laid open on the
   1st September, - - - - - - 42

Duncan's island and Lewistown section,—
   Navigation throughout to be laid open on
   the 1st November, - - - - - $44\frac{1}{2}$

The North branch sections, from Nanticoke downward, and the Delaware sections, from Easton downward, to be vigorously prosecuted.

Of the Philadelphia and Columbia rail road, a section to be accomplished forthwith.

December, 1829.

Relative to the waters of the Delaware river, the commissioners appointed by the states of Pennsylvania and New-Jersey, have agreed upon the terms of a convention, to be ratified by each legislature, for the mutual use of the waters of the Delaware.

It provides for the successful completion of the Pennsylvania canal, in the valley of the Delaware on one side, and the supply of the New-Jersey canal, between the Delaware and the Rariton on the other side. It also provides for maintaining the river stream navigation, and for the interest of the river fishery.

By the 1st article, the state of Pennsylvania is at liberty to erect a dam across the river at the head of Wells's falls, and to construct a feeder therefrom, for the Pennsylvania canal, not exceeding 40 feet wide at the water line, 25 feet wide at the bottom, and 5 feet in depth, with a guard lock and other works as needful.

By the second article, the state of New-Jersey is at liberty to erect a dam across the river at the head of Warford's falls, at Eagle island, or Bull's island, and to construct a feeder therefrom for the contemplated Delaware and Rariton canal, not to exceed 40 feet in width at water line, 25 feet at the bottom, and 5 feet in depth perpendicular.

By the third article, it is provided, that either state may erect dams at other places therein specified.

JANUARY, 1830.

Owing to insufficiency in the provisions of the legislature at their last session, the works of the past season have been chiefly confined to the sections of canal which were under contract, and had been commenced; and upon them, not any very rapid progress has been made; and not only so, but some embarrassment in duly discharging the demands of sundry of the contractors, has ensued.

The commissioners reported, on the 18th of last month, to the legislature, as follows:—

That the whole distance of the Pennsylvania canal, authorized to be constructed by the several acts of assembly, and placed under contract prior to the 1st of June, 1829, is $419\frac{1}{2}$ miles: 9 miles have been placed under contract since that period; making a total, now finished or under contract, of $428\frac{1}{2}$ miles; viz.

	Miles.
From Pittsburg to Johnstown,	104
From the mouth of the Juniata, to Smith's mills, above Huntingdon,	90
From Middletown to Muncy hills, upon the West branch of the Susquehanna, and including 10 miles placed under contract between Middletown and Columbia,	100
From Northumberland, up the North branch of the Susquehanna, to Nanticoke falls,	55
From Bristol to Easton,	60
From Bemis's mill, on French creek, to Muddy run,	$19\frac{1}{2}$
	$428\frac{1}{2}$

Of which aggregate distance, 195 miles are now finished for navigation; viz.

From Pittsburg to the head of the dam at Blairsville,	75
From the mouth of the Juniata to Lewistown,	45
From Middletown to Clarke's ferry,	24
From the mouth of the Juniata to Northumberland,	41
On the French creek feeder,	10
Miles,	195

And a great portion of the remaining 233½ miles pretty well advanced; also that there are 40 miles of the Philadelphia and Columbia rail road under contract, and in progress, as to preparatory formation.

The report states; that,

The sum required to pay the debts due upon the respective divisions of the canal, and portion of rail road, according to the reports of the acting commissioners and superintendents, amounts to	$ 1,398,791
The whole amount of work, of every description, yet to be done upon the several divisions above specified, as estimated by the principal engineers,	2,060,742
The amount already expended, - - - -	6,406,000
Making the total expense, for 428½ miles of canal, and 40 miles of rail road formation, - -	$ 9,865,533

As expressed above, 195 miles of the canal to be laid open for navigation as soon as the season commences, and the rest, in such a train, as for the greatest part, if not all, to be finished off and made navigable in the course of the summer; if, as there can hardly be a doubt, adequate legislative provision be made for the same.

The location of route, for an extension of the canal from the city of Pittsburg to Presque Isle on Lake Erie, was in the contemplation of the legislature at their last session, but has not yet been effected. Some additional examinations of the ground have, however, taken place, and have decided the commissioners in recommending, that the route by the Beaver and Shenango valleys, Conneaught lake, the Elk and Walnut creeks, be adopted, in preference to the Alleghany river and French creek route, or any other.

The Portage rail road, across the Alleghany mountain, has likewise had additional attention; and the engineer, in his report, recommends passing the summit by a tunnel of one mile long, and overcoming the elevation by 5 lifts and 5 levels on each side. The Portage, according to this plan, measures 38 miles 51 poles; and, for a complete execution of it, the engineers' estimate of cost is 936,005 dollars.

To decide on the precise means of accomplishing this connexion, is a thing of no inconsiderable magnitude; for, on the decision, right or wrong, may depend, besides lesser considerations, the great one of a successful or unsuccessful competition of the Pennsylvania canal with other avenues for the trade of the western states to the Atlantic.

SUMMARY FOR NEW-JERSEY, DELAWARE, MARYLAND, PENNSYLVANIA, AND OHIO STATES.

ARTIFICIAL NAVIGATION.

Page.	No.		Miles.
93	54.	The Delaware and Rariton canal,	60
100	55.	The Morris canal,	101½
106	56.	Delaware river canals, and stream improvements,	220
108	57.	Schuylkill river canals, and slackwater improvements,	110½
120	58.	The Union canal,	105
127	59.	The Lackawaxen canal and rail road,	41
129	60.	Carbondale and Pittstown canal,	22
130	61.	Lausanne and Wilkesbarre canal,	40
130	62.	Lehigh river canals, and stream improvements, and rail road to the mine,	93
145	63.	Nescopec and Lehigh canal,	35
147	64.	Pittstown and Water Gap canal,	60
149	65.	The Perkiomen canal,	40
149	66.	The Catawissa canal,	50
151	67.	Upper Schuylkill valley canal,	
152	68.	Mahanoy creek canal,	
152	69.	Shamokin creek canal,	
153	70.	Chesapeake and Delaware canal,	14
163	71.	Patapsco and Susquehanna canal,	100
169	72.	Patapsco and Potomac canal,	44¾
171	73.	Susquehanna river canals, and stream improvements,	288
181	75.	Peters's camp canal,	
182	76.	Port Deposite canal,	10
182	77.	Conestoga river canals, and stream improvements,	18
183	78.	Conewago canals,	2¼
265		The Pennsylvania state canal and rail road,	1022⅛
186	80.	Chester creek canal or rail road,	25
204	89.	Kiskimenetas and Conewango canal,	70
205	90.	The Conococheague canal,	120
207	91.	Potomac river canals, and stream improvements,	182

Amount carried forward, 2874⅓

INTERNAL NAVIGATION

Page.	No.		Miles.
		Amount brought forward,	$2874\frac{1}{8}$
215	92.	Chesapeake and Ohio canal,	341
224	93.	Savage river branch canal,	30
233	94.	Ohio and Erie canal, by Big Beaver valley,	154
236	95.	Ohio state canals, Scioto division,	322
236	96.	Ohio state canals, Miami division,	290
241	97.	Sandy creek canal,	60
241	98.	Portage summit canal,	75
			$4146\frac{1}{8}$
		Deduct for so much rail road included at articles 59, 62, 79, 80, 81,	$183\frac{1}{2}$
		Total of artificial navigation,	$3962\frac{5}{8}$

NATURAL NAVIGATION.

93	New-York harbour to Rariton bay,	35
100	Rariton bay to the Passaick,	30
108	Lower Delaware river,	155
108	Lower Schuylkill river,	9
163	Frenchtown to Baltimore; bay navigation,	60

To which add:—

For all other streams; viz. Of the rivers, creeks, and bays in these five states, some of which are particularized below; there are in number about 475, affording an average natural navigation of 15 miles each. This makes, 7125

Total of natural navigation, 7414
Total of artificial navigation, $3962\frac{5}{8}$

Total of both, *Miles*, $11376\frac{5}{8}$

IN NEW-JERSEY STATE; VIZ.

The Hackinsack river, rises in New-York, and passes, by a southern course, into Newark bay. It is navigable 15 miles.

Great and Little Egg Harbour rivers, rise in Gloucester and Burlington counties, and fall into Great and Little Egg Harbour bays, on the Atlantic coast. They are navigable, together, 100 miles.

Other small rivers and creeks, and the bays and sounds into which they discharge, on the east of the state, between Sandy Hook and Cape May.

Morris river, rises in Salem, and runs through Cumberland county into Delaware bay. It is navigable 30 miles.

Cohanzy river, runs also through Cumberland county, into the bay, and is navigable 25 miles.

Creeks, tributary to the River Delaware, on the west border of New-Jersey, from the bay upwards.

IN DELAWARE STATE; VIZ.

Christiana creek, runs from Pennsylvania, into the north of the state, and after being joined by the Brandywine, falls into the Delaware river. It is navigable 13 miles.

Creeks, falling into the Delaware river and bay, between the Christiana and Cape Henlopen.

Nanticoke river, flows south-westwardly, through this state, into Maryland.

IN MARYLAND STATE; VIZ.

The Elk, the Sassafras, the Chester, the Choptank, the Nanticoke, the Wycomico, the Pocomoke, and other streams, tributary to Chesapeake bay, from the Eastern shore.

The Patuxent river, rises west of Baltimore, and falls into the Chesapeake, between Drum and Cedar points. It is navigable 60 miles.

The Severn, the Patapsco, and other short streams and bays, on the west of the Chesapeake.

Rivers and creeks, tributary to the Potomac, on the east and the north-east.

IN PENNSYLVANIA STATE; VIZ.

Confluents of the Delaware river, from the west and northwest; they are many, but streams of inferior magnitude in general, except those already noticed.

Confluents of the Susquehanna; from Tioga point to Sunbury, the Towanda, the Wyalusing, the Tunkhannock, the Lackawannock, Fishing creek, and some others, are mountain streams of short natural navigation.

West branch, Susquehanna, receives some considerable streams, as the Sinnemahoning, the Bald Eagle, Pine creek, Lycoming, the Loyalsock, and others; partly navigable.

The Juniata branch, receives the Frankstown, which is considerable, and many streams of limited navigation.

Creeks, falling in below the mouth of Juniata.

The Pennsylvania confluents of the Potomac river; these are not considerable.

Confluents of the Alleghany river; these are very considerable, as the Kiskimenetas, French creek, Clarion river, Red Bank, Mahoning, and others; affording much natural navigation.

Confluents of the Monongahela river, in Pennsylvania; the Youghioghany, and some minor streams.

IN OHIO STATE; VIZ.

The Great Miami river, navigable to Dayton, in Montgomery county.

Its confluents; the White water, South-west branch, Mad river, and others.

Little Miami river, meanders 100 miles, between its main source in Greene county, and its mouth at six miles above Cincinnati, on the Ohio: it is precipitous, but receives a branch from the east, and several small streams, partly navigable.

Scioto river, navigable up to Columbus, where it receives the Whetstone river.

Other confluents of the Scioto; the Big Belly, the Walnut, the Alum, the Darby, the Deer, the Paint, the Salt.

The Hockhocking river, rises in Fairfield county, and is navigable 70 miles from its mouth, at Troy.

Whitewoman's river, formed by the junction of the Owl and the Mohegan, unites with Killbuck creek, at 5 miles above Cochocton, and forms that branch of the Muskingum.

Tuscarawas river; by this and the Whitewoman's uniting, at Cochocton, the Muskingum river is formed.

The Muskingum, is navigable from its mouth, at Marietta, up to Cochocton; a natural obstruction, at Zanesville, having been overcome by a lock improvement at that place.

The principal tributaries of the Muskingum, are navigable at high water, each 40 or 50 miles.

Big Beaver river, has its source in this state, partly; its mouth in Pennsylvania.

The Sandusky river and bay, the Huron, the Vermillion, the Black, the Rocky, the Cuyahoga, the Chagrin, the Grand, the Ashtabula; these discharge into Lake Erie.

PORT AND CITY OF PHILADELPHIA.

As a companion to the *Note* inserted upon the active state of ship-building in the port of New-York, this note serves to record, that, in the ship yards on the Delaware, there are at this time constructing, more than 10,500 tons of shipping, which includes a man of war of the largest size.

But the CITY itself, though not now claiming, as to commerce, to be ranked as the prime emporium of the Union, is still possessed of incidents of high, if not higher grade, for the subject of a NOTE; as, for instance, the journals announce to the public about fifty courses of scientific lectures, proposed to be delivered in the city, in the approaching winter; including nine courses at the university.

Besides the University of Pennsylvania, as of old, relative to which, it may be remarked, that a more efficient organization in the cause of academical learning, than of late years, is in contemplation by the trustees,—besides this university, the city of Philadelphia now cherishes other institutions, which have their standing professors, and lecturers on science and the arts; *law, commerce,* and the *mechanical operations* inclusive.

1828.

If the Pennsylvania capital be not, at the present day, to be ranked as No. 1, in foreign and domestic commerce, yet she has the virtue and the glory of maintaining a no little conspicuous eminence in another point of view: in brief, she still is the DISTINGUISHED CITY; and likely long to continue so, in her splendid institutions of beneficence, literature, science, and the arts, and especially, not omitting those of elementary character, in favour of the multitude of her citizen sons and daughters, most needing elementary aids and primary instruction.

By the *State*, the sums expended, in various improvements, apart from public education, from the year 1791, to the year 1828, have been stated, as follows;—

Schuylkill and Susquehannna rivers, Schuylkill and Delaware,	$ 440,000
Conewago, east and west,	220,000
Chesapeake and Delaware; old canal,	100,000
Ditto ditto. new canal,	2,028,600
Schuylkill navigation,	2,490,176
Lehigh navigation, exclusive of purchases of land, stocks, &c.	1,100,719
Union canal,	1,600,000
Lackawaxen canal and rail road,	440,000
State canals and railways, to the 1st July, 1828,	2,160,000
Legislative appropriations for clearing rivers, erecting piers, harbours, &c. and private expenditures,	440,000
	$11,019,495
102 turnpike roads, extending 2380 miles,	8,431,059
49 bridges, constructed by companies,	2,560,000
Total, expended on roads, bridges, and inland navigation, from 1791, to 1st July, 1828,	$22,010,554

To which may be added, by anticipation, 8 or 10 millions, to complete the state canal and railway now in hand.

But, as to the coasting trade of Philadelphia, it appears by an official report made to the chamber of commerce, that the same, for the year 1827, comprising—

1. The value of vessels and their cargoes, regularly employed in the said trade alone, has amounted to, - - - - - $27,895,000
2. The value of what was carried on in transport vessels, estimated at, - - - - 20,000,000

Amount in total, for 1827, - - - $47,895,000

Whereof, 2,090,000 dollars employed in the coal trade.

And it may here be noticed, that the *Port* is about to receive an improvement of vast universal importance, in the erection of a breakwater, at the entrance of the Delaware, on a comprehensive scale; the site whereof, near Cape Henlopen, is designated on the map.

1829.

The following account, given by a visitant, of the Philadelphia navy-yard, and its contents of *burthen*, is presented verbatim, as an apposite notice just at this place.

A little inflation of style in the description, it is not doubted, will generously be overlooked by the reader, in favour of what may be deemed not a little glorious to the arts of the nation; and possibly too, may be viewed as something a little curious, by many persons whom this particular piece of information may not as yet have reached.

THE NAVY YARD.

This establishment, which boasts the possession within its borders, of the largest vessel in the world, deserves a passing notice, both from its location and its value, as furnishing the nation with the means of defence, on which we pride ourselves more than on any feats of arms on land. The *Pennsylvania*, is the greatest curiosity in naval architecture of which the world can boast; and we are proud that she drew the name of the state, which we have always considered the key-stone of the federal arch. She has three decks, independent of the spar deck, and is pierced for 160 guns, but will probably carry 200. With her complement of men, which will not be less than 13 or 1400, her giant dimensions, rounding stern, and an able commander, she may literally sweep the seas ; and wo be to the enemy who attempts to cope with her single handed. There are 40 or 50 carpenters at work upon her at present, and our readers may form some idea of the work yet to be executed to render her fit for service, when we inform them that it would take 500 carpenters six months to accomplish all that is necessary. She is built after a model of Mr. Humphreys, naval architect, who was at great pains and expense in visiting the European navy yards, before he adopted the present plan. Mr. James Keen is the architect who has superintended the work generally.

In the adjoining building is the *Raritan*, a frigate of the first class, nearly completed, also built with a round stern.

In the yard is the enormous ordnance, 42 pounders, for the Pennsylvania, which lie in sullen silence, ready to have their fury roused at the call of the nation. The best bower anchor of the Pennsylvania weighs 10,171 pounds!! The yard itself, to which has lately been added extensive brick buildings, for the accommodation of the various artisans employed, is in excellent order; the marines were undergoing an examination during our visit, and appeared to advantage; their muskets were as neat as if just from the mint. In the stream lies the Cyane, which has passed through the hands of three European nations, and finally, through the agency of Commodore Stewart, came in our possession. She was originally built in Denmark, from which nation she was captured by the French, who again lost her to the English; the well known engagement where Commodore Stewart captured the Levant in her company, which vessel, however, escaped, placed her on the list of American vessels. She is to be hauled up and repaired, her upper deck taken off, and converted into a single decked sloop of war. Farther out lies the Sea Gull, celebrated for her expedition against the pirates, under Commodore Porter. She is now a receiving vessel, being past active service. There are few places more worthy of being visited by strangers than our Navy Yard; and those who make the proper application, may be assured of a polite reception, either from Commodore Bainbridge or his officers.

There is a rumour in circulation, and it rests apparently on good foundation, that a compliment of no mean character, and curious enough to be the subject of reflection, is about being paid to the United States in her maritime and naval capacity. It is no less a compliment, than that of a deputation from the third naval power of Europe, of a certain number of officers, for the purpose of seeing some service, on board our ships of war, and, together with a knowledge of the mode of ship building as practised by us, to acquire that of our mode of discipline, and our tactics.

This is an incident that may well be placed on the historic page, along side of the well known anecdote of the first Czar Peter of Russia, with various additional circumstances of curiosity, as food for reflection.

VIRGINIA NAVIGATION.

N.—From Washington city, down the Potomac river, and down Chesapeake bay, to Hampton roads; thence up James river, to Bermuda hundred, or City Point; thus far there being a passage for ships; and thence, 20 miles, up to Richmond, a sloop navigation.

Distance from Washington, *Miles*, 310

M.—From City Point, on James river, up the Appomatox, 10 miles, to Fisher's bar, above Broadway's, and thence, by canal, round the falls, to five or six miles above Petersburg; from whence, up the river channel improved, to Farmville, in Prince Edward county.

Distance, by the meanders, *Miles*, 110

No. 99.

APPOMATOX RIVER CANALS.

These useful works were, in part, long since executed by the Appomatox company of Virginia.

By canal and other improvements in connexion, a boat navigation on the Upper Appomatox is laid open to the distance specified. The amount of capital expended on the works of the Upper Appomatox, down to the 31st August, 1825, was 88,416 dollars; and since then, 9,929 dollars have been added; making 98,345 dollars to the 31st August, 1827. In 1825, the tolls and water rents amounted to 5,497 dollars, but owing to accidental causes, and particularly the carrying away of a large aqueduct by a freshet, the company's income during the last two years has been very small.

In January 1825, a "Lower Appomatox company" was organized, and great improvements have since then been effected in the navigation below Petersburg. The company's object, in the undertaking, was to enable vessels, drawing 7 feet of water, to come up to this town.

The obstructions, extending about 5 miles, consisted in accumulations of sand, gradually deposited; and the remedy was, to straighten the channel, by cuts through several of the shoals, and to contract and deepen it, by means of jetties, made of fascines, united by wattles, and loaded with alternate courses of gravel.

The probable expense of this undertaking, was estimated at 28,500 dollars, exclusive of superintendence and contingencies, making a considerable addition. A final report is expected.

A.—From a point of the Appomatox river, below Little Goose creek, by canal, down the valley, and across to Deep creek, at 1½ mile above its junction with James river, in Powhatan county.   Distance, *Miles*, 19

No. 100.

THE POWHATAN CANAL.

This route of connexion between the Upper Appomatox and James river, which may be considered as a continuation of the line between the Roanoke and the Appomatox, here below specified, has been surveyed, by direction of the state legislature; and, provided circumstances can be brought to favour the execution of the "Junction canal," then, it is likely, this proposed work will also be gone into.

The distance above stated, includes a tunnel of 911 yards, to be opened through the dividing ridge; also, of deep cutting,

1192 yards on the Appomatox side,
1612 yards on the James river side.

Descent from summit level, 32 feet to the Appomatox, 72½ feet to Deep creek, by the valley of Hudsmouth creek, making 104½ feet of lockage. The engineer's estimate of cost is 258,853 dollars.

A.—From a point on James river, south side, at or near Bosher's mill dam, by canal, down to the town of Manchester, and thence to the tide water of the river.
    Distance, *Miles*, 10

No. 101.
THE MANCHESTER CANAL.

In pursuance of a resolution of the legislature, 14th February, 1825, a survey of the ground for this projected work has been made. The object of it, principally, is to facilitate the coal trade; the plan suggested, being, to enable the coal boats to proceed to a point of the river below the falls, and there, with the aid of machinery, to deliver their lading of coal at once into sea or bay vessels.

The engineer's report states, that, the canal as proposed, may be brought into a basin immediately above the town of Manchester, at an expense of 218,479 dollars, and thence be continued, as far as the river bank; thus,

By means of 11 locks, to overcome 91 feet of fall, cost, $81,900
Excavation of intermediate basin, - - - - 6,000

making a total cost of 306,379 dollars, for the canal down to the river bank, which, at this place, is about 18 feet above the surface of the water, and to which is to be applied such mechanical means as will effect the transshipment from boat to vessel. The estimate is framed on a canal 30 feet wide, 3½ deep, with a bank of 10 feet wide, raised 2 feet above the water surface; the locks 76 feet long, 10½ feet wide in the clear.

NOTE.

It has been proposed to construct a rail road, to run from an intermediate point between the coal pits of Beverly Randolph, and Nicholas Mills, Chesterfield county, to tide water opposite Rockett's, in the city of Richmond.

A.—From the mouth of Buffalo river, a little above Farmville, by canal, up the Buffalo valley, and across the dividing ridge, to the Little Roanoke river; down the valley whereof to the River Staunton. Distance, by canal, or by canal and stream improvement together, *Miles*, 30

No. 102.
APPOMATOX AND ROANOKE;—OR JUNCTION CANAL.

This proposed connexion between the Appomatox and the Roanoke or Staunton river, has been styled "The Junction canal;" and has been a favourite project, in the view of its leading a considerable trade to Richmond and to Petersburg. But, it is now thought, that the route of the Roanoke river and Dismal swamp canal, after the improvements in progress on these latter shall be finished, will be pretty generally preferred, and will lead the trade under consideration, consequently, to Norfolk; and a recent re-examination of the ground by the state engineer, seems to have decided that a thorough water communication between the Appomatox and the Staunton, as above specified, would be a work of greater expense, than any prospects of advantage, under present circumstances, can justify.

A good road of 8 miles, across the ridge, is to be established; and the water improvements of the Junction company, will, for the present, be confined to the rendering the Buffalo river navigable up from its mouth, a distance of 18 or 19 miles, upon the sluicing principle, by jetties and falling gates.

NOTE.

A rail road is proposed to be constructed by the corporation of Petersburg, between that town and the Roanoke river; and a survey for the same is on foot.

M.—From tide water, at the foot of Richmond falls, by canal, and by the stream of James river, rendered boatable by various improvements, up to Covington, at the mouth of Dunlap's creek, Jackson's river. Distance, by the river course, *Miles*, 257½

No. 103.

JAMES RIVER CANALS.

The navigation improvements effected up this stream prior to the execution of the Maiden's Adventure falls canal, as inserted in the article next below, are thus described, viz.—

The river is navigable for vessels of 125 tons, to Rocket's landing, a little below Richmond. At the city, there are 12 locks, overcoming an ascent of 80 feet, and connecting the tide water with a basin on Shockoe hill.

From this basin, proceeds a canal of 25 feet wide and 3 feet deep, for 2½ miles, where it enters the stream; at 3 miles farther, are 3 locks, overcoming an ascent of 34 feet, and a short canal leading to Westham, at the upper end of Great Falls.

These works, and certain improvements in the bed of the

river above this place, as far up as Lynchburg, to facilitate a boat navigation of about 12 inches draft of water, were executed many years ago, by the old James river company, chartered in the year 1784.

It is now proposed, to extend in distance as far up as Covington, at the mouth of Dunlap's creek, Jackson's river, and to augment considerably, the existing improvements on the stream navigation, by means of a series of locks and dams, and to add thereto the advantages of steam-power; that is to say, it is proposed to adapt the improvements to this mode of navigation; which may be introduced both upon this river and upon the Kanhaway, with prospects of great advantages accruing from it. On this subject, as also on that of *sluice navigation*, the engineer of the state, who very recently made a survey of the whole line, has introduced into his report, the striking remarks, and useful systematic calculations, which are here transcribed. He says,—

"I should say but little on the subject, if I had to make a comparison between the navigation of rivers by boats managed by men, and that of canals with boats propelled by horses. Experience has long since decided the question in favour of canals; and the principal objection to the improving of the beds of rivers, has always been the want of a suitable propelling power. But the introduction of a new agent, powerful and locomotive, will lead me to consider the various modes of improvement, under a different point of view.

In this age of discovery, the application of steam as a moving power, has produced a revolution in the mechanical arts. To this powerful agent we owe the advantage of a convenient, expeditious, and safe mode of navigation: but its application, as yet, has been confined to deep and comparatively still waters. Of late, however, some attention has been given to its introduction in the various systems of internal improvements. On the Susquehanna, experiments have recently been made to ascertain the practicability of applying the steam-engine to sluice navigation. A steam-boat (the Codorus) has ascended the Susquehanna up to the mouth of the Chenango. Of the capability of steamboats to ascend a river, there could have been no doubt: for, the question being reduced to this simple statement, if a steamboat would move in still water at the rate of 10 miles an hour, for instance, could it stem a current of 4, 5 or 6 miles an hour, and how fast would it do it? the answer could not be doubtful. The possibility of ascending a stream is not, therefore, the principal question to be investigated; but, rather, whether the application of steam-power to sluice navigation will, in all cases, be attended with real benefit; and also, whether it could, advantageously, be introduced on a river improved by locks and dams.

As to canals, experience has taught, that steam is not easily applicable to their navigation, and that it would require that they should be made of dimensions and in a manner different from their usual construction; and also on a more expensive plan.

The principal aim of all the improvements in navigation, is to obtain the most advantageous application of the most economical propelling power: and the chief advantage of a canal, consists in the facility of using horses in the towing of boats, which cannot be employed in sluice navigation, and are seldom advantageously so in lock and dam navigation: the power of a horse being equal to that of at least six men, and much cheaper, this circumstance alone would make canal transportation a great deal less expensive than the navigation of a river. But, if steam could be used as a propelling power, it is obvious that a lock and dam improvement might be advanced towards an equality with a canal. It is this important question that I now purpose to investigate. As the suggestion is of recent date, experience has not yet furnished precedents from which to draw positive deductions: it is necessary, therefore, to recur for information, on this head, to the very fundamental principles and data on which it depends, and to proceed in this investigation with cautious steps.

INTRODUCTORY REMARKS ON THE USE OF STEAM IN NAVIGATION.

The most advantageous way of applying steam-boats to the transportation of produce in open waters, is evidently in towing lighters: the propelling boat in this way draws less water; and the whole train experiences less resistance, than if all the load was collected in the leader. Of the possibility of using steam-boats in this way, there never could have been any doubt. They have been employed for some years past on the Savannah river, on the Cayuga lake, on Lake Champlain, on the Hudson, and probably on other waters. The only inquiry to be made is relative to their convenience and expense.

Steam-boats of ten horse power may be made of such dimensions as not to require locks of an inconvenient size. I suppose that they might easily be made to pass through a width of 14 feet, which would not be too great for locks made through dams. This, or even a smaller size of steam-boats, appears eligible, not only as regards the dimensions of locks, but for other reasons which I will advert to in the sequel.

I will, therefore, make all my calculations for a boat of this capacity. The process would be the same for other dimensions.

The price of transportation by steam-boats of all sizes, in open waters, (that is, without locks,) seems to be established generally at about one dollar per ton per hundred miles. On the Hudson, Mississippi, and other waters, this is said to be very nearly the rate of freight: the velocity of the boats used, averages about eight miles an hour. This speed is far from being the most advantageous in the transportation of produce or merchandise; and it is probable that it is assumed for the accommodation of travellers. But, here, the subject of inquiry being the carriage of produce, it is proper to determine what should be the speed adopted, and how it would affect the price of transportation.

When a vessel moves in a fluid, it experiences from it a *resistance* which is well known to be *proportional to the square of the velocity;* and consequently, since the propelling power must be increased in proportion to the resistance, it follows, that it would require a four-fold power to move a boat through water with a two-fold velocity; a nine-fold power for a three-fold velocity, &c.; that is, *the propelling power must be increased in proportion to the square of the velocity intended.*

Hence, if two equally loaded boats perform the same trip, one with a velocity of 8 miles, and the other with a velocity of 4 miles an hour, the former will require four times the propelling power of the latter; and, because it will perform two trips while the other makes but one, the expense of its moving power will be double that of the slower boat, and this expense must of course be paid by the freight.

In the same way, if the speed of the first boat was accelerated to 12 miles, the propelling power must be nine times as great; but, on the other hand, performing three trips during the same time, its expense would be three times as great, and so on for any rate of velocity.

From this it must be concluded, that *the expense of a propelling power to move a loaded boat is in direct proportion to the velocity given;* or, in other words, *the expense of transporting freight is proportional to the velocity with which it is carried.*

An augmentation of speed may be obtained, either by an increase of power, or by a proportional reduction of weight: but it does not quite follow, that the actual quantity of freight carried would always be exactly in the inverse ratio of the speed of transportation; that is, that exactly half the freight, for instance, would be transported by the same power with double the velocity: in all cases, part of the power is lost in moving the boat and engine (if steam is used) and other things, whose weight must be deducted to obtain the *useful effect* produced by the propelling power; by which deduction, the ratio of the freights corresponding to different velocities is altered to the still greater disadvantage of rapid motion. All these conclusions are verified by daily experience, and instinctively applied to transportation.

The useful effect of a propelling power is, in general, estimated by the product of the freight carried multiplied by the distance to which it is transported in a certain unit of time. The measure of the power itself is usually estimated by the height to which it is capable of raising a certain weight in a certain time. Thus, in steam-engines, whose power is generally compared to that of horses, the horse power is most commonly estimated to be equal to 33,000lbs. raised one foot in one minute; or, in another way, 150lbs. raised 2½ miles in one hour. According to this standard, and the foregoing remarks, the freight transported by a steam-boat of 10 horse power at different velocities, would be as follows:—

Velocity in miles.	Useful tons moved.	Useful effect in tons moved 1 mile.
2	400	800
2½	255	638
3	175	525
3½	127	445
4	95	380
5	58	290
6	38	228
8	18	144
10	9	90

The numbers in the second column do not include the weight of the apparatus: it has been deducted from the actual freight which would be moved, if the engine was stationary and had not to transport its own weight.

This table shows how much less is to be expected from steam-boats moving with a great velocity, than from slower rates. These important results, which are not generally duly appreciated, apply to any other kind of propelling power.

In this, consists the chief disadvantage of sluice navigation; for, if a current run through a sluice at the rate of 5 miles an hour, for instance, it must be stemmed by a power capable of a velocity of at least 6 miles an hour; so that the ascending boat is actually in the same situation as if it moved at that last rate, and consequently is not capable of carrying more than 38 tons, as shown in the table, if propelled by a 10 horse power; or 3.8

tons by one horse power; or, at the highest estimate, 1 ton if moved by 3 men; and, with that weight, it advances only one mile an hour through the sluice; so that, though there may be many long ponds of smooth water, the intervening of such sluices forbids large loads to be carried on them.

The daily expense of a steam-boat of 10 horse power may be estimated as follows :—

30 per cent. on the cost of the boat and engine, valued at $3,500, for interest, decrease of value, hazard, renewals and repairs, allowing only 300 working days,	$3 50
For captain,	3 00
Engineer,	2 00
Two hands,	1 00
Fuel, 1½ cord of wood per day of 12½ hours, or from 15 to 20 bushels of coal,	3 00
Total for working each day,	$12 50

Which, since the boat would perform 100 miles in a day, and carry 18 tons, would be about 70 cents per ton per 100 miles.

To this must be added the expense occasioned by delays, stoppages, loading and unloading, which depend on many uncertain circumstances, and on the distance of uninterrupted transportation. Supposing the time lost by these causes to be about one-half the time of travelling, which I think very ample, 35 cents per ton must be added to the above, which will give $1 05 cents for the expense of transporting one ton a hundred miles on slack and open waters. Indeed, some deduction should be made for some fuel saved while the boat is stopped for any length of time; but it is better to err on the safe side. This result agrees nearly with the rate of freight above stated; it would be still less for boats of greater burden, on which the expense of attendance does not increase in proportion to the size.

Having now established the price of transportation in a boat moving at the rate of 8 miles an hour, it is proper to inquire how much it will be reduced by lower rates of velocity.

The expense of delays, stoppages, &c. will evidently be less in proportion, when the boat moves slower and carries much freight; but my object being to make a safe estimate, I will still continue to state it at 35 cents per ton per 100 miles.

The expense of transportation alone, being inversely, as the quantity of freight transported during the same time, may be easily calculated by dividing the expense per hour, by the useful effect expressed as above, in tons transported one mile in an hour. The cost of the hour is $1 for the steam-boat; and may be estimated for each lighter and the man in it, at 8 cents. Each lighter is supposed to carry from 25 to 30 tons.

The following table exhibits the cost of transportation per ton per 100 miles for different rates of velocity.

Velocities in miles per hour.	Useful effect in tons moved one mile in one hour.	Number of lighters.	Expense of transportation per ton per 100 miles.	Do. with the addition of 35 cents per ton per 100 miles allowed for delays, stoppage, &c.
8	144	0	70 cents.	105 cents.
6	228	1	47 "	82 "
5	290	2	40 "	75 "
4	380	3	33 "	68 "
3½	445	5	31 "	66 "
3	525	7	30 "	65 "
2½	638	10	28 "	63 "
2	800	15	28 "	63 "

This table shows that much is gained by reducing the velocity to 3½ or 4 miles an hour; but a smaller speed, when the load is distributed among lighters, does not seem so advantageous: a train of 7, 10, or 15 lighters, would add more to the incumbrance than to the profit.

The expense of transportation here exhibited, would be still less if the distance travelled without interruption was greater, and the trade well regulated; for then, lighters might be loading while the steam-boat would perform a trip, and be ready to be taken in tow upon its arrival at each place. By this means, the sum of 35 cents per ton allowed for delays, stoppages, loading, and unloading, would be greatly diminished.

I do not think that I have underrated the expense of the steamboat and lighters; but, even if I had, from the last remark it is obvious, that much might yet be gained by judicious management.

The most eligible degree of speed will of course depend on the nature and quantity of the trade; within the limits, however, of 3½ and 8 miles an hour, which seem to be fixed by the preceding table.

The size of the steam-boat itself must depend on the trade, the distance of the extreme points, &c. Large steam-boats would, in proportion, be less expensive; but, unless plying between two large and commercial places, they could not make a load so easily. On this account small boats suit best on a river where the trade is not concentrated, as is the case on James river.

In a system of locks and dams, the size of the locks is another consideration which advises smaller dimensions. Boats of moderate size require, besides, less capital, and are on this account more likely to be preferred. I have supposed that boats of 10 horse power would be used; they would, I think, be of a very eligible size; smaller ones would likewise be advantageous, especially in the beginning of this system of navigation.

Having obtained these preliminary data relative to open and slackwater, I will proceed to apply them in the first place to

SLUICE NAVIGATION.

In the infancy of a country, the first improvement in navigation which suggests itself, is that of the natural bed of rivers, by clearing their channel and opening sluices through their shoals. So far as this goes to remove obstructions, and to enable small boats, under the management of about 3 or 4 men, with a load of a few tons, to move down the stream, and to return with a light load, it is attended with benefit; and, with all its imperfections, this navigation is even preferable to a road. But, beyond this degree, I think that it is an error, on a rapid river, to incur an additional expense for the enlargement of sluices; for, the strength of the current increasing with the size of the sluice, and moreover, the power necessary to move a larger boat increasing likewise with its dimensions, a proportional number of hands is requisite in the boat, and consequently, nothing is gained either in point of time or power. It generally happens, therefore, that when a river has much fall, the increased expense of its numerous sluices soon proves disproportionate to the result obtained; and that, after many fruitless attempts, this kind of navigation is abandoned, and a more perfect improvement resorted to.

Sluice navigation has ever been objected to, not only on account of its uncertainty and danger, but also of the impracticability of applying to it a cheap and uniform power. But, what I conceive to be its greatest defect, is the waste of power, of whatever nature it may be, which it necessarily occasions.

In ascending a sluice, a boat must be propelled with a power capable of giving to it a velocity superior to that of the current; and consequently, though its progress is slow, the power exerted is exactly the same as that which would give to the boat, in still water, a velocity equal to that of the current in the sluice, added to the actual speed with which the boat stems it. The propelling power, according to what has been said before, must then be proportional to the square of this *virtual* or *relative* velocity of the boat; or else, if, as is usually the case, the power remains the same, the weight moved must be reduced in the same rapid ratio; and indeed to even a much lower rate, when the power of men is used; for it is well known that this power, like the strength of animals, decreases rapidly when the speed, whether *real* or *virtual*, is increased. In going up, therefore, on account of the sluices to be stemmed, only very light loads can be transported, and but little useful effect is produced. In going down the stream, on the contrary, rapid sluices add to the danger of navigation, without increasing the useful effect, since prudence forbids large loads, which, besides, would lessen the speed in the ponds of still water, for which the load must then be calculated.

These remarks apply likewise to steam navigation. A current running at the rate of 5 miles an hour, for instance, may be stemmed by a steam-boat capable of a velocity of 8 miles an hour; but then, though the actual velocity of the boat is only 3 miles an hour, its load must be suited to its *virtual* velocity of 8 miles an hour; and consequently, the useful effect of a 10 horse power will be, according to the above table, 18 tons; which being moved only 3 miles an hour, will be the same as 54 tons moved 1 mile; and the expense for the distance in which this current has to be stemmed, will be to that through still water, as the useful effect, 144, of the same steam-boat, moving 8 miles an hour in slackwater, is to 54; that is, almost three times as great. On a river, therefore, which has a rapid fall, the multiplied delays resulting from the current in sluices, and the consequent diminution of useful effect, would materially increase the expense of steam navigation in ascending; while, on the other hand, the frequent and dangerous rapidity of the current in descending, would so often forbid the operation of steam as to render it an almost useless agent.

But, on a sluggish river, which has but few rapids improved by sluices, though the current of the sluices would, for the above reasons, prevent the carrying of large loads, still this would in part be compensated by a degree of speed, which would be but little affected by the occasional check of a few sluices. On such a river also, the operation of steam would so seldom be interrupted in descending, that it would be found an efficient and economical agent.

The cost of the improvement of a river of this nature by sluices, would be inconsiderable when compared to that of a canal; and might, frequently too, be much cheaper and otherwise more expedient than a lock and dam navigation.

Of this kind is, I think, *the Kanhaway river;* and it was chiefly in reference to it, that I have been induced to make the preceding remarks. I have heard the opinion expressed, that the improvement had rather injured than benefited the navigation; and, even that steam-boats would not answer *on the Kanhaway.*

From what I have said above, it will appear, that I do not think the making of large sluices an advantage, so long as men are employed as the propelling power; and especially with large, heavy, and unmanageable boats, as those used on the Kanhaway: in coming up the sluices, the crew of the boat has to give to it a virtual velocity, which, as remarked just above, lessens the useful effect in a rapid ratio; and, though there may be much still water, the load must, notwithstanding, be suited to the swiftness of the sluices; and but little can be transported; and here, besides, we have not, as with steam, the advantage of speed in the ponds, because the day's work of men is limited, and is rapidly shortened by an accelerated muscular action.

At high water, when the current is swift, these large boats must be very difficult, and I may say, impossible to push up; for then, a virtual velocity would be requisite, which men cannot give.

In descending, on the contrary, the current impels the boat forward with a rapidity, which takes the control of its motion from the men: and a false manœuvre, a change of direction of the current, produced by a casual circumstance, may prove fatal to the cargo.

I, therefore, am ready to admit, that, if to be navigated by boats propelled by oars or poles, the Kanhaway river would have been nearly as useful, by merely clearing out the principal obstructions; but, with the use of light steam-boats obeying readily the rudder, the advantages obtained will, I think, be considerable.

Only one of the sluices was as swift as $4\frac{1}{2}$ miles an hour when I measured their current (there being then a slight rise in the river.) How then can it be doubted, that steam-boats capable of a velocity of ten miles an hour could stem them; and, if they could, why should they not answer as good a purpose on that river as they do on others? Steam-boats have ascended the Susquehanna, which is a more rapid river, at the rate of from four to five miles an hour, at different stages of its waters; and some benefits are expected from their use in navigating it. But the Kanhaway offers by far greater advantages. It has little fall; the sluices are but few; the ponds of still water very long; hence a steam-boat might move up generally at the rate of eight miles an hour, in the long ponds of still water of this river, and though occasionally its velocity would be reduced to four or five miles an hour at a sluice, it would be but for a short distance; and, therefore, if the cost of transportation would be (as calculated above, and also established by facts,) $1 05 per ton per 100 miles, for a velocity of 8 miles an hour, I question much whether the sluices would raise it to as much as $1 25.

All this, of course, applies to a low stage of the river. In times of floods, the steam-boats would have to encounter a continuous current. But, the time of these swells constitutes but a small proportion of the year; and, when they are somewhat considerable, the present ascending navigation is at an end; whereas, steam-boats might yet ascend at the rate of three or four miles an hour, and bring freight for perhaps $2 or $2 50 a ton, from Point Pleasant to Charlestown.

In going down, the boats would move in the ponds of still water at the rate of four or five miles an hour, according to their load; in coming to sluices, they would check their steam and obey the current. The danger of being wrecked would easily be guarded against with a power both so active and perfectly under control, and which is capable of an almost instantaneous retrograde motion. The danger would likewise be much lessened by the circumstance that the leader and lighters might be made to draw but 20 or 24 inches of water, if not less. A steam-boat of 25 tons is now building at Philadelphia, which will have a draught of only $2\frac{1}{2}$ feet.

In conclusion, I do not think that the improvement of the Kanhaway navigation will be found by far as valuable, until steam-boats be introduced on it; and then, I am convinced, that, coal and labour being cheap there, freight, after a short time, will be transported at very nearly the above average rate of one dollar per ton per hundred miles: at present it is only the descending navigation which is facilitated ; but, in connexion with the great scheme of communication, we must look to the ascending trade on that river.

As regards the *James river*, its fall is much greater than that of the Great Kanhaway. It is only in the lower part, and in short sections, that a sluice improvement might be made, of such proportions as would facilitate the passage of steam-boats. But, it may be doubted whether the same fall might not be overcome at less expense by dams, than by well regulated and large sluices. The sluice at *Red-house Shoal*, on the Kanhaway, for example, which is intended to regulate a fall of not quite four feet, will certainly have cost much more than would on James river a dam to raise the water four feet, with a lock in it.

James river, moreover, is frequently studded with rocks, among which the path of boats is very devious and difficult : it would be impossible for a light steam-boat, animated with a velocity of eight or ten miles an hour, or for the same boat moving at a reduced speed, but with several lighters in tow, to pursue, without danger, these crooked channels. The necessity of straightening them, and making them, as well as the sluices, of enlarged dimensions to suit steam-boats, would render this a very expensive improvement: and it may be questioned, besides, whether it would be expedient to make a navigation exclusively applicable to steam-boats.

Dams will in general furnish, at less expense, a proper depth of water over the obstructions of the natural bed; by their means a slackwater navigation is obtained; the trade is made more constant and regular; the delays may be more correctly estimated, and are the same, whether in ascending or descending; and the time of arrivals may be anticipated with some degree of certainty.

An improvement by sluices, on the contrary, produces an inequality between the ascending and descending trade, which may frequently be a great inconvenience. The delays are uncertain; and, in a common rise of the river, when dams check the current, sluices, on the contrary, increase it: the loss of time or waste of power in ascending becomes considerable; and the descending navigation is attended with greater danger.

The delay experienced at each dam, to pass through its lock, is often represented as an objection to the lock and dam system of improvement; but the delay produced by sluices is still greater: in a sluice, for instance, a quarter of a mile in length and three feet deep, having a fall of four feet, the current would be at the rate of about four miles an hour: a steam-boat, moving at the rate of eight miles an hour, would consequently stem it with a velocity of four miles; and, therefore, it would lose in the sluice nearly four minutes: a lock of four feet lift would hardly stop a boat this length of time. But, if the load be supposed to be increased, and consequently the speed of the boat lessened, its progress in ascending the sluice will be more and more retarded, until the load being increased to such a degree that it would reduce the speed to four miles an hour, the boat would actually be unable to move up the sluice. Whereas, under the same circumstances, it would not only proceed on through the lock of a dam, but the velocity of four miles an hour would continue to be the most advantageous, as will be shown below.

Hence, sluice navigation would only suit light and swift ascending boats capable of but little useful effect; when, on the contrary, heavy loaded boats, *which might be altogether stopped by sluices*, would not only move with facility on a river improved by locks and dams, but actually prove *much more profitable* than lighter ones.

It appears, consequently, that the relative inferiority of sluice navigation, when compared to a lock and dam improvement, would be about the same after the introduction of steam-boats, as it was before; and, in fact, the same propelling power having been used heretofore in both cases, and the application of the new power proposed being likewise the same for both improvements, there does not appear any reason, why their relative merits should be changed by it; and consequently, experience would decide now, as formerly, in favour of locks and dams.

LOCK AND DAM NAVIGATION.

The principal objection to this mode of navigation has ever been the expensiveness and inefficiency of the only propelling power which was applied to it; that of men, instead of horses which were used on canals. The first subject of inquiry appears, therefore, to be, what influence the introduction of steam in lock and dam navigation, would have on the cost of transportation.

I have already presented calculations and results applicable to navigation by steam on slackwater, with different velocities and loads. In order to extend these results to a lock and dam navigation, it is only necessary to inquire how much should be added for detention at the locks to the prices heretofore stated.

In the same view of the subject that I have taken all along, I will suppose each boat to be detained at a lock one minute per foot lift; a position which I suppose will be admitted to be quite safe: it might, perhaps, at first appear, that the necessity of raising steam after having passed a lock might add more to the delay; but the steam-boat passing first, might raise her steam while the lighters are passing.

In the preceding pages I have given the load corresponding to each rate of velocity in slackwater, and the number of lighters requisite to carry it, (each lighter being supposed to contain from 25 to 30 tons.)

The following diagram, constructed according to these data, exhibits, besides the data, the time lost at the locks for each foot lift by the whole train.

Velocity in slack-water in miles per hour.	Load in tons as before.	Number of lighters.	Leader and lighters will be detained by each foot lift, at the rate of one minute per foot lift, per boat.
2	400	15	16 minutes.
2½	255	10	11 "
3	175	7	8 "
3½	127	5	6 "
4	95	3	4 "
5	58	2	3 "
6	38	1	2 "
8	18	0	1 "

The cost of the steam-boat of ten horse power, which is supposed to be used, being $1 per hour, and that of each lighter eight cents; the expense occasioned by detention at the locks for any fall and rate of speed, may now be readily calculated, and in the same way also might the investigation be extended to steam-boats of different power.

Having established previously, that velocities less than 3½ or 4 miles an hour, would not be advantageous, I will confine myself to calculations for the rates of 4, 5, 6 and 8 miles an hour. The process of computation is sufficiently explained by the following table:

A TABLE,

Showing the cost of transportation by steam-power, of ONE TON *a distance of* ONE HUNDRED MILES, *on a river improved by locks and dams,*

FOR DIFFERENT FALLS AND RATES OF VELOCITY.

1st—FOR A VELOCITY OF FOUR MILES AN HOUR.

One steam-boat of 10 *horse power,* 3 *lighters, freight* 95 *tons, expense per hour* $1 24.

(Each foot fall per mile adds 6 2-3 hours to the transportation per hundred miles, and $8 27 to the whole expense, or 8.70 cents per ton.)

Lockage in feet per mile.	Delay per mile in minutes.	Rate to which the speed is actually reduced by the passage of locks. In miles per hour.	Cost of transportation of one ton per 100 miles.	Do. with the addition of 35 cents per ton for delays, stoppages, &c.
0	0	4	33 cents.	68 cents.
1	4	3.15	42 "	77 "
2	8	2.60	50 "	85 "
3	12	2.20	59 "	94 "
4	16	1.95	68 "	103 "
5	20	1.70	77 "	112 "
6	24	1.55	85 "	120 "
8	32	1.30	103 "	135 "
10	40	1.10	120 "	155 "

2d—FOR A VELOCITY OF FIVE MILES AN HOUR.

One steam-boat, 2 *lighters, freight* 58 *tons, expense per hour* $1 16.

(Each foot fall per mile adds 5 hours to the whole time, $5 80 to the expense, or 10 cents per ton.)

0	0	5	40 cents.	75 cents.
1	3	4	50 "	85 "
2	6	3.33	60 "	95 "
3	9	2.85	70 "	105 "
4	12	2.50	80 "	115 "
5	15	2.20	90 "	125 "
6	18	2	100 "	135 "
8	24	1.66	120 "	155 "
10	30	1.45	140 "	175 "

OF THE UNITED STATES.

3d—FOR A VELOCITY OF SIX MILES AN HOUR.

One steam-boat, 1 lighter, freight 38 tons, expense per hour $1 08

(Each foot fall per mile adds 3 1-3 hours to the time, $3 60 to the whole expense, or 9 1-2 cents per ton.)

Lockage in feet per mile.	Delay per mile in minutes.	Rate to which the speed is actually reduced by the passage of locks. In miles per hour.	Cost of transportation of one ton per 100 miles.	Do. with the addition of 35 cents per ton for delays, stoppages, &c.
0	0	6	47 cents.	82 cents.
1	2	5	57 "	92 "
2	4	4.30	66 "	101 "
3	6	3.75	76 "	111 "
4	8	3.33	85 "	120 "
5	10	3	95 "	130 "
6	12	2.75	104 "	139 "
8	16	2.30	123 "	158 "
10	20	2	142 "	177 "

4th—FOR A VELOCITY OF EIGHT MILES AN HOUR.

One steam-boat, no lighter, freight 18 tons, expense per hour $1.

(Each foot fall per mile adds 1 2-3 hour to the trip, $1 67 to the whole expense, or 9.60 cents per ton.)

0	0	8	70 cents.	105 cents.
1	1	7	80 "	115 "
2	2	6.30	89 "	124 "
3	3	5.70	99 "	134 "
4	4	5.20	108 "	143 "
5	5	4.80	118 "	153 "
6	6	4.45	128 "	163 "
8	8	3.85	147 "	182 "
10	10	3.40	166 "	201 "

This table exhibits the following results:—

1st. That *the additional expense occasioned by each foot lift per mile, may be averaged at 9½ cents per ton per hundred miles.*

2dly. That if the train travel in slackwater at the rate of 4 miles an hour, with a full load of 95 tons, its speed will be reduced to about the usual canal rate of from 2 to 2½ miles an hour, by an average lockage of 3 feet per mile, and the cost of transportation will be 94 cents per ton per hundred miles, which is very little more than transportation on a canal in the case also of a full load.

3dly. That if the velocity in still water be 5 miles an hour, it will be reduced to canal speed by a fall of 4 feet, and transportation will be increased to 115 cents per ton.

4thly. That a velocity of 6 miles an hour will be reduced to the common canal rate by a fall of about 7 feet, and the expense will then be about 149 cents.

5thly. That the fall must be more than 10 feet per mile to reduce a velocity of 8 miles an hour to the usual rate of travelling on a canal.

These are the principal conclusions necessary for the present purpose. With the preceding table, calculations may be extended to any particular modification of load, speed, or power.

CONCLUSION.

After having, pursuant to your order, considered every circumstance relative to the Independent canal, I have laid down introductory principles, and obtained data necessary to the examination of the question relative to the best mode of improving the navigation of James river: The well and long established superiority of canal navigation over that of rivers, precluded the idea of investigating the question with a view to the common mode of propelling boats; but its features are altogether changed by the introduction of steam power.

From the 3d of the preceding remarks, it appears that 95 tons may be transported 100 miles, for 94 cents per ton, on a river having a lockage of 3 feet per mile, by a steam-boat of 10 horse power, moving at the rate of 4 miles an hour in still water; whose velocity would be reduced by the lockage, to the common rate of speed on canals. The expense of transportation in a boat with full load, would be very nearly the same as on a canal.

If the steam-boat was made to move faster than 4 miles an hour, it would carry less; and consequently, the expense of transportation would be greater: this would necessarily happen if the boat did not obtain a full load; but of course, it would also be the case with boats on a canal; or rather, it would be still more disadvantageous: for with a half load, for instance, a canal boat, though it would move faster than when fully loaded, could, nevertheless, not be propelled as fast as a steam-boat carrying an equal proportion of load; for it is well known, that, on one hand, animals cannot usefully increase their speed beyond a certain degree; and that, on the other, a velocity exceeding 4 miles an hour is injurious to a canal. Hence, if we were to compare cases when small loads will be carried, we should obtain a result greatly favourable to steam power.

If, for instance, a canal boat with a back load of one-fourth of its descending freight, that is, 5 tons, would perform 100 miles in 4½ days (including a due proportion of its delay at both ends of the trip,) the cost of transportation of the 5 tons, would be in all, - - - - - - - - $13 50
Or per ton for 100 miles, - - - - 2 70

Supposing now, that a steam-boat has come down with a full load of 95 tons, and has to carry back its three lighters, (which is the most unfavourable case,) its back load, being also one-fourth of its descending freight, would consist of 24 tons; which, together with the weight of the lighters, would make a whole load of about 38 tons. With this load, a steam-boat would advance 6 miles an hour in still water, according to the table; and its velocity would be reduced to $3\frac{3}{4}$ miles an hour on a river having a fall of 3 feet per mile. The expense of the steam-boat and three lighters would be $1 24 per hour, or for $3\frac{3}{4}$ miles, (see the table.) Which is, per 100 miles for the 24 tons of freight actual-
ly transported, - - - - - - - $33 10
Or per ton, - - - - - - - 1 38
To which adding as usual 35 cents per ton for delays,
   loading, &c. the cost of transportation of a ton 100
   miles, will be - - - - - - 1 73

Which is 97 cents cheaper than on the canal. So that this conclusion may safely be adopted, that, *on a river improved by locks and dams, and which has a fall of about 3 feet per mile, transportation by steam would be cheaper than on a canal:* this will again be adverted to."

The beneficial project of an easy, safe, and expeditious communication between the waters of James river and the Great Kanhaway, as a first great step towards facilitating commercial intercourse between the eastern and western portions of the state;— a measure so obviously important to both, and essential even to the very settling of, and consequent prosperous cultivation of many of the counties beyond the Alleghany mountains, has long been a subject of deep legislative concern, and one in which the public interest was the more strongly felt, as it was not doubted there would, eventually, through this channel, be established an extensive commercial intercourse with the *states* of the west: so that, in these latter years, views of improvement have gone to the extent of suggesting the expediency, if practicable, of a *thorough water communication* by means of a canal. The difficulties, however, of the mountain pass, so far as examinations have gone to ascertain the matter, though not as yet denoting absolute impracticability, have been of a nature to suspend, for the present, any final decision upon the point. Very possibly, renewed researches, and minute explorations of the ground, may bring to light some route less difficult, for a thorough canal, than has hitherto been discovered; and in that event, it will only remain to be seen, what influence, for, or against the execution of this great Virginia project, the completion of more northerly water communications between the east and the west, may or ought to have: The engineer of the state, Mr. Crozet, observes,—

"The surveys of the first year, (of the Chesapeake and Ohio canal route) did not disclose the most advantageous and important circumstances of this route; yet three parties, or *brigades* of engineers were employed in the operation: two of these consisted of sixteen officers, the third was composed of one civil engineer and five assistants; in all, twenty-two engineers, or surveyors.

"Had the Alleghany mountains in Virginia been searched for two successive years with the same persevering diligence, and by a party as numerous, the result, perhaps, might have been as different from what is now known, as the survey made by the United States engineers, the second year, was different from their first examination. I have heard it affirmed, that there is a much lower place through the mountain, than that through which the survey was conducted; and that a sufficiency of water may be had.

"Should it be confirmed by an actual survey, that such a low place exists, and that it could be supplied with water, the connexion of James river and the Kanhaway, in point of practicability, would not yield to the projected Chesapeake and Ohio canal; for the difficulties of the ground would most probably be rather less than greater here, and the length of the canal could not differ much on either route."

The history of what has been effected, stands as follows:—

In 1819, pursuant to a resolution of the general assembly of Virginia, surveys were made, to ascertain "the best practicable communication between the waters of the James and Kanhaway rivers; viz. James river, Kanhaway river, Craig's creek, Sinking creek, Dunlap's creek, Ogley's creek, Howard's creek, Greenbriar river, and New river; also, for an independent canal along the valley of James river; and for a road, from the mouth of Dunlap's creek to the falls of the Kanhaway river."

Which, being reported, with maps and estimates, the board of public works recommended, that the same should be gone into, by sections, and completed on a scale commensurate with the objects specified. They proposed, namely,

1. An independent canal from the basin at Richmond, up the valley of James river, and of its branch, Jackson's river, to the mouth of Dunlap's creek; a distance of 250 miles.

2. A good road, from the mouth of Dunlap's creek, across the Alleghany mountain, to the Great Kanhaway river, at the foot of Great falls; a distance of 90 miles.

3. From the foot of Great falls to the mouth of this river, at Point Pleasant on the Ohio; along this distance, 94 miles, the river bed to be made navigable.

Which plan was adopted by the legislature; and in 1820, an act was passed in consequence, by the terms of which, and in virtue of an agreement with the James river company, the chartered privileges thereof were annulled, and the company became, from this period, an agent, holding in trust for the *use and benefit of the commonwealth*.

The company received authority, viz.

1. To render the Kanhaway river navigable at all seasons, for boats drawing at least 3 feet of water, from Great falls down to its junction with the Ohio.

2. To improve the navigation of James river, from tide water to Pleasant's island, by locks and navigable canals, affording at all times 3 feet depth of water, and so as to navigate boats carrying 1000 bushels of coal.

3. To make the best practicable road, from the mouth of Dunlap's creek to Great falls of the Kanhaway river, in conformity to the suggestions of the chief engineer, in his report.

4. To make independent or lateral navigable canals, from Pleasant's island to the mouth of Dunlap's creek, in conformity to the same report, as nearly as may be, affording 3 feet depth of water at all seasons.

5. To make safe and convenient branch communications from the river, at such points as will afford ample accommodation to the trade of the river.

In pursuance whereof, this series of improvements was commenced; and so much of the same has been accomplished, as is specified in the articles which here follow.

A.—From Richmond basin, by canal, up the James river valley, to the head of Maiden's Adventure falls, Goochland county. Distance, *Miles*, 30½

No. 104.
JAMES AND JACKSON'S RIVER CANAL;—MAIDEN'S ADVENTURE SECTION.

Under act of the general assembly, 17th February, 1825, the

James river company commenced this section of an entire independent or lateral canal; purposing to make such additions, in distances from place to place along the valley line, as the legislature should find it expedient to direct; and by a report of the state commissioner, 10th December, 1825, it appears, that this section was then finished throughout, and brought into use. It comprises,

>4 dams across the river,
>10 lift locks, including those in the dams,
>5 guard locks; 3 guard gates,
>5 aqueducts; 9 culverts,
>15 waste weirs,
>1 set flood gates, besides those in the weirs,
>2 foot bridges; 2 road bridges,
>34 farm bridges.

Width of the canal 40 feet. Depth of water 3½ feet. Expense 623,295 dollars.

NOTE.

Additional disbursements, to the 1st January, 1828, make the cost of this section of canal amount to 637,607 dollars; and repairs and alterations are yet needed.

A.—From the lower end of Irish falls, or Piney island, in Amherst county, by canal, along the margin of James river, up to the mouth of North branch, Rockbridge county. Distance, *Miles,* 7

No. 105.

JAMES AND JACKSON'S RIVER CANAL;—BLUE RIDGE SECTION.

This section, commenced in 1824, and which passes through a gap of the Blue ridge mountain, has been reported on as nearly finished. Fall overcome by lockage 96 feet; the locks of stone, 10½ feet wide, 76 feet long in the clear. Cost of this section about 340,000 dollars.

NOTE.

Additional disbursements, to the 1st January, 1828, make the cost of this mountain section of canal amount to 365,013 dollars. And considerable repairs and alterations are yet needed.

A.—From James river, at or near the Cow Pasture branch, up the valley of Jackson's river, to Covington, at the mouth of Dunlap's creek.   Distance, *Miles,* 24

No. 106.

JAMES AND JACKSON'S RIVER CANAL;—JACKSON'S RIVER SECTION.

Along this extreme portion of the water communication, intended to meet the Kanhaway turnpike road at Covington, the ground is very rough and difficult of improvement; so that a canal construction at this section, as was intended, has not been carried into effect. It appears, by estimate, that an independent canal to fill up these 24 miles of distance along the route, would cost upwards of 600,000 dollars. And it is now proposed to substitute, at least for the present, an improvement of the Jackson's river navigation, by the lock and dam method. Which, it is calculated, may be effected at the expense of 55,000 dollars, thus:—

In the 24 miles of distance, there is a fall of 220 feet; and the mean width of the river at such sites as would be eligible for dams is probably 225 feet; each dam suitable for which is estimated at 500 dollars, and each lock suitable for batteaux, estimated also at 500 dollars. That is, together, 1000 dollars required for every 4 miles of fall; which makes, for the whole, an expense of only 55,000 dollars.

NOTE.

In regard to filling up the whole distance between Richmond and Covington on Jackson's river, with one uninterrupted canal, as has been contemplated, the period of its accomplishment may yet be at a distance. The plan of yet improving the natural channel of James and Jackson's rivers, by means of locks and dams, it is likely will still for most of the distance be preferred. On the 17th December, 1824, however, the general assembly passed a resolution, directing an entire new survey to be made, from Maiden's Adventure falls upward, and estimates to be formed and reported; in order that a full and undoubted knowledge of local circumstances may not be wanting, for them to come to a decision as to the course most expedient to be pursued.

In consequence whereof, the state chief engineer has made an elaborate report, under date of July 1, 1826. From which report, the following particulars are extracted.

From Covington,
To Rich Patch ford

 Length by canal, 16.06 ⎱ Lockage, 191.88   Estimate.
      river, 21.06 ⎰ $585,850

To North branch,
 Length by canal, 53.99 ⎱ Lockage, 332.27
      river, 60.50 ⎰   1,363,076

To Judith's creek,
 Length by canal, 16.45 ⎱ Lockage, 76.40
      river, 16.00 ⎰   473,761

To Tye river,
 Length by canal, 43.50 ⎱
      river, 43.50 ⎰   890,000

To Seven Island falls,
 Length by canal, 37.75 ⎱ Lockage, 133.21
      river, 38.34 ⎰   594,086

To Maiden's Adventure falls,
 Length by canal, 44.41 ⎱ Lockage, 95.35
      river, 44.00 ⎰   758,999

  Allow for damages to property, and fencing,   84,228

Total estimate, for these sections, $4,750,000
To which is to be added, viz.—
For the Maiden's Adventure section, finished,   623,295
For the Blue ridge section,   -   -   -   -   340,000
For contingencies extra,   -   -   -   -   36,705

And we have,
Total probable cost, of an uninterrupted canal, from
 Richmond to Covington at the mouth of Dunlap's
 creek,   -   -   -   -   -   -   - $5,750,000

The distance being 249 miles, and this estimate allowing the dimensions of 3½ feet depth of water; 30 feet wide, generally, above the Maiden's Adventure section, which has 40 feet width. The towing paths 10 feet wide, and 2 feet above the water-surface. In some difficult places of the route, the supposed canal-width is reduced to 22 feet.

The whole continuous water-distance, to the Ohio river, including the mountain-pass, by the route surveyed, is as follows ;—

From below Richmond basin to the mouth of Dunlap's creek,   -   -   -   -   -   -   *Miles*, 251
Thence to lowest point on the dividing ridge,   -   16

       Amount carried forward,   267

OF THE UNITED STATES. 307

Amount brought forward,	267
Thence to mouth of Howard's creek, on the Greenbriar river,	12
To the mouth of the Greenbriar,	50
Down the Kanhaway to Bowyer's ferry,	46
Thence to foot of Great falls,	21
Thence to mouth of the Kanhaway at Point Pleasant on the Ohio,	94
Miles,	490

The summit of the ridge, 2478 feet above tide water level. The mouth of Dunlap's creek ascertained to be 1238 feet above tide, and 649 above the foot of Great falls of the Kanhaway. Now, supposing, in the event of a canal along this route, that a tunnel were opened through the mountain ridge, at 227 feet below the summit, it follows, that such canal, between tide water at Richmond, and Great falls of the Kanhaway, would require 3913 feet of lockage.

A lower base line, or summit level, however, which has been had in view; say at 1918 feet above tide; makes the amount of lockage to be 3267 feet; with a tunnel of 3 miles 440 yards long; an eastern deep cut of 395 yards; a western deep cut of 932 yards.

M.—From the mouth of Great Kanhaway river, at Point Pleasant, on the Ohio, by a series of lock and dam, and of sluice improvements, up the river stream, 89 miles, to Loophole shoal; whence, by turnpike road, up to Great falls; and, through Nicholas and Greenbriar counties, across to Covington, at the mouth of Dunlap's creek, Alleghany county. Distance,

By river improvements,	89
By turnpike,	99
Miles,	188

No. 107.

KANHAWAY RIVER NAVIGATION AND TURNPIKE.

The sluicing mode of improvement has been followed on the Kanhaway, as appearing to be adapted to the circumstances of the case; for, on this river, the ascent is only 108 feet in 94 miles; and, of this, for the 57 miles distance from Point Pleasant up to Charlestown, the difference of level is no more than 48 feet.

By means of sluices, the several shoals, up to the Loophole, within about 4 miles of Great falls, have in consequence frequently been overcome. It was intended, the turnpike road from Covington should terminate at the foot of Great falls, but afterward found advisable for it to be extended about 5 miles lower; that is, to 1 mile below the Loophole shoal of the river; at which point, the water improvements are, by act of the legislature, 1st March, 1826, directed to stop for the present.

The turnpike passes through a portion of very rugged difficult country; it is generally 22 feet wide, with the centre raised by a curve from each side, and sloped ditches.

The Greenbriar river is crossed over by an elegant bridge; and the Ganley river by another,* of a similar construction, but not equal in dimensions. The Greenbriar bridge, (says a report on the subject) is one of the most splendid wooden bridges ever built: it consists of

Two spans of 211 feet each, supported by 2 abutments, and a middle pier very handsomely built of hewn stone. The under part of the bridge is 25 feet above the river; each span, composed of two strong lateral frames, and with a middle one, forming between them 2 road ways, each $10\frac{1}{2}$ feet in width; the whole width of the bridge being 26 feet. The frames are connected together, at their lower part, by the cross horizontal ties which support the flooring, and at their top, by horizontal cross ties, and by the framing of the roof, which covers the whole bridge; the sides are planked over. Each one of the frames is composed of 2 ribs, or rather of a double rib, rising about 20 feet in the middle, and whose extremities are held together by a tie-beam or chord, also double, forming a slight bow of 3 feet sagitta. The double ribs and chords embrace strong upright posts, to which they are firmly bolted. The uprights are capped, the whole length of the bridge, by a strong beam, and braced by crosses halved together in the middle, with wedges at their junction, by means of which they may be stiffened when wanted. The cross horizontal ties already mentioned, are placed at top, between the caps, and at the base, between the chords or longitudinal ties of the opposite frames. On the timbers which connect the chords, rests a double floor, which is itself laid diagonally, and acts thereby as an additional horizontal brace; so that the whole bridge is carefully and firmly secured against lateral motion, so often fatal to bridges. In a word, it is built on the best principles; the architect, Mr. James Moore.

The expense of the improvements comprised in this article, is stated to be as follows;—

* Since burned down.

For the Kanhaway river works,	- - -	$ 76,503
The turnpike road,	- - -	125,692
Bridge over Ganley river,	- - -	18,400
Bridge over the Greenbriar,	- - -	19,000
Salary and contingencies,	- - -	2,381
	Total,	$241,976

The quantity of salt now manufactured at the Kanhaway salt works, above Charlestown, is computed at upwards of a million of bushels annually.

It is remarked of the turnpike, which has opened to a certain degree the communication sought after with the beautiful valley watered by the Kanhaway, and of the river navigation set of improvements, that both together have already given a great impulse to business; the valley exhibiting an activity not known before, partly in the lively trains of wagons now engaged in transporting salt to Lewisburg. The principal part, however, of the salt manufactured, descends the river as yet to Point Pleasant, in flat boats, which load from 400 to 500 barrels of 360 *lbs.* each. Horse boats also navigate the river, and it is quite probable that light steam-boats will, ere long, be introduced.

NOTE.

Additional disbursements, to the 1st of January, 1828, including part rebuilding of Ganley river bridge, make the Kanhaway river and turnpike works of this article amount to $253,414.

M.—From a point on the Potomac river, in Berkeley, or Jefferson county, along the Shenandoah valley, through the counties of Frederick, Shenandoah, Rockingham, and Augusta, by canal and river improvements, to the Lexington branch of James river, in Rockbridge county; or by way of the Lexington or North river valley, to form a junction with the Blue ridge canal, at the mouth of North river.

Distance, *Miles*. 250

No. 108.

THE SHENANDOAH CANALS.

Should the Chesapeake and Ohio canal communication, by the Potomac, be realized, as it is hoped; there will, at some period not very remote, be another efficient communication attempted, through the central counties of Virginia, from the Potomac to the waters of James river. It is the one here specified, through the Shenandoah valley, by which the most fertile district of all the state will be immeasurably benefited, in the facility of transporting its produce. The river has long since been made navigable for boats up to Port Republic, in Augusta; near which place, a fall of 50 feet was overcome by six short canals with stone locks.

A.—From the mouth of the Rivanna river at Columbia on James river, by canal, or by the stream of the Rivanna, improved after the lock and dam method, up to Moore's ford, opposite Charlottesville, Albemarle county. Distance, *Miles*, 37

No. 109.

THE RIVANNA RIVER CANALS.

The recent survey of the course of this tributary of James river, flowing through a limited but very important tract of country, has been made by the state chief engineer, with a view to improve the navigation thereof. It is proposed to adapt it to the passing of light steam boats; and to effect this improvement by means of a series of locks and dams; together with a canal or two round the principal falls, as the falls at Milton, and at the Palmyra mill.

The engineer's estimate for this object is,—

For lockage, by locks of 14 feet width, 127 feet, at 500 dollars per foot,	$63,500
For dams and various particulars,	51,700
Superintendence and contingencies, 15 per cent.,	17,300
Total probable cost,	$132,500

NOTE.

A survey is directed to be made of the Meherrin river, with a view to the improvement thereof from Murfreesboro' upwards; also a survey of the country between the waters of the Roanoke river and the New river branch of the Great Kanhaway. It is thought that a junction of the Eastern and Western waters, by this route, may be not impossible, but rather probable. A new survey is likewise directed, to ascertain the best mode of improving the James and Jackson's rivers, up to Covington.

NOTE 2.

In 1826, surveys were commenced by a brigade of United States' engineers, to determine, co-operatively with the surveys on foot by the state, as to the practicability of uniting the waters of the James and the Kanhaway rivers, by a canal, and this year, 1827, the same have been concluded. The engineers have discovered a practicable route, and have, in consequence, marked out or located a line of canal, from Covington, on Jackson's river, to the foot of Great falls, on the Kanhaway, with summit level, and the several works appertaining, as feeders, reservoirs, &c.

The engineers have, moreover, ascertained the practicability of uniting the waters of the Roanoke and New rivers, and have pointed out a line of route from Salem, in Bottetourt, or from Christianburg, in Montgomery county, to the head of boat navigation, on the Great Kanhaway. The engineers' reports are expected.

JUNE, 1828.

By a report made to the United States war department, as well as one to the legislature of Virginia, it is now thoroughly confirmed that a connexion of the James and the Kanhaway rivers, by a continuous canal, is really practicable, but would be very expensive to execute. On the other hand it is ascertained, that a connexion, by canal, of the waters of the Roanoke river and the New river branch of the Kanhaway, is not only practicable, but easy, and is highly promising of advantages ; and further, that a union of the waters of the Roanoke river and James river, near the point where the connexion last mentioned is proposed to take place, is also of easy practicability.

Which important discoveries, embracing the project of a *double connexion*, by canal, are in consequence made the subjects of the two next inserted articles, No. 110 and No. 111.

A.—From tide water of the Roanoke river, at Weldon, by canal, up the valley thereof, and the South fork valley, to a point of a dividing summit, at about 5 miles south of Christianburg, in Montgomery county,

Virginia, between the heads of Elliott's creek on the east, and Meadow creek on the west; whence across, and down the valleys of Little river and New river, and that of the Great Kanhaway, to the foot of Great falls. Distance, viz.

Tide water to east end of summit level,
Ascent, 2049 feet in 260 miles.
Length of summit, $\frac{5}{8}$ to $\frac{3}{4}$ "
West end of summit to mouth of Little river,
Descent, 309 feet in 11¼ miles.
Little river to mouth of Greenbriar,
Descent, 358½ feet in 83½ miles.
Mouth of Greenbriar to foot of Great falls,
Descent, 741 feet in 67¼ miles.

Total lockage, 3457½ feet in 422¾ miles.

No. 110.

ROANOKE AND KANHAWAY CANAL.

According to what is here stated, the desideratum of a route to connect the Eastern and Western waters of the country, by canal, appears to be realized, and this after a manner quite unexpected, both in regard to facility of construction, and the easy communication it will afford when constructed. It is a route far superior to either of the others hitherto discovered; there being at this situation a depression in the Alleghany ridge, and a flat summit level is presented after some deep cutting, at only 30 feet below the top of the mountain; to which summit, a most abundant supply of water can be brought, by a feeder, 9½ miles in length, from Little river, a copious tributary of New river, and brought in such a manner, winding round the mountain, as to throw all the waste water on the side of the Roanoke. Which feeder will include a tunnel of 1 mile and 290 yards through the Pilot mountain; but this there will be no need of making navigable; and no reservoir at all is needed; neither will any tunnel along the main canal be needed. The deep cutting required is only 1083 yards; and the declivities from the summit on both sides, except the first mile of each, are gradual, making the ground favourable for excavation and arrangement of the locks: so that no difficulties whatever appear to exist, or be in the way of constructing a canal from one of the two great rivers to the other.

But there exists a section of the route, on the Kanhaway river valley, where the case is different. It lies between Bowyer's ferry and Great falls: the ground here is represented as being too rough and difficult for canal constructions, and it has been conjectured, that, along this section, a rail road may be resorted to with advantage, as a substitute.

Further examinations are now on foot, by the which, a proper decision may be come to on this point, and all other essential points likewise, of this interesting project.

Near the summit level, or the point of connexion as above, *hydraulic limestone* has been found. Small locks are recommended, say 10 feet in width, by 75 feet long in the clear.

1829.

From the deep cutting on the summit, eastward, the route descends, to the junction of the two forks of Elliott's creek, and passes to the mouth thereof, and to the south fork of Roanoke; thence to the north fork, at the site of an aqueduct 100 feet long, by which to cross the same, and thence, about 4½ miles farther, to the entrance of a proposed tunnel of 850 yards at a bend of the Roanoke river. After which, and a deep cutting of 240 yards long, the route proceeds 7 miles to the pond at Salem; at which point the examinations down the Roanoke were suspended for the season. Distance from summit level to Salem, by the canal route, 36 miles.

The Roanoke navigation company have carried their improvements on the stream navigation as far up as Salem.

The following enumerated distances and elevations are referred to. To which is added, a comparative view, taken at large, of the great routes between the eastern and western navigation of the country, as stated by Mr. Crozet, the able engineer of Virginia.

DISTANCES AND ELEVATIONS,

Referred to the top of the Alleghany, at the depression between the heads of Meadow creek and the North fork of Elliott's creek.

WESTWARDLY.

	Miles.	Chains.	Feet.
From the top of the Alleghany,			
To the end of the Deep cut,	0	26.06	30.00
To the end of the next mile,	1	26.06	80.00
To the mouth of Meadow creek,	7	68	300.05

	Miles.	Chains.	Feet.
To New river, at the mouth of Little river,	11	23	338.81

EASTWARDLY.

	Miles.	Chains.	Feet.
To the end of the Deep cut,	0	23.15	30.00
To the end of the next mile,	1	23.15	113.00
To the junction of the two forks of Elliott's creek,	4		268.44
To the mouth of Elliott's creek,	13		684.00
To the South fork of Roanoke, at the head of the cliff just above the first crossing of the stage road,	18	16	774.31
To the end of the cliff above the second crossing,	21	74	845.70
To the North fork at the site of the aqueduct, which will be 100 feet long,	24	11	896.16
Level in the aqueduct and James river feeder,			857.70
To the forks of Roanoke,	24	27	900.58
To the entrance of the short tunnel,	28	62	
To Roanoke, nearly opposite the mouth of the tunnel, and at the last crossing of the road,			939.27
To the river opposite E. White's,			1009.73
To the pond at Salem, (by the route of the canal,)	36	12	1076.59

The following elevations of different points above tide water, computed either from my own surveys, or other documents, may likewise be of some interest in the inquiries relative to the connexion of the eastern and western waters.

ELEVATION ABOVE TIDE WATER.

Of James river,	at Maiden's Adventure,	141
	at Columbia,	178
	at Scottsville,	255
	at Lynchburg,	500
	at the North branch (head of the canal,)	700
	at Pattonsburg,	806
	at Covington,	1,222
Of Greenbriar,	near the Droop mountain, 39 miles above Howard's creek,	1,986
	at the mouth of Anthony's creek,	1,779
	at the mouth of Howard's creek,	1,669
	at the mouth of Second creek,	1,629

Of Greenbriar,	at its mouth, or New river mouth,	1,382
Of New river,	at the mouth of Sinking creek,	1,627
	at the mouth of Little river,	1,740
Of the Kanhaway,	at Bowyer's ferry,	982
	below the Great falls of Kanhaway,	641
	at the mouth of Kanhaway in the Ohio,	535
Of the Ohio,	at Pittsburg,	648
	at the mouth of Big Beaver,	691
Of Lake Erie,		563
Of the Champion swamp, dividing summit between Lake Erie and Big Beaver,		905
Of the Roanoke,	at the mouth of Elliott's creek,	1,399
	at the Forks,	1,178
	at Salem,	1,002
Of the Alleghany,	at the head of Second creek,	2,596
	between the South prong of Fork run and Tuckahoe, (the best route in this quarter,)	2,315
	at the North prong of Fork run,	2,445
	at the Turnpike,	2,512
	at the Old road,	2,476
	between Brush creek and the North fork of Howard's creek,	2,758
	between the Middle fork of Ogley's creek and Anthony's creek,	2,996
	in Montgomery county, Virginia, between Meadow creek and the North fork of Elliott's creek,	2,079
	in the same county, between Stroubler's and North fork of Roanoke,	2,072
On the route of the Ohio and Chesapeake canal by Deep creek,		2,567
	by Casselman's route,	2,759

This comparative table shows, that the depression of the Alleghany in Montgomery county, is considerably the lowest of any yet recommended for a connexion of the eastern and western waters.

In my report of last year, I had established a tabular comparison between this and the Ohio and Chesapeake canal routes. The operations of last season having elicited some results somewhat different from those then presented, many of which had been obtained by mere computation, I do herewith submit similar corrected tables; discarding, however, the Deep run route of the Ohio and Chesapeake canal, which is no longer thought of.

COMPARATIVE VIEW

Of several Routes for a Canal connexion of the Eastern and Western waters.

OHIO AND CHESAPEAKE CANAL.

CASSELMAN'S ROUTE.

	Distances in miles.	Lockage in feet. Ascent.	Lockage in feet. Descent.	Lockage in feet. Average per mile.	Lockage in feet. Total.	Length of Tunnel.	Deep cut 35 feet next to the tunnel. in yards.	Elevation of the ridge above the assumed base line. in feet.	Length of feeder in miles.	Minimum supply of water at the origin of the feeders, in cubic feet per second.
From tide water to Cumberland,	185 5-8	578	—	3.11						
Thence to the mouth of Little Will's creek,	13 7-8	309	—	20.43						
Thence to the eastern end of the summit level,	15 1-4	1016	—	66.62						
Summit level,	5 3-4	0	0	0		navigable.	Eastern. 140 Western. 1060			
From the western end of the summit level to the mouth of Middle Fork creek,	16 1-8	—	216	13.40						
Thence to the mouth of Casselman's river,	19 5-8	—	420	26.75						
Thence along the Youghiogany to Connelsville, one of the worst sections of the line, the river breaking through the Briery and Laurel mountains: (In one mile of this section, the fall is as much as 96 feet, and the ground bad,)	27 1-2	—	432	15.70						
Thence to the mouth of the Youghiogany,	43 3-4	—	152	4.50						
Thence to Pittsburg,	14	—	35	2.50						
Total amounts,	341 1-2	1903	1255		3158	mls. yds. 4—80	1200	856	5¼	18

ROANOKE AND NEW RIVER CANAL.

	Distances in miles.	Lockage in feet. Ascent.	Lockage in feet. Descent.	Lockage in feet. Average per mile.	Lockage in feet. Total.	Length of Tunnel. Navigable.	Length of Tunnel. For feeder.	Deep cut, 30 feet at the deepest. in yards.	Elevation of the ridge above the assumed base line. in feet.	Length of feeder in miles.	Minimum supply of water at the origin of the feeder, in cubic feet per second.
From tide water to Salem, (computed,)	224	1002	—	4.47							
Thence to the forks of Roanoke,	11 3-4	176	—	14.98							
Thence to the mouth of Elliott's creek,	11 1-4	221	—	19.64							
Thence to the end of the summit level,	12 3-4	650	—	51.53							
Summit level,	5-8	0	0	0		none.	mil. yds. 1—200	Eastern. 510 Western. 573			
From the western end of the summit level down Meadow creek and Little river to New river,	11 1-4	—	309	27.46							
Thence to the mouth of Greenbriar,	83 5-8	—	358	4.26							
Thence to Bowyer's Ferry,	45 1-2	—	400	8.79							
Thence to the foot of the Great Falls of Kanhaway,	22		341	15.50							
Total amounts,	422 5-4	2049	1408	—	3457	none.	mil. yds. 1—200	1083	30	9½	50	Taken from Little river.

By a tunnel two miles long, as stated in the body of the report, the rapid descent at the beginning, and 220 feet of lockage, might be saved, which would reduce it to be little more than that of the Ohio and Chesapeake Canal: a further lowering of the level might give the same lockage, and a tunnel of about the same length, but only 170 feet below the top, and succeeded by an easy declivity, and favourable ground on both sides.

JAMES RIVER AND KANHAWAY CANAL.

I.—BY WAY OF COVINGTON AND GREENBRIAR RIVER.

	Distances in miles.	Lockage in feet.				Length of Tunnel.			Elevation of the ridge above the assumed base line.	Length of feeder in miles.	Minimum supply of water at the origin of the feeder, in cubic feet per second.
		Ascent.	Descent.	Average per mile.	Total.	Navigable.	For feeder.	Deep cut 50 feet next to the tunnel.	in feet.		
From tide water to Pattonsburg,	199	806	—	4							
Thence to Covington, (by the improvement,)	58 1-2	416	—	7.11							
Thence to the mouth of Fork Run,	16 1-2	432	—	26.18							
Thence to the end of the summit level,	2 5-8	264	—	100.50							
Summit level,	4 1-2	0	0	0				Eastern. 458 yds. Western. mil. yds. 1—177		311.8 fm. Greenbriar.	43 from Greenbriar.
From the western end of the summit level, down Howard's creek, to Greenbriar,	8 1-8	—	249	30.65							
Thence down Greenbriar to New river,	49 1-8	—	287	5.90						17-8 from Anthony's creek.	11 from Anthony's creek.
Thence to Bowyer's ferry,	45 1-2	—	400	8.80							
Thence to the foot of the Falls of Kanhaway,	22	—	341	15.50							
Total amounts,	405 7-8	1918	1277	—	3195	ms. yds. 2—1120	ms. yds. 5—958	mil. yds. 1—635	397	33 miles.	54

If a tunnel of the same length, with the same depth of cutting at each end, were made here, the lockage would be reduced to 3,155 feet, which is about the same as on the Ohio and Chesapeake canal.

JAMES RIVER AND KANHAWAY CANAL.

II.—BY WAY OF PATTONSBURG, ROANOKE, AND NEW RIVER.

	Distances in miles.	Lockage in feet.				Length of Tunnel.		Deep cut 50 feet next to the tunnel.	Elevation of the ridge above the assumed base line.	Length of feeder, in miles.	Minimum supply of water at the origin of the feeder, in cubic feet per second.
		Ascent.	Descent.	Average per mile.	Total	Navigable.	For feeder.				
From tide water to the mouth of the Catawba,	212 3-4	886	—	4.16							
Thence to the Forks of Roanoke, (computed,)	51	292	—	5.72		Tunnel from Mason's to Carvin's creek, 2 miles. Another through Tinker's mountain 3 3-4					
Thence as before to summit level,	24	871	—	36.29							
Summit level,	5-8	0	0	0							
Thence as before to the mouth of Greenbriar,	94 7-8	—	667	7			mil. yds. 1—200				
Thence to the foot of the Falls of Kanhaway,	67 1-2	—	741	11			1—200				
Total amounts,	450 3-4	2049	1408	—	3457	5 3-4		Not ascertained for the 2 navigable tunnels.	Ditto.	9½	50

These tables show, that the James river and Greenbriar connexion is all considered fully as practicable as the Casselman's route, or Ohio and Chesapeake canal; but that the route between New river and Roanoke is by far superior to both.

Here we have a most abundant supply of water, at such an elevation, that we are compelled to let it fall a great number of feet, in order to admit it into the summit level; rendering it thereby useful for mechanical purposes, even before it reaches the canal, and leaving, moreover, there, a surplus applicable to the same object.

Whereas, on the other routes, a rather scanty, if not a doubtful supply, is obtained at the expense of vast reservoirs, long tunnels, &c. On the Ohio and Chesapeake canal especially, the supply is secured by passing the tunnel through the Alleghany, at the enormous depth of 856 feet, requiring, therefore, shafts to be sunk close to each other to this extraordinary depth at least, (for, it is not improbable that many points of the ridge would be much higher above the tunnel than the lowest point under which, according to the map, its direction passes,) and, after all, only 18 feet of water are obtained at the origin of the feeder. On the Kanhaway route, the quantity of water is much more abundant, (54 feet,) but it has to travel such a distance over difficult and broken ground, that unless the feeder was constructed and regulated with unusual care, it is doubtful whether the supply would not be exhausted in droughts before reaching the canal, which would have then to depend altogether upon the reservoirs.

No such difficulty is encountered on the Roanoke and New river route; no navigable tunnel is required. If one should be made, it would be only as a matter of expediency or economy; but not, as on the other routes, from indispensable necessity: and then its depth below the ridge would not necessitate shafts of an objectionable length: 150 feet would be the extent of the deepest.

Reservoirs, likewise, are perfectly unnecessary, and would be made only, if at all, for the purpose of collecting more water power.

Here again, it is only for one mile on each side, that the declivity is too great to allow a sufficient distance between the locks; but it has been seen that the valley is quite favourable to the formation of intermediate basins, which, by occupying the middle of it, would make up in width their deficiency in length, or else that a tunnel, at a moderate depth under the ridge, would at once obviate this rapid descent, and save lockage.

A.—From the upper waters of the Roanoke river, near the point of their connexion with those of New river, as in the preceding article, as, suppose at or near Salem, in Bottetourt county, by canal, across the said county, and through Fincastle, to a point of the James river improvements, at or near Pattonsburg.

Distance, *Miles*, 30

No. 111.

ROANOKE AND JAMES RIVER CANAL.

A cursory examination of the ground, sufficient to ascertain the practicability of this important connexion, has taken place; but a more regular survey, with accurate levellings, &c. is yet to be made. The which, however, will soon be accomplished. The engineer of Virginia, in his report, observes, as to this two-fold connexion of the Roanoke, the James river, and the Kanhaway waters, that,—

"The trade of New river and its tributaries, the trade of the Holston river and of the Upper Roanoke, as also that of James and Jackson's rivers and tributaries, will be likely all to meet in Bottetourt. A concentration of trade, this, if it takes effect, which will have immense influence on the prosperity of the state."

New river, for more than 100 miles above the mouth of Little river, flows through a country rich in mineral as well as agricultural products, and is reported as susceptible of having its navigation greatly improved. Moreover, the direction of Reed creek, which discharges, from the west, at a few miles above the mouth of Little river, would seem strongly to invite a connexion, by canal, with one or other of the forks of the Holston; which is understood not to be at all a work of difficulty, from the nature of the ground. It is supposed that by means of 50 miles of canal, or less, an eligible communication may be formed between New river and Middle branch of the Holston.

So that, when all this shall have been accomplished, the chain, it appears, will be complete, for a very direct internal water passage from Albemarle sound, or from Chesapeake bay, to the Gulf of Mexico, as follows:—

From Norfolk, on Elizabeth river,
 Through the Dismal Swamp canal,
  Through the Murfreesboro' canal to the Roanoke river,
  Up the Roanoke improvements,
  Through the Roanoke and Kanhaway canal to New river,

Through Reed creek canal to the Holston,
Thence, through the Tennessee, the Black Warrior, and the Tombecbee, or the Cahawba and Alabama river improvements respectively, to Mobile harbour, in the Gulf of Mexico.

Or, the communication may pass thus:—

From the Chesapeake bay,
Up James river, and through the improvements thereof, to Pattonsburg, in Bottetourt county,
Thence through the Roanoke and James river canal,
Through the Roanoke and Kanhaway canal, to New river,
Through Reed creek canal, and so on through the Holston river, the Tennessee, &c. as above, to the Gulf of Mexico.

NOTE.

The anticipations of Mr. Crozet, who stated in one of his former reports, the belief he entertained that hydraulic limestone would be discovered in Virginia, have been realized to the full; this valuable formation actually existing there in great abundance. The facility this will give to the many works of improvement there in contemplation, requiring water cement, is most acceptable. It will, in short, create a vast saving of expense annually to the state, (besides encouraging works, which, without it, might not have been undertaken,) in the construction of such works as may be thought absolutely needful, and the repairing of those that already exist in the state.

The stone, at different places, has a variety in its appearance; and probably some also in its adhesive quality, when properly reduced into cement; which, experiments will determine. A series of these must be the only means of ascertaining the best process of reduction, including a knowledge of the exact proportion of sand to be mixed with it.

Mr. John H. Cocke, Jr. a gentleman of Fluvanna, made the fortunate discovery last year, near James river, at the nearest point of the limestone district, and within a short distance of the Blue ridge canal; there he found the substance to exist. This was not, however, like as many other useful discoveries in the world have been; one of mere *chance;* but was the fruit of a laborious research, devoted *expressly to the object.* Since then, it has been found at other places, but, as noticed above, is not uniform, as to colour or appearance.

1829.

The very important and very diligent surveys effected at the last season, in reference to the James river and Roanoke connexion, have resulted in disappointing the hopes which had been formed; so far, that is to say, that, instead of a project of easy or moderately expensive practicability, it turns out to be one of the first magnitude in point of difficulty; owing to a greater depression of the water than was expected in the vicinity of the dividing ridge between Looney's and Tinker's creeks, near Amsterdam, the place that was proposed for crossing, and the necessity therefore of seeking a sufficient head at a long distance, and establishing a feeder or feeders over a most rugged country, besides having recourse to tunnelling; so that the work, if executed, and it can be executed, will be costly.

The plan at present is;—That a feeder be taken out of each of the Roanoke forks, at a level of 43 feet above that of their junction, and be brought to unite their supplies at the aqueduct of 100 feet long, by which the New river canal crosses the North fork; and after the tunnel of 850 yards on the north bank of the Roanoke, together with the deep cutting attached to it eastwardly, has been passed, then a division to be made; that is to say, from this point the two routes diverge; one of them passing, according to what has been stated, down the course of the Roanoke river; and the other route, or junction route, which is the particular subject of this article, striking off towards James river, according to what is pointed out by the survey effected. On this plan, the route winds round from the said point of deep cutting, to the head of the east prong of Mason's creek, there entering a tunnel of 2 miles long, which conducts into the valley of Carvin's creek, by which, in 3 miles, it reaches a long tunnel of 3¾ miles under Tinker's mountain, and emerging from this, enters the valley of the Catawba, and pursues it down to the mouth of this stream, on James river. The lockage in this distance, with suitable deduction for some contemplated improvements as regards elevations, will be 320 feet. Distance, from the said point of divergence, by the winding route surveyed, to the mouth of the Catawba, on James river, about 46 miles. The cost of this "Junction" canal would be not less than 1,200,000 dollars.

The construction of a rail road in this quarter, the engineer observes, would present no great difficulty; with some few deviations from the canal line of route specified, it might be graduated so as not to exceed any where an inclination of 1°, and the length of it would be about 35 miles. Its cost, on a cheap plan, about 400,000 dollars, or on a perfect plan, 800,000 dollars.

NOTE.

Elevations referred to James river at the Pattonsburg bridge.

Mouth of the Catawba, - - - - 80.40 *Feet.*
Head spring of Looney's creek, - - 520

Depression of the dividing ridge.	At its western extremity between Tinker's creek and the Catawba,	645	Feet.
	At Howrietown,	605.16	
	At its eastern end, between Looney's creek and Little Buffalo,	595.75	

Height of Bottetourt spring, - - - 230
Mill pond at Salem, - - - - 196.19
North fork, at site of the aqueduct, - - 380 21
Assumed level of the feeder, - - - 415.08
Length of feeder to ⎰ to the ridge, by Amsterdam, 60   *Miles.*
  follow the hills, ⎱ to the Catawba, - 48
Length of the latter, shortened by a tunnel of 2
  miles, between Mason's and Carvin's creeks, 33
Supply of water to be obtained from both forks of
  the Roanoke, exclusive of reservoirs, per second, 34   *Feet.*
Supply from the Catawba,   do. do.   8   do.

No. 103. (CONTINUED.)

JAMES RIVER CANALS, AND STREAM IMPROVEMENTS.

Pursuant to a resolution of the general assembly of Virginia, 9th March, 1827, directing additional surveys on James and Jackson's rivers, with a view to the improving of the navigation of the same, by locks and dams, or by sluices, or both modes; according to whichever plan is found to be most advisable, the same was, in the course of last season, effected by the principal engineer; and his report on the subject, at the commencement of the present year, 1828, is on record.

By this, it appears satisfactorily proved, that the river course can be improved, to most advantage, for the present at least, by the method of locks and dams almost the whole of the way ; the same so calculated as to admit the application of steam-power. Short canals will be necessary at a few places, viz.—

At the *Seven Islands;* length 3½ miles; beginning at the mouth of Hardware river, and ending at Big Bremo ; the river at this place being too wide to allow of the raising of dams to a proper height.

Through the *Blue Ridge.* A canal is, indeed, already made, along this distance, of 7 miles ; but its dimensions were not calculated for steam-navigation ; and alterations will be needed.

At the *gap of the Rich Patch mountain;* where a tunnel of 167 yards in length will be advisable also ; the latter passing through a narrow neck below Ritchie's land, in order to save a distance of 3 miles.

At other points, where the fall of the river is great, short canals may be resorted to also, for the sake of acquiring the water power which they create; although generally of much more expensive construction than dams.

The following is a summary estimate of the whole plan, as now proposed, comprising distances, lifts, and cost. The locks calculated to be 15 feet wide, 85 feet long from gate to gate. Longer boats than can cross through these would be less manageable; and besides, could not pass through the present locks of the lower canal.

RECAPITULATION

Of the estimate of the improvement of James river; including the length and lift of the sections already completed.

	Distances.	Lifts.	Cost.
	miles. chs.	*feet.*	*Dollars.*
From tide-water to Maiden's Adventure, the canal is completed; but the series of connected locks, from the basin to the dock, are in bad order. They should be re-placed by more permanent locks, better suited to an active intercourse,	29—00	140.50	Completed.
From the dam at Maiden's Adventure, to Columbia, locks and dams,	30—07	39.28	70,340
From Columbia to Big Bremo, do.	11—00	29.22	32,830
From Big Bremo to Hardware river, the Seven Islands falls, canal,	3—37	33.27	109,424
From Hardware river to Scottsville, locks and dams,	8—00	15.11	42,700
From Scottsville to Warminster, do.	19—10	58.37	94,810
From Warminster to Lynchburg, do.	50—03	185.88	253,660
From Lynchburg to the Blue ridge canal, do.	20—15	103.47	117,220
Canal through the Blue ridge, On south side of the river,	2—15	34.75	Completed.
On the north side,	4—45	60.00	ditto.
From the head of the canal to Pattonsburg, locks and dams,	21—64	106.23	122,140
From Pattonsburg to the Cow Pasture, do. (In this section, there is purposed a tunnel 167 yards long, which will save very nearly three miles.)	33—50	189.10	209,800
From the Cow Pasture to Covington, (Jackson's river,) locks and dams, This section includes two short canals; one of them, 18½ chains long, through the Rich-patch gap; the other, 1 mile and 35 chains long, below the Cave rock.	24—25	229.50	238,030
Total amounts,	257—31	1224.68	1,290,954

Total cost,	$1,290,954
And supposing an additional 10 per cent. for contingencies,	129,046
	$1,420,000
And adding thereto, for the Maiden's Adventure and Blue ridge sections of canal,	1,080,000
This makes, altogether,	$2,500,000

Which is a very reduced amount, in comparison with 5,750,000 dollars, the estimated cost of an independent, or continuous canal, along the whole distance, from Richmond to Covington, as already stated. How far the very important discovery now made, of a route for uniting, with unexpected facility, the waters of the Roanoke and Kanhaway rivers by a navigable canal, and of the Roanoke and James rivers by another navigable canal, may operate in manner and degree, to occasion the former project, at so much greater an expenditure, to be undertaken, is a question, which, if not as yet quite at maturity for solution, the existing circumstances of the case are nevertheless on the very eve of bringing to a decision ; and this decision, there is little doubt, will be such as to favour a system of improvements, on the widest scale that can possibly be justified by the rules of a well considered public economy. Such is the spirit of the times !

NOTE,—1829.

The principal engineer having been instructed to make a survey of the Rappahannock river, has effected it, and reported ; and his report states, in detail, the improvements that are desirable ; beginning at Fox's mill on the North branch, otherwise called Hedgeman's river, and descending, step by step, to Falmouth race, in tide water ; a distance of 43¼ miles, in which the fall of level is 242.24 feet.

Cost of the proposed improvements estimated at 52,670 dollars ; including, on the side of Fredericksburg, a basin and canal, above the town, recommended by the engineer.

The engineer is required to survey the Maherrin river from Murfreesboro' up to the highest point susceptible of navigation. Likewise the Nottoway river, from the mouth thereof to the highest point of navigation.

SUMMARY

Of proposed Virginia state improvements, for connecting the eastern and western navigation ;

Whereof, however, the respective plans, or precise modes of execution, remain as yet to be settled ; and some additional surveys and estimates yet to be made, in order to decide upon and fill up details.

The entire course of James river, from tide water at Richmond dock, to Covington, Jackson's river; upon the plan laid down and recommended, of dams and locks generally, but comprising canals at certain distances, besides those already constructed, which are to be altered and made more perfect; and a series of new connecting locks between the basin above Richmond and the dock, to be located, suitable to an active commerce.
Ascent of water level 1224 feet; distance, *Miles*, 257½

The Roanoke and New river connexion, beginning at tide water, Weldon, and passing up the Roanoke valley to Salem in Bottetourt county; whence to a summit between the heads of Elliott's and Meadow creeks in Montgomery; and from said summit down the valleys of Little river and New river, and that of the Kanhaway, to the foot of Great falls.

But, it is to be observed, that along the section between Bowyer's ferry and the falls, a rail road is recommended. Ascent and descent, 3457½ feet, 422¾

A junction canal between the James river and the Roanoke navigation as above; beginning at the mouth of Catawba river, in Bottetourt county, and striking off to a summit at Tinker's mountain; and thence proceeding to a point of the navigation as above, where it emerges from a tunnel of 850 yards, or near to the same, on the north bank of the Roanoke.
Lockage along this route, 320 feet, 46

Total, *Miles*, 726¼

To which, adding, viz.

The section of route between Great falls of Kanhaway and the mouth thereof, at Point Pleasant on the Ohio river; this section, already improved in stream navigation, being now likely to receive a superior improvement, as coming into immediate connexion with the foregoing. Descent 106 feet, 94

Making, for the double route between tide water and the Ohio river at Point Pleasant; namely, one route taking the course of James river, the other route that of the Roanoke river, and both routes that of New river; a distance of, *Miles*, 820¼

NOTE.

This includes an extra distance of 45 miles between the mouth of Catawba river and Covington.

SUMMARY FOR VIRGINIA.

ARTIFICIAL NAVIGATION.

Page.	No.		Miles.
282	99.	The Appomatox river canals, and stream improvements,	110
283	100.	The Powhatan canal,	19
284	101.	The Manchester canal,	10
284	102.	Appomatox and Roanoke, or Junction canal,	30
285	103.	James and Jackson's river canals, and stream improvements,	257½
303	104.	James and Jackson's river canal, Maiden's Adventure section,	..
304	105.	James and Jackson's river canal, Blue ridge section,	..
305	106.	James and Jackson's river canal, Jackson's river section,	..
307	107.	Kanhaway river navigation and turnpike,	188
309	108.	Shenandoah river canals, and stream improvements,	250
310	109.	Rivanna river canals, and stream improvements,	37
312	110.	Roanoke and Kanhaway canal,	422¾
321	111.	Roanoke and James river canal,	46
		New river and Holston canal,	50
			1420¼
		Deducting turnpike road, included at article 107,	99
		Total of artificial navigation,	1321¼

NATURAL NAVIGATION.

282		Between Washington city and Richmond,	310
	To which add :—		
		For all other streams and navigable waters; viz. Of the rivers, creeks, and bays of the state, some of which are particularized below, there are 100, affording an average natural navigation, 10 at 100 miles each, 90 at 20 miles. This amounts to,	2800
		Total of natural navigation,	3110
		Total of artificial navigation,	1321¼
		Total of both,	4431¼

Rappahannock river, rises in the Blue ridge; its general course south-east, to the Chesapeake bay. It is navigable up to Fredericksburg.

York river, is formed by the junction of the Mattapony and the Pamunkey; which rise in the mountains, and unite at Delawar town. Pursuing a course between the Potomac and Rappahannock rivers, to Chesapeake bay, it is navigable by both branches, and the main.

Pianketank, and other minor tributaries of the Chesapeake, from the west.

Tributaries of the Potomac, viz.

The South branch, rises by numerous creeks, in Pendleton county, and joins the main Potomac, at Cumberland. It is navigable 150 miles.

The Shenandoah rises by several forks in Augusta county, and is augmented by many streams, in its course to Frederick county; where it receives a north branch, and whence it pursues a north-east course to the Potomac, at Harper's ferry. It has been noticed, relative to a canal.

Tributaries of James river; the Chickahominy, the Rivanna, Tye river, North river, and many minor streams discharging from the north: the Nansemond, the Appomatox, and others, from the south and the south-west.

The upper waters of the Roanoke and Staunton rivers, and their tributaries, the Smiths rivers, Goose creek, Big and Little Otter, Big and Falling Cub, Little Roanoke, Banister.

Big Sandy river, the Guyandot, Great and Little Kanhaway, and other tributaries of the Ohio in Virginia: these afford considerable navigation.

NOTE.

A List of Surveys for Navigation Improvements, made by the public Engineer of the State of Virginia.

In the year
1817, Survey of the Rappahannock and Rappidan rivers; for ascertaining as to the practicability of rendering these streams thoroughly navigable.
" Survey of the James and Jackson's rivers, between the mouth of Looney's creek and the mouth of Dunlap's creek.
" Survey of the Kanhaway river, from Great falls thereof to its confluence with the Ohio.
" Survey for the route of a canal, to connect the waters of the Roanoke and Appomatox rivers.

1818, Survey and examination of James river, from Rockett's to Warwick; and digesting plans and details for the Richmond dock.

" Survey for the route of a canal, from Goose creek to Alexandria.

" Survey of James river, and its branch, North river, and the Rivanna.

1819, Surveys for a canal on the south side of James river, from Westham to tide water.

" Surveys to ascertain the best practicable communication between the waters of the James and Kanhaway rivers; viz. James river, Kanhaway river, Craig's creek, Sinking creek, Dunlap's creek, Ogley's creek, Howard's creek, Greenbriar river, and New river: also, for an independent canal along the valley of James river, and for a road from the mouth of Dunlap's creek, to the foot of the Great falls of the Kanhaway river.

1820, Examination of the Pamunkey river, and its principal branches, North Anna and South Anna, with a view to render them navigable.

" Survey of the Monongahela river, and its branches.

" Examination of the Potomac and its tributary waters, and of the country between them and the Ohio river; with the view of a communication by canal.

" Examination of New river, to ascertain the nearest navigable points between it and the North fork of the Holston; and the nearest navigable points between said New river and the Roanoke river.

" Examination of the Middle and North forks of the Holston river, with the view of improving the navigation thereof.

" Examination of the Chickahominy river, with a view to improve the navigation thereof.

1821, Survey for the route of a canal to connect the waters of the Appomatox and Staunton rivers; and examination of the Appomatox river from tide water up to Farmville.

" Examination of Little Kanhaway river, from Great falls thereof, to its junction with the Ohio.

" Examination of Clinch and Powell's rivers, from the state line of Tennessee, up to the highest point susceptible of navigation.

1822, Surveys of the Roanoke, Dan, and Staunton rivers, with a view to improvement by a sluice navigation.

" Survey of the Potomac river, under direction of commissioners appointed by Maryland and Virginia.

1823, Examination of Slate river, to the highest practicable point of improvement.
" Examination of the South branch of Potomac, the Great Cucapehon river, North river, and Patterson's creek; with a view to improve their navigation.
1824, Location of a canal at the Blue ridge.
" New survey of James and Jackson's rivers, from Maiden's Adventure falls to the mouth of Dunlap's creek, to ascertain and to adopt the best mode of improvement.
1825, Surveys for a canal to connect the waters of the Appomatox with the South branch of Willis's river; or with Deep creek and Hudsmouth's creek, in Powhatan county.
" Survey of a canal route, from Bosher's dam to Manchester.
" Examination of Tygart's valley river, from the mouth of West fork to the highest point susceptible of navigation.

Subsequent to these, the principal of the state surveys have been designated at the articles to which they belong, as here inserted.

INDIANA NAVIGATION.

M.—From the south-west extremity of Lake Erie; or from that point up the Maumee river, which may be struck by the Ohio state canal works; by the course of the Maumee and Wabash rivers, to the confluence of the latter with the Ohio, at Shawneetown, in Gallatin county, Illinois; this line of route cutting the north-west angle of Ohio state, and passing through the state of Indiana. Distance, by canal and river navigation combined, *Miles,* 600

No. 112.

LAKE ERIE AND OHIO CANAL;—*via* WABASH RIVER.

This communication has long been projected; and the proper examinations are now on foot. The upper waters of the two rivers approach to within a few miles, at the Maumee village, or Fort Wayne. The Wabash, in its course, will probably, with some works of improvement, afford a steam-boat navigation of between 400 and 500 miles, and the Maumee nearly 100 miles, exclusive of the Ohio state canal works; so that it is thought the principal or connecting canal, may not require to be so much as 50 miles in length. The legislature have appointed a committee of survey upon the subject. On the part of the general government, there is, by law, an assignment of 100,000 acres of the public lands towards the execution of the project, whenever it shall be gone into.

NOTE.

Since the above was written, application has been made to congress, by the state of Indiana, for a grant of three sections in width of the public lands on each side of this contemplated canal; in order to further the execution of the work, by the state. It will probably be complied with.

In 1824, a bill was passed by congress, authorizing the state of Indiana to open a canal through the public lands, between the waters of the Wabash and the Maumee rivers; and it was stated, that the project could be executed at the expense of 300,000 dollars.

The said bill granted to Indiana a strip of the public land, 90 feet wide on each side of the intended canal; and it required of the state, that the survey should be completed within 3 years; the canal itself within the period of 12 years.

To promote the execution of the work, congress have now granted sections of land on each side; that is to say, the quantity granted is equal to one half of five sections in width on each side of the canal; each alternate section being reserved by the United States, from one end to the other.

NOTE.

Comprehensive surveys are now set on foot, under a detachment from the United States corps of engineers, having in view to connect, by a series of canals, the waters of Lake Michigan with those of the Wabash river; the upper waters of White river with the Wabash, by way of the Mississineway valley, as also with the Miami navigation in Ohio state; and the St. Mary's and St. Joseph's rivers, in a line of navigation with the Wabash and the Ohio. These surveys, as soon as completed, to be reported on to the war department.

SUMMARY FOR INDIANA.

ARTIFICIAL NAVIGATION.

Page.	No.		Miles.
332	112.	Wabash and Maumee connecting canal,	50
		Series of canals, to connect the waters of Lake Michigan, with those of the Wabash river; the upper waters of White river with the Wabash, by way of the Mississineway valley, as also with the Miami navigation in Ohio state; and the St. Mary's and St. Joseph's rivers, in a line of navigation with the Wabash and the Ohio rivers,	350
		Total of artificial navigation,	400

NATURAL NAVIGATION.

Along the streams of these rivers,	550

To which add :—

> For all other streams and navigable waters; viz. Of the rivers and creeks in this state, some of which are particularized below, there are 20 affording an average natural navigation of 50 miles each, and 100 an average of 10 miles each.

These make, together,	2000
Total of natural navigation,	2550
Total of artificial navigation,	400
Total of both, *Miles*,	2950

White river, the main stream of which falls into the Wabash, 30 miles below Vincennes, watering the country to a vast extent, by its branches and sub-branches. The northern branch rises in the heart of the state, by a number of creeks, and is in length 150 miles; the eastern branch 150 miles.

The Petoka river, falls into the Wabash 4 miles south of White river, after meandering about 100 miles.

These, and some other tributaries of the Wabash river, afford together a natural navigation of more than 500 miles.

Whitewoman's river, a considerable stream of the south-east of the state, flowing into the Great Miami.

Other streams intersect the land in all directions, and some, having their courses within the Indian possessions, are as yet imperfectly explored.

OHIO RIVER AND KENTUCKY NAVIGATION.

N.—From Pittsburg, in Pennsylvania, down the Ohio river, to Louisville, in Kentucky, above the rapids; and from the foot of the rapids, down to its junction with the Mississippi, at Cairo, in Illinois, above Fort Jefferson. Distance, taken by stations, *Miles*, 945

NOTE.

By act of congress, 3d March, 1827, a further appropriation of 30,000 dollars is made, towards clearing away obstructions to the safe navigation of this river. A survey of the Kentucky river also, by a party of the United States engineers, is immediately to take place, with a view to remove obstructions. As likewise of Green and Cumberland rivers.

DECEMBER, 1828.

A report is in preparation at the war department, to lay before congress, showing the progress made in removing obstructions to the navigation of the Ohio, in conformity to the act above mentioned, of 3d March, 1827. And it appears that an appropriation, of the sum of 50,000 dollars, is now called for, as needful for prosecuting the works of improvement, in the Ohio and Mississippi rivers together, during the ensuing year of 1829.

A.—From the River Ohio at Louisville, by canal, to a point of the same below the rapids, near to Portland. Distance by the bend of the river 3; across, *Miles*, 2

No. 113.
LOUISVILLE AND PORTLAND CANAL.

An act was passed, and a sum voted by congress in 1824, for a removal of the obstructions to the navigation of the Ohio and the Mississippi rivers. Examinations were directed to be gone into by a detachment from the United States corps of engineers, in order to ascertain the particulars, and point out, by a report to the department of war, the means for a complete removal of difficulties, or at the least, a thorough improvement of the same; and one of the consequences of this salutary measure, was that of accelerating an actual commencement in the long projected undertaking which is the subject of the present article; the full accomplishment whereof, it is expected, will take place at an early period.

It had been ascertained, by skilful engineers, that, on either the Indiana or the Kentucky side of the river, a canal around the falls was practicable; but on the Kentucky shore, it appeared, the work would be attended with least expense: and, in consequence, a company received a charter from the legislature of Kentucky, in January last, 1825, as the "Louisville and Portland canal company," who commenced the work. Capital stock 600,000 dollars, of which amount an act of congress has authorized a subscription, on the part of the general government, for 100,000 dollars, and the rest was readily filled up.

It is however believed, that the expense of this very desirable improvement will not exceed the sum of 500,000 dollars, including two capacious docks or basins; and, if no extraordinary accident happen, that it will be completed by the year 1828. The descent of the river, from Louisville to the foot of the rapids, to be overcome by lockage, is $22\frac{1}{2}$ feet.

This canal will of course be on a scale to pass large vessels. It commences from the lower end of a basin or estuary, which extends along the shore of the river for the whole length of the village of Louisville, and is connected with the river at its upper end. From the lower part of this basin, the canal traverses the point formed by the bend of the river at the falls, and re-enters the river at the little village of Shippingsport. Its length, taken thus from the lower end of Louisville, across the curve of the river, will be about 2 miles. It is proposed that the bottom of it shall be 50 feet wide, and be sunk 4 feet below the level of the basin at Louisville at the time of low water; the banks to be elevated 2 feet above the highest high water mark known at Louisville, which makes 42 feet from the bottom of the canal, and to be sloped, as $1\frac{3}{4}$ base to 1, so far as respects the upper or earthen portion; underneath which there lies a natural solid bed of stone, for a foundation the whole length of the canal, and this will be cut into, perpendicularly, to the requisite depth, varying along the 2 miles from 1 to 10 feet; the slope above which, to the top of each bank, to receive a substantial facing of stone work. This is necessary to prevent the abrasion of the banks by the motion of the water, produced by the wheels of steam-boats. The excavation of rock is done by drilling and blasting, and removal of the fragments effected by means of a newly invented crane.

There will be 3 lift locks of 7 feet lift each, and a guard lock at the lower end of the canal; dimensions 190 feet long by 50 wide, in the chamber.

MARCH, 1829.

Longer time than was expected, is found to be necessary for the accomplishment of this great work, which, however, is steadily advancing, and may be finished in about two years from the present time. But at a cost, it is now apprehended, considerably beyond the estimate of the engineer as above stated. In consideration whereof, and of the vast public utility expected from the work when complete, congress have concluded to make a second subscription to the funds of the company, to the amount of 135,000 dollars.

Mr. Darby, in his "Geographical view of the United States," observes,—"In the accelerated advance of canal improvement, another line of incalculable value will meet public attention. The Ohio river, at some stages of the water, is a very safely navigable stream; but is annually, in autumn, rendered unnavigable, from drought. This impediment continues, with diminished extent, as low as Louisville, and can be obviated only by a *canal along the entire bank of the river*, or by dams and sluices. The former, infinitely the most eligible mode, will no doubt be ultimately adopted, and will secure at once more safety, and a steady conveyance at that season of the year when most necessary."

The following table shows the ratio at which the trade of the Ohio has increased from year to year, since 1823;—

1823,	arrivals	98	whereof steam-boats	42	tons	19,453
1824,	"	120	" "	36	"	20,651
1825,	"	140	" "	42	"	24,969
1826,	"	182	" "	51	"	28,914
1827,	"	277	" "	62	"	48,744
1828,	Tonnage estimated at					50,000

Indicating the quantity of employment the locks of the Louisville and Portland canal are likely to command when complete.

JANUARY, 1830.

Surveys are directed by the legislature upon the Green and Barren rivers of the state of Kentucky, and a grant of 10,000 dollars made towards improving their navigation. A charter is also granted to a company as the "Lexington and Ohio rail road company," with privilege to construct a rail road from Lexington, to any point of the Ohio river, at their selection; capital stock 1,000,000 dollars.

SUMMARY.

The distance, as above, - - - - *Miles,* 947
To which add:—
    The natural navigation of Kentucky; viz. Of the rivers and creeks in this state, some of which are particularized below, there are 10 affording an average navigation of 100 miles each, and 80 an average of 20 miles each.
    This makes, together, - - - 2,600

Total, - - - - - - 3,547

The Cumberland river, which falls into the Ohio, 60 miles above the mouth of the latter, and which is navigable 500 miles; whereof the upper and lower sections lie within the state of Kentucky, a distance of *Miles,* 200

Green river, rises in the centre of the state, in Lincoln and Mercer counties, and discharges into the Ohio, near Evansville, Indiana. It is navigable, - - 150

Salt river, which falls into the Ohio, 30 miles below Louisville, is navigable for boats, - - - - 60

Kentucky river, rises in the south-east angle of the state, and falls into the Ohio, at Port William. Navigable, - - - - - - - - - 130

Licking river, rises between the sources of the Kentucky and Big Sandy rivers, and falls into the Ohio at Newport, opposite Cincinnati. It is navigable, - 70

Big Sandy river, has its sources in Cumberland mountains; they interlock with those of the Licking, the Cumberland, and other rivers; and this stream, which forms the eastern boundary of the state, falls into the Ohio at Catletsburg, - - - - - - - - ..

Of these several rivers, the branches and their sub-streams are very numerous, pervading every part of the state, and supplying a great extent of natural navigation, ..

THE MIDDLE GREAT LAKES, AND THE STATES OF ILLINOIS AND MICHIGAN NAVIGATION.

N.—From Buffalo, on Lake Erie, by the lake, to its extremity west, at the Maumee bay. Distance, by stations on the coast, *Miles*, 350

A.—From the west of Lake Erie, or from the Maumee bay or river, by canal, across, westward, to the south or the south-eastern extremity of Lake Michigan.
Distance, *Miles*, 150

No. 114.

THE ERIE AND MICHIGAN CANAL.

This projected canal will become hereafter no unimportant link in the chain of general water communication. As yet, no precise surveys and levelling have been gone into; but, from what is asserted of the capacity of the intermediate water courses, a junction of the lake waters this way, would appear to be quite practicable. A line of route has been suggested, by the head waters of the two St. Joseph's: a part of it lying in the (as yet) Indian country.

The St. Joseph's river of Michigan, which discharges into that lake near its southern extremity, is stated as being navigable, for boats of three feet water, to the distance of 130 miles from its mouth, free from rapids, or obstruction of any kind. But should a part of this river navigation be included in the route, the length of canal must still be great.

N.—From Maumee bay, across Lake Erie, up Detroit river, to Lake St. Clair, across which, and up St.

Clair river, to Fort Gratiot; whence, up Lake Huron to Michilimakinac, and thence through Lake Michigan to the south-western extremity thereof, near Fort Dearborn, or the mouth of Chicago river. Distance, by stations, or the indentations of the coast, as follows:—

Maumee bay to the mouth of Raisin,		35
Mouth of Detroit river,	15	50
Detroit city,	21	71
Peach island,	6	77
Gross island,	3	80
Huron of St. Clair,	15	95
St. Clair river,	8	103
Belle river,	18	121
Delude river,	9	130
Fort Gratiot,	2	132
White rock,	55	187
Elm creek,	10	197
Black river,	12	209
Pointe aux barques,	12	221
Pointe aux chesnes,	18	239
Shawangunk island,	11	250
Sable river,	30	280
Thunderbolt island,	40	320
Flat-rock point,	18	338
Presqu' isle,	20	358
Blancbois isle,	60	418
Michilimakinac,	12	430
Chicago river mouth,	350	*Miles*, 780

A.—From Lake Michigan at Fort Dearborn, or from Chicago river, at or near the mouth thereof, by canal, to a point on the Illinois, below obstructions; which may be attained at the confluence of the latter with the River Vermillion. Distance, *Miles*, 120

No. 115.
CHICAGO CANAL.

The route for this canal has been examined by commissioners of the state of Illinois, and a report on the subject been by them rendered to the legislature; but nothing of the canal itself is yet done. The work will probably be gone into as soon as there shall be a certain further advance made in improvements at other points. A company is incorporated by the state, as the "Illinois and Michigan Association;" their capital 1,000,000 of dollars, with a reserve in the law, that, after 50 years from the completion of this canal, the state may become the proprietor thereof, on refunding to the company the whole cost, and six per cent. per annum interest. The commissioners' report states the surface level of Lake Michigan to be about 158 feet above the surface level of Illinois river, at the mouth of the Little Vermillion, which is contemplated for the point of connexion; and the engineers' estimate of cost, is about 7000 dollars average per mile; making, for 100 miles, 700,000, or for 120 miles, 840,000 dollars. Towards the object, there is a grant by the United States, of 100,000 acres of land, besides the space through which the canal will run, and 90 feet on each side of it.

Below the lower rapids, near the mouth of Vermillion river, the current of the Illinois is deep and gentle, and the navigation unobstructed through the year.

Congress has passed a new bill, to aid the construction of this canal. It grants to the state of Illinois, a quantity of the public lands equal to one-half of 5 sections in width on each side of the canal; each alternate section being reserved to the United States, from one end to the other.

N.—From the mouth of the Vermillion river, down the Illinois, to the confluence of this with the Mississippi, near the town of Monroe, in Illinois state, and 30 miles above St. Louis, Missouri. Distance, by the river course, *Miles,* 250

SUMMARY FOR THE MIDDLE GREAT LAKES, AND THE STATES OF MICHIGAN AND ILLINOIS.

ARTIFICIAL NAVIGATION.

Page.	No.		Miles.
339	114.	Erie and Michigan canal, distance,	150
340	115.	The Chicago canal,	120
		Total of artificial navigation,	270

NATURAL NAVIGATION.

Page.		Miles.
339	Coast of Lake Erie,	350
340	From the mouth of Maumee river to Detroit, and by the St. Clair, and the coast of Lakes Huron and Michigan, to the Chicago river,	780
341	Illinois river, below the Vermillion,	250
	To which add,— For all other streams and navigable waters, viz. Of the rivers and creeks in these states, some of which are particularized below, there are 50 affording an average natural navigation of 20 miles each, and 50 an average of 10 miles each. These make, together,	1500
	Total of natural navigation,	2880
	Total of artificial navigation,	270
	Total of both,	3150

IN MICHIGAN STATE, VIZ.

The Raisin river, after a course of about 100 miles, falls into Lake Erie, below Monroe town.

The Huron of Lake Erie, rises by several branches, and flows parallel to the Raisin: it discharges at the outlet of Detroit river.

The Huron of St. Clair; north of the above; rises, like them, in the dividing ridge, and flows through a lake: it receives in its course a number of streams, and falls into Lake St. Clair.

OF THE UNITED STATES. 343

Saganaw river and bay, of Lake Huron, and Ottoway river and bay, of Michigan: these each include a considerable extent of coast.

Carp river, Platte river, the Betsy, the Manistic, the Sandy, the Marquette, the Pentwater, the White, the Mascogon, the Grande, the Iroquois, the Kikolanozo, the Blackwater, and the St. Joseph's rivers, are tributary streams to the Michigan lake on the east.

Tongnamon river, the Sheldrake, the Twohearted, the Hurricane, the Miners, the Trains, the Laughing Fish, and the Chocolate, are tributaries of Lake Superior, in this state.

IN ILLINOIS STATE; VIZ.

Tributaries of the Illinois; the Spoon and Crooked rivers, rising in the west of the state, and after a course of 80 to 100 miles each, falling into the Illinois; which also receives on the east bank, a number of smaller streams.

Henderson river, rises in the same ridge with the Spoon. This, as well as several rivers and creeks not here named, enters the Mississippi at the west line of the state.

The Kaskaskias river, rises in the prairies between the Illinois and the Wabash: it falls into the Mississippi, midway between the Ohio and the Illinois: it is 150 miles and more in length, and navigable for boats 130 miles.

The Cahokia river, falls into the Mississippi four miles below St. Louis; navigable not far.

Vaseuse, or Muddy river, falls into the Mississippi above Cape Giraudeau.

Saline river, falls into the Ohio, 20 miles below the Wabash: navigable to some miles above the salt-works.

The Little Wabash, and other streams falling into the Wabash, afford natural navigation, more or less, each. The waters lying within the Indian possessions of this state, are not yet fully explored.

NOTE.

The privilege of being stiled "state," in regard to Michigan, has, above, been anticipated. It will very soon be acquired.

LAKES ONTARIO AND SUPERIOR, AND NORTH-WEST TERRITORY NAVIGATION.

N.—From the point on the St. Lawrence river, struck by the contemplated "Champlain and St. Lawrence canal," of New-York, up the said river, to Sackett's harbour, Lake Ontario, and thence up the Lake, to Fort Niagara and Lewistown, on the Niagara strait. Distance, as follows:

St. Regis, lat. 45°, to		
Hamilton,		35
Great Gallop islands,	10	45
Ogdensburg,	14	59
Morrisville,	12	71
Cape Vincent,	50	121
Sackett's harbour,	20	141
Oswego river,	40	181
Great Sodus bay,	28	209
Genessee river,	35	244
Fort Niagara,	74	318
Lewistown,	7	*Miles*, 325

N. 648.
A. 1. } From Michilimakinac, through Lake Superior, to the western extremity thereof, at Fond du Lac, and thence up St. Louis' river, to the establishment of the "American Fur Company." Distance, by stations, viz.

To Detour,		40
Sault St. Marie,	45	85
Pointe aux Pins,	6	91
Pointe Irroquoise,	9	100
Tonguamanon bay	15	115
Sheldrake river,	9	124

White Fish point,	9	133
Two-hearted river,	24	157
Grande Marais,	21	178
Pointe Grand Sable,	9	187
Picture rocks,	12	199
Doric rock,	6	205
Grand isle,	12	217
Train's river,	9	226
Train's island,	3	229
Laughing Fish island, (river,)	6	235
Chocolate river,	15	250
Dead river,	6	256
Grand point,	6	262
Garlick river,	9	271
St. John's river,	15	286
Burned river,	12	298
Pine river,	6	304
Huron river,	9	313
Around Keweena point,	90	403
Little Trout river,	9	412
Graverod river,	6	418
Misery river,	12	430
Fire-steel river,	18	448
Onontagon, or Coppermine river,	6	454
Iron river,	15	469
Carp river,	15	484
Presqu' isle river,	6	490
Blake river,	6	496
Montreal river,	21	517
Bad river,	12	529
Chegomigon point,	6	535
Isle St. Michael,	3	538
Raspberry river,	15	553
Sandy river,	6	559
Detour,	3	562
Cranberry creek,	30	592
Fond du Lac, (Boisbrulé river,)	15	607
Fond du Lac,	21	628
Chippeway village,	3	631
Fur company's establishment,	18 *Miles*,	649

No. 116.

ST. MARY'S CANAL.

The navigation between the Lakes Huron and Superior, especially upward, is interrupted by the Falls of St. Mary, but the distance is short; and it is stated that a side canal at this place, which would render the navigation continuous, need not be near a mile in length, and would not be at all of difficult construction.

N.—From the head of Noguet's bay, Michigan, through that and Green bay, to Fort Brown, at the mouth of Fox river. Distance, *Miles*, 90

A.—From Fort Brown, at Green bay, Michigan, by canal, in the direction of Fox river, upward, and along a series of rapids between the mouth thereof and Winnebago lake. Distance, *Miles*, 50

N.—From the extremity of this canal, at the outlet of Winnebago lake, through the said lake, and up Fox river channel, to its fork; whence, by the main south branch, 15 miles, to a portage. Distance, *Miles*, 190

A.—From the point on Fox river, last above specified, by canal, westward, to the opposite water of the Ouisconsin river. Distance, *Miles*, 2

No. 117.

THE FOX AND OUISCONSIN CANAL.

The ground for the location and particulars of these projected works, has yet to be more minutely examined than it has hitherto been, with a view to the undertaking: but effective attention will no doubt be drawn to the object; if not forthwith, within the course of a very few years, as the territory around becomes more dense in population. That is to say, *white* population; for, as yet, the proprietorship of the soil, both around and through this important district of country, remains chiefly with the aborigines.

NOTE.

A passage has been effected by a flotilla of boats, having on board a body of the United States infantry, from Green bay, Michigan, by way of the Fox and Ouisconsin rivers, to St. Louis, Missouri; and this, without there having been encountered more than 2500 yards, or 1½ mile, of portage, before the flotilla reached the Ouisconsin river.

This channel of communication from the great lakes, it is not a little probable, will, ere long, no less than the Illinois and Wabash ones, be improved to the utmost, for the facilities that it may afford to the defences of the country; it leads most directly to the Upper Mississippi; as the others do, one to a middle point, and one to the Lower Mississippi. The central military station of St. Louis, is destined, no doubt, to become of surpassing importance, and greater historical note, than that of the celebrated Fort Chartres, under the French, in times of old: which was, however, with them, the chief position of a cordon, stretching from Canada to the Gulf of Mexico, through New-Orleans.— A cordon, or chain of posts, conceived by the French government, for opening a line of water communication between their possessions in Canada and Louisiana, and in the end to lead to an intimate union of the one with the other; populating the wilderness border from Quebec to New-Orleans, along the whole course of the northern lakes and the Mississippi river. This chain, it was intended, should secure to them all the extensive territory of the west, in thorough union and reciprocal intercourse with the one no less extensive or less important, (though of a different character) in the north; their only civilized neighbours were the English, at 1,000 miles distance, (if neighbours they might be termed,) confined to the shores of the Atlantic, and separated by the Alleghany range of mountains, then an insurmountable barrier between the east and the west.

It has so happened, that the execution of the French plan was not on a scale worthy its conception, and far less commensurate with the mighty objects, which, had the plan succeeded, it would have been found to embrace.

It was in August, this year, 1826, that the boats found a passage, as above, from Green bay.

The tract of country between the two rivers, and south of the Portage, and perhaps the whole between Lake Michigan and the Mississippi, possesses a rich store of lead mines; which it is an object to enter into immediate negotiation with the Indians for. A treaty with the Winnebagoes and others, the present proprietors, is to be set on foot, for a cession of the district; which being accomplished, population will at once flow to this point with rapidity; and improvements of every description speedily follow. Considerations of the highest importance will invite the establishment of a new military station on the very site of the present portage ground. Its name, probably, Fort Winnebago. It is thought this large "mining district," a name it now bears, has not any where an equal, for abundance in lead ore, and ease with which the miner can obtain it. No estimate can be formed of the quantity of lead that may here be produced.

December, 1828.

A deputation of Winnebago chiefs, now on their way home from a first visit to Washington, have been induced to engage to use their influence to induce the nation to make a cession to the United States, of a *small portion* of the "mining district" of country!!!

In the mean time, two recent treaties have been effected, viz. one with the Winnebagoes and the united tribes of the Potowatomy, Chippeway, and Ottoway Indians, bearing date 25th August, 1828. The other with the Potowatomy tribe apart, bearing date 20th September, 1828. And there cannot be any doubt whatever, but the United States government will be completely successful, in obtaining from the Indians, possession of *all* the lead mine region, as well as the important "portage," so needful in order to complete a military communication between the Mississippi valley and the Canada frontier. By the former of said two treaties, a boundary line is agreed on for possession on the part of the United States provisionally, until such time as a regular cession can be made, in full Indian council, of a tract of country lying between the Ouisconsin river, the waters of Rock river, and the Mississippi; which includes the mines of Fever or Fêve river, sometimes called Bean river, Illinois state.

By the September treaty, a cession is actually obtained of the Indian title to two tracts of country, whereof one is bounded by the River St. Joseph, the northern line of Indiana state, and the shore of Lake Michigan; the other lying south of a line drawn eastward, from the south extremity of the lake, and east and west between the head of a branch of Kankakee river, and the boundary line of the states of Indiana and Ohio. The whole extent of territory which the government of the United States at present look forward to, by an early regular cession from the Winnebagoes, the Potowatomies, and other Indians conjointly, lies on both sides of Rock river, and is bounded west by the Mississippi, east in part by Lake Michigan, in part by a strip yet reserved to the Indians on the lake shore, north by the Ouisconsin and Fox rivers, and may amount to $7\frac{1}{2}$ millions of acres of land.

The white population, including that of Fever river district, Illinois, is computed already at 15,000, partly occupying the villages of Galena, Cassville, Prairie des Chiens, Green Bay, and others, but mostly engaged in extracting mineral wealth from the earth; (lead for the present, but the country is also rich in copper ore.) It is expected that congress, at their next session, will separate from the territorial government of Michigan, and erect into a new territory, as the "Huron territory," all the district bounded by the upper and head waters of the Mississippi on the west, by Canada and Lake Superior on the north, by

Lake Michigan on the east, and the state line of Illinois on the south. After which, the territory of Huron will no doubt soon become a "state."

1829.

All has been executed as above signified, and confirmed by the Indians in regular council, and the Indian title to the lands is now extinct. By which measure, the benefits accruing to the United States may be summed up as follows :—

1. The pecuniary value of the lands, which may extend to 8 or even 10 millions of acres.

2. Rendering the Winnebago and Potowatomy Indians powerless and harmless for hostile purposes, cut off as they now are from any intercourse with the tribes of Indians more to the west and to the north-west; because now surrounded by a white population on three sides, and the Michigan lake on the fourth.

3. The advantages, in a military point of view, of securing safe communication to and fro, between the Mississippi valley and the great lakes, as already noticed.

4. The power of immediately completing a thorough navigation between Green bay, Michigan, and the Mississippi river at Prairie des Chiens, which, as already stated, is interrupted by only 2500 yards of dry ground, situate between the Fox and Ouisconsin rivers, at their two great bends; the United States being, by the treaties effected, placed in possession of this spot of ground. Steam-boats now run from the New-York canal at Buffalo, through the several lakes, to Green bay, and Fox river, notwithstanding the rapids below Winnebago lake; and there is only needed a canal of 2500 yards in length, at the portage in question, for the same to pass on, through the Ouisconsin, to the Mississippi at Prairie des Chiens, and thence, if requisite, down the stream to New-Orleans; thus forming a single line of internal steam-boat navigation of more than 3000 miles in length.

5. In this ceded country, possession is obtained of an unknown number of lead mines, the richest probably in all the world; in so much so, that lead is now selling, at the places where dug from, at the rate of $1\frac{1}{2}$ cent, and in St. Louis, at $2\frac{1}{4}$ cents per pound. But besides lead, indications are dispersed over the face of the country, of there being copper in abundance.

6. An extensive farming country is likewise obtained, there being exhibited the singular spectacle, of wheat land of the richest quality being in combination with mines the most productive.

Thus, whether the cession be regarded in a money point of view, as the means of opening a large amount of revenue into the national treasury; or in a military point of view, as conquering the Winnebago and Potowatomy Indians without bloodshed, and opening a secure and easy road, upon any emergency, into Canada; in a commercial point of view, as connecting the lakes and the Mississippi, and uniting New-York and New-Orleans; or in a manufacturing point of view, as it presents an abundant cheap domestic supply of lead, and probably of copper, but certainly of lead, the chief ingredient in a variety of manufactures, and highly useful purposes; or in an agricultural point of view, as presenting as fine a wheat country as is to be found in the United States,—it is difficult, under either of these aspects, to estimate the worth of the acquisition; and, taken in the aggregate view, the advantages to be derived from it to the nation at large, are certainly invaluable. In its character of a BARGAIN, it may well rank alongside the celebrated convention with Bonaparte himself, for the great territory of Louisiana.

Produce of lead in 2 years from Fever river mines.

	Pounds.
Made there, from 30th September, 1827, to 30th September, 1828,	11,105,810
Made there, from 30th September, 1828, to 30th September, 1829,	13,343,150
Together,	24,448,960

N.—From the termination of the canal at the Ouisconsin river, down the river stream, to the mouth thereof at Prairie des Chiens, Fort Crawford, on the Mississippi.
Distance, *Miles*, 182

SUMMARY FOR LAKES ONTARIO AND SUPERIOR, AND THE NORTH-WEST TERRITORY.

ARTIFICIAL NAVIGATION.

Page.	No.		Miles.
345	116.	St. Mary's canal,	1
346	117.	The Fox and Ouisconsin canal,	52
		Total of artificial navigation,	53

NATURAL NAVIGATION.

Page.		Miles.
344	St. Regis on the St. Lawrence river, to Lewistown on the Niagara, - - - -	325
344	Michilimakinac to Fond du Lac, by the coast of Lake Superior, - - - - -	648
346	Noguet's bay, through Green bay, to the mouth of Fox river, - - - -	90
346	Winnebago lake and Fox river navigation,	190
350	The Ouisconsin river, to the Mississippi,	182

To which add:—

For all other rivers and creeks, some of which are particularized below and above; and of which, exclusive of those flowing into the Mississippi, (hereafter noticed,) there are 50, affording a natural navigation of 10 miles average each,   This makes,   500

Total of natural navigation,   1935
Total of artificial navigation,   53

Total of both, - - - 1988

The Coppermine river, the Montreal river, and many streams of less note on the south shore of Lake Superior. The first two are each connected, through a short portage, with the Ouisconsin river, north branch.

The St. Croix river, formed of several branches rising in the northern swamps: it expands into a lake near the Mississippi, and discharges at 50 miles below St. Anthony's; the Chippeway, the Black, and some lesser streams, which discharge into the same, farther south.

NOTE.

Upon Lake Superior, and within the United States section of it, there are several islands reputed for being very productive in copper ore. The late Dr. Franklin related, that when resident in Paris, he was favoured with the perusal of a set of unpublished journals and maps of a corps of French engineers; who had sloops, and visited and examined those islands, when the French had possession of Canada; and that, according to their account, the quantity of copper ore was inexhaustible.

MISSISSIPPI NAVIGATION; AND CONFLUENTS FROM THE WEST.

N.—From Fort St. Peters, below the Falls of St. Anthony on the Mississippi, latitude 45°, down the river stream, to the mouth thereof, at the Balize, in the Gulf of Mexico. Distance, by stations, on the windings of the river, *Miles*, 2250

No. 118.
MISSISSIPPI RIVER BED.

This navigation, through the natural channel of the river, from the rapids at St. Anthony, down to the sea, although it may be considered as open and unimpeded in all the distance, yet contains some hidden dangers, which now and then occasion serious accidents to vessels on their passage. These consist in sunken trees, brought down by the floods; some kept in motion by the current, others immovable; and are denominated "Planters," or "Sawyers," or "Snags," according to their respective position and circumstance to occasion damage, or the manner in which they happen to have partially imbedded themselves beneath the water.

To clear away a few of these dangers from along this great highway of the country, at places where they can be discovered, an appropriation was made by congress last year, 1824, and the work is at present in prosecution. The sum voted was 70,000 dollars, the river Ohio being included in it for the like improvement along its channel, where similar dangerous obstructions exist; and contracts, passed to individuals by the commissioners of government, for certain distances of the one and the other, are now in execution. Further appropriations for the object, will, no doubt, be required and made.

NOTE.

It has been suggested, that the construction of an entire side canal, along the west of the Mississippi, from the mouth of the Ohio river down to some point not far distant from New-Orleans, or from the Missouri river downwards into Louisiana state, will be required ; and Mr. Darby remarks, (*Geographical View,*) that if steam-boats had never been invented, this same idea might possibly by this time have arrested serious attention, and that notwithstanding all existing steam power advantages, great canal improvements on the west of the Mississippi are but postponed for a season. He says, "The advance of population along the Mississippi will no doubt eventuate in opening many of those natural but obstructed channels, which wind over the great alluvial plain from Missouri to Louisiana. The Arkansas, Red, and Washitto rivers are to unite, and an immense circuit, down the Mississippi, and up the two latter, will be avoided."

To this distance, - - - - - *Miles*, 2250
Add as follows,—

Above the Falls of St. Anthony, the Mississippi river receives from the west; the Corbeau, the Pine, the Elk, the Sac, and some other streams; the Corbeau is navigable about 200 miles. - - - - - -

The St. Peter's river, enters the Mississippi at the United States fort below the Falls of St. Anthony; it has been ascended : its extreme sources approach and interlock with those of the North Red river; it receives in its course a number of streams, and affords a passage for canoes, or in flood season for boats, of about 500 miles, interrupted by two short portages. This navigation is susceptible of improvement. - - - -

The Occano, the Ioway, the Turkey, the Moines, besides other rivers falling into the Mississippi below the mouth of St. Peter's river, and above that of the Missouri, afford together a navigation to an unascertained extent, especially in the season of flood. The Moines has a course south-east, of 800 miles, and receives the contribution of two great branches; the Raccoon, and the North fork; together, - - - - - - - 1500

The Missouri river, from its mouth near St. Louis, is navigable up to the Great falls, 2532 miles, and above the falls to its sources, 500 miles in addition, - - 3032

The Merrimeg, and its branch, the Big river, navigable, - - - - - - - 200

The St. Francis river flows from the highlands in Madison, Washington, and St. Francis counties, Missouri; it receives Bear creek and many other streams, and passes, in a southern course of 400 miles, through an immense swamp, entering the Mississippi at latitude 34° 33', some miles south of the Chickasaw Bluffs. The lowermost part of this river is checked by a large stationary raft: its comparative course is about 250 miles.

The White river is derived from a number of sources in the Ozark mountains, latitude 37° 30', and after a long circuitous course, falls into the Mississippi at 20 miles above the mouth of the Arkansas. The White is navigable 400 miles, to Harding's ferry, and during some part of the year, 500 miles. Its greatest north-east branch, the Big Black, and the numerous tributaries of the latter, as the Spring, the Strawberry, the Currant, and others, are navigable about the same distance; together, - 800

Tributaries of the Missouri, viz.

Gasconade river enters from the south, 79 miles above St. Charles: it is navigable 150 miles, - - - 150

The Osage river has its source in the Ozark mountains. It receives several fine rivers, and enters the Missouri at 120 miles from the Mississippi. It is navigable, by estimation, from 500 to 600 miles. - - - - 500

Chariton rivers; east and west; they unite on approaching the Missouri; and are navigable more than 300 miles, 300

Grand river, from the north, is navigable for boats, 250

The Kanzas river is made up of two branches, heading between the Platte and Arkansas; namely, the Republican and Smoky hill forks, and the branches of these. From either extreme source to the Missouri, is a distance of 700 or 800 miles eastward; yet so shallow is the river bed, that the Kanzas is not navigable more than 200 miles, except for a short interval in the height of flood season, 200

The Platte river rises in the Oregon or Rocky mountains, and, like the Kanzas, crosses the Great Sandy Desert. After a course of 800 or 900 miles, it falls into the Missouri, at 600 miles thence to the Mississippi. At midway it branches into two great forks, north and south, besides receiving, in its course below, the Long fork, the Elkhorn, and other rivers of note. Through most of its length, however, the bed of the Platte is quite dry, in summer, for hundreds of miles, and the same is the case with its main tributary rivers; so that through most of this great extent, there is no navigation, except for a very limited time in flood season; and in the upper parts of these rivers, the Indian navigation is carried on by canoes of skin, floating lightly, - - - - - ...

The Yellow Stone river, is of a different character; it enters the Missouri from the south, in latitude 48°, and is navigable, in its main stream and branches, by estimation, 800 miles, - - - - - - 800

Numerous other tributaries, from on both sides, swell

the Missouri in its course; some of them perpetual streams of hundreds of miles in length, affording, in the aggregate, navigation to a vast extent: this, notwithstanding very many of the Missouri rivers are, by the circumstance of situation, condemned to have their outlets obstructed by annual formations of bars of mud. The floods of the great river coming down later, are apt to back up the currents of the others,

The Arkansas river;

Is made up of two great branches; viz. the main Arkansas, and the Canadian river; the first whereof has its source within the Oregon or Rocky mountains, and pursues a long south-east course to its confluence with the Mississippi, in latitude 34°, which, taking in the meanders, comprehends a distance of about 2000 miles. Amongst its tributaries are these ;—

The Negracky, or Red fork, rises near the mountains, and after an eastwardly course of 400 or 500 miles, joins the Arkansas at 900 miles above its mouth,

Newsawkatonga, or Grand Saline, on the south, has its source between the Arkansas and the Canadian, and joins the Arkansas at 150 miles below the Red fork,

Little Arkansas, has its head waters near the Smoky-hill fork of the Kanzas river, and discharges at 860 miles above the mouth of the Arkansas,

Stinking-fork, rises near the head waters of the Neocho, and falls into the Arkansas at 800 miles above its mouth,

Neocho, or Grand river, has its head waters in Missouri territory, west of the Ozark mountains, and pursues a southern course by several branches. It falls into the Arkansas at 600 miles from the Mississippi,

Illinois river, of Arkansas, rises in the Ozark mountains, state of Missouri, and falls into the Arkansas river, east of the Neocho,

The Canadian branch, has its source at the base of the Oregon mountains, and after a course eastward, of 1000 miles, joins the Arkansas at 550 miles thence to the Mississippi; and a little below the mouth of Illinois on the opposite bank,

The Canadian has two forks, viz.

North fork, at 50 miles from its mouth; this meanders eastwardly 800 or 900 miles, and receives in its course, Little North fork,

South fork, at six miles above the North: length of the
South 400 to 500 miles, - . - - ...

Notwithstanding the almost immensity of these river distances, described by the Arkansas and its parallel tributaries, they are comparatively very little navigable. Along the beds of them all, across the Great Desert, the water disappears entirely in the summer season, as in the case of the Platte river. The Arkansas is, however, most generally navigable for boats, as high as the mouth of the Neocho, otherwise Grand river, 600 miles, - - 600

Miles, 10,582

For the many rivers not here extended in miles, together with a multitude of sub-streams not here enumerated, affording each a length, more or less, of natural navigation; moreover, the streams falling into the Upper Mississippi on the eastern bank; of all these, the aggregate distance may be taken to be equal to that formed by as much as is extended above of the Mississippi's western tributaries; namely, - - - - - 8,332

Total of natural navigation, - - *Miles*, 18,914

NOTE.

Near the heads of the St. Peter's river, is situate Lake Travers, one of the sources of the Red river of the north, and separated from the St. Peter's by two or three miles of ground, very little elevated above either the lake or the river. On the north, Lake Traverse sends its waters through an outlet, called Swan river, into the Red river, and in times of flood, it also communicates with the St. Peter's, on the south. So that here is presented one out of the number of striking exemplifications in this part of the continent, of the fact that it is not high ridges of mountains, generally or altogether, which have determined the course of river streams from their sources, into one or another channel or direction. Here we have the head waters of two mighty streams; one of them taking a direction nearly north, and discharging into Hudson's bay, in latitude 57°; the other a southern course, and discharging into the Gulf of Mexico, in latitude 29°. They rise in a valley, far from any mountain; on the contrary, amidst lakes and swamps, within a short distance of each other, and during seasons of flood are in actual contact. The Mississippi has its extreme source, or rather, one of its extreme sources, in Turtle lake, north of Little Winnepec, and close to Red lake; which is another of the sources of Red river, by way of Red fork.

In the tract of country lying between latitude 45° and 48° north; longitude 93° and 97° west from Greenwich; that is to say; in 200 miles square of surface, we have an interlockage of the head waters of a number of large rivers, terminating in three of the mightiest streams that are known. The Mississippi river, and many of its great tributaries, proceed from the same lakes and swamps, which go to swell the waters of Nelson's river, and of the St. Lawrence. There are places where a spectator may stand and see the streams running from him in the three directions; towards the north, the south, and the east.

At Lake Traverse, the "Columbian fur company," established since 1822, have their principal station: the latitude of it is 45° 40'. The lake is 15 miles in length. From whence, at 400 miles of navigation distance, taking the Swan river outlet, and the course of Red river, which is winding, you arrive at the town of Pembina; which lies within the United States domain; but at the north outskirt of this town there is affixed a boundary mark with Upper Canada, latitude 49°.

The whole length of Red river, from the Swan channel, to its entrance into Lake Winnepec, counting after the same manner, is probably 600 miles. Besides receiving the waters of Otter tail river, the eastern source of which is Otter tail lake, it has many tributaries, whereof the Pse or Rice river, the Chienne, the Buffalo, the Elm, the Wild Rice, the Plane, the Sandhill, the Goose, the Red fork, the Turtle, the Big Saline, the Pack, and some others, lie within the United States: several of the latter affording navigation through lakes and swamps, towards the heads of the Mississippi, and including in that general course, each one, a large circuit. The Assiniboin river, in the British territory, is one of much importance, and navigable, at all stages of the water, to a great distance.

The heads of the Mississippi, and of course the heads also of those other streams diverging from the same swampy spot; some towards Lake Winnepec to swell the Nelson, and some towards Rainy lake river and Lake Superior, and ultimately the St. Lawrence; are computed to be 1300 feet above tide water.

From the frontier settlement of Pembina, on Red river, latitude 49°, the distance to York factory, on Hudson's bay, by water, with 25 portages, is, by estimation, 845 miles.

From the same, to New-Orleans, by water, with three portages, 3000 miles.

From the same, to Buffalo, on Lake Erie, by the way of Red lake, by water, but with many portages before reaching Lake Superior, 1963 miles.

Such is the aspect of the natural navigation of the country, north, south, and east, from this spot.

The following table, showing the extent and position of the

Mississippi basin, is taken from Darby's "Geographical View." It is exclusive of the smaller river basins of West Florida, in the vicinity of the Mississippi delta.

Table of the Extent and Geographical position of the respective Valleys of the Mississippi Basin.

Natural sections.	Length.	Mean width.	Area in sq. miles.	Between lat. N.	Between lat. N.	Between long. W.	Between long. W.
Ohio valley, - - -	750	261	196,000	34° 00'	42° 30'	1° 00'	11° 40'
Mississippi valley, above Ohio, including the minor valley of Illinois, but exclusive of Missouri, - - -	650	277	180,000	37 00	48 00	9 00	20 00
Lower valley of the Mississippi, including White, Arkansas, and Red river valleys,	1,000	200	200,000	29 00	42 00	11 00	30 00
Missouri proper, including Osage, Kansas, Platte rivers, &c.	1,200	437	523,000	37 00	50 00	13 00	35 00
Total area,			1,099,000				

The tributaries of the Upper Mississippi, are enumerated by the same author, thus:—

From the right bank, the Mississippi receives, advancing from source to mouth, Leech lake river, Vermillion, Pine, Corbeau, (Crow river,) Elk, and Sac, above the Falls of St. Anthony; below the latter point are the confluents, St. Peters, Upper Iowa, Little Maquaquetois, Galena, Great Maquaquetois, Lower Iowa, and Lesmoines. From the left, in descending, enter Thornberry, Round lake, Turtle, Portage, Chevreuill, Prairie, La Crosse, Ouisconsin, Sissinawa, Riviere au Fevre, Rock, Henderson, and Illinois.

"The confluents of the Mississippi," says Mr. Darby, "are given in great part on the respectable authority of Mr. Schoolcraft, who estimates the elevation of the sources of that stream at 1330 feet. From comparative length of course with the Ohio, and from other data, the statement of Mr. Schoolcraft approaches, it is probable, very near the real elevation of that marshy tableland, which gives source to the southern branch of Assiniboin, and to the Mississippi.

"Vast as is the above basin in extent, it can only, however, on true geographical principles, be considered as a section of that system of rivers which flow into the Gulf of Mexico, and regard that inland sea as their common recipient. It is very remarkable, that if every stream, great and small, which enters this gulf, from Cape Sable, of Florida, to Point Gorda, of Yucatan, were supposed to be continued in the line of their course, they would unite with each other in a common estuary, not far outside of the centre of the gulf. But from the great superiority in quantity of water and of surface drained by the Mississippi, that river well deserves to give name to the system of which it forms so conspicuous a part."

Of the progress in population of this great central valley, some notice may be here allowed.

It was not until the year 1764, that even Daniel Boone, whose flight from wilderness to wilderness forms a kind of hegira in the west, made his appearance in East Tennessee. The first cession of land, obtained by treaty of the Indians, is of no older date than April, 1775, and therefore becomes most strikingly remarkable, as simultaneous with another momentous event;—the blow is now struck, from which American Independence was to be achieved, and simultaneously the portals of the western mountains are for the first time thrown open to a white population; prior to this period, settlements beyond the river Ohio having, by authority from the Crown, been forbidden. It is related, that in 1766, a party descended the Great Tennessee and Cumberland rivers, and not one white man was then found settled thereon.

In 1810, the western population is stated, by census returns, at - - - - - - - 1,078,325 souls,

In 1820, thus:—

Alabama,	143,000
Arkansas,	14,273
Illinois,	55,211
Indiana,	147,178
Kentucky,	564,317
Louisiana,	153,407
Michigan,	10,000
Mississippi,	75,448
Missouri,	66,586
Ohio,	581,434
Tennessee,	422,813

2,233,667 souls, without including the western portions of Virginia, Pennsylvania, and New-York states. So that it may fairly be affirmed, the Mississippi valley now contains (1829) a population more than equal to that with which the old 13 United States plunged into the revolutionary war; and there appears a strong probability, that after the census of 1830, not more than three other periods, of 10 years each, will run, ere the said 13 old states (now 15) shall commence to be outnumbered, and consequently outvoted in the councils of the nation. The "sceptre shall depart from Judah, never to return." In 38 years, from 1790, the central population in question has risen from 100,000 to 3,500,000; that of the United States at large, from 4,000,000 to 13,000,000.

"But it is not merely the rapid growth of the western settlements into populous states, that surprises the traveller from the seacoast. For this growth he must be prepared, because he finds it set down in the statistical tables of the country, and because, as a mere matter of figures, he cannot but comprehend it. That which strikes him with astonishment is the advanced state of the community,—the social improvement which he witnesses. He finds this great region abounding not merely with fertile lands, but with highly cultivated farms; filled, not with wild hunters, but with a substantial yeomanry. The forests are interspersed, like the region he has left, with villages active with all the arts of life:—he descends the mighty rivers in one of those floating castles—half ware-house and half palace—which the genius of Fulton has launched on all our waters; built here in greater numbers than in the East, and with at least equal magnificence; and on these rivers, he finds, from Pittsburg down to New-Orleans, a succession of large towns, surpassed only by a few of the Atlantic cities; growing fast into a rivalry with some of them;—and already rich, not merely in wealth, but in all the refinements of life, and in all the institutions that adorn the nature of social, intellectual, moral, and religious man." *Everett.*

Of Pittsburg city, the Pennsylvania great western emporium, it may here be noticed, that within the remembrance of thousands of individuals now living at or occasionally visiting the place, it was a mere frontier village, of small extent and little value for the trade it carried on; now it has so risen, as, in point of commerce, to employ 300 of those large steam-boats above spoken of, in the exchange of the commodities it commands; and in point of manufacturing consequence, is actually styled the "Birmingham of America." Cut flint-glass, there wrought, adorns at present the table of the President at Washington. Pittsburg, too, is ambitious to become the seat of a flourishing university; and is taking measures accordingly.

The account of steam-boat navigation in the west, its sudden rise, and almost miraculous results in so short a time; with, moreover, the most assured prospects of still increasing benefits to be derived from it, to an indefinite extent, in favour of the social system, throughout the expansive and abundantly watered territory of these United States, is too apposite not to be here inserted, after what has been stated above. The account has claims, too, from the very circumstance of being taken from a recent publication, issued in *Cincinnati, Ohio,* as being, therefore, incidentally illustrative of certain facts, the knowledge of which, with all the deductions they irresistibly suggest, is here intended to be conveyed to the yet uninformed *stranger;* for it is a knowledge which, at this day, has, indeed, by the force of familiarity, ceased to excite in the minds of most well informed Americans, any great emotion of the *wonderful;* but the mention of which things, some 40 or 50 years ago, could they by supernatural powers have been foreseen by any individual, would not have escaped from being denounced, at once, by every reasonable man of cultivated understanding, as ravings or dreams of the fancy, *not destined for fulfilment.*

STEAM-BOATS IN THE WEST.

To a native of the West, the rapid improvement which has taken place in almost every thing that strikes the eye, is a subject of the most intense interest. In retrospecting through the last thirty years, the changes have more the appearance of the extravagant shiftings of a dream, than the usual progress of reality. Strangers describe us as having a powerful propensity for self-praise and boasting; no doubt we deserve much of this censure; the cause of it, however, is not to be sought in any peculiarity of national feeling, but may be traced to the circumstances of the period and region in which we live. A few years will be sufficient to correct this sentiment of pride; and the habit of looking at the existing state of improvement, will shortly involve in oblivion those days of toilsome suffering and inconvenience, which every middle aged native of the valley of the Ohio remembers, and has felt.

It is little more than thirty years since the then frontier village of Fort Pitt (now Pittsburg) was subject to frequent alarms from the appearance of the red man on the western shore of one of her rivers; it is little more than thirty years since one of the first necessaries of life was packed from the eastern side of the mountains, by the individuals themselves who consumed it; it is little more than thirty years since the canoe of the savage gave place to the scarcely less inconvenient flat boat of the emigrant, which in its turn was to yield to the open keel of the trader, and the flat roofed ark of the Mississippi. What is the revolution which has occurred? Pittsburg has earned the name of the American Birmingham; Fort Washington, under the name of Cincinnati, has become one of the most beautiful and attractive cities of the Union; and the Ohio river, which, within the memory of many of us, presented a navigation as dangerous as that of the mysterious Niger, is now visited for its picturesque charms, by travellers from the Rhine, the Rhone, and the Danube.

Of all the various subjects of interesting speculation which have combined in producing these almost incredible advancements in the West, the steam-boat is, probably, the one of the greatest moment. A review of the rise and progress of this item in the catalogue of the causes of our prosperity, may not be unimportant, and a statement of facts connected with it, will be likely to surprise ourselves, not less than strangers.

The first boat built on the Western waters, of which the writer of this article has any record, was the New-Orleans, built at Pittsburg in 1811;—he has no account of more than seven or eight built previously to 1817 ; from that period they have been rapidly increasing in number, character, model, and style of workmanship, until 1825, when two or three boats, built about that period, were declared by common consent to be the first in the world. Since that time, we are informed, that some of the New-York and Chesapeake boats rival, and probably surpass us in richness and beauty of internal decoration. As late as 1816, the practicability of navigating the Ohio with steam-boats, was esteemed doubtful ; none but the most sanguine augured favourably. The writer of this well remembers, that in 1816, observing, in company with a number of gentlemen, the long struggles of a stern-wheel boat to ascend Horse-tail ripple, (five miles below Pittsburg,) it was the unanimous opinion, that "such a contrivance" might conquer the difficulties of the Mississippi, as high as Natchez, but that we of the Ohio must wait for some more happy "century of inventions." In 1817, the bold and enterprising Captain Shreve, (whose late discovery of a mode for destroying snags, and improving western navigation, entitles him to the reputation of a public benefactor,) made a trip from New-Orleans to Louisville in 25 days. The event was celebrated by rejoicing, and by a public dinner to the daring individual who had achieved the miracle. Previous to that period, the ordinary passage by barges, propelled by oars and sails, was three months. A revolution in Western commerce was at once effected. Every article of merchandise began to ascend the Mississippi, until we have seen a package delivered at the wharf of Cincinnati, from Philadelphia *via* New-Orleans, at one cent per pound. From the period of Captain Shreve's celebrated voyage, till 1827, the time necessary for the trip has been gradually diminishing: during that year, the Tecumseh entered the port of Louisville, from New-Orleans, in 8 days and 2 hours from port to port !

Since the introduction of the steam-boat, the memorandum before me furnishes a list of 323, whose united tonnage may be estimated at about 56,000 tons, employed during this period, on the waters of the Mississippi and Ohio. The largest size rated about 500 tons, but a large majority of them are under 250 tons.

The average first cost of a steam-boat is estimated at one hundred dollars per ton; the repairs made during the existence of the boat, amount to one-half the first cost. The average duration of a boat has hitherto been about 4 years; of those built of locust, lately, the period will probably be 2 years longer. The amount of expenditure in this branch of business, on the Western waters, then, for the last ten years, will in some measure be shown by the following calculation:—

56,000 tons, costing 100 dollars per ton, amount to $5,600,000
Repairs at the end of the present *generation* of
    boats, say 3 years hence, - - - - 2,800,000

                                          Total, $8,400,000

Amount of money expended in building and repair-
    ing, in ten years, - - - - - $8,400,000

The annual expenditure of steam-boats is very difficult to be arrived at; the importance of this expenditure, however, to the towns on our rivers, and to the whole extent of country, running along their shores, may be estimated from the following calculation of the item of fuel alone, for one year. Take the present year of 1829. We have now in commission above two hundred boats, the average tonnage of which may be stated at 175 tons; this will give the whole amount now employed, 35,000 tons.

It is calculated that the business season of each year lasts eight months; deduct one-fourth for the time lost in port, and we have 6 months, or 180 days of running time. Each boat is presumed to consume one cord of wood, for every 12 tons, every 24 hours.

  The 35,000 tons, then, consume per day,   2,917 cords.
  Or during the six months, - - - 525,060 cords.

The price of wood varies from one dollar and a half to five dollars per cord; a fair average would place it about $2 25 per cord. This makes the expenditure for fuel alone, on the banks of our rivers, 1,181,385 dollars. The other expenditures, while running, are calculated by the most experienced and intelligent owners, to be equal to 1,300,000 dollars, which gives the total expenditure per annum (1829) at - - - $2,481,385

This calculation and estimate, then, which are both made lower than the facts justify, present these results—first,

The amount of first cost of steam-boats since
    1817, - - - - - - - $5,600,000
* Repairs on the same, up to 1832, - - 2,800,000

---

* Allowing the present amount of tonnage, 35,000 tons, to be the average amount to be employed for the next eight years, and allowing the generation of a boat to be 4 years, boats to the amount of 70,000 tons, including those of this

Total amount of expenditure of capital produced by
 the introduction of steam-boats, - - $8,400,000
Amount of expenditure in fuel and other expenses,
 exclusive of repairs, per season of 8 months, 2,481,381

We cannot better illustrate the magnitude of the change in every thing connected with Western commerce and navigation, than by contrasting the foregoing statement with the situation of things at the time of the adoption of steam transportation, say in 1817. About twenty barges, averaging 100 tons each, comprised the whole of the commercial facilities for transporting merchandise from New-Orleans to the "Upper country;" each of these performed one trip down and up again to Louisville and Cincinnati, within the year. The number of keel boats employed in the Upper Ohio cannot be ascertained, but it is presumed that 150 is a sufficiently large calculation to embrace the whole number. These averaged 30 tons each, and employed one month to make the voyage from Louisville to Pittsburg, while the more noble and dignified barge of the Mississippi made her trip in the space of 100 days, if no extraordinary accident happened to check her progress.

Not a dollar was expended for wood in a space of 2000 miles, and the squatter on the banks of the Ohio, thought himself lucky if the reckless boatman would give the smallest trifle for the eggs and chickens, which formed almost the only saleable articles on a soil whose only fault is its too great fertility. Such was the case 12 years since. The Mississippi boats now make five trips within the year, and are enabled, if necessary, in that period, to afford to that trade 35,000 tons. Eight or nine days are sufficient, on the Upper Ohio, to perform the trip from Louisville to Pittsburg and back. In short, if the steam-boat has not realized the hyperbole of the poet in "annihilating time and space," it has produced results scarcely surpassed by the introduction of the art of printing.

So far goes this interesting Cincinnati statement. A brief recapitulation and estimate, will exhibit as here follows:—

Amount of first cost of steam-boats, since the year
 1817, - - - - - - - $5,600,000
Repairs on same, down to 1832, - - - 2,800,000

Amount carried forward, $8,400,000

year, must be built during this time; first cost would be 7,000,000, and repairs, 3,500,000 dollars! The greatest part if not the whole of this last item might be secured to Cincinnati by the creation of dry-docks, and other conveniences as now contemplated.

Amount brought forward,	$8,400,000
For fuel and other necessaries, besides repairs, expended per season of 8 months, $2,481,385; and taking 10 such seasons to form an aggregate for the past, we have, for this head of expenditure,	24,813,850
Amount of first cost of 70,000 tons of steam-boats, required further to be built, to maintain the course of the trade, down to the year 1840, at $100 per ton,	7,000,000
Repairs on same,	3,500,000
For fuel and other necessaries, besides repairs, during 8 seasons of business, at $2,481,385 per season,	19,851,080
Amount, total,	$63,564,930

Or thus:—

Capital created and circulated, by the business of building and navigating steam-boats, on the Mississippi and Ohio rivers, from the first introduction thereof, in 1817, down to 1832,	$33,213,850
Further capital to be created and circulated, by the same business in continuation, from the year 1832, down to 1840,	30,351,080
Amount, total,	$63,564,930

There has lately appeared in one of the literary periodicals of the other side of the Atlantic, an able sketch of the most striking peculiarities, exhibited by the social condition of Europe at the present time, in contrast with former times. A quotation of the passages, it is hoped, will be acceptable, partly as a companion sketch to what has just been stated as belonging properly to *our side;* but in greater part, for the sake of what it contains as historical facts, so curious and so universally interesting. They are curious, because they intimate, that to a very small number of very humble, if not simple discoveries, in private or domestic life, working as ultimate causes, it is highly probable the social system of mankind, throughout the whole world, is destined to advance and attain its highest degree of perfection; and they are interesting, in the light of coming home to the feelings of almost every operative individual of the present day, and every mere beginner in his new career of knowledge, who at every turn of his mind to reflection, if he be but made acquainted with facts, cannot but take a feeling interest, in comparing times gone by, with present opportunities, and both the past, and the present, with what he may conclude the course of events is preparing to be, the state of things hereafter, in his children's day.

The London reviewer observes;—

There was no part of the Roman policy which so effectually promoted the good of mankind, or which has transmitted such exalted ideas of the imperial grandeur, as the number and magnificence of their roads. Though constructed principally for military purposes, they were of vast utility to the districts which they traversed, and proved the most efficacious means of promoting the comfort and civilization of the conquered peoples. As an instance of the extraordinary celerity in travelling which occasionally took place in ancient times, we are informed by Pliny, that Tiberius travelled 200 Roman miles in a day and a night, on being despatched by Augustus to console his sick brother Germanicus. But the ordinary rate of travelling, even in those days, was slow in comparison of what it is at present.

It is not easy to ascertain, from one period to another, what the state of the roads was, but they must have improved as trade increased. We know that the amelioration of them was slow; that the arts of constructing and directing them were for a long time understood very imperfectly; and that the first kingdom in which the condition of the great roads at all approached the present standard of excellence, was Sweden—where, from its want of wealth, and remote situation, no such occurrence could reasonably have been looked for.

The new arrangement for the arrival and departure of mails, which took place in England, in 1793, greatly forwarded that improvement of the principal roads which had been going on through the eighteenth century; and, from 1793 to the present moment, the highways, cross-roads, bridges, and ferries, throughout the whole extent of this country, are decidedly superior to those which are to be seen anywhere else. There are few places where the materials for making roads are so excellent and plentiful as in England; and as good roads conduce so much to the comfort as well as profit of those who use them, it is probable that this is an advantage which the inhabitants of this country will for a long period possess in greater perfection than their neighbours.

A remarkable improvement has, however, recently taken place in roads and bridges all over Europe. Materials for road making have been found where formerly they were not believed to exist, and the skill with which they are employed is surprising. Neither clay, sand, morasses, torrents, precipices, nor any other obstacles, are deemed insurmountable. A terrace has been conducted along the whole face of the Apennines, from Nice to the Gulf of Spezzia. The finest carriage roads cross the Alps, over Mount Cenis, St. Bernard, the Simplon, St. Gothard, the Splugen, from the Lake of Como to the source of the Inn, from Trent to Brixen, and where the road from Vienna to Venice crosses them at Ponteba. An entirely new road has been formed in the kingdom of the Netherlands, from Namur to Luxembourg; another runs along the banks of the Rhine, from Mentz to Nimeguen; another, from Hamburg to Hanover, and from Hanover to Deventer. Two more are under consideration, one from Hamburg to Lubeck, and the other from Berlin to Hamburg, through sands which appear almost impassable. Another has been made from Warsaw to Kalisz, which is to be continued to Breslaw; another runs from Berlin, by Wittemberg, to Leipzig; and the whole way from Berlin, by Kustrin, Konigsberg, and Riga, to Petersburg, either does or will speedily present an admirable line of communication between the Prussian and Russian capitals. Baron Pasquier has just laid before the Chambers in France, a detailed report on the state of the roads of that country, a circumstance which of itself demonstrates the growing importance attached to internal communication in that kingdom. In short, the traveller can nowhere direct his steps without seeing bridges building, and roads opening, widening, levelling, and repairing; and it is difficult to determine what states or districts at present show most zeal and judgment in this branch of national improvement.

The progress lately made in water conveyance is still more remarkable. The first canals known in this part of the world, were those which were formed in Italy and the Low Countries, and served in several cases both to drain the ground and for the conveyance of merchandise. France followed their example, and, by means of the canal of Languedoc, (which is now acknowledged to have failed in the objects for which it was constructed) joined the Channel and the Mediterranean. Several others have since been completed, and others are in progress; but that country is never likely to place much dependence on its canal communications. About the middle of the last century, the commercial prosperity of this country induced it to turn its attention to canals, and from its abundance of water, and the moderate elevation of its surface, it has now pushed canal navigation beyond every other country. Austria has now got rail roads, and it, as well as Prussia and Sweden, possesses canals; and Russia, both within her old limits and in Poland, is zealously encouraging canals to connect her rivers, and transport the produce of the soil. The application of steam to shipping, which deserves to be ranked among the greatest discoveries, theoretical or practical, which ever were made, has, however, done more within the last twenty years to facilitate the communication between different places by water, than all the contrivances that went before it. Steam-vessels are now found permanently or occasionally plying from the bottom of the Mediterranean all round to the top of the Baltic. No place in this part of the world has derived so great advantage from the discovery of steam-vessels as England. Its situation, coal, and commerce, enable it to shoot forth these vessels in every direction; and, by means of the certainty and celerity of their passage, they have diminished its distance, and multiplied its means of access to every part of the European continent. To these accommodations in travelling must be added the variety, excellence, and cheapness of public conveyances, and the quick and sure transmission of letters by post. The combination of these discoveries and improved arrangements has produced an ease, certainty, and rapidity of intercourse, exceeding all past experience or imagination. We are, perhaps, not far enough removed from these changes to estimate them at their proper value. Though few in number, and simple in their operation, they have yet done more to change the face and multiply the comforts of society, than all the inventions which have taken place from the earliest ages to the present day.

The increase in the number of travellers, which these facilities have caused, is another of the chief peculiarities of the present period. The inhabitants of every country, but particularly of England, who travel for their improvement or gratification, have multiplied fifty or a hundred fold, and their numbers are continually augmenting.—One now thinks as little of going into another kingdom, as fifty years ago he would have done of going into a neighbouring county. In time of peace, Europe may now be said to compose but one family; and whenever a stranger of established character or extensive information is received from abroad under an hospitable roof, instead of fruitlessly endeavouring to overcome the obstacles which the want of community of manners, language, and ideas presented in former times to all easy and agreeable intercourse, he finds himself engaged at once in animated conversation with persons of congenial habits, on topics of mutual and equal interests. It is scarcely possible to estimate these advantages too highly. They break down the artificial distinctions which separate one man from another, remove misapprehensions, ignorance, and prejudice, and bind together the inhabitants of different countries by endearing ties of recollection.

Another characteristic of the present time is the extraordinary increase of education and knowledge which has taken place within the last forty years. That a much larger proportion of the people of Europe now read and write than formerly, is indisputable. Those parts of it which are Protestant were early distinguished from those which continued Roman Catholics, in respect of education, and they have ever since retained their superiority. But, with the exception of Spain and Portugal, it is impossible not to perceive that the means and habit of reading have of late increased every where. The multiplication of newspapers and periodical publications; the number of booksellers' shops; and the profusion of literary institutions and circulating libraries, are infallible indications of the extraordinary spread of education and reading. What effect this change may eventually produce on society, it is too soon to decide; but we cannot help expressing an apprehension, that both education and reading have been pushed too far among the lower classes, and that, among the higher, they are not taking a very desirable direction. With regard to labourers and mechanics, experience has already proved to demonstration, that the instruction which consists merely in being taught to read and write, will by no means insure that proper regulation of the mind and conduct which some enthusiastic friends of education expected from it. To render reading and writing really useful, that moral and religious discipline, which parents, pastors, masters, and relatives can alone bestow, must be superadded; and yet, strangely enough, this is a branch of education which those who are most solicitous about mere reading and writing have almost totally neglected.

STATES OF TENNESSEE, MISSISSIPPI, LOUISIANA, ALABAMA, AND GEORGIA NAVIGATION.

N.—From the confluence of the Tennessee and Ohio rivers in Callaway county, Kentucky, up the stream of Tennessee, to the foot of the Muscle shoals, near Florence, in Alabama.   Distance, *Miles*, 250

A.—From Florence, by canal, or else by the channel of the river, rendered at this place navigable to Marathon, or Brown's ferry, on the Tennessee, above the Muscle shoals.   Distance, *Miles*, 25

No. 119.

THE MUSCLE SHOAL CANAL.

This proposed improvement may, it is said, consist either in canal, or in a removal of the existing obstructions from the bed of the river, in such a way as to contract and deepen the channel. The obstructions are an immense collection of loose stones and shells, besides fresh water clams, and turtles; the river at this place spreading out, and forming several islands.

NOTE.

Since the above was written, preliminary examinations have been gone into by the United States board of engineers, for the accomplishment of this improvement; and a detailed report thereof, including rough plans and estimates, is in preparation. The examinations extend from Brown's ferry down to the foot of Colbert's shoals, below the Muscle shoals proper, and are to be followed by regular surveys, embracing three several routes for a canal; namely, one along the margin of the river, north; one along the southern margin; and one through the country, south side, at some distance from the river bank; in order to determine, should the canal mode of improvement be adopted, which of these routes will be most advantageous for the purpose. A grant of public lands is expected from congress, to aid the state of Alabama in making this improvement.

An act of congress, 2d May, 1828, has passed, granting 400,000 acres of public land, situate in the counties of Jackson, Madison, Morgan, Limestone, Lawrence, Franklin, Lauderdale, to enable the state of Alabama to effectuate the improvements here contemplated, as also any other navigation improvements along the course of the Tennessee river, within the state of Alabama, which the legislature thereof may deem advisable.

The said improvements to be commenced within two years from the passing of this act, and to be completed within ten years thereafter. They are also to be competent to steam-boat navigation, and to embrace, if possible, a connexion with the navigation of Elk river, from the state of Tennessee.

The property of the general government, to be exempt from tolls along these improvements; and all citizens of the United States exempt from tolls, unless congress should hereafter authorize a toll.

January 1830.

The legislature of Alabama have appointed commissioners to superintend the operations, which are immediately to be commenced, at the Muscle shoals.

N.—From the head of the Muscle shoals of the Tennessee, up the river stream, to the suck, or whirl, at Cumberland mountain, Hamilton county, and thence up to the head of navigable water, at Tellico blockhouse. Distance, by the windings of the river, *Miles*, 625

M.—From Tellico blockhouse on the Tennessee, by canal, or by a mixed navigation, to the navigable waters of Savannah river; taking for route, up the main Tennessee valley, or up the Tellico and Hiwassee valley, and down that of the Tugaloo,
Distance, to Augusta, *Miles*, 250

No. 120.

TENNESSEE AND SAVANNAH CANAL.

Surveys to determine the line of route for the projected connexion of these two rivers are to be made. But in case this ground for a canal should prove unfavourable, another route of connexion is suggested, as referred to at Art. 139, namely, between the head waters of one or more of the Georgia streams, and a head branch of the Coosa river, and between this latter and the Hiwassee; by means whereof, a communication of the Atlantic seaboard of Georgia with the Tennessee river may be effected.

N.—From Augusta, down the river stream, to Tibee point, 18 miles below the port of Savannah.

Distance, *Miles*, 158

M.—From Augusta, by canal and other water improvements, up the course of the Upper Savannah and the Tugaloo, and across to the valley of Chatahootchee and Flint rivers, and to the heads of their natural navigation; down which streams into the Appalachicola, and down the latter, 70 miles, to St. George's sound. This sound communicates, at 50 miles eastward, with Appalachee bay.

Distance, by a mixed navigation, *Miles*, 550

No. 121.

SAVANNAH AND APPALACHICOLA CANAL.

The ground, for this also, is to be regularly surveyed. As yet, the Chatahootchee river passes through Indian possessions; but the removal of the Indians to another district of the country, it is expected, is at hand.

In the mean time, the navigation of the Savannah river itself is undergoing considerable improvement in its upper waters, where the sluicing mode has been pretty much adopted by the state engineers of South Carolina; also a bill is at this moment before congress, appropriating 60,000 dollars, towards the removing of obstructions generally to the free navigation of this river.

A.—Canals are proposed between the Savannah and Ogatchee, and the Ogatchee and Alatamaha rivers; and surveys for the same have been, in part, effected.

Distance, together, *Miles,* 66

Nos. 122, 123.

SAVANNAH AND OGATCHEE CANAL.—OGATCHEE AND ALATAMAHA CANAL.

February, 1826.

An act of incorporation passed the Georgia legislature, on the 20th of December, 1825, in favour of Mr. Ebenezer Jenckes and associates, or representatives; authorizing him or them to construct a canal between the Great Ogatchee and Savannah rivers; and vesting in him, or them, a proprietary interest therein, for the term of 60 years; he, Jenckes, being bound to have the said canal finished and complete, within six years from the date of this act; and likewise bound to convey, at the expiration of the term of 60 years, if so required, to the state of Georgia, all right and title to the canal and appurtenances, upon receiving from the treasury, a sum of money, reimbursing the whole amount of expenses, together with an interest, above all charges, of eight per centum, on such part of the stock as shall not have afforded such an interest.

An act likewise passed the legislature, in favour of the same, for another canal, extending the communication after the manner contemplated, from the Ogatchee river to the Alatamaha; with a grant of privileges, and under conditions the same as in the above instance, nearly.

In virtue of which two acts of the state, an engineer was immediately engaged; and there has been a regular survey of the ground, in order to fix a route for the first of these undertakings; also a reconnoissance or preliminary examination, in regard to the other.

The report states, that the proposed canal between the Ogatchee and Savannah rivers, may be eligibly located, so as to strike from Jones's lake to the upper end of the city of Savannah; distance 16 miles; lockage 29 feet; the engineers' estimate of cost 162,676 dollars. And taking the distance between the Ogatchee and Alatamaha rivers, at 50 miles; that is to say, from Fort Argyle, in a straight line, to strike upon a point at or near the mouth of the Great Ohoopee river, the estimate for this is 480,000 dollars; making, for the whole canal distance of 66 miles, between the Alatamaha river, and the Savannah river, at the city of Savannah, the sum of 642,676 dollars. Width of canal at bottom, to be 33 feet; locks 18 feet wide, 90 feet long.

By the construction of this line of canal, of 66 miles, there will be saved in distances, between the upper navigable waters of the Oakmulgee, the Oconee, the Ohoopee, the Ogatchee, the Canoochee, &c. &c., and the port of Savannah, many hundreds of miles. The route at present taken, is to descend to the sea border, and there enter the sounds or inland passage leading to Savannah; and vice versa from thence, returning upwards. Through the said passage, from Darien, on the north channel of Alatamaha, to the port of Savannah, is 150 miles.

But, moreover, the line of communication once perfected as far as the Alatamaha river, there will, no doubt, soon afterwards, be a continuation of it to Appalachee bay, in the Gulf of Mexico. To connect the port of Savannah thus with the gulf, there is a distance of not more than about 230 miles; and it is likely to be a thoroughfare of not inferior importance to the one that may be accomplished by the St. Mary's river, or the St. John's.

We shall thus have, between Savannah harbour and Appalachee bay, a canal passage of 230 miles, or thereabout; viz.—

From Savannah to the Great Ogatchee,	16
Great Ogatchee to the Alatamaha,	50
Thence to Appalachee bay,	164

Miles, 230

A.—From a point of the Alatamaha river, where it is entered by a canal from the Great Ogatchee, as expressed in the article last above inserted, by canal, south-westward, to St. Mark's, or Appalachee bay.

Distance, *Miles,* 164

No. 124.

ALATAMAHA AND APPALACHEE CANAL.

As already specified, the proposed line, running south-westwardly, is intended to strike upon the bay of St. Mark's, which opens into Appalachee bay.

A.—An act of incorporation has passed the legislature of Georgia, empowering the "Mexican and Atlantic company of Georgia," to construct canals, or rail roads, between the navigable waters flowing into the Atlantic ocean, and those flowing into the Gulf of Mexico. Capital stock, 2,000,000 of dollars.

No. 125.

ATLANTIC AND MEXICAN CANALS OF GEORGIA.

It is rendered probable, that either a canal or a railway construction, between Augusta on Savannah river, and a point of Flint river, as at Fort Lawrence, the line of route passing through Milledgeville, will ere long take place. Distance, 150 miles.

The board of public works are instructed to make surveys, and report upon the subject.

NOTE—1829.

A bill of incorporation is now before the Georgia legislature, for the "Georgia central rail road company" to construct a rail road between Augusta on the Savannah river, and Columbus on the Chatahootchee, to pass through Milledgeville on the Oconee, and Macon on the Oakmulgee river. The cost estimated at 2,000,000 of dollars.

A.—By an act of the legislature of Georgia, 29th December, 1825, which instituted a board of public works for that state, the said board is required to make surveys, and estimates for the construction of canals, or rail roads, or both, between the navigable waters of the state entering the sea, and the western parts of the state; with the view of forming hereafter a junction of such canals, or rail roads, with the waters of the Tennessee and Mississippi rivers. The board is likewise required to make examinations of the principal river-courses of the state, particularly the Oakmulgee, Oconee, and Alatamaha rivers, for the purpose of improving the channel-navigation thereof as much as practicable.

Required, moreover, to effect surveys of the several outlets of the Atlantic rivers to the sea, including their bars, their harbours, and sounds.

No. 126.

TENNESSEE, OAKMULGEE, AND OCONEE CANALS.

January, 1827.

The duties assigned to the board of public works of Georgia, could not all be gone through with in the past year; but, the board has reported progress to the legislature, and the operations will be resumed as the season opens.

It appears, that a transverse line has been run from Augusta on the Savannah river, to Fort Lawrence on the Flint, with the view of locating a rail road between those points.

The board also examined portions of the ground for a central canal, to commence from a point of the Chatahootchee river, in Hall county, and strike upon the navigable water of one or other of the great rivers crossed by the transverse line above mentioned, and there to terminate; or else, to continue on to the sea coast, according to whichever mode of improvement shall be found to be most eligible.

The examinations, commenced on the Chatahootchee, in the Cherokee country, have rendered it probable that this river can be advantageously connected, by canal, with the waters of the Tennessee; but, the engineers' survey, on this occasion, was interrupted by the Indians, and all certainty on the point of a good practicable connexion is, in consequence, postponed for a season.

The important surveys on the Atlantic, and along the river-channels, will proceed forthwith, and these will decide with regard to the expediency of any extension of the proposed central canal, beyond, or south of, the transverse rail road line.

An appropriation of 125,000 dollars, has been voted by the legislature, to commence these improvements upon. Distance of canal, from a point of the Chatahootchee river, in Hall county, to the point of intersection, as, suppose, at Milledgeville, 120 miles.

A.—From Fort Deposite, on the Tennessee river, 20 miles south-east of Huntsville, by canal, to the navigable water of the Tuscaloosa, or Black Warrior river, below the falls thereof, at Tuscaloosa town.

Distance, *Miles*, 150

No. 127.
TENNESSEE AND TOMBECBEE CANAL.

The ground, or line of route, for this proposed communication, is included in the course of surveys now on foot, between Mobile bay and the upper country. The increasing productiveness of this district, will ensure the execution of the best plans of improvement that can be devised, to facilitate transportation to a plurality of markets, of the commodities produced.

The state of Alabama has obtained from congress a grant of public lands, for the purpose of defraying the expense of improving the navigation of the Tennessee, the Coosa, the Cahawba, and the Black Warrior rivers. The grant is for 400,000 acres, situate in Jackson, Madison, Morgan, Limestone, Lawrence, Franklin, and Lauderdale counties of the state.

Should this suggested connexion, by canal, between the Tennessee river and the Black Warrior, leading to Mobile harbour, prove not to be practicable, a rail road, it is possible, might be resorted to, with advantages to recommend it; and there is suggested another route of connexion, by canal, as referred to at Art. 139, namely, between the waters of an upper branch of the Coosa river, and a branch of the Hiwassee; by means of which, a communication of the Tennessee river with the Alabama, and thence with Mobile harbour, may be accomplished.

N.—From below the falls of the Black Warrior, down the river stream, to the mouth thereof, at Demopolis, and down the Tombecbee river, to Fort St. Stephen, which, so far, is a boat navigation, and thence, by a sloop and schooner navigation, down to Fort Stoddart; whence, through the river and bay of Mobile, to Fort Bowyer, at Mobile point.

Distance, *Miles*, 340

NOTE.

A regular steam-boat line is now established between Mobile port, at the head of Mobile bay, and Tuscaloosa town. Distance, 319 miles of the 340.

N.—From Mobile point, last above mentioned, by Pascagoula bay, and Lake Borgne, westward, to the mouth of Pearl river, at Fort Rigolets.
Distance, *Miles*, 70

M.—From the mouth of West Pearl river, state of Louisiana, up the stream of the same, and of the main river, by improvement thereof, to a point in Lawrence county, Mississippi; and thence, by canal, across to the Big Black river valley; down which, to the Mississippi river. Distance, by river navigation improved, and canal, together, *Miles*, 240

No. 128.
PEARL RIVER AND MISSISSIPPI CANAL.

For this suggested connexion, there is not any regular survey made as yet; but, improvements in the Pearl river channel are in the mean time taking place, and will probably give occasion, before the lapse of any long period, to more than one canal of communication, and other improvements too, in the waters of the Mississippi state.

NOTE.

The works of improvement along the Pearl, are already of that degree of consequence, that a steam-boat passage has been obtained up to Monticello, in Lawrence county, Mississippi, 150 miles from the mouth of the Pearl. The clearing of this river's channel, is, however, as yet imperfect: what chiefly obstructs the Western branch below the forks, is a range of old cypress trees, of 4 or 5 miles long, still standing across the channel. From appearances, these trees must have been original tenants of a swamp in this place, at a time when there was no West branch of the River Pearl.

A.—From the mouth of the River Amite, on Lake Maurepas, up the stream thereof, by channel navigation improved, to the point where it is entered by the Comite river. Distance, *Miles*, 70

No. 129.

AMITE RIVER CANALS.

This river rises in Mississippi state, and, after a winding course of 150 miles, first southwardly and then south-east, discharges into Lake Maurepas. Its navigation is obstructed by fallen timber, and a number of sharp angular points influencing the channel. The which it is proposed to remedy, by removing the former, and cutting off, or cutting through, the latter. A steam-boat passage may thus be effected; and hereafter the improvements may be extended to the boundary line of the state. At which period, this beautiful river will command a flourishing trade between St. Helena, East Baton Rouge, New river, East Feliciana, a part also of the neighbouring state of Mississippi, and the port of New-Orleans.

A.—From the mouth of Tangchepahaw river, on Lake Pontchartrain, up the stream thereof, by channel navigation improved, to the point of confluence with the Chapeau Pilier. Distance, *Miles*, 43

No. 130.
TANGCHEPAHAW RIVER CANALS.

This river also rises in Mississippi state, and has a course between the Pearl and the Amité, nearly equi-distant. Its navigation is similarly obstructed, and is consequently to be improved, after the same mode, up to the point specified: what is furthermore said of the Amité, applies in a degree to this river.

NOTE.

The board of commissioners have reported to the legislature of Louisiana, in favour of opening, by means of improvements, a steam-boat navigation up the Boguechitto, which is a tributary of the Pearl river; and they remark, that, when the several works recommended shall be accomplished, navigable water, for the benefits of transportation, will have been brought up to the very precincts of almost every occupier of a plantation in this north-east section of Louisiana.

A.—From a point of the Mississippi river, opposite New-Orleans, by canal, taking the way of Verret's or Dugay's cut and bayou, to Lake Barataria, and thence, by the Grand Catahoula and the Cher Ami cut, to La Fourche river; whence, by the Solet and Lake Long, to Bayou Terrebonne; up which, and across to and along the course of the Black river, to the waters which unite with the Teche river at Berwick's bay. Distance, *Miles*, 100

No. 131.

NEW-ORLEANS AND TECHE RIVER CANAL.

There has been a regular survey of the route for this proposed canal, which is to be a steam-boat navigation, and will tend much to enhance the value of property, particularly the rich lands situate along the Teche and La Fourche rivers, by giving to them an easy conveyance of their productions to the market of New-Orleans. It will obviate some very inconvenient portages now existing; in so much, that, to effect one continuous navigation between New-Orleans and Berwick's bay of the Teche, is regarded as an undertaking of the first magnitude in point of utility; and it is proposed to solicit the aid of congress for its execution, in the form of *a grant of public lands, of a few miles extent, on each side of the intended water communication, between La Fourche river and Berwick's bay.*

The expense of the works, consisting of a number of short canals of connexion, and other improvements, and including an improvement of the Bay of Barataria, it is estimated will not exceed the sum of 150,000 dollars.

The two present routes of communication between the Mississippi and the waters of the Teche, namely, one by the Bayou Plaquemine, Grand river, and Grand lake, and the other by La Fourche river to the lower part of the Atakapas, are both not only circuitous as respects New-Orleans, but very imperfect, and not either of them susceptible of being easily, if at all, improved into a good passage for all the year round; the latter indeed is only navigable for barges or keel boats, and any hitherto purposed improvement along the same, will probably be superseded, by the now projected line between New-Orleans and Berwick's bay, as above described, going into effect. The Plaquemine route is navigable for steam-boats the entire distance, but only during high water in the winter season; at low water of the Mississippi, this bayou is dry; and in time of flood, the channel is much encumbered with drift wood, forced in by the rapidity of the current at the Mississippi pass, where is a bend of the river; there is, besides, a considerable raft accumulation at Bayou Pigeon, which is a deep water, communicating directly between Grand river and Grand lake. To render this route a good navigation during the period of high water, such improvements as will deepen the Plaquemine bayou channel, and keep it free from floating timber, also clear away the rafts of the Pigeon bayou, are highly desirable, and are recommended by the board of commissioners on internal improvement for the state of Louisiana, to be immediately set on foot.

December, 1828.

The governor of Louisiana, on a communication just made to the legislature, observes, that a portion of the contemplated canal from New-Orleans to Atakapas, to wit; from La Fourche to Terrebonne, has been nearly completed by individual enterprise: evincing with what facility such improvements in this state may be effected.

A.—From Lake Barataria, by canal, southward, by way of Petit Lake Barataria, to the Bay of Barataria, at the West pass of Grandterre. Distance, *Miles*, 40

No. 132.

BARATARIA BAY CANAL.

This proposed canal, to diverge from the one specified in the foregoing article, at Lake Barataria, towards the sea, may be regarded as an equally important branch of the whole communication. At the distance of 66 miles from New-Orleans, a new seaport may be thus acquired, through which, at all seasons of the year, the gulf trade, up to the extent of 6½ feet draft of water, may pass, in lieu of taking the circuitous route of the Balize.

NOTE.

It is proposed, likewise, to remove existing impediments to a thorough navigation of La Fourche river, which flows along a most fertile district of country. Besides much drift-wood at many places, there is at one place, in this river, a range of willow trees growing, to the distance of 17 miles, which have produced the effect of shoaling the water quite across the stream, by deposites of intercepted sand, with other matter; and would, through the continued action of growing in width, and causing fresh deposites, very soon be sufficient, if no preventive were applied, to fill the channel entirely up.

The combined canal works of this and the article preceding, the commissioners on internal improvement consider to be of great importance to the state. They recommend them, as such, to the attention of the legislature, and they suggest, that at a future day there may be effected a prolongation of the Teche canal, westward, to the Vermillion, the Mermenteau, the Calcasieu, and the Sabine rivers, quite across the state, and perhaps even to the Bay of Galvestown, in the adjoining Mexican province of Texas.

A.—From Concordia, west of the Mississippi river, opposite Natchez, by canal, ascending to Bullit's bayou, and thence, by the way of Bayou Crocodile, Turtle lake, Grassy bayou, the Cane and Brushy bayous, and Tensaw river, to the Washitta river, at or near Catahoula Courthouse. Distance, *Miles*, 66

No. 133.

CONCORDIA AND CATAHOULA CANAL.

This is the route of the mail during high water, and, on that account, therefore, of much importance; and, moreover, a perfect water communication between the points is regarded as essential to the interests of the parishes of Concordia and Catahoula, and those even of the whole country on the Upper Washitta, for the sake of giving an easy access, by boats or steam vessels, to that growing region, and to connect it with the Mississippi, through a more direct and prompt navigation, than by the mouth of the Red river, now in use.

The works recommended, though so eminently useful in their nature, and in the application of them here, will not, in this alluvial country, be expensive. They consist of some connecting canal, a general clearing of the bayous of sunken timber, &c. and at certain places deepening the present channel.

M.—From the confluence of the Red river with the Mississippi, up the stream of the former, to the point of interception by the *Great Raft* in Nachitoches district, Louisiana; from whence, by lateral canals, to the upper termination of the raft impediment, and thence. up the stream improved, to the point where it enters the state from the territory of Arkansas. Distance, by a mixed navigation, *Miles*, 500

No. 134.

RED RIVER CANALS.

It is now becoming an important object to the nation, and especially to the state of Louisiana, most immediately interested, to obtain, if practicable, an uninterrupted navigation along the course of this vast river; that is to say, to surmount, if it be possible, amidst a few other obstacles, that most formidable one of the "Great Raft," which is supposed to have been accumulating for ages.

There are, however, at this moment, sanguine hopes entertained of success. They are derived from a recent preliminary survey, made by order of the United States government. By an official report on the subject, it appears, that *parallel lakes and streams* have been discovered or better explored, which, by means of being united by short canals, and the clearing of some of these streams or bayous, it is thought may be reduced to an effective, good navigation for steam-boats, all the way around the raft. It is said, that besides the difficulties of this place, it does not appear that any serious obstacles exist to a steam-boat navigation along a distance of 1500 miles of the Red river course, or more.

Surveys have been directed by the legislature, of various bayous and water courses of Upper Louisiana, with a view to their being cleared of obstructions, and improved for convenient navigation. The which kind of improvements, including all canal communications, are, in this alluvious country, effected with great comparative facility, and at little expense. Here no strata of rocks are to be encountered, rendering the process of excavation tedious and costly; neither do any great or abrupt declinations of the surface occur. To return to the Red river:—

Extract of a Report.

" The commissioners (of Louisiana) consider it immensely important to the state, and particularly so to the commercial interests of the great capital. There is, too, another consideration; that, in all the commerce of the Red river, New-Orleans will be *without a rival.* Our efficient brethren of the North will here find a stream beyond the reach of their enterprise; for no line of canal can send its waters refluent to the shores of the Hudson, the Delaware, or the Potomac. Of the Red river we can ever boast, as our own exclusive property; and its banks are capable of sustaining a population greater than that of the Rhine or the Danube."

It is strenuously urged on the general government to construct a road, through the public lands, from St. Louis, Mississippi, to Alexandria, at Red river rapids, not far from the Mexican frontier.

NOTE.

The presumed Mississippi export of products for the present year, 1828, through the port of New-Orleans, is thus caluclated:

           350,000 bales cotton,
            60,000 hogsheads sugar,
            20,000 hogsheads molasses,
            40,000 hogsheads tobacco,
           100,000 barrels flour,
           100,000 barrels pork,
           150,000 kegs lard,
                   staves, lead, castings, &c.

Which will have required 360,000 tons of shipping, or 1200 vessels of 300 tons each.

A.—From a point of the Mississippi river, at or below New-Orleans city, by canal, calculated for sloop navigation, to a point of Lake Pontchartrain.

Distance, *Miles*, 5 to 10

No. 135.

MISSISSIPPI AND PONTCHARTRAIN CANAL.

The board of the United States engineers for internal improvement, were directed to cause a survey of the ground between the Mississippi river and Lake Pontchartrain, with a view to these waters being connected by a sloop-of-war navigation; and they have reported two routes as being favourable for the purpose, viz. One from the city of New-Orleans, to enter Lake Pontchartrain at two miles east of the mouth of Bayou St. John; the other from a point of the Mississippi, about two miles below New-Orleans, to enter the lake at about five miles east of Bayou St. John; along either of which, a canal of the description required may be readily constructed.

This canal, in case adequate dimensions be given to it, will embrace, not only military purposes in the event of war, and the purposes of a commercial shortened route to and from the city, but the still more important object, under actual circumstances, of forming an outlet towards the sea for a portion of the great volume of Mississippi water, when it hurries down in the flood season.

There is now existing, a canal, named the "Carondelet," between the basin in the rear of the city, and the Bayou St. Jean, a small but navigable water of six miles, emptying into Lake Pontchartrain; but it is quite inadequate to the present occasions. It appears, however, that at the *infant* period (1805) of granting canal charters, in that part of the country, then "territory," some exclusive and rather extraordinary privileges were inadvertently conferred upon the navigation company who undertook the construction of the canal; which privileges it has now become necessary to extinguish *by consent*, in case that be practicable, before a new canal, such as occasions require, can be set on foot.

It is highly essential to the prospective commerce of this district, apart from other considerations, that such a canal be here constructed, as shall form a sufficient avenue, not only for all vessels navigating the rivers of this vicinity, but likewise competent to the whole coasting trade of the eastern shore of the Gulf of Mexico.

NOTE.

The inhabitants of New-Orleans have had a meeting, in order to take into consideration the project of constructing a rail road between that city and Lake Pontchartrain.

It is also proposed to petition congress for a grant of 500,000 acres of the public lands, towards facilitating the construction of a canal, by the state, and some other works of improvement.

Besides the important advantages already stated to be derived from a capacious canal between Lake Pontchartrain and the Mississippi, it is quite obvious, that new commercial markets will be opened by it to the whole western country. The interior valley of the Ohio river, and the Mississippi valley, may alike have their rich products floated down, through a direct short passage to Mobile and to Pensacola, as often as such a course for the same shall be preferred to the Balize outlet. A canal, promising such advantages as these, and apparently almost essential to the safety of this section of the union, has been estimated, by the engineers, to cost about 900,000 dollars.

M.—From the point of efflux into the Ibberville, or Manchac channel, on the Mississippi river, 100 miles above New-Orleans, down the said channel improved, as also the Lower Amite river, and thence, by a mixed navigation, including a series of canals, with intermediate lakes and bays, to the River Appalachicola, at the mouth of Chipola, West Florida.

Distance, *Miles*, 350

No. 136.

MISSISSIPPI AND APPALACHICOLA CANALS.

It has been represented, that by cutting merely about 12 miles of canal, an inland tide water and steam-boat navigation may be obtained, between these two rivers, as here specified, a distance of 350 miles; the route being as follows:—

From the Mississippi, through the Ibberville, the obstructions of which are to be removed, to Lake Pontchartrain; thence through Lake Borgne and Pascagoula bay, between the islands and the shore, to Mobile bay; which may be connected with the Perdido by a cut of 4½ miles, and this with the Pensacola bay, through the Grand Lagoon, by a cut of half a mile; thence through Santa Rosa sound and bay, 40 miles, to the Choctowatchee river, which may be connected, by a cut of 5 miles, with the St. Andrew's bay; through which you pass 24 miles, and thence, by a cut of 2 miles, to the Chipola river, which discharges into the Appalachicola.

This important passage will have the attention of the United States board of internal improvement. It is to be regarded as a section, completing, most eligibly, the vast chain of border navigation, extending from the rivers of New-England quite to the river Mississippi; as thus,—

From Boston harbour,
  Through the canal, to Taunton and Narraganset bay,
  Thence, through Long Island sound to New-York harbour, and Rariton bay,
  Through the Delaware and Rariton canal, to the Delaware river,
  Through the Chesapeake and Delaware canal, to Chesapeake bay,
  Down the Chesapeake to Elizabeth river, and through the Dismal Swamp canal, to Albemarle sound,

Through Albemarle and Pamlico sounds, and the Clubfoot and Harlow creek, or Adams creek and North river canal,
Through Bogue, Stumpy, and Tooner's sounds, to Cape Fear river, below Wilmington,
Through the Waccamaw canal, and Waccamaw river, to Winyaw bay, below Georgetown, South-Carolina,
Through Charleston and Georgetown canal, to Wando river, and to Charleston harbour,
Through the canals of connexion, and the bay and sound navigation between Ashley river and the Edisto, and between the Edisto and Savannah rivers,
Through the Savannah and Ogatchee canal, to Great Ogatchee river,
Through the Ogatchee and Alatamaha canal, to the Alatamaha river,
Through Ossabaw, St. Catharine's and other Georgia sea island sounds, to St. Mary's bay and river,
Through the Florida isthmus canal, and continuation thereof, to Appalachicola river,
Thence to the Mississippi river, through the Great lakes, as specified in the present article; or the Mississippi may be gained from Lake Pontchartrain, through the contemplated Pontchartrain canal, near New-Orleans, as specified at Article 135.

NOTE.

Application is made to the governor and legislative council of Florida territory, for an act of incorporation, instituting a company as the "Chipola canal company," with privilege to cut a canal between the Chipola river and the eastern arm of St. Andrew's bay; the act to be confirmed by congress, as regards the said canal passing through the public lands.

N.—From Fort Bowyer, up the bay, and up the Tensaw branch of Mobile river, to the confluence of the Tombecbee and the Alabama; whence, up the latter, to the head of schooner navigation at Claiborne; and thence, by boat navigation, to its extremity at Fort Jackson, where the Coosa and Talapoosa rivers unite to form the Alabama. Distance, by the serpentine course of the river stream, *Miles,* 360

NOTE.

A steam-boat line is established also on this route to Montgomery, within about 15 miles of Fort Jackson. They touch at Canton, Cahawba, Vernon, plying to and from Mobile and Montgomery. Distance, 331 miles of the 360.

M.—From the point last designated, up the course of the Coosa river, and across the valley at Wills creek, to a point of the Tennessee, east of Fort Deposite, where, or near where, the Tombecbee canal, as inserted at Article 127, is supposed to unite. Distance, by canal and improved channel together, *Miles*, 250

No. 137.

TENNESSEE AND ALABAMA CANAL.

Surveys and levelling are yet to be gone into, to decide respecting this projected undertaking, like as to the foregoing, and to the next also here inserted.

In case the ground for this suggested connexion, by canal, to form so direct a communication between the Tennessee river and the Bay of Mobile, through the Alabama, should prove not to be favourable, then possibly a rail road might be resorted to, with advantages to recommend it; and there is suggested another route of connexion for a canal, as referred to at Article 139 ; namely, between the waters of an upper branch of the Coosa, and a branch of the Hiwassee river.

M.—From the confluence of the Black Warrior river with the Tombecbee, at Demopolis, or Eagleville, by canal, or a mixed navigation, up the Tombecbee valley, to a navigable point of Bear creek, and thence to the mouth thereof, on the Tennessee river, below Havana, in Lauderdale county, west of the Muscle shoals. Distance, *Miles*, 240

No. 138.

BEAR CREEK CANAL.

The northern part of this projected communication is, as yet, within the boundaries of the Chickasaw Indians.

In case the ground for a connexion, by canal, between the waters of Bear creek and the Tombecbee, leading so directly from the Tennessee river to Mobile harbour, should prove not to be favourable, then, possibly, a rail road may be resorted to with success, and under circumstances of sufficient weight to recommend it, in the object of obtaining a straight communication between the Lower Tennessee river, and the Gulf of Mexico at Mobile. The following inserted article suggests a route between the upper waters of the Tennessee and Mobile harbour.

A.—From a point of the Okou, a navigable branch of the Hiwassee river, to a point of the Conesaugo, a navigable branch of the Coosa river, near the Georgia and Tennessee line, where these waters approach each other to within about 10 or 12 miles, and where the ground, it is said, is favourable to a connexion, by canal, at a moderate expense. Distance, *Miles*, 12

No. 139.

HIWASSEE AND COOSA CANAL.

At a meeting held in Cahawba, Alabama, on the 20th of May, 1823, the project was recommended, as a means of laying open forthwith, a passage for boats, from the head waters of the Tennessee river, in Virginia, through the Coosa and Alabama rivers, to Mobile and the Gulf of Mexico.

NOTE.

A survey by the United States board of engineers, on this article, is in course of accomplishment; the report thereof to be laid before congress.

JANUARY, 1829.

A communication from the chief engineer, and report of the board of internal improvement, on this subject, in consequence of preparatory examinations in the course of the past season, have been made to congress; from which it appears, that a route has been levelled and surveyed for the proposed communication, as passing by the most favourable depression of the ridge dividing the two tributary valleys, viz. between Hiltebrand's boat yard on the Okou, and M'Nair's boat yard on the Conesaugo; the heads respectively of a descending navigation. Distance, by the line of survey, near 12 miles. The line rises from M'Nair's to the head sources of the Chestoe creek, whence it descends by a ravine into the Okou at Hiltebrand's; which is found to be 159 feet below the summit point of the intermediate high ground.

The supply of water, for the whole canal, must be derived from one or other of these two sources, or both. The Conesaugo, at the head of its navigation, being 46.60 feet higher level than the Okou head of navigation, would, on that account, be a more eligible stream to feed the summit level; but the banks of the Okou, and vicinity, proving to constitute far more favourable ground for the erection of a dam, and formation of a reservoir, it is proposed to select for the purpose, the spot where that stream breaks through the Unica or Round mountain. The surface of the water, however, proves here to be 134 feet below the said intervening ground summit, and, therefore, it becomes necessary to adopt, besides the dam mentioned, a certain deep cutting, to effect the communication required. If the height of the dam be assumed at 64 feet, this, and supposing a deduction of 4 feet for inclination of a feeder, would fix the surface of the water at the summit level, 74 feet below the summit point of the ground; 85 feet above Hiltebrand's boat yard; and 38.40 feet above M'Nair's boat yard. On this supposition, and assuming for the canal a width of 50 feet at the water surface, and a depth of 5 feet, the length of the summit level would be 10 miles 1320 yards; and the amount of its excavation, 5,823,560 cubic yards. Ten locks would be necessary to descend from the summit level into the Okou, and five to descend into the Conesaugo; in all fifteen locks.

A line of levels was taken from the Round mountain to the summit level, but the route of the feeder not located; its length may be 6 or 7 miles. Length of canal and feeder together, 18 miles, or thereabout.

In regard to a supply of water, the Okou stream appears to be fully adequate. It was gauged in the month of May, and found to yield 1,755.54 cubic feet per second. The Conesaugo, though not navigable in summer, yet can afford during spring and winter a good supply of water. It was gauged also in the month of May, and then yielded 210.32 feet per second.

These facts ascertain the feasibility of accomplishing the object, although, on account of the requisite deep cutting at the summit level, together with the great elevation of the dam, and other local difficulties to be overcome in leading a feeder from Round mountain to the main canal, the expense may be great.

Such a connexion, however, once effected, or supposed to be effected, it immediately suggests a question as to a prolongation of the canal down the valley of the Okou, and down that of the Hiwassee, as far as where steam-boat navigation reaches or can be made to reach, on the latter ; also down the Conesaugo valley, to the head of steam-boat navigation on the Coosa river.

It has been said, that the Coosa, being improved, might afford, at all seasons, 3 feet draft of water, as far up as the mouth of the Conesaugo ; and that the Hiwassee, from Calhoun down to the Tennessee river, is navigable at all times. Should this really be the case, a canal of 100 miles long in all, or thereabout, it is probable might be sufficient to connect, by this route, the navigation of the Tennessee and Alabama rivers: and it becomes therefore extremely desirable to have the inquiry, began as above, as soon as practicable prosecuted to the end, by means of regular and minute examinations and surveys. The view that may be taken of it, and has been taken of it, as follows, falls nothing short of bringing it within the class of *great national objects*.

1. A report on the Muscle and Colbert's shoals, states that this pass of the Tennessee river can be improved. After which shall have been effected, there will be a free steam-boat navigation, for at least eight months out of the twelve, from the mouth of the Tennessee, up to the Whirl, or Suck; a distance, by the windings of the stream, of 500 miles ; and, with a few works of improvement above, a like navigation be obtained up to Kingston, and to Knoxville on the Holston. Therefore, there needs only what is stated, to be accomplished, on the Tennessee, the Hiwassee, and the Coosa waters, for the great valley of the Tennessee to have the choice of two clear routes for the transportation of its products to the Gulf of Mexico ; and, vice versa, for its returns from the seaports of the gulf, viz. One route through the Coosa and Alabama, to Mobile ; the other, through the Mississippi and New-Orleans. As to comparative distance, we have, from the mouth of Tennessee river, down the Mississippi to its mouth, 1145 miles : and from the same point, up the Tennessee, and by the bends of that, the Hiwassee, Conesaugo, Coosa, and Alabama, we have about the same distance. In this instance, the Mississippi route, being altogether *descending*, is of course preferable ; but if we suppose a point of departure from any part high up the Tennessee valley, the case becomes widely different ; and much time as well as distance may be saved, by taking the Coosa and Alabama route, to the Gulf of Mexico.

2. It may be remarked, that, from Fort Deposite on the Tennessee, to St. Louis on the Mississippi, these two streams form almost a straight line of steam-boat navigation. Now, if the

Muscle and Colbert's shoals improvement, also the Hiwassee and Coosa improvements, be effected, then will St. Louis, Missouri, and Montgomery, Alabama, become united by an uninterrupted water communication of 1200 miles and upwards. And thus, the states of Alabama and Georgia be brought into commercial communication with the states of Missouri and Tennessee; as also with the states bordering on the Ohio river : for, in regard to Georgia ;

3. Should a connexion be formed between some of the Georgia streams emptying into the Atlantic, and one of the head branches of the Coosa, then will the valleys of the Upper Mississippi, the Ohio, and the Tennessee, become, through the proposed Hiwassee and Coosa canal, connected with the sea-board of Georgia. See Articles 120, 125, 126.

4. It being ascertained that Pensacola harbour can easily be connected, by canal, with Mobile bay, should it so happen that war breaks out, and, by the chances of it, that the outlets of the Mississippi, by the Balize and by Lake Pontchartrain, should both of them be blockaded, the important naval station of Pensacola, would, notwithstanding, receive, in perfect safety, its supplies from the Upper Mississippi, and the valleys of the Ohio and the Tennessee. In the event of a blockade, as here supposed, the water communication between the Tennessee and Alabama rivers would be of the highest degree of importance, in relation both to *supplies* and *protection*.

In regard to other suggested lines of communication between the Tennessee river and the sea-board, across the states of Alabama and Georgia, as specified at Articles 120, 127, 137, 138, sufficient examinations have not, as yet, been gone into, to ascertain as to the ground admitting, or not admitting, in either case, the construction of canals competent to unite the head navigable waters. Supposing this to be found impracticable, possibly rail roads, in one, or other, or all, of the cases, may be resorted to, with useful effect, in the important object of forming a direct transport communication between the Tennessee river valley, and southern sea coast, especially the harbour of Mobile.

OF THE UNITED STATES. 393

SUMMARY FOR THE STATES OF TENNESSEE, MISSISSIPPI, LOUISIANA, ALABAMA, AND GEORGIA.

ARTIFICIAL NAVIGATION.

Page.	No.		Miles.
370	119.	The Muscle shoal and Colbert's shoal canal,	37
372	120.	Tennessee and Savannah canal,	250
372	121.	Savannah and Appalachicola canal, and stream improvements,	550
373	122.	Savannah and Ogatchee canal,	16
373	123.	Ogatchee and Alatamaha canal,	50
374	124.	Alatamaha and Appalachee canal,	164
375	125.	Savannah and Flint rivers canal,	150
376	126.	Chatahootchee and Milledgeville canal,	120
377,	127.	Tennessee and Tombecbee canal,	150
378	128.	Pearl river and Mississippi canal, and Pearl stream improvements,	240
379	129.	Amité river canals, and stream improvements,	70
379	130.	Tangchepahaw river canals, and stream improvements,	43
380	131.	New-Orleans and Teche river canal,	100
381	132.	Barataria bay canal,	40
382	133.	Concordia and Catahoula canal,	66
383	134.	Red river canals, and stream improvements,	500
384	135.	Mississippi and Pontchartrain canal,	10
386	136.	Mississippi and Appalachicola canals of connexion, and the Ibberville and Lower Amité improvements,	52
388	137.	Tennessee and Alabama canal, and Coosa stream improvements,	250
389	138.	Bear creek and Tombecbee canal and stream improvements,	240
389	139.	Hiwassee and Coosa canal,	100

Total of artificial navigation, 3198

NATURAL NAVIGATION.

370	The Tennessee river,	875
372	The Savannah river, up to Augusta,	158

Amount carried forward, 1033

Page.		Miles.
	Amount brought forward,	1033
377	The Mobile, the Tombecbee, and the Black Warrior, up to Tuscaloosa,	340
378	From Mobile point, through Pascagoula bay, to the mouth of Pearl river,	70
387	The Tensaw of Mobile, and Alabama rivers,	360
386	Passage, from Appalachicola bay, westward, through Lakes Borgne, Pontchartrain, and Maurepas, to the Mississippi river, at the Manchac,	350

Deducting the line of canals, and stream
   improvements, included,   52
Also, the above inserted 70 miles,   70
                                     —122

                                          228

To which add :—

For all other streams and navigable waters; viz. Of the rivers, creeks, bays and sounds within these five states, some of which are particularized below, there are 50, affording an average natural navigation of 125 miles each, and 1000 an average of 20 miles each,

        These make, together,   26250

Total of natural navigation,	28281
Total of artificial navigation,	3198
Total of both,	31479

IN TENNESSEE STATE ; VIZ.

The Cumberland river, its middle section lying within this state, navigable 300 miles.

The Holston branch of the Tennessee river, navigable 150 miles.

Tributaries of the Holston ; the Watauga, the French Broad, and some others, and sub-branches.

The Clinch branch of the Tennessee river, a part whereof, lying in Virginia, is navigable 200 miles.

Powell river, a branch of the above; this and sub-branches.

Duck river, falls into the Tennessee in lat. 36°, is navigable 90 miles.

The Hiwassee river, enters the Tennessee 70 miles above the Whirl, is navigable 80 miles.

Tributaries of the Cumberland ; the Caney fork, the Red river, the Marpeth, the Obeds, and their branches, some of which are navigable to a great distance, for boats.

The Wolf river, the Big Hatchie, the Forked Deer, and the Obions, flow westwardly into the Mississippi river: they are all navigable, as are some of their branches; many of the sub-branches to the larger streams here situated, are also navigable.

IN MISSISSIPPI STATE; VIZ.

The Yazoo river, rises in the Cherokee country, and falls into the Mississippi river at 12 miles above the Walnut Hills: it is navigable for boats 150 miles.

The Big Black, rises in the Choctaw country, and falls into the Mississippi at 15 miles above Natchez.

The Homochitta river, receives many streams, in a long south-western course, and enters the Mississippi near to a junction with the Red river.

The Buffalo river, from Amité county, winds to its discharge at Loftus Heights, 2 miles above Fort Adams.

Pearl river; has a number of sources in Hinde county, near the centre of the state; its remote sources in the Choctaw country, not far south of the Big Black. It flows, first south-west, then south, and then east of south, a distance of more than 300 miles, and discharges by two principal branches at Fort Rigolets, or the strait between the Lakes Pontchartrain and Borgne.

Below lat. 31°, the main river, and afterwards its eastern branch, forms the boundary line between the states of Louisiana and Mississippi. On this East branch, the navigation, for many miles upward from Lake Borgne, is difficult and dangerous.

The Leaf and Chickasahas rivers, which unite in lat. 31°, and form the Pascagoula: they rise from several sources, and are navigable 100 miles.

NOTE.

It is suggested, as desirable, that a grant of public lands be made by the general government, to enable the state of Mississippi to improve the navigation of the rivers Pearl, Pascagoula, Leaf, Big Black, Homochitta, and Yazoo; as also to construct a canal to unite the waters of the Homochitta and Buffalo rivers. A bar at the Homochitta mouth prevents, at present, a steam-boat passage up from the Mississippi.

IN LOUISIANA STATE; VIZ.

The Red river, is, in this state, the main tributary of the Mississippi: it enters the state at the north-west angle, lat. 33°. Its sources are in the mountains of Mexico, at lat. 35°; and, counting from where it strikes upon the western line of Arkansas territory, it has a course, within the United States, of near 1000 miles; it joins the Mississippi, in lat. 31°. It is navigable, during part of the year, up to the Great Raft, near 500 miles; but the lower navigation still is liable to stoppages, by trees and floats of timber choking up the channel.

Near the latitude, as above, of 33°, on the border of Red river, there commences a prodigious chain of lakes, and swamps, and channels, or an intricate maze of islands and inlets, occasioned by periodical overflowings; and which follows the course of this river, to a greater or less extent and width, down to where the stream is met by the highlands of the Avoyelles, a few miles below the rapids at Alexandria; but the principal inundated tract, which has occasionally been denominated the raft region, lies between Grandecor, 4 miles above Nachitoches, and a point of the Red river, 30 miles below the north-west angle of the state, and is 60 miles in length. From points of the Red river, near to where it is deflected towards the Mississippi, and from points of the latter below the junction, various great river or bayou courses, together with numerous lesser bayous or channels, strike off and spread southward and south-eastward, and go to form what is called the Mississippi delta, bounded by a remarkable curve line on the coast, extending from Achafalaya bay, round to the efflux of Lake Pontchartrain, at Fort Rigolets. The long *claw-footed* protrusion of this delta into the ocean, in a south-eastern direction, to its extremity below the Balize, is singular in physical geography.

The Achafalaya river, issues from the Mississippi near to where the Red river enters, and thence diverging, with numerous inflexions, towards the gulf, discharges into Achafalaya bay, after a course of 200 miles. The channel is encumbered by a natural raft, or a succession of rafts, the accumulations of drift timber from the Mississippi, of many miles in extent.

The Crocodile and the Bœuf, both of which rise in the hilly pine forests, between Red river and head of the Calcasieu, are, together with their united stream the Courtableau, as also the Teche river, all tributaries of the Achafalaya, and of the great Lake of the Atakapas, called Lake Chetimaches. They are remarkable for their tortuous courses, especially the Teche river, the entire length of which, by comparative courses, is about 150 miles; but, following the windings of the stream, is nearly 300 miles.

The Teche river, rises in the northern prairies of Opelousas, at lat. 30° 40′, and flows in a general course of south-east, to its confluence with the Achafalaya. At New-Iberia, lat. 30° 02′, it meets the tide, and there it widens from 30 yards to 100, and deepens from 5 feet to 30 or 40 feet.

"New-Iberia, at the head of tide water in the Teche, is a

port of entry, and vessels frequently clear out from thence; but the general commercial communication is with the city of New-Orleans, through the Achafalaya, Plaquemine, and Mississippi, or from the Lower Teche, through Lakes Palourde and Verret, and their connecting inlets, and the La Fourche and Mississippi rivers.

Boats from 15 to 60 tons, are conveyed from New-Orleans, by the Plaquemine, into the Achafalaya. Those destined for the lower part of Atakapas, descend the latter river, and enter their points of destination by the Teche. Those bound to the centre of Atakapas, ascend the Achafalaya about 20 miles, and are thence transported, by an outlet, and Lake Chetimaches, to Fausse Point landing. Here is a portage of 10 or 12 miles, to St. Martinsville, seat of justice for the parish of St. Martin's, or Upper Atakapas. Vessels destined for the higher and central parts of Opelousas, ascend the Achafalaya to the mouth of Courtableau, and thence by the latter stream to Lemell's landing, 6 miles, or into Bayou Carron, 4 miles from the village of St. Landré."*

La Fourche river, or Mississippi outlet, the efflux of which is at Donaldsonville, lat. 30° 6', by a north-east course of 90 to 100 miles, falls into the gulf at lat. 29° 5'. It has 9 feet water over the bar, and vessels of 5 feet draft may ascend this stream to within 30 miles of Donaldsonville.

Beyond La Fourche, is formed an intricate net-work of lakes and bayous, which are mostly discharged into Barataria bay.

The Ibberville, or upper drain of the Mississippi, leaves the main volume near the termination of the eastern high land, and, following its base in a north-east direction, receives the Amité from the north; from whence, inflecting to the east by a winding channel, it opens into Lake Maurepas, thence communicating with the gulf through Lakes Pontchartrain and Borgne, also with the Bay of Mobile through the pass Au Héron.

The chief water courses serving to drain the western division of the lower plains of Louisiana, are the Sabine river, the Calcasieu, the Mermenteau, and the Vermillion. They spread out into lakes, and interlock with their branches, and communicate by numerous bayous; and traversing, in a general southern course, the great prairie country of Opelousas and Atakapas, they discharge into the gulf, on the line of coast nearly due east between the Sabine and Vermillion outlets.

The Sabine river, which forms the United States western boundary up to lat. 32°, has its source in the prairies of Texas ; after flowing through a long winding channel, it dilates into a shallow lake of 30 miles in length, and 5 in width, which, at the southern extremity, again contracts to a river stream, that passes

* Darby.

to the sea at lat. 29° 28'. Neither the lake, nor river, afford any navigation of commercial importance.

The Calcasieu, rises in the angle between the Sabine and the Red rivers, at lat. 31° 30'; from its sources to its mouth, it flows with similar features, emerging from the same forest into open prairies and marshes; and, like the Sabine, expanding to a lake, again contracts into a river, before it reaches the gulf.

The Mermenteau, rises in lat. 31° 53', draining in its course the centre of the Opelousas prairies, by a number of branches. It expands to the lake form, and again contracts, and, like the other two streams, is defective in its navigation.

"From the outlet of the Mermenteau, a distance of about 60 miles is altogether unbroken by a single stream originating in the solid prairie; and crossing the marsh, this inaccessible line of coast is followed by the Vermillion, a fine but small river, rising in Opelousas, but flowing through Atakapas into the Gulf of Mexico. The source of the Vermillion is near the village of St. Landré, the seat of justice of Opelousas, at lat. 30° 31', and with a general southern course of about 80 miles, falls into a large bay, which again opens, by several passes, into the Gulf of Mexico, at lat. 29° 35'. Though somewhat more navigable than the small rivers, already noticed, as entering the Mexican gulf west of that stream, the Vermillion will not admit vessels of above 5 feet draft."*

The Red river, at 30 miles above its junction with the Mississippi, receives its great tributary or north-east branch, the Washitta, which has its sources in the mountainous prairies of Arkansas, between the Red and Arkansas rivers, lat. 34° 40'. In a course southward of 400 miles, it receives the Darbone, the Salutar, the Bartholomew, the Bœuf, and other rivers, some of which are 200 to 300 miles in length. The general features of the Washitta are similar to those of the Red river itself, particularly in what regards its annual inundations, and the vast tracts of alluvious country formed in consequence, along its course through the upper plains of Louisiana.

IN ALABAMA STATE; VIZ.

The Talapoosa river, rises in the Upper Creek district of this state, which it bisects, running south, and joining the Coosa at Fort Jackson.

The Cahawba river, has its sources, by several branches, in Jefferson and St. Clair counties: after a course of 150 miles south, it falls into the Alabama river at Cahawba city, the centre of the state.

* Darby.

NOTE.

A company is incorporated by the state, as the "Cahawba navigation company," for the purpose of rendering this river navigable.

Also, in virtue of an application to congress, a grant of public lands has been made, for the purpose of defraying, or to aid in defraying the expense of improving the navigation, both of this river, and of the Tennessee, the Coosa, and the Black Warrior rivers; that is to say, the Muscle shoal improvements of the Tennessee being first in order effected out of the grant. This grant amounts to 400,000 acres; with a prospect of being extended to 500,000.

The St. Andrews, the Choctaw, the Yellow Water, the Connecuh, the Perdido, and other streams flowing south, from this state into West Florida.

Tributaries of the Tombecbee river, of the Black Warrior, of the Coosa, and of the Tennessee in this state; they are numerous.

Passage from Mobile bay, westward, by the pass Au Héron, or Pascagoula bay, through Lake Borgne, Lake Pontchartrain, Lake Maurepas, and the River Ibberville, to Baton Rouge; a navigable distance of 150 miles.

IN GEORGIA STATE; VIZ.

The Great Ogatchee river, runs nearly parallel to the Savannah; and discharges, at 18 miles south-west thereof, into the Atlantic. It receives, in Bryan county, the Canoochee river, and is navigable, with some interruptions, 300 miles.

The Canoochee river, tributary to the Great Ogatchee, is navigable for rafts and boats, up to its confluence with Cedar creek.

The Alatamaha river, is formed of two great branches, the Oakmulgee and the Oconee rivers; which have their sources near to those of Chatahootchee; from whence diverging, they afterwards pursue a long parallel course south-east, and in latitude 32° unite; the joint stream continuing that course. It receives the Great Ohoopee river, and enters the sea by several mouths; from whence, up to Milledgeville on the Oconee branch, the navigation is 220 miles.

The Great Ohoopee, tributary to the Alatamaha, has its sourse in Washington county, taking a course east of south, to its mouth in Tatnall; whence it is navigable 40 miles.

The Oakmulgee river, has an inflected course of 300 miles; in which it receives many tributary streams. It is navigable, up from its confluence with the Oconee, 150 miles.

The Great Santilla river, is formed of three forks from the Cypress Swamp, each of which has a long winding course: the united stream falls into the Atlantic, at Cumberland island.

St. Mary's river, rises in Eokefanokee swamp, and after a very crooked course of 150 miles, enters the sea at Amelia island. It is deep, and generally navigable. See *Florida.*

The Lappapaha river, and the Ocolocconee river, flow southwardly from this state, into West Florida.

Broad river, Little river, Bear creek, Beaver dam, and other waters; tributaries of the Savannah river.

Tributaries of the Oconee, of the Oakmulgee, of the Flint river, and of the Chatahootchee, on the east. Together very numerous.

The Warsaw sound, the Ossabaw sound, St. Catharine's sound, Sapelo sound, Doby sound, Alatamaha sound, St. Simon's sound, Jekyll sound, St. Andrew's sound, Cumberland sound: these, along the coast of the state, between Savannah river and St. Mary's, afford a navigation of 250 miles.

NOTE,

Illustrative of the General Progress making in Useful or Physical Science.

A Mr. Phillips, a teacher, in Savannah, has at present before the executive of the United States, five or six scientific plans; some of which, he thinks, from correspondence already had with the department, may come before congress this session. He enumerates them as follows:—

1. A plan for erecting telegraphs throughout these United States, and have promised to convey any sort of signal, or even the contents of letters, by my system, from New-York to Philadelphia, in 8 minutes. I have composed a book (in part only) which will consist of words in the first part of it, and sentences in the second part, and will contain a million or more of signals.

2. A code of signals to be used in the ships of the United States navy, containing a different signal for each day in the year.

3. The outlines of a plan for building dry docks, large enough to dock the largest ship in our navy—and having an apparatus attached to it that will be of essential service in the dock yard.

4. A method for loading and firing, with great accuracy and quickness, red-hot shot, from guns of any calibre, by mathematical projection.

5. A method to lay garrison guns so correctly, that the second shot must take effect.

6. A gun carriage, made upon a plan that will fire in every direction, being on a moveable pivot, the loading of which keeps the men under cover.

NOTE,

Illustrative of Prospects on the Advancement of Intellect, as well as Physical Science, throughout the United States.

The population of the Union for 1830, is, by a report to congress, computed at 13 millions; and the following list shows the number of students, at the principal colleges actually existing therein, to be 3400; or one college student in every 3800 inhabitants, taking the whole together; viz.

States.	Students.	Population.	Proportion.
Maine,	126	420,000	1 in 3,300
New-Hampshire,	119	300,000	1 in 2,500
Vermont,	135	280,000	1 in 2,000
Massachusetts,	449	580,000	1 in 1,300
Rhode-Island,	33	90,000	1 in 2,700
Connecticut,	191	290,000	1 in 1,500
New-York,	540	2,000,000	1 in 3,700
New-Jersey,	96	330,000	1 in 3,400
Pennsylvania,	310	1,300,000	1 in 4,500
Delaware,	7	80,000	1 in 11,000
Maryland,	171	450,000	1 in 2,600
District of Columbia,	21	50,000	1 in 2,400
Virginia,	401	1,180,000	1 in 2,900
North-Carolina,	88	720,000	1 in 8,000
South-Carolina,	196	600,000	1 in 3,000
Georgia,	100	410,000	1 in 4,000
Alabama,	31	380,000	1 in 12,000
Mississippi,	23	130,000	1 in 5,600
Louisiana,	12	300,000	1 in 25,000
Kentucky,	141	650,000	1 in 4,600
Ohio,	148	1,000,000	1 in 6,700
Tennessee,	75	600,000	1 in 8,000
United States,	3,400	13,000,000	1 in 3,800

Whence, it will be seen, that in New-England there is, on an average, 1 student in college for every 2000 inhabitants; in the middle states, 1 for 4000; and in the states south and west of Pennsylvania, 1 for 6000; and this of course includes nothing of the faculty departments in the several universities.

SOUTHERN ATLANTIC COAST; ALSO, NORTH CAROLINA AND SOUTH CAROLINA NAVIGATION.

N.—From Hampton Roads, on the Chesapeake, up Elizabeth river, to Deep creek, on the southern branch thereof; the entrance of the Dismal Swamp canal, at 10 miles above Norfolk. Distance from the Roads,
Miles, 25

A.—From the point of Deep creek, last above specified, by canal, to Joyce's creek, at the head of Pasquotank river, a water of Albemarle sound.
Distance, *Miles,* 22¼

No. 140.

THE DISMAL SWAMP CANAL.

This canal of connexion between Virginia and North-Carolina, was finished, after a temporary plan and manner, and so as to be in the receipt of tolls, in the year 1822. It is cut through the Great Swamp, and is fed with water from a lake in the midst, named Drummond's lake, by means of a channel 3¼ miles long, the fall of which is about 5 feet. It is mostly 5½ to 6 feet deep, and 38 feet wide at the water surface, with recesses for admitting vessels to pass one another. The locks, originally of wood, are now building of stone; length 96½ feet, width 18.

An extension of this canal is in contemplation; as also an enlargement of its dimensions; and congress have now, 1826, a bill before them, authorizing the secretary of the treasury to subscribe, on behalf of the United States, $150,000, equal to 600 shares in the company's capital stock, with a view to enable them to compass the object eligibly and promptly.

Amount of capital expended on the work, to the present time, and present state thereof,	$499,456
Tolls for the year just expired,	11,110

The bill in congress has passed.

NOTE.

Proposals are invited for contracts to be entered into with the company, for completing the canal upon the plan now adopted; which is in conformity to a survey and report thereupon, made by a board of the United States engineers on the occasion; the said report including an estimate of the several improvements proposed to be accomplished, as here follows:—

Estimate of probable Expense of finishing the Dismal Swamp Canal.

Drawbridge at the road over Pasquotank river,	$ 800
Deepening and improving Joyce's creek, and the river Pasquotank, 1 mile 240 yards,	3,410
Lock at the south outlet into Joyce's creek, as particularized,	18,700
Finishing 2d lock,	5,000
Excavation of the trunk to 32 feet wide, and 6½ feet deep: 2° height to 3° base,	25,869
Excavation of recesses at each half mile,	4,144
Additional embankments,	10,604
Lock in Deep creek, to give approach to the canal at low water, and to debouche in 8 feet, the same as with regard to the south outlet lock,	18,700
Extra, for copper, damming, &c.	1,300
Improvement of the feeder, and construction of a wooden lock for the passage of lighters to Lake Drummond, and regulating the supply of water, &c.	10,000
Opening a communication between the canal and Currituck sound, to debouche on North-west river, in 7 feet water: 2760 yards,	5,364
Lock for the same, for the passage of small craft. Lift 4½ feet,	10,000
Bridges and contingencies,	36,109
Total; being equal in amount to 600 shares of stock, newly created by the Dismal Swamp canal company, and subscribed for by the United States,	$150,000

The whole is expected to be gone through with in the seasons of 1827 and 1828.

A connexion with the Sound of Currituck, it will be perceived, forms a part of the new plan.

It would have been desirable, were the thing possible, to give to this section of the whole proposed inland Atlantic chain, a depth of navigation correspondent to that observed in the Chesapeake and Delaware communication now in progress; and to what is to be observed in the Delaware and Rariton one; that is to say, to give a depth of 8 or 10 feet water, so as for it to comprise, without interruption, all the coasting trade navigation up to that draft of water, and thus to render the system uniform, as well as more comprehensive. But to this desideratum of the arrangement, there are opposing circumstances, in the shallowness of the water of almost all the sounds and inlets of North Carolina, which have not been found susceptible, in this respect, of any adequate or lasting improvement. For a continuous navigation into and through the Albemarle and other sounds, 6½ to 7 feet of water is all that can be calculated upon, and therefore it becomes unnecessary to give to the Dismal Swamp canal a greater depth than this, for as much as the North Carolina coasting trade is concerned. The original plan, for much of the distance, had it down to five feet, and some part less than five.

December, 1828.

By an official report of the 1st of this month, it appears the works have advanced near to a completion, and a canal is now obtained, having no where less than 6½ feet depth of water, and a width of 40 feet, save for a few miles where recesses at short distances have been formed. Many essential improvements, besides the proposed particulars as enumerated, have, during the progress of operations, presented themselves, and been duly attended to; particularly in constructions forming a new debouche on the south, into Joyce's river, at 400 yards from Pasquotank. But the proposed communication between the Dismal Swamp canal and the North-west river has not yet been opened: the company require $40,000 additional funds to perfect this object, giving to it locks of stone. The distance is nearly 6 miles. The locks newly constructed, of the Dismal Swamp canal, have been made to correspond in dimensions with the Chesapeake and Delaware canal locks; and the old ones can be so altered, when it shall be found requisite. The summit level of the canal is 16½ feet above the Atlantic at mid tide, and supplied by a feeder of 5 miles from Lake Drummond. See *engraved profile.*

March, 1829.

Congress have effectually aided the completion of the work, in having now voted an additional subscription of $50,000 to the company's stock.

NOTE.

It is in contemplation to introduce the water of Lake Drummond to the navy-yard at Gosport, either directly from the lake, or through the Dismal Swamp canal; and surveys are on foot in regard to it. If found practicable, at a moderate expense, and provided government see proper to maintain this as a naval establishment, the advantages to be derived are obvious, in reference to the docks, the machinery, and various other wants of the yard, including the watering of our ships.

N.—From the south termination of the canal at Pasquotank, down this river, to Albemarle sound; down which, and through Pamplico sound; also, through Core sound to Beaufort, and Bogue sound to Swansborough, and thence through Stumpy and Toomer's sounds; the head of which last is at a very trifling distance from New inlet, or Federal point, Cape Fear river.   Distance, *Miles*, 270

NOTE.

The straits south of Neuse river, or entrance from Pamplico to Core sound, frequently, however, affords not more than 3½ to 4 feet of water; which being insufficient for general coast navigation, the difficulty is obviated by ascending the Neuse as far as South river thereof, or Adams creek, and thence passing, by a projected canal, of 3 miles, as specified at Article 143, to North river; which leads to Beaufort harbour.

M.—From the mouth of Roanoke river, on Albemarle sound, up the river stream, by a sloop passage, 90 miles, to the foot of Great falls, above Halifax; thence, by a boat navigation, about 200 miles, to near the Blue ridge, in Bedford county, Virginia.

Distance, *Miles*, 300

No. 141.

THE WELDON AND ROANOKE RIVER CANALS.

This long and rapid river, which has its principal source west of the Blue ridge, and discharges by several channels into Albemarle sound, takes the name of Staunton river after having passed the mountain; between Charlotte, Halifax, and Mechlenburg counties, Virginia, however, where it receives the Dan river from the south-west, it resumes the name of Roanoke. Sundry improvements are made and making in the stream below the Weldon falls, by which the lower navigation of this river is much facilitated, and will be more so ; and the improvements carrying forward on its upper waters, which are mostly by the sluicing method, will open a boat navigation to the distance here specified. The sluicing on Staunton river, at present extends to Clark's ferry, 88 miles above Rock landing.

At the Weldon, or Great falls, the descent, in 12 miles, is 100 feet; which is overcome by the Weldon canal.

December, 1828.

By official report, it appears that the labours of the Roanoke company, Virginia, the past season, have extended their improvements on the stream navigation, as far up as Salem, in Bottetourt county, Virginia ; a distance of 244 miles, by the course of the river, from Great falls at Weldon.

M.—From the confluence of the Dan and Staunton rivers, as above described, up the stream of the Dan, to Danville, in Pittsylvania county, Virginia; and thence, through the Danville canal, and up the stream improved, into Rockingham and Stokes counties, North Carolina. Distance, by a mixed navigation, *Miles*, 150

No. 142.

DANVILLE AND DAN RIVER CANALS.

On this branch of the Upper Roanoke, besides the canal at Danville, which is a work of importance, a series of sluicing improvements already extend as far as Leaksville, in Rockingham county, North Carolina, which is 152 miles above Rock landing.

The expenditure of capital, by the Roanoke navigation company, to the present time, (November, 1826,) on the lower and upper works of improvement together, and including real estate and negroes held by the company, amounts to 341,283 dollars.

NOTE.

The expenditure on the Upper and Lower Roanoke improvements, down to the 12th November, 1827, including real and moveable property held by the company, amounts to 357,156 dollars, and down to the 5th November, 1828, to 365,991 dollars.

Locks are forthwith to be located at Weldon, of a description to connect the Upper and Lower Roanoke navigation, suitably for an active commerce.

A.—From Plymouth, on the Roanoke river, 5 miles above the mouth thereof, by canal, southward, across the counties of Washington, Beaufort, Craven, Carteret, and through the towns of Washington and Newbern, to Beaufort harbour, on Core sound, coast of North Carolina. Distance, by canal, or in part by Neuse river navigation, and North river,   *Miles,* 100

No. 143.

PLYMOUTH AND BEAUFORT CANAL.

On the 9th March, 1826, the engineer department of the United States made a report, through the secretary of war, to congress, in reference to the proposed system of inland navigation, near the Atlantic coast of Virginia and North Carolina.

The report states, that incidentally to certain examinations made by the board of engineers, for selecting a site for a naval depot, and projecting fortifications, it was ascertained that those states possess great capability for the internal navigation in question, on an extensive scale, so as, besides conferring other benefits, to be essentially connected with the defences of the country.

The board recommends, in case the plan be adopted, that the Dismal Swamp canal should be extended, and have its dimensions enlarged. The board suggests a line of navigation from Norfolk, to Beaufort in North Carolina, including the Dismal Swamp as a part of that line; and, for the remainder, to connect the Roanoke, the Pamplico, and Neuse rivers, by canal, passing through Plymouth, Washington, and Newbern; whence, proceeding on to Beaufort.

The great line of interior communication along the sea board having reached Albemarle sound, North Carolina, the question is here presented, by what route it may most advantageously be continued;—whether through the sounds to Beaufort, as designated at page 320, and thence southwardly, &c., or, as proposed in the present Article, by connecting the Roanoke, Tar, and Neuse rivers, make the line pass through Washington and Newbern, to Beaufort harbour? This latter is considered as highly eligible in reference to the defences of the country, and in a commercial point of view, it may, no doubt, be said, that both routes will be used to advantage.

The Sound route might, however, require to be defended; and, exposing the boats which use it on a broad sheet of water, to the accidents of the sea, cannot, in point of security, be compared to the other.

From Tar river, opposite Washington, to Swift creek, at Dawson's bridge, is about 16 miles, through a flat country, and across some swamps capable of supplying a canal with water; from Dawson's bridge to Newbern, the navigation is good for steam-boats, or sloops, at all seasons. From Newbern, the line proceeds down the Neuse river to Adams creek; up which, and by a canal of 3 miles, across to North river, leading by a good navigation to Beaufort harbour. Adams creek affords 12 feet water.

This canal, it may be seen, between Adams creek and North river, will be common to both routes, the one by the Sounds, and the more interior one just described, passing through Washington and Newbern.

The great importance of Beaufort in time of war, recommends it to notice, for a complete line of improvements of the nature suggested. Besides being a considerable rendezvous, during the last war, for armed vessels and their prizes, Beaufort became a great depot of the produce of Virginia, previously collected at Richmond, at Petersburg, and at Norfolk. It was transported thither, for both home consumption and exportation.

The inlet leading from the sea to Beaufort harbour, was in old times called Topsail inlet. Both inlet and harbour have continued to the present day without material change; the description given of them in the year 1701, being applicable nearly to circumstances at this moment.

NOTE.

The Dismal Swamp canal referred to, is now undergoing alterations and enlargement, as particularized at Article 140, and the United States government are subscribers for 600 shares of the company's stock, or 150,000 dollars, equal to the computed expense of the improvements now in progress.

By an act of congress, 20th May, 1826, there was required to be made, "a survey of Roanoke inlet and sound, with a view to ascertaining as to the practicability of making a permanent ship channel, between Albemarle sound and the Atlantic ocean at Roanoke inlet."

1829.

A recent report on this subject, prepared by the engineer department of the United States, has been submitted to congress, which in some measure still leaves the matter in a state of doubt and suspense. The report, at its outset, remarks, that "*it is impossible to enter upon the discussion of the proposed project, involving such important consequences to the populous and productive portions of the country watered by the Roanoke river, without feeling deeply sensible of the difficulties in effecting so desirable an object, and the degree of uncertainty attending the result of any operations where the causes to be governed are so infinite and powerful. Wherever the course of Nature, in her marine operations, is to be governed, there is probably no subject within the range of the science, where so much is deduced from hypothesis, and where, necessarily, in the result, there is so little certainty."*

It is recorded in topographical history, that there existed originally at Roanoke, or the point of coast called Nag's Head, an inlet capable of receiving sloops and small brigs, or having 10 feet water over the bar, which has been filled up, by deposits, in consequence, it seems, of Albemarle sound having found new vents for its waters lower down. About nine years ago, however, a comprehensive plan of operations was devised and recommended by the civil engineer of the state of North-Carolina, for the purpose of restoring the original state of the navigation, or even, as it was hoped might be practicable, of improving upon the original, and surpassing its advantages. The plan, which has not been acted on, may in some degree be judged of from the engineer's estimates of the cost thereof, as follows; he says,—

In order to open a communication between Albemarle sound and the sea, near Nag's Head, and keep that communication permanently navigable, it will be necessary to cut off all connexion between Albemarle sound and Pamplico, by embankments across Croatan and Roanoke sounds.

Since the closing of the Roanoke inlet, a deposition of soil has taken place in the former channel to the inlet. This, as well as the bed of the new inlet, must be removed by dredging.

The sides of the new inlet must be protected by a facing of rough stone, from the bottom to 5 feet above high water, and not less than 10 feet thick. There must likewise a facing of stone extend from each side of the inner end of the inlet, for a quarter of a mile, in opposite directions, along the shore of Roanoke sound.

Should the estimate for this work, of the above materials and dimensions, exceed the sum which can be appropriated, I have submitted a plan for its construction of

TIMBER AND SOIL.

This, I am of opinion, may be effected by two rows of piles, 20 feet apart. The piles to be of pine logs, of not less dimensions than such as would square to a foot. They are to be hewn or sawed perfectly straight on two sides, the face and back to be left rough, with the bark upon them. These piles are to be driven quite close together, and to be connected longitudinally and transversely by string and cross pieces, with a trenail driven through the string pieces into every pile. The piles are to be driven as far into the bottom of the channel as possible; in no instance to be less than 6 feet. The intermediate space between the rows of piles to be filled with the most tenacious soil which can be had on the spot, for 6 feet on the inside of each row; the incumbent vegetable soil of the marshes and islands may be used for this purpose: the remainder of the space may be filled with the soil from the dredging machine.

Estimate for Stone Embankments.

Stone for the embankment of Croatan sound,	$1,274,182 00
Do. do. Roanoke sound,	251,469 00
Stone for protecting the inlet, - - -	132,000 00
Dredging the channel, - - - - -	493,166 00
Dredging the inlet, - - - - -	212,666 00
	$2,363,483 00

Estimate of Timber and Earth Embankment.

CROATAN SOUND.

Timber for piles, string and cross pieces, - - - - -	$40,576 00	
Pile driving, - - - -	40,392 00	
Fixing string pieces and trenailing,	13,225 00	
Fixing cross pieces, - -	1,575 00	
Earth between the rows of piles,	74,037 00	
Earth for sloping banks, - -	180,204 00	
Stone for piers and embankment,	69,816 00	
		$419,825 00

ROANOKE SOUND.

Timber for piles, string and cross pieces, - - - - -	$18,793 00	
Pile driving, - - - -	27,720 00	
Fixing string pieces and trenailing,	9,260 00	
Fixing cross pieces, - - -	1,050 00	
Earth for embanking inside and outside of the piles, - -	37,772 00	
		94,595 00
Amount carried forward,		$514,420 00

Amount brought forward, $514,420 00

CHANNEL AND INLET.

Excavating the channel, (after deducting the quantity used in the embankments),	$347,211 00	
Excavating the inlet,	212,666 00	
Stone for protecting the inlet,	132,000 00	
		691,877 00
		$1,206,297 00

Recapitulation.

Total for stone embankments,	$2,363,483 00
Total for timber and earth embankments,	1,206,297 00
Difference,	$1,157,186 00

The engineer of the present day, not entirely confident of a successful execution of the scheme as above, in all its plenitude, so as for the works to resist the assaults of the elements, and be permanent; or, should it so far be crowned with success, not still perceiving a great probability, that the country could, in consequence, be benefited in its intercourse, and home and foreign trade, to an extent that would counterbalance the heavy expense involved in erecting and maintaining the needful works; but especially dubious as to the possibility of guarding the proposed usefulness of them against future encroachments or accidents of impediment, induced by an unsettled ocean, whose operations are in the "deep," and "secret," and, though governed by fixed laws, are yet placed far beyond our sphere of ability to calculate beforehand;—the engineer, under such impressions as these, recommends a substitute, as here follows,

He observes,—

The general features of the plan now presented for consideration are, the excavation of a channel through the shoal ground in the sound, cutting across the sands between it and the sea, and, by the intervention of a tide lock, secure to the trade an outward navigation at all times, between half tide and high water. In submitting this plan, we must regret the entire impracticability of giving to the import trade the benefits of the same channel. This will be evident at once in the smallness of the sea mouth of the cut, thereby causing great risk in attempting its entrance, with a lee-shore, as it must always prove—and in the immediate vicinity of a cape, the most dangerous, with one exception, of our extended coast, without the protection of a breakwater in case of unfavourable weather. The hopelessness of combining such an auxiliary, however, is most conclusive, when we reflect upon the unremitting tendency of the currents of the ocean on the southern coast, and the abundance of the elements which go into the formation of the shoals, and which, in this instance, would endanger the safety, if not, indeed, the very existence of the proposed inlet.

The reasons for the adoption of the plan now proposed, are,

1st. The comparatively small expense attending its execution;

2d. That, although its benefits will be confined to the export trade, to successfully prosecute which requires greater draft and despatch, yet, in consequence of the absence of the current of the tide in the still water of the sound, a navigation of greater depth may be maintained ; and

3d. That, in case the plan should, in the execution, be found not to answer the ends intended, the measures in its adoption, with one exception of the tide lock, make up in part the project connected with the stoppage of the sounds, and which might then be adopted as a dernier resort.

No. 1.

Estimate showing the first cost of a dredging machine, steam-engine, scows, &c. complete, and the current expenses of the same for one year.

Purchase of a vessel,	$6,000	00
steam engine of eight horse power,	2,800	00
four receiving scows, at $450 each,	1,800	00
Cost of one machine, &c. complete,	$10,600	00

Pay of a superintendent, at $75 per month, for one year,					$900	00
steam engineer,	30	do.	do.		360	00
four hands,	15	do.	do.	each,	720	00
six hands,	12	do.	do.	do.	864	00
Subsistence twelve hands,	6	do.	do.	do.	864	00
Purchase of 437½ cords of wood for engine, for one year of 250 working days, at $3 per cord,					1,312	50
Repairs of engine, &c. and contingencies,					600	00
Current expenses of a dredging machine for one year,					$5,620	50

No. 2.

Estimate of the cost of clearing out the proposed channel in Roanoke sound, 300 feet wide, for a draft of 10 feet at the common stage of the water; supposing six dredging machines be employed for that purpose, and that each will lift 250 cubic yards of deposite every working day of 10 hours, estimated at 250 in the year.

First cost of six dredging machines complete, at $10,600 each—See No. 1.	$63,600 00
Current expenses of the same for 2 years and 106 days, or 573 working days, the time required for the removal of 859,762 cubic yards, at $5,620 50 each per year—See No. 1; or $12,873 25 each machine, to the completion of the excavation,	77,239 50
Total cost of excavating the channel in Roanoke sound,	$140,839 50

No. 3.

Estimate of the cost of the cut through the banks between Roanoke sound and the ocean, including lining, &c. for a depth of 10 feet below the common level of the sound.

Excavation of 25,584 cubic yards of sand, &c. above the level of high water, at 15 cents per cubic yard,	$3,837 60
Excavation of 69,553 cubic yards of sand, &c. below the level of high water, at 50 cents per cubic yard,	34,776 50
Purchase of 44,480 perches of stone to line the cut, including the bottom, five feet thick, to the height of storm tides, or 2½ feet above ordinary high tides; the wall to be 10 feet thick at bottom, and 5 at top, at $5 per perch,	222,400 00
To lay the same as a dry wall, at $1 50 per perch, including scowing, pumping, &c.	66,720 00
Total cost of the cut,	$327,734 10

HARTMAN BACHE,
Capt. Top. Engineers.

An act was passed last year, by the legislature of North Carolina, confirming and amending an act of the same of the year 1821, granting corporate powers to a company as "the Roanoke inlet company," for the purpose of effecting the improvement contemplated; the state to become a subscriber to the company's stock, and the governor required to transmit a copy of the act to congress, in order to receive their concurrence to one or more of its clauses ; as likewise to solicit congress for a subscription to the stock thereof, in furtherance of the object.

A.—From a point of the Roanoke river, at or near the head of Weldon falls, or from the Weldon canal basin, by canal, eastward, and bordering on the Virginia line, to Murfreesboro' on the Meherrin river; and thence, down that and the Chowan river, to Bennet's creek; up which, and across to the Dismal Swamp canal, and Elizabeth river.

Distance, *Miles*, 80

No. 144.

MURFREESBORO' CANAL.

This suggested undertaking has, for direct and immediate object, to shorten the distance to market, of the rich produce of the Roanoke lands; which, at present, is generally transported quite down the river, and thence, by way of Albemarle sound and the Dismal Swamp canal, to Norfolk.

The projected route, now under consideration, was examined in the year 1818, by a board of commissioners of the states of North Carolina and Virginia, jointly, and was reported upon as practicable, at the expense of 761,522 dollars.

M.—From New inlet, at Smith's island, at the mouth of Cape Fear river, up the stream, to Wilmington, and thence, by a course of lock and dam and other improvements, up to the head thereof, formed by the union of Deep and Haw rivers, below Haywoodsborough, in Chatham county. Distance, *Miles*, 200

No. 145.

CAPE FEAR RIVER CANALS.

This work, so highly important for the interests of North Carolina, is prosecuting by the state, and is among a series of useful objects, to which the growing prosperity of the country has, within some years past, called forth an increase of attention; much has already been effected, in creating facilities of commercial transportation within the state; and much will yet be attempted, to improve the natural communications between the rivers of North Carolina and the sea. The present undertaking, goes as well to deepen and clear the ship channel below the port of Wilmington, as to render, if practicable, the river, upwards from thence, thoroughly navigable for steam vessels with boats in tow.

NOTE.

By a report of the board of internal improvement, 22d January, 1827, to the legislature of North Carolina, it appears, that the work of improving the river upwards from Wilmington, as far as Fayetteville, was prosecuted during the past season with considerable effect. The boat channel has been cleared of great quantities of floating and embedded logs, at the most prominent shoals, in the distance between Campbelltown and the mouth of Black river; but a great deal yet remains to be done, even along the same ground, and a dredging machine is to be employed for removing sand and mud; also jetties, at favourable points, will be made. The sluicing system, it is likely, will be brought into operation pretty extensively on the upper waters of this river; that is to say, between Fayetteville and Haywood, to produce in this distance a good batteau navigation. At Smiley's falls, however, a dam and locks will have to be constructed. It is expected, that, from Wilmington up to Fayetteville, a steam-boat passage may be effected, that will be in activity during 10 months of the year.

As to the flats below Wilmington, the dredging machine was last season to have been applied, with a hope of partly removing that obstruction to the navigation of ships from sea; but, an error being committed by the agent, in attaching machinery to an unsuitable vessel, in place of building one for the purpose, there is, in consequence, a delay of this operation. Preparations are now making, to commence with it as the season opens again. It is, however, apprehended, that, to have this desirable object complete and satisfactory, may be a work of labour and time.

NOTE.

A detachment from the corps of United States engineers, have been engaged in surveying these flats, to ascertain the best mode to obtain a permanent ship channel through them; but no conclusive report on the subject is yet made.

M.—From Haywoodsborough, Cape Fear river, by the valley of Deep river, across to a point on the Yadkin, below the Narrows, in Montgomery county, at or near Blakeley, and thence down the course of the Yadkin river, into the Great Pedee, at Cheraw, South Carolina; from whence, down to the mouth thereof, and to Winyaw bay point, 13 miles below the port of Georgetown, South Carolina. Distance, by a mixed navigation, *Miles*, 275

No. 146.

CAPE FEAR AND PEDEE CANAL.

The projected communication between these two rivers, is dependent upon regular examinations of the ground, yet to be made; and dependent also on the degree of success that may attend the efforts making to clear the Cape Fear channel downward. In the meantime, much attention has been bestowed on clearing the Pedee river channel, from Cheraw downward to Georgetown. This work of improvement is still going forward, with a prospect of being finished very soon. The distance from Cheraw down to Georgetown, is, by the winding of the river, 270 miles. Short canals, at the different bends, will reduce it to 180 miles.

M.—From that point of the Yadkin river, struck by the canal of the article last above specified, up the river stream, by an improved boatable navigation, to Wilkes Courthouse, at the mountains. Distance, *Miles*, 200

No. 147.

YADKIN RIVER CANALS.

This river, the upper part of the Great Pedee, traverses the state south-east from the Alleghany ridge, into South Carolina. Its navigation has received considerable improvements: in 1818, a survey was made, under the Yadkin navigation company, from Wilkes Courthouse, down to Cheraw Hill, at 6 miles south of the state line, a distance of 247 miles; the whole of which, it was estimated, might be rendered navigable, for boats of 10 tons, at the expense of 250,234 dollars; exclusive, however, of the narrows at Montgomery; at which place, an improved road was recommended.

NOTE.

A rail road has been proposed, between this point and Fayetteville, on Cape Fear river; and between the same and a point of the Catawba river: in furtherance whereof, a detachment will be made from the corps of United States engineers, if applied for to the general government; that is to say, to make surveys, in order to ascertain the best line of route for a rail road from Fayetteville to a point of the Yadkin above the Narrows, and from the Yadkin to a point of the Catawba; thus connecting the Catawba and Yadkin valleys, both, with that of Cape Fear river.

N.—From the mouth of Santee river, up the stream, to its head, formed by the confluence of the Wateree and Congaree rivers, and up the latter to Columbia. Distance, by the meanders, *Miles*, 175

M.—From the point of confluence of the Congaree and Wateree rivers, up the course of the latter, as also of the Catawba river, into and across the state of North Carolina, to near the source thereof, in the mountains. Distance, by the river channel improved. and lateral canals, together, *Miles*, 275

No. 148.

WATEREE RIVER AND CATAWBA RIVER CANALS.

In South Carolina, many series of river navigation improvements have been undertaken, and are some part finished, others in progress of execution, under a superintendent of public works. The Wateree river, below the falls, was, last year, 1825, to be cleared of obstructions in its channel through a distance of 84 miles, into the Santee, and a canal at the falls, near Camden, expected also to be finished: a canal above that, on the Catawba, was completed two years ago; and above that, at Rocky Mount,

Chester county, there is constructing another work,—a great one of the kind,—that is to say, one section of it is soon to be finished, at the expense of 40,000 dollars; but there are six or seven other sections not yet begun upon; the which, however, it is important should be expedited, in order to overcome, by an efficient lockage, the Rocky Mount falls. These sections will require from 180,000 to 200,000 dollars additional, to be voted by the legislature, for their construction; and well will the sum be applied; for, when this work shall be finished, a complete navigation, by the Catawba and Wateree, will be laid open, all the way from the extensive iron works of North Carolina, down to the Santee river, and thence, of course, to sea, if so required, through the Santee canal, and the port of Charleston. The Catawba river improvements, and Broad river improvements, up to the foot of the mountains in North Carolina, will reach within a few miles of the navigable waters of the Tennessee. More than 1500 miles of inland navigation has already been improved, and laid open, by the state of South Carolina.

M.—From Columbia, through the Columbia canal, into Broad river, and through the Saluda canal, from Broad into Saluda river, up which, and through Drehr and Lorick's canals, on to the Abbeville county line, near Cambridge: also, from Santee river, by the Santee canal, into Cooper's river; down which, to the port of Charleston. Distance, by a mixed navigation, *Miles,* 150

No. 149.

THE SANTEE, COLUMBIA, AND SALUDA CANALS.

This article, of 150 miles of a mixed navigation, comprises five canals, with 28 locks, overcoming 217 feet of fall; all complete, except on the Saluda, towards Abbeville, which is to be completed, either by canal, or by dam and sluice works, this year, 1825. The Santee canal, which opens from the point of the Santee river, where Sumpter, Williamsburg, and Charleston counties unite, and runs southwardly to Cooper's river, and which is of very great importance to the trade and intercourse between the port of Charleston and a large section of the state, as also a part of North Carolina, was completed in 1802, at an expense of 650,667 dollars. It is 22 miles in length, 35 feet wide, and 4 feet deep.

M.—From the point of confluence of the North and South Edisto rivers, up the course of the latter, by improvements of the stream navigation to this point.
Distance, *Miles*, 70

No. 150.

SOUTH EDISTO RIVER CANALS.

Attention has been directed to a re-opening and amending the navigation of the South Edisto stream, up the distance of 70 miles from its junction with the North Edisto, by clearing away obstructions, and making cuts to straighten in some degree the tortuous abrupt channel.

M.—From the mouth of Seneca river, at Andersonville, on the Savannah, up the stream of the Seneca, also the branches thereof, to the North Carolina line at the Blue ridge of mountains. Distance, by improved stream navigation, *Miles*, 200

No. 151.

SENECA RIVER CANALS.

The Seneca river was to be, in the course of last year, or at the farthest this year, 1826, rendered navigable, by means of dam and sluice works, from opposite Pendleton Courthouse down to its mouth on the Savannah, 150 miles above Augusta; and the sluicing mode is to be extended still upwards, along the Seneca and its tributaries, from Pendleton to the Blue ridge, or the boundary line with North Carolina; the feasibility thereof, at a moderate expense, having been ascertained by a regular examination. In this corner of the state, these improvements are likely to open an easy and valuable extra navigation into the Savannah river, of not less than 200 miles extent.

A.—From Winyaw bay, below Georgetown, by canal, westward, to Wando river, communicating with Cooper's river and the port of Charleston.
Canal distance, *Miles*, 45

No. 152.

CHARLESTON AND GEORGETOWN CANAL.

A canal communication between these ports, on a broad scale, is an object to which the attention of the general government has been solicited, as to one of great national importance. This canal, when once accomplished, will hold a prominent place, during both peace time and war, in the general system of border tide navigation. It probably will not be delayed. The line pointed out, is from Winyaw bay to Wando river, to run parallel with the sea coast; which, therefore, includes the existing cut between Winyaw bay and the Santee river. Wando river dicharges into Cooper's river, a little above Charleston. Length of canal, 45 miles.

M.—From the mouth of Waccamaw river, opposite Georgetown, up the river stream, to near the source thereof, or about 70 miles, and thence, by canal, to a point of Cape Fear river, at or near the port of Wilmington. Distance, together, *Miles*, 100

No. 153.

WACCAMAW CANAL.

This is proposed as a continuation of the line specified in the Article last above inserted, extending the communication, by river stream and canal together, from Winyaw bay to Cape Fear river, North Carolina. The Waccamaw is navigable the distance specified, for vessels of 100 tons. It has its source in a lake of the same name; and, after the first few miles of its course, runs in a line parallel with the Atlantic coast nearly. The Waccamaw lake is relied on for a very convenient as well as abundant supply of water to the canal.

M.—From Ashley river, a little above Charleston, southwestward, on a line nearly parallel to the coast, to strike on the Lower Edisto, and thence on the Savannah river. Distance, by canals of connexion, and bay and river navigation, together, *Miles*, 100

Nos. 154, 155.

ASHLEY AND EDISTO CANAL.—EDISTO AND SAVANNAH CANAL.

The proposed canal-works between these points, when realized, in addition to those particularized in the foregoing Articles, will complete the connexion along the whole of the Carolina border; and there will be established so much of that kind of safe and unimpeded tide navigation, so very desirable for the interests of the country.

It is supposed, that by using the most convenient of the many sounds and bays lying between the Ashley and Savannah rivers, and cutting at places from one to another, there will not be more than 40 miles of canal requisite, in all the distance between Charleston and Savannah, if indeed so much.

NOTE.

The establishing a rail road between Charleston and Hamburg on the Savannah river, opposite Augusta, has been suggested; and the city of Charleston having memorialized the South Carolina legislature on the subject, a charter has been granted for the construction. Distance, about 120 miles.

The company is stiled "the South Carolina canal and rail road company." They have made application to the United States war department, for engineers, to survey the country and mark out a line of route between Charleston and Hamburg, to perform which, a detachment of officers are to go forward in November next, 1828.

A second rail road, of about the same distance, is also proposed, and embraced within the objects of the said company; viz. between Charleston and Columbia; both lines of route to pass through or near the town of Orangeburgh; which thus is proposed to become the central point of three great sections, into which the whole will be divided. The railways to be of wood, with tracks of iron.

SUMMARY FOR NORTH CAROLINA AND SOUTH CAROLINA.

ARTIFICIAL NAVIGATION.

Page.	No.		Miles.
402	140.	The Dismal Swamp canal. Distance, including the North-west river branch,	28
405	141.	Roanoke river canals, and stream improvements,	334
406	142.	Dan river canals, and stream improvements,	150
407	143.	Plymouth and Beaufort canal,	100
414	144.	Murfreesboro' canal,	80
414	145.	Cape Fear river canals, and stream improvements,	200
416	146.	Cape Fear and Pedee canal, and Pedee stream improvements,	275
416	147.	Yadkin river canals, and stream improvements, and extension across, by canal or rail road, through Anson and Mechlenburg counties, to the Catawba,	200
417	148.	Wateree and Catawba river canals, and stream improvements,	275
418	149.	Santee, Columbia, and Saluda canals, and Saluda stream improvements,	150
419	150.	South Edisto river canals, and stream improvements,	70
419	151.	Seneca river canals, and stream improvements,	200
420	152.	Charleston and Georgetown canal,	45
420	153.	Waccamaw canal,	30
421	154.	Ashley and Edisto canal, }	40
421	155.	Edisto and Savannah canal, }	
		Total of artificial navigation,	2177

NATURAL NAVIGATION.

		Miles.
402	From Hampton Roads, up Elizabeth river, to entrance of Dismal Swamp canal,	25
405	Sound navigation, from Pasquotank to Cape Fear,	270
	Amount carried forward,	295

OF THE UNITED STATES. 423

Page.		Miles.
	Amount brought forward,	295
417	The Santee river,	175
420	Waccamaw river,	70
420	Bay and sound navigation between Charleston and Savannah,	60

To which add:—

For all other streams and navigable waters; viz. Of the rivers, creeks, bays, and sounds within these two states, some of which are particularized below, there are 10, affording an average natural navigation of 100 miles each, and 200, an average of 15 miles each.

This making, together, - - - 4000

Total of natural navigation, 4600
Total of artificial navigation, 2177

Total of both, *Miles,* 6777

The Chowan river, which is formed of the Meherrin, the Nottaway, and the Black rivers; all rising in Virginia, and, in their course, watering several counties: the Chowan falls into Albemarle sound: its branches afford a boat navigation of 200 miles.

Tar river, rises in the north of the state, and by a general south-east course, falls into Pamplico sound: it is navigable up to Tarborough, 90 miles.

Neuse river, rises also in the north of the state, and has a like general, but more winding course: it falls into Pamplico sound at 70 miles below Newbern, and is navigable, for boats, 200 miles.

The Yadkin, or upper part of the Great Pedee, traverses the state south-east from the Alleghany ridge, into South-Carolina. This river was surveyed, in 1818, from Wilkes Courthouse, in the mountains, down to Cheraw, a distance of 247 miles; and it was estimated that the sum of 250,234 dollars would render the whole of this distance navigable for boats of 10 tons, except at the Narrows in Montgomery; where a good road of 7 miles was recommended.

The Catawba river, also crosses the state, and enters South-Carolina as the Wateree.

Tributaries of the Catawba, of the Yadkin, of the Neuse, of Tar river, of the Roanoke, are many, each affording navigation.

IN SOUTH CAROLINA; VIZ.

The Waccamaw river, rises from Waccamaw lake, in North-Carolina, and runs south by west 70 miles, into Winyaw bay.

Little Pedee river, rises by several branches, in North-Carolina, and flows into the Great Pedee, at Yahany ferry.

Lynch creek, a considerable river, rising in North Carolina, and flows south-east into the Great Pedee.

The Wateree branch of the Santee river, or a continuation of the Catawba, from North Carolina to its junction with the Congaree river, below Columbia.

The Broad river, reinforced by several considerable streams from the north-west, as the Ennoree, the Tigre, the Pacolet rivers. It is improved and rendered navigable from its confluence with the Saluda at Columbia, up into North-Carolina; to which distance, it is in consequence navigable for boats; and the other streams are navigable into the counties of Newberry, Union, and Lawrens, for boats also.

The Seneca river, is formed of numerous streams from the Blue ridge of mountains, west of the upper waters of the Saluda; it augments the Tugaloo, or Savannah river, at Andersonville, Pendleton county.

The Edisto river, rises by two branches, in Edgefield county, and discharges at Edisto island, south-west of Charleston, by outlets north and south. Navigation, together, for boats, 150 miles, since 70 miles of the South Edisto river have been cleared of drift timber.

The Ashpoo river, the Combahee, and the Coosaw, which run south-eastwardly, into St. Helena sound.

The Coosahatchie river, rises in Barnewell county, and runs south-east, through Beaufort, into Broad river, an arm of the sea, west and north-west of Beaufort island. Navigable, together, 75 miles.

Raccoon sound, Moultrie sound, James island sound, Kiawaw sound, Hilton head, or Cahbogan sound, and various channels on the coast of the state, between the Santee and Savannah rivers; they afford a navigation of 200 miles.

FLORIDA NAVIGATION.

N.—From Appalachicola bay, eastward, through St. George's sound, to an oyster bank of 4 feet water, (across which, a deeper channel if required can be cut), and onward to the bay of Appalachee, up which, and up St. Marks' bay, or Appalachee river, to Fort St. Marks, at the mouth of St. Marks river.
Distance, *Miles*, 80

A.—From the point last above specified, by canal, eastward, crossing the rivers Oscilla, and Amazura, or Suawnee, and passing south of Eokefanokee swamp, to the navigable water of St. Mary's river, at or near the south point of the Great bend. Distance, 100 miles; or from a point of the Appalachicola river to the south bend of St. Mary's, *Miles*, 180

A.—From St. Mary's river, at the point last mentioned, by canal, south-eastwardly, to strike upon St. John's river, at or near Jacksonville, and thence, in continuation, to the bay and harbour of St. Augustine.
Distance, *Miles*, 70

Nos. 156, 157.

FLORIDA CANALS.

This suggested passage, between the Atlantic sea and the Gulf of Mexico, by means of a series of canals, when the time for its execution shall arrive, will most probably be realized in *a thorough conveyance for ships;* which, in such event, must confer on the trade of the country, benefits hardly calculable, in obviating the delays and perils of a navigation round the coast of the great peninsula of Florida, not less than 1000 miles; with all the dangers of the Tortugas bank, the Florida reefs, the Bahama shoals, and the depredations of pirates attendant, and combined with the want of good harbours in all the distance, some two or three points perhaps excepted, as St. Augustine on the east coast, Tampa bay on the west.

NOTE.

An article on the Isthmus (Peninsula) of Florida, has appeared lately, in some newspapers, purporting to be a translation from a manuscript in French, found on board of some piratical vessel, captured 16 years ago. It gives a short description of the peninsula; and the object of the editors who publish the translation, is to show that the country possesses an internal navigation, of which we have hitherto been kept in ignorance; that there does exist a passage, or passages, across, from the Atlantic to the Gulf of Mexico; and which, by way of lakes, and rivers, and channels, can be traversed without danger or difficulty. One of these communications, as pointed out and partly described, is between the Bay of St. Esprit, now called Tampa bay, and the St. Lucie river outlet, or Mosquito river outlet; both north of Cape Carnaveral. Another communication is between the Amazura river and the Atlantic side of the peninsula. The account, moreover, speaks of a canal from the river St. John, direct to one of the western outlets.

The details given are not very intelligible, owing apparently to inaccuracy in the translation; but, the Florida peninsula is a very interesting spot to this Union, and, having so happily for herself become a member, there can be no doubt that the country will soon be thoroughly explored; her exact situation and capacties known, and all her resources laid open.

An appropriation has been made by congress, for surveys being gone into; and engineers are engaged in the object. $20,000 are appropriated, and the board of engineers are directed to make accurate and minute examinations of the country south of St. Mary's river, and including said river, with the view of determining as to the most eligible route for a canal, to admit the transit of boats to connect the Atlantic with the Gulf of Mexico; and also with a view to ascertain as to the practicability of a ship channel: also a particular examination of the line of route from St. Mary's river to the Appalachicola river or báy; and from St. John's river to Vacassar bay, with a view to both the above objects. Estimates of cost, likewise, for each project; and plans.

February, 1827.

The surveys directed as above were made, or partly made, in the past season; the details of which, however, are not as yet sufficiently digested and arranged, it may be presumed, to admit of a circumstantial, regular report; but it is understood, that the result of these preliminary examinations will appear favourable, and be satisfactory. The principal object in view, that of a canal across the peninsula, to connect the waters of the Atlantic and the gulf, it is understood can be accomplished by an easy excavation, and at a very moderate expense, compared with canal works in most other parts of the country. Losses sustained under existing circumstances, in amount of property, (not here to speak of lives,) by wrecks on the coast in the course of a single year, amount probably to a sum not less than sufficient to answer the expense of accomplishing an entire protection and security against those special disasters, and do away the danger of them (now recurring annually) for ever.

As it would appear that Vacassar bay, which receives the Suawnee river, is not a very eligible outlet or inlet, wanting both depth of water over the bar and security as a harbour, there is but little doubt the canal will be made at once to proceed on, and communicate with the Appalachicola river, passing either through the sound of St. George as already described, or else, and as is more probable, keeping to the north of Appalachee bay, be made to strike the Appalachicola river, at some point below the mouth of the Chipola, which is 35 miles from the sea, as perhaps at Fort Gadsden, now named Colintown; or the route may be directed to the Bay of Appalachicola, and this bay can, if required, be easily joined to St. Joseph's bay, on the west of it.

The line of route for which communication, as it will pass through a country abounding in lakes and natural channels, so the work of excavation will, in a considerable degree, be found to be already done; and for the rest, it will be through clay, and argillaceous soil, as clay, shells, and sand mixed, and occasionally limestone; and where, it is said, will be found an abundance of good materials for embankments, &c. Distance from the south point, at the bend of St. Mary's river, 180 miles. An estimate of somewhere between $500,000 and $1,000,000 for the full accomplishment of this grand canal communication, it is supposed, cannot lead to any undue or exaggerated expectation. Vessels drawing 12 feet of water may enter the bay of Appalachicola; and St. Joseph's bay, with which it can be made to communicate, is a safe and desirable harbour for ships of war.

The possession of this fine harbour of St. Joseph, with the advantages of which it is but just now that the country has been, through the researches and examinations of our engineers, made acquainted, may be regarded as invaluable, in reference to all that is here proposed or alluded to, and the best projects of the nation. Situate due north of Cape Blass, it has two entrances;

the western one affording 30 feet water; the eastern, 22. A very short cut will connect it with Appalachicola bay.

It has been shown, at Article 136, that by cutting merely about 12 miles of canal, and clearing the Manchac or Ibberville outlet of the Mississippi, of an obstruction that has been but recently formed, an entire steam-boat navigation of 350 miles may be pursued, between the Appalachicola river and the Mississippi at Baton Rouge district; and for the execution of this branch of the improvements on foot, which is essentially connected with the main project, or Isthmus canal, it is calculated that the sum of $100,000 expense need not be exceeded. The line of navigation will also communicate with the Mississippi river at New-Orleans, by means of the contemplated canal from Lake Pontchartrain, as designated at Article 135.

The Florida navigation is continued as here follows.

N.—From the south point of St. Mary's river, above designated, down the stream of the river, to the mouth thereof, or Bay of St. Mary's, at Amelia island. Distance, *Miles*, 70

No. 158.
AMELIA ISLAND DIVISION.

A.—From the Bay of St. Mary, by canal, or by channel improved, along the rear of Amelia island, to the mouth of St. John's river. Distance, *Miles*, 15

N.—From the mouth of St. John's river, at Talbot island, up the stream thereof, south, by a steam-boat navigation, as far as Lake Munroe, in lat. 28° 38', and beyond. Distance, *Miles*, 150

No. 159.
ATLANTIC COAST DIVISION.

M.—From the mouth of St. John's river, by canal, and

by inland tide channel navigation, along the eastern border of the peninsula, as far as Cape Florida, or Bocca Ratones. From which point, a steam-boat may pursue, within the keys and sheltering islands, a safe and easy passage to the Tortugas. Distance to Cape Florida, including 20 miles of connecting canals, *Miles*, 350

FLORIDA CANALS.

No.		Miles.
159.	Distance of canal, as above,	20
156.	Distance from St. Mary's river to the Appalachicola,	180
157.	Distance from St. Mary's river to the Harbour of St. Augustine,	70
158.	Distance of canal, or channel improved, in the rear of Amelia island,	15
136.	Distance of connecting canals between the Appalachicola river and the Mississippi,	12

This collective article, according to the specifications above, now comprises five heads; namely,—

1. The main project of a canal, and, if practicable, a ship canal, from the Atlantic to the gulf. The new lights thrown upon this subject by the recent examinations made, and all circumstances hitherto known, appear to be more than commonly favourable and encouraging, for the execution of it, on the broadest scale that the nation's interests may require.

It does not, however, appear, that the disemboguement of this canal can be made to take place at the heretofore suggested point of Vacassar bay. A harbour, with all the requisite advantages, not being here presented, the plan in all probability will be, to continue the canal on to Appalachicola river, or bay, as above stated.

2. The proposed improvements, in continuation, from the Appalachicola river to the Mississippi, consisting in about 12 miles of excavation, thereby to obtain, between those points, an interior steam-boat navigation of 350 miles, as particularized at Article 136. This in continuation of the main projected canal as above.

3. The proposed prolongation, or branch canal, from the south point of St. Mary's river to the harbour of St. Augustine, intersecting the St. John's river at Jacksonville.

4. A subsidiary work of improvement, consisting in straightening, at several places, the tortuous channel behind Amelia island, between St. Mary's river mouth and St. John's, and cutting through an obstruction at the middle, to the distance of 1½ mile, and depth of 4 feet; or otherwise, constructing a lateral canal along this distance, on the main land. This work, opening a free passage inland to the River St. John, and of course up to its head navigation, will not, it is estimated, require more than 10,000 dollars expense for its execution. The St. John's river is described as a magnificent stream, pursuing an average breadth of 2 miles, along a distance of 100 from its mouth, and often spreading into lakes of 4 or 5 miles wide; its banks thickly lined with forests of the finest timber, composed of cypress, pine, live oak, and cedar, not equalled in quality in the United States. Its navigation unimpeded, affording generally 8 feet of water, and more, up to Lake George, which is a lake 18 miles long, by 12 wide, and the bar whereof has 6 feet water. After passing which, an increased depth is again maintained up to Lake Munroe, 40 miles or thereabouts above Lake George. A south-west branch of the St. John flows out of Lake Apopka, situate near the centre of the peninsula, in lat. 28° 15'; and under the name of Ocklowaha river, in a course of 80 miles, at first nearly north, then curving eastward, unites with the St. John proper, at some miles below Lake George; from whence the stream has a very tortuous course of 100 miles, to its mouth on the Atlantic. The Ocklowaha is also navigable for a considerable distance, if not its whole length; and both branches are represented as bearing a nearer resemblance to irregular canals than to rivers in general.

5. Another subsidiary work, consisting in effectuating a secure line of inland navigation along the Atlantic Florida border, by means of a few connecting short canals, between the natural channels, or rivers, or lagoons, running parallel with the coast. Less than 20 miles of canal, it is understood, will suffice for the whole; as, for example;—a canal of 7 miles long, will connect, by means of Pablo river and North river, the mouth of St. John's, with the harbour of St. Augustine; a second canal, of 6 miles, will connect the Matanza and Mosquito waters; and a cut of ½ a mile will extend thence to Indian river, from which a communication by the Jupiter, with the Potomac and Ratones river waters, will complete the line to Cape Florida: and thence exists an easy steam-boat passage to the Tortugas. To which point, it is quite probable, the attention of the general government will be drawn, for effecting a thorough nautical examination; and, should requisite facilities here be found, then to make this a naval station for the United States West India squadron. The canal grounds to be excavated, are stated as being, at a mean

elevation, only 17 inches above tide water level, and composed of marl, clay, sand, and vegetable deposite; and the estimate of expense, for the whole of this work, is 50,000 dollars. Which is truly a consideration of but small account, taking into view the great extent of easy steam-boat navigation to be laid open by its accomplishment, and the great advantages that must result to the country out of this improvement. It has been remarked, that *the surveys of the St. Mary's and St. John's rivers, and the Atlantic coast of Florida to Bocca Ratones, expose to view a field for internal navigation and intercourse, of a magnitude and interest wholly unexpected.*

It results, then, that at the small expense of 60,000 dollars, the River St. John may be made approachable through an inland channel, and its treasures available, and 350 miles besides of interesting inland border navigation be laid open, down to the very southern extremity of the coast, or even to the Tortugas. Also, that, for a further expense, not exceeding 1,100,000 dollars, and perhaps a great deal less, the leading great project itself, and the one in continuation, westward, to the Mississippi river, may be accomplished; whereby a further distance of 530 miles of inland border navigation will be obtained; and with a probability that so much of this line of communication as regards a passage from the waters of the Atlantic into those of the Gulf of Mexico, may be made a passage for *ships.*

Of which canal of communication, between the Atlantic and the gulf; to revert for another moment to this object; the demonstration of its being, if not at the very head, certainly one of the number of that class of improvements of the very highest interest to every section of the country, needs not the slightest allusion to any of that description of advantages, in the anticipation of which, the speculative political genius of the times has been latterly wont to indulge a little; namely; such advantages as, it has been supposed may, by possibility, accrue to the nation out of the bearing or relation this Florida canal may happen to have upon or with the projected South American cut through to the Pacific, in the event of this latter ever taking place. And it moreover has been said, that, instead of our navigation and commerce passing, as now it does pass, to a vast extent, along the shores of Cuba, not only will this hazard and many others be avoided, but the United States be enabled to lay some portion of the commerce, between Europe and America, under contribution, in the form of tolls, for the sake of a passage across a portion of the United States territory.

Placing, however, these speculative contingent incidentals quite out of view, it is sufficient at present, (seeking only to set forth how promptly the work claims to be executed for our own commerce sake) to consider the striking additional facilities and benefits which it will immediately, and to a certainty, confer, directly or indirectly, upon the established trade of the nation at large.

"It is evidently the sense of the national legislature, that, whilst the proposed canal will, in its first operation, benefit the country through which it passes, open the public domain to rapid population, bring to a ready sale the public lands, and add to the aggregate of national wealth, the products of a region probably not equalled in the United States, in the number and variety of articles to the growth of which it is adapted; it will, in its indirect operation, afford the most important facilities to the whole coasting trade of the northern and eastern states, and the whole inland navigation of the western waters."

Should the channel be for ships, the greater will be the benefit; but whether for ships, or for smaller vessels merely, our southern Atlantic seaports, as, for instance, Charleston, Savannah, St. Mary's, will consequently rise in importance, as places of deposite for the exportable staples of the interior, to an increased extent not at present calculable.

For a continuation of the navigable channel quite to the Mississippi at the Manchac, as well as at New-Orleans; by way of St. Andrew's bay, the Choctawatchee, Santa Rosa, Pensacola, Mobile, and Pascagoula bays, and the Lakes Borgne and Pontchartrain, it would seem that the few works needful to accomplish this, have additional claims to a prompt execution, in another point of view;

To explain this point;—It is regarded as of the highest importance, that the Manchac, or Ibberville channel, should be reopened, and the dimensions of it be enlarged, for the purpose of carrying off some of the superabundant water of the Mississippi, at every annual flood. It is thought that it may even be requisite to lay open other capacious channels also to the sea, as a measure of caution against the threatened danger of absolute inundation along the banks of the river for many miles upward; the very safety of New-Orleans itself requiring it. As the dyke system has already been rather unduly extended up this mighty stream, and is still in some degree extending, so the danger of some great unmanageable disruption in the lower situations is becoming, from year to year, more and more imminent; for nothing can be more evident, than that the more the high water is confined, by levées above, the higher will the waters rise every year in the lower country, and the levées of the latter must go on proportionately increasing in height, unless some expedient be found to remove the danger and counteract the evil.

There exist, it is well known, several points below the Manchac, at either of which a communication with Lake Maurepas, or with Lake Pontchartrain, might be formed, by cutting a distance of about 5 to 10 miles merely; and where the river, at low water, is said to be 10 feet above the level of the lake. At the city of New-Orleans, a canal has been projected and surveyed, from the river to the lake, as specified at Article 135. Moreover, at Bayou Dupré, 12 miles below the city, the Mississippi approaches within 4¼ miles of Lake Borgne, where the declivity to the level of the lake is 11 feet. Besides which, the lakes of Barataria approach the Mississippi on the west side, seemingly located for a natural receptacle of a portion of its surplus water, to be thence carried off to the sea. Millions of acres of fertile land are susceptible of being reclaimed and brought under cultivation, if an effectual plan for draining the rich Mississippi delta were adopted.

A report of the board of commissioners on internal improvement, made to the legislature of Louisiana, recommends that the subject be submitted to the consideration of the general government.

December, 1828.

The governor of Louisiana, in a communication to the legislature, has just reiterated his recommendations in regard to the important objects above noticed; "to diminish the evils arising from the periodical inundations of the Mississippi; which become every year more alarming." And, he observes, "by opening canals, morasses to a large extent may be reclaimed."

January, 1829.

Since the above was written, a very able report on the subject of the inundated lands on the Mississippi, has been made by the commissioner of the general land office, through the secretary of the treasury, to congress. It is dated 12th of this month.

In the course of the river, between the northern boundary of the state of Louisiana, latitude 33°, and the Gulf of Mexico, it is computed that the tracts of country inundated in the height of flood season, amount to a superficial area of 5,429,260 acres. Whereof, that portion which lies below the 31st degree of latitude, may be estimated at 3,183,580 acres; and that portion lying between the 31st and 33d degrees of latitude, at 2,245,680 acres, of which last, 398,000 acres lie within the state of Mississippi.

This computation includes the whole of the country subject to inundation, by the Mississippi and the waters of the gulf.

A portion, however, of the above area, including both banks of the Mississippi, from a certain distance below New-Orleans up to Baton Rouge, and the west bank up to near the 31st degree of latitude; also both banks of La Fourche for a distance of about 50 miles from the Mississippi at Donaldsonville, has, by means of levées or embankments, been reclaimed, at the expense of individuals. These strips of land, so reclaimed, taken all together, may be estimated as equal to the depth of 40 acres on each side of the Mississippi and La Fourche, along the distances specified, and, by consequence, as amounting on the whole to about 500,000 acres; which, deducted from 3,183,580, leaves the quantity of 2,683,580 acres of land, below the 31st degree of latitude, still subject to inundations, annually or occasionally, and the whole quantity of lands within the area stated, and not protected by embankments, equal to 4,929,260 acres.

Now, it is suggested and believed, that, by clearing out and deepening the existing natural channels, and opening some artificial ones, the whole surplus of waters which the Mississippi river channel is not of sufficient capacity to carry off, may be made to pass through these, and be discharged into the gulf; and, with the aid of embankments, together with natural or artificial reservoirs, and the use of machinery, worked in the first instance by steam, and afterward, as the country becomes cleared, by wind-mill power, to carry off the rain-water falling when the Mississippi waters happen to be high; by these means, all combined, it is not doubted that the whole extent of country in question, as above, may be reclaimed, and rendered in the highest degree productive. No calculation, that could at present be made, would perhaps convey any tolerably correct idea of the comparative state of productiveness, in rich commodities, of by far the greater part of the whole of this extent of land, which is hereafter, and that too, perhaps, very shortly, to be realized by the Mississippi cultivator. Strikingly similar in many local circumstances to the plain of the Nile, and derived from the successive deposites of a still mightier river, the alluvious plain of the Mississippi reclaimed, may possibly become an object of as much celebrity for the benefits it will have been destined to confer upon mankind. Benefits, however, to be attained, free from the charge of resorting to any thing similar to those difficult, but admirable and durable works which have signalized the Egyptian plains, and were employed, and so are still employed, for the purpose of not only controlling and restricting within its banks the stream of the great river, to the extent that was desirable, but likewise for the purpose of irrigating the soil periodically. The application of a few simple mechanical and hydraulic contrivances, of no expensive character, in addition, occasionally, to the rains from heaven, it is quite probable, and cheering to believe, will, in the Mississippi case, always be sufficient to effectuate the last mentioned important purpose. Blessings will not be the less blessings, although no stupendous monuments of the art and labour of man, should be transmitted to the wonder of posterity, as having produced them.

The alluvial lands of Louisiana, from the overflowings of the Mississippi river, may be divided into two great portions; viz. The first, or upper plain, extending from the 33d degree down to the 31st degree of north latitude, 150 miles in length, in a direction west of south, and generally from 25 to 30 miles in breadth, but at some places is much broader.

The second portion, or lower plain, extending from latitude 31°, about 250 miles, in a general south-east direction, down to the principal mouth of the river, which protrudes into the Gulf of Mexico; and there is formed a semi-circular base of 200 miles extent, from the Achafalaya river round to the Rigolets. The elevation of the plain, at the 33d degree of latitude, above the waters of the gulf at common tide, may be about 130 feet.

The Mississippi river, on entering this plain, at latitude 33°, crosses it diagonally to the highlands, below the mouth of the Yazoo; from whence it winds round the highlands in the states of Mississippi and Louisiana, to Baton Rouge; leaving, in this distance, the alluvial lands on its western bank; from some distance below Baton Rouge, it takes an eastern course through the plain, parallel nearly to the shores of the gulf, until, reaching English turn, it bends to the south-east, and through six or seven different channels, disembogues into a shallow ocean. The banks of the Mississippi, near the mouth thereof, are not more than 2 or 3 feet above common tide water: they gradually ascend with the plain, up to the 33d degree of latitude, but at that point have arrived at no greater elevation than 30 to 40 feet above low water mark of the river. Throughout the whole of this distance, the river banks are subject to be overflowed, with the exception of those places, as already mentioned, that are protected by levées or embankments.

Exclusive of a number of small bayous, there exist three large natural canals or bayous, by which these floods, composed of the surplus waters of the Mississippi, are, in a measure, carried off towards the gulf. These outlets, above New-Orleans, are;—

1. La Fourche, leaving the Mississippi river at Donaldsonville, and reaching the sea, by a tolerably direct course, of 90 to 100 miles. Its banks are high, and chiefly protected by levées; and, in high floods, it carries off a large column of water; after such improvements as are already on foot along its whole course, shall have been effected, it will carry off a greater column. It is the only natural channel, in its present state, that takes off the waters to the ocean so rapidly and directly as to admit of embankments being erected by individuals along the whole course of the same.

2. Above La Fourche, the bayou Manchac, or Ibberville,

leading to the Lakes Maurepas and Pontchartrain, takes off into the gulf, through the Rigolets and other passes, a considerable body of water. Besides, however, the bed of this bayou being 14 feet above the level of the Mississippi low water, the channel of the same is at present very much obstructed; otherwise, reaching tide water in a very short distance compared with that the river channel has to traverse, this outlet would prove a mighty drain. The difference between the highest elevation of the waters at the afflux of the Manchac, and the lowest level of the tide in Lake Pontchartrain, is from 27 to 30 feet.

3. A little below the Manchac, on the opposite side, Bayou Plaquemine strikes off, and communicates with the Achafalaya. It being unobstructed in its channel, and there being a considerable declination in this part of the plain of the alluvion, it in consequence is rapid, and carries off much water into the Achafalaya. At leaving the Mississippi, however, the bed of Bayou Plaquemine is 5 feet above the level of low water. At about 88 miles above Plaquemine, and just below the 31st degree of latitude, the Achafalaya itself strikes off. This is one of the ancient channels of the Mississippi river, and, being deep, carries off at all times large quantities of water; yet this passage is greatly encumbered with timber, and considerable improvements are requisite to render it as powerful a drain as it may be.

As the distance from the point whence the Achafalaya leaves the Mississippi, along its channel to the gulf, is only 132 miles, and the distance traversed by the great river, from the same point to the gulf, is 318 miles, it is evident that a given column of water will, velocities equal, be passed off to the gulf, by the former, in a proportionately less length of time. But this, in the case before us, is not the whole consideration; for, from the topographical description given of the Louisiana plain south of the 31st degree of latitude, it is also evident, that, besides the general and gradual declination of this plain as it descends with the Mississippi, it has a declination more abrupt, both towards the Lakes Maurepas and Pontchartrain on the east, and towards the great lake of Attakapas on the west; and that streams passing off each of these ways, will have the greater velocity. Which facts established, it would seem, that by following the suggestions of nature, and aiding and enlarging the operations which she has commenced, there are strong grounds to believe *the whole plain may be recovered from inundation.*

In point of form and configuration, this lower alluvious plain has been compared to the convex surface of a scollop-shell, flattened and trimmed so as to have one of its sides much curved, and the surface of the other somewhat indented.

It has been shown, that the quantity of water drawn off by the Ibberville, the Bayou Fourche, and the Achafalaya, inadequate as these three drains are to the whole object desired, has yet had so much effect in restraining the volume of water passing through the Mississippi proper, and diminishing the floods of former times, as to enable embankments to be thrown up along this river, from a point just below where the Achafalaya leaves it, to some distance below New-Orleans, as also along the greater part of Bayou La Fourche; the consequence of which operation is, that about 500,000 acres of formerly inundated lands are now kept free; and whereof, it is estimated, 400,000 acres, consisting of tracts on each bank, to the average depth of 40 acres, are fit for cultivation ; and, so far as cultivation already extends, alleged to be the most productive bodies of land in the United States.

If the waters drawn off, in any given time, from the Mississippi, through the natural channels now formed, could be delivered into the gulf, through the same channels, in the same given time, then all the adjacent lands would be reclaimed; but the fact being different, inasmuch as the banks of these channels themselves are subject to regular overflowings, it follows, that the object in question can only be attained by increasing the capacity of these natural water courses, and if need be, adding artificial ones, or by both means; so that, the volume of water entering, in any given time, the lower plain of Louisiana, may be discharged into the Gulf of Mexico within the same given time. What the actual contents of such a volume of water may be, becomes therefore an important question; for, this point ascertained with any tolerable degree of precision, the number and capacity of the channels needful to carry it off, will then admit of being calculated with sufficient certainty.

At the 31st degree of latitude, and near to the point where the Red river flows into, and that whence the Achafalaya is discharged from, the Mississippi, the waters of this are compressed into a narrower compass than at any other point below latitude 33°. This may be considered as the apex of the lower plain; and it is thought probable, that, at this point, a series of experiments could be made, by which the question would be solved ; that is, for as much as respects the lower plain, in the present state and course of things.

With regard to the upper plain ; the contraction just above spoken of, occasioned by the elevated lands of the Avoyelles, where the Red river is arrested in its general course, and deflected circuitously, across the plain, to the Mississippi ;—this contraction has a strong tendency to, and in fact does, back up all the waters of the upper plain ; and therefore it is, that, immediately above this point, there is a vast accumulation of alluvious lands, more deeply covered with water than the alluvions at other places ; and below this point, the embankments of the

Mississippi terminate. To enable individuals to advance with these embankments, and besides, to erect others along the various water-courses of the upper plain, it would seem to be indispensably necessary, first to drain off all the said superabundance of water, and to have recourse to artificial means to effectuate this purpose.

The Red river, arrested as already stated, in its general course, and turned to the Mississippi, there are appearances for believing, did at some period or other convey, if not the whole of its stream, at least a large portion thereof, through Bayou Bœuf, and the lake of the Atakapas, to the ocean. At present, in high floods, some of the Red river waters are discharged into Bayou Bœuf, at different points between Avoyelles and the rapids. Now, it is not improbable, that if the existing channels by which these waters, in high floods, find their way to Bayou Bœuf, were improved, and in addition thereto, that a *deep cut* were effected, from the Red river, through the tongue of elevated alluvious land, to the Achafalaya; it is not improbable that by this combined operation, the object of drawing off the waters from the upper plain might be accomplished; that is to say, that these channels together, might be sufficient to take off with rapidity the waters which now accumulate at the base of the upper plain; or, at the least, to reduce the elevation of them so much as to enable individual enterprise and capital to continue the embankments upward, not only along the course of the Mississippi, but along all those extensive water courses running through the upper plain. By which means, conjointly, and provision being made, by machinery, to take off the rain water, and that occasioned by leakage and accidental crevasses, the whole plain may be reclaimed and be preserved from inundation in future.

But, it is next to be considered, that the whole of the upper plain, once reclaimed in the manner here suggested, and the waters thereof, contracted into narrow channels, being consequently thrown, at greater elevation, and with proportionate rapidity, upon the lower plain, the necessary consequence of this would be, unless properly guarded against, that such accessions would again deluge the lower plain, and perhaps lay vast tracts of the Atakapas and Opelousas under water. To prevent this from happening, it will be needful to have the outlets from the lower plain into the gulf, natural and artificial together, of such capacity as to be sufficient to carry off the joint superabundant waters of the Red river and the Mississippi, belonging to both the upper and the lower plain, through the channels provided for the same, without overflowing their banks. This precaution attended to, and the other suggested means adopted, it is likely that both plains may be recovered from the floods, permanent or occasional, and committed to a beneficial cultivation. The outline of the only effectual plan that can be adopted, for the accomplishment of the entire object, is,

1. To enlarge to the utmost the capacities of the several existing natural channels between the Mississippi river and the Gulf of Mexico, in all the distance of each one, from their points of outlet respectively, to the sea. 2. To make tappings of the Mississippi by artificial canal works, such as may aid, to the extent required, the operation of the natural channels therefrom, in their improved state; as likewise tappings of the Red river, for the purpose of drawing off the present accumulation, just above the 31° of latitude, and of preventing in future the refluent waters at that point from rising beyond a certain height; and, 3. To secure an adequate regular discharge into the sea, of all the surplus waters thrown into the lower plain, through the several channels, natural and artificial, assigned or to be assigned for that purpose, without overflowing the banks thereof; which is to be effected by clearing from existing obstructions certain natural outlets to the gulf, particularly the Manchac pass of the Rigolets, and the pass of Berwick's bay, by which the copious waters of the Achafalaya, the Teche, and the Atakapas lakes, are at present imperfectly conveyed, and by the construction of artificial outlets to the extent requisite, in addition to the improved natural ones, for accomplishing this object. Outlets by artificial cuts, from the great lake of the Atakapas, across the Teche river, for a distance of 15 or 20 miles above its mouth, to the nearest convenient points of the gulf, at the same time embanking the lake to the height of 3 feet above its present surface, it is supposed would be competent to drain off the present superabundance of water there, together with such additional volume as, in the course of operations, it might be found expedient to throw into that lake. It has been suggested, that three or four brigades of the topographical corps of engineers might most beneficially be employed, for a few seasons, from the 1st of November to the 1st of July, in examining and surveying the two plains; as it is believed sufficient data would be obtained to enable them to lay down an eligible connected plan for the accomplishment of the whole purpose; with estimates, upon probable ground, of the expense attending it. The quantity of lands belonging to government, within the alluvial limits, is computed at 3,000,000 of acres; which, at a minimum price of 10 dollars, would of course amount in value to $30,000,000.

A tapping of the Mississippi, on the south side, at or near New-Orleans, to communicate with Lake Barataria, and thence with the gulf, has been projected, as noticed at Articles 131 and 132.

NOTE.

Mr. Darby, in his "*Geographical View,*" lays down a plan, founded on examinations and admeasurements made by himself, for deepening the bar at one or other of the passes of the Mississippi. He observes, "Besides three or four of little consequence, the Mississippi has four passes or outlets; these are, the west pass, with about 8 feet water; south-west pass, with 12 feet water; south pass, with 8 feet; the south-east, or main pass, with 12 feet water. These depths are given at ordinary tides. At either of the two greater of which passes, you have, at a distance of two cables length from the bar, 50 feet of water." And he adds, after describing his plan of improvement, "I am convinced, that long before 50 years expire, ships of any draught of water may be navigated to and from New-Orleans." Probably indeed long within the period here supposed, will such navigation be realized, not only in respect to the largest class of merchant ships, but likewise compassing a greater object in reference to the country's defences in time of war. The immensely increasing commerce of the Mississippi, will not suffer the measure to be delayed, after it shall be once well ascertained that a safe and adequate port of entry for line-of-battle ships can here be formed, according to hopes at present entertained. Could the bar of the Mississippi be sufficiently deepened, a safe and capacious harbour would indeed be afforded, for any number of vessels of war, at all seasons of the year.

July, 1829.

FLORIDA CANAL, No. 156, CONTINUED.

A more circumstantial trace of the Appalachicola route is now given; and its length, it appears, will extend to 250 miles. The route leaves St. Mary's river at 3 miles above St. Mary's town, and taking a western course along the valley, crosses it at a few miles south-west of Ellicot's mound, and enters the marshes of Eokefanokee swamp, along the ravine of Alligator creek. Leaving the swamp, the route takes a south-west direction, and passing through Hamilton county into the valley of Alapha river, pursues this to the mouth of the Withlacuchee. From this point, it proceeds westward, parallel with and near to the great road leading from St. Augustine to Tallahassee, crosses the Oscilla river at Evans's ferry, through Jefferson county, and intersects St. Mark's river at the new town of Rock-haven. Thence, pursuing this river valley by the town of Magnolia and Old Fort St. Marks, the route proceeds to cross the Ocolockonee, and along James island sound to its termination at Appalachicola bay, opposite the town of Appalachicola. Distance, 250 miles.

Greatest elevation, 217 feet, which was found between the Oscilla and Ocolockonee rivers. See the *engraved profile* of this canal route.

A branch canal from the above is suggested; to commence at the intersection of the Suawnee river, and pursue the valley thereof as far as the Indian Cow Pens; there uniting with said river, at 10 miles from its discharge into Vacassar bay. Length of this branch 75 miles.

Another communication is suggested, viz. The route to leave St. Mary's river, at the same point with the Great main canal above specified, and taking a south-west direction, cross the Nassau ridge, and pass by Jacksonville, and the ravine of Black creek; whence, by Santa Fé pond, (which is proposed as a feeder,) pursue the valley down to the mouth of Santa Fé river, on the Suawnee, 17 miles above the Cow Pens. Length of this canal, 120 miles.

The preliminary examinations made, mark out a further route of canal communication, as of importance, viz. To commence on the St. John, at the mouth of Pablo river, and crossing the Twelve mile swamp, intersect the St. John at the mouth of Black creek, and pass along the creek valley, and by the Tampa bay road, to Orange lake; which lake, and the River Ocklowaha, as far as Indian pond, it is proposed to convert into a part of the communication; and from Indian pond pass on, parallel with and near to the Augustine and Tampa bay road, to its intersection with Hillsborough river; whence to Tampa bay, near to the United States cantonment. Distance, between the mouth of St. John's river and Tampa bay, 225 miles.

NOTE ON NEW MEXICO.

A project is now on foot for establishing a regular intercourse with the interior of the state of Chihuahua, by means of steamboats.

In consequence of a grant made to certain individuals, of the exclusive privilege of navigating the Rio del Norte, with steamboats and horse-boats, during the term of 15 years, a steam-boat is at present equipping in New-York, and expected soon to sail, for the purpose of commencing operations. The boat for this first voyage is not large; say 100 tons. Her engine is of 36 horse-power; and she moves at the rate of $11\frac{1}{2}$ miles per hour, drawing only 3 feet 4 inches water. A voyage from New-Orleans to Matamores or Refugio can, it is said, be made in 3 or 4 days, and thence, by steam, up to the city of Chihuahua, in the same time: and, at high water, this schooner, the Ariel, will be able to reach within 15 leagues of Santa Fé. (She sailed and arrived.)

SUMMARY FOR FLORIDA.

ARTIFICIAL NAVIGATION.

Page.	No.		Miles.
440	156.	The Isthmus and Appalachicola canal, distance,	250
425	157.	Branch to St. Augustine,	70
428	158.	Amelia island canal, and channel improvement,	15
428	159.	Florida Atlantic coast canals,	20
		Branch to Vacassar bay,	75
		Santa Fé canal,	120
		Tampa bay canal,	225
		Total of artificial navigation,	775

NATURAL NAVIGATION.

		Miles.
425	Appalachicola river to Fort St. Marks,	80
428	St. Mary's river navigation,	70
428	St. John's river navigation,	150
428	Sound and bay navigation along the Atlantic coast of the Peninsula,	330

To which add :—

The Perdido, or Sinking river; of no importance, however, but as forming the boundary, in part, with Alabama state, . . .

The Connecuh river; rises in the south-east of Alabama, running south-west to its junction with the Escambia, which falls into Escambia bay through a deep channel. The principal tributaries to it are, the Sepulgas, Murder creek, the Big and Little Escambia, . . .

The Yellow Water; rises also in Alabama, and, by a south-west course, enters Yellow Water bay: it receives Shoal river and Tile creek, . . .

The Alaqua; rises north of Choctawatchee bay, into which it discharges: it is navigable for boats 15 miles, to Vaughan's, . . .

Amount carried forward, 630

	Miles.
Amount brought forward,	630

The Choctawatchee river; rises near the east line of Alabama, and runs a general course, west of south, down to Cow ford; and thence west, to Choctawatchee bay, which it enters through numerous channels. It receives

Pea river and Uchee creek, from the west;

Big Barren, the Holmes, and the Pond creeks, from the south-east.

Boats can ascend 100 miles,   -   -   -   -   ...

The Econfina; has a short course into St. Andrew's bay, and is navigable 15 miles,   -   -   -   ...

The Chipola river; a branch of the Appalachicola; has its sources in several large springs at the north line of the state, and falls into the Appalachicola river, at 9 miles above Colintown, or Fort Gadsden, after passing through a lake of 20 miles long, formed recently by the bursting of an arm of the Appalachicola into the Chipola. It is navigable 60 miles, up to a point in Jackson county, where two head branches, after having disappeared for some distance under ground, and then re-appeared, unite, - - - - - ...

The Appalachicola river; is formed by the union of the Chatahootchee and Flint rivers at the Georgia line, and is navigable for large schooners to the sea, near 100 miles, - - - - - - ...

The Ocolockonee river; rises in Georgia, and after a general course west of south, falls into the gulf on both sides of James island, Gadsden county.

Little river, Robinson's creek, and Rocky Comfort, are branches thereof, - - - - - ...

The Appalachee river; is formed by the union of the Wakully and St. Mark's rivers, at Fort St. Mark, 9 miles from the sea. It is navigable; and vessels of 7 feet draft, ascend the Wakully to 7 miles above the fort, and the St. Mark's river 4 miles, - - - ...

The Oscilla river; rises a little south of the state line: it passes through the centre of Leon county, and enters the sea, east of the Appalachee: it has, over the bar, 5 feet water only, but thence, is deep for 12 miles upward, - - - - - - ...

The Occonohatchee, and the Chatahatchee; falling into the gulf, east of the Oscilla, are said to be considerable streams, but are not much known, - - ...

Amount carried forward,	630

	Miles.
Amount brought forward,	630

The Histahatchee; enters Histahatchee bay at a few miles west of the Suawnee river: it is navigable 9 miles, up to where it branches into creeks, . . .

The Suawnee, or Amazura river; opening amongst a number of low keys, with scarcely 5 feet water, into Vacassar bay; would, but for this shoalness of its entrance, afford a most important outlet of the projected canal between the Atlantic and the Gulf. This river has not been thoroughly explored, but is said to afford much good navigation, . . .

The central parts of West Florida are interspersed with many lakes and ponds: amongst the number are; Mickasukee lake, north-east of Tallahassee, 12 miles long, 2 broad; Lake Jackson, north-west of Tallahassee, of 8 miles long and 2 or 3 broad; Lake Ioamony, north of Tallahassee, 8 miles long, 3 broad; the Old Tallahassee lake, Lake Wimico, in Washington county, 7 miles by 2 or 3; the Inundation or Horts lake, 20 miles long by 7 broad,—forests therein still standing in 20 feet depth of water; and Dennard's lake, 12 miles long by 5 broad, . . .

The Perdido bay, Pensacola bay, the Grand lagoon, Big bayou, Bayou Chico, Bayou Texas, Bayou Mulatto, Escambia bay, Santa Rosa sound, 40 miles in length, Choctawatchee bay, St. Andrew's bay, St. Joseph's bay, Appalachicola bay, Ocolockonee, Appalachee, Histahatchee or Dead Man's, and Vacassar bays; these afford, in the aggregate, an extensive navigation, . . .

The interior waters of the peninsula, navigable and tributary to the St. John's river, are considerable. The St. John receives, in its course, the waters of many rivers, and bayous, and detached lakes, and is itself in several places enlarged to the lake form, . . .

For the aggregate natural navigation above specified or referred to, and not above extended, by computation, 2500

Total of natural navigation,	3130
Total of artificial navigation,	775
Total of both,	3905

EXPOSÉ

Of the great base lines of internal navigation improvements.

The United States, taken as far as the shores of the Mississippi, being, by nature, divided into two distinct portions; namely; the Atlantic division on one side of the Alleghany mountains, whence the water courses are eastward, and the *western country* on the other side, the waters whereof flowing westward, the two portions bounded on the north by the great lakes and River St. Lawrence, which separate the country from Canada; and bounded on the south by the Gulf of Mexico, into which the western and southern waters flow; it thence follows, that the subject of a *general intercommunication by water*, is, most methodically, to be considered under three heads, or referable to three series of improvements, as a basis for all the rest, now intended, or that may be brought into contemplation: each of the three, embracing the several respective works effected, or to be effected, as follows; viz.

1. Those within tide water, and tending to form a curved parallel line immediately upon, or at no great distance from the seacoast.

2. Those connecting the western country with the seaboard, either by artificial canals, forming a complete union of the eastern and western waters, or else, by efficient roads, such as railroads, between the heads of navigation east and west of the Alleghany range of mountains.

3. Those connecting both the eastern and western water courses with the great lakes on the north.

And to which, may be added,

4. Intermediate partial communications, serving either to give variety to parts of one or other of the above great lines of route, or else, for confined local occasions and limited objects.

To one or other of these heads, every article, whether general or partial in its scope, that has in this book been inserted, will, at first view of the reader, be referred. The plan of description has been, to commence at the north-east, or New-England extremity of the country, and to pursue one continuous, though diversified, line of navigable water communication, through the interior, to the extremities both on the west and on the south, as well as to the northern, or Canada frontier of the country: this, of course, comprising *canals of connexion*, and the *improvements of river stream navigation*, as well on the seaboard, as at a distance from, and in other directions than parallel to it.

At pages 15 and 22, the routes extending from the Atlantic ports of Maine, New-Hampshire, Massachusetts, through a series of improvements, to the confines of the United States, at the Lower Canada line, have been specially noticed.

It will have been observed, too, that, at New-York, there centers three all-important routes of the improved navigation described; viz. First,—By the Hudson river, up to Albany, and thence, by the Northern Champlain canal, to the village of Whitehall, at the head of Lake Champlain; through which lake, to the northern frontier of the United States; or, branching from Albany and Troy, eastward, through the proposed Connecticut and Hudson canal, and the Boston and Connecticut canal, to the harbour of Boston; or, otherwise, by a rail road between the Hudson river and Boston harbour, as described at Article 23. Or, again, branching from Albany, westward, through the Erie canal, to the great lakes, and thence, by actual and contemplated improvements, to the western country, and the south. Secondly,—By Long island sound, as far as New-Haven bay; whence, along the Farmington canal, and the Hampshire and Hampden canal, and thence, by the improvements of the Connecticut river, above Northampton, and by the Memphramagog canal in Vermont, to the northern frontier of the United States, at Lake Memphramagog, lat. 45°. Also, branching from the Connecticut river, eastward, as above, to Boston harbour. Thirdly,—Up Rariton bay, and through the proposed Delaware and Rariton canal, to the Delaware river, and thence, by actual and contemplated improvements, to the Schuylkill and Susquehanna rivers, and to the western country, and the south.

In reference to the connexion across,

Of the eastern and western waters of the country; the state of New-York, it has been shown, stands pre-eminent in having executed her canal, from the Hudson river at Albany, to Lake Erie at Buffalo, with complete success in the objects of it; in as much as this *line*, besides having passed the mountain, and already opened to the state a lucrative unimpeded navigation to the very extremity of the lakes, north-westward, is also in a fair train of being extended, in virtue of new improvements, south-westwardly, to the Ohio river and the Mississippi; thus connecting the ports of New-York and New-Orleans, by a variety of routes through the interior.

Southward of the New-York western canal, will be the "Pennsylvania state canal and rail road," a magnificent undertaking, now in spirited progress. As described at page 265, it strikes from Philadelphia, westward, on the Susquehanna river, and thence, by the Juniata and the Conemaugh, and Alleghany valleys, strikes upon the Ohio river at Big Beaver; and will, including its several branches, particularly an extension of it from the River Ohio to Lake Erie, measure the distance of 1022 miles. Southward of this, will be the "Chesapeake and Ohio canal," striking from Washington, along the Potomac valley, up to Cumberland; and, on the other side of the Alleghany ridge, by the Youghioghany and Monongahela valleys, to its point of termination, at Pittsburg, on the Ohio river, as described at Article 92.

Southward of this again, there already exists the Virginia western communication, as described at Articles 103, 104, 105, 106, 107, comprising a series of improvements along the valley and the stream of James river; one other series of improvements along the Great Kanhaway river, from Point Pleasant, at the mouth thereof, on the Ohio, up to near Great Falls; and a state road, traversing the Alleghany mountain between the highest points of the water navigation improvements, east and west; save, however, a proposed improvement along Jackson's river, which is to form a part of this great line. But, besides this Virginia line *across*, consisting partly of *road*, a thorough *water communication* across to the Great Kanhaway of the west, by the Roanoke river line of improvements, and a connexion of the same with New river, as described at Articles 110, 111, is in contemplation.

In reference to the inland coast,

Or tide water navigation, free from the dangers of the sea, and tedious passages round promontories and projecting shoals avoided, the particular improvements embraced in *this line*, may be summed up as here follows; viz.

	Miles.
From Boston harbour, to avoid having the Cape Cod peninsula to weather, a canal has been proposed, across the isthmus between Barnstable bay and Buzzard's bay, or between Barnstable and the harbour of Hyannis, as described at Article 21. Or, if circumstances render this ineligible, then, a canal between Weymouth landing and Taunton on Taunton river, as described at Article 20, leading to Narraganset bay. Length thereof,	26
From Taunton, down the river, and through Mount Hope and Narraganset bays, and Long island sound, to New-York harbour. The distance is,	250

	Miles.
From New-York harbour, up Rariton bay, to Brunswick bay, New-Jersey,	35
Between Brunswick, or Rariton bay, and the Delaware river below the falls at Trenton, the "Delaware and Rariton canal" has been projected, as described at Article 54, page 100, length, including a navigable feeder,	60
Down the Delaware river, from below Trenton falls to the basin of the Chesapeake and Delaware canal, at Newbold's landing, opposite Pea Patch island,	80
Length of the Chesapeake and Delaware canal, from the basin at the Delaware, to Back creek on the Chesapeake bay, Maryland, as described at Article 70, page 152,	14
From Back creek, Maryland, down the Chesapeake bay, to the entrance of the Dismal swamp canal, on Elizabeth river, above Norfolk,	250
Length of the Dismal swamp canal, between Elizabeth river, and the head of Pasquotank river, Albemarle sound, with a cut to Currituck inlet, as described at Article 140, page 403,	24
Down Pasquotank river, and through Albemarle and Pamplico sounds, to Neuse river, up which, to the entrance of the "Adams creek and North river canal," the distance is,	150
Length of the Adams creek and North river canal, leading to Beaufort harbour, North Carolina, as described at Article 143, page 408,	3
Through Bogue, Stumpy, and Toomer's sounds, from the head of which last, a cut, of not more than 2 miles, will effect a communication into Cape Fear river, at 10 miles below Wilmington ; page 405,	90
Length of the Toomer sound canal, opening into Cape Fear river,	2
Up Cape Fear river, to the entrance of the Waccamaw canal, at or near the port of Wilmington,	10
Length of the Waccamaw canal, between the port of Wilmington, North Carolina, and a point of the River Waccamaw, as described at Article 153, page 420,	30
From this canal, down Waccamaw river, to Winyaw bay,	70
Length of Charleston and Georgetown canal, between Winyaw bay and Wando river, leading to	

OF THE UNITED STATES.   449

	Miles.
Cooper's river and the port of Charleston, as described at Article 152, page 420,	45
From this canal, down Wando river, to Charleston harbour,	10
Length of sundry proposed short canals, from one river, bay, or sound, to another, to complete a direct passage, between Ashley river, above the port of Charleston, and the Lower Edisto river; and the like between the Lower Edisto and the Savannah river at the port of Savannah, as described at Article 155, page 421,	40
The bay and sound navigation, proposed thus to be connected, between the ports of Charleston and Savannah,	60
Length of the "Savannah and Ogatchee canal," opening at the port of Savannah, and communicating from the Savannah to the Great Ogatchee river in Georgia, and, by continuation, the "Ogatchee and Alatamaha canal," terminating at a point of the Alatamaha river, as described at Articles 122, 123, page 373, together,	66
From this canal, down the Alatamaha river to Darien, and thence, through St. Simon's and other sounds, opening southward, in the rear of the Georgia sea islands, to St. Mary's, the distance is,	120
Up St. Mary's river, to the south point of the Great bend, at the opening of the proposed Florida isthmus canal,	70
Length of the Florida isthmus canal, between the bend of St. Mary's river, and the Appalachicola on the Gulf of Mexico, as described at Article 156,	180
Length of short canals, proposed to connect the bays and sounds between the Appalachicola and the Bay of Mobile, as described at Article 136, page 386, together,	12
The bay and sound navigation thus united, between the Appalachicola river and Mobile harbour, and thence, by Pascagoula bay, and the lakes Borgne, Pontchartrain, Maurepas, to the Mississippi river. Distance, together, including the Ibberville or Manchac channel,	338
	502 1533
Miles,	2035

                                                                Miles.
Or thus ;—
To St. Mary's, as above, - - - - - 310 1125
From St. Mary's to Appalachicola, by the Florida
  canal route, described at page 440, - - - 250
Length of short canals, as above, - - - 12
The bay, sound, and lake navigation, as above, -   338
                                                      ─────────
                                                      572 1463
                                                      ─────────
                                            Miles, 2035
                                                      ─────────

Whence it appears, that, when these enumerated canal works shall all have been completed, there will then be accomplished a safe, continuous, border navigation, extending from Boston harbour to St. Mary's river, East Florida; and thence, across the peninsula and along the border of the Gulf of Mexico; and, by Pascagoula bay, through the lakes Borgne, Pontchartrain, Maurepas, to the Mississippi river:—a distance, in all, of 2035 miles, whereof 572 miles designated as canal.

And these 2035 miles of SAFE navigation, will then hold the place of a sea passage from Boston harbour, round Cape Cod, and along the Atlantic coast, and round the Florida peninsula, to the Mississippi river, and up that, to the same point; namely, the Manchac, or Ibberville outlet;—a distance of 2500 to 3000 miles, and sometimes more, of HAZARDOUS navigation.

But, further; we beg leave here to state, if it may be stated without transcending probabilities, and it is hoped it may, a few particulars, by *anticipation*, of voyages through the interior of the United States, the practicability of which, at a future day, is in a train of soon being ascertained.

	Miles.
From Boston harbour, by the Chickapee canal, or otherwise, by the Massachusetts rail road, to Albany on the Hudson, as designated at page 41,	200
Enter Erie canal, and proceed to Buffalo on Lake Erie. Art. 26, page 53.	363
Enter Conewango canal, and proceed to Portland. Art. 40, page 77,	60
Enter Detroit canal, and proceed to Cleaveland. Art. 33, page 73,	119
Thence to Maumee bay, and to Detroit. Art. 33, page 73,	150
Enter Michigan canal, and proceed to the southern extremity of Lake Michigan, or at or near the mouth of Chicago river. Art. 114, page 339,	150

Enter Chicago canal, and proceed by that and the

Illinois navigation, to the Mississippi river. Art.
115, page 341. - - - - - - 370 Miles.
By the Mississippi navigation, to New-Orleans, 1,160

                 2,572

From Boston harbour, as above, to Cleaveland on
Lake Erie, - - - - - 742
Enter Ohio state canal, and proceed to the Ohio
river at the mouth of Scioto. Art. 95, page 237, 322
By the Ohio and Mississippi navigation, to New-Orleans, - - - - - 1,583

                 2,647

From Boston harbour, as above, to Albany, on the
Hudson, - - - - - 200
By the Hudson navigation, to New-York, - 145
By bay navigation to Brunswick, and thence proceed
by Delaware and Rariton canal; or—enter the
Morris canal, and proceed to the river Delaware.
Art. 55, page 103, - - - - - 100
Enter the Pennsylvania state canal, at Easton, and
proceed to Philadelphia. Art. 84, page, 266, 77
Enter Schuylkill canal, and proceed to near Reading. Art. 57, page 108, - - - 65
Enter Union canal, and proceed to Middletown, on
the Susquehanna river. Art. 58, page 126, 82
Enter the Pennsylvania state canal, and proceed to
Duncan's island, and thence westward, to Pittsburg. Art. 88, pages 267, 268, - - - 317
By the Ohio and Mississippi navigation, to New-Orleans, - - - - - - 1,929

                 2,915

From Boston harbour, as above, to Philadelphia, 522
By the Delaware navigation, to Newbold's landing, 42
Enter Chesapeake and Delaware canal, and proceed
to Chesapeake bay. Art. 70, page 153, - 14
By the bay and Potomac navigation, up to Washington, - - - - - - 262
Enter Chesapeake and Ohio canal, and proceed to
Pittsburg, Art. 92, page 221, - - - 341
By the Ohio and Mississippi navigation, to New-Orleans, - - - - - - 1,929

                 3,110

452 INTERNAL NAVIGATION

	Miles.
From Boston harbour, as above, to Chesapeake bay,	578
By the bay and river navigation, up to Richmond,	336
Enter the James river line of canal, and proceed up to Covington. Art. 110, page 318,	257
Enter the Catawba junction canal, and proceed to a point of the Roanoke river, 7 miles above Salem, in Bottetourt county, Virginia. Art. 111, page 323,	46
Enter Elliot's creek canal, and proceed to the mouth of Little river, or New river. Art. 110, page 317,	41
By the New river and Kanhaway line of canal, to the foot of Great falls. Art. 110, page 317,	151
By the Great Kanhaway navigation, thence to Point Pleasant on the Ohio river, page 307,	94
By the Ohio and Mississippi navigation, to New-Orleans,	1,506

3,009

From Boston harbour, as above, to Chesapeake bay,	578
By the bay navigation, to Elizabeth river, above Norfolk,	245
Enter the Dismal swamp canal, and thence the Murfreesboro' canal, and proceed to Weldon on the Roanoke river. Art. 144, page 414,	80
Enter on the Roanoke line of canal, and proceed up to the outlet of the Catawba junction canal, 7 miles above Salem. Arts. 110, 111, page 317,	231
Enter the Elliot's creek and Little river canal, and proceed, as above, to Point Pleasant on the Ohio river, as above,	286
By the Ohio and Mississippi navigation, to New-Orleans,	1,506

2,926

From Boston harbour, as above, to the outlet of the Catawba junction canal,	1,134
Enter Elliot's creek and Little river canal, and proceed to New river, at the mouth of Little river. Art. 110, page 317,	41
Enter Reed creek canal, and proceed to a navigable point of the Middle branch of Holston river, in Wythe county. Art. 111, page 321,	50

By the Middle branch and Main Holston navigation,
and thence by the Tennessee navigation to a point
at or near Fort Deposite, in Alabama state, - 800
Enter the Tennessee and Tombecbee canal, and
proceed to a point of the Black Warrior river below Tuscaloosa falls. Art. 127, page 377, - 150
By the Black Warrior, the Tombecbee, the Mobile
river and bay navigation, down to Mobile point.
Page 377, - - - - 340

2,515

From Boston harbour, as above, to a point of the
Tennessee river, at or near Fort Deposite, 2,025
Enter the Tennessee and Alabama canal, and proceed
to a point of the Coosa river, at or near the mouth
of Wills creek. Art. 137, page 388, - - 50
By the Coosa, the Alabama, and the Tensaw navigation, to Mobile bay and point. Pages 387, 388, 560

2,635

From Boston harbour, as above, to Buffalo, on Lake
Erie, - - - - - 563
Steam-boat navigation from Buffalo, through the
lakes, to Green bay, Michigan, and thence through
the Fox and Ouisconsin rivers, and down the
Mississippi stream to New-Orleans, as designated
at pages 339, 340, 346, 350, - - 3,000

3,563

THE

INTERNAL NAVIGATION

OF

THE UNITED STATES.

Distance, 103,202½ miles.

Which includes, of artificial or improved navigation, partly finished, or in progress, and partly contemplated, 16,397½ miles, as here follows ;—

LIST A.

IN THE STATES OF NEW-ENGLAND.

Page.	No.		Miles.
10	1.	Merrimack river canals, and stream navigation improved, from Haverhill upward, distance,	110
11	2.	Baker's river and Oliverian canal; between the Merrimack and Connecticut rivers, by the Baker and Oliverian valleys,	39¾
12	3.	Connecticut river canals, and stream navigation improved, from Hartford up to Barnet,	220
14	4.	The Connecticut and Memphramagog canal; between a point of the Connecticut river, and the Lake Memphramagog,	50
16	5.	Memphramagog and Champlain canal; between the Lakes Memphramagog and Champlain, by La Moelle and Black river valleys,	75
17	6.	The Winnepiseogee canal; between the Piscataqua river at Dover, New-Hampshire, and the Pemigewasset, or Upper Merrimack, by the Lake Winnepiseogee,	40
18	7.	Oxford and Cumberland canal; between Portland harbour and Bear pond, in Waterford, Maine, via the Sebago lake,	50
18	8.	Waterford and Bethel canal; between Bear pond and the River Androscoggin, at Bethel,	20

OF THE UNITED STATES.

Page.	No.		Miles.
19	9.	Kennebeck and Androscoggin canal; and the Cobbassee Contee river and pond navigation improved, - - -	30
		Brunswick canal and feeder, - -	7⅜
21	10.	Androscoggin and Connecticut canal, and stream navigation of the Androscoggin river improved, from Leeds upward, -	130
23	11.	Kennebeck river canals, and stream navigation improved, from Augusta upward, and canal to the Chaudiere, - - -	200
25	12.	The Pushaw canal; between the Penobscot river at Bangor, and the Pushaw lake, -	6
26	13.	The Farmington canal; between New-Haven and Southwick ponds, and from the mouth of the Farmington river to New-Hartford, Connecticut, - - - -	73
28	14.	Hampshire and Hampden canal; between Southwick ponds and the Connecticut river above Northampton, Massachusetts,	29
29	15.	Connecticut and Champlain canal; or Montpellier canal and rail road, between the mouth of Onion river on Lake Champlain, and the mouth of White river on the Connecticut, - - - -	103¼
30	16.	Rutland and Whitehall canal; between the Otter river at Rutland, Vermont, and Whitehall on Lake Champlain, -	25½
31	17.	The Otter river canals, and stream navigation improved, - - -	100
31	18.	Otter and Battenkill canal; between the head waters of the Otter river, in Bromley, Vermont, and the New-York line, down the Battenkill valley, - - - -	20
32	19.	The Middlesex canal; between Boston harbour and the Merrimack river at Chelmsford, - - - -	27
34	20.	Boston and Narraganset canal; between Boston harbour at Weymouth, and Taunton, on Taunton river, - -	26
35	21.	Cape Cod canal; across the isthmus, between Barnstable and Hyannis harbours, -	7
36	22.	The Chickapee, or Boston and Connecticut canal; between Boston harbour and the Connecticut river, - - -	100
40	23.	Connecticut and Hudson canal; between points of these rivers, in continuation of the canal preceding, - -	78

Page.	No.		Miles.
44	24.	The Blackstone canal; between Providence harbour, R. I. and Worcester, Massachusetts,	45

IN NEW-YORK STATE.

54	25.	The New-York Champlain canal, and navigable feeder, from Glen's falls,	70½
53	26.	The Erie and Hudson canal, between Albany city and Buffalo,	363
66	27.	The St. Lawrence and Champlain canal, between points of the river and lake, at or near the New-York and Canada line; or otherwise, between Plattsburg and Ogdensburg,	130
67	28.	The Oswego canal, between Lake Ontario at the port of Oswego, and the Erie canal at Salina,	38
67	29.	Great Sodus canal; between Lake Ontario at Great Sodus bay, and a point of the Erie canal,	25
68	30.	Cayuga and Seneca canal; between the river Seneca and the Erie canal at Montezuma,	21
69	31.	Delaware and Hudson canal; between tide water on the Waalkill river, near Kingston, and a point of the Delaware river, opposite the mouth of the Lackawaxen,	81
70	32.	The Lackawaxen and Cookquago canal; between the terminating point of the canal preceding, in continuation along the Delaware river valley, and Deposite town on the Cookquago,	60
71	33.	Cookquago and Canisteo canal; between the town of Deposite, on the Cookquago, and Hornellsville, on the Canisteo river,	150
		Portland and Detroit canal,	269
73	34.	Newburgh and Water Gap canal; between the Hudson and the Delaware rivers at these points,	88
74	35.	Rochester and Olean canal; between the Genessee river and the Alleghany at these points,	111
74	36.	The Genessee and Chemung canal, and stream navigation of the Genessee river improved,	139
75	37.	The Chenango canal; between the Erie canal, at Whitesborough, and the Susquehanna river at Binghamton,	96

OF THE UNITED STATES.

Page.	No.		Miles.
76	38.	Seneca and Tioga canal, } between the heads of Lakes Seneca and Cayuga, and the Susquehanna river at those points; or Seneca and Tioga canal and rail road,	
76	39.	Cayuga and Owego canal,	66
77	40.	The Conewango canal; between Lake Erie at Buffalo, and the Conewango branch of the Alleghany river at the Pennsylvania line, - - - - - -	89
77	41.	Portland and Maysville canal; between Lake Erie, at Portland, and the head of Chatauque lake, at Maysville, - - -	10¼
78	42.	Black river of Ontario canals, and stream navigation improved, - - - -	136
78	43.	Ogdensburg and Boonsville canal; between the Erie canal, at Rome, and the St. Lawrence river, at Ogdensburg, or mouth of the Oswegatchie, through the village of Boonsville, - - - -	114
79	44.	The Overslaugh canal; between Albany and Coeymans, on the Hudson river, - -	12
80	45.	Long-Island canals; uniting the principal bays of the island, - - - - The Hurl-Gate canal, - - - -	11
81	46.	Port Watson canal; between the Erie canal, at Syracuse or Salina, and the Tioughnioga branch of the Susquehanna river at Port Watson, - - - - - -	47
81	47.	Unadilla canal; between a point of the Erie canal, at Herkimer, and the Susquehanna river, at Bainbridge, or at the Pennsylvania line; or Otsego canal and rail road,	100
82	48.	The Batavia canal; between the Erie canal and the River Alleghany, at Olean, through the Tonnewanto valley and the village of Batavia, - - - -	90
82	49.	Buffalo and Olean canal; between Lake Erie, at Buffalo, and the Alleghany river, at Olean, through the valleys of Buffalo and Ischua creeks, - - - - -	75
82	50.	The Battenkill canal; between the New-York Champlain canal and the Vermont state line, up the valley of the Battenkill river, - - - - - -	20
82	51.	The Sharon canal; between the Erie canal and the Hudson river, at the mouth of	

Page.	No.		Miles.
		Croton, passing through Sharon, in Schoharie county,	140
83	52.	The Catskill canal; between a point of the Erie canal and the Hudson river, at Catskill, by the Schoharie and Catskill valleys,	60
83	53.	The Niagara canal; between the mouth of Tonnewanto creek and Lewistown, along the Niagara river valley,	15

IN THE STATES OF NEW-JERSEY, DELAWARE, MARYLAND, PENNSYLVANIA, OHIO.

100	54.	The Delaware and Rariton canal; between the Delaware river, below Lamberton, and the Rariton, below Brunswick, with navigable feeder,	60
103	55.	The Morris canal; between the Delaware river, opposite Easton, and the Hudson, at Powles hook,	101½
106	56.	Delaware river canals; and stream navigation improved, from Trenton falls upward,	220
118	57.	Schuylkill river canals, and slackwater improvements, between Philadelphia and Mount Carbon, in Schuylkill county, Pennsylvania,	110½
126	58.	The Union canal; between the Schuylkill river, below Reading, and the Susquehanna, at Middletown, with navigable feeder up to Pine Grove,	105
128	59.	The Lackawaxen canal; between the mouth of Lackawaxen river and the upper water thereof, at Keen's pond, near the coal mines; or canal and rail road to Carbondale,	41
129	60.	Lackawaxen and Pittstown canal; between the Lackawaxen river, at Keen's pond, and the Susquehanna, at Pittstown, or from Carbondale to Pittstown,	22
130	61.	Lausanne and Wilkesbarre canal; between the Lehigh river and the Susquehanna at these points,	40
141	62.	The Lehigh river canals, and stream navigation improved, from Easton up to Stoddartsville, and coal mine rail road,	93

OF THE UNITED STATES. 459

Page.	No.		Miles.
145	63.	Nescopec and Lehigh canal; between the Susquehanna river, at Berwick, and a point of the Upper Lehigh, by the Nescopec valley, - - - -	35
147	64.	Pittstown and Water Gap canal; between the Susquehanna river and the Delaware, at those points, - - - -	60
149	65.	The Perkiomen canal; between the Lehigh river, at Allentown, and the Schuylkill river, at Norristown, by the Perkiomen valley, - - - - -	40
149	66.	The Catawissa canal; between the Schuylkill river and the Susquehanna, by the Little or East Schuylkill, and the Catawissa valleys, - - - -	50
151	67.	Schuylkill valley canal; between the mouth of Mill creek on Upper Schuylkill river, and George Reber's mill, - -	
152	68.	Mahanoy creek canal; between the Susquehanna river, and the coal mines on the Mahanoy creek, - - -	
152	69.	Shamokin creek canal; between the Susquehanna river, and the coal mines on the Shamokin creek, - - -	
153	70.	The Chesapeake and Delaware canal; between the Delaware river, opposite Fort Delaware, Pea Patch island, and the Chesapeake bay at Back creek, Maryland,	14
163	71.	Patapsco and Susquehanna canal; between the port of Baltimore, and the Susquehanna river at the mouth of the Swatara,	100
170	72.	Patapsco and Potomac canal; between the port of Baltimore, and the Chesapeake and Ohio canal at Washington, or at Little falls of the Potomac river; say, between Baltimore and Georgetown, - -	44¾
179	73.	Susquehanna river canals, and stream navigation improved, from tide water up to the New-York line, above Tioga point,	288
181	75.	Peter's camp canal; between the Susquehanna river, near Tioga point, and the Peter's camp coal mine, - - -	
182	76.	Port Deposite canal; along the Susquehanna rapids, at the Maryland and Pennsylvania line, - - - - - -	10
182	77.	The Conestoga river canals, and stream navi-	

Page.	No.		Miles.
		gation improved, between Lancaster city and Safe harbour on the Susquehanna,	18
183	78.	The Conewago canals; along the Conewago rapids of the Susquehanna river,	2¼
266		The Pennsylvania canal and rail road, Delaware or Eastern division; Connecting the Delaware river, at Philadelphia, with the same at Carpenter's point, on the north-east boundary line of the state, by canal navigation along the river valley, viz.	

Philadelphia and Bristol section,
Distance by survey, — — 17½
Bristol and Easton section,
Distance by survey, — — — 60
Easton and Carpenter's point section,
Distance by survey, — — — 66½

144

266 The Pennsylvania canal and rail road, Ohio and Lake Erie, or Western division;
Connecting the Ohio river, at Pittsburg, with Lake Erie at Presqu' isle harbour, by way of the Beaver and Shenango valleys, and across the valley of Elk creek.
Distance, — — — — 167½

266 The Conneaught summit navigable feeder, from French creek, — 21½

189

267 The Pennsylvania canal and rail road, Susquehanna or Middle division,
Connecting the Susquehanna river at Columbia, with the same at the New-York line, 4 miles above Tioga point, along the Susquehanna valley; and comprising the sections as follows; viz.
Columbia and Middletown section, 18
Middletown and Juniata section, 24
Juniata and Northumberland section, 37½
Northumberland and Tioga section, 165½

245

267 The Pennsylvania canal and rail road,
Juniata and Alleghany, or Transverse division,
Connecting the Delaware river at Philadelphia, with the Susquehanna at Columbia, through Chester and Lancaster counties;

OF THE UNITED STATES. 461

Page. No.   Miles.

and the Susquehanna river at Duncan's island, with the Ohio at Pittsburg, by the Juniata valley, and the Conemaugh, Kiskimenetas and Alleghany valleys, including a probable distance of 50¾ miles of rail road across the Alleghany mountain : this division comprising the sections as follows; viz.

Philadelphia and Columbia road section, not including the proposed extension of road from Columbia to the west end of the borough of York, in York county, - 82¾
Duncan's island and Lewistown section, - - - - - - 44½
Ohio and Kiskimenetas section, - 30⅞
Kiskimenetas and Blairsville section, 51
Blairsville and Johnstown section, - 28½
Lewistown and Frankstown section, 87½
Frankstown and Johnstown road section, - - - - - - 50¾

                                                         375⅞

186 80. The Chester creek canal, or rail road; between the Pennsylvania canal or rail road, and the River Delaware, by the Brandywine and Chester creek valleys, - -   25

269 85. West branch Susquehanna canal; between the Pennsylvania canal at Northumberland, and the Bald Eagle river, or a point near the same, in Lycoming county, by the West branch Susquehanna valley, - -   68¼

205 89. Alleghany and Conewango canal; between the mouth of French creek, and the Conewango at the New-York line intersection, - - - - - - -   70

205 90. The Conococheague canal; between the Susquehanna river at the mouth of the Conodogwinnet, and the Potomac river, by the Conococheague valley, - - -   120

207 91. Potomac river canals, and stream navigation improved, from tide water up to Cumberland, - - - - - - -   182

221 92. Chesapeake and Ohio canal; between Washton city and Pittsburg, by the Potomac valley, the Casselman summit, the Youghioghany and the Monongahela river valleys, - - - - - - -   341

462   INTERNAL NAVIGATION

Page.	No.		Miles.
224	93.	Savage river branch canal; between the main canal at Cumberland, and the mouth of Savage river on the Potomac, by the Potomac valley,	30
		Ohio and Erie canal,	
233	94.	By Beaver and Cuyahoga; between Pittsburg and Cleaveland, by the Big Beaver and Cuyahoga river valleys,	154
		Ohio state canals,	
237	95.	Muskingum and Scioto division; between Lake Erie at Cleaveland, and the Ohio river at the mouth of the Scioto, with navigable feeders,	322
		Ohio state canals,	
238	96.	Miami valley division; between Lake Erie at Maumee bay, and the Ohio river at Cincinnati, with navigable feeders,	290
241	97.	Sandy creek canal; between the Ohio river at the mouth of Little Beaver, and the Ohio state canal, by the Sandy creek valley,	60
241	98.	Portage summit canal; between a point of the Ohio river in Pennsylvania state, and the Portage summit of the Ohio state canal,	75

IN VIRGINIA STATE.

282	99.	The Appomatox canals, and stream navigation improved, from tide water up to Farmville,	110
283	100.	The Powhatan canal; between a point of James river and a point of the Upper Appomatox, by the Hudsmouth creek valley,	19
284	101.	Appomatox and Roanoke, or the "Junction" canal; between the Upper Appomatox and Staunton river, by the valleys of the Buffalo and Little Roanoke,	30
283	102.	The Manchester canal; between Bosher's mill on James river, and tide water of the same, through the town of Manchester,	10
285	103.	James river canals, and stream navigation improved, from tide water below Richmond, upward to Covington,	257½
307	107.	Kanhaway river navigation and turnpike; stream improved from the Ohio at Point	

OF THE UNITED STATES. 463

Page.	No.		Miles.
		Pleasant, up to Loophole shoal below Great falls, - - - 89	
		Turnpike thence across the mountain to Covington, - - - - 99	
			188
309	108.	The Shenandoah canals, and stream navigation improved, between the Potomac and the Lexington branch of James river,	250
310	109.	The Rivanna river canals, and stream navigation improved, from Columbia on James river, up to a point opposite Charlottesville, - - - -	37
312	110.	Roanoke and Kanhaway canal, between tide waters of the Roanoke river and the foot of Great falls of the Kanhaway; by the valley of the Roanoke south fork on the east, and of Little river and New river on the west, leading to the Great Kanhaway and to the Ohio, - - -	422¾
323	111.	Roanoke and James river canal, between a point of the upper waters of the Roanoke, above Salem, in Bottetourt county, and the James river navigation, at the mouth of the Catawba, - - - -	46
321		New river and Holston canal, connecting the navigation of New river with that of the Holston, through Reed creek valley,	50

IN INDIANA STATE.

332	112.	Lake Erie and Ohio canal,	
		By the Wabash; between points connecting the lake at Maumee bay with the navigation of the Maumee river, and this latter with the Wabash river, - -	50
335	113.	Louisville and Portland canal; along the rapids of the Ohio river, between those points, on the Kentucky side, -	2
339	114.	Erie and Michigan canal; between Lake Erie at or near Maumee bay, and a point towards the south-east extremity of Lake Michigan, - - -	150
333		Series of canals to connect the waters of Lake Michigan with those of the Wabash river; the upper waters of White river with the Wabash, by way of the Mississineway valley, as also with the Miami	

Page.	No.		Miles.
		navigation in Ohio state; and the St. Mary's and St. Joseph's rivers in a line of navigation with the Wabash, and the Ohio,	350

IN ILLINOIS STATE.

340   115. The Chicago canal; between the Chicago river, of Lake Michigan, and a point of the Illinois river, at or near the mouth of the Little Vermillion, - - 120

IN THE NORTH-WEST TERRITORY.

345   116. St. Mary's canal; along the falls, between Lake Huron and Lake Superior, - 1

346   117. Fox river and Ouisconsin canals; between Fort Brown at Green bay, Michigan, and Lake Winnebago, and between the Upper Fox river and the Ouisconsin, - - 52

IN THE STATES OF TENNESSEE, MISSISSIPPI, LOUISIANA, ALABAMA, AND GEORGIA.

370   119. The Muscle shoal canal; between Brown's ferry and Florence, Alabama, along the Muscle shoal obstructions of the Tennessee river; also Colbert's shoals, - 37

371   120. Tennessee and Savannah canal; between points of the upper waters of these rivers, and stream navigation of each improved, 250

372   121. Savannah and Appalachicola canal; between the upper waters of these rivers, and stream navigation of each, also of Flint river, improved, - - - 550

373   122. Savannah and Ogatchee canal; between the port of Savannah on the Savannah river, and Jones's lake, leading to the Ogatchee river, - - - - - 16

374   123. Ogatchee and Alatamaha canal; between Fort Argyle on the Great Ogatchee, and the mouth of the Great Ohoopee river, on the Alatamaha, - - - - 50

374   124. Alatamaha and Appalachee canal; between the Alatamaha river and the Bay of St. Mark, communicating with Appalachee bay, - - - - - - - 164

375   125. Augusta and Flint river canal, or rail road; between the Savannah river at Augusta,

OF THE UNITED STATES. 465

Page.	No.		Miles.
		and the Flint at Fort Lawrence, passing through Milledgeville,	150
376	126.	Chatahootchee and Milledgeville canal ; between a point of the upper waters of the Chatahootchee river, and the Oconee river at Milledgeville,	120
377	127.	Tennessee and Tombecbee canal; between Fort Deposite on the Tennessee river, Alabama, and Tuscaloosa town on the Black Warrior branch of the Tombecbee,	150
378	128.	Pearl river and Mississippi canal; between a point of the Pearl in Lawrence county, Mississippi state, and the Mississippi river, by way of the Big Black valley ; and the Pearl river navigation below improved,	240
378	129.	Amité river canals, and stream navigation improved, from Lake Maurepas up to the mouth of Comité river,	70
379	130.	Tangchepahaw river canals, and stream navigation improved, from Lake Pontchartrain up to the mouth of Chapeau Pilier river,	43
380	131.	New-Orleans and Teche river canal ; between the Mississippi river opposite New Orleans, and Berwick's bay, by way of Lake Barataria and La Fourche,	100
381	132.	Barataria and Grandterre canal; between a point of the lake and the pass of Grandterre, at Barataria bay,	40
382	133.	Concordia and Catahoula canal ; between the Mississippi river at Concordia, opposite Natchez, and the Washitta river at Catahoula Courthouse,	66
383	134.	Red river canals, and stream navigation improved to, at, and beyond, the Great Raft,	500
384	135.	Mississippi and Pontchartrain canal; between New-Orleans, and a point of the lake near to Bayou St. Jean,	10
386	136.	Mississippi and Appalachicola canals, and the Ibberville and Lower Amité river navigation improved,	52
388	137.	Tennessee and Alabama canal; between points of the Coosa and Tennessee rivers, and stream navigation of the Coosa improved,	250

Page.	No.		Miles.
388	138.	Bear creek canal; between points of the Tombecbee river and Bear creek, and stream navigation of each improved, - -	240
391	139.	Hiwassee and Coosa canal; between the Okou and the Conesaugo, navigable branches of these rivers, approaching the Georgia and Tennessee boundary line; or between Calhoun, on the Hiwassee river, and the mouth of Conesaugo, on the Coosa,	100

IN THE STATES OF NORTH CAROLINA AND SOUTH CAROLINA.

404	140.	The Dismal swamp canal; between a point of Elizabeth river above Norfolk, and the head of Pasquotank river, leading to Albemarle sound; and branch to Currituck, by the North-west river, - - -	28
406	141.	The Weldon canal; at Great falls, Roanoke river, and stream navigation of the river improved up to Salem, in Bottetourt county, Virginia, - - - -	334
406	142.	The Danville canal, at the falls of Dan river, and stream navigation improved, below and above, - - - - - -	150
407	143.	Plymouth and Beaufort canal; between the Roanoke river at Plymouth, and Beaufort inlet on the coast, passing through Washington and Newbern, - - -	100
414	144.	Roanoke and Elizabeth river or Murfreesborough canal; between the Weldon canal at Great falls of the Roanoke river, and the Dismal swamp canal, leading to Elizabeth river and the port of Norfolk, - -	80
414	145.	Cape Fear river canals, and stream navigation improved, from below Wilmington up to Haywoodsborough, - - -	200
416	146.	Cape Fear and Pedee canal; between points of the upper waters of these rivers, and stream navigation of each improved; and extension across, by canal or rail road, to a point of the Catawba river, - -	275
416	147.	The Yadkin river canals, and stream navigation improved, up to Wilkes Courthouse, North Carolina, - - - - -	200

OF THE UNITED STATES. 467

Page.	No.		Miles.
417	148.	The Wateree and Catawba river canals, and stream navigation improved, up to near the source thereof, in the mountains,	275
418	149.	The Santee, Columbia, and Saluda canals, and stream navigation of the Saluda river improved, up to the Abbeville county line, South Carolina,	150
419	150.	South Edisto river canals, or stream improved, from the North Edisto junction upward,	70
419	151.	The Seneca river canals, or stream navigation improved, of the Seneca and branches, from Andersonville on the Savannah river, up to the mountains,	200
420	152.	Charleston and Georgetown canal; between Winyaw bay below Georgetown, and Wando river, leading to Cooper's river and the port of Charleston,	45
420	153.	The Waccamaw canal; between Waccamaw river at a point 70 miles from Winyaw bay, and Cape Fear river at the port of Wilmington,	30
421	154.	Ashley and Edisto canal, } between Lower Edisto river, and the Ashley above Charleston, and between the same point of the Edisto, and the Savannah river at the port of Savannah,	
421	155.	Edisto and Savannah canal, }	40

IN FLORIDA STATE.

440	156.	The Florida isthmus canal; between a point of the Atlantic river of St. Mary, and a point of the Appalachicola, on the Gulf of Mexico,	250
429	157.	The Isthmus prolongation, or Branch canal; between St. Mary's river at the South bend, and the Bay of St. Augustine, intersecting the St. John's river at Jacksonville,	70
429	158.	Amelia island canal, or channel improved; between the Bays of St. Mary and St. John,	15
429	159.	Atlantic Florida canals; connecting the sound and bay navigation, along the east coast of the peninsula, from the mouth of	

INTERNAL NAVIGATION

Page.	No.		Miles.
		St. John's river, to Bocca Ratones, or Cape Florida, a distance of 350 miles, -	20
441		Branch canal to Vacassar bay; between the point of intersection of the Suawnee river, by canal, No. 156, and the Indian Cow Pens, near the mouth of Suawnee,	75
441		Santa Fé canal; between St. Mary's river, at a point above the town of St. Mary, and the Suawnee river, at the mouth of the Santa Fé, - - - - -	120
441		Tampa bay canal; between the St. John's river, at the mouth of the Pablo, and Tampa bay, on the western coast, - -	225

Total, not including the 282½ miles of road, as expressed at Articles 59, 62, 79, 80, 81, 107, - - 16397½

Which 16397½ miles of artificial navigation, is composed of,
1. Canals of connexion, as enumerated in List B, - - - - - - - 10742½
2. River navigation improvements, with and without the aid of canals, and whether by lock and dam, or by the sluice mode, as enumerated in List C, - - - - - 5655
——— 16397½

The improvements along the Ohio river stream, not included in this distance; neither those of the Mississippi channel.

LIST B.

List of Navigable Canals, Connecting Rivers and other Navigable Waters of the United States.

y refers to a yellow line traced on the map; r to a red line.

Page.	No.		Miles.
11	2. *y*	Baker's river and Oliverian canal; connecting the Merrimack river with the Connecticut, by the Baker and Oliverian valleys. Distance, - - - -	39¾
14	4. *y*	The Connecticut and Memphramagog canal; connecting the river and lake, by the Nulhegan river valley, -	50
16	5. *y*	Memphramagog and Champlain canal; connecting these lakes, by the valleys of La Moelle and Black river, - -	75
17	6. *y*	The Winnepiseogee canal; connecting the Upper Merrimack or Pemigewasset river, with the Piscataqua at tide water, below Dover, New-Hampshire, through Lake Winnepiseogee, - -	40
18	7. *y*	Oxford and Cumberland canal; connecting Portland harbour with Bear pond in Waterford, Maine, by way of the Sebago lake, - - - - - -	50
18	8. *y*	Waterford and Bethel canal; connecting Bear pond with the Androscoggin river at Bethel, in continuation of the canal preceding, - - - - -	20
19	9. *y*	Kennebeck and Androscoggin canal; connecting these rivers, by way of the Cobbassee Contee pond and river, - -	4½
	y	Brunswick canal; connecting Casco and Merrymeeting bays, - - -	7¾
21	10. *y*	Androscoggin and Connecticut canal; connecting these rivers, between Guildhall on the Connecticut, and a point of the Androscoggin above Shelburne, - -	31½
23	11. *y*	The Kennebeck and Chaudiere canal; connecting the upper waters of these rivers in the highlands, between the state of Maine and Lower Canada, - -	

Page.	No.		Miles.
25	12. *y*	The Pushaw canal; connecting the Penobscot river at Bangor, Maine, with the Pushaw lake,	6
26	13. *r*	The Farmington canal; connecting New-Haven with Southwick at the Massachusetts' line, also the town of Farmington with New-Hartford, Connecticut,	73
28	14. *r*	Hampshire and Hampden canal; in continuation of the Farmington canal, up the Connecticut valley, to a point above Northampton, Massachusetts,	29
29	15. *y*	Connecticut and Champlain canal, or Montpellier canal and rail road; connecting Lake Champlain with the Connecticut river, by the valleys of Onion and White rivers,	103¼
30	16. *y*	Rutland and Whitehall canal; connecting the Otter river at Rutland, Vermont, with Lake Champlain at Whitehall,	25½
31	18. *y*	Otter and Battenkill canal; connecting the head water of the Otter river in Bromley, Vermont, with the New-York Battenkill canal, down the Battenkill valley,	20
32	19. *r*	The Middlesex canal; connecting Boston harbour with the Merrimack river at Chelmsford,	27
34	20. *y*	Boston and Narraganset canal; connecting Boston harbour at Weymouth, with Taunton on Taunton river, leading to Narraganset bay,	26
35	21. *y*	Cape Cod canal; connecting Barnstable and Hyannis harbours, across the Cape Cod peninsula,	7
36	22. *y*	The Chickapee or Boston and Connecticut canal; connecting Boston harbour with the Connecticut river, by the Chickapee, or by Miller's river valley,	100
40	23. *y*	Connecticut and Hudson canal; connecting these rivers, in continuation of the canal preceding,	78
41	24. *r*	The Blackstone canal; connecting Providence harbour, Rhode-Island, with Worcester, Massachusetts, by the Blackstone valley,	45

OF THE UNITED STATES. 471

Page.	No.		Miles.
54	25. r	The New-York Champlain canal; connecting the Erie and Hudson canal with Lake Champlain, and navigable feeder from Glen's falls, - - -	70½
53	26. r	The Erie and Hudson canal; connecting Lake Erie at Buffalo, with the Hudson river at Albany, - - - -	363
66	27. y	St. Lawrence and Champlain canal; connecting the St. Lawrence river with Lake Champlain, at points as between Ogdensburg and Plattsburg, - -	130
67	28. r	The Oswego canal; connecting Lake Ontario at Oswego harbour, with the Erie canal at Salina, - - -	38
67	29. y	Great Sodus canal; connecting Lake Ontario at Great Sodus bay, with the Erie canal, - - - -	25
68	30. r	Cayuga and Seneca canal; connecting the Seneca river, with the Erie canal at Montezuma, - - -	21
69	31. r	The Delaware and Hudson canal; connecting these rivers, between tide water of the Waalkill at Eddy's factory, and the mouth of the Lackawaxen river on Delaware, - - - -	81
70	32. y	Lackawaxen and Cookquago canal; connecting these rivers, between the mouth of Lackawaxen and the town of Deposite on the Cookquago, in continuation of the canal preceding, - - -	60
71	33. y	Cookquago and Canisteo canal; connecting these rivers, between the towns of Deposite and Hornellsville, in continuation of the canal preceding, - -	150
	y	Portland and Detroit canal; round the southern shore of Lake Erie, - -	269
73	34. y	Newburgh and Water-gap canal; connecting the Hudson and Delaware rivers at these points, - - - -	88
74	35. y	Rochester and Olean canal; connecting the Genessee and Alleghany rivers at these points, - - - -	111
74	36. y	Genessee and Chemung canal; connecting the Genessee river, on the Erie canal at a point near Rochester, with the Chemung river at or near Newtown, -	100

INTERNAL NAVIGATION

Page.	No.		Miles.
75	37. y	The Chenango canal; connecting the Erie canal at Whitesborough with the Susquehanna river at Binghamton, by the Chenango valley,	96
76	38. y	Seneca and Tioga canal, } connecting the	
76	39. y	Cayuga and Owego canal, } heads of Seneca and Cayuga lakes, with the Susquehanna river at Newtown and at Owego, or Seneca and Tioga canal and rail road to the coal mines,	66
77	40. y	The Conewango canal; connecting Lake Erie at Buffalo, with the Conewango branch of the Alleghany river, at the Pennsylvania line of intersection,	89
77	41. y	Portland and Maysville canal; connecting Lake Erie at Portland, with the head of Chatauque lake,	104
78	43. y	Ogdensburg and Boonsville canal; connecting the St. Lawrence river at Ogdensburg, with the Erie canal at Rome, through Boonsville,	114
79	44. y	The Overslaugh canal; connecting the deep water navigation of the Hudson at Albany, with that below the obstruction, at a point of the river near Coeymans,	12
80	45. y	Long Island canals; connecting the principal bays of the island,	11
	y	The Hurl gate canal,	
81	46. y	Port Watson canal; connecting the Erie canal at Syracuse or Salina, with the Tioughnioga branch of the Susquehanna river at Port Watson,	47
81	47. y	The Unadilla canal; connecting the Erie canal below Herkimer, with the Susquehanna river at Bainbridge, or at the Pennsylvania line, through the Unadilla valley; or Otsego canal and rail road,	100
82.	48. y	The Batavia canal; connecting the Alleghany river at Olean, with the Erie canal, through the Upper Tonnewanto valley and the village of Batavia,	90
82	49. y	Buffalo and Olean canal; connecting Lake Erie at Buffalo, with the Alleghany river at Olean, through the valleys of Buffalo and Ischua creeks,	75
82	50. y	The Battenkill canal; connecting the New-	

Page.	No.		Miles.
		York Champlain canal, with the Otter and Battenkill canal of Vermont, by the Battenkill valley,	20
82	51. *y*	The Sharon canal; connecting the Erie canal at a point west of Schoharie creek, with the Hudson river at or below the mouth of the Croton, passing through Sharon in Schoharie county,	140
83	52. *y*	The Catskill canal; connecting the Erie canal at a point west of Schoharie creek, with the Hudson river, by the Schoharie and Catskill valleys,	60
83	53. *y*	The Niagara canal; connecting the Erie canal at the mouth of Tonnewanto creek, with the Niagara river at Lewistown, below the falls,	15
100	54. *y*	The Delaware and Rariton canal; connecting the Delaware river at or below Lamberton, with the Rariton below Brunswick, New-Jersey, and navigable feeder,	60
103	55. *r*	The Morris canal; connecting the Delaware river opposite the mouth of the Lehigh at Easton, with the Hudson river at Powles hook, New-Jersey,	101½
118	57. *r*	The Schuylkill canal works; between Philadelphia and Mill creek,	110½
126	58. *r*	The Union canal; connecting the Schuylkill river below Reading, with the Susquehanna river at Middletown or mouth of the Swatara, and navigable feeder up to Pine Grove,	105
128	59. *r*	The Lackawaxen canal; connecting the Delaware navigation, also the Delaware and Hudson canal, with the head water of the Lackawaxen river, at Keen's pond, near the Lackawannock coal mines; or canal and rail road up to Carbondale,	41
129	60. *y*	Lackawaxen and Pittstown canal; connecting the upper water of the Lackawaxen river, with the Susquehanna at the mouth of Lackawannock, in continuation of the canal preceding; or otherwise, improvement from Carbondale to Pittstown,	22
130	61. *y*	Lausanne and Wilkesbarre canal; connecting the Susquehanna and Lehigh rivers at these points,	40

Page.	No.		Miles.
141	62. *r*	Lehigh river canal works, and rail road to the mine,	56
145	63. *y*	Nescopec and Lehigh canal; connecting the upper water of the Lehigh with the Susquehanna river at Berwick, by the Nescopec valley,	35
147	64. *y*	Pittstown and Water Gap canal; connecting the Susquehanna and Delaware rivers at these points,	60
149	65. *y*	The Perkiomen canal; connecting the Lehigh river at Allentown, with the Schuylkill river at Norristown, by the Perkiomen valley,	40
149	66. *y*	The Catawissa canal; connecting the Schuylkill river with the Susquehanna, by the Little or East Schuylkill, and Catawissa valleys,	50
151	67. *y*	Schuylkill valley canal; connecting the navigation of Upper Schuylkill river at the mouth of Mill creek, with that at George Reber's mill,	
152	68. *y*	Mahanoy creek canal; connecting the Susquehanna river with the coal mines on the Mahanoy,	
152	69. *y*	Shamokin creek canal; connecting the Susquehanna river with the coal mines on the Shamokin,	
153	70. *r*	Chesapeake and Delaware canal; connecting the Delaware river, opposite Fort Delaware, Pea Patch island, with the Chesapeake bay, at Back creek, Maryland,	14
163	71. *y*	Patapsco and Susquehanna canal; connecting the port of Baltimore with the Susquehanna river at the mouth of the Swatara,	100
170	72. *y*	Patapsco and Potomac canal; connecting the port of Baltimore with the Chesapeake and Ohio canal at or near Little falls of the Potomac river, through the district of Columbia; say, between Baltimore and Georgetown,	44¾
181	75. *y*	Peter's camp canal; connecting the Susquehanna river, near Tioga point, with the Peter's camp coal mine,	

OF THE UNITED STATES. 475

Page.	No.		Miles.
182	76. r	Port Deposite canal; connecting the Susquehanna river navigation, at the rapids south of the Pennsylvania line,	10
182	77. r	Conestoga canal works, from Safe harbour up to Lancaster city,	18
183	78. r	The Conewago canals; connecting the Susquehanna navigation at the Conewago falls,	2¼

266   r The Pennsylvania canal and rail road, Delaware or Eastern division; connecting the Delaware river at Philadelphia with the same at Carpenter's point, on the north-east boundary line of the state, along the Delaware valley; viz.

Philadelphia and Bristol section,
    Distance, by survey, - - 17½
Bristol and Easton section,
    Distance, by survey, - - - 60
Easton and Carpenter's point section,
    Distance, by survey, - - 66½

                                                                             144

266   r The Pennsylvania canal and rail road, Ohio and Lake Erie, or Western division; connecting the Ohio river at Pittsburg, with Lake Erie at Presqu' isle harbour, by way of the Beaver and Shenango valleys, and across the valley of Elk creek. Distance, - - - 167½
The Conneaught summit navigable feeder, from French creek, 21½

                                                                             189

267   r The Pennsylvania canal and rail road, Susquehanna, or Middle division; connecting the Susquehanna navigation at Columbia, with the same at the New-York line, 4 miles above Tioga point, along the Susquehanna valley, and comprising the sections as follows; viz.

Columbia and Middletown section,
    Distance, - - - - 18
Middletown and Juniata section,   24
Juniata and Northumberland section,   37½
Northumberland and Tioga section,   165½

                                                                             245

267   r The Pennsylvania canal and rail road, Juniata and Alleghany, or Transverse di-

Page.	No.		Miles.
		vision; connecting the Delaware river at Philadelphia, with the Susquehanna at Columbia, through Chester and Lancaster counties; and the Susquehanna river at Duncan's island, with the Ohio at Pittsburg, by the Juniata valley, and the Conemaugh, Kiskimenetas, and Alleghany valleys, including a probable distance of 50¾ miles of rail road across the Alleghany mountain; this division comprising the sections as follows; viz.	

Philadelphia and Columbia road section, and extension of road, from Columbia to the west end of the borough of York, in York county, - - - 82¾
Duncan's island and Lewistown section, - - - - - 44½
Ohio and Kiskimenetas section, - 30⅞
Kiskimenetas and Blairsville section, 51
Blairsville and Johnstown section, 28½
Lewistown and Frankstown section, 87½
Frankstown and Johnstown section, 50¾

375⅞

186 80. *y* Chester creek rail road; connecting the Pennsylvania rail road last above specified, with the Delaware river, through the Brandywine and Chester creek valleys, 25

269 85. *r* West branch Susquehanna canal; connecting the Pennsylvania canal at Northumberland, with the mouth of the Bald Eagle river, or a point near the same in Lycoming county, along the West branch valley, - - - - - 68¼

205 89. *y* Alleghany and Conewango canal; connecting the mouth of French creek, with the New-York Conewango canal, at the state line intersection, by the Alleghany river valley, - - - - - 70

205 90. *y* The Conococheague canal; connecting the Susquehanna and the Potomac rivers, by the Conodogwinnet and Conococheague valleys, - - - - - - 120

221 92. *r* Chesapeake and Ohio canal; connecting the eastern and western waters, between Washington city and Pittsburg, by the Potomac valley, Casselmans summit, the

OF THE UNITED STATES.

Page.	No.		Miles.
		Youghioghany and Monongahela valleys,	341
224	93. *r*	Savage river branch canal; connecting at Cumberland, the main canal last specified, with the mouth of Savage river, along the Potomac valley,	30
233	94. *y*	Ohio and Erie canal, By Beaver and Cuyahoga; connecting the Ohio river at Pittsburg, with Lake Erie at Cleaveland, by the Big Beaver and Cuyahoga river valleys, in continuation of the Chesapeake and Ohio canal,	154
237	95.	Ohio state canals, *r* Muskingum and Scioto division; connecting the Ohio river, at the mouth of the Scioto, with Lake Erie at Cleaveland, by the Scioto, Muskingum, and Cuyahoga river valleys,	322
238	96.	Ohio state canals, *r* Miami valley division; connecting the Ohio river with Lake Erie, between Cincinnati and Maumee bay,	290
241	97. *y*	Sandy creek canal; connecting the Ohio river, at the mouth of Little Beaver, with the Ohio state canal, by the Sandy creek valley,	60
241	98. *y*	Portage summit canal; connecting the Ohio river, at a point in Pennsylvania, with the Portage summit of the Ohio state canal,	75
283	100. *y*	The Powhatan canal; connecting James river with the Upper Appomatox, by the Hudsmouth creek valley, Powhatan county, Virginia,	19
283	101. *y*	The Manchester canal; connecting the navigation of James river, at Bosher's mill, with the tide water below Manchester,	10
284	102. *y*	Appomatox and Roanoke canal, or "Junction" canal; connecting the Upper Appomatox and Staunton rivers, by the Buffalo and Little Roanoke river valleys,	30
285	103. *r*	James and Jackson's river canals; from tide water at Richmond dock, up to Covington,	257½
309	108. *y*	The Shenandoah canal; connecting the	

Page.	No.		Miles.
		upper water of the Shenandoah river with the Lexington branch of James river, or with James river by the Lexington valley,	50
312	110. r	Roanoke and Kanhaway canal; connecting the eastern and western waters; or the Roanoke river at tide water, by the valley thereof, and the valley of South fork, with New river and the Kanhaway, at the foot of Great falls, by the valleys of Little river and New river,	422¾
323	111. r	Roanoke and James river canal; connecting the Roanoke river, also the canal last above specified, at a point above Salem, in Bottetourt county, with the navigation of James river at the mouth of the Catawba,	46
	y	New river and Holston canal; connecting the navigation of New river, in the direction of Reed creek valley, with the navigation of the Middle branch of the Holston river at a point in Wythe county, Virginia,	50
332	112. y	Lake Erie and Ohio canal,	
		By the Wabash; connecting Lake Erie with the navigation of Maumee river above the obstructions, and this latter with the Wabash river,	50
	y	Series of canals, to connect the waters of Lake Michigan with those of the Wabash river; the upper waters of White river with the Wabash, by way of the Mississineway valley, as also with the Miami navigation in Ohio state; and the Rivers St. Mary and St. John's, in a line of navigation with the Wabash and the Ohio,	350
335	113. r	Louisville and Portland canal; connecting the navigation of the Ohio river above, with that below the rapids, between those points,	2
339	114. y	Lakes Erie and Michigan canal; connecting these lakes across the Peninsula of Michigan, from Maumee bay to St. Joseph's river,	150
340	115. y	The Chicago canal; connecting Lake Michigan with the Illinois river, between	

OF THE UNITED STATES.

Page.	No.		Miles.
		the Chicago river, and the mouth of the Little Vermillion,	120
345	116. *y*	St. Mary's canal; connecting the navigation above and below the Falls of St. Mary, between Lakes Huron and Michigan,	1
346	117. *y*	Fox river and Ouisconsin canal; connecting Lake Michigan with the Ouisconsin river; that is to say, Green bay with the Lake Winnebago, and the Upper Fox river with the Ouisconsin,	52
370	119. *y*	The Muscle shoal canal; connecting the navigation above and below this obstruction in Tennessee river, between Brown's ferry and Florence, Alabama, as also Colbert's shoal, below the Muscle shoal,	37
371	120. *y*	Tennessee and Savannah canal; connecting the upper waters of these rivers,	50
372	121. *y*	Savannah and Appalachicola canal; connecting the upper waters of the Savannah river with those of the Chatahootchee, leading to the Appalachicola,	100
373	122. *r*	Savannah and Ogatchee canal; connecting the port of Savannah with the Great Ogatchee river, through Jones's lake,	16
374	123. *r*	Ogatchee and Alatamaha canal; connecting these rivers, between Fort Argyle on the Great Ogatchee, and the mouth of the Great Ohoopee river on the Alatamaha,	50
374	124. *y*	Alatamaha and Appalachee canal; connecting the Alatamaha river with the Bay of St. Mark, leading to Appalachee bay,	164
375	125. *y*	Augusta and Flint river canal, or rail road; connecting the Savannah river at Augusta, with Flint river at Fort Lawrence, passing through Milledgeville,	150
376	126. *y*	Chatahootchee and Milledgeville canal; connecting the upper water of the Chatahootchee river with the Oconee river at Milledgeville,	120
377	127. *y*	Tennessee and Tombecbee canal; connecting the Tennessee river at Fort Deposite, with the Black Warrior branch of the Tombecbee, below the falls at Tuscaloosa,	150

Page.	No.		Miles.
378	128. *y*	Pearl river and Mississippi canal ; connecting the upper water of the Pearl in Lawrence county, Mississippi, with the Mississippi river, by the valley of the Big Black,	90
380	131. *y*	New-Orleans and Teche river canal ; connecting the Mississippi river at New-Orleans, with the Teche at Berwick's bay, by way of Lake Barataria and La Fourche,	100
381	132. *y*	Barataria and Grandterre canal ; connecting the lake with the bay of Barataria, at the pass of Grandterre,	40
382	133. *y*	Concordia and Catahoula canal ; connecting the Mississippi river at Concordia opposite Natchez, with the Washitta river at Catahoula Courthouse,	66
384	135. *y*	Mississippi and Pontchartrain canal ; connecting the Mississippi river at New-Orleans, with Lake Pontchartrain, at or below Bayou St. Jean,	10
386	136. *y*	Mississippi and Appalachicola canals; connecting the bays and sounds between Mobile bay and Appalachicola river,	12
388	137. *y*	Tennessee and Alabama canal ; connecting the Tennessee river at or near Fort Deposite, with the Coosa branch of the Alabama, by the Wills creek valley,	50
388	138. *y*	Bear creek canal ; connecting this water of the Tennessee river, with the Tombecbee river, at the heads of their stream navigation improvements,	40
391	139. *y*	Hiwassee and Coosa canal ; connecting the Okou and the Conesaugo, navigable branches of these rivers, at points near the Georgia and Tennessee state line; or, between Calhoun on the Hiwassee river, and the mouth of Conesaugo on the Coosa,	100
404	140. *r*	The Dismal swamp canal ; connecting Elizabeth river above Norfolk, with the head of Pasquotank river, leading to Albemarle sound; and branch to Currituck by the North-west river,	28
406	141. *r*	The Weldon canal ; connecting the navigation of the Roanoke river at Great falls, Halifax county, North Carolina,	12

OF THE UNITED STATES. 481

Page.	No.		Miles.
407	143. *y*	Plymouth and Beaufort canal; connecting the Roanoke river at Plymouth, with Beaufort inlet on the North Carolina coast, passing through Washington and Newbern, - - - -	100
414	144. *y*	Roanoke and Elizabeth river or Murfreesboro' canal; connecting the Weldon canal at Great falls of the Roanoke river, with the Dismal swamp canal leading to Elizabeth river and the port of Norfolk,	80
416	146. *y*	Cape Fear and Pedee canal; connecting the Cape Fear river at or near Haywoodsboro', with the Upper Pedee or Yadkin below the Narrows in Montgomery, North Carolina, by the Deep river valley; also extension across, by canal or rail road, through Anson and Mechlenburg, to a point of the Catawba river, - - - -	125
418	149. *r*	The Santee canal; connecting the Santee river with Cooper's river, leading to the port of Charleston, - - -	22
420	152. *y*	Charleston and Georgetown canal; connecting Winyaw bay below the port of Georgetown, with Wando river, leading to Cooper's river and the port of Charleston, - - - -	45
420	153. *y*	The Waccamaw canal; connecting the Waccamaw river at a point 70 miles from the mouth thereof on Winyaw bay, with Cape Fear river at the port of Wilmington, - - - -	30
421	154. *y*	Ashley and Edisto canal,	
421	155. *y*	Edisto and Savannah canal; connecting the Lower Edisto river with the Ashley at the port of Charleston; and the same point of the Lower Edisto with the Savannah river at the port of Savannah,	40
425	156. *y*	The Florida Isthmus canal; connecting the Atlantic river of St. Mary, at the south bend, 70 miles above the mouth thereof, with the Appalachicola river or bay, on the Gulf of Mexico; or otherwise, from St. Mary's town to Appalachicola bay, - - - -	250
425	157. *y*	The Isthmus prolongation or branch canal;	

Page.	No.		Miles.
		connecting the St. Mary's river at the south bend as above, with the harbour of St. Augustine, intersecting the St. John's river at Jacksonville,	70
428	159. *y*	Atlantic Florida canals; connecting the sound and bay navigation along the east or Atlantic coast of the peninsula, between the mouth of St. John's river and Bocca Ratones, or Cape Florida, a distance of 350 miles,	20
	y	Branch canal to Vacassar bay; between the point of intersection of the Suawnee river, by canal No. 156, and the Indian Cow Pens, near the mouth of Suawnee,	75
	y	Santa Fé canal; between St. Mary's river, at a point above the town of St. Mary, and the Suawnee river at the mouth of the Santa Fé,	120
	y	Tampa bay canal; between St. John's river at the mouth of the Pablo, and Tampa bay on the western coast,	225

Total distance, without including the $183\frac{1}{2}$ miles of road as expressed at Articles 59, 62, 80, 81, $10,742\frac{1}{2}$

The letter *r* prefixed, denoting a red line upon the map, signifies that the work is either finished or well advanced. The letter *y*, denoting a yellow line on the map, signifies either that the work is not yet commenced, or, if commenced, not as yet actively prosecuted. Of these two descriptions, the distances are, viz.—

Canals finished or well advanced (*r*) $3908\frac{5}{8}$
Canals contemplated or not advanced, (*y*) $6833\frac{7}{8}$
                                                  $10,742\frac{1}{2}$

LIST C.

List of River Stream Navigation Improvements, with and without the aid of Canals, and whether by means of Lock and Dam, or by the Sluice mode; a large proportion of which is either finished or gradually prosecuting.

Page.	No.		Miles.
10	1.	Merrimack river improvements, from Haverhill, Massachusetts, upward,	110
12	3.	Connecticut river improvements, from Hartford, Connecticut, up to Barnet, Vermont,	220
19	9.	Cobbassee Contee pond and river improvements; between the Kennebeck and Androscoggin rivers, Maine,	25½
21	10.	Androscoggin river improvements, from Leeds up to or above Shelburne,	98½
23	11.	Kennebeck river improvements; from Augusta upward, by the West, or Dead river branch, to the highlands between Maine and Lower Canada,	200
31	17.	Otter river improvements; from the mouth thereof, at Ferrisburg, on Lake Champlain, up to head water, in Bromley, Vermont,	100
74	36.	The Genessee river improvements,	39
78	42.	Black river, of Ontario, improvements,	136
106	56.	Delaware river improvements; from Trenton falls upward,	220
141	62.	The Lehigh river improvements; in continuation from the Mauch Chunk coal mine, up to Stoddartsville,	37
179	73.	Susquehanna river improvements; from tide water up to the New-York line, above Tioga point,	288
207	91.	The Potomac river improvements; from tide water up to Cumberland,	182
282	99.	The Appomatox river improvements; from tide water of James river, up to Farmville, Prince Edward county, Virginia,	110
307	107.	The Kanhaway river improvements, and turnpike; Stream navigation improved from the Ohio at Point Pleasant, up to Loop	

Page.	No.		Miles.
		Hole shoal below Great falls of the Kanhaway, — 89	
		Turnpike thence, across the mountain to Covington, — 99	
			188
309	108.	The Shenandoah river improvements; from the mouth thereof to its upper waters, above Port Republic, Augusta county,	200
310	109.	The Rivanna river improvements; from the mouth thereof, at Columbia, on James river, up to Moore's ford, opposite Charlottesville,	37
371	120.	The Upper Tennessee river, and Upper Savannah river improvements; to points of each for a canal of communication,	200
372	121.	The Appalachicola, Flint river, and Chatahootche river improvements; up to a point of the latter river, to meet a canal of communication with the upper waters of the Savannah river,	450
378	128.	Pearl river improvements; from the mouth thereof, at Lake Pontchartrain, up to Monticello, in Lawrence county, Mississippi state,	150
378	129.	Amité river improvements; from the mouth thereof, at Lake Maurepas, up to the junction of Comité river,	70
379	130.	Tangchepahaw river improvements; from the mouth thereof, at Lake Pontchartrain, up to the Chapeau Pilier river,	43
380	131.	La Fourche river improvements; from Donaldsonville, on the Mississippi, down the course of the La Fourche,	
383	134.	The Red river improvements; up to, at, and beyond the Great Raft, in Nachitoches district, Louisiana,	500
386	136.	Ibberville channel, and Lower Amité river improvements; between the point of outlet from the Mississippi, and the mouth of Amité river, at Lake Maurepas,	40
388	137.	The Coosa river, of Alabama, improvements; from Fort Jackson up to a point for a canal of communication with the Tennessee river,	200
388	138.	The Tombecbee river, of Alabama, from Demopolis upward, and Bear creek improvements; to points of each, for a canal of communication with the Tennessee river,	200

OF THE UNITED STATES. 485

Page.	No.		Miles.
405	141.	Roanoke river improvements; from the mouth thereof, at Albemarle sound, up to Salem, in Bottetourt county, Virginia,	322
406	142.	The Dan river improvements; from the junction of this river with the Roanoke, up to the Danville falls canal, and thence up to Rockbridge and Stokes counties, North Carolina,	150
414	145.	Cape Fear river improvements; from below the port of Wilmington, up to Haywoodsborough, Chatham county, North Carolina,	200
416	146.	Great Pedee river, and Lower Yadkin improvements; up to the point for a canal of communication with Cape Fear river,	150
416	147.	The Yadkin river improvements; from the Narrows, in Montgomery county, North Carolina, up to Wilkes Courthouse,	200
417	148.	The Wateree and Catawba river improvements; from the Santee fork, South Carolina, up the Wateree river to the Catawba, and up this to near its source in the Blue ridge, North Carolina,	275
418	149.	The Saluda river improvements; from Columbia, at the Congaree fork, up to near the Abbeville county line, South Carolina,	128
419	150.	South Edisto river improvements; from the fork made with the North Edisto, upwards, 70 miles,	70
419	151.	Seneca river improvements; from Andersonville, on the Savannah river, up the main Seneca and branches of the same to near their sources in the mountains,	200
429	158.	Channel in the rear of Amelia island improvements; between the bays of St. Mary and St. John,	15

Total of river stream or channel improvements, without including the 99 miles of road, as expressed at Article 107, - - - - - - - 5655

In which distance of 5655 miles, the rivers Ohio and Mississippi are not included, although works of improvement for the safety and facility of their navigation are going forward upon each. Not only to the Mississippi and Ohio, but to other great river courses, besides those above designated, improvements will be extended from year to year successively, as occasions may point out: that is to say, in carrying on the needful works, to clear away or overcome obstructions to a safe navigation, whether they be of old standing, or newly caused by floods of annual occurrence; and yearly appropriations by government, for this division of internal navigation improvement, will, probably, in some degree or proportion, always be requisite.

GRAND SUMMARY.

Being an approximation to the aggregate distance of the internal navigation of the United States, composed of the natural navigation within the several states, partly ascertained, and partly by computation; together with sundry canals of communication, and sundry series of river stream improvement, both with and without canals attached, viz.

Page.		Artificial. Miles.	Natural. Miles.	Total. Miles.
45.	In the New-England states,	$1611\frac{7}{8}$	5395	$7006\frac{7}{8}$
84.	In New-York state,	$2626\frac{3}{4}$	5051	$7677\frac{3}{4}$
275.	In New-Jersey, Delaware, Maryland, Pennsylvania, and Ohio states,	$3962\frac{5}{8}$	7414	$11376\frac{5}{8}$
328.	In Virginia,	$1321\frac{1}{4}$	3110	$4431\frac{1}{4}$
333.	In Indiana,	400	2550	2950
338.	In Kentucky,	2	2600	2602
338.	Ohio river channel,		945	945
342.	Middle great lakes, and the states of Illinois and Michigan,	270	2880	3150
350.	Lakes Ontario and Superior, and North-West territory, east of the Mississippi,	53	1935	1988
352.	Mississippi river channel,		2250	2250
356.	Confluents from the west, and the Upper Mississippi, east and west,		16664	16664
394.	In the states of Tennessee, Mississippi, Alabama, Louisiana, and Georgia,	3198	28281	31479
444.	In Florida,	775	3130	3905
422.	In North Carolina and South Carolina,	2177	4600	6777
		$16397\frac{1}{2}$	86805	

Total computed distance of inland navigation, not including the river courses west of the Oregon or Rocky mountains, — — — — — — — $103202\frac{1}{2}$

Which 16397½ miles of artificial navigation, treated of in the inserted Articles, No. 1 to 159, and whereof the foregoing list marked A is a recapitulation, is composed of, viz.

1. Canals of communication, as enumerated and particularized in another list, marked B.
2. River stream navigation by improvements, with and without the aid of canals; and whether by lock and dam, or by the sluice mode, as enumerated and particularized in a third list, marked C.

Say, B. *Miles,* 10742½
    C.   5655 together, *Miles,* 16397½, equal to A.

In these 5655 miles of river stream improvements, as per list C, the beds of the Mississippi and Ohio rivers are, however, not included, although works are in prosecution for the clearing away obstructions in them: and besides, improvements will be extended to the navigable condition of other rivers than those already designated, successively, from year to year: other connecting canals also will be projected, and, in due course of time, be executed, by boards of public works or internal improvement, now established by law in many of the states of the Union, or by individual enterprise.

Of the 10742½ miles of canal in the List B. as above, some further analysis may be given; namely;

	Miles.
In New-England:	
The Middlesex canal; long since finished,	27
The Farmington canal; and its prolongation, the Hampshire and Hampden canal: now well advanced,	102
The Blackstone canal: nearly finished,	45
In New-York state:	
The Champlain canal, and Glen's falls feeder,	70½
The Erie canal,	363
The Oswego canal; finished,	38
The Delaware and Hudson canal; finished,	81
The Cayuga and Seneca canal; finished,	21
In New-Jersey state:	
The Morris canal; now well advanced,	101½
In Pennsylvania:	
The Schuylkill works, up to Mill creek,	110½
The Union canal, and Pine Grove feeder,	105
The Lackawaxen canal and rail road, up to Carbondale; nearly finished,	41
Amount carried forward,	1105½

	Miles.
Amount brought forward,	1105½
The Lehigh canal works, and raid road to Mauch Chunk coal mine,	56
The Chesapeake and Delaware canal,	14
The Conestoga canal,	18
The Conewago canal,	2¼
The state canal and rail road. Many sections of the principal divisions now in active progress. 192 miles of canal along several of the sections are preparing for open navigation, between the 1st of September and the 1st of November next, or spring of 1830; though some demur is occasioned by a want of due legislative provision,	1022⅛
The state canals of Ohio: In active progress. Of these, the Cleaveland and Scioto division measures 322 miles, whereof 250¼ miles are now finished, or under contract; and the Miami division measures 290 miles, whereof 67¾ miles are finished,	612
The Chesapeake and Ohio canal: In satisfactory progress: and whereof 50 miles, on the Eastern section, expected to be finished next spring,	371
The Baltimore and Ohio rail road: In active progress: and whereof 66 miles expected to be finished this year, 1829, or in the ensuing spring,	350
The Maryland Deposite canal,	10
In Virginia, The state project of a two-fold communication, east and west; viz. from tide water, through the James river course, across by New river, to Great falls of the Kanhaway; and through the Roanoke river course, to the same; with a canal of connexion between the two. Of this project, 37 miles along the James river section are finished,	726¼
In North Carolina, The Dismal swamp canal; now nearly finished,	28
The Weldon canal,	12
In South Carolina, The Santee canal,	22
Amount carried forward,	4349⅛

OF THE UNITED STATES. 489

	Miles.
Amount brought forward,	4349⅛
In Georgia state, The Savannah and Ogatchee canal, and the Ogatchee and Alatamaha canal; in progress, and, by terms of charter, to be finished by the year 1832,	66
In Kentucky state, The Louisville and Portland canal,	2
Making a total now finished, or in a course of execution, including 548½ miles of rail road,	4417⅛

The routes of which, (excepting the Baltimore and Ohio rail road route; which nearly corresponds with the Chesapeake and Ohio canal route,) are traced on the map in RED LINES. The remaining 6833⅞ miles of canal, being merely contemplated, are traced on the map in YELLOW LINES.

This is the canal and rail road state down to July, 1829. There are a few other canals of the book than those above stated, on which small beginnings have been made; and other projected or contemplated ones; also rail roads, especially the great project of New-England; these will successively be taken up, prosecuted, and made to become realities.

After closing for the United States, in regard to the present subject, and the several incidental matters which follow, the reader will perceive, that the Canada canals have claimed to be brought under notice, as somewhat pertinent to the occasion, and recommending their admission as a finishing stroke to this book.

Much has latterly been done by the general government in the cause of internal improvement. Since a wider range, than formerly was the case, has happily been taken, in construing some of the provisions of the federal constitution which have a bearing upon the subject, the consequences have been, so to speak, as an electrical stimulant to the body of the nation. In 1824, congress passed an act, authorizing the organization of a board of military and civil engineers, to make surveys and estimates of such roads and canals as the president should deem of national importance for *mail*, or *military*, or *commercial* purposes: since which time, a United States board of internal improvement has therefore been in existence, and sundry appropriations, to a large amount, out of the nation's income, have been made by congress, to assist the execution of improvements of general utility.

Applications to the president, or to the war department of state, for engineers, to make preliminary surveys, in regard to proposed undertakings of *national importance,* are a necessary consequence; and parties are appointed to the service accordingly, on every application, whether by state authority, or by individuals of any of the states, where such proposed works are respectively to be gone into, or desired.

It appears, by an official statement, that the United States board of internal improvement, have been occupied, during the season now expired, (1827) on the following objects;—

A report of a mail route between the cities of Baltimore and Philadelphia.

A report, plan, and estimate of a canal to connect Lake Pontchartrain with the Mississippi river at New-Orleans.

Examination of the Florida peninsula, for a canal across.

Examination between the bays of Mobile and Pensacola, for a canal to connect them.

Examination of the country from New-Orleans to Knoxville, for a national road, via Baton Rouge, from Washington city to New-Orleans, through West Tennessee.

Examination for an improved communication, between St. Mary's harbour and the mouth of St. John's river.

It also appears, by a report from the engineer department, that the distribution of duties to the topographical and civil engineers, during the season, was as here follows;—viz.

One brigade on the survey to connect the Atlantic sea with the Gulf of Mexico, by canal across the Florida peninsula; which the party have accomplished, and a report is preparing.

One brigade on the surveys hereunder;—

1. For removing obstructions to the navigation of the Piscataqua river, state of Maine.

2. For deepening the channel at the bar of Merrimack river.

3. For removing obstructions in the Saugatuck river and harbour.

4. For removing obstructions in Mill river harbour, Connecticut.

5. For the erection of a beacon in Black Rock harbour, Fairfield, Connecticut.

6. For the construction of piers at Little Compton harbour, Rhode Island.

7. For improving a part of the harbour of Newport, Rhode Island.

8. For the erection of a pier in Warren river, Rhode Island, at the entrance of the harbour.

9. For the erection of a pier in Stonington harbour, Connecticut.

10. For the examination and survey, by different routes, to

locate a canal between Taunton and Weymouth, Massachusetts, not yet finished.

One brigade on the examinations and surveys for connecting the waters of Lake Erie with the Ohio river at Pittsburg, viz.

1. Surveyed a route from the head of the main feeder, Conneaught reservoir, along the valley of French creek, to Miles's branch, up Le Bœuf, and across the Tamarack swamp and Beaver dam summits, to the port of Erie.

2. Surveyed a feeder, from the junction of Miles's branch and French creek to both these summits.

3. Surveyed an experimental line for the establishment of the Conneaught and Elk route, from the valley of the latter creek to the town of Erie.

4. Surveyed the route from Pittsburg to Conneaught lake, by the valley of the Alleghany river and French creek.

5. Surveyed and determined the position of a canal from the Akron summit of the Ohio state canal, to the eastern side of the ridge dividing the waters of the Mahoning from those of the Cuyahoga; with the lines of feeders for conducting supplies of water to the same.

6. Examined the ground east of the Shenango river, and the valley of the Mahoning, to Ravenna.

One brigade, on completing the surveys of different routes for a canal between Lake Memphramagog and Lake Champlain, by way of La Moëlle and Black rivers; and for a canal from Lake Champlain to the Connecticut river, by the valley of Onion river.

A topographical engineer and assistant, on examinations for a national road between Washington city and Buffalo, and another one from Zanesville in Ohio state, to Florence in Alabama.

One brigade, on surveys to determine as to the practicability of uniting the waters of the Great Kanhaway with those of James river, by a canal.

Three brigades, on examinations and surveys for the Baltimore and Ohio rail road, in co-operation with the Company's surveyors.

One brigade, on surveying the swash in Pamplico sound, North Carolina, and the flats of Cape Fear river, below Wilmington; also in part, a route for the proposed canal between the Neuse and North river leading to Beaufort harbour.

A topographical party, on surveying, in part, the obstructions of the Muscle shoals in the Tennessee river; also a route for the proposed canal between the waters of the Hiwassee and Coosa rivers in Alabama.

One brigade, on surveying a route for the proposed canal between Baltimore and the intended Chesapeake and Ohio canal;

and an extension of the same from Baltimore, or from some intermediate point to the city of Annapolis.

One brigade, on surveying a route for the proposed canal to connect the Maumee river of Lake Erie with the Wabash.

Commissioners, under act of congress, 3d March, 1825, on marking out a road from the western frontier of Missouri state, to the confines of New-Mexico.

A civil surveyor, on surveying divers routes for a continuation of the national road from Cumberland to Washington city.

A special commissioner, on preliminary and experimental surveys for a continuation of the national road from Zanesville, westward, and an actual location thereof as far as the boundary line between Indiana and Illinois states. The section of national road between the Ohio river and Zanesville is partly completed.

Two civil engineers, on making a re-examination of the Chesapeake and Ohio canal route, for the purpose of forming new estimates of the cost of the canal.

Engineers and agents, on the several objects as follows;—

Under act of congress, 2d March, 1827, for repairs of the national road from Cumberland and Wheeling, in part.

Under the same act, the construction of a road between the Maumee river of Lake Erie and Detroit; also a road from Detroit to Saganaw river and bay, and another one from Detroit to Fort Gratiot.

Under act of congress, 26th May, 1824, for deepening the channel leading to the harbour of Presqu' isle, Lake Erie; and for the preservation of Plymouth beach.

Under acts of congress, 24th May, 1824, and 3d March, 1827, for improving the navigation of the Ohio and Mississippi rivers.

Under act of congress, 2d May, 1827, for the erection of a pier in Dunkirk harbour, New-York, and for the improvement of Cleaveland harbour, Lake Erie; also for the construction of two piers at the mouth of Oswego harbour, Lake Ontario.

For removing obstructions to the navigation of Saugatuck river, and protecting the harbour.

For the erection of a pier at the mouth of La Plaisance bay, Michigan.

For the erection of piers, placing of beacons, and removing of obstructions at and near the entrance of Saco harbour, state of Maine.

For the erection of piers at the mouth of Buffalo creek, Lake Erie.

For the erection of piers at the mouth of Ashtabula creek, Lake Erie.

For the erection of piers at Cunningham's creek, at Grand river, and at Huron river, state of Ohio.

The improving the navigation of Sackett's harbour, Lake Ontario.

For the erection of a pier at Belfast harbour, state of Maine.

For the erection of new piers and repairing of old ones at Newcastle harbour, in the River Delaware.

For removing of obstructions and deepening the harbour of Mobile, in the Gulf of Mexico.

Under act of congress, 20th May, 1826; surveying the public piers at Chester, on the river Delaware, and estimating the expense of needful repairs.

Under act of congress, 2d March, 1827, examining the public piers at Marcus hook, and Fort Mifflin, Delaware river; and forming plans for improvements, with estimates.

Inspection of the Chesapeake and Delaware canal, by a military and a civil engineer.

The president, in his message to congress, with obvious propriety, observes;

"All the officers of both corps of engineers, with several other persons duly qualified, have been constantly employed on these services, since the passage of the act of 30th April, 1824, to this time. Were no other advantages to accrue to the country from their labours, than the fund of topographical knowledge which they have collected and communicated, that alone would have been a profit to the Union, more than adequate to all the expenses which have been devoted to the object. But the appropriations for the repair and construction of the Cumberland road, for the construction of various other roads, for the removal of obstructions from rivers and harbours, for the erection of light houses, beacons, piers, and buoys, and for the completion of canals undertaken by individual associations, but needing the assistance of means and resources more comprehensive than individual enterprise can command, may be considered as treasures laid up from the contributions of the present age, for the benefit of posterity."

The document next presented, is a statement, as transmitted on the 28th April, 1828, by the secretary of war, to congress, and embraces the *whole* subject, down to this period, of the works of internal improvement on the part of the federal government, since the time referred to, i. e. 30th April, 1824, viz.—

A LIST of the different works of Internal Improvement, comprising routes for Roads and Canals; attempts to improve the Navigation of Rivers, Lakes, Creeks, and Bays; and to protect Coasts and Islands, that have been undertaken or projected by the Federal Government within the different States and Territories, from the year 1824 to the year 1827, inclusive: showing how many works, and of what kind, have been undertaken or projected in each State and Territory within that time; the amount intended, or deemed necessary, to be expended in the execution of each work, so far as the same has been estimated; and the time which each will probably require for its completion, as far as practicable.

Designation of the different works.	In what state or territory located.	Estimated cost of execution.	Estimated time for completion.	Remarks.
ROADS.				
A national road from Washington city, district of Columbia, to New-Orleans, Louisiana,	-	-	-	Four routes examined; not surveyed—not projected.
A mail road from Baltimore, Maryland, to Philadelphia, Pennsylvania,	Maryland, Delaware, and Pennsylvania,	-	-	Reconnoitred—not projected.
A national road from Washington city, district of Columbia, to Buffalo, New-York,	District of Columbia, Maryland, Pennsylvania, New-York,	$1,877,063 92		
A road from a point opposite to Memphis, in Tennessee, to Little Rock, in Arkansas territory,	Arkansas territory,	-		
Extension of the Cumberland road to the district of Columbia,	Virginia, district of Columbia,	-	-	Survey not completed.
Continuation of the construction of the Cumberland road, from Canton to Zanesville, Ohio,	Ohio,	595,000 00		
Surveying and locating the continuation of the Cumberland road, from Zanesville to the permanent seat of government of Missouri,	Ohio, Indiana, Illinois, Missouri,	-	-	Located to dividing line between Indiana and Illinois.
A road from the Black swamp road to Cadiz, in Ohio, and thence to Wheeling, in Virginia, and Washington, in Pennsylvania,	Ohio, Pennsylvania,			
A road from the Black swamp road, through Wooster, Canton, New-Lisbon, and Beavertown, to Pittsburg, Pennsylvania,	Ohio, Pennsylvania,			

OF THE UNITED STATES. 495

ROADS	A road from a point in the north-west boundary of Ohio, near the foot of the rapids of the Miami of Lake Erie, to Detroit, Michigan,	Michigan,	41,500 00	in 1828
	A road from Chicago, Illinois, to Detroit, Michigan territory,	Illinois, Michigan,		
	A road from Little Rock to Cantonment Gibson, Arkansas,	Arkansas territory,		
	Marking a road from the western boundary of Missouri to the confines of New-Mexico,			
	Repairing the Cumberland road, between Cumberland, Maryland, and Wheeling, Virginia,	Maryland, Pennsylvania, Virginia,		
	A road from Detroit to Saganaw river and bay, Michigan,	Michigan territory,		
	A road from Detroit to Fort Gratiot, in Michigan,	Do. do.		
	A road from Zanesville, Ohio, to Florence, Alabama,	Ohio, Kentucky, Tennessee, Alabama,		
	A rail road from Baltimore to the Ohio river,	Maryland, Pennsylvania, Virginia,		
ROUTES FOR CANALS	Chesapeake and Ohio canal,	Maryland, dist. of Columbia, Pennsylvania, Virginia,	22,375,427 69	
	Continuation of the Chesapeake and Ohio canal to Lake Erie,	Ohio, Pennsylvania,	-	Surveys not completed.
	Continuation of Chesapeake and Ohio canal to Alexandria, in the district of Columbia,	District of Columbia,	158,673 00	
	Canal from the Alleghany river to the Susquehanna and Schuylkill rivers,	Pennsylvania,		
	Canal to connect the Delaware and Raritan rivers,	New-Jersey,		
	Canal to connect Barnstable and Buzzard's bays, Mass.	Massachusetts,		
	Canal from the Mississippi river to Lake Pontchartrain, La.	Louisiana,	-	Surveyed—not projected.
	Chesapeake and Delaware canal,	Maryland, Delaware,	1,935,000 00	
	Canal from Lake Memphramagog to Connecticut river,	Vermont, New-Hampshire,		
	Brunswick canal, to connect the Merrymeeting and Casco bays,	Maine,		
	Cobbasse Contee canal, to connect the waters of the Kennebec, at Gardner, with those of the Androscoggin, at Leeds,	Maine,		

496 INTERNAL NAVIGATION

LIST OF WORKS—CONTINUED.

Designation of the different works.	In what state or territory located.	Estimated cost of execution.	Estimated time for completion.	Remarks.
ROUTES FOR CANALS.				
Ammonusuck canal, to unite the waters of the Connecticut with those of the Androscoggin, by Ammonusuck and Dead rivers,	New-Hampshire,			
Sunapee canal, to connect the Connecticut with the Merrimack river near Concord,	Do. do.			
Oliverian canal, to connect the waters of the Connecticut, near Haverhill, with those of Merrimack, near Plymouth,	Do. do.			
Winnepiseogee canal, to connect the Winnepiseogee lake, with the navigable waters of Cocheco, at Dover, and from thence by the Piscataqua, to effect a connexion with the harbour of Portsmouth,	Do. do.			
Pasumpsick canal, to unite the waters of the Connecticut with those of Memphramagog lake,	Do. do.			
Rutland canal, to connect, by water communication, the town of Rutland, Vermont, with the northern canal at Whitehall,	Vermont, - Maryland, district of Columbia,			
Canal between Baltimore and the Potomac river,				
Canal to connect the Chesapeake and Ohio canal, with the Pennsylvania canal,	Pennsylvania,	2,980,815 00	-	Surveys not completed.
Canals to connect the head waters of the Kanhaway, with James and Roanoke rivers,	Virginia, -	-		
Canals to connect the waters of Lake Michigan with those of the Wabash,		-		
Canal to connect the Wabash with White river, by Mississineway river, and by Ponceaupecheau river,	Indiana, Ohio,	2,368,731 21	-	Estimate in part—surveys not completed.
Canals to connect the St. Mary's, St. Joseph's, and Wabash rivers, with the Ohio river,				

OF THE UNITED STATES. 497

ROUTES FOR CANALS.	Canal to overcome the obstructions presented by the Falls of Ohio,	Indiana,	-	Surveyed—not projected.
	Canal to connect the Tennessee with the Coosa river,	Alabama,	-	Surveyed—not projected.
	Canal to connect the Atlantic with the Gulf of Mexico, across the Peninsula of Florida,	Florida territory,	-	Examined.
	Canal to unite the waters of the Potomac and Rappahannock rivers,	Virginia,	-	Examined.
	Canal from the Mahoning river at Warren, to the portage summit of the Ohio canal,	Ohio,	-	Examined.
	Canal to connect the Mississippi river with Lake Borgne,	Louisiana,	-	Examined.
	Canal from Taunton to Weymouth,	Massachusetts,	-	Survey not completed.
	Montpelier canal, to connect the waters of Lake Champlain with those of the Connecticut, by Onion and White river valleys,	Vermont,	-	
	La Moëlle canal, to connect Lake Memphramagog with Lake Champlain, by the valleys of La Moëlle and Black rivers,	Do.	-	
	Canal between the Neuse and North rivers, in North Carolina,	North-Carolina,	-	Surveyed—not projected.
	Canal to unite the waters of Elizabeth river with Lockwood's folly, North Carolina,	Do. do.	-	Surveyed.
ATTEMPTS, &c.	Improvement of the navigation of the Connecticut river, from Barnet, Vermont, to Lake Connecticut,	Vermont, New-Hampshire,	-	
	Improvement of the navigation of Kennebeck river, from Bath to Scowhegan,	Maine,	-	
	Survey and level of the Androscoggin river,	Do.	-	
	Surveys of the mouth of Black river and Conneaught creek, on Lake Erie, with a view to their improvement,	Ohio, Pennsylvania,	-	
	Improving the navigation of the Tennessee river,	Tennessee,	-	
	Improving the navigation of the Ohio and Mississippi rivers,	Pennsylvania, Virginia, Ohio, Kentucky, Tennessee, Mississippi, Missouri, Arkansas T. Louisiana,	-	

LIST OF WORKS—CONTINUED.

Designation of the different works.	In what state or territory located.	Estimated cost of execution.	Estimated time for completion.	Remarks.
Deepening the channel leading into the harbour of Presqu' isle, on Lake Erie,	Pennsylvania,	35,223 18	in 1828	
Repairing Plymouth beach,	Massachusetts,	38,896 90	1828	
Building a pier at Steele's ledge, near the harbour of Belfast, Maine,	Maine,	1,200 00	1828	
Preservation of a point of land forming Provincetown harbour,	Massachusetts,	3,500 00	1828	
Removing obstructions to the navigation of Piscataqua river,	New-Hampshire,			
Building a lighthouse at the harbour of Edgartown, and preventing the harbour from filling up with sand,	Massachusetts,	4,273 56	1828	
Deepening the channel over the bar at the mouth of Merrimack river,	Maine,	32,080 27		
Improvements in the harbour of Hyannis, for the safe anchorage of vessels,	Massachusetts,	10,650 00	1828	
Building a pier and repairing the old one, at the mouth of Buffalo creek, New-York,	New-York,	49,000 00	1828	
Cleaning out and deepening the harbour of Sackett's harbour, New-York,	Do.	3,000 00	1828	
Improving the navigation of the bay and harbour of Oswego,	Do.	33,348 64	1828	
Building piers and repairing old ones, and deepening the water around them, at New-Castle, Delaware,	Delaware,	25,000 00	1828	
Survey of the public piers at Chester, in the River Delaware, to determine upon the expediency of accepting the cession thereof from Pennsylvania,	Pennsylvania,			
Removing obstructions at the mouth of Grand river, Ohio,	Ohio,	14,755 11	1828	
Removing obstructions at the mouth of Ashtabula creek, Ohio,	Do.	14,403 50	1828	

ATTEMPTS TO IMPROVE THE NAVIGATION OF RIVERS, LAKES,

Removing obstructions at the mouth of Cunningham creek, Ohio,	Ohio,	3,517 76	1828
Removing obstructions at Huron river, Ohio,	Do.	9,413 35	1828
Improving the navigation of La Plaisance bay, Michigan,	Michigan territory,	3,977 81	1828
Survey of Sandusky bay, to ascertain the expediency and expense of constructing piers to improve the navigation thereof,	Do. do.		
Removing obstructions to the navigation of Saugatuck river,	Connecticut,	1,500 00	1828
Survey of the swash in Pamplico sound, near Ocracock inlet, for the purpose of ascertaining whether the channel through the same can be deepened,	North-Carolina,		
Survey of Cape Fear river, below the town of Wilmington, North-Carolina, with a view to its improvement,	Do. do.		
Survey of Roanoke inlet and sound, with a view of ascertaining the practicability of making a permanent ship channel between Albemarle sound and the Atlantic ocean, at Roanoke inlet, or elsewhere,	Do. do.		
Removing obstructions and deepening the harbour of Mobile,	Alabama,	8,000 00	1828
Surveys of Marblehead and Holmes' hole,	Massachusetts,		
Erecting a pier at the mouth of Dunkirk harbour, N. Y.	New-York,	9,000 00	
Improving Cleaveland harbour, Ohio,	Ohio,	10,000 00	1828
Improving the harbour at the mouth of Pascagoula river,	Mississippi,	25,500 00	1828
Surveys to ascertain the expediency and expense of constructing piers to improve the harbour of Church's cove, in the town of Little Compton,	Rhode-Island,	24,062 85	
Surveys to ascertain the expediency and expense of erecting a pier in Stonington harbour,	Connecticut,	37,145 00	
Examining the public piers at Port Penn, Marcus hook, and Fort Mifflin, in the River Delaware, with a view to repairing and improving the same,	Pennsylvania, repairing, $4,412 43; improving,	91,689 33	

LIST OF WORKS—CONTINUED.

	Designation of the different works.	In what state or territory located.	Estimated cost of execution.	Estimated time for completion.	Remarks.
ATTEMPTS, &c.	Removing the Colbert shoals in Tennessee river,	Tennessee.			
	Removing the obstructions in the Kennebeck river, at Lovejoy's Narrows,	Maine,	6,500 00	1828	
	Erecting piers and removing obstructions at and near the entrance into the harbour of Saco,	Do.	7,000 00	1828	
	Survey of the harbour of Mill river, with a view to the erection of a beacon on a ledge of rocks about one mile from the town,	Connecticut,	6,201 20		
	Survey of the shoal at the north end of Goat island, in the harbour of Newport, Rhode Island, with a view to building a wall to the extremity of that shoal,	Rhode-Island,	13,669 12		
	Survey of the river and harbour of Warren, with a view to erecting a pier in Warren river, near the entrance into Warren harbour,	Do. do.	3,953 25		
	Examination and survey of the Muscle shoals in Tennessee river, with a view to the improvement of its navigation,	Tennessee.			

Engineer Department, *April 28, 1828.*

ALEX. MACOMB, *Maj. Gen. Chief Engineer.*

January 1st, 1830.

The attention of the engineer department of the United States, during the past year, in relation to civil constructions and improvements, has been directed to the several heads, as follows; viz. at

1. La Plaisance bay, Michigan territory.
2. Huron river, Ohio.
3. Black river, Ohio.
4. Cleaveland harbour, Ohio.
5. Grand river, Ohio.
6. Cunningham's creek, Ohio.
7. Ashtabula creek, Ohio.
8. Conneaught creek, Ohio.
9. Presqu' isle bay, Pennsylvania.
10. Dunkirk harbour, New-York.
11. Buffalo harbour, New-York.
12. Black Rock harbour, New-York.
13. Genessee river, New-York.
14. Big Sodus bay, New-York.
15. Oswego harbour, New-York.
16. Sackett's harbour, New-York.
17. Lovejoy's narrows, Kennebeck river, Maine.
18. Harbour of Saco, Maine.
19. Kennebeck river, Maine.
20. Berwick branch of Piscataqua, Maine.
21. Merrimack river, Massachusetts.
22. Deer island, Boston harbour, Massachusetts.
23. Plymouth beach, Massachusetts.
24. Princetown harbour, Massachusetts.
25. Hyannis harbour, Massachusetts.
26. Nantucket harbour, Massachusetts.
27. Edgartown harbour, Massachusetts.
28. Warren river, Rhode Island.
29. Stonington harbour, Connecticut.
30. Mill river, Connecticut.
31, 32, 33. Marcus Hook, Fort Mifflin, Port Penn, Pennsylvania.
34. New-Castle, Delaware.
35. Ocracock inlet, North Carolina.
36. Cape Fear river, North Carolina.
37. Inland passage between the St. Mary's river, Georgia, and St. John's river, Florida.
38. St. Mark's river, Florida.
39. Appalachicola river, Florida.
40. Bay of Mobile.
41. Pass Au Héron.
42. Pascagoula river.

43. Red river, Louisiana and Arkansas.
44. Mississippi river.
45. Ohio river.
46. Repairs of the Cumberland road, between Cumberland and Wheeling.
47. Road from Canton to Zanesville.
48. Road westwardly, from Zanesville, in Ohio.
49. Road through Indiana.
50. Road from Detroit to Chicago, Michigan territory.
51. Road from Detroit to Fort Gratiot, Michigan territory.
52. Road from Detroit to Saganaw, Michigan territory.
53. Road from Detroit to Maumee.

Also, the surveys here enumerated :—

SURVEYS UNDER SPECIAL ACTS AND RESOLUTIONS OF CONGRESS.

Of the surveys enumerated under this head, as in progress at the time of my last annual report, all have been completed, and were reported to congress last year, except the survey of the Wabash river, and the examination of sites for an armory on the western waters, on which a report will be made this winter.

Those ordered at the last session of congress, are—

1. Survey of the ship channel of Penobscot river, Maine, from Whitehead to Bangor, and ascertaining the cost of improving the navigation of the same, and proper sites for spindles and buoys.

2. Survey of the Cocheco branch of Piscataqua river, New-Hampshire, from Dover falls to its confluence with the Piscataqua, for the purpose of ascertaining the practicability of removing obstructions to navigation, and the cost.

3. Survey of North river, between Scituate and Marshfield, Massachusetts, to ascertain the expediency of removing obstructions at the mouth of the same, and to make an estimate of cost.

4. Survey of the piers erected at Sandy bay, Massachusetts; to report the condition of the same, and what works are necessary to make a good and safe harbour at that place, together with an estimate of the cost.

5. Survey of the harbour of Bass river, between Yarmouth and Dennis, Massachusetts, to ascertain the practicability and expense of improving the said harbour.

6. Survey of the River Thames, Connecticut, with a view to improve the navigation of the same, and estimating the cost of such improvement.

7. Survey of the harbour of West Brook, near the mouth of Connecticut river, Connecticut, with a view to the improve-

ment of said harbour, and for ascertaining the cost of such improvement.

8. Survey of the harbour of Norwalk, Connecticut, with a view to its improvement.

9. Survey of the harbour of Stamford, Connecticut, with a view to its improvement.

10. Survey of the bars at the mouth of Sag harbour, New-York, to ascertain the best method of preventing the harbour being filled up with sand, and the cost of the same.

11. Survey of Flat beach, alias Tucker's island, New-Jersey, with a view to preserve the anchorage of the port, and to report an estimate of the cost of such improvements as may be necessary to effect those objects.

12. Survey of Deep creek, a branch of the South branch of Elizabeth river, Virginia, for the purpose of improving the navigation of the same, and an estimate of the cost.

13. Survey of Pasquotank river, North Carolina, for removing bars and obstructions in the same, and an estimate of cost.

14. Survey of the harbour of St. Augustine, and the bar at or near the entrance of the same, with a view to remove the latter, and to render the access to the harbour safe at all times, and to make an estimate of the cost of accomplishing that object.

15. Survey of the water tract between Lake Pontchartrain and Mobile bay, with a view to the erection of light-houses, and placing buoys.

16. Survey of the passes at the mouth of the Mississippi river, with a view to the improvement of the navigation, and building light-houses and placing buoys.

17. Survey of the entrance of the River Teche, with a view to improve and shorten the navigation of the same, and an estimate of the cost of such improvement.

18. Survey of certain sites on the Ohio river, to ascertain the practicability of erecting bridges over said river.

These surveys have been made; and the reports, some of which have been already received, will be presented as soon as practicable.

19. The surveys for continuing the location of the national road to the seat of government of Missouri, have been diligently prosecuted this season. At the date of my last annual report, the location had been effected as far as Vandalia: since that time, experimental surveys have been made from Vandalia, through St. Louis, along the south side of the Missouri, to Jefferson; thence, in returning, along the north side of the Missouri, back to Vandalia, which place the commissioners expected to reach about the 25th of October. In the course of this winter, therefore, such a report may be expected, as will afford the means of

deciding on the most advantageous route for the road beyond Vandalia.

SURVEYS UNDER THE ACT OF THE 30th APRIL, 1824.

The operations under this head, during the year past, in addition to those reported to congress at its last session, have been as follows :—

1. Preparing copies of various maps required by the commissioners for settling the north-east boundary of the United States. Maine.
2. Surveys, with a view to connect the waters of Lake Champlain with those of the Connecticut river, by the valleys of Onion and Wills' rivers. Vermont.
3. Survey, with a view to unite the Connnecticut and Pemigewasset, by the valley of the Oliverian. New-Hampshire.
4. Survey of a canal route from Taunton to Weymouth. Massachusetts.
5. Survey of a route for a rail road from Catskill to Ithaca. New-York.
6. Survey to connect the Pennsylvania and Ohio canal, by the valleys of the Big Beaver and Mahoning. Pennsylvania and Ohio.
7. Survey of the Alleghany river, from French creek to Pittsburg. Pennsylvania.
8. Surveys for the location of a canal round the Muscle and Colbert shoals, in the Tennessee river. Alabama.
9. Surveys for the location of a rail road from Charleston to Hamburg. South Carolina.
10. Preparation of a map of Pensacola bay. Florida.
11. Survey of the country between the Tennessee and Alatamaha rivers, and preparation of a report on the same. Georgia and Tennessee.
12. Surveys of Licking and Green rivers, in Kentucky, with a view to improve their navigation. Kentucky.
13. Surveys, with a view to connect the waters of Lakes Erie and Michigan with those of the Ohio and Illinois rivers. Indiana.
14. Survey of a canal route to connect the waters of Lake Michigan with those of the Illinois river. Illinois.
15. Surveys of the Des Moines and Rock river rapids, in the Mississippi river. Illinois.
16. Survey and examination of the concerns of the Louisville and Portland canal, made at the request of the secretary of the treasury. Kentucky.
17. The aid previously afforded by the department to the

Baltimore and Ohio rail road company, has been continued during the year. Maryland.

"The necessity of withdrawing some of the officers from the duties in which they were engaged, for the purpose of making the surveys enumerated in the preceding class, has prevented the completion of some of the reports on those of this class, which would otherwise have been rendered."

To these objects of permanent benefit, which by their nature constitute so many real solid additions to the wealth of the nation, and become, moreover, the surest foundation that can be laid for an accelerated increase of the aggregate national wealth taking place in periods to come, between three and four millions of the income of this Union have, by laws enacted at the three last sessions of congress, been applied ; and this has been done, as is justly remarked by the president, without intrenching upon the necessities of the treasury for other occasions, and without adding a dollar to the debts of the community. There has, on the contrary, within the same three years, been discharged, of the public debt, contracted in former days, upwards of 16 millions of dollars !*

The plan laid down, of a total liquidation of this debt, now reduced to 60½ millions, is steadily adhered to, and the object will undoubtedly be accomplished, nothing sinister happening, within a very short period of years. Against which change of things, ways and means are yet to be devised for the "putting out to usury," or (in other terms to speak of the approaching difficulty) for the proper distribution and employment of a considerable annual surplus of the nation's income. It is as yet a question of much doubt, as to what may finally appear to the wisdom of the nation's councils to be the best mode or modes of applying her yearly surplus treasures for the most salutary, and withal, increasingly beneficial purposes. A truly interesting topic for discussion !

In the mean time, the United States' yearly revenue, incumbered, as it still is, with payments on account of some subsisting debt, will yet be abundantly sufficient for an unremitted prosecution of a certain regular system of *national defence*, commensurate with the wants of the country, which, other objects not neglected, has now been in very successful progress for some years past.

To the perfecting of, and maintaining this system of national defence, in the first place ; and secondly, to the objects of progressive permanent improvement alluded to, together with the necessary regular expense of administering the government through its legislative, executive, and judiciary branches, the

---

*$16,297,210—the exact sum.

whole of the public revenue will, in the course of a few years, in virtue of the nation being discharged from debt, be at liberty to be applied without reserve or diminution. The national debt once liquidated, no other legitimate objects of expenditure than the necessary one of administering the government, and the two all important ones of defence and improvement, can have existence. The mode of distributing, or applying that portion of the treasure which may annually go to effect improvements, will be the only question at issue.

Now, by reference to the reports of the treasury, it will be seen, that under present circumstances, the expenditure needed per annum, for all the objects above designated, amounts, at extreme allowances, especially as to the military establishment, to about thirteen millions of dollars, including about one million for internal improvements; so that all the difference between this sum of thirteen millions and what may prove to be the amount annually of the nation's income, will be so much additional means to the million which the community will possess for the purposes of improvement.

The thirteen millions here referred to, may be classed thus;—

Military establishment, including the construction of fortifications, acquisition of ordnance, and other permanent preparations of national defence, from 4½ to 6 millions, say,	$6,000,000
Navy, including a standing appropriation of 500,000 dollars per annum towards its gradual increase,	4,000,000
Civil, diplomatic, and miscellaneous, including objects of internal improvement,	3,000,000
	$13,000,000

The nation's income is composed of two items; namely;—

1. The net amount accruing from duties on imports and tonnage.
2. Sales of public lands, which are, by law, pledged to the creditors of the nation.

Of these two items, the aggregate amount, under the circumstances of the year expired, 1827, is about $22,000,000; but, if an average of the three years, 1825, 1826, 1827, be taken, as a better index to the truth we would arrive at, then the said aggregate revenue, for the year, appears to be about $23,000,000; as thus,

Customs.

Net amount in 1825,	$24,358,202
Do. in 1826,	20,248,054
Amount carried forward,	$44,606,256

Amount brought forward, $44,606,256
Net amount in 1827, estimated on a certainty of this sum, and great probability of more, - - - - 20,248,054

$64,854,310

One third of which sum is, - - - - $21,618,103
Sales of lands, for a year; 1 to 1½ million; suppose, 1,500,000

$23,118,103

This, consequently, giving an excess (public debt apart) of 11,000,000 dollars, over and above the hypothecated 12,000,000 for administration and defence. But, to pursue the calculations a step farther, with a view to arrive at, or, if not arrive at, to approach to a correct or very probable estimate as to what may be the nation's annual income, from the same sources, at any given period yet to come, (sinister accidents not intervening, and especially no such alteration, in the impost, or tariff system, taking place, as may have the effect of deteriorating the revenue of the nation) it is here, with deference, submitted, as perhaps not being a very exceptionable criterion, or rule, to calculate by, viz.—

To take the *ratio of the increase* of the last three years over the preceding three years, and apply that as a ratio of increase for the next following three years, and so onward from one period of three years to another.

How near to the truth this rule may approach, experience alone can verify; the plausibility it is at present presumed to have, is chiefly, if not altogether, derived from a consideration of the country's steadily advancing state in point of population, and the great probability of a long, a very long continuance of that state of advancement; sufficient, it is presumed, for giving scope, at one and the same time, both to an increase of manufactures at home, and an increase of dutyable importations under a tariff judiciously graduated.

Assuming, for the present, the rule to be a good one, the following figures will serve to exemplify its application, showing what the annual revenue of the United States may amount to, at the expiration of six years from the 1st January, 1828; the epoch at which it is thought not unlikely the extinguishment of the whole national debt will be effected, with the exception perhaps of a small sum, not redeemable but by consent, before the year 1835; and perhaps, too, government may choose to except the 3 per cent. stock from being paid off; but this is not absolutely certain.

To proceed with the rule,

The net customs on imports and tonnage,		
for the year 1822, amounted to		$20,500,775
The same, for	1823,	17,008,570
The same, for	1824,	20,385,430
	Making, together,	$57,894,775
The same, for 1825, 1826, 1827, as above stated,		$64,854,310

The ratio of which is,—as 9 to 10 and a fraction.

Now, the average annual revenue on the 1st January, 1828, being about $23,000,000; therefore,

As 9 to 10, so is $23,000,000 to $25,555,555, average annual revenue, on the 1st January, 1831.

As 9 : 10 : : $25,555,555 to $28,395,061, average annual revenue, on the 1st January, 1834.

At which epoch, consequently, the present rule holding good, and if it be assumed that the public debt will then have been paid off, and no sinister event taking place to disturb this course and order of things, there will be set at liberty the whole excess of this amount of revenue over and above the twelve millions requisite for the administration of the government, and works of defence: and this excess, which here rises to upwards of sixteen millions, and all subsequent, and still increasing, annual surpluses, will claim to be applied, after such mode and form as shall be agreed on, to the purposes of improvement, as above stated.

It would seem, at this place, not irrelevant to observe, (and be it done with respect and deference) that a different course from the one presupposed in the present calculations, does lie open for choice. Should it, indeed, appear to the majority in the national councils, preferable for the nation to have no surplus revenue at all; no annual balances in the treasury; rather than to surmount all the alleged difficulties in the way of disposing of the same, this state of things can with readiness be brought about by certain regulations of the tariff; as, for instance, let the duties on some foreign articles of importation be reduced or abolished, and the duties on some others be raised to a pitch operating almost to prohibition, for the sake (as it is termed by a multitude of individuals, who have been led to regard little or no more than one side of the question) of fostering and encouraging our home fabrics ;—let this be done, and then the receipts of the custom house will soon sink down to the standard required. But, such a course of policy it is not to be expected can prevail. It may at least with great confidence be relied on, that if experimental measures be adopted, which, after experience had, shall be found, in their practical effect, as regards the nation at large, to be detrimental in the room of being beneficial, they will not be allowed to subsist.

The president has made a pointed declaration of his sentiments to congress, on this important topic.

The great interests, he observes, of an agricultural, commercial, and manufacturing nation, linked in union together, are alike under the protecting power of the legislative authority; and the duties of the representative bodies are to conciliate these interests in harmony. "If the tariff adopted by congress, shall be found, by experience, to bear oppressively upon the interests of any one section of the Union, it ought to be, and I cannot doubt will be, so modified as to alleviate its burthen." "The object of the tariff was, to balance the burthens upon native industry, imposed by the operation of foreign laws, but not to aggravate the burthens of one section of the Union by the relief afforded to another. To the great principle sanctioned by the tariff act, one of those upon which the constitution itself was formed, I hope and trust the authorities of the Union will adhere. But, if any of the duties imposed by the act, only relieve the manufacturer by aggravating the burthen of the planter, let a careful revisal of its provisions, enlightened by the practical experience of its effects, be directed to retain those which impart protection to native industry, and to remove, or supply the place of those provisions which only subserve one great national interest by the depression of another."

NOTE.

The net revenue from customs, for the year 1827, is ascertained to be 22,472,067 dollars.

An official exhibit from the treasury department of the United States, furnishes an instance of custom house punctuality and adroit management, not a little striking in its character. It is as follows; viz.

That the aggregate gross amount of duties, on merchandise imported, received at the various United States custom houses, from 1st January, 1790, to the 1st January, 1828, a period of 38 years, is - - - - - - - $658,361,563
And that, during the same period, the aggregate of bonds which have required to be put in suit, is - - - - - - - $4,369,617

Consequently, the whole defalcation upon the entire amount of duties, for this period of 38 years, amounts to no more than a two-third part of one per cent. Which it is presumed is equal to any thing of the kind in the class of custom house operations, or that of even any other official results, where paying and receiving is the business, to be found now passing, or upon record, in any other part of the commercial world. When it is considered, too, that extensive credits have all along been granted to the payers of this revenue, the result may seem a little marvellous, and give rise to a few satisfactory reflections and deductions.

The subjoined extract, from an English publication on the "Elements of Political Economy," may be regarded as not inappositely inserted at this place.

It leads to a consideration of the question, whether the principle of a total abolition of the restrictive laws and governmental regulations touching matters of commerce, manufactures, and agriculture, now subsisting throughout the world; and a universal and absolute freedom of trade and intercourse to take the place thereof, can, or cannot safely be trusted; and, if the principle can be trusted, whether or not such a state or course of things can or will be produced.

This may be sub-divided and extended, as follows;—

Whether, provided it be allowed that such a state of universal freedom, would have the effect of increasing the productions, the riches, and consequently the physical enjoyments and comforts of the whole world, collectively taken, as an aggregate, *the establishment of such universal freedom be, or be not, practicable,* consistent with, and necessarily productive of an increase of the physical enjoyments of every individual nation and state composing the whole, each one considered in its distinct and separate capacity? If which should be decided in the affirmative, then the most immediate question remaining for solution, stands thus;—what are the preliminary steps to be taken to *enlighten the understandings of each and all communities and nations* upon the point of their own true solid and permanent interests, as well individually as collectively, going hand in hand with universal freedom of intercourse, one with another; and in regard to the separate internal economy of each one within itself:—In other words, so to enlighten mankind, as to produce, in time, *perfect human freedom,* and that freedom to be consistent with the maintenance of a plurality of nations and states as now subsisting through the world. Nations and states, though partaking each of a general increase of *good,* yet, not on that account, to lose their characteristic identities and individualities?

EXTRACT.

We have often been surprised at the manner in which, in parliament, the manufacturing, commercial, and agricultural interests are opposed to each other, as if the interests of all these classes were not one and the same. It is as absurd to suppose that one of these can flourish without the other, or to suppose that the prosperity of one can be increased by the suffering of the other, as to suppose that the legs are injured by the strength of the arms, and would benefit by the diminution of such strength. In a new country, every man is agriculturist and manufacturer. In the course of time it is found that by one man confining himself to cultivating the soil, while others exercise their industry as artisans, all will be gainers. The merchant, as a middle man, connects together the cultivator and the manufacturer. But the demands of the manufacturers and the agriculturists limit each other. There cannot be more food raised than the manufacturers can take off, as there cannot be more goods made than the agriculturists require.

We are supposing a country cut off from all intercourse with other countries. In that case, the manufacturers, the agriculturists, the merchants, must bear a proportion to each other. This is not affected by the existence of a class of state annuitants, by clergy, servants of the state, &c. These merely diminish proportionally the receipts of the producers.

But foreign commerce makes the matter a little more complicated. A densely peopled country employs itself in manufacturing for a country that can employ its industry more beneficially in the cultivation of land. The condition of the intercourse between the two countries is the importation of agricultural produce in return for the exportation of manufactures. To say that no food shall be imported, is to say that no manufactures shall be exported. The agriculturists of England had the wild idea that foreign commerce could be carried on without returns. They imagined that the manufacturing population could be increased, while the ports were shut against food.

Supposing England were to import freely in return for her manufactures, the increasing manufacturing population would always demand more and more animal food from the agriculturists, and all such produce as cannot conveniently be imported. Corn is but one of the productions of the soil, and even corn would not fall much by the importation; because, in all those places which produced for our market, a great rise of price would be experienced on a free intercourse.

Jacta est alea. It has been otherwise decreed. The continent of Europe is becoming every day more and more manufacturing. Even North America—between which and this country, a beneficial commerce of raw produce in return for manufactures might have taken place for ages—has been forced to act on an unprofitable restrictive system. We shall by and by have no other foreign commerce but that with the countries from which we import wines, spices, sugar, tea, and other luxuries, that cannot be cultivated to advantage in England.

In the meantime, as our manufacturing population is excessive, the diminution of beneficial employment must be felt in the diminished demands from the farmer. But misery cannot be extensive in any branch of the population, without affecting all the other branches. Things find their level, except through a process entailing much misery on large classes. Each endeavours to throw the suffering on his neighbour, by means of fraud and artifice, for the path to poverty always abounds in vice and crime. Those who cannot subsist by industry must be maintained, and hence new burdens on the owners of land.

It would be amusing, could one be amused with what has reference to so painful a subject, to hear the evils caused by restrictions on free trade, placed to the account of free trade.

The habits of the country are all formed on a different state of things from that which now prevails. The extension of trade caused by the extraordinary improvements in British machinery, gave, from the demand for labour, and the increased reward for it, an astonishing impulse to our population. Hence the early marriages—hence the miraculous increase of our cities and towns.

The next revolution will, probably, be the destruction of the most of the present land-owners. A diminished demand for manufactures, and decay of the manufacturers, must be felt in a fall of the value of land. This must, to a great extent, place the mortgagee in the room of the nominal owner.

There are countries in which the population remains nearly stationary, from the resources being stationary. In Balbis's elaborate account of Portugal, we are told, " that on the estates which have seigneurs, (*donatarios*) the condition of the cultivators is as miserable as that of the ancient serfs of Russia. Innumerable imposts, known under the name of *raçoes de terco & quarto*, of *jugadas, octaves dizmo coimas;* the harshness of receivers, &c.; all this absorbs almost all the gain of the labourers, to whom there remains hardly enough to support a miserable existence. The young people of both sexes, instead of yielding to the inclinations of nature, by uniting in the sacred bands of marriage, pass their life in libertinism ; others wait till they have made a little fortune." In a list which he gives of the males above seventeen, there appear 310,914 celibatories, and 631,371 married, and of the married, 143,829 had wives above the child-bearing age.

This country is not Portugal ; but we must lay our account, we fear, with changes for the worse.

PUBLIC LANDS.

With regard to this item of revenue under review, as above, although the sales effected by government have not, from the nature and situation of things, been sufficiently productive hitherto, to bear any large proportion in amount to the other item, or customs, from year to year, yet it is obvious, the time must arrive, when, from increased demands for immediate occupancy, if not from increased prices, the article will be an efficient source of revenue.

Hitherto, in 40 years, not more than twenty millions of acres have been sold, because this quantity has sufficed to supply the demand, according to the increase of population within the period, for bringing these new lands into *settlement*. They are sold by government at low prices, and taken up just as fast as the country furnishes new hands, by an increase of people, to take them up and bring them under cultivation.

The lands acquired by the United States, amount to near two hundred and sixty millions of acres, whereof, as above stated, only twenty millions or thereabout have hitherto been sold. About twenty-nine millions have been appropriated as military bounties, donations to colleges, &c.; so that there are now remaining two hundred and eleven millions of acres, held by government as the common property of the Union.

To which if there be added fifty-five millions of acres, the quantity computed of unceded Indian lands within the present limits of the states and territories, also seven hundred and fifty millions lying north and west of the states and territories, we have here one thousand and sixteen millions of acres of land, as an aggregate.

This, it will be perceived, taken in connexion with the provisions of the constitution, with the acts of cession from the old states, and compacts with the new states, all combined; and a condition stipulated, by which, all parties other than the United States government are precluded from becoming the original purchasers from the native Indians, is a treasure of no mean consideration. It is solid capital as well as revenue, which may well constitute a guarantee during ages to come, for the furtherance and eventual accomplishment of any legitimate national enterprises likely to be contemplated and set on foot. How essential, upon this, if on no other ground, does it not appear, that the United States government should continue to be *landed trustee for the Union?* A point, however, that is strenuously contested!!

Besides the lands of Louisiana and Florida, acquired through the purchase of those provinces from France and Spain, the acquisition, it is well known, of the right of soil as to those other regions, in favour of the general government, arose out of voluntary cessions on the part of the states, made chiefly to the old confederation, and which were termed as consisting of their "wild" lands, to be as a source of revenue to meet the expenses of the revolutionary war then prosecuting. The old congress, in 1780, passed an act recommending these cessions, and the cessions were accordingly made to the Union, to pay the debt of the revolution; and it was stipulated that new states were to be formed out of the territories so ceded, whenever a certain quantum of population shall require it; that is to say, 60,000 free inhabitants of a division of territory, should be entitled to claim admisssion into the Union as a new state.

In the year 1802, stipulations on the subject, between Georgia and the United States, took place, so that the public lands of the United States have been derived from four sources; viz.—

1. Cessions made to the old confederation, at the recommendation of the old congress.
2. The compact with Georgia in 1802.
3. The purchase of Louisiana in 1803.
4. The purchase of Florida in 1819.

Now, on the admission, as provided for, of the several new states, which have grown up since that memorable epoch, into the Union, under the present federal constitution, *compacts* were made with each of these new members; by virtue of which the tenure of their lands respectively, or right of soil, remains at this day unaltered, and as it was by the acts of cession from the old states to the Union; to wit; The cessions were made on three substantial conditions, or trusts;—

1. That the ceded territories should be formed into *states*, and admitted in due time into the Union, with all the rights belonging to other states.
2. That *the lands should form a common fund, to be disposed of for the general benefit of all the states.*
3. That *they should be granted, or sold and settled, under such regulations as congress shall direct.*

Thus, then, the new states of the federal Union are circumstanced, so as not to hold, in sovereignty, their own soil. It is contended by many, that political justice, and they think public expediency, abstractedly, both require at present retrocessions or grants by congress, in favour of these states, of the portions of public lands contained within their limits respectively.

But it is nevertheless possible, that the conditions of cession from the old states, and a scrupulous fulfilment of trusts solemnly undertaken in consequence, on the part of the Union, are considerations which may determine the question otherwise.

This public domain, or "national inheritance," has cost, including every charge of purchase, surveying, and sale, 32,911,813 dollars.

But, this sum covers the purchase money of Louisiana and Florida, 20,000,000 dollars paid to France and Spain, which was paid for *sovereignty* of that state and territory, rather than for the soil.

If, therefore, the latter sum be deducted, the total aggregate of public lands, amounting, by measurement in part, and estimate in greater part, to one thousand and sixty-five millions of acres, have really cost the United States, in reference to soil, and including every charge hitherto incurred for surveying, &c. &c. no more than the sum of 12,911,813 dollars;—whilst, on the other hand, the financial advantages which already they have produced to the United States, are as is here stated;—viz.—

Amount of actual sales, to the 30th June, 1828,	$41,950,247
Amount granted in military bounties and private claims, 18,285,777 acres, which, if estimated at 2 dollars per acre, is - - - - -	36,571,554
Amount granted for support of schools and colleges, 7,841,947 acres, which, at the same estimate, is - - - - - -	15,683,894
Amount granted for roads and canals, 1,934,537 acres, which, at the same estimate, is -	3,869,074
	$98,074,769

Balance in favour of the treasury to the 30th June, 1828, 85,162,956 dollars.

CHICKASAW AND CHEROKEE INDIANS.

A *nook* in the rear of " public lands," it is hoped will not be considered as unprofitably intruded upon, if briefly occupied with the *Indian* topic.

The contingent event of the aborigines of the country, or even of selections from among their numerous tribes, being led to that state of pure civilization, or social condition, in virtue of which they may come ultimately to be *secured* in an unmolested retention of any large proportion of the yet unceded Indian lands, it is believed, (and in honest truth is no subject for exultation,) is but visionary. There is, with reference to this subject, a recent "talk" of the Chickasaw Indians, which merits to be recorded. It is cited below. They speak, it will be perceived, *something* for themselves. There is, too, a different occurrence, claiming a short notice, as having, perhaps, the more important bearing of the two; namely, in the tribe of the Georgia Cherokees, having actually commenced, and made some advance in, the administration of a regular, organized, constitutional system of government. Of these Indians, the language is now *in print*, and a newspaper, in Cherokee and English, has found support, and is issued under the title of " *The Cherokee Phœnix,*" or

"New-Echota Gazette." The alphabet of this now written language, consists of 86 different characters, representing so many different sounds, or syllables, the combinations of which make up the language, and to which printing type have been adapted. A system, it would seem, partaking of the nature of the Chinese written language, in as much as these characters are significative of so many simple sounds, or monosyllabic words, in the language as it is spoken, and these syllables or words, possessing each one, a specific determinate meaning; but is a system of language differing from the Chinese in its structure afterward, by a polysyllabic formation out of the 86 elementary sounds or syllables, represented by the 86 newly invented characters or symbols. It is the invention of a Cherokee, not acquainted previously with any language but his native one. His name is Guess, and it is stated, that, within a few months' time from Mr. Guess beginning to teach his countrymen, the acquisition of reading and writing spread through the whole nation, and became common to this people, without the aid of schools or of money.

Council Room, October 9, 1827,
Chickasaw Nation.

Brother! We have opened our ears wide to your talk; we have not lost a word of it. We came together to meet you as an old friend, and to shake hands with you. We were happy, and our hearts grew big, when we heard you had come to our country. We have always thought of you as our friend; we have confidence in you; we have listened more close, because we think so much of you. We know well you would not deceive us, and we believe you know what is best for us and for our children.

Brother! Do not forsake us. Our friends, as you told us, are few; we have none to spare; we know that brother; you think it will be better for us to take your advice. It has truly made deep impressions on our hearts. Without making a long talk, as you are to leave us in the morning, we will state our terms for an exchange of country. We have no objection to our country; if we could be left alone, we might do well; but we are great sufferers; every thing seems against us, and we will agree to almost any thing that can make our condition better. We believe if the government of the United States is honest towards us, and wish us to be a people, and not outcasts always, that we may yet do better. We will now tell you what we will do.

Brother! You would not wish us to move away, and into a country where we could not live, and as well as we live here. Then, as you have pointed us out a country on the north of the state of Missouri, and between the Missouri and Mississippi rivers, and speak well of it; we agree, first and foremost, to go and look at it, and any other country that we may choose. When twelve of our people, three from each district, have examined it, assisted by a scientific doctor, to see to our health, and by three good white men, to be selected by ourselves, and three of your men of science from Washington, or elsewhere—we say, when we have examined it, if we like it, if its soil is good and well wooded, if water is plenty and good, we will agree to exchange, acre for acre: provided, you, on your part, will mark out the country, and divide it into counties, and leave a place in the centre for a seat of government, and then drive every body off of it, and guaranty it to us for ever; and, as soon as may be, divide it for us into farms, and give us a parchment for them to be recorded, with a right to sell to our brothers, with the consent of our father, the president of the United States: and provided also, that in addition, you examine our houses, and mills, and fences, and our workshops here, also our orchards, and build and put up and plant as good there, at such places within the territory as we may choose; also, provided you count our stocks here, and put an equal number, and of each kind, within their respective owners' limits there; also, provided you establish schools in all the counties, sufficient for the education of our children, and to teach our girls how to spin and manage household affairs; and provided, also, you send a sufficient force there to ensure our protection, and organize our people into companies like your militia, to be commissioned by our father, the president of the United States: and provided, that you establish a government over us in all respects like one of your territories, Michigan, for example, and give the right of suffrage to our people, as they shall be prepared, by education, to vote and act, and allow us, after the territory is organized, a delegate, like your territories enjoy, in congress: and provided, there be allowed to some of our people, reservations, not exceeding twenty, to be surveyed and given to them on parchment, to sell, if they please, like the white men.

Brother! Grant us these terms, better our condition as a people, give us the privileges of men, and if the country you point us to, or any other we may find, turns out to be acceptable to us, we will treat for exchange upon the above basis. We ask, also, for a millwright, and three blacksmiths; they will be needed by us.

Brother! We are willing to go, next May, in steam-boats, from Memphis to St. Louis, and thence over the line, and examine the country thoroughly, and, on the following spring, then we shall know all the seasons, and how the climate is. Should you think proper to take us at our offer, provide the means, and let us know in time, say by the 1st of April next. The cost is to be yours, and every thing, and each of our people who may go, must have a fine rifle, and horn, and powder, and lead, and plenty of things for an outfit in provisions, and tobacco, and blankets, and the like.

Brother! Should our offer not be accepted, then we are done. We hope to be let alone where we are, and that your people will be made to treat us like men and Christians, and not like dogs. We tell you, now, we want to make our children men and women, and to raise them as high as yours in privileges. We will have inducements then, to do so ; now, we have not.

Brother! Understand nothing is done, unless the country we go to look at suits, and not then, unless all we require is agreed to on your part.

Brother! We shake hands with you, and our hearts go with you.

    Tisho Mingo, his x mark.
    William M'Gilvery, his x mark.
    Levi Colbert, his x mark.
      Committee of the Nation.
    Stimoluct, his x mark.
    Pus-ta-la-tubbee, his x mark.
    Ma-tash-to, his x mark.
   Witness, PITMAN COLBERT, Secretary.
To Col. Th. L. M'Kenney.

Since the notice above on the Chickasaws was written, there has appeared the *state paper* here annexed, which well merits to be preserved. It is termed a "phenomenon" of its kind.— After the organization of the two houses of the Cherokee congress, or council, it is stated, "The national committee, comprising 16 members, and the national council 24 members, a code of rules was adopted, evidently framed from the rules which governed the proceedings of the United States congress."

From the New-Echota Gazette.

GENERAL COUNCIL OF THE CHEROKEE NATION.

MESSAGE

Of the principal Chiefs of the Cherokee Nation to the General Council.

To the members of the committee and council, in general council convened:—

Fellow citizens,—In addressing you on this momentous occasion, we cannot, in justice to our feelings, forbear a solemn pause, and with grateful feelings, meditate on so many blessings which a kind providence has conferred on us as a people.—Although we have had trials and tribulations to encounter, and in some instances the sad effects of intemperance have been experienced within the circle of our citizens, yet, there is every reason to flatter us in the hope, that, under wise and wholesome laws, the preponderating influence of civilization, morality, and religion, will secure to us and our posterity, an ample share of prosperity and happiness.

Occupying your seats by the free suffrage of the people, under the privileges guarantied by the constitution, the various subjects requiring your deliberation the present session, will necessarily be important. The organization of the new government, the revision and amendments of the old laws, so as to make them in unison with the principles of the constitution, will require your attention; and it cannot escape your wisdom, that the laws should be short, plain, and suitable to the condition of the people, and to be well executed. The judiciary system demands your serious deliberation, and the mode for conducting suits in courts should be free from all complicated formalities, and no other *form* should be required than to let both parties know distinctly what is alleged, that a fair trial may be had.

A law should be passed requiring managers and clerks of all public elections, to register the names of the persons voting, as well as the names of the candidates to whom the votes are given. By observing such a course, illegal voters will be detected, and the elections conducted with more regularity, harmony, and satisfaction.

The public press deserves the patronage of the people, and should be cherished as an important vehicle for the diffusion of general information, and as a no less powerful auxiliary in asserting and supporting our political rights. Under this impression, we cannot doubt that you will continue to foster it by public support. The only legislative provision necessary for conducting the press, in our opinion, is to guard against the admission of scurrilous productions of a personal character, and also against cherishing sectarian principles on religious subjects. The press being the public property of the nation, it would ill become its character, if such infringements upon the feelings of the people should be tolerated. In other respects, the liberty of the press should be as free as the breeze that glides upon the surface.

From the accompanying memorial, signed by several of our respectable citizens, together with the public treasurer, you will discover, that further indulgence is called for in behalf of the public debtors, and it is for your wisdom to determine whether it would be just and proper that the law requiring the treasurer to call in all the money loaned out, should be amended, so as to give further indulgence to the borrowers, that the payments may be made by reasonable instalments. Owing to the extreme scarcity of money, from the general pressure in business, such indulgence would, no doubt, be a great relief; and the probable distress and ruin, from the sacrifices of property, consequent from public sales, may be averted.

After receiving the treasurer's report, and ascertaining the true condition of the public funds, it will also be your province to determine the expediency of making suitable provisions for the erection of a national academy at New-Echota. This subject, for some time past, has been agitated, and is anticipated with the warmest zeal by the reflecting part of our citizens, and it should receive your particular attention. By the treaty of 1819, four tracts of land, equal to fifteen miles square, were reserved for the purpose of creating a revenue for a school fund, to be applied, under the direction of the president of the United States, for the education of the youth of this nation. The lands were to have been sold under the direction of the president, in the same manner as the public lands of the United States; and notwithstanding the repeated and urgent requests which have been made for the sale of these lands, and the no less repeated promise on the part of the general government to attend to it, for reasons unknown, they are not yet sold. We would recommend you to memoralize the president on this important subject, and respectfully to request, that the available funds may be applied to the support of the contemplated national academy.

The several charity schools in this country, under the immediate patronage of benevolent societies of the several states, should not escape your notice. Although the superintendents of these schools, under the direction of respective societies, have the right of conducting them according to the dictates of their own discretion and judgments, yet, without presuming any disparagement to their regulations, we would suggest the expediency of selecting a visiting committee on the part of the nation, for the purpose of inspecting their public examinations, and at such other times as said committee may deem proper, and that they should be required to make a general report on the state of improvement, &c. to be laid before the session of each general council. Such a course, pursued by the authorities of the nation, in relation to these institutions, would no doubt excite an interest among the pupils, and add to the vigilance of their preceptors, and at the same time produce a general satisfaction. An indifferent course, perhaps, might eventually produce relaxation and apathy in their operations; and we should endeavour to avoid the dishonour of any circumstances which might possibly take place, that would defeat the fondest expectations of those upon whose benefaction they are founded.

The circumstance of our government assuming a new character, under a constitutional form, and on the principles of republicanism, has, in some degree, excited the sensation of the public characters of Georgia, and it is sincerely to be regretted that this excitement should have been manifested by such glaring expressions of hostility to our true interests. By the adoption of the constitution, our relation to the United States, as recognised by existing treaties, is not in the least degree affected; but, on the contrary, this improvement in our government is strictly in accordance with the recommendation, views, and wishes of the great Washington, under whose auspicious administration our treaties of peace, friendship, and protection, were made, and whose policy, in regard to Indian civilization, has been strictly pursued by the subsequent administrations.

The pretended claim of Georgia to a portion of our lands, is alleged on the following principles.—First, by discovery; secondly, by conquest; thirdly, by compact.

We shall endeavour briefly to elucidate the character of this claim. In the first place, the Europeans, by the skill and enterprise of their navigators, discovered this vast continent, and found it inhabited exclusively by Indians of various tribes; and by a pacific courtesy and designing stratagems, the aboriginal proprietors were induced to permit a people from a foreign clime to plant colonies; and, without the consent or knowledge of the native lords, a potentate of England, whose eyes never saw, whose purse never purchased, and whose sword never conquered the soil we inhabit, presumed to issue a parchment, called a "Charter," to the colony of Georgia, in which its boundary was set forth, including a great extent of country inhabited by the Cherokees and other Indian nations.

Secondly, after a lapse of many years, when the population of their colonies had become strong, they revolted against their sovereign, and by success of arms, established an independent government, under the name of "the United States." It is further alleged, that the Cherokee nation prosecuted a war at the same time against the colonies.

Thirdly, Several years after the treaties of peace and friendship, and protection, which took place between the United States and the Cherokee nation, and by which the faith of the United States was solemnly pledged to guaranty to the Cherokee nation for ever, a title to their lands, a compact was entered into between the United States and the state of Georgia, by which the United States promised to purchase for the use of Georgia, certain lands belonging to the Cherokee nation, so soon as it could be done on *reasonable* and *peaceable terms.*

Thus stands the naked claim of Georgia to a portion of our lands. The claim advanced under the plea of discovery, is preposterous. Our ancestors, from time immemorial, possessed this country, not by a "Charter" from the hand of a mortal king, who had no right to grant it, but by the Will of the King of kings, who created all things, and liveth for ever and ever.

The claim advanced under the second head, on the ground of conquest, is no less futile than the first, even admitting that the Cherokees waged a war with the colonies, at the time they fought for their independence. The Cherokees took a part in the war *only* as the allies of Great Britain, and not as her subjects, being an independent nation, over whose lands she exercised no rights of jurisdiction; therefore nothing could be claimed from them, in regard to their lands, by the conqueror, over the rights of Great Britain. At the termination of the war, the United States negotiated with the Cherokees on the terms of peace as an independent nation, and since the close of that war, other wars took place, and at their terminations other treaties were made; and in no one stipulation can there be found a single idea that our title to the soil has been forfeited or claimed as the terms of peace; but, to the contrary, we discover that the United States solemnly pledged their faith, that our title should be guarantied to our nation for ever.

The third pretension is extremely lame. The United States enters into a compact with Georgia, that they will purchase certain lands, which belong to us, for Georgia, so soon as they can do it on *peaceable* and *reasonable terms*. This promise was made on the part of the United States, without knowing whether this nation would even consent to dispose of those lands on any terms whatever; and the Cherokees not being a party in the compact, their title cannot be affected in the slightest degree. It appears astonishingly unreasonable, that all those hard denunciations, which have been unsparingly lavished against our sacred rights and interests, by interested politicians, have arose from no other circumstance, than our honest refusal to sell to the United States, lands, for the fulfilment of their compact with Georgia. Although our views and condition may be misrepresented—although we may be stigmatized with the appellation of "*Nabobs*," and should be represented as *ruling* with an "*iron rod*," and "*grinding down into dust the wretched and abject mass*" of our citizens; and although we may be called *avaricious* for *refusing to sell our lands*, we should not be diverted from the path of rectitude. In all our intercourse with our neighbouring white brethren, we should endeavour to cultivate the utmost harmony and good understanding, by strictly observing the relations which we sustain to the United States.

Owing to the various misrepresentations respecting us, we have been frequently called upon to make a treaty of cession; and under the hope of succeeding with us, a treaty has been entered into by the United States, with that portion of the Cherokees who have absolved themselves from all connexion with us, by removing west of the Mississippi, and establishing themselves there as a distinct community, stipulating that all those Cherokees residing east of the Mississippi, who will consent to emigrate west of that river, shall receive a bounty consisting of a *rifle gun*, a *blanket*, a *steel trap*, a *brass kettle*, and *five pounds of tobacco.* Such are the temptations offered to induce us to leave our friends, our relatives, our houses, our cultivated farms, our country, and every thing endeared to us by the progress of civilization—for what? To tread the barren wilds and dreary waste on the confines of the Rocky mountains, with those necessary accoutrements and appendages of the hunter on our backs, in pursuit of the buffalo and other wild animals. With the view of carrying this burlesque on our happiness into effect, the United States' agent for this nation has been instructed, by the secretary of war, to visit us at our firesides, accompanied by James Rogers and Thomas Maw, two of the Cherokees residing west of the Mississippi, and who composed a part of the chiefs that negotiated the late treaty. This extraordinary movement has been made, though without any effect; and we are happy to state, that our citizens generally have treated the agent and his associates with civility, and have with great propriety restrained their indignant feelings from committing any violence on the persons of the two Arkansas chiefs, for the indignity offered by the design of their visit. We would recommend you, as the immediate representatives of the people, to submit a respectful memorial to the congress of the United States, expressive of the true sentiments of the people respecting their situation, and praying that measures may be adopted, on the part of the United States, for the adjustment of their compact with the state of Georgia, otherwise than to anticipate any further cession of land from this nation.

WILLIAM HICKS,
JOHN ROSS.

New-Echota, C. N., Oct. 13, 1828.

In reference to this subject, the president, in his general message to congress, of 2d December, 1828, observes as here follows;—

The attention of congress is particularly invited to that part of the report of the secretary of war, which concerns the existing system of our relations with the Indian tribes. At the establishment of the federal government, under the present constitution of the United States, the principle was adopted, of considering them as foreign and independent powers; and also as proprietors of lands. They were, moreover, considered as savages, whom it was our policy and our duty to use our influence in converting to Christianity, and in bringing within the pale of civilization.

As independent powers, we negotiated with them by treaties; as proprietors, we purchased of them all the lands which we could prevail upon them to sell; as brethren of the human race, rude and ignorant, we endeavoured to bring them to the knowledge of religion and of letters. The ultimate design was to incorporate in our own institutions, that portion of them which could be converted to the state of civilization. In the practice of European states, before our revolution, they had been considered as children to be governed; as tenants at discretion, to be dispossessed as occasion might require; as hunters, to be indemnified by trifling concessions, for removal from the grounds upon which their game was extirpated. In changing the system, it would seem as if a full contemplation of the consequences of the change had not been taken. We have been far more successful in the acquisition of their lands, than in imparting to them the principles, or inspiring them with the spirit of civilization. But in appropriating to ourselves their hunting grounds, we have brought upon ourselves the obligation of providing them with subsistence; and when we have had the rare good fortune of teaching them the arts of civilization, and the doctrines of Christianity, we have unexpectedly found them forming, in the midst of ourselves, communities claiming to be independent of ours, and rivals of sovereignty within the territories of the members of our Union. This state of things requires that a remedy should be provided. A remedy, which, while it shall do justice to those unfortunate children of nature, may secure to the members of our confederation their rights of sovereignty and of soil. As the outline of a project to that effect, the views presented in the report of the secretary of war, are recommended to the consideration of congress.

The outline drawn by the secretary of war, is a masterly sketch. It is replete with the most interesting facts, and sensible observations. A colonization system, on a very broad scale, is recommended, accompanied by legislative enactments, defining clearly the nature of the relations to stand between the whites and the Indian tribes, and especially defining, or prescribing, what shall be the reciprocal rights, both as to property and government, over all the tracts of country which the Indians claim and inhabit. The secretary's concluding paragraph is this, viz.—

"It is, in my opinion, worse than useless to impart education and the arts to the Indians, without furnishing them, at the same time, with appropriate subjects on which to employ them."

A previous passage in the secretary's report, is in these words:

If the project of colonization be a wise one, and of this I believe no one entertains a doubt, why not shape all our laws and treaties to the attainment of that object, and impart to them an efficiency that will be sure to effect it?

Let such of the emigrating Indians as choose it, continue, as heretofore, to devote themselves to the chase, in a country where their toils will be amply rewarded. Let those who are willing to cultivate the arts of civilization, be formed into a colony, consisting of distinct tribes or communities, but placed contiguous to each other, and connected by general laws, which shall reach the whole. Let the lands be apportioned among families and individuals in severalty, to be held by the same tenures by which we hold ours, with perhaps some temporary and wholesome restraints on the power of alienation. Assist them in forming and administering a code of laws adapted to a state of civilization. Let the 10,000 dollars appropriation be applied, within the new colony exclusively, to the same objects for which it is now expended; and add to it, from time to time, so much of our other annual contributions, as can be thus applied without a violation of public faith.

In regard to such Indians as shall still remain within the states, and refuse to emigrate, let an arrangement be made with the proper authorities of the respective states in which they are situated, for partitioning out to them, in severalty, as much of their respective reservations as shall be amply sufficient for agricultural purposes. Set apart a tract, proportioned in size to the number of Indians, to remain in common, as a refuge and provision for such as may, by improvidence, waste their private property; and subject them all to the municipal laws of the state in which they reside. Let the remainder of the reservation be paid for by those who hold the paramount right, at such prices as shall be deemed, in reference to the uses which Indians are accustomed to make of lands, reasonable; and the proceeds to be applied for the benefit of those of the tribe who emigrate, after their establishment in the colony, or to be divided between those who emigrate and those who remain, as justice may require.

It may, perhaps, be fairly doubted, whether the 10,000 dollars appropriation (independently of its tendency to prevent emigration) produces, under the circumstances in which it is now expended, any useful results. These schools, it is true, impart to a certain number of Indian youths, so much information, and so far change their habits, as to inspire them with all the passions and desires, and particularly the passion for accumulating individual wealth, peculiar to a state of civilization; and then these half educated men are turned loose among their respective tribes, without any honourable means of satisfying the desires and wants which have been thus artificially created. The lands of the tribe being common and unalienable, they have no motive to cultivate and improve them; there is no floating wealth to attract their ambition, and the only and usual means of gratifying their cupidity for money, is by employing the advantages acquired by their education, to appropriate to themselves more than their just share of the large contributions annually made by the government: and in this way, they, with some few honourable exceptions, render not only themselves, but the very arts they have acquired, obnoxious to the nation at large.

An official estimate of the number of Indians now within the United States, is reported, as follows:—

- 2,573 within the states of Maine, Massachusetts, Rhode Island, Connecticut, and Virginia.
- 4,820 within the state of New-York.
- 300 within the state of Pennsylvania.
- 3,100 within the state of North Carolina.
- 300 within the state of South Carolina.
- 5,000 within the state of Georgia. (and upwards.)
- 1,000 within the state of Tennessee.
- 1,877 within the state of Ohio.
- 23,400 within the state of Mississippi.
- 19,200 within the state of Alabama.
- 939 within the state of Louisiana.
- 4,050 within the state of Indiana.
- 5,000 within the state of Illinois.
- 5,631 within the state of Missouri.
- 9,403 within the peninsula of Michigan.
- 7,200 within the territory of Arkansas.
- 4,000 within the territory of Florida.
- 20,200 within the country *east* of the Mississippi, *north* of the state of Illinois, and *west* of the three upper lakes.
- 94,300 within the country *west* of the Mississippi, *east* of the Rocky mountains, and not included in the states of Louisiana, or Missouri, or the territory of Arkansas.
- 20,000 within the Rocky mountains.
- 80,000 west of the Rocky mountains, between latitude 44° and 49°.

313,130 Total, by computation.

This statement is not to be taken as an exact census, even for as much of it as respects most of the federal states; and, as to the vast territories not received into the Union, it is evident that the best information obtainable, can do no more than furnish a probable conjecture of the remaining Indian population.

February, 1829.

Another very interesting publication, from the Cherokee *press*, is now selected; as follows;—

From the New-Echota (Cherokee) Phœnix, of January 28.

It is frequently said that the Indians are given up to destruction; that it is the will of heaven that they should become extinct, and give way to the white man. Those who assert this doctrine, seem to act towards these unfortunate people in a consistent manner, either in neglecting them entirely, or endeavouring to hasten the period of their extinction. For our part, we dare not scrutinize the designs of God's providence towards the Cherokees. It may suffice to say, that his dealings have been merciful and very kind. He inclined the heart of George Washington, when we were in a savage state, to place us under the protection of the United States, by entering into a treaty of peace and friendship with our forefathers, on the 2d day of July, in the year of our Lord 1791, in which treaty is the following provision.

"That the Cherokee nation may be led to a greater degree of civilization, and to become herdsmen and cultivators, instead of remaining hunters, the United States will, from time to time, furnish gratuitously the said nation with useful implements of husbandry."

He furthermore inclined that illustrious man, and his successors in office, and the agents of the United States, to carry the said provision into execution. By His overruling providence, a door was opened for the introduction of those implements of husbandry; and at this day, were Washington living, he would find that his expectations and wishes were realized. He would rejoice, and those who compassionated the Indians with him, would rejoice, to see that the Cherokees have in a great measure become herdsmen and cultivators. Where they were accustomed to hunt the deer, the bear, and the beaver, are seen their farms; and they labour peaceably, for the troubles of warfare do not now molest them.

But we cannot enumerate all the dealings of God towards us, in a temporal point of view. They are gracious, and to our minds would convey the belief that he has mercy still in store for us. But what are his dealings in a spiritual point of view! "If the Lord was pleased to destroy us, he would not have shown us all these things, nor would, as at this time, have told us such things as these." We have heard great things indeed; salvation by Jesus Christ. To what purpose has God opened the hearts of Christians of different denominations to commiserate not only the Cherokees, but all the other tribes? To what purpose are contributions freely made to support missionaries and schools? To what purpose is it that these missionaries meet with such remarkable success, and that preachers are arising from among the Cherokees themselves? To what purpose is it that hundreds have made a public profession of religion, and that the number is rapidly increasing? To what purpose is it that the knowledge of letters has been disseminated with a rapidity unknown heretofore; and that eight hundred copies of a Cherokee hymn book is now issuing from our press? What do all these indicate? Do they indicate the displeasure of God against us, and the certainty of our extinction? It is not for man to pry into the designs of God, where he has not expressly revealed them; but from past blessings we may hope for future mercies.

The causes which have operated to exterminate the Indian tribes, that are produced as instances of the certain doom of the whole aboriginal family, appear plain to us. These causes did not exist in the Indians themselves, nor in the will of Heaven, nor simply in the intercourse of Indians with civilized man; but they were precisely such causes as are now attempted by the state of Georgia; by infringing upon their rights; by disorganizing them, and circumscribing their limits. While he possesses a national character, there is hope for the Indian; but take his rights away, divest him of the last spark of national pride, and introduce him to a new order of things; invest him with oppressive laws, grievous to be borne,—he droops like the fading flower before the noon-day sun. Most of the northern tribes have fallen a prey to such causes, and the Catawbas of South Carolina are a striking instance of the truth of what we say. There is hope for the Cherokees, as long as they continue in their present situation; but disorganize them, either by removing them beyond the Mississippi, or by imposing on them "heavy burdens," you cut a vital string in their national existence.

Things will no doubt come to a final issue before long, in regard to the Indians; and, for our part, we care not how soon. The state of Georgia has taken a strong stand against us, and the United States must either defend us and our rights, or leave us to our foe. In the former case, the general government will redeem her pledge solemnly given in treaties; in the latter, she will violate her promise of protection, and then we cannot in future depend, consistently, upon any guarantees made by her to us, either here or beyond the Mississippi.

By those who experience a difficulty, in reconciling within their breasts, one code of rights for the white man, and another for the Indian, the memorial of *Robert Campbell*, a resident of Savannah, and citizen of the state of Georgia, addressed and presented to the senate of the state, may be perused with no small degree of interest. The memorial is brief. It is dated, Savannah, 24th November, 1828. It did not reach to the stage of a discussion in that assembly.

December, 1829.

Having given above the Indians' representation of their case, and the sentiments of president Adams on the subject, communicated in his message to congress, on the 7th of December last, impartiality requires that president Jackson's views of the same ground, as they are now presented to congress, in his message opening the present session, should here be noticed. His words are as follows:—

The condition and ulterior destiny of the Indian tribes within the limits of some of our states, have become objects of much interest and importance. It has long been the policy of government, to introduce among them the arts of civilization, in the hope of gradually reclaiming them from a wandering life. This policy has, however, been coupled with another, wholly incompatible with its success. Professing a desire to civilize and settle them, we have, at the same time, lost no opportunity to purchase their lands, and thrust them farther into the wilderness. By this means, they have not only been kept in a wandering state, but have been led to look upon us as unjust, and indifferent to their fate. Thus, though lavish in its expenditures upon the subject, government has constantly defeated its own policy; and the Indians, in general, receding farther and farther to the west, have retained their savage habits. A portion, however, of the southern tribes, having mingled much with the whites, and made some progress in the arts of civilized life, have lately attempted to erect an independent government within the limits of Georgia and Alabama. These states, claiming to be the only sovereigns within their territories, extended their laws over the Indians; which induced the latter to call upon the United States for protection.

Under these circumstances, the question presented was, whether the general government had a right to sustain those people in their pretensions? The constitution declares, that "no new state shall be formed or erected within the jurisdiction of any other state," without the consent of its legislature. If the general government is not permitted to tolerate the erection of a confederate state, within the territory of one of the members of this Union, against her consent, much less could it allow a foreign and independent government to establish itself there. Georgia became a member of the confederacy, which eventuated in our federal union, as a sovereign state, always asserting her claims to certain limits; which having been originally defined in her colonial charter, and subsequently recognised in the treaty of peace, she has ever since continued to enjoy, except as they have been circumscribed by her own voluntary transfer of a portion of her territory to the United States, in the articles of cession of 1802.

Alabama was admitted into the Union on the same footing with the original states, with boundaries which were prescribed by congress. There is no constitutional, conventional, or legal provision, which allows them less power over the Indians within their borders, than is possessed by Maine or New-York. Would the people of Maine permit the Penobscot tribe to erect an independent government within their state? and unless they did, would it not be the duty of the general government to support them in resisting such a measure? Would the people of New-York permit each remnant of the Six Nations within her borders, to declare itself an independent people, under the protection of the United States? Could the Indians establish a separate republic on each of their reservations in Ohio? And if they were so disposed, would it be the duty of this government to protect them in the attempt? If the principle involved in the obvious answer to these questions be abandoned, it will follow, that the objects of this government are reversed; and that it has become a part of its duty to aid in destroying the states which it was established to protect.

Actuated by this view of the subject, I informed the Indians inhabiting parts of Georgia and Alabama, that their attempt to establish an independent government would not be countenanced by the executive of the United States, and advised them to emigrate beyond the Mississippi, or submit to the laws of those states.

Our conduct towards these people is deeply interesting to our national character. Their present condition, contrasted with what they once were, makes a most powerful appeal to our sympathies. Our ancestors found them the uncontrouled possessors of these vast regions. By persuasion and force, they have been made to retire from river to river, and from mountain to mountain, until some of the tribes have become extinct, and others have left but remnants to preserve, for a while, their once terrible names. Surrounded by the whites, with their arts of civilization, which, by destroying the resources of the savage, doom him to weakness and decay, the fate of the Mohegan, the Narraganset, and the Delaware, is fast overtaking the Choctaw, the Cherokee, and the Creek. That this fate surely awaits them, if they remain within the limits of the states, does not admit of a doubt. Humanity and national honour demand that every effort should be made to avert so great a calamity. It is too late to inquire whether it was just in the United States to include them and their territory within the bounds of new states, whose limits they could control. That step cannot be retraced. A state cannot be dismembered by congress, or restricted in the exercise of her constitutional power. But the people of these states, and of every state, actuated by feelings of justice, and regard for our national honour, submit to you the interesting question, whether something cannot be done, consistently with the rights of the states, to preserve this much injured race?

As a means of effecting this end, I suggest, for your consideration, the propriety of setting apart an ample district west of the Mississippi, and without the limits of any state or territory now formed, to be guaranteed to the Indian tribes, as long as they shall occupy it: each tribe having a distinct control over the portion designated for its use. There they may be secured in the enjoyment of governments of their own choice, subject to no other control from the United States, than such as may be necessary to preserve peace on the frontier, and between the several tribes. There the benevolent may endeavour to teach them the arts of civilization; and by promoting union and harmony among them, to raise up an interesting commonwealth, destined to perpetuate the race, and to attest the humanity and justice of this government.

This emigration should be voluntary: for it would be as cruel as unjust to compel the aborigines to abandon the graves of their fathers, and seek a home in a distant land. But they should be distinctly informed, that if they remain within the limits of the states, they must be subject to their laws. In return for their obedience, as individuals, they will, without doubt, be protected in the enjoyment of those possessions which they have improved by their industry.—But it seems to me visionary to suppose, that, in this state of things, claims can be allowed on tracts of country on which they have neither dwelt nor made improvements, merely because they have seen them from the mountain, or passed them in the chase. Submitting to the laws of the states, and receiving, like other citizens, protection in their persons and property, they will, ere long, become merged in the mass of our population.

Moreover, in order to be thoroughly communicative, both abroad and at home, as well as strictly impartial; on the principle, that is, of stating the whole of the truth relative to this momentous Indian question, and of not drawing, or at least not setting forth any conclusion from the premises whatever, on one side or the other, it is deemed proper, in this place, to quote from one other writing of the day, because it refers to ex-president Monroe's opinion on the subject, as formerly addressed to congress. Here follows the quotation :—

THE GEORGIA INDIANS.

That the reader may know what measures are contemplated in Georgia, we subjoin a few leading features of a bill now pending in the legislature of that state, to take effect from and after the 1st day of June next.

"Sect. 8. That all laws, usages, and customs, made, established, and in force in the said territory, by the said Cherokee Indians, be, and the same are hereby, on and after the 1st day of June, 1830, declared null and void.

"Sect. 9. That no Indian, or descendant of Indian, residing within the Creek or Cherokee nations of Indians, shall be deemed a competent witness, or a party to any suit, in any court created by the constitution or laws of this state, to which a white man may be a party."

There are other sections, extending the criminal laws over the Indians, apportioning their lands among the counties of Carroll, De Kalb, Gwinnet, Hall, and Habersham; another section imposes full taxes upon every Indian 21 years of age and upwards, &c. &c.

This act, if passed, and if allowed by the federal government to be enforced, will inflict a wound upon our national honour, which all the waters of the Mississippi would be insufficient to wash away. It was our intention to have referred to the special message of president Adams upon this subject, every word of which deserved to be written upon the walls of the capitol in letters of gold. But we have not time. The opinion of president Monroe upon this great question, however, was no less open and explicit, than that of his illustrious successor. The following is from his last message :—

"I have no hesitation, however, to declare it as my opinion, that the Indian title was not affected in the slightest circumstance by the compact with Georgia, and that there is no obligation on the United States, to remove the Indians by force. The express stipulation of the compact, that their title should be extinguished at the expense of the United States, when it may be done *peaceably* and on *reasonable* conditions, is a full proof that it was the clear and distinct understanding *of both parties to it*, that the Indians had a right to the territory ; in the disposal of which they were to be regarded as free agents. An attempt to move them by force, would, in my opinion, be unjust. In the future measures to be adopted in regard to the Indians within our limits, and in consequence, within the limits of any state, *the United States have duties to perform, and a character to sustain, to which they ought not to be indifferent.*"

On general politics, as regards the country's condition at this moment, the sentiments of speaker Stevenson, in his address just delivered to the house of representatives, at Washington, on the occasion of congress opening their session, are so very cogent and luminous, and withal so happily expressed, that it is thought they may be perused and re-perused with increased pleasure and profit; and therefore, it is concluded, that an insertion of them at this place will prove acceptable, and not need other apology than the remark just made.

In assembling again to consider the condition of our beloved country, I seize the occasion to offer you my cordial congratulations upon its prosperity and happiness, and the still more exalted destinies that await it. Whilst our relations with foreign powers are distinguished by alliances and good will, which serve but to render our friendship more valuable to each, and more courted by all, our situation at home, under the influence of virtuous and patriotic councils, is peaceful, united, and happy. How long these blessings are to be enjoyed by us, and secured to our children, must depend upon the virtue and intelligence of the people; the preservation of our happy Union; and the virtuous, liberal, and enlightened administration of our free institutions.

That our confederated republic can only exist by the ties of common interest and brotherly attachment—by mutual forbearance and moderation, (collectively and individually,) and by cherishing a devotion to liberty and union, must be apparent to every candid mind; and as our fathers united their counsels and their arms, poured out their blood and treasure, in support of their common rights, and by the exertions of *all*, succeeded in defending the liberties of *each*, so must we, if we intend to continue a free, united, and happy people, profit by their counsels, and emulate their illustrious example.

How much will depend upon the conduct and deliberations of the national legislature, and especially of this house, it is not needful that I should admonish you. I need not, I am sure, remind you, gentlemen, that we are here the guardians and representatives of our entire country, and not the advocates of local and partial interests: that national legislation, to be permanently useful, must be just, liberal, enlightened, and impartial: that ours is the high duty of protecting all, and not a part—of maintaining inviolably the public faith—of elevating the public credit and resources of the nation—of expending the public treasure, with the same care and economy that we would our own—of limiting ourselves within the pale of our constitutional powers, and regulating our measures by the great principles contained in that sacred charter, and cherishing in our hearts the sentiment, that the union of the states cannot be too highly valued, or too watchfully cherished.

These are some of the great landmarks, which suggest themselves to my mind, as proper to guide us in our legislative career. By these means, gentlemen, we shall not only render ourselves worthy of the high trust confided to us, but we shall endear to our people the principles of their constitution and free institutions, and promote a sentiment of union and action, auspicious to the safety, glory, and happiness of our beloved and common country.

The public debt referred to, is composed, as here stated; viz.

6	per cent. stock, redeemable	in 1826,	-	$ 2,744,423
6	do.	do.	in 1827,	-	13,096,543
6	do.	do.	in 1828,	-	9,490,099
4½	do.	do.	in 1829,	-	769,668
4½	do.	do.	in 1830,	-	769,668
5	do.	do.	in 1831,	-	18,902
5	do.	do.	in 1832,	-	18,902
4½	do.	do.	in 1832,	-	10,000,000
5	do.	do.	in 1832,	-	999,999
5	do.	do.	in 1833,	-	18,901
4½	do.	do.	in 1833,	-	2,227,364
4½	do.	do.	in 1834,	-	2,227,364
5	do.	do.	in 1835,	-	4,735,296
3	do. at the pleasure of government,				13,296,248
5	do. issued in payment of Bank United States shares,	-	-	-	-	7,000,000

Total of funded debt, 1st January, 1828, $ 67,413,377

Deduct the last item of 5 per cents; government holding, in bank shares, a convertible equivalent, - - - - - - - 7,000,000

Total of debt, $ 60,413,377

On the 1st January, 1816, after sundry floating claims, growing out of the late war, had been funded, the debt amounted to about 126½ millions. To which may be added, five millions created afterwards, as the stipulated price paid to Spain in purchase of the Florida territory; making, together, 131½ millions of dollars, and showing, that besides the interest during the twelve years last past, there has been 71 millions principal of the debt paid off. There existed, likewise, at the close of the war, certain direct internal taxes of the general government, to the amount of 12½ millions of dollars ; from which burthen, the people were forthwith relieved; these taxes all surrendered up and extinguished.

These two or three facts stated, it follows, that the receipts of the United States custom house have been made equal to *great* objects in these twelve years ; and may well, under similar management, be relied on for the future. Without any additional revenue, save the limited sum derived from sales of land, they have been rendered sufficient, in the hands of government, for all the affairs of state, including *extraordinaries*, such as payment of old debts, appropriations to an extension of the nation's defences, also to works of internal improvement, facilitating general trade and intercourse, and six millions of dollars surplus at this day in the treasury.

The magnitude and importance of these twelve years' operations, will perhaps be made tolerably apparent, by the sketch of an enumeration here presented ; namely,—

Principal of debt paid off, 71,000,000 of dollars.

Aggregate of annual interest paid, 60,000,000 of dollars.

Claims that grew out of the war, to a considerable amount, besides the funded items, satisfied.

The navy maintained, and increased.

An army establishment supported.

A regular system of national defence, commensurate with the wants of the country, instituted, and prosecuted.

Appropriations for works of internal improvement, favouring general trade and intercourse.

Discharge of a debt of gratitude, in favour of surviving soldiers of the revolution.

Annuities to Indian tribes.

Augmented expense of foreign intercourse.

Expenses of the whole legislative, judiciary, and executive branches of the government, comprising state, treasury, war, and navy departments, the post-office establishment, mint establishment, light-houses, and various miscellaneous items appertaining to the Union of *twenty-four* states and *three* territories.

As above stated, the amount of debt, exclusive of the 3 per cents., and the Bank of the United States stock subscription, is	$47,117,129
The quarterly accruing interest on these stocks, from 1st January, 1828, down to the 31st December, 1835, when, if not previously redeemed by consent, every part will have become redeemable, amounts to	16,225,828
Principal and interest together,	$63,342,957

Or, average annual amount required for the payment of both principal and interest, being one-eighth, is 7,917,869 dollars.

Consequently, the existing annual appropriation of ten millions to the sinking fund, is more than sufficient, by 2,082,131 dollars annually, for the object of extinguishing the whole of this debt by the period here specified. The same appropriation, during six years only, would, with consent of parties, be nearly equal to the object. But, as most probably will be the case, should no item of the debt be redeemed prior to its full term of maturity; then, and in that case, the annual appropriations to the sinking fund may be curtailed ; for, as appears by this calculation, there would accumulate, supposing it were continued at the present rate for the eight years, a surplus in the sinking fund treasury, to the amount of 16,657,543 dollars.

The accumulation, from the annual ten millions, is shown as follows ;—

Required for payments of principal and interest,

in 1828,	$9,079,375	surplus $	920,625
in 1829,	8,725,996		1,274,004
in 1830,	8,372,618		1,627,382
in 1831,	8,019,240		1,980,760
in 1832,	7,672,059		2,327,941
in 1833,	7,491,042		2,508,958
in 1834,	7,126,009		2,873,991
in 1835,	6,856,618		3,143,382
Total payments,	$63,342,957	total surplus,	$16,657,043

If it be assumed, that the ten millions to the sinking fund be continued down to the latter period, for the purpose of buying in, or paying off the 3 per cent. stock along with the rest ; government deciding to do so, it is evident this also can be done, without absorbing the whole surplus as above. There will, on the contrary, still remain of it between three and four millions of dollars, upon the extreme supposition, that no portion of the said 3 per cents. were obtainable, by the commissioners, at a less price than par.

So that the sinking fund, on its present footing, is thus much more than competent to the extinguishment of the whole national debt, by the 31st December, 1835. And then,

In 20 years from the 1st January, 1816, debts to the amount of 207½ millions of dollars, as above shown, principal and interest, will have been liquidated, and extraordinary objects besides accomplished.

December, 1828.

In a further review of the national debt, extended down to the end of the present year, and reported to congress, the secretary shows, that in 12 years, counting from the 1st January, 1817, the year in which the act establishing the sinking fund passed, to the 1st January next, there will have been made payments, besides *extra sums* paid on account of principal, comprehending certain amounts obtained on loan at a lower rate of interest than 6 per cent., to replace stock at that interest paid off, as also certain amounts accumulated in the treasury under the effect of the double-duty system ; that besides these latter, there will have been made payments, by which, in these said 12 years, the national debt will have been positively lessened in amount of principal, by means of surplus funds in the treasury, to the extent of $65,129,829. And during the same period, the payments on account of interest, will amount to $57,835,664, making together, in these 12 years, $122,965,493.

Which, consequently, exceeds the allotted sum of ten millions of dollars per annum, to the sinking fund, for these purposes, in the amount of 2,965,493 dollars.

All which goes to corroborate the statements made above, in regard to 12 years operations, counting from the 1st January, 1816, to the 1st day of last January.

For the last 4 years, the payments stand thus ;—

in 1825,	-	$12,099,045
in 1826,	-	11,039,444
in 1827,	-	10,001,586
in 1828,	-	12,163,567
Making, in these 4 years,		$45,303,642
Whereof,	$14,930,454	is interest,
	30,373,188	principal paid off.

Of the 12,163,567 dollars for 1828, 9,061,496 dollars is principal, consisting all of 6 per cent. stocks, save a small balance of treasury notes, and minute fraction of old registered debt, both together, 10,254 dollars. This year's payments, therefore, reducing the whole debt of 60,413,377 dollars, as it stood last January, down to 51,362,135 dollars, which the nation will owe on the 1st January, 1829. The particular stocks composing it are noted below.

The secretary wisely observes, that assuming the stated sinking fund appropriation of ten millions, to be forerun in the same proportion in future years, as it has been this year, the debt may in effect be totally paid off in little more than 4 years to come. That is to say, exclusive of the 3 per cent. stock. The secretary, on stating that the market price of this portion of the public stocks has ranged, during the last 4 years, at from 80 to 85, at the same time remarks, that as a sure evidence of the stable resources of a country, actual and prospective, is to be found in the prices which its funded debt bears in the money market ; so the stocks of the United States, keeping at an elevation above par, is an indication of the high credit of the United States government; and the more decidedly so, from the consideration that these stocks are redeemable at short periods, and, as experience declares, will be as quickly redeemed, in fact, as the periods arrive. The heavy fall of stocks in England, towards the close of 1825, affected those of the United States less than might have been expected from the connexion of business between the two countries.

Debt of the United States on the 1st January, 1829, viz.—

6 per cents. now redeemable,				$16,279,824
4½	do.	redeemable	in 1829,	769,668
4½	do.	do.	in 1830,	769,668
5	do.	do.	in 1831,	18,901
5	do.	do.	in 1832,	18,902
4½	do.	do.	in 1832,	10,000,000
5	do.	do.	in 1832,	999,999
5	do.	do.	in 1833,	18,901
4½	do.	do.	in 1833,	2,227,364
4½	do.	do.	in 1834,	2,227,364
5	do.	do.	in 1835,	4,735,296
3	do.	at the pleasure of government,		13,296,248
5	do.	issued in payment of Bank of the United States shares,		7,000,000

Total of funded debt, 1st January, 1829, $58,362,135
Deduct the last item of 5 per cents. ; government possessing, in bank shares, an equivalent convertible into money at pleasure - - 7,000,000

True total of debt, 1st January, 1829, $51,362,135

to be the subject of a " phenomenon," and undergo complete extinction in the year 1835 ; nothing very extraordinary happening to prevent.

NOTE.

The national debt of 16 kingdoms and 44 principalities in Europe, is stated as amounting to 744,000,000 of pounds sterling.

The national debt of Great Britain, is 777,000,000 of pounds sterling.

To recur to the topic of *surplus revenue ;*—

It has been said, on the floor of congress, that, when our public debt shall be paid off; when the great works for national defence shall be completed; and when the demands upon our treasury, growing out of the consequences of the revolutionary and late wars, shall be extinguished, or reduced within a small amount; that then, the whole expenses of the federal government, which may be termed *ordinary expenses;* civil, military, naval, diplomatique, miscellaneous, all included; will be reduced to less than 9 millions of dollars per annum. If which view be taken as a correct anticipation, and be coupled with another one, in the flattering prospect, from calculations stated, of a revenue of not less than 25 to 28 millions, accruing from customs, about the year 1835,—that is likely to be the period, not only for an occurrence which the world, according to an expression used, will behold with astonishment; namely, "*the spectacle of a great nation without a national debt;*" but the occurrence likewise, of a huge annual balance being introduced into the national treasury, claiming to be disposed of; its employment to be for general benefit, or that of all the states composing the Union, in as much as each state of the Union, and every individual thereof, will have contributed to produce the said treasury surplus, by their consumption, respectively, of foreign commodities imported.

How the great object can best and most satisfactorily be attained, or, in other words, after what mode and manner the country at large will, through her representatives, consent to become enriched, is, as yet, matter of doubt; yet is a subject that begins already to stir up some warmth of public debate.

The questions to be decided are, however, not numerous; but may be said to array around them a certain degree of intricacy, not favourable to perfect harmony of sentiment among the parties; arising, as it would seem, out of the predominance of state or sectional feeling, over a well balanced comprehensive survey of the general prosperity of the nation, and the objects best suited to it. The questions, nevertheless, with whatever of difficulty they carry about them, are to be legislatively pronounced upon, and a choice must be the consequence;—there is no alternative: they appear to be in substance, as here follows:—

1. Whether such annual surpluses as may accrue in the United States treasury, shall remain wholly at the disposal of the general government; and be, as in all cases of surplus hitherto, from time to time appropriated by congress, in the soundness of their discretion, to objects of the highest national importance, calculated to subserve the best interests of the Union, and of *all its component parts;* as, for instance, the establishing and endowing, or efficiently supporting seminaries of elementary and progressively useful education, throughout all the states and territories; again, such improvements over the face of the country, as will most effectually facilitate intercourse between the great

geographic divisions of the Union;—whether this mode of directing the application of the nation's annual surplus treasure, arising as at present out of duties on importations, is to be adopted; or not?

2. Whether the duties now in force on certain articles of importation from abroad, shall be repealed, or modified in such a way as to prevent, as much as possible, the accumulation of any surplus money annually in the United States treasury, over and above the ordinary and necessary expenses of the general government; or not?

3. In case of a repeal of certain duties taking place; and if, after all the reductions that can be made, the event should prove to be such, that there still be found surplus revenue in the United States treasury; shall congress retain the power, which it is contended she possesses, of appropriating the same, *at her discretion*, to fulfil the best interests of the nation at large, to the extent of all the means in hand? or, will it appear preferable, that some rule be devised, according to which, a distribution of all surplus revenue found in the United States treasury, may annually be made, among the several states of the Union; to be employed on such objects as the state authorities of each one respectively shall decide to be proper?

It is evident, that if the tariff does not admit of being so cut down as to liberate the nation entirely from the occurrence of any annual surplus from duties; then such surplus money, be the amount more or less, must either be employed by the general government for the people, or return in kind to the people, from whom it has been collected, by means of a distribution among the several states.

4. Admitting the discovery of some rule, not otherwise onerous to the nation than in its power of reduction, by which all the surplus receipts into the treasury, over and above the ordinary expenses of the general government, may be prevented; the question here is, as to the sound, or the safe policy of adopting such a measure?

It has been remarked in congress, that the internal improvements, facilitating intercourse between the great geographical divisions of the country, towards which the fostering attentions of the general government hitherto have been called, embrace a few great works only; and that a majority of these will be executed by private companies, requiring but small additional aid from government. The range of canals along the coast is gradually advancing. A canal, and a railway, each to connect the Atlantic with the Ohio, are commenced, and will not require very great aid from congress. The extension of the Cumberland road, through the north-western states, now in progress, will require small annual appropriations. And to complete the *sys-*

tem of roads, so called, there must be a road from the capital to the lakes; one other from the capital to New-Orleans, and branching through the capitals of Ohio, Kentucky, Tennessee, and Mississippi; the annual appropriations for which roads will not be large. In short, the whole system, it is supposed, of canals and roads, to the extent it has thus far been taken up by the general government, or contemplated, will not, for its accomplishment, require over the sum of $2,000,000 a year; and this probably for no great number of years. The which once provided for, it is added, a distribution of the surplus revenue among the states, if that should be resorted to, will effect every thing else which is desirable.

In this year, 1829, there will have been paid, of the public debt;—

Amount of interest,	$2,563,994	
On account of principal in the 6 per cents.,	9,839,265	
		12,403,259

And the residue will therefore consist of; viz.

6 per cents., now redeemable,		$ 6,440,556
4½ per cents., redeemable in 1830,		1,539,336
5 do. do. in 1830,		18,901
5 do. do. in 1831,		18,902
5 do. do. in 1832,		1,018,901
4½ do. do. in 1832,		10,000,000
4½ do. do. in 1833,		2,227,364
4½ do. do. in 1834,		2,227,364
5 do. do. in 1835,		4,735,296
3 do. redeemable at the pleasure of government,		13,296,249
5 per cents., issued in payment of Bank United States shares,		7,000,000
Total of funded debt, that will remain due on the 1st January, 1830,		48,522,869
Deduct the last item of 5 per cents.; government possessing, in bank shares, its equivalent, convertible into money at pleasure,		7,000,000
True total of funded debt, 1st January, 1830,		$41,522,869

"The fortification of the coasts, and the gradual increase of the navy," observes the president, "are parts of a great system of national defence, which has been upwards of 10 years in progress, and which, for a series of years to come, will continue to claim the constant and persevering protection and superintendence of the legislative authority."

In another communication too, to congress, the president observes, on this subject, with additional emphasis ;—

"The first of these great systems, is that of fortifications, commenced immediately after the close of our last war, under the salutary experience which the events of that war had impressed on the nation in favour of its necessity.

"This, combined with corresponding exertions for the gradual increase and improvement of the navy, prepares for our extensive country a condition of defence adapted to any critical emergency which the varying course of events may bring forth. Our advances in these concerted systems have, for the last ten years, been steady and progressive.

"The next of these cardinal measures of policy, is the preliminary to great and lasting works of public improvement, in the surveys of roads, examination for the course of canals, and labours for the removal of the obstructions of rivers and harbours, first commenced by the act of congress of 30th April, 1824."

The present navy list, 27th November, 1828, stands thus:—

Including the vessels built, and building, it consists of,

Ships of the line,	12
Frigates,	20
Sloops of War,	16
Schooners,	4

For what remains to be finished of this, as also gradual additions to it, provision being made by law.

The secretary of the navy remarks, "no condition of either our commercial or political relations, will permit its diminution ; no probable change can demand a large augmentation. Under a wise and efficient administration, our coasts and commercial interests may always be protected by an active force, not much, if any thing, beyond, 15 ships of the line, 20 frigates, 30 sloops, a few smaller vessels, and 10 or 12 steam-batteries. Our safety lies in the nation's peculiar position, and in having our small navy in the most perfect state for efficiency and action."

The secretary calls the attention of congress, to some topics of deep and increasing interest ; viz.

A survey of the coast.

An organization of both the navy and marine corps.

A criminal code.

An increase of rank.

A naval school.

A change in the form, not the substance, of the appropriation.

A suitable provision for naval hospitals.

A passage across the Isthmus, to the Pacific.

A system for forming and educating American seamen, sufficient for our wants.

The establishment of a naval academy, that shall furnish the youth of the country entering the service, with theoretic instruction; and especially, that shall lay a suitable foundation for the higher attainments appropriate to the profession and its contingent circumstances; or, the attainment of such qualifications as shall prove to be equal to a proper discharge of any, or of all the great trusts, in various situations, to which the duties of the service may lead;—is a measure very forcibly recommended by the actual position of the United States, as a member of the community of nations; and will, in all probability, take effect as speedily as the plan and details of such institution can be thoroughly considered, and the proper arrangements made.

The distinguished, and apparently, in every respect, merited reputation, to which the infant institution of the United States military academy, has thus early attained, is of itself no slender recommendation in favour of the other proposed one.

The president's language, addressed to congress, on the West Point academy, is in the highest degree exhilarating to the country:—

"It is the most important undertaking in itself, and the most comprehensive in its consequences. It is the living armory of the nation. While the other works of improvement are destined to ameliorate the face of nature; to multiply the facilities of communication between different parts of the Union; to assist the labours, increase the comforts, and enhance the enjoyments of individuals, the instruction acquired at West Point, enlarges the dominion, and expands the capacities of the mind. Its beneficial results are already experienced, in the composition of the army, and their influence is felt in the intellectual progress of society."

A measure that may aptly be considered as a correlative, in as much as it may most happily lay open an area of the widest dimensions, for all the *budding* science of the country, here referred to, military as well as nautical, to be freely exercised upon, is now as strenuously called for, and most likely on the eve also of being adopted. It is, apart even from the high consideration spoken of, of the very first importance to the national interests, in both a political and a commercial point of view. The measure is, that of effecting a complete systematic survey of the whole coast of the United States, designating the islands, shoals, roads, and anchorage, situate within 20 leagues of any given point of the coast; the courses, distances, &c. between conspicuous points or head lands, one with another; and extending such examinations to St. George's and other banks, to the

Gulf stream, and generally to all places as well beyond as within the said 20 leagues, the examinations whereof, accompanied with accurate delineations, can in any wise promote the benefits of navigation, or safety of the navigator.

The plan, as far as regards the coast, and both in its military and its nautical character, was digested many years ago; and valuable instruments were provided for its execution. This was done about the year 1807, under the administration, and the immediate patronage, of Mr. Jefferson; congress voting 50,000 dollars for the object.

Instruments for two observatories were in consequence imported, and some preparatory operations took place; but the country's becoming politically convulsed, interfered; and of late years, even the whole, in the shape of a regular system, has been suspended. Detached, unconnected, surveys, have been relied on for occasional purposes.

The plan is this:—

1. The ascertaining, by means of a series of astronomical observations, the true position of a few prominent or remarkable points on the coast; such as are, or probably will be, the sites of forts, of light-houses, &c.

2. Astronomical survey, by a chain of triangles, of the line of coast between those points; marking therein the position of every prominent object distinguishable at a distance.

3. A nautical survey of the shoals and soundings; of which, the trigonometrical land survey *to be the base;* depending as little as may be on the astronomical observations made on board of ship.

Mr. F. R. Hassler was the learned gentleman, who, in 1807, devised plans, with a view to an accurate survey of the coast of the United States, and who, in virtue of his communications, made in the first instance to Mr. Secretary Gallatin, was engaged by government, upon the then proposed service. Mr. Hassler embarked for England, to procure instruments; and, on his return, a slight commencement, as above mentioned, was made in the scientific operations. But at the utmost, they were merely preparatory for what the plan intended, and particularly in the establishment of two observatories, one either in the state of Maine, or else at Washington, and the other at New-Orleans. A full view of Mr. Hassler's arrangements and methods, may be had, on consulting the Philosophical Transactions of Philadelphia; the paper which comprises the account of them having been communicated by the gentleman himself. Professor Silliman's Journal, Vol. 16. contains a note in the words here following;

"The suspension of the operations of the survey of the coast of the United States, begun in so admirable a manner, by Mr.

Hassler, may be considered as a national misfortune. It is such, in truth, not so much for the loss of the previous expenditures, in consequence of the delay, or from the deferring of its advantages to a future period, as from the fact, that the principles and methods proposed, and some of them actually used by Mr. Hassler, were in advance of the science of Europe at that period. As these principles and methods require the highest proficiency in mathematical and physical science, their application to practice originally in the United States, would have redounded to the national honour."

NOTE.

The aggregate number of seamen, &c., now (1829) in the United States service, at sea, is 4745, employed at 4 stations; viz.

Mediterranean,	2230 men.	224 guns.
Pacific, -	800 "	90 "
Brazil coast,	705 "	78 "
West Indies,	1010 "	120 "
	4745 men.	512 guns.

Of the United States army, the official returns are;
Eastern department, 2530 troops.
Western   do.   2203 do.

Making an aggregate of 4733 in the two departments, composed of 44 posts. One department under the command of a brevet major general, the other under that of a brevet brigadier general.

November, 1829.

United States Army and distribution;—

Fort Brady,	Sault St. Mary,	Michigan Terr.
Fort Mackinack,	Michilimackinac,	Do.
Fort Howard,	Green Bay,	Do.
Fort Dearborn,	Head Lake Michigan,	Do.
Fort Gratiot,	Outlet Lake Huron,	Do.
Fort Niagara,	- - - -	New-York.
Madison Barracks,	Sackett's Harbour,	Do.
Hancock Barracks,	Holton Plantation,	Maine.
Fort Sullivan,	Eastport,	Do.
Fort Preble,	Portland,	Do.
Fort Constitution,	Portsmouth,	N. Hampshire.

Fort Independence,	Boston,	Massachusetts.
Fort Wolcott,	Newport,	Rhode Island.
Fort Trumbull,	New-London,	Connecticut.
Military Academy,	West Point,	New-York.
Fort Columbus,	New-York,	Do.
Fort Delaware,	Near Newcastle,	Delaware.
Fort M'Henry,	Baltimore,	Maryland.
Fort Severn,	Annapolis,	Do.
Fort Washington,	On the Potomac,	Do.
Fortress Monroe,	Old Point Comfort,	Virginia.
Bellona Arsenal,	Near Richmond,	Do.
Fort Johnson, N. C.	Near Smithville,	North Carolina.
Fort Moultrie,	Charleston,	South Carolina.
Augusta Arsenal,	Augusta,	Georgia.
Oglethorpe Barracks,	Near Savannah,	Do.
Fort Marion,	St. Augustine,	Florida.

Eastern department, 27 posts; 2895 troops.

Fort Snelling,	Upper Mississippi.
Fort Crawford,	Prairie des Chiens, Michigan Terr.
Fort Winnebago,	Portage, Fox, and Ouisconsin rivers, Do. do.
Fort Armstrong,	Rock Island,
Cantonment Leavenworth,	Right bank of the Missouri, near the Little Platte, Missouri.
Jefferson Barracks,	Near St. Louis, Do.
Cantonment Gibson,	- - - - Arkansas Terr.
Cantonment Jessup,	Near Nachitoches, Louisiana.
Baton Rouge,	Baton Rouge, Do.
Fort Wood,	Chef Menteur, Do.
Fort Pike,	Petite Coquille, Do.
Fort St. Philip,	Near New-Orleans, Do.
Cantonment Clinch,	Near Pensacola, Florida.
Cantonment Brooke,	Tampa Bay, Do.
Fort Mitchell,	Near Creek agency, Alabama.

Western department, 15 posts, 2463 troops.

EXPORT TRADE AND NAVIGATION.

"In England, fifty years ago, the whole value of our exported produce, both native and foreign, was just 15 millions of money. Now, the value of exported British produce alone, is upwards of 50 millions of money." *Edin. Obs.*

The United States export, for the twelve months ending on the 30th of September, 1825, has been, in value, as follows:—
It is true, this has been a year of great speculation in trade:—

Domestic commodities, - $ 66,944,745
Foreign do. reshipped, 32,590,643
Total,————$99,535,388
15,000,000 pounds sterling are equal to - 66,666,666

So that it appears, the export of the United States, in domestic articles alone, for the year lately expired, has exceeded in value, the whole export of Great Britain fifty years ago; and further it appears, that the domestic articles of the United States so exported, exceed in value, two-sevenths of the exports of Great Britain in domestic articles, during the last year; and that the United States foreign export during the same, amounts to one-seventh more, making three-sevenths.

The United States export for the last twelve months, of 99,535,388 dollars, as above stated, shows an excess in amount over that of the year preceding, of 24,600,000 dollars, and an excess over the average amount of the three preceding years of 1822, 1823, 1824, of 25,600,000 dollars;

The exports of those years having been as follows:—

1822. Domestic, - - - $49,874,079
Foreign reshipped, - 22,286,202
———— $72,160,281
1823. Domestic, - - - $47,155,408
Foreign reshipped, - 27,543,622
———— 74,699,030
1824. Domestic, - - - $49,684,709
Foreign reshipped, - 25,248,779
———— $74,933,488

For these three years, the average proportion of the domestic exports, to the foreign, was as two to one nearly: for the year last past, it has been somewhat more in favour of domestic. Furthermore it appears, that out of the whole export of 99½ millions for the past year, 88¾ millions have been exported in United States bottoms; which shows the preponderating state of our navigation, over foreign, in a competition of equal tonnage duties and charges in our ports; an equality that now prevails, according to treaties with foreign nations, without material exceptions, as a rule.

The navigation of the United States, by which this trade is carried on, may be reviewed as follows:—

From 1792, the year immediately preceding the revolutionary war of France, down to near the end of 1807, the United

States commercial marine rose from 564,457 tons, to 1,268,548; an increase of 704,091 tons: that is to say:—

In the year 1792, vessels engaged in foreign voyages,	411,438
Coasting trade and fisheries,	153,019
Tons,	564,457
In the year 1807, vessels in foreign voyages,	848,306
Coasting trade and fisheries,	420,242
Tons,	1,268,548

At this epoch, there commenced a series of restrictions, such as embargo, &c., and war ensued, till 1815. In which opening year of peace, the United States commerce was eagerly resumed, and the tonnage engaged in its navigation surpassed even that of former prosperous times: it stood thus;—

Vessels in 1815, engaged in foreign voyages,	854,294
Do. in coasting trade and fisheries,	513,833
Tons,	1,368,127

But this sudden spring from fetters into activity, very naturally carried things, for the moment, beyond their maintainable bounds. In a little while from that period, navigation received a shock, as might have been expected, and during three or four years, a decrease was experienced. In 1821, however, commerce with us was no longer languishing; it had taken a decided start again; and the tonnage was as follows:—

Vessels engaged in foreign voyages,	593,825
Do. in coasting trade and fisheries,	705,132
Tons,	1,298,957

At the close of 1824, it stood thus:—

Vessels engaged in foreign voyages,	636,806
Do. in coasting trade and fisheries, whereof 33,345 tons in the whale fishery,	752,357
Tons,	1,389,163

At the close of 1825, thus:—

Vessels engaged in foreign voyages, including the whale fishery,	700,788
Vessels in the coasting trade and fisheries,	722,323
Tons,	1,423,111

On the 31st December, 1826, the aggregate mercantile tonnage was, - - - Tons, 1,534,190

So that, upon the whole, it appears the commercial marine of the country has increased, in the course of 34 years from 1792, near a million of tons; and, although after the first year of peace, 1815, had expired, there was a retrogradation, occasioned by excessive importations during that year, combined with some other causes, the reaction of which was felt for three or four years, yet, the commercial tonnage of 1826 has risen, it appears, above that of the active year 1815, by 166,063 tons, and it continues on the rise. Since the year 1792, the fisheries and coasting trade have increased five-fold, and more.

The tonnage, on the 31st December, 1827, is officially reported at, viz.—

Registered vessels employed in foreign voyages, 747,170
Enrolled and licensed vessels, including 84,278 tons
  employed in the fisheries, and 40,097 tons of steam-
  navigation, - - - - - 873,437

Total merchant tonnage of the United States, 31st
  December, 1827, - - Tons, 1,620,607

Of British merchant foreign tonnage, the total amount is stated, on the 5th January, 1828, at 2,150,605 tons, composed of 18,035 ships.

The British export of produce and manufactures, in the year 1826, amounted, according to official valuation,
  to £46,453,021 sterling.
  in 1827,   40,332,254
  in 1828,   51,276,448

December, 1828.

The United States importations, during the four years, 1825, 1826, 1827, 1828, amount in value to $350,202,469.

Those, however, for a small fraction of the present year yet to expire, being of course given on probable estimate, in place of actual knowledge.

The United States exportations for the same years, calculated in the same way, amount in value to $337,202,426, of which export, $233,069,035 is composed of domestic produce and manufactures, and $104,133,391 composed of foreign commodities re-exported.

Importations during the four preceding years of 1821, 1822, 1823, 1824, value $303,955,539.

Exportations during the same, $287,820,350, of which export, $191,350,881 is composed of domestic produce of the soil and manufactures, and $96,469,469 composed of foreign commodities re-exported.

Average import annually for the years, 1821, 1822, 1823, 1824,		$75,988,884
Average export; domestic,	$47,837,720	
Foreign, reshipped,	24,117,367	
		71,955,087

Average import annually, for the years, 1825, 1826, 1827, 1828,		$87,550,617
Average export; domestic,	$58,267,258	
Foreign, reshipped,	26,033,347	
		84,300,605

The *receipts into the treasury*, which are always chiefly dependent upon the importations as subject to custom house dues, but which, besides the customs and the regular sales of public lands and dividends on bank shares, include likewise, occasionally, some accidental items of receipt, have amounted, for the last four years of 1825, 1826, 1827, 1828, to near 98 millions of dollars; of which, however, the sum of 5 millions consisted in a new loan, obtained in 1825, at a low rate of interest, for the purpose of paying off a like sum of old existing stock bearing a higher interest, and not otherwise from any deficiency of assets in the treasury; this allowance made, the aggregate receipts, from the regular sources, including a probable estimate as regards the fraction of a year yet unexpired, appear to be about 93 millions; out of which, about 14 millions of dollars have been expended on internal works, designed to improve the condition of the country, or otherwise, expended on objects not belonging to the mere annual support of government in its civil, military, and naval establishments.

The said 93 millions of dollars, aggregate receipts into the treasury for these four years, is found to exceed, by 18 millions, the aggregate receipts for the preceding period of four years, namely, 1821, 1822, 1823, 1824, and shows, consequently, one period compared with the other, an average annual increase of 24 per cent.

Now, whilst the increase in receipts has been at this rate of proportion, the increase of expenditure, aside from what has been paid towards reducing the old debt, has been less than 10 per cent., and this latter occasioned chiefly in planning and giving effect to internal improvements. The average annual increase in the consumption of foreign articles, one period compared with the other, has been 18 per cent.

In a word, it is thus made apparent, in regard to the flow of prosperity, these periods compared together, that, the general foreign commerce of the country has been steadily advancing;— First, in the value of her exports, at the average rate of 17 per cent.; and, taking that portion of exports, the productions of the soil and of manufacture, apart from re-exportations of foreign commodities, the advance has been nearly 22 per cent. In foreign articles merely, at the rate of 8 per cent. Secondly, in the value of her importations, at the rate of 12 per cent.; and in her actual consumption of foreign articles, at the rate of 18 per cent.

During all which, it is to be well remarked, that, although the nation's revenue passing in to the public treasury, has been increased, by this course of things, at the rate of 24 per cent., yet, the nation's annual expenditure, aside from payments made in liquidation of former debt, has not increased more than, or so much as, 10 per cent.; and that this is principally laid out in extra improvements of the country.

It is believed too, as the secretary observes, that the shipping of the United States will be found to have increased in a fair ratio with commerce and revenue. The returns, however, under this head, are not yet sufficiently complete to speak with precision.

But, more than all, as a source of wealth flowing in to the national community, though without being indicated by corresponding riches in the public treasury, is to be distinguished, the advanced state of domestic manufacture, throughout several states of the Union, improved, in the course of these eight years, in almost every useful branch, and at this moment advancing in improvement with accelerated energy. Did it fall within the scope of the present article to enter into particulars on this head, or, were it in fact susceptible of being appreciated and described, like the increase of foreign trade, with a per centum accuracy, the picture might, perhaps, startle those taking a lively interest in such things, who have not rendered themselves familiar with the past and present circumstances of the country's condition.

The secretary of the treasury's report to congress, which embraces a lucid retrospect of the principal financial operations, and their results, contains the following emphatical passage, apposite to what has been here stated;—

The foregoing statements indicate a steady advance in the national prosperity. The reality of this advance is only to be measured by aggregate results, ascertained at proper intervals of time. It is useful to present such results. They show the general condition of the country, viewed not in parts, but under one undivided whole. They attest the positive growth of its riches and the rapidity of growth by comparison. They afford resting points for doubtful opinions, when all desire to arrive at those that may appear best supported by results. No single eye can take them all in, unassisted by the authentic returns which it is the province of the government, and chiefly of the department of the treasury, to watch over and promulgate, endeavouring also to trace them to their causes. A state whose natural resources and territory are abundant, whose institutions are free, and whose interests are diversified, may witness occasional and temporary pressure upon some one of those interests, whilst all the great branches of its industry are in course of sure development. But transient inconvenience is lost in the aggregate prosperity, and must, in the end, participate in that prosperity. It is thus that great states, under successful systems of legislation, go onward in their career of riches and power. Not only has there been a marked increase of importations and revenue in the United States during the last four years, and of exportations of domestic commodities, but a like diminution in re-exportations. The latter is very striking, and justifies the inference not merely of an increased desire to import for the purpose of meeting the contingencies of trade or speculation, but of an increased ability in the country to purchase and use foreign fabrics. The increased consumption of the latter, and the increase in revenue, have exceeded the ratio of the increase of duties under the tariff of 1824, and the presumed increase of population also. The exports of domestic products have increased more than four-fold faster than the increase of population, as given by the census at periods the most favourable. These facts cannot mislead. They point to an unequivocal increase, so far, in the prosperity of the nation. Statistical testimonials, for a single year, or for more than one, may rise or fall in amount, from causes that postpone all permanent conclusions; but where they are seen to go on in an increasing train, throughout a succession of years, it is rational to ascribe them to causes beginning to assume a fixed character. If we review the last four years, as a period of time in commercial history, we find little in the circumstances of the world, either from general war or otherwise, to affect foreign markets beyond the ordinary fluctuations incident to trade at all times. The extraordinary operations in the cotton market, that fell upon the first of these years, viz., 1825, are not conceived to impair the applicability of the remark, because there has been time enough for diminished exportations, as a consequence of the large exportations of that year. No term, indeed, of eight years, since the establishment of the government, has been so exempt from the influence of external events, that disturb the regular operations of national industry and commerce, as the last eight. None, therefore, could be so fairly taken for the comparative statements that have been made.

It does not escape recollection, that from 1781 to 1815, there were epochs when the foreign commerce of the country advanced with even more rapidity than is here stated; when it was greater, absolutely, and therefore greater in proportion to the population of the country. But during that long interval, there prevailed in Europe, with scarcely a perceptible interruption, desolating wars, which created an unparalleled demand for our staple productions, and brought them up to extravagant prices. This, with our neutral attitude, which gave to our carrying trade a scope almost unbounded, raised exportations and importations to an artificial pitch, that can never be recurred to as a standard of comparison for commerce, under circumstances more ordinary and regular. It is known, that during portions of that interval, our trade in foreign produce far exceeded that in domestic. It is wholly otherwise now. The mere profits on our tonnage, at that earlier day of the republic, by the capital which it introduced, gave, of itself, the capacity for an enlarged consumption of foreign articles, on a comparatively smaller basis of population.

A WORD ON SILK,

Is here solicited, on the ground of this beautiful production being destined to become, one day, an item that will go to swell very perceptibly the export bill of the United States. That day will arrive promptly, after the mulberry trees, of approved kind, now planting and about to be planted, shall be in full bearing.

On this matter, the following *extract* is presented for the anticipations of the reader, as pleasing, circumstances weighed and considered, as his best judgment will allow them to be. Those of our community, already somewhat conversant in this eastern staple, and who may now be at the most pains to scrutinize the subject, will perhaps be those precisely having the most reason to be pleased with the results presented to their imaginations.

AMERICAN SILK.

An extract of a letter from a gentleman of Lyons, in France, containing the proceedings of the Chamber of Commerce in relation to American silk, &c.

The proceedings were originally published in the "Precurseur," a paper published at Lyons, January 3d, 1830.

Chamber of Commerce.—The chamber had requested one of its members to cause to be assayed at Lyons, the silk that has lately been prepared at Philadelphia.

The assay took place recently upon a sample prepared by Mr. d'Homergue, of Nismes, son of Louis d'Homergue, late proprietor of a splendid filature of silk, in the said town.

It results from that assay, publicly executed at Lyons, by

Pierre Mazel, licensed assayer of silks, that the raw silk obtained in Philadelphia, is of an extraordinary quality, and is admirably adapted to the uses of fabrication. Its degree of fineness is 16 dwts., so that it would produce singles of 50 dwts., organzine of 32, and tram or woof silk of 30; a quality of silk extremely rare in our country. American silk is fine, nervous, good, regular, clean, of a fine colour; in a word, it unites all the qualities that can be wished for. Its market price in the state of raw silk, well reeled, according to its different qualities, well prepared, would be 26 francs a pound, and the sale of it at Lyons would be very easy, particularly if there was a constant supply of bales, weighing from 100 to 150 pounds.

The chamber of commerce loses no time in publishing information so satisfactory. They ought, more than ever, to excite the Americans to plant mulberry trees and raise silk, a kind of industry that will afford great advantage to both countries, and may in future give birth to establishments of various kinds, and be a new source of wealth to the United States.

POST OFFICE AND POST ROADS.

The revenue of the general post office, this year, 1827, will exceed its expenditure, by upwards of 100,000 dollars, with every prospect of the receipts, which this year have amounted to near 1,500,000 dollars, being from year to year considerably increased. The number of post offices within the United States, now amounts to 7000. And, so admirable, not to use the term *perfect*, is the organization of the establishment all together, that, it is thought not too much to say of *it*, and of *good roads* for travelling, viewed in connexion, *the facilities of intercourse between fellow-citizens, in person or by correspondence, will soon be carried to the door of every villager in the Union.* The president himself observes, "of the indications of the prosperous condition of our country, none can be more pleasing than those presented by the multiplying relations of personal and intimate intercourse, between citizens of the Union dwelling at the remotest distances from each other."

On the 1st of July, 1828, the number of post-offices within the United States, which in the year 1792 was less than 200, is found to have swelled to 7,651.

And the year's revenue, which, in 1792, was - $67,444
amounts, for the 12 months last past, to - - $1,598,134

The length of post-roads, which, in 1792, was no more than 5,642 miles, has advanced to - - - *Miles,* 114,536

The transportation of the mail, for the year last past, has amounted in distance to 13,610,039 miles;

Whereof, in mail stages,	6,439,594
On horseback and in sulkeys,	7,170,445

In the year 1812, the whole revenue of the post-office amounted to $649,208

Consequently,—

The increase of revenue, since then, has been   948,926

Making, for 1828, as above, - - - $1,598,134

It is remarked, in the postmaster-general's report, that the extension of the mail has been accompanied by great increase of expedition, on almost all the important routes. On many of them, it is now conveyed at the rate of 100 miles per day; and, in some instances, more.

From the year 1789, *to the* 1*st of July*, 1829,

The whole amount of postages received, has been $26,441,496

Expenses, viz.

For transportation of the mail,	$16,052,513	
Compensation to post-masters,	7,829,925	
Incidental,	896,967	
Together,		$24,779,405

Producing, consequently, an aggregate revenue into the treasury, to this time, of $1,662,091.

1830.

It is in agitation to extend a mail route, from St. Mark's, Florida, via Key West, to the Havana, and establish a regular mail-intercourse, to and from; at least, the citizens of Tallahassee are petitioning congress to this effect.

It appears, from a Spanish document, that the United States commerce with the Island, for the year 1829, has amounted as follows:—

Imports from the United States, in vessels of the
United States, - - - - - $4,086,230
Imports from the United States, in Spanish vessels,   610,797

                                                                $4,697,027

Imports from Spain, in vessels of the United States, $2,065,060
Imports from other countries, in vessels of the United States, 974,996

$3,040,056

The amount of all imports, for the year 1829, stated at - - - - - - - $14,925,414

Roads of various descriptions, appertaining to the several states, it need not here be observed, are incessantly multiplying; but it is satisfactory to notice, that, at the present day, many of those which are planned, and some in actual execution, are on a grand scale, and of the highest importance, as respects both partial and general intercourse. It is not too much to expect, that a lapse of years, greater or less, will supply occasion for the whole settled country to be pervaded by turnpikes, or other travelling-roads as good; and for every important district being besides intersected by canals or railways, in as much as one or other of these two modes of improvement, or both, can be applied with any advantageous results.

A national military road, striking from Washington city, westward, is now in a respectable state of progress: a portion of it, called the "Cumberland road," long since completed, has latterly been added to, and a location by the United States' engineers is at present made, as far west as the boundary line between Indiana and Illinois states; the line of road from Cumberland passing through Brownsville, Wheeling, Canton, Zanesville, Columbus, Little Darby, Springfield, Richmond, Indianapolis; from whence the location will be continued through Illinois state, to the permanent seat of government in the state of Missouri, and the road itself, it is supposed, may be constructed in three years from this time, 1828. From the western frontier of Missouri, a road of intercourse has, pursuant to act of congress, 3d March, 1825, and with permission of the Indians, been marked out to the confines of New-Mexico.

Another division of national road is to extend from Washington city to New-Orleans; and for this, four routes have been examined, but neither one as yet projected or surveyed; possibly the route through Knoxville, and through West Tennessee, and by way of Baton Rouge, in Louisiana, may receive a preference; and, in that case, a great branch may strike off from Zanesville, in Ohio state, to Florence, in Alabama, passing through Lexington of Kentucky, and Nashville, Tennessee.

A third division of national road will strike northward from Washington city, and terminate at Buffalo, on lake Erie; for which an examination of the ground has been made by engineers of the United States, and a circumstantial report thereof exists.

A great variety of routes, between the two points, are pointed out, with their geographical and local peculiarities and distinctions. One of them, denominated "Painted Post route," appears to offer advantages over some of the others; but a minute survey and levelling, yet to be made, additional to what is already done, will have influence in finally deciding the choice.

Distance of National Road, viz.

	Miles.
From Washington, district of Columbia, westward, to the permanent seat of government in Missouri state; passing through Cumberland, Wheeling, Zanesville, Columbus, Indianapolis, Vandalia, St. Louis. Distance,	1,350
From the same, south-westward, to New-Orleans; passing through Knoxville and West Tennessee, also Baton Rouge, in Louisiana,	1,200
From the same, northward, to Buffalo, on Lake Erie; passing through Westminster, Williamsport, Peter's camp, Painted post,	372½
Branch, from Zanesville, in Ohio state, to Florence, in Alabama; passing through Lexington, Kentucky, Nashville, Tennessee,	600
National road,	3,522½

Other branches are proposed, to various points of the Union, where it may be of importance for a military road to centre or to terminate; but any conclusive designation in regard to these, is necessarily postponed, until a location of the main stems, north-west, west, and south-west, as above, from Washington, shall be completely fixed. "To connect the seat of the federal government, by the shortest lines of communication, with the capitals and great cities of the several states; and the most exposed and remote frontiers of the United States; is deemed a primary object, because essential to the national safety, and one of the most efficient preparations for war."

The graduation of these roads is not to exceed 4° with the horizon. The one to Buffalo, as above, it is calculated, will run thus:—

Miles, 282½ of 2°
66 of 3°
24 of 4°
———
372½

Cost of construction, agreeably to the M'Adam system, this section, estimated $1,855,171; or, about $5000 per mile.

JANUARY, 1830.

An actual location of the road westward, has taken place as far as Vandalia, Illinois state, and experimental surveys have been carried, by the United States' engineers, from Vandalia, through St. Louis, along the south side of Missouri river, to the town of Jefferson, Missouri state.

1830.

RATES OF CANAL TOLLS BY THE LATEST REGULATIONS.

Rules for the Collection of Toll on the Schuylkill Navigation, and Rates of Toll for 1829:

I. The toll is to be charged on the weight of articles in boats (except boats for passengers), marked with their tonnage, as herein provided; the master or owner exhibiting a list of them, with their quantities and weights, and complying with the provisions of the laws and the regulations of the board of managers. Toll is to be charged on boats passing up, in addition to the toll on the articles.

II. All boats, whose owner or skipper shall refuse or neglect to have them marked with their tonnage, as herein provided, or shall refuse to exhibit a list of the articles on board, with their quantities and weights, shall be charged $6\frac{1}{4}$ cents per ton, for the whole tonnage, for each lock the boat may pass through below Reading, and 4 cents above, as authorized by the act of incorporation.

III. The tonnage of boats to be ascertained by loading on board, in the canal at Fair Mount, kentledge provided and marked for the purpose, and the boat to be marked with copper nails for every 2 tons put on board.

IV. In every case where a boat is offered to pass a lock, without having the tonnage marked upon her, or a special permit, the collectors or lock-tenders are to take the following course:—

1st. To propose to the owner or master of the boat, to name

a person resident within two miles of the lock, to unite with one to be named by the collector or lock-tender, to measure and mark the boat.

2d. If the owner or master declines, then the collector or lock-tender himself to choose a person to ascertain the tonnage, and by the tonnage so ascertained, to charge the toll as mentioned in the second article.

V. The places for the "general offices" of collection are at Fair Mount, Reading, and Mont Carbon; those for the "intermediate offices" are at Flat Rock, Oakes canal, Vincent canal, Hamburg canal, and Waterloo. At the general offices, the toll may be paid, and a permit issued, to pass to the next office of collection, or to the place of destination, 5 per cent. being deducted; the intermediate offices can grant permits, and allow the same discount to the next office or place of destination, provided it be not farther than to the next general office in any case. No further allowance will be made, at any other time or place, on any account whatever, nor shall a permit be issued until the money be paid. No boat which has passed a "general office" without taking out a permit, can be allowed a discount at any "intermediate office."

VI. The rates of toll are fixed by the lock, and are to be paid at each lock or set of locks, unless a permit is taken out as provided in the fifth article. Between Philadelphia and Reading, toll will be charged for 36 locks, being the whole number, except 3 at Fair Mount, for passing which toll will not be charged, except on boats and articles which pass those locks only; and toll between Reading and Port Carbon will be charged for 76 locks, being the whole number, except the 10 upper locks, for the passage of which toll will not be charged, except on boats and articles which pass those locks only, or some of them.

On boats or vessels passing up, except boats for passengers.	Between Philadelphia and Reading.	Four cents per lock,	144 cents.
	Between Reading and Port Carbon.	Two cents per lock,	152 cents.

On coal, limestone, stone, plaster of Paris, iron ore, sand, manure, and clay.	Between Philadelphia and Reading.	One and a half cent per ton per lock,	54 cents per ton.
	Between Reading and Port Carbon.	Three-fourths of a cent per ton per lock,	57 cents per ton.

On coal, *from Port Carbon to Philadelphia*, one dollar nett per ton.

On bricks, lumber, lime, marble, bark, cord-wood, cider, fruits, vegetables, hay, straw, oysters, beer, and porter.	Between Philadelphia and Reading.	Two cents per ton per lock, - -	72 cents per ton.
	Between Reading and Port Carbon.	One cent per ton per lock, - - - -	76 cents per ton.

On flour, grain, and seeds of all kinds; salt, salted beef, pork, and fish; lard and butter.	*Between Philadelphia and Reading.*	Two and a half cents per ton per lock,	90 cents per ton.
	Between Reading and Port Carbon.	One and a quarter cents per ton per lock,	95 cents per ton.

On all articles not enumerated.	*Between Philadelphia and Reading.*	Three cents per ton per lock,	108 cents per ton.
	Between Reading and Port Carbon.	One and a half cents per ton per lock,	114 cents per ton.

On boats or vessels, made and used for the transportation of passengers.	*Between Philadelphia and Reading.*	Twenty cents per lock,	7 dolls. & 20 cents.
	Between Reading and Port Carbon.	Ten cents per lock,	7 dolls. & 60 cents.

Passage boats to be allowed to carry seventy-five pounds of baggage for each passenger on board, without charge for tolls.

On lumber in rafts, passing down through a canal where there is a slope to the dam, -- -- -- -- -- -- -- -- Four cents per 1000 feet per lock.

On lumber in rafts, passing down where there is no slope to the dam, -- -- -- -- -- -- -- -- -- -- Toll free.

On lumber and logs in rafts, passing up, -- -- -- -- Four cents per 1000 feet per lock.

List of the Quantities of various Articles which are to be deemed and estimated as a Ton, in Collecting the Tolls, viz.

Flour, Ten barrels and a half.
Whiskey, Eight barrels, or two hogsheads.
Wheat, Rye, Indian Corn, Flaxseed, Forty bushels.
Oats, Eighty bushels.
Barley, Fifty bushels.
Stone, Four-fifths of one perch.
Salt Fish, Seven barrels and a half, or fourteen half barrels.

Lumber,
- 2,000 3 feet shingles.
- 3,000 2 feet shingles.
- 5,000 1 foot 6 inch shingles.
- 1,000 barrel staves and heading.
- 700 hogshead staves and heading.
- 500 pipe staves and heading.
- 100 rails or posts.
- 1,000 hoop poles.

Cord-Wood, Half a cord.
Bricks, Five hundred.
Salt, Liverpool Fine, Forty-five bushels.
All other kinds, Thirty-two bushels.
Tar, Seven barrels.
Rosin, Eight barrels.
Oysters, Four thousand.
Lime, Twenty-eight bushels.
Window Glass, Two thousand eight hundred feet.

Rates of Toll upon the Union Canal.—1830.

ARTICLES.	PER TON, &c.	Toll per Mile.	Toll the whole Distance.
		Cents	Dolls. Cts.
Ashes, pot and pearl,	Per Ton of 7 barrels,	1½	1 20
Bark,	Cord,	1	0 80
Do. ground,	Ton,	1¼	1 00
Bricks,	Ton of 500	¾	0 60
Beef, salted,	Ton of 8 barrels,	1½	1 20
Boards and other sawed stuff,	1000 feet, board measure,	1¼	1 00
Barley,	Ton of 50 bushels,	1½	1 20
Butter,	Ton,	1½	1 20
Clay,	Ton,	½	0 40
Cider,	Ton of 8 barrels, or 2 Hhds.	1½	1 20
Coal,	Ton,	¾	0 60
Corn, Indian,	Ton of 40 bushels,	1½	1 20
Earth,	Ton,	½	0 40
Fish, salted,	Ton of 7½ barrels, or 14 half-bbls.	1½	1 20
Flour,	Ton of 10½ barrels,	1½	1 20
Furniture, household,	Ton,	2	1 60
Grindstones,	Ton,	1	0 80
Gypsum,	Ton,	1	0 80
Hay,	Ton,	1	0 80
Hoop poles, for barrels,	Ton of 400		
Do. for hogsheads and pipes,	Ton of 200	1	0 80
Heading for do.	Ton of 400		
Do. for barrels,	Ton of 500		
Iron, bar, blooms, or wrought,	Ton,	1¼	1 00
Do. castings,	Ton,	1¼	1 00
Do. ore,	Ton,	½	0 40
Do. pig,	Ton,	1	0 80
Lard,	Ton,	1½	1 20
Lime,	Ton of 28 bushels,	¾	0 60
Limestone,	Ton,	½	0 40
Manure,	Ton,	½	0 40
Marble, unwrought,	Ton,	¾	0 60
Do. manufactured,	Ton,	2	1 60
Merchandise,	Ton,	2	1 60
Mill stones, and French burrs,	Ton,	1¼	1 00
Oats,	Ton of 80 bushels,	1½	1 20
Oysters,	Ton of 4000,	2	1 60
Pork, salted,	Ton of 8 barrels,	1½	1 20
Posts, and rails, split,	Hundred,	1	0 80
Rye,	Ton of 40 bushels,	1½	1 20
Rosin,	Ton of 8 barrels,	2	1 60
Salt, fine,	Ton of 45 bushels,	2	1 60
Do. coarse	Ton of 32 bushels,		
Seed, clover,			
Do. flax,	Ton of 40 bushels,	1½	1 20
Do. of all other kinds,			
Shingles,	Thousand,	¾	0 60
Straw,	Ton,	½	0 40

562 INTERNAL NAVIGATION

ARTICLES.	PER TON, &c.	Toll per Mile.	Toll the whole Distance.
		Cents	Dolls. Cts.
Staves, for pipes,	Per Ton of 400	1	0 80
Do. for hogsheads,	Ton of 500		
Do. for barrels,	Ton of 600		
Stone,	Ton of four-fifths of a perch,	½	0 40
Tar,	Ton of 7 barrels,	2	1 60
Timber, round and square,	90 solid feet,	1¼	1 00
Wheat,	Ton of 40 bushels,	1½	1 20
Whiskey, and other domestic distilled spirits,	Ton of 2 Hhds. or 8 barrels,	1¾	1 40
Window glass,	Ton of 2800 feet,	2	1 60
Wood,	Cord,	1	0 80
On all articles, not enumerated, passing eastward,	Ton,	1½	1 20
On all articles, not enumerated, passing westward,	Ton,	2	1 60
On passage boats,	Mile,	20	16 00
On boats used for transportation, carrying over 5 tons,	Mile,	2	1 60
On boats, if empty, or carrying not more than 5 tons, besides the toll on cargo,	Mile,	4	3 20
For passing the outlet locks at Middletown, (except such boats as have come or are going immediately on the Union Canal,)			
On every loaded boat,			0 75
On every empty boat,			0 50

Union Canal Office, Philadelphia, January 1st, 1830.

Recapitulation of the Rates of Toll.

ARTICLES.	Toll per Ton, per Mile.	Toll the whole Distance.	PER TON, &c.
	Cents	Dolls. Cts.	
Ashes, pot and pearl,	1½	1 20	Per Ton of 7 barrels.
Beef, salted,	1½	1 20	Ton of 8 barrels.
Barley,	1½	1 20	Ton of 50 bushels.
Butter,	1½	1 20	Ton.
Cider,	1½	1 20	Ton of 8 barrels.
Corn, Indian,	1½	1 20	Ton of 40 bushels.
Fish, salted,	1½	1 20	Ton of 7½ barrels, or 14 half-bbls.
Flour,	1½	1 20	Ton of 10¼ barrels.
Lard,	1½	1 20	Ton.
Oats,	1½	1 20	Ton of 80 bushels.
Pork, salted,	1½	1 20	Ton of 8 barrels.
Rye,	1½	1 20	Ton of 40 bushels.
Seed, clover, Do. flax, Do. of all other kinds,	1½	1 20	Ton of 40 bushels.
Wheat,	1½	1 20	Ton of 40 bushels.
On all articles, not enumerated, passing eastward,	1½	1 20	Ton.

ARTICLES.	Toll per Ton, per Mile.	Toll the whole Distance.	PER TON, &c.
	Cents	Dolls. Cts.	
Bark,	1	0 80	Per Cord.
Grindstones,	1	0 80	Ton.
Gypsum,	1	0 80	Ton.
Hay,	1	0 80	Ton.
Hoop poles, for barrels,	1	0 80	Ton of 400.
Do. for hogsheads and pipes,	1	0 80	Ton of 200.
Heading, for do.	1	0 80	Ton of 400.
Do. for barrels,	1	0 80	Ton of 500.
Iron, pig,	1	0 80	Ton.
Posts and rails,	1	0 80	Hundred.
Staves, for pipes,	1	0 80	Ton of 400.
Do. for hogsheads,	1	0 80	Ton of 500.
Do. for barrels,	1	0 80	Ton of 600.
Wood,	1	0 80	Cord.
Bricks,	$\frac{3}{4}$	0 60	Ton of 500.
Coal,	$\frac{3}{4}$	0 60	Ton.
Lime,	$\frac{3}{4}$	0 60	Ton of 28 bushels.
Marble, unwrought,	$\frac{3}{4}$	0 60	Ton.
Shingles,	$\frac{3}{4}$	0 60	Thousand.
Ground bark,	$1\frac{1}{4}$	1 00	Ton.
Boards, and other sawed stuff,	$1\frac{1}{4}$	1 00	1000 feet, board measure.
Iron, bar, blooms, or wrought,	$1\frac{1}{4}$	1 00	Ton.
Do. castings,	$1\frac{1}{4}$	1 00	Ton.
Mill stones, and French burrs,	$1\frac{1}{4}$	1 00	Ton.
Timber, round and square,	$1\frac{1}{4}$	1 00	90 solid feet.
Furniture,	2	1 60	Ton.
Marble, manufactured,	2	1 60	Ton.
Merchandise,	2	1 60	Ton.
Oysters,	2	1 60	Ton of 4000.
Rosin,	2	1 60	Ton of 8 barrels.
Salt, fine,	2	1 60	Ton of 45 bushels.
Do. coarse,	2	1 60	Ton of 32 bushels.
Tar,	2	1 60	Ton of 7 barrels.
Window glass,	2	1 60	Ton of 2800 feet.
On all articles, not enumerated, passing westward,	2	1 60	Ton.
On boats used for transportation, carrying more than 5 tons,	2	1 60	Each boat.
Clay,	$\frac{1}{2}$	0 40	Ton.
Earth,	$\frac{1}{2}$	0 40	Ton.
Iron ore,	$\frac{1}{2}$	0 40	Ton.
Limestone,	$\frac{1}{2}$	0 40	Ton.

ARTICLES.	Toll per Ton, per Mile.	Toll the whole Distance.	PER TON, &c.
	Cents	Dolls. Cts.	
Manure,	½	0 40	Per Ton.
Straw,	½	0 40	Ton.
Stone,	½	0 40	Ton.
Whiskey, and other domestic distilled spirits,	1¾	1 40	Ton of 2 Hhds. or 8 barrels.
Passage boats,	20	16 00	Each boat.
Empty boats for transportation, carrying not more than 5 tons,	4	3 20	Each boat.
Outlet locks at Middletown,			
A loaded boat, not using the Union canal,		0 75	
An empty boat,		0 50	

State of New-York,
Canal Room, Albany, March 18th, 1830.

Rates of Toll established by the Canal Board, to be collected on the New-York State Canals.

Provisions, &c.

Cts. M.

On flour, salted beef and pork, butter and cheese, beer and cider, per ton per mile, 1 5
On bran, and ship stuffs, in bulk, per ton per mile, 1 0

Iron, Minerals, Ores, &c.

On salt manufactured in this state, per ton per mile, 0 5
On gypsum, the product of this state, do. 0 5
On brick, sand, lime, clay, earth, leached ashes, manure, and iron ore, per ton per mile, 0 5
On pot and pearl ashes, mineral coal, charcoal, pig iron, broken castings, and scrap iron, per ton per mile, 1 0
On stove, and all other iron castings, going to or from tide water, per ton per mile, 3 0
On copperas, going towards tide water, per ton per mile, 1 0
On bar and pig lead, going towards tide water, do. 1 0

Furs, Peltry, Skins, &c.

On furs and peltry, (except deer, buffalo, and moose skins,) per ton per mile, 3 0
On deer, buffalo, and moose skins, per ton per mile, 1 3
On sheep skins, and other raw hides of domestic animals, per ton per mile, 1 5

Furniture, &c.

On carts, wagons, sleighs, ploughs, and mechanic's tools, necessary for the owner's individual use, when accompanied by the owners, emigrating north or west, for the purpose of settlement, per ton per mile, 1 0

Stone, Slate, &c.

	Cts.	M.
On slate and tile, for roofing, per ton per mile,	1	0
On all stone, entirely unwrought, do.	0	5
On all other stone,	1	0

Lumber, Wood, &c.

	Cts.	M.
On timber, squared and round, per 100 cubic feet per mile,	1	0
On the same, if carried in rafts, per 100 cubic feet per mile,	1	5
On boards, plank, scantling, and sawed timber, reduced to inch measure, and all siding, lath, and other sawed stuff, less than one inch thick, (except such as is enumerated in regulations Nos. 21 and 30,) per 1000 feet per mile,	1	0
On the same, if transported in rafts, per ton per mile,	2	0
On sawed lath, of less than 5 feet in length, split lath, and hoop poles, per ton per mile,	0	5
On staves and heading, per ton per mile,	0	5
On the same, if transported in rafts, per ton per mile,	1	0
On shingles, per M. per mile,	0	2
On the same, if conveyed in rafts, per M. per mile,	0	4
On split posts and rails, for fencing, do.	4	0
On the same, if conveyed in rafts, do.	8	0
On wood, for fuel, (except such as may be used in the manufacture of salt, which shall be exempt from toll,) and tan bark, per cord per mile,	1	0
On the same, if transported in rafts, per cord per mile,	2	5
On sawed stuff, for window blinds, not exceeding one-fourth of an inch in thickness, per ton per mile,	1	0

Agricultural Productions.

	Cts.	M.
On cotton, per ton per mile,	1	5
On live cattle, sheep, and hogs, per ton per mile,	1	0
On horses, (and each horse, when not weighed, to be computed at 6 cwt.) per ton per mile,	1	5
On rags, per ton per mile,	1	5
On hemp and tobacco, going towards tide water, per ton per mile,	1	0
On all other agricultural productions of this state, not particularly specified, per ton per mile,	1	5

Articles not enumerated.

	Cts.	M.
On all articles not enumerated or excepted, passing from tide water, per ton per mile,	3	5
On all articles not enumerated or excepted, passing towards tide water, per ton per mile,	1	5

Boats and Passengers.

	Cts.	M.
On boats used chiefly for the transportation of persons, and navigating the Erie canal between Schenectady and Utica, per mile,	15	0
On boats used chiefly for the transportation of persons and navigating the Erie canal west of Utica, per mile,	6	0
On boats used chiefly for the transportation of persons, and navigating the Champlain or Champlain and Junction canal, per mile,	6	0
On boats used chiefly for the transportation of persons, and navigating the Oswego canal, per mile,	6	0
On boats used chiefly for the transportation of persons, and navigating the Cayuga and Seneca canal, and the lateral canal to East Cayuga village, or either of them, per mile,	6	0
On boats used chiefly for the transportation of persons, and navigating the Junction canal, and not connected with regular lines of boats for the transportation of persons, on the Erie or Champlain canals, per mile,	50	0

	Cts.	M.
On boats used chiefly for the transportation of property, per mile,	2	0
On each person over eight years of age, transported in a boat used chiefly for the transportation of persons, per mile,	0	2
On each person over twelve years of age, transported in a boat used chiefly for the transportation of property, per mile,	2	0

Resolved, In pursuance of the provisions of the revised statutes, part first, chapter 19, title 2, section 35, that in levying, charging, and collecting tolls, upon all the canals of this state, "the hundred weight shall consist of one hundred pounds avoirdupois, and twenty such hundreds shall constitute a ton."

Resolved, That the foregoing rates of tolls be, and they are hereby established, and that the same be hereafter charged and collected on the several canals of this state, in lieu of all rates of toll heretofore established upon any or either of the said canals, or any part thereof.

S. YOUNG,
WILLIAM C. BOUCK, } *Canal Commissioners.*
H. SEYMOUR,

SILAS WRIGHT, Jun.
A. C. FLAGG,
GREENE C. BRONSON, } *Commissioners of the Canal Fund.*
A. KEYSER,

RAIL ROADS.

1826—1829.

Much of the public attention has been turned of late to the subject of rail roads. It was, a year or two ago, attracted and fixed to it, in so much, that a kind of controversy ensued, upon the point of *which mode of improvement is entitled to a preference; whether canals or railways?* The solution of the problem may be said to be at present tolerably well settled, indirectly; that is to say, both of them seem destined to become highly useful in their proper places, and each one, on every occasion where a proper choice between them shall have been made in reference to local circumstances, the *most* useful mode, on a comparison with the other.

The most discriminating and sifting of our investigators in relation to such important matters, did perceive at the beginning, that the question, in the way propounded, was of too general a form for any direct conclusive answer to it to be expected, or, if it did admit of one at all, that, at least it was prematurely ushered into discussion; and it turns out now to be generally admitted that such was the case. Whilst in the science of canal construction, this country had already the advantage of much practical experience, and of having become in a degree familiar with the subject, that of rail roads was a new topic, which had not then, nor has it yet, with us at least, if any where, undergone the test of a sufficient experience in all the variety of circumstances and detail ; and besides this deficiency, there is now evidence enough, that, of what was really known abroad of the latter, a large portion was introduced to public notice on this side of the water, under the disguise of high colouring, or exaggerated comparisons. There was, in fact, a delusion in the case, in England, with regard to the expense of railway construction and maintenance. Since the clearing away of which, most of the formerly projected railway undertakings there, whereof the list was long, have been either quite abandoned or suspended ; a judicious selection only, small in number, being at this moment in prosecution with assurance of success. There is, under the auspices of so favourable a circumstance as the being located between the towns of Manchester and Liverpool, a magnificent work of the kind, going forward with spirit ; the results of which, when once finished, will, no doubt, form a better standard to judge from, of comparative merits or defects, in most other instances of railway construction that are or may be contemplated, than any of the works already in existence can be allowed to form.

It will perhaps be found, as to expense, where the purposes of a general transportation are in view, and allowing the competency of a rail road to execute those purposes, that, taken all in all, the cost of this latter construction, and maintenance of it for any long period of time, will not be vastly different from the cost of constructing and maintaining, during the same long period, a canal of the like character, over the same length of ground ; whilst, in every particular instance, the local circumstances, it is more than probable, will favour in some degree, one of the two kinds of improvement in preference to the other one.

For these reasons, it may, with confidence, be affirmed; viz.—

1. That the canal system is not, in this country, likely to be superseded by that of rail roads, as, by some of the advocates of this latter, was, at one period, not long since, contended, must be the case.

2. That nevertheless, the rail road cause itself has suffered injury, throughout the last year or two, by a premature zeal in its partisans; but that, now that its true character, both as to cost and capabilities, is likely to be soon thoroughly known, there is an almost certainty of this mode of improvement being adopted to a considerable extent ; and of its proceeding, upon the principle of concurrent usefulness, with the canal system.

Two of the current advantages that have been insisted on, of rail roads over canals, are obvious enough, as respects some portions of this country ; they are these ;—

1. That rail roads can be kept in use throughout the year ; whereas, during the prevalence of hard frosts, canal conveyance is suspended.

2. That rail roads are practicable in various situations, where, from scarcity of water or other disadvantageous localities, canals cannot so easily be constructed, or be made thoroughly serviceable during all the good season of the year.

Since the discussions referred to were at their height, there has been something substantial realized in two distinct quarters; namely ; the Quincy rail road, as noticed at Article No. 23, New-England head, and one at the Lehigh, Mauch Chunk, coal mountains, as noticed at Article No. 62, both of them brought into operation, attended with complete success as to their respective objects ; and, although each one is but limited in point of distance, yet, taken together into view, may be considered in the light of an experiment, affording the most encouraging prospect in favour of what is now brought into a fair train of being prosecuted, in more than one district of the country, upon a broader scale. The question upon the all important point of rendering a rail road competent to general transportation, it would seem, is now in a measure settled, by the evidence of what has been done in these instances, though not embracing much extent or variety or ground.

Something very conclusive, however, upon the point, will soon open to view, as a few of the numerous works now proposed to be undertaken, come to be prosecuted. They are as follows ;—

But, before proceeding to our enumeration, permission is asked, to lay before the reader a perspicuous exposition of the theory of railway power, and remarks on the two modes of transportation improvement, in question, as applicable to the circumstances in particular, of the James river valley, the insertion whereof, just at this place, upon a subject of such universal interest, it is believed will not prove unacceptable or devoid of use, although it be not either a first or a second quotation from the writings of the scientific author whose name is affixed.

ON RAILWAYS.

Having concluded my report on the navigation of James river, I will add a few words on this mode of improvement, which has of late excited much public attention, and is now very deservedly in great favour in England.

The accounts that have been given on this subject have been very contradictory. They appeared, for a long time, more in the shape of opinions dictated by private interest or partiality, than as results of sound principles and actual experience. Like every thing new, they have had enthusiastic admirers and warm opponents.

It is surprising, however, that such a diversity of opinions should have existed in regard to railways, whose properties depend on the most elementary principles in the application of power. What is, in fact, a railway? A mere road, made of materials by which the resistance of friction is considerably reduced, whereby a propelling power is capable of more useful effect.

Friction and inertia are, it is well known, the two great obstacles that engineers or mechanicians have to overcome in the application of power. If it was not for the constant resistance opposed by friction, bodies once set in motion on a plane would never stop. A common road counteracts the pulling of horses by the considerable friction of the wheels; *M'Adamized* roads enable horses to draw heavier loads, because of their greater smoothness; and a road made of iron, offering still less resistance, will of course admit of much heavier loads being transported by the same power.

The resistance opposed by friction varies according to the nature of the substances placed in contact; it is proportional to the weight moved, *and remains the same whatever may be the velocity given;* in this last peculiarity consists the advantage of railways.

On a canal, on the contrary, *the resistance increases as the square of the velocity of the boat,* and consequently, as I have remarked in speaking of navigation, a rapid rate of velocity, besides the injury it does to the banks of the canal, will allow of but small weights being carried on it.

Whereas, on a rail road, if a power be capable of overcoming the resistance opposed by friction, it will, without any additional exertion, not only keep the body in motion, but, since friction is independent of velocity, it will continue to accelerate the speed, without any other limits than the extent of velocity of which the propelling power itself is capable.

Because, the power of horses decreases rapidly when their speed is increased, it follows, that on a railway as well as on a canal, their velocity cannot be considerable; and that the advantage of railways, *that velocity does not increase resistance,* is counteracted by the diminution of the power of exertion of horses when their speed is increased.*

---

* The following table is given in a recent and valuable work by Thomas

Still, owing to the circumstance that railways cost less than canals *in England*, transportation is found to be nearly the same there by either mode of conveyance, even when horse power is employed.

But, recently, a new propelling power has been introduced, which, like friction, remains the same, whatever may be the velocity: this is the locomotive engine. After having once set a train of wagons in motion, the engine will continue to act with constant and undiminished power, and will accelerate the speed of the whole train, until it has attained the maximum velocity that can be given to the wheels by the strokes of the piston. By increasing, therefore, the velocity of the rim of the wheels by any means whatever, the speed of transportation on railways might be increased *without limits*, by a propelling steam-engine. Prudence alone fixes a limit to the velocity: a great swiftness on a straight road might occasion very serious accidents; but in curves it would be particularly dangerous. It seems admitted, that a rate of speed of more than 6 miles an hour, would exceed the bounds set by prudence, though some of the sanguine advocates of railways extend this limit to 9 miles an hour. I should think, however, that this ought to depend on local circumstances which may increase or lessen the danger.

The advantage of railways over canals, as to transportation, is, therefore, that with the locomotive engine, an increase of speed neither lessens the moving power, nor requires a diminution of the weight transported: whereas, on a canal, great velocities are inadmissible.

At slow rates, however, the same power will transport more

Tredgold, to show the length of time that horses are capable of different velocities.

Duration of labour in hours, -	1	2	3	4	5	6	7	8	10
Maximum velocity in miles per hour, the horse being unloaded, - - - - -	14.7	10.4	8.5	7.3	6.6	6	5.5	5.2	4.6

In the same work, another table shows their power of exertion when moving at different rates of velocity. The following is an extract from it:—

Speed in miles per hour, - - -	2	3	4	5
Moving force, - - - - -	166	125	83	41 2-3

The rapid decrease of the power of horses is evident from these tables, which are entitled to perfect confidence, and agree both with calculations and experience.

on a canal than on a railway. The ratio is variously stated by those who have given comparative accounts of these two sorts of improvement; and in fact it could hardly be otherwise, for it would be almost impossible, that in two successive experiments, the numerous elements on which the comparison depends could be the same.

The statement most advantageous to railways, makes the useful effect on a canal double that on a railway, when the velocity is 2 miles an hour; and it makes it equal with a velocity of 3 miles; beyond which, the superiority of railways increases rapidly with the speed.

Other statements, which I should be inclined to think more correct, make the useful effect on canals about three times as great when the velocity is 2½ miles an hour.
Double when it is   3   miles   "
Equal for a velocity of   4½ miles   "
Beyond this degree of speed, while the useful effect decreases on canals, it increases rapidly on railways. Hence it appears, that this mode of conveyance is particularly calculated for a fixed trade, in which celerity is an object, as may be the case between two commercial and manufacturing places; and, in this respect, it must be very advantageous in a great many situations in England.

Railways have, besides, the advantage, that they are not liable to interruptions from floods or droughts, and but little from frosts; they can be made to extend their ramifications to any desired important point; and, in this respect, they suit particularly for the transportation of such objects as are constantly supplied from a fixed centre, because in this case they avoid the change of conveyance. The transportation of coal, for instance, by their means, may be made from the coal mine to the point of destination; whereas, if carried by water, it generally happens that it has to be transferred from wagons into boats, and sometimes again from boats into wagons. But a trade which is not concentrated, and has to seek the main artery of conveyance, is not so much benefited by a railway.

But what contributes principally to the superiority of railways over canals *in England*, is, that they are found in most instances to be cheaper. From an average of the expense of a number of these works taken in England, it is estimated that the medium cost of railways is -   -   -   -   -   -   £5,000
and that of canals -   -   -   -   -   -   9,000

From their acknowledged superiority in a great many instances in England, railways have obtained warm advocates in this country; though the opinion seems most generally to prevail, that they are not applicable here. Without attempting to judge of what is expedient in other states, I am of opinion, that, at least in Virginia, railways could not be extensively introduced.

A rail road has been spoken of as a substitute for the navigation of James river; and, it is with a view of analyzing this opinion, that I have introduced the foregoing observations on this mode of improvement.

In the first place, not only the expense of a railway here, would not bear to that of a canal the same ratio it does in England, but it would actually cost more than a canal, as I will demonstrate.

In the making of a railway, we have two things to consider: the *rails* and the *foundation*. The dimensions and strength of the rails are determined by the weight they have to support: hence the quantity of iron wanted is the same every where; but, from an estimate I have seen, cast rails in England cost $62 a ton delivered. Here, on the contrary, before delivery, they would probably cost at least $112, and their price might be advanced by a greater demand : so much for the iron.

In regard to the foundation, it will be sufficient to enumerate its principal difficulties, to give an idea of its considerable expense. For a double railway, a road must be made about 30 feet wide ; it must be graduated with mathematical precision, not inclining more than $\frac{1}{8}$th of an inch to the running yard : it must not form abrupt curves ; hence numerous deep cuts and expensive embankments : or, if these are not adequate to the object of avoiding great curvatures, expensive stationary engines and inclined planes must be constructed, to carry the road in a direct line, over such elevations as could not be graduated at the maximum angle, which will allow the operation of the locomotive engine. Along cliffs, the rail road must be kept above highwater, and held up by walls or paved banks, as expensive as along a canal.

It must be carried over *every creek* by *stone* or *iron* bridges, which would be a serious cause of expense along the valley of a large river, which receives a great many tributaries of all sizes, none of which should be suffered to reach the railway ; whereas, a canal may receive many of the minor runs. It is of the utmost importance, that a rail road should be dry and firm : this requires side ditches to drain it, and trenches filled with broken stones, under the foundations of the rails; for this reason, also, the expense of deep cuts would be increased, by the difficulty of draining them, and that of embankments, by the necessity of placing in their body, masses of broken stones, to act as sinks, and prevent water from being retained by them.

If all these difficulties, and many others, which it would be too minute to detail, are properly weighed, how could a railway cost less than a canal, in a valley so broken and intersected by streams and drains as that of James river? And how could it cost less than in England, when the expense for iron alone would be double?

The comparison which was made in England, between railways and canals, cannot apply to the James river canal:

1. Because the canals of England are of much larger dimensions, than those which have been prescribed by law for the canal along James river.

2. Because stone and wood in England are dearer, and iron cheaper, than in this country.

3. Because the valley of James river presents great difficulties to the construction of a regular and uniformly graduated work.

Admitting the average cost of a railway in England to be correctly stated at £5000, or $22,000, (though some recent railways are said to have cost much more) it is probable that here the expense of such a work would be greater than this sum.

If a railway, then, would be more expensive than a canal, it would be still more so than a lock and dam improvement. And as transportation, with small velocities, is admitted to be much cheaper on a canal than on a railway, there can be no doubt, that, upon every consideration of expense, a railway along James river is not advisable.

As to its expediency in other respects, it will be sufficient to observe, that railways are advantageous only when great speed is a desirable object. But along James river, the trade is of a miscellaneous nature, the articles are bulky, more easily loaded in boats than in small wagons. The objects to be transported are scattered, and speed is not of so much consequence as economy of transportation. Though short interruptions of the navigation may be occasioned by floods, droughts on James river will never have this effect, and frosts hardly ever: so that the advantages of railways, in this respect, are of no weight in this instance.

The making of a railway across the mountains has been also mentioned; but it would there be attended with still greater practical difficulties.

In the first place, the mountains are so rugged and broken, that the only practicable way to carry this plan into execution, would be to follow the valley of some creek which leads up to the top of the dividing ridge. But here, all the difficulties presented in the valley of James river, would be greatly multiplied. The graduation of the road must be almost every where among cliffs; its windings would be more numerous and considerable; the deep cuts would be enormously expensive; and the stationary engines and inclined planes very frequent, &c.: after having, at an immense expense, established the foundation of the railway, blocks of stone must be obtained, shaped, and transported into a complete wilderness, and put in their places. Then castings must be obtained from a foundry, at the rate of at least $112 per ton, and transported an immense distance to this same wilderness, to form a railway, perhaps 100 miles in length, at the rate of nearly 100 tons of iron per mile, exclusive of fixed steam-engines or machinery.

In England, where facilities of all sorts are concentrated, where there exists an extensive practical knowledge of these things, the nice adjustment of railways may not be thought an object capable of having a material influence on the expense; but, among the mountains of Virginia, far from foundries, rails would have to be procured of particular shapes to suit each of the numerous curves of the road, and counteract the centrifugal force of the wagons in the turns.

What the expense of railways, made under circumstances so unfavourable, would be, I am not prepared to say; but certain it is, that it would be immense; and that the present state of things would not justify it.

All which is repectfully submitted.

C. CROZET, *P. Engineer.*

Richmond, July 1st, 1826.

RAIL ROADS PROJECTED.

A magnificent undertaking is resolved on, and actually on foot, to extend from Baltimore to Wheeling, or to some other eligible point of the river Ohio; the surveys for which, under the Baltimore and Ohio rail road company, chartered by the state of Maryland, being in progress, as noticed at Article No. 71. Locomotive steam-engines to be applied. Computed distance 250 miles, or more.

NOTE.

On the 4th July, 1828, this work actually commenced, and it is in spirited progress.

The plan and preliminary measures for another magnificent project, are advancing to maturity. It is to consist in a main line of rail road, commencing at Boston, and extending westward to the Connecticut river, and thence to the Hudson, with various branches from the main road, into the districts of country along the route. The examinations are reported upon in part, and satisfactorily. Distance in all, 308 miles, more or less, as noticed more particularly at Article No. 23.

A measure not yet decided on, but under present consideration, with a prospect of being carried, is a rail road across New-Jersey state, to be executed either by the state or by individual means. The route to be, between a point of the Delaware river, near Philadelphia, as Camden, and some favourable point of the Rariton; or otherwise, between the Delaware, and the Bay of Amboy.

The project has been brought before the legislature, by a convention of delegates on "internal improvement," and it recommends itself to favour, and an early execution, by many considerations; one of them, the unlucky suspension of the long contemplated construction of a canal across this part of the state. But, the vast importance of this 30 or 40 miles of route, in the scale of intercourse, is alone a sufficient indication that the undertaking, calculated for a general transportation, can scarcely fail of being attended with great success; both in profit as an individual or state concern, and in much public benefit. The undertaking is noticed at Article No. 54.

A plan is submitted to the New-Jersey legislature, for a rail road, between Patterson, on the Passaic, and the Hudson river; and an act of incorporation applied for.

The project of a complete rail road, between Philadelphia and Columbia, on the Susquehanna; which many cogent reasons concur in to urge the propriety of being immediately set on foot; always supposing that the mode of its construction will be such as to prove competent to the demands of a *general* transportation.

NOTE.

This has been adopted into the plan, and made part of the great "Pennsylvania state canal and rail road," now in execution; which is also to comprise about 50 miles of rail road, more or less, across the Alleghany mountain, connecting points of the Juniata and Conemaugh rivers, in the transverse line of canal. They are noticed at Articles Nos. 79, 81.

A rail road, between Boston, and Providence, Rhode Island, as is noticed at Article No. 20. The examinations of the ground to form a route for this, were some time since effected, and a route has been chosen. Between Boston and the Connecticut river at Brattleboro', a rail road is proposed.

A rail road is proposed, by an association to be styled the *Vermont Rail Road association*, to commence at Ogdensburgh, in New-York, and cross to Lake Champlain, from whence to a point of the Connecticut river; thence to Concord, New-Hampshire, and through Lowell to Boston. The general government to be requested to effect a survey for this undertaking.

In New-York, in Pennsylvania, in the southern states, numerous rail roads are projected, and recommended to the public attention : the following are chiefly sanctioned by legislative enactments, viz :—

Between Ithaca, at the head of Lake Cayuga, and Owego, on the Susquehanna river ; for which a company is chartered, as stated at Article No. 39. Also, south of the Erie canal, a rail road is proposed between Albany and Schenectady, to be constructed by the Mohawk and Hudson rail road company ; and one other, between Catskill, on the Hudson river, and Ithaca, on Lake Cayuga; that is to say, this latter to commence at Catskill, and pass across an angle of Schoharie county, to the head waters of the Delaware, and thence, either direct to Ithaca, or, down the Susquehanna valley to Owego ; joining, consequently, the Ithaca and Owego rail road, at one of the two points. Distance, 160 miles : rough estimate of cost, 1,500,000 dollars.

Between the head of Lake Otsego and the Erie canal, as noticed at Article No. 47.

A rail road is proposed, from Painted Post, up to the coal mines at the head waters of the Tioga, to form a connexion with the proposed Chemung canal, through its feeder, at Painted Post, as noticed at Article No. 38.

A rail road is also proposed, between the waters of West branch Susquehanna, in Centre county, and of the Juniata, at Huntingdon, to pass through Philipsburgh. A survey is directed by law, with a view of connecting the West branch Susquehanna state canal with the Juniata section.

Connecting the Schuylkill canal with the Susquehanna river, by the Catawissa valley, or to strike the Susquehanna, at some point between Catawissa and the town of Sunbury, as stated at Article No. 66.

From the head of the Schuylkill navigation company's works at Pottsville, or Port Carbon, up the valley, over a tract of 10 miles, through a rich body of coal land, as noticed at Articles Nos. 57, 67. Moreover, a company is organized, as the *Mine hill and Schuylkill haven Rail road company*, for the object of constructing rail roads between those points, and along the valley of the Schuylkill west West branch, to the coal mines in that direction.

Between the Union canal navigation, and the coal mines at the heads of the Swatara river and branches. See Article No. 58.

Between Harrisburg bridge, west extremity, and Chambersburg, by way of Carlisle ; or, from the west end of Columbia bridge, through York and Gettysburg, to Chambersburg, in Franklin county, Pennsylvania, as noticed at Article No. 90 ; and from Columbia down to the mouth of the Conestoga.

Between the Susquehanna river, North branch, and the River

Delaware at the Water Gap, by the heads of the Lehigh navigation, and along Brodhead's creek valley, as noticed at Articles Nos. 63, 64.

Branch from the Pennsylvania state rail road, by the Brandywine and Chester creek valleys, to the River Delaware, as noticed at Article No. 80.

Between Baltimore and York Haven, on the Susquehanna river. Distance, 69 miles, as noticed at Article No. 71.

Between the cities of Baltimore and Washington, as stated at Article No. 72. The Maryland act of incorporation in favour of which, is confirmed by congress, for as much as concerns its passing into the District of Columbia.

Between the Delaware river, at the termination of the Delaware and Hudson canal, 4 miles above the mouth of the Neversink, and the Lackawaxen coal mines, as noticed at Article No. 59. Or, probably, only between the Dyberry forks of the Lackawaxen, at Honesdale, and the Carbondale coal mines. Distance, 16 miles.

Between the town of Newcastle, on the Delaware river, and Frenchtown, on the Elk, as noticed at Article No. 70.

Between Charleston, South Carolina, and Hamburgh, on the Savannah river, opposite Augusta, as noticed at Article No. 152; also, between Charleston and Columbia.

Between Augusta, on the Savannah river, and Columbus, on the Chatahootchee, in Georgia; passing through Milledgeville, on the Oconee river, and through Macon, on the Oakmulgee. See Article No. 125.

Between the Yadkin river, at Montgomery, North Carolina, and Fayette, on Cape Fear river, as noticed at Article No. 147; and from the Yadkin river to the Catawba.

Between the Mississippi river, at or near New-Orleans, and Lake Pontchartrain, as noticed at Article No. 133.

Between Beverly Randolph's and Nicholas Mills's coal mines, in Chesterfield county, Virginia, and tide water of James river, opposite Rockett's, in the city of Richmond. See Article No. 101. Also, a rail road is proposed to be constructed by the corporation of Petersburg, between that town and the Roanoke river, as noticed at Article No. 102.

Between Lexington, in Kentucky, and a point of the Ohio river, as noticed at Article No. 113.

Between Steubenville, on the Ohio, and the Ohio state canal; for the construction of which, a company is chartered by the legislature of the state.

A huge railway construction is proposed, and very strenuously recommended for public consideration; to extend from New-York city, westward, to the Mississippi river; on the plan of intersecting the principal improvements now existing or on foot, and of being as a basis also, for future rail roads in this quarter of the country.

The route and circumstances are here described, in the projector's own words; and on the map of the United States, a green coloured line is traced to correspond.

The ingenious projector does not, however, allow his magnificent ideas to stop at this point;—he proceeds to suggest a second great rail road, to hold the place of the present contemplated government road from Washington to New-Orleans; which, he observes, being carried nearly parallel to the Blue ridge, would serve as a base line for the great system of improvements along this division of the country, and be intersected by the southern rail roads now on foot, as well as numerous others, which are, sooner or later, to proceed from various points of the Ohio river and of the borders of the Atlantic, and be extended across.

Sketch of the geographical route of a Great Railway, by which it is proposed to connect the canals and navigable waters of New-York, Pennsylvania, Ohio, Indiana, Illinois, Michigan, Missouri, and the adjacent states and territories; opening thereby a free communication, at all seasons of the year, between the Atlantic states and the great valley of the Mississippi.

The construction of a GREAT WESTERN RAILWAY, on the route which is traced on the annexed map, is recommended to the attentive consideration of every citizen who feels an interest in the prosperity of his country, and wishes to promote its rapid advancement in wealth and power, by the multiplication of those physical resources which constitute national greatness, and best promote individual happiness and prosperity.

The proposed railway has, for its object, not only the connexion of the great cities on the borders of the Atlantic, with the magnificent lakes and rivers of the west, by a channel, available at all seasons of the year, but also the development of the latent wealth and resources of large and valuable tracts of country, which are not now traversed by any of the great works which have been constructed, or are in progress, under the patronage of the several states. It affords happy facilities for accomplishing these great objects, in a manner that will best subserve the interests of the whole community; and by connecting the canals of New-York, Pennsylvania, Ohio, Indiana, and Illinois, in one great system, will give increased value and efficiency to the plans of internal improvement, which have been adopted in these several states.

The route commences on the Hudson river, in the vicinity of the city of New-York, at a point accessible at all seasons to steam ferry-boats, and from thence proceeds through a favourable and productive country, to the valley of the Delaware river, near the north-west angle of the county of Sullivan. From thence the route ascends along the Delaware, to a point that affords the nearest and most favourable crossing to the valley of the Susquehanna, which it enters at or near the Great bend of that river.

Pursuing a westerly and almost level course through the fertile valleys of the Susquehanna and Tioga rivers, the route crosses the head waters of the Genessee, having in its course intersected the terminations of the Ithaca and Owego railway, and the Chenango and the Chemung canals in New-York, the great Susquehanna canal in Pennsylvania, and several other points that afford important facilities for intercommunication.

From the Genessee river, our route enters the valley of the Alleghany, and proceeds along that river, which affords a navigable communication with Pittsburg, the Pennsylvania canals, and the Ohio river. From the Alleghany, the route intersects the outlet of the Chatauque lake, by which a communication may be established with Lake Erie, and proceeds to the head waters of the French creek, in Pennsylvania, from whence it again communicates with the Alleghany and the Pennsylvania canals, on the one hand, and may be connected with the harbour of Erie on the other.

The benefits which would result from the construction of a railway, on the route which we have thus far followed, and its capacity to multiply the elements of individual and national prosperity, can be best appreciated by those who have carefully observed the effects of such improvements: but that portion of the route which remains to be considered, offers to our view results of the highest and most invaluable character.

From the Western branch of the Alleghany, we proceed in a direction nearly parallel to the shore of Lake Erie, and entering the northern counties of Ohio, intersect the great canal of that state on the portage summit. A free and rapid communication is thus established both with the lakes and the Ohio river.

From the Ohio canal, the route proceeds in a western direction, near the forty-first parallel of latitude, along the fertile table lands which separate the tributary streams of the Ohio from those of the great northern lakes. Having entered the state of Indiana, we pass the head waters of the Wabash, intersect the route of the canal which is to unite the Wabash river with the lakes, enter the state of Illinois, and passing near the course of the Kankakee, *arrive at the head of steam-boat navigation on the Illinois river.*

The Illinois, which is soon to be connected by a canal with Lake Michigan, affords good depth of water for steam-boats, with a current so slight, as to be, in many places, hardly perceptible. It affords excellent navigation for 250 miles, through a country of unbounded fertility, to the Mississippi river, which it enters near the mouth of the Missouri, and a short distance above the flourishing and important town of St. Louis.

Having accomplished this grand object, our railway continues from near the bend of the Illinois, and at a distance of little more than 60 miles, *reaches the banks of the Mississippi.*

The proposed point of junction with that immense river, is immediately above the Rock island rapids, from whence the navigation is at all seasons uninterrupted to the River St. Peters, and the Falls of St. Anthony. The country bordering on the Mississippi, for a great distance above the termination of the railway route, besides its immense fertility, contains inexhaustible quantities of lead ore, and is supposed also to abound in copper.

The whole distance from the Hudson river to the Mississippi, at the junction of Rock river, is less than 1000 miles. The route extends along one of the best parallels of temperate latitude, and in great part through the most fertile and valuable portions of our country. A railway, constructed upon this route, would connect, in the most advantageous manner, the agricultural, navigating, and commercial interests of the regions bordering on the numerous rivers, canals, and lakes, with which it communicates; and would extend the production and dissemination of valuable commodities throughout the most distant portions of our common country.

In a military, as well as commercial point of view, the results of such a railway would surpass the power of calculation. With such ample means for throwing any amount of military force and material, at any time, to almost any point of our frontier, with a rapidity resembling that of an express-rider, we should have little occasion to claim the respect of our proudest foes, whether savage or civilized.

The whole extent of the proposed railway could be constructed for a sum not greatly exceeding that which the state of New-York has expended on its justly celebrated canals; and its cost would be trifling, in comparison with its benefits, or even to the increased value, which it would give to the lands which border on the route. It would, when completed, be far more beneficial in its effects on the intervening country, and on our national prosperity, than to turn the Mississippi itself into the same course. Free from the inundations, the currents, the rapids, the ice, and the sand-bars of that mighty stream, the rich products of its wide-spread valley would be driven to the shores of the Atlantic, with greater speed than if wafted by the wings of the wind; and the rapid return of commercial equivalents would spread life and prosperity over the face of the finest and fairest portion of the habitable world.

Without inquiring whether such a work could be best accomplished by the several states through which the route extends; or by incorporations, aided by grants of money or lands from the general government; or by appropriations from the surplus funds, which will soon be at the disposal of that government; it is sufficient to assert, that our citizens have only to appreciate the value of the enterprise, and raise their voices in its favour, and it will be accomplished.

TOPOGRAPHICAL AND OTHER MEMORANDA.

The various and aggregate distances, on the route described in these pages, may be estimated as in the following tables, in which an average of about 10 per cent. is added to the supposed rectilinear distances, which, on some parts of the route, it is supposed, will more than compensate for the sinuosities of the railway.

From the Hudson river at Tappan, to the Delaware and Hudson canal,	55	*Miles.*
Delaware river above Kalikoon creek,	35	
Up the Delaware, to Stockport,	15	
Across Starucca summit to the Great bend,	20	
		125
Binghamton, (mouth of Chenango,)	20	
Owego,	20	
Head of Pennsylvania canal, (on the Tioga,)	20	
Newtown, or Elmira, (Chemung canal,)	12	
		72
Genessee river,	65	
Alleghany river, at Olean,	28	
Chatauque outlet, (near Pa. line,)	45	
Meadville, Pa.,	62	
State line of Ohio,	28	
Warren, O.,	20	
Ohio canal, Portage summit,	42	
		290
Whole distance to Ohio canal,	487	
New-Haven, O.,	60	
Sandusky river,	30	
Fort Finley,	25	
Fort Brown,	35	
State line of Indiana,	25	

Fort Wayne,	15
Tippecanoe river,	75
State line of Illinois,	55
Pinkamink river,	32
Vermillion river,	44
Illinois river,	24
	420
Rock river,	56
MISSISSIPPI RIVER,	7
	63
Miles,	**970**

Elevations of different portions of the route above the surface of Lake Erie.

	Feet.
Passage of the Shawangunk ridge,	227
Stockport on the Delaware,	345
Susquehanna river at the Great bend,	315
Chenango bridge at Binghamton,	290
Tioga river at Newtown, (Chemung canal,)	265
Olean, on the Alleghany river,	845
Meadville, on French creek, Pa.	500
Ohio state line,	450
Ohio canal summit,	395
New-Haven, Ohio,	414
Illinois river, near the mouth of Robinson's river,	000
Mississippi river, head of Rock Island Rapids,	125

Great extent of Internal Navigation united by the Railway.

The actual extent of internal communication, by the various rivers, lakes, canals, and railways, connected with this route, and with each other, cannot be estimated at less than *thirty thousand miles*, and probably much exceeds that distance.

A writer at St. Louis, estimates the whole river navigation above that town, at a fraction short of 30,000 miles. The navigation below St. Louis, he estimates at 20,000 miles, including the Ohio and all its tributaries; which would make the whole navigable waters of this great valley equal to near 50,000 miles.

These estimates are said to be the result of "careful and accurate calculation," and if we were to add to this the entire line of the lakes and their tributaries, and all the artificial communications to be connected by the proposed work, the whole would probably exceed 60,000 miles.

The greater part, however, of the river navigation, included in this writer's estimate, is more or less imperfect. Even the

Ohio affords good navigation, according to the best authorities, only four months in the year, and the navigation of the Mississippi is greatly obstructed by the Des Moines and Rock island rapids, which obstructions could be entirely avoided by the use of the Illinois river, and the terminating section of the proposed railway.

How immensely might the commerce of these great rivers be enlarged, by the construction of such a railway as is here proposed!

To effect such an extensive connexion of these waters, by means of a canal, would, if practicable, be of much less utility than the railway, by reason of the interruption of its navigation in the winter season, and in times of drought, which would be much more detrimental than on an ordinary canal, through a less extensive country, and calculated for less general purposes. To this must be added, the advantage afforded by the railway, of conveying passengers and the public mails, in the most rapid manner, through such an extensive and important region of country.

The business of the grand canal of New-York, which connects with the great lakes, and the country on their borders, *is chiefly derived from the country through which it passes;* and owing to the interruptions of winter, and the hazards and delays of lake navigation, answers, but very imperfectly, the wants of the great western country. In the present state of knowledge, it would be absurd to rely alone upon canals, valuable as they are, for a communication with our surpassingly rich and extensive interior. And in opening its resources, and its extensive river navigation, to free access by a railway, it would be equally absurd to locate its eastern termination on the inland portion of a river or canal that should be liable to obstruction by ice. To realize the full value of our canals, rivers, and lakes, we must unite them by a grand arterial communication, which shall promote the rapid circulation and exchange of all products, at all seasons, throughout the whole region of country in which they extend.

Further description of the Route to the Ohio Canal.

The route here proposed, is believed to furnish the most practicable passage from the Atlantic to the western states, that is to be found between the Erie canal and the state of Georgia.

Leaving the Hudson, about 20 miles from the city of New-York,[*] it paases the high ground which constitutes the west-

---

[*] To this point, the channel of the Hudson is rarely obstructed by ice in winter, and as the river must be crossed by means of steam-boats, nothing is lost by making this the eastern termination of the route; or, it might otherwise be extended along the margin of the river, beneath the Palisado rocks, to a point opposite the city of New-York.

ern shore of that river, through the valley of Tappan creek, the only suitable pass that is to be found in a range of near 100 miles along the river. From this pass, we proceed north-westerly, crossing the range of the highlands, through the *clove*, or Ramapough gap, ascend the valley of the Ramapough, proceed through the county of Orange, and near the town of Goshen, to the Shawangunk ridge. We pass this ridge by the Deer Park gap, cross the Delaware and Hudson canal, near its summit, and, proceeding through the county of Sullivan, and near the town of Monticello, we reach the valley of the Delaware. We then proceed up this valley, about 15 or 18 miles, to Stockport, in Pennsylvania.

Here we cross the Delaware, and ascend the dividing ridge, through the valley of Stockport creek, and in proceeding a few miles, arrive at the summit dividing the Atlantic slope from the Susquehanna basin. This summit, though of moderate elevation, compared with other routes, on which important public works are now in progress, *is probably the highest which this route presents, if pursued even to the vicinity of the Rocky mountains.* From it, we descend through the Starucca valley, and soon reach the fertile borders of the Susquehanna river.

Most of the natural difficulties which attend the proposed work, are to be found on that portion of the route which we have just passed in review. These obstacles, it is believed, are not of a serious nature, and can be correctly estimated only by actual surveys, made by competent engineers. It is thought that stationary power, if required, will only be found necessary in a very few instances, and from this point our progressive range is apparently unobstructed.

We now cross the Susquehanna, a short distance below the mouth of the Starucca, at the angle of the Great bend, and pass on to Binghamton, where we unite with the contemplated Chenango canal, which, commencing at this place, is to terminate in the Erie canal, near Utica. We thence continue about due west, through this fertile and beautiful valley, and unite at Owego with the railway, which is to extend from that place to Ithaca, at the head of the Cayuga lake, and thus form another communication with the Erie canal. Arriving at the Tioga river, we unite directly, or, by a short lateral branch, with the great Susquehanna canal, which opens to us, through the heart of Pennsylvania, a communication with the cities of Philadelphia and Baltimore.

We then proceed along the Tioga, and unite at Elmira with the contemplated Chemung canal, and the Seneca lake, which forms our third connexion with the Erie canal and Lake Ontario. Passing onward, we arrive at the western summit of the Susquehanna basin, and crossing the Genessee river, near its sources, we enter upon the great basin, or valley, which is drained by the Mississippi and its tributaries. On a great part of the route along the Susquehanna and Tioga, it is supposed that almost a perfect level can be obtained ; and, in passing from thence to the Alleghany river, no serious obstruction is apprehended, as the Alleghany ridges here run under the surface of the great table land of the interior. The surface of the country is described as not broken, but consists of large swells of land, with broad shallow valleys intervening.

We now enter the valley of the Alleghany river, or northeast branch of the Ohio, which forms our first communication with the almost endless ramifications and extent of the Mississippi, and its tributary streams. We proceed along the Alleghany, till, in order to preserve a more westerly course, we diverge from that river, and cross the outlet of the Chatauque lake, through which an easy communication can be opened with Portland, on Lake Erie. We continue in a course indicated by the general level of the country, and nearly parallel to Lake Erie, and crossing the navigable waters of French creek, near Meadville, we proceed through this fine portion of Pennsylvania, and intersect the canal, which is to extend from Pittsburg to Erie, near its summit level. This opens a third or fourth avenue to the important manufacturing city of Pittsburg, and also another route to the waters of Erie and the upper lakes. Continuing our range along this fertile summit, we enter the state of Ohio, pass through the flourishing counties of Trumbull and Portage, and near the towns of Warren and Ravenna, to the summit of the Ohio canal. This great canal is a work which confers lasting honour upon the well guided enterprise of a young, but intelligent and powerful member of our national confederacy. It unites us again with the Ohio and the lakes, as well as with the flourishing and extensive country through which it passes.

Western Division of the Route.

A more determinate specification of the route to be pursued, from the Ohio canal to the head waters of the Maumee and Wabash, and from thence, across the states of Indiana and Illinois, to the Mississippi river, is rendered unnecessary, by the favourable nature of the country to be traversed, which presents no obstacles to a free choice of surface and location. A large portion of the country comprised in the states of Ohio, Indiana, and Illinois, together with the Michigan peninsula, and the country between Lake Michigan and the Mississippi, constitutes an extensive table land, or *plateau*, of pretty even character and surface, and of great general fertility. This great district may, with propriety, be called *the great plateau of Michigan*, and constitutes, probably, the finest portion of the vast region which is drained by the tributaries of the Mississippi and the Canadian lakes. It is almost surrounded by navigable waters; having the Ohio on the south, the Mississippi on the west, the Wisconsin and Fox rivers, and the lakes Michigan, Huron, St. Clair, and Erie, on the north. It is intersected by several valuable tributaries of the Ohio and Mississippi; the most important of which, are the Wabash and Illinois; the latter enters the Mississippi 20 miles above the junction of the Missouri, and 35 miles above the town of St. Louis. This river occupies the lowest portion of the plateau, and from the head of its navigation to Lake Michigan, there is but little elevation; so that, in forming a canal, to communicate with that lake, the water of the latter can, by means of a moderate excavation, be had to supply the canal, and may be drawn in sufficient quantity to supply and quicken the current of the river during the dry season.

The Illinois is described as one of the best rivers in our country for steam-boat navigation; its channel being good for more than 250 miles, to its junction with the Mississippi, and its current being so gentle, as to be, in many places, hardly perceptible. The canal in question, is, probably, one of the few which ought to be constructed in full view of the advantages of railways, as its navigation would be always open, during the season in which the lake itself is navigable; and therefore, like the proposed improvements in the bayous of Louisiana, it deserves support under all circumstances. The construction of a breakwater harbour, to protect the entrance of the canal into the lake, would perfect its utility.

The great section of country which we are describing, is intersected, centrally, by the route of the proposed railway, which will not only lay open its valuable resources, and connect its rich interior with the navigation of the surrounding rivers and the Atlantic markets, but offers a base line, of unequalled utility, for lateral railways and intercommunications, which may be hereafter established. A railway may ultimately be found extending through the centre of the Michigan peninsula, from the straits of Mackinaw to the Ohio river, and also from the falls of that river to Lake Michigan. This great plateau will, indeed, one day, be intersected by thousands of miles of railroad communications; and so rapid is the increase of its population and resources, that many persons, now living, will probably see most or all of this accomplished.

The general character of the whole region is, as before observed, that of a great table land, with its surface gently undulating, and presenting shallow valleys, and deeper grooves, which have been worn down by the streams that carry off its surplus waters. These streams, as they increase in length and magnitude, produce a greater effect upon the aspect of the country on their borders; and towards their junction with the Ohio, or other recipients, are bounded by the numerous river hills, which form so marked a feature in western scenery. As the portion of country passed over by our route, lies near the sources of the principal streams, much advantage is afforded to the railway, by avoiding the deep grooves or valleys, which are formed by these streams. The extent of this advantage will be appreciated by those who are conversant with the physical character of the great valley of the Mississippi.

Parallel to the proposed line of rail road, and at the most advantageous distance between it and the Ohio river, is found the great national road, which is extending from Wheeling, on the Ohio, through the capitals of these states, and to the seat of government of Missouri. This road happily coincides with the proposed work, in supplying the wants of this extensive and valuable region of country. The Miami canal, which is completed from Cincinnati to Dayton, will soon be either extended to Maumee bay, on Lake Erie, or connected by a railway with the Ohio canal, or the harbour of Sandusky, thus forming one of our most important lateral communications.

In the state of Indiana, the contemplated Wabash and Miami canal, will form another invaluable auxiliary to our system of intercommunication. Its length will be 280 miles, through a fertile region; and the Wabash itself is represented as navigable by boats for nearly 400 miles. Many other important communications will eventually be established in this great and flourishing state, which possesses a more homogeneous character than Ohio. Should the construction of its great canal be neglected, it will only be for the purpose of establishing a railway of equal or greater importance.

The advantages of connecting our railway with the navigation of the Illinois, and thus obtaining an unobstructed railway and steam-boat route to St. Louis and New-Orleans, are sufficiently obvious. The short western section of the railway, by which it is proposed to connect the Illinois with the Upper Mississippi, is also of high importance, and offers advantages sufficient to justify the execution of that section without delay. It touches the north-west corner of the military bounty lands, which will be greatly enhanced in value thereby, and it offers an excellent communication between St. Louis and the lead mine country, on the Upper Mississippi, through the Illinois river, during the dry season, thus avoiding the obstructions which are occasioned by the Des Moines and Rock river rapids in the Mississippi. It would be the principal line of communication with that extensive and invaluable country, on both sides of the Mississippi lying north of Rock river and the state of Missouri, and which is now but little known.

The great lead mine district, on the Upper Mississippi, situated between the Rock river and the Wisconsin, is no less remarkable for its fine aspect and general fertility, than for the inexhaustible quantities of lead ore, with which it abounds. Although no part of this tract has yet been surveyed and opened for sale by the government, and although the means of communication are, at present, imperfect, yet 13,000,000 pounds of lead were obtained in the year 1828; and, it is said, that 5,000,000 of pounds were reported for three months in the year 1829. At Galena, the principal depot of the mines, there were 99 arrivals of steamboats, and 74 of keel boats, in 1828. The diggings have already been scattered over different portions of a district, containing 3,000 square miles, and no limit can be assigned to the future extent of the mining operations. Copper ore has also been found in its original deposite, in such quantities, and over such an extent of this country, as to justify the expectation of that metal being produced in considerable quantities.

The inventive genius of Mr. Gurney, and others in England, will abundantly promote the usefulness of rail roads, and multiply consequently the construction of them, if it be found that the newly invented *steam-carriages* of these gentlemen be equal, in practice, to the extraordinary character given of them, on the strength, it would seem, of some very careful experiments. The qualities of Mr. Gurney's locomotive machine, are stated to be as follows;—

1. It can be stopped *dead*, within the space of 2 yards, though going at the rate of 18 or 20 miles per hour; and this without any inconvenient shock to passengers, or to the machinery.

2. It is capable of dragging a carriage, weighing 3 tons, and having 100 passengers, over a level road, at the rate of 8, 9, or 10 miles per hour.

3. It is capable of dragging the same carriage, with 25 passengers, up the steepest road in England, at the same rate.

4. In ascending hills, for every cwt. that is shifted, from the front to the hind wheels, the carriage acquires an additional drawing power of 4 cwt., and on level ground, an additional one of 10 cwt.

5. On descending hills, the contrivance by which the carriage is retarded at pleasure, acts independently of the wheels, so that the sliding and cutting effect of ordinary drags is avoided.

The Liverpool and Manchester railway company, offered a

premium of £500 sterling for the most improved steam-emgine, not weighing more than 6 tons, that should be capable of drawing after it, on a well constructed level rail road, with a pressure of steam on the boiler not exceeding 50 pounds to the square inch, day by day, a gross weight of 20 tons, or, at the least, a weight equal to three times that of the engine itself, at the rate of 10 miles per hour or more; and this has produced a number of very ingenious and beautiful locomotive carriages on trial. The velocity gained, is stated to be 25 miles to a certainty, and more, per hour, on level rail road, with a load three times the weight of the carriage itself.

Thus, then, it is, that the great rail road question, in reference to general transportation, which but a little while since was somewhat doubtful, may now be regarded as completely and most satisfactorily decided, in virtue of these extraordinary inventions in steam-power apparatus.

A day of trial was appointed; and three carriages started in competition; not together, but successively; and for several days, by adjournment, the experiments were continued. The *Rocket*, belonging to Mr. Robert Stephenson, weighing 4 tons 3 cwt., and drawing a load of 12 tons 9 cwt., travelled 35 miles in 2 hours and 52 minutes, including all stoppages at the ends of the course, which was exactly 1½ mile long, with an additional length of 220 yards, in which to stop the engine. Her speed, when in full motion, with this load, was from 14 to 17 miles per hour. She also drew a carriage, with a number of passengers, (about 30) up an inclined plane, rising one foot in 96, at the rate of 12 miles per hour.

After the Rocket, a lighter carriage, called the *Novelty*, appeared, weighing, with her complement of fuel, tank of water, &c., two passengers included, 3 tons 14 cwt. Thus accoutred, she darted off at the rate of 28 miles per hour, increasing her velocity, and actually performing the first mile in 1' 53", and, had the railway from Liverpool quite to Manchester been complete, there appeared nothing of a nature to have prevented her proceeding along the whole distance at that average rate, and more. Indeed, the owners of this engine entertain an opinion, that when the rail road shall be finished, they will be able to ensure the conveyance of passengers from one place to the other, 34 miles, by the power of this engine, in one hour!

Next, with a load attached, weighing, several passengers included, about 6 tons 12 cwt., total, consequently, engine and apparatus inclusive, about 10 tons 6 cwt., the Novelty again set off at the rate of 12 miles per hour, and, increasing her speed so as to equal 17½ miles per hour; not leaving in the minds of spectators, any doubt but that her travelling for a distance, thus loaded, and provided with level rail road, would have amounted to the average of 20 miles per hour, at the least.

In consequence of these things, the Liverpool and Manchester railway company's stock rose in value more than 50 per cent. on the price of subscription, and, by the latest accounts received, was still rising.

It is reported that Mr. Winans, (an American,) has made new discoveries in locomotives, of so very important a character, that, should they be fully confirmed, they may go far towards excluding the use of horse-power for transportation, even along the common high-ways. Such are the reports ; trials of new inventions and improvements are at least daily going forward ; and the extraordinary expectation is attributed to Mr. Winans, that he will be able to furnish engines of any weight and power required, and to suit all the irregularities of road, both as to ascent and descent. However this may prove, in the event, to be, the rail road car of this gentleman, already experimented upon, is allowed to be highly important, in its principle, for overcoming friction ; the carriages and wheels, weighing 11¼ cwt., were loaded with three tons of pig iron, making together, weight, 3 tons 11¼ cwt., and all was moved along the roads, and kept moving, at different velocities, by the force of 10, 12, 14, 17, 19 pound weights, applied in succession.

Some experiments on the carriages of Sir J. C. Anderson and W. H. James, Esq., have been made, on the Croydon high road, and have averaged full 12 miles per hour ; and arrangements of the machinery, it is said, can be made, to increase the speed to 20 miles, or more ; but this, however it may hold good in theory, can certainly never be reduced to practice on a common crowded road, where there are various difficulties to be counteracted or overcome, besides the circumstances of its being crowded. On a good rail road, it is added, as much as 100 miles per hour may be run, by introducing a blast to the fuel. One of the carriages tried, with a supply of water for 20 miles travelling, and fuel sufficient for 50 miles, does not, it is stated, weigh more than 26 cwt.

A blowing machine, to act on the fuel, and produce the velocity of 100 miles per hour, as above, although asserted to be quite practicable, is yet not recommended, because of the injurious effects such a blast, it is known, would have on the metal composing the boiler.

In the number of benefits to accrue to the civilized world, from the increased celerity and ease of conveyance by means of rail roads and steam-power, the reduction of *standing armies* is now calculated on as one, and a very important one.

More recently ;—

The following letter, a consequence of the very last experiments in England, will be found to be highly important. The price of coke, at Liverpool, is 10 shillings sterling per ton.

(*Copy.*)

To the Chairman and Directors of the Liverpool and Manchester Railway Company.

Gentlemen,—

The result of the experiments with the "Novelty," which were made on Tuesday last, by Mr. Vignoles, in order to ascertain the capability of that engine, are contained in the accompanying abstract:—

Grounding our proposals upon these results, we submit to the board the following offer, viz.—"To deliver locomotive engines, not exceeding 5 tons weight, capable of drawing 100 tons gross weight, at the rate of 15 miles an hour, on perfectly clean and level rails. The consumption of fuel not to exceed one-third of a pound of coke per gross ton per mile; the price of the engines to be determined by the proportion of work they do, as compared with the performance and price of the best engine on the road at the time of delivery.

We have the honour to be, gentlemen,
Your obedient servants,
[Signed] BRAITHWAITE & ERICKSON.

Liverpool, Feb. 1st, 1830.

CANADA, NEW-BRUNSWICK, AND NOVA-SCOTIA CANALS.

A.—From the mouth of Grande, or Ouse river, on Lake Erie, by canal, north-eastward, to strike at a point of the Welland, or Chippeway river, and, taking the course thereof downward, 11 miles, proceed from thence northward, across the mountain ridge, and down to the mouth of Twelve mile creek, on Lake Ontario. Distance, from lake to lake,   *Miles*, 43

No. 1.
THE WELLAND CANAL.

This canal, intended to connect Lakes Erie and Ontario, or to remove the natural barrier caused by the wonderful falls of Niagara, will, in the wide spread surface of its waters, exceed any other now in the world. The width afforded, in consequence of numerous ravines converted into extensive reservoirs, will give to this canal more the appearance of a large river, than an artificial navigation.

In 1824, an act was passed by the legislature of Upper Canada, incorporating a company with power to cut a canal, for boat navigation, round the cataract of Niagara; but, at the following session, the charter was, upon petition, amended, so as to increase the company's stock, and render it competent to the enlarged project of uniting the waters of Lake Erie and Lake Ontario, by a direct communication, on a scale of sloop or schooner navigation.

As much of the capital stock as was thereupon offered to the public, was readily taken up, and a large proportion of it subscribed for in the state of New-York, which gave occasion to the work, upon the enlarged plan, being immediately commenced upon, and prosecuted with spirit; and, it appears by a report on the subject to the legislature, of January, 1827, that very satisfactory progress to that time was made.

The canal is divided into three sections.—

Sect. 1. Commences at a harbour on Lake Ontario, at the mouth of Twelve mile creek, and, passing up 5 miles, to St.

Catherine's, proceeds, by two ravines of the mountain, and by means of a quick succession of locks, up to a summit level; where, at a distance of 4¼ miles from the point gained, commences a deep cut of 1 mile 54 chains, through the dividing ridge. Along this, and along some lesser cutting, through a winding ravine of 66 chains, the line passes to the Welland river, at about 10 miles above the mouth thereof, on the Niagara.

This is section No. 1. Length of it, 16½ miles. Down the mountain descent to St. Catherine's, in a distance of 4 miles 72½ chains, are 32 locks, with a declension of 322 feet. The dimensions of them, 100 feet long, and 22 feet wide in the pool, calculated to pass vessels of 125 tons burthen. From St. Catherine's to Lake Ontario, are 3 locks, including 1 at the harbour, of 32 feet in width, and 125 feet long, made so for the purpose of admitting steam-boats from Lake Ontario. At the termination of this section, a guard gate will control the admission of the waters from Lake Erie.

The deepest cutting of the summit, is of 56 feet of excavation; it is sloped above the towing-path, at an angle of 45°, which is steep, but the banks are composed of firm, stiff clay.

The general dimensions of the canal, 8 feet depth of water, 26 feet width at bottom, with a slope of 2 to 1; giving a surface of 58 feet water; this is sufficient to allow vessels of 22 feet beam to pass each other; and wider vessels than these cannot pass through the locks, according to the present plan of the canal; but there is already provision made for an enlargement of the plan at a future day, if requisite, at a small additional expense.

With a velocity of half a mile per hour, nearly 10,000 cubic feet of water per minute will pass through this section of the canal; which will afford an ample supply, at a number of advantageous sites for hydraulic machinery along the descent, over and above the occasions of the canal itself.

Sect. 2. Consists of a distance upon the Welland river, which, for about 30 miles from its mouth, resembles a canal, in the circumstance of having scarcely a perceptible current; and it being from 12 to 30 feet deep, there will consequently be nothing more requisite, but to form a towing-path along its bank for the distance specified, that is, 11 miles, ascending the river course from the point struck by section 1.

Sect. 3. Is a cut of 14 miles, from the upper point, on the Welland river, to the Grande, or Ouse river, at or near Sherboro', within a mile or two of the outlet into Lake Erie, at a flat, swampy tract of country, called Wainfleet marsh; the surface of which is 8 feet above the level of the lake. This marsh, containing 13,400 acres, has been granted by the Crown to the company.

The execution of this section, as it will not be attended with any difficult or laborious work, so the expense of it will be easy in proportion; and, once the all-important northern section accomplished, this portion of the work will of course be gone into, and carried through with rapidity. In the mean time, the navigation through into Lake Erie will be laid open, by way of the Welland, and the Niagara river above the falls; and may be used while the works on sections 2 and 3 are going on.

Thus it appears, that the Welland canal will always have two outlets for vessels ascending from Lake Ontario, one by the Niagara river, and the other by Grande river: the latter, however, cutting off a distance of 40 miles on Lake Erie. Considerably more than half the work on the No. 1., or northern section, is now gone through with, and the whole is under contract, and probably will, according to the report of the engineers, be completed this year, (1827) including a capacious harbour at the Twelve Mile creek entrance into Lake Ontario; which harbour is constructing on a scale to afford 12 feet depth of water, and to be a construction of durability: it is estimated to cost 30,000 pounds; and, if a break-water be added, then 1000 pounds more. The general canal estimate is, viz.

There has been expended hitherto, including about 15,000 pounds on the harbour,	£89,000
There is required, to complete the section to the Welland river,	80,000
Additional for the harbour,	15,000
For a break-water at the harbour,	1,000
For the section between the Welland and Grande rivers,	37,500
Towing-path on the river bank, 11 miles, and contingencies,	12,500
Total estimate,	£235,000

The capital stock of the company is 200,000 pounds, divided into 16,000 shares.

A calculation has been made, as follows, to show what amount of revenue it is thought the Welland canal may produce immediately after its completion; toll descending, for the whole 41 miles, taken at 7s. 6d. per ton, except lumber; toll ascending, at 10s. per ton.

1,500,000 staves, at £1 per 1000,	£1,500 00
Boards, plank, and other lumber, at 3s. 9d. per 1000 feet, board measure,	5,625 00
Masts, spars, &c.,	750 00
Amount carried forward,	£7,875 00

OF THE UNITED STATES.

	Amount brought forward,	£7,875	00
Stone, gypsum, &c.,		750	00
1250 tons potash, at 7s. 6d. per ton,		468	15
Flour and wheat, equal to 100,000 barrels, or 10,000 tons, at 7s. 6d.,		3,750	00
5000 barrels pork,		187	10
Whiskey, cider, lard, butter, cheese,		187	10
100 hogsheads tobacco, and other articles,		187	10
	Tolls descending,	£13,406	05

Salt in barrels, 1800 tons at 10s.,	£ 900 00	
Merchandise of all sorts, including hardware, mill stones, &c., at $\frac{1}{10}$th in weight of the quantity sent down, at 10s. per ton,	1,787 10	
Amount of toll, on operations on the canal, the erection and conducting of buildings suited to the hydraulic advantages, computed at 10,000 tons, at 3s. 9d. per ton,	1,875 00	
Toll on tonnage of vessels, at £1 5s. per trip: say 50 vessels, at 14 trips each,	875 00	
Rent from hydraulic situations, to be received after the expiration of 3 years,	2,500 00	
Tolls ascending, &c.,		£7,937 10
Total of estimated gross income,		£21,343 15

Which is exclusive of a gratuity to come from government, and the benefit to accrue from a tract of 13,400 acres of land.

It is, moreover, the opinion, that a certain amount will be added to the yearly revenue, by produce from the United States side, passing through the Welland canal; for it will be profitable for United States merchants along Lake Erie, to use in some measure this canal, even for a New-York market: in support of which position, a calculation is made, as follows;—

Transit from Lake Erie to Syracuse, by the Erie canal, and by the Welland canal; compared;

Distance from Buffalo to Syracuse, 200 miles;

Toll on which, at 1½ cent per mile,		$3 00
The same for transportation,		3 00
Toll on boats,		7
		$6 7

41 miles Welland canal; toll,	$1 50	
32 miles Oswego canal; toll at 1½ cent,	48	
73 miles transportation, at 1½ cent,	1 9	
Tonnage on vessels,	7	
Freight from Welland canal harbour to Oswego, in continuation of the voyage,	50	
		3 64

Difference, in favour of the Welland canal route; descending; per ton, — $2 43

From Syracuse to Buffalo, 200 miles;
Toll at 3 cents per mile,		$6 00
Transportation at 1½ cent per mile,		3 00
Toll on boats,		7
		$9 7

Syracuse to Oswego, 32 miles;
Toll at 3 cents per mile,	$ 96	
Welland canal,	2 00	
Tonnage,	7	
Transportation,	1 59	
		4 62

Difference, in favour of Welland canal route; ascending; per ton, — $4 45

The facility of travelling by way of Oswego and the Welland canal, will besides be great; and steam-boats will be put up, and cause another addition to the canal revenue.

It is proposed, whenever the company shall find the state of trade such as to require it, to cause a branch canal to be cut, from a point below the mountain ridge, direct to the harbour of Niagara, on Lake Ontario. It is believed that great advantages will hereafter accrue from this double harbour and double entrance upon the lake. Dimensions to correspond with the main canal. Distance, from a point near St. Catherine's, to Niagara, 11 miles. No regular survey has yet been made, but the expense is computed at £35,000.

The company have already power to construct a towing-path on the Niagara river, from Fort Erie to the Welland, and along this, 10 miles, to its intersection of the canal. By which means, together with a ship lock that will soon be constructed at Black Rock, vessels will be enabled to pass and repass from lake to lake without obstruction, and in a very direct manner.

JANUARY, 1828.

The board of managers have made their report of operations for the past year, which, although there has not been accomplished during the season, on section No. 1, which includes the summit level and deep cut, all that the engineer had conjectured might be done, exhibits, notwithstanding, a satisfactory progress made in this great work, under the circumstances of the weather and other occurrences, and a prospect decidedly encouraging as to the complete ultimate success of it. The report says,—

"The public advantages to be derived from it, are developing themselves, not only by the rapid improvement of the country on its immediate borders, but by the spirit of enterprise and exertion which it calls forth among the more remote inhabitants, who seek to avail themselves of the benefits this canal is likely to afford, by already improving various natural streams leading into Lake Erie."

From St. Catherine's to Lake Ontario, a distance of 5 miles, the canal is finished, and filled with water; and, it appears, that by the 1st of June next, no accident happening, 15 miles will be complete, leaving only about 1½ mile to be finished, in order to have, by way of the Welland river and the Upper Niagara, a thorough communication between the Lakes Ontario and Erie. The locks, down the mountain descent to St. Catherine's, 32 in number, are in great forwardness; they are located in a distance of 4 miles 72 chains. Of the 2,333,706 cubic yards of excavation originally on this No. 1, or northern section, there now only remains 406,553 to be removed.

Moreover, the board of directors have concluded that it is advisable now to proceed with the No. 3, or southern section, lying between the Welland river and Lake Erie ; and accordingly the same is already placed under contract, for a preliminary clearing and draining of the marsh land ; which last, though not difficult to effect, may prove somewhat tedious. A re-survey of route has been made, and the line adopted gives a distance of 12½ miles, between a point of the Welland river and the mouth of Grande river; or rather, to terminate on Broad creek, near the entrance thereof into Grande river. It is proposed to execute this section on the thorough-cut plan. The engineer's estimate of cost, including a safe harbour, is £61,934. The expense for the entire canal, it is now ascertained, will, ere it be complete, exceed the estimate above cited ;—perhaps by £50,000 or more.

The line just referred to, as decided on for the southern section, passes directly through the lower part of the great Wainfleet marsh, with the company's lands, granted by the crown, lying on either side. These will in consequence be drained, and become very valuable.

July, 1828.

The Grande river, or No. 3 section, of the Welland canal, may now be designated, as follows:—

	Miles.	Chains.
From the mouth of Grande river, on Lake Erie, up that stream, by a towing-path,	1	48
Thence, up Broad creek,		70
Thence, by a cut through the marsh,	10	00
Thence, down Mill creek,	2	40
Descending into the Welland river, by a ship lock of 8 feet lift. Total distance, Miles,	15	

To this, add for

Sect. 2. A track way along the Welland river this distance,	10
Sect. 1. As described,	16½
Total, Miles,	41½

The first idea of all and every canal, is suggested by the direction of natural water courses; but, in no instance, perhaps, has there ever been a route for a canal more plainly laid down, than this one through the Niagara peninsula.* It affords great geological information touching this part of the country.

December, 1829.

On the 2d of this month, the anniversary of the commencement of the Welland canal five years previous, two schooners arrived at Buffalo, Lake Erie, from Lake Ontario; having ascended the heights of the cataract, by the northern division of this canal.

A.—From the village of Hull, on the Great Ottawa, by the course of the River Rideau, and a chain of lakes, to the Gannanoqui river, on the St. Lawrence, at the Kingston mills, 5 miles from the city of Kingston. Distance, *Miles*, 122

No. 2.

THE RIDEAU CANAL.

This canal, or rather, series of canals, and branches thereof,

* Silliman.

is in active progress. Its object is to connect the two great rivers at the points specified, and by that means obtain a passage from Montreal into Lake Ontario, by way of the Ottawa ; or obtain safe and easy water communication between Upper and Lower Canada ; avoiding, consequently, the formidable rapids on the St. Lawrence, between the mouth of the Ottawa and the mouth of the Oswegatchie river, opposite Prescott.

The connexion is formed principally by damming up the Rideau and the lakes mentioned, so as to create still-water in the first, and greater depth in the latter, which are naturally shallow, but are sufficiently extensive to induce an establishment of steam-boats on them, for the purpose of towing across sloops and other canal craft.

The plan of communication has not been calculated for more than a sloop passage ; but, there is reason to think, it will be enlarged to a steam-boat navigation throughout, so as to correspond in that respect to the Welland canal.

The expense of this undertaking was estimated at £650,000; but, it is supposed, may, ere it be finished, amount to £1,000,000. It traverses, as above stated, a space of 122 miles of country.

The Articles Nos. 3, 4, 5, which here follow, designate the works of improvement needful to overcome the natural obstructions in the way from Montreal, up the Ottawa river, as far as the point specified.

July, 1828.

Parliament, at home, last year, passed a vote for the sum of £45,000 towards completing the Rideau canal, and have this session voted £135,000 to defray the expense for the present year ; these two sums, making a part of £527,000, estimated as needful to a full execution.

A.—From the city of Montreal, on the St. Lawrence, a canal direct to Upper La Chine, on Lake St. Louis; cutting off a bend in the river, and the rapids of St. Louis.   Distance, across, *Miles*, 10

No. 3.
LA CHINE CANAL.

This has but lately been finished. It is a fine piece of workmanship, and has cost £220,000, paid in part by a joint stock company, in part by a vote of the house of assembly, and in part by a grant from government, at home.

The construction of this canal is, however, only on a scale of sloop navigation.

It is on foot likewise to improve the river navigation between Montreal and La Prairie, in blasting and cutting away rocks, by means of the diving-bell: an engine that will work to much advantage in the pellucid waters of the St. Lawrence.

A.—From Lake St. Louis, at the foot of St. Anne's rapids, to the head thereof, by a canal, passing either at the back of St. Anne's, or else, which appears preferable, across the Isle Perrault.

Distance, *Miles*, 5

No. 4.

L'ISLE PERRAULT CANAL.

This cut will be accomplished at small expense, a natural channel across the island already existing, which at one period or another has formed a branch of the river.

The rapids, by this means to be avoided, are those celebrated by Moore, in his " *Canadian Boat Song.*"

A.—From the head of Long Sault, or Ottawa falls, at the village of Grenville, by a lateral canal, to the foot of Carillon rapids, opposite Point Fortune.

Distance, *Miles*, 12

No. 5.

THE GRENVILLE CANAL.

This work is advancing; but, from the nature of the ground, the excavation is a tedious process; all of it that has thus far been done, or examined, being through solid rock. The present plan of this canal is for a sloop navigation.

No regular estimate of its cost appears as yet to have been made, but it is conjectured the same may amount to £250,000.

A.—From the foot of Carillon rapids, at Hawkesbury, on the River Ottawa, the point last above-mentioned, across the Peninsula, obliquely, to the St. Lawrence, at Prescott.   Distance, (supposed,) *Miles*, 50

No. 6.

LA PETITE NATION CANAL.

A survey has been made for this proposed communication, between the Ottawa and the St. Lawrence, at points of each, lower than those of the Rideau canal.

Prescott, at the mouth of the Oswegatchie river, the point here struck on the St. Lawrence, is 70 miles below Kingston, and is immediately above the St. Lawrence rapids.

A.—From a point of La Petite Nation canal, last above specified, down the valley of the St. Lawrence, to a point of the Isle Perrault canal; forming a junction therewith.   Distance, (supposed,) *Miles*, 50

No. 7.

THE ST. LAWRENCE CANAL.

The ground for this projected lateral canal, was surveyed last year, and a report made thereon. It will form a more direct route of communication between Montreal and the Lakes Ontario and Erie, than by passing up the Ottawa river, and through either the Rideau or the Petite Nation canal, in as much as, by this additional improvement, the line along the St. Lawrence valley will be preserved, and the formidable rapids of this river be equally avoided. It is, in short, contemplated, to have a direct steam-boat navigation from Prescott to Montreal, a distance of 132 miles: which may be effected by means of about 60 miles of canal, and 196 feet of lockage.

A.—From a point of Lake Simcoe, along the direction of Talbot river, and a chain of shallow waters, eastward and south-eastward, to the River Trent, and thence, passing on to the Bay of Quinty, and to Lake Ontario. Distance, by a series of canals and lake navigation together, and including a branch canal of 10 miles, to strike from Rico lake upon Port Hope, Ontario, where a fine harbour is to be constructed,

Miles, 190

No. 8.

LAKE SIMCOE CANAL.

This very important project, which is to be carried into execution by the Canada company, opens, by way of Trent river and the Severn, a passage to Lake Huron and its borders, and ultimately to Lake Superior, and adds, consequently, in this direction, an almost unbounded range of country, in Upper Canada, to be brought into an easy commercial intercourse with Lower Canada, by a line of water communication the most direct.

At or near the city of Kingston, some day or other, will be seen, the trade arriving by the St. Lawrence river and by the Rideau canal, and passing up, one portion to Lake Simcoe, Lake Huron, and the north-west, and another portion to Lake Ontario, and thence, by the Welland canal, to Lake Erie; and vice versa, the trade arriving from these two divisions, and passing on towards Lower Canada.

It is to be hoped the mother country will neither look indifferently, nor in vain, to this side of the Atlantic, for a safe, commodious, and happy asylum, for a part, not inconsiderable, of the present superabundance of her population.

The extensive peninsula between the Ottawa and the St. Lawrence, including the tract of country traversed by the Rideau canal route, which is characterized as being of the greatest fertility, there can be but little, if any doubt, will become, ere long, the support of a dense population.

A.—From the head of the Rideau canal on the River Ottawa, up the course of this river, by canal, and a series of other improvements, and a canal to connect the south-west branch of the same with Lake Nipissing, at or near the extreme east point thereof; and from the south point of this lake, by a canal, to the north shore of Lake Huron. Distance, by canal and other improvements, and lake navigation, together,

Miles, 400

No. 9.

LAKE NIPISSING CANAL.

A project is on foot, or at least is suggested, to effect the addition of what is here specified to the mass of improvements already going forward. It will, when the day of its accomplishment comes, afford a precious variety in the navigable water-route between Lower Canada and the West, and there will be included within the great chain of improved communication, the range of country on the upper waters of the Ottawa river, of unbounded extent, besides giving access to Lake Huron, and thence to Lake Superior, in this new direction.

GREEN BAY CANAL.

A canal of about 12 miles, in New-Brunswick, will connect the Gulf of St. Lawrence with the Bay of Fundy. It will strike from Vert or Green bay, in the Straits of Northumberland, across to the NE. branch of the Bay of Fundy.

THE SHUBENACADIE CANAL.

This Nova-Scotia canal will connect the Bay of Fundy, SE. branch, with Halifax harbour.

NOTE.

In Upper Canada, besides the sundry specifications of the foregoing Articles, various and extensive works of improvement are suggested, and a portion thereof, of no inconsiderable importance, decided on, and more or less in actual progress of execution.

A canal route along the line of the river Thames, continued to Detroit, has been surveyed. A steam-boat canal, up the Niagara river, by means of tunnel locks, is proposed. Navigation improvements between Lakes Huron and St. Clair, are on foot. Coots' Paradise is to be dammed at the neck, and a lock constructed in the dam, to enable ships to float up to the town of Dundass. At the head of Dundass river, the city of Guelph is building; from within which city, run rivers into four lakes;—namely;—Lake Huron, Lake Simcoe, Lake Erie, Lake Ontario: which rivers are each to receive improvements in their navigation; they will be dammed and locked by the Canada company.

THE END

INDEX.

A.

	Page.
Abolition of restrictions,	510
Acquisitions from the Winnebago and Potowatomy Indians, by treaty,	349
Act of congress, authorizing a board of United States engineers for internal improvement,	493
Advanced state of the western community,	360
Advantages pointed out, public and private, to accrue from connecting, by canal, the head waters of the Tennessee and Coosa rivers,	391
Advantages to arise from a union of the Roanoke and James river waters; also the Roanoke connexion with New river, and the Holston of Tennessee,	321
Alphabet of the Cherokee tongue, recent invention of	516
American seamen, plan to form and educate a number sufficient for the country's wants,	543
Annual income and expenditure of the United States,	506
Anthracite coal, and mineral powder; inquiries concerning the formation of, and on the applicability of either to the smelting furnace,	143
Anthracite coal mountain,	131
Appropriations by congress, to works of internal improvements,	505
Area of Schuylkill county coal district,	117
Army and navy forces compared,	545
Arnold's route of march to Quebec,	24

B.

Ballendine, John, his project of improving the James river and Potomac navigation, in the year 1773,	213
Baltimore and Ohio rail road, the progress of, to December, 1829,	167
Barataria; proposed new seaport of Louisiana,	381
Beaufort harbour, North Carolina, the importance of, in time of war,	408
Bishop Berkeley's prophecy,	231
Board of Internal Improvement of the United States, institution of, in 1824,	489
Boone, Daniel	349
Breakwater at entrance of the Delaware,	280

INDEX.

	Page
British documents in 1773, on projected improvements from the Atlantic to the Ohio,	209
British mercantile tonnage and exports,	549
(NOTE.—In 1829, the tonnage amounted to 2,184,000 tons.)	

C.

Cahawba river, Alabama, in a course of improvement,	399
Canada, New-Brunswick, and Nova-Scotia canals,	592
Canal proposed along the bank of the Ohio, uninterruptedly, from Pittsburg to Louisville,	337
Canal proposed along the west border of the Mississippi river,	352
Canal proposed to connect the navigation of the Penobscot and Kennebeck rivers, from near their sources,	48
Canal proposed to encircle Lake Erie, from Portland to Detroit,	72
Canals already finished, or well advanced, distance $3908\frac{5}{8}$ miles, a recapitulation list of	482
Canals contemplated merely, or not advanced, distance $6833\frac{7}{8}$ miles, a recapitulation list of	482
Canals of Scotland,	174
Canals proposed in prolongation, from the Teche river, westward, across the state of Louisiana, to Galveston bay, Texas,	382
Canal to avoid the pass of Hell gate, or Hurl gate,	80
Capacity of the Delaware and Chesapeake canal, and a view taken of the commerce it will connect,	158
Capacity of the Lehigh river, for the improved navigation thereof,	133
Capacity of the Union canal,	124
Capital created and circulated, by the mere operations of building and navigating steam-boats,	365
Carbondale coal mines,	128
Carondelet canal company, Louisiana; the unadvised privilege of, to be annulled,	385
Carrollton viaduct,	168
Cayuga marshes, on draining the	68
Central military station,	347
Ceremonies at commencing the Chesapeake and Ohio canal, and the Baltimore and Ohio rail road, on the 4th of July, 1828,	230
Cherokee and other Indian tribes; view taken of their case by the president of the United States,	523
Chesapeake and Delaware canal; contemplated, and route for it surveyed, in the year 1769,	155
Chickasaw and Cherokee Indians,	515
Chickasaw and Cherokee state papers,	516
Civil constructions and surveys, by the engineer department of the United States, since 20th April, 1824,	494
Clinton, General James	173
Coal, anthracite; mode of using to advantage in the furnace; a question,	131

INDEX.

	Page.
Coal district of the Schuylkill, the Swatara, and the Lehigh mountains,	117
Coal trade in prospect, by the Chesapeake and Ohio canal, and prosperity connected with it,	224
Coasting and inland trade, between the cities of New-York and Philadelphia, and the ports and places upon the waters of the Chesapeake, computed,	97
Coast tide water inland navigation, between Boston harbour and the Mississippi river,	386
Coking of coal,	226
Columbia; trade of the Susquehanna, passing through	160
Commerce of United States; the periodical advancement of	557
Commercial tonnage of Great Britain,	549
Communication between the waters of Lake Ontario and the shores of the Atlantic, by the Kennebeck, the Androscoggin, and Piscataqua rivers,	22
Compacts, by which, and in virtue of previous cessions, the public lands have been acquired by the federal government,	514
Competency of territories to claim admission into the Union of States,	514
Connecticut rapids,	13
Convention between the states of Pennsylvania and New-Jersey, for the use, mutually, of the waters of the Delaware,	272
Convention of Delegates on the Chesapeake and Ohio canal,	221
Coosa and Black Warrior rivers, Alabama, in a course of improvement,	399
Cotton factories at Dover, New-Hampshire,	17
Cuba; a mail establishment with, through Tallahassee, St. Marks, and Key West,	555
Cuba, commerce of the United States with	555
Cuba, the annual imports of	556
Culture of silk,	551
Cumberland river, in a course of improvement,	335
Custom house punctuality,	509
Customs of the United States,	506

D.

Delaware and Rariton canal,		
Branches of trade connected with,		97
Contemplated to be a state concern,		98
Estimate of revenue from tolls,		99
Delaware breakwater,		280
Delaware falls and rapids, between tide water and Easton,		107
Delta of the Mississippi; importance of draining the		432
Deputation of foreign naval officers, to see service on board of United States ships of war,		281
Differences of level, and distances of coal districts to a market,		133
Discovery of the use of coke, by Dudley,		226
Distances by stations, Buffalo to Detroit,		72
Domain of the United States,		513
Domestic arts and industry; the great advances of		551

INDEX.

D.

Dry docks, and other conveniencies, contemplated for a vast internal emporium, at Cincinnati, Ohio, - - - 361

E.

Education, elementary and practical, to form a complete American marine, - - - - - - - - 543
Elements of political economy, - - - - - 510
Elevations of various points above tide level, - - 314
Elk river navigation of Tennessee state, to communicate with the Tennessee in Alabama, - - - - - 371
Emigration from Europe, on the subject of - - - 232
Events in Europe, operating great changes in the social condition, - - - - - - - - - - 366
Expenditures of Pennsylvania, on improvements, since 1791, 279
Expense of constructing canals in the south, very moderate, 427
Experiments on steam carriages, - - - - - 588
Export trade and navigation, - - - - - - 546
Exports of Great Britain, - - - - - - 549
Exposé of the great base lines of internal navigation improvements, - - - - - - - - - - 445
Extreme productiveness of the lower plain of Louisiana, when reclaimed from floods, - - - - - - 434

F.

Fair Mount water works, - - - - - - 116
Financial operations, - - - - - - - 550
Fisheries of Nantucket and New-Bedford, - - - 44
Forces, naval and military, compared, - - - - 545
Foreign commerce; rate of its advancement, - - - 551
Fort Chartres of the French, and St Louis, Missouri, - 347
Freedom of trade and intercourse, - - - - 510
French ancient military posts, the chain of - - - 347
Future canal, along the western border of the Mississippi, from the mouth of Missouri river, to a point opposite New-Orleans, - - - - - - - - - 352
Future prolongation of the Teche canal, westward, across the state of Louisiana, to the river Sabine; and to Galveston bay, in Texas, - - - - - - - - 382

G.

General politics, or national policy, - - - - 533
General public funds, and other funds of New-York state, 92
Georgia board of works, and "Mexican and Atlantic canal company." Capital, $2,000,000, - - - - 375
Glasgow collieries, - - - - - - - 225
Grand summary of the navigation of the United States, - 486
Grant by congress, towards improving Kentucky river, - 337
Grant of public lands to Alabama, - - - - 371
Grant of public lands to Illinois, - - - - - 341
Grant of public lands to Indiana, - - - - - 333
Grant of public lands to Louisiana, - - - - 385
Grant of public lands to Mississippi, - - - - 395

INDEX.   609

	Page.
Grants of public lands to Ohio state,	243
Green bay, New-Brunswick, canal,	603
Greenbrier bridge, in Virginia, architectural description of	308
Greenock and Whin hill aqueduct,	173
Green river of Kentucky, in a course of improvement,	335
Guelph city, and its four rivers,	604
Gurney and others; their new invented steam carriages,	588

H.

Hassler, F. R., his arrangements for astronomical surveys,	544
Havana; commerce of the United States with	555
Hurlgate canal, proposed,	80
Hydraulic advantages, at Cincinnati,	240
Hydraulic improvements, for saving water,	173
Hydraulic limestone; discovered on the James river,	322
Hydraulic limestone; discovered on the Susquehanna and Potomac rivers,	235

I.

Ibberville, or Manchac channel; the importance of clearing out, and enlarging of	432
Improvement on canal locks, so as to save one half the usual time requisite to pass through,	236
Improvements in transportation; official estimate of	42
Imports of the United States,	549
Inclined plane system, adopted in the Morris canal,	102
Indian case, the president's view of	523
Indian lands, not yet ceded by the Indians,	513
Indian population,	526
Indian state papers,	518
Institutions of Philadelphia,	279
Internal improvements undertaken by the general government; the sudden favourable effects of	489
Internal trade of the country; the several great branches of it, in relation to the Delaware and Rariton canal,	97
Inundations of the Mississippi,	432
Inventions of note,	400

J.

Jetties on the Appomatox, constructed of fascines, similar to the fascine work on the Rhine, and in Holland,	283

K.

Kanhaway valley salt works,	309
Kentucky river, in a course of improvement,	335

L.

Lake Drummond; its connexion with the Navy Yard at Gosport,	404
Lake Travers, fur company establishment,	357

INDEX.

	Page
Lake Travers; the Table land of	356
Language of the Cherokees; newly invented written characters,	515
Latent riches, to be developed, and brought into circulation,	185
Lead and copper mines, in the newly acquired territory,	349
Lee, Richard Henry,	218
Lehigh coal; proposed contracts for, to supply the New-York market,	103
Lehigh works; the completion of, and the extensive prospect of the company,	140
Lehman, William; the legislative father and constant supporter of the "Pennsylvania canal and rail road,"	252
Lines of connexion between the eastern and western waters, also the border navigation of the country; a recapitulation of	445
Liquidation of public debt,	505. 535
List A, recapitulating all the artificial, or improved navigation, treated of; distance, 16,397½ miles; referred to at p. 486,	454
List B, recapitulating all the canals of communication; distance, 10,742½ miles, constituting a part of List A, referred to at p. 486,	469
List C, recapitulating the river stream navigation improvements, finished or proposed; distance, 5655 miles, constituting the remainder of List A, referred to at p. 486,	483
Lock and dam navigation; remarks on, and tables,	297
Locomotive steam carriages; recent extraordinary improvements in	588
Louisiana alluvious lands, plan for reclaiming the	433
Lycoming coal mines,	200

M.

Mail conveyance to and from the Havana,	555
Manchac or Ibberville outlet, and the Mississippi floods,	432
Marsh lands in France,	69
Matawaska settlement; a subject of negotiation between the United States and Great Britain, in regard to boundary line,	49
Mauch Chunk creek, and mountain,	131
Mercantile tonnage,	548
Merrimack rapids,	10
Military academy,	543
Military avenues to St. Louis, Missouri,	347
Military, or trigonometrical survey of the coast,	544
Military, pecuniary, commercial, manufacturing, and agricultural importance of lands newly acquired from the Indians,	349
Military roads,	556
Military stations,	545
Mississippi channel; plan for deepening the bar of, at its entrance,	440
Mississippi natural basin; the extent and geographical position of,	358
Mississippi navigation dangers,	352

INDEX.

	Page.
Mississippi proposed side canal, from the Ohio, or the Missouri, to New-Orleans,	352
Mississippi river; export of productions through New-Orleans,	384
Mississippi valley; progress of population,	359
Modern improved communication through the principal states of Europe,	368
Mountains of the United States, a great source of income to canals crossing east and west,	227
Mount Carbon,	108
Mule anecdote,	139

N.

Nantucket and New-Bedford whale fisheries,	44
National debt,	536
National defence, the great systems pursuing towards a completion thereof,	542
National military roads of the United States,	556
National objects accomplished in twelve years,	535
National policy, adapted to the times,	525
National prosperity, the steady advance of	551
Naval academy, a desideratum,	543
Navigable communications between the waters of Lake Ontario, and the Atlantic ports of the states of Maine,	22
Navigable water, reaching the precincts of every occupier of a plantation in the north-east quarter of Louisiana,	379
Navigation between Boston harbour and the Mississippi,	386
Navigation between Boston harbour and the river St. Lawrence, Lower Canada,	15
Navigation between Portland harbour and the same,	22
Navigation by various routes, through the interior, from Boston harbour to New-Orleans; and from the same to Mobile point in the Gulf of Mexico,	450
Navigation, direct, from the Chesapeake, or from Albemarle sound, through the interior, to the Gulf of Mexico,	321
Navigation in the south; the easy and cheap means of improving, and extending,	383
Navigation lines through the United States recapitulated,	446
Navigation of the Rio del Norte, New-Mexico, by exclusive privilege,	441
Navigation through New-York, between the Hudson, Lake Erie, and the Ohio, on two parallels of canal,	71
Navy augmentation, the probable limit of	542
Navy list of United States,	542
Navy Yard at Philadelphia, and ship Pennsylvania,	280
New British colony on the Ohio, in the year 1773,	209
New-Echota, capital of the Cherokees, in Georgia,	518
New-England; the vast capacity of, for still increasing business; officially stated,	42
New-York, general state fund, and other funds,	92
New-York port; activity in the ship yards of	91
New-York, variety of improved routes to the coal districts,	106

O.

	Page.
Observatories proposed,	544
Ohio river navigation; grant by congress for improving the	335
Ohio river, the trade thereof,	337
Ohio state canals; aids from the United States government, and progress of the works to December, 1829,	245
Opening of the Chesapeake and Delaware canal,	162
Opening of the Union canal navigation,	125
Opinion in England in 1775, on the military enterprise against Quebec,	25
Opinions declared, of Presidents Adams, Jackson, and Monroe, on the Indian question,	529
Original military, and commercial plans of the French; their expansive views,	347

P.

Pacific, proposed connexion, by canal, across the isthmus,	431
Pembina frontier settlement, on Red river,	357
"Pennsylvania," line of battle ship,	280
Pennsylvania state canal and rail road, a summary view of it, its present state, and works coming into immediate connexion with it,	265
Pennsylvania state; her expenditure on improvements,	279
Philadelphia; prosperous condition of science in	279
Philadelphia; value of the coasting and coal trade thereof	280
Picture of the west,	360
Pittsburg; its advancement,	360
Plan of reclaiming the alluvial lands of Louisiana, both upper and lower plains,	435
Plan of the secretary of war, for a final disposition of the Indians,	525
Portage at Ouisconsin, needful to complete a military communication between the Mississippi valley, and the Canada frontier,	348
Post office establishment, and post roads,	554
Potomac navigation company, their operations, and surrender of charter,	208
Preliminaries to great and lasting works of public improvements, commenced under act of congress 30th April, 1824,	493

Profiles inserted viz;—

Boston and Albany rail road,
Hudson and Erie canal,
Ohio state canal,
Morris canal,
Union canal,
Schuylkill canal,
Pennsylvania canal,
Columbia rail road,
Baltimore and Ohio rail road,
Chesapeake and Ohio canal,
Florida canal,

} These eleven projected on a uniform scale.

INDEX.

	Page.
Dismal swamp canal, Chesapeake and Delaware canal, Lehigh canal, Welland canal, — These four, on a larger uniform scale.	
Progress making generally in useful science,	365
Progress of population in the west,	359
Prospects as to intellectual and moral advancement,	401
Prospects of the nation, in connexion with the coal trade, and attendant circumstances,	224
Public debt of the states of Europe,	538
Public debt of the United States,	541
Public domain to the 30th June, 1828, creditor with the treasury in the sum of $85,162,956,	515
Public lands of United States,	512
Public lands, vested in the general government, by cession and compact, for the benefit of the Union,	514
Public resources, and individual wealth; manifestations of their periodical advancement,	551

Q.

Question on the two lines of route from Plymouth to Beaufort harbour, North Carolina,	407
Questions on universal freedom of trade and intercourse,	510
Quincy rail road,	41

R.

Raft in Red river,	383
Raft in the Achafalaya,	396
Rail road proposed, from New-York city to the Mississippi river at Rock island,	578
Rail roads enumerated,	574
Railway conveyance, remarks on	568
Recapitulation of canals finished or in course of execution,	487
Recapitulation of the great lines of navigation improvements, opening communications, the east with the west; also from Boston harbour, by tide water, to St. Mary's river, East Florida, and to the Mississippi river,	445
Red river, importance of, in the view taken of it by the legislature of Louisiana,	383
Reduction of standing armies, connected with rail road and steam power improvements,	590
Retrospect of financial operations,	550
Revenue from the proposed Delaware and Rariton canal, from tolls; estimate of	98
Revenue of United States, whence derived,	550
Rio del Norte, navigation of, by exclusive privilege,	441
Road proposed, from St. Louis, Missouri, to Alexandria, on Red river,	584
Roanoke inlet, or connexion at Nag's head of Albemarle sound, with the Atlantic; measures in relation to	409

614 INDEX.

	Page.
Route of communication between Philadelphia and Fort Pitt, now Pittsburg, on the Ohio, and Presqu' Isle, Lake Erie, surveyed in 1762,	156
Routes of communication, by water improvements, through the interior, from the Atlantic to the Gulf of Mexico,	321
Russian deputation of naval officers,	281

S.

Savage river coal mines,	224
Saving water system,	173
Schedule of internal improvements, undertaken or aided by the general government,	494
Schuylkill navigation works, summary view of, and proposed rail road branches,	118
Scientific discoveries,	400
Scotland, the canals of	174
Sheet iron steam-boats,	172
Shubenacadie canal. Nova-Scotia,	603
Silk; its culture recommended,	553
Sinking fund; its operation,	536
Sluice navigation, remarks on, and tables,	292
Social improvement in the west,	360
Sources of the Mississippi, the Hudson, and St. Lawrence rivers,	357
South Carolina, her extensive river improvements,	417
Speculative, or contingent advantages, to arise out of the Florida canal,	431
Steam-boat navigation, the introduction and present state of, on the Ohio and Mississippi rivers,	360
Steam carriages of extraordinary power,	588
Steam engines of Pittsburg manufacture, for the Union canal water works,	124
Steam navigation, from Buffalo, on Lake Erie, to New-Orleans,	349
Steam power navigation, remarks on, and tables,	287
St. Joseph's bay, north of Cape Blas, West Florida; its importance as a harbour for ships of war,	427
Summary of inland coast navigation,	447
Summary of	
The Florida navigation,	444
Indiana navigation,	333
Kentucky navigation,	338
Lakes Ontario and Superior, and the North-West territory navigation,	350
Middle great lakes, and Illinois and Michigan navigation,	342
Mississippi river, and confluents,	352
New-England states navigation,	45
New-Jersey, Delaware, Maryland, Pennsylvania, Ohio, navigation,	275
New-York navigation,	84
North Carolina and South Carolina navigation,	422

INDEX.   615

	Page.
Tennessee, Mississippi, Louisiana, Alabama, Georgia, navigation,	394
Virginia navigation,	328
Surplus funds in the treasury, how to dispose thereof,	538

Surveys directed by legislative authorities, to be made, or to be completed,

Alleghany stream and valley, between the Kiskimenetas and French creek,	251
Genessee river, New-York,	501
Ground and stream for connecting the upper water of White river with the Wabash,	333
Ground and streams for a connexion of the waters of Lake Michigan, and the waters of the Wabash river,	333
Ground and streams for connecting the St. Mary's and St. Joseph's rivers, in a line of navigation with the Wabash and the Ohio,	333
Kennebeck and Androscoggin river streams, and the valleys thereof,	23
La Fourche river, or outlet from the Mississippi, in Louisiana,	381
Little Schuylkill river, in order to an improved slack water navigation, down to its junction with the Big Schuylkill,	150
Meherrin river, in Virginia, from Murfreesboro' upwards,	326
Mill river, and Thames river, Connecticut,	500
Muskingum river, Still water and Killbuck creeks, in Ohio state,	244
Nottoway river, in Virginia, up from the mouth thereof,	326
Ohio river stream and valley, between Pittsburg and the mouth of the Beaver,	251
Pascagoula river, Florida,	501
Rappahannock river, from tide water at Fredericksburg, upward,	326
Red river, through Louisiana state and Arkansas territory,	502
Rivers and creeks of the state of Ohio,	501
St. Marks and Appalachicola rivers, in Florida,	501
Stream of the Boguechitto, flowing into the Pearl river in Louisiana,	379
The Green and Barren rivers of the state of Kentucky, also the Licking river, and Kentucky river,	335
The Upper Merrimack river, New-Hampshire,	501
Valley and stream of the Codorus, from its mouth in the Susquehanna, up to a point above the borough of York,	184
Valley and stream of the Kanhaway river, below Great falls, for additional improvements,	326
Valley and stream of the Monongahela river,	251
Warren river, Rhode Island,	500

616   INDEX.

	Page.
Surveys directed, of various bayous and water courses of the northern division of the state of Louisiana, to be cleared of obstructions,	383
Susquehanna river, the descending trade of, passing Columbia,	160
Susquehanna river, the descending trade of, passing Harrisburg,	180
Swatara coal mines, prospects in regard to	126
System proposed, for forming and educating American seamen,	543

T.

Table of distances, Buffalo to Detroit,	72
Table of the Mississippi basin; its extent and geographical position,	358
Tables, exhibiting a comparative view of the canal routes, east and west,	316
Tables of elevations,	313
Tariff operations,	508
Tariff; the true governing principles for its graduation,	509
Tennessee river, Alabama, in a course of improvement,	371
Theory of power applied to railways,	569
Theory of steam power navigation, and tables,	287
The Tortugas; Atlantic coast inland-passage to, by steamboats,	429
The Tortugas to be rendered a naval station for the United States West India squadron,	430
Tide level heights, and distances of anthracite coal districts to a market for the coal,	133
Tolls, payable on the Schuylkill, Union, and Erie canals,	558
Tonnage employed in the trade between New-York and Philadelphia, and other ports and places on the Delaware river and bay; as also between New-York and all ports and places upon the waters of the Chesapeake,	99
Tonnage of the United States, the fluctuation and ultimate increase of	548
Trade, descending, of the Susquehanna, passing Columbia,	160
Trade, descending, of the Susquehanna, passing Harrisburg,	180
Trade of the Mississippi, through New-Orleans,	384
Trade of the river Ohio; rate of its increase,	337
Transit of foreign trade, by the Florida canal,	431
Treasury surpluses, question on the mode of employing them,	538
Trigonometrical surveys of the whole coast of the United States,	544
Tunnels, finished, or in execution, or intended, viz:—	
The Casselman's intended tunnel, 4 miles 80 yds.	219
The Conemaugh tunnel, 750 feet,	268
The Grant's hill Pittsburg tunnel, 800 feet,	245
The Schuylkill tunnel, 450 feet,	109
The Union Canal tunnel, 850 feet,	123
The Virginia proposed tunnels,	317

INDEX.

U.

Union, by proposed canal, of the Penobscot and Kennebeck rivers, near their sources, ... 48
Union canal, its completion, character, and the ultimate prospects arising, ... 125
Union canal, the origin of, in the year 1792, and previous projects, ... 120
Union of the Roanoke and James river waters; also of the Roanoke with New river, and the Holston of Tennessee; the advantages to arise from, ... 321
Union proposed, of the Alabama, and Tennessee river navigation, and advantages, public and private, to be derived, 391
United States army and navy forces, and distribution of, . 545
United States, in the next century, to be the greatest smelter of iron ore in the world, ... 226
University of Pennsylvania, ... 279

V.

Virginia state canals, connecting the eastern and western navigation, ... 326
Virginia state surveys, since 1817, ... 329
Voyages through the interior, by various routes, from Boston harbour to New-Orleans, also to Mobile bay, . . 450

W.

Wabash river, in a course of improvement, . . . 333
Washington, General George, and River Potomac, . . 208
Wealth of the nation, manifestations of its advancement, 551
Western country, the first settlement of, and rapid advancement, ... 359
Whin hill, and Shaw's burn water works, at Greenock, described, ... 173
Winnebago lands, lead and copper mines, . . . 349
Works of internal improvement, by the engineer department of the United States, for 1829, ... 561

FINIS.